HISTORICAL DICTIONARY

The historical dictionaries present essential information on a broad range of subjects, including American and world history, art, business, cities, countries, cultures, customs, film, global conflicts, international relations, literature, music, philosophy, religion, sports, and theater. Written by experts, all contain highly informative introductory essays of the topic and detailed chronologies that, in some cases, cover vast historical time periods but still manage to heavily feature more recent events.

Brief A–Z entries describe the main people, events, politics, social issues, institutions, and policies that make the topic unique, and entries are cross-referenced for ease of browsing. Extensive bibliographies are divided into several general subject areas, providing excellent access points for students, researchers, and anyone wanting to know more. Additionally, maps, photographs, and appendixes of supplemental information aid high school and college students doing term papers or introductory research projects. In short, the historical dictionaries are the perfect starting point for anyone looking to research in these fields.

HISTORICAL DICTIONARIES OF LITERATURE AND THE ARTS

Jon Woronoff, Series Editor

Science Fiction Literature, by Brian Stableford, 2004.
Hong Kong Cinema, by Lisa Odham Stokes, 2007.
American Radio Soap Operas, by Jim Cox, 2005.
Japanese Traditional Theatre, by Samuel L. Leiter, 2006.
Fantasy Literature, by Brian Stableford, 2005.
Australian and New Zealand Cinema, by Albert Moran and Errol Vieth, 2006.
African-American Television, by Kathleen Fearn-Banks, 2006.
Lesbian Literature, by Meredith Miller, 2006.
Scandinavian Literature and Theater, by Jan Sjåvik, 2006.
British Radio, by Seán Street, 2006.
German Theater, by William Grange, 2006.
African American Cinema, by S. Torriano Berry and Venise Berry, 2006.
Sacred Music, by Joseph P. Swain, 2006.
Russian Theater, by Laurence Senelick, 2007.
French Cinema, by Dayna Oscherwitz and MaryEllen Higgins, 2007.
Postmodernist Literature and Theater, by Fran Mason, 2007.
Irish Cinema, by Roderick Flynn and Pat Brereton, 2007.
Australian Radio and Television, by Albert Moran and Chris Keating, 2007.
Polish Cinema, by Marek Haltof, 2007.
Old Time Radio, by Robert C. Reinehr and Jon D. Swartz, 2008.
Renaissance Art, by Lilian H. Zirpolo, 2008.
Broadway Musical, by William A. Everett and Paul R. Laird, 2008.
American Theater: Modernism, by James Fisher and Felicia Hardison Londré, 2008.
German Cinema, by Robert C. Reimer and Carol J. Reimer, 2008.
Horror Cinema, by Peter Hutchings, 2008.
Westerns in Cinema, by Paul Varner, 2008.
Chinese Theater, by Tan Ye, 2008.
Italian Cinema, by Gino Moliterno, 2008.
Architecture, by Allison Lee Palmer, 2008.
Russian and Soviet Cinema, by Peter Rollberg, 2008.
African American Theater, by Anthony D. Hill, 2009.
Postwar German Literature, by William Grange, 2009.
Modern Japanese Literature and Theater, by J. Scott Miller, 2009.
Animation and Cartoons, by Nichola Dobson, 2009.
Modern Chinese Literature, by Li-hua Ying, 2010.
Middle Eastern Cinema, by Terri Ginsberg and Chris Lippard, 2010.

Spanish Cinema, by Alberto Mira, 2010.
Film Noir, by Andrew Spicer, 2010.
French Theater, by Edward Forman, 2010.
Choral Music, by Melvin P. Unger, 2010.
Westerns in Literature, by Paul Varner, 2010.
Baroque Art and Architecture, by Lilian H. Zirpolo, 2010.
Surrealism, by Keith Aspley, 2010.
Science Fiction Cinema, by M. Keith Booker, 2010.
Latin American Literature and Theater, by Richard A. Young and Odile Cisneros, 2011.
Children's Literature, by Emer O'Sullivan, 2010.
German Literature to 1945, by William Grange, 2011.
Neoclassical Art and Architecture, by Allison Lee Palmer, 2011.
American Cinema, by M. Keith Booker, 2011.
American Theater: Contemporary, by James Fisher, 2011.
English Music: ca. 1400–1958, by Charles Edward McGuire and Steven E. Plank, 2011.
Rococo Art, by Jennifer D. Milam, 2011.
Romantic Art and Architecture, by Allison Lee Palmer, 2011.
Japanese Cinema, by Jasper Sharp, 2011.
Modern and Contemporary Classical Music, by Nicole V. Gagné, 2012.
Russian Music, by Daniel Jaffé, 2012.
Music of the Classical Period, by Bertil van Boer, 2012.
Holocaust Cinema, by Robert C. Reimer and Carol J. Reimer, 2012.
Asian American Literature and Theater, by Wenying Xu, 2012.

Historical Dictionary of Asian American Literature and Theater

Wenying Xu

Historical Dictionaries of Literature and the Arts

The Scarecrow Press, Inc.
Lanham • Toronto • Plymouth, UK
2012

Published by Scarecrow Press, Inc.
A wholly owned subsidiary of The Rowman & Littlefield Publishing Group, Inc.
4501 Forbes Boulevard, Suite 200, Lanham, Maryland 20706
www.rowman.com

10 Thornbury Road, Plymouth PL6 7PP, United Kingdom

British Library Cataloguing in Publication Information Available

Library of Congress Cataloging-in-Publication Data

Xu, Wenying.
Historical dictionary of Asian American literature and theater / Wenying Xu.
p. cm. — (Historical dictionaries of literature and the arts)
Includes bibliographical references.
ISBN 978-0-8108-5577-9 (hardback : alk. paper) — ISBN 978-0-8108-7394-0 (ebook)
1. American literature—Asian American authors—Bio-bibliography—Dictionaries. 2. Asian American authors—Biography—Dictionaries. I. Title.
PS153.A84X83 2012
810.9'895—dc23

2011049876

∞™ The paper used in this publication meets the minimum requirements of American National Standard for Information Sciences—Permanence of Paper for Printed Library Materials, ANSI/NISO Z39.48-1992.

Printed in the United States of America

Contents

Editor's Foreword *Jon Woronoff*	ix
Preface	xi
Acknowledgments	xiii
Chronology	xv
Introduction	1
THE DICTIONARY	21
Bibliography	303
About the Author	389

Editor's Foreword

There are numerous strands in the literature of the United States and this web has become increasingly variegated with time. Among the latest additions are Asian American writers, this broad term making considerably more sense when broken down by national origin, as they do tend to vary from Chinese American, to Japanese American, to South Asian American, to Vietnamese American, just to mention the main ones. This group does not speak with one voice, since the origins and time of arrival vary considerably, and along with first, there are now second and third generations. On top of this, even among those from the same contingent, there is considerable variety because each writer has his or her own concerns and sensibility and writes on different themes. Among these are such general ones as adapting to a new culture without shedding the old one, somehow forming a bridge between the two, facing challenges like assimilation, liminality, and real or perceived racism, but also more specific issues faced by women or gays. Most of the writing deals with the here-and-now but some of it also harks back to earlier times in the homeland. The output is now sufficiently large that it is hard to keep track of, and, along with novels and short stories, there is a steady flow of poetry and plays.

After consulting this *Historical Dictionary of Asian American Literature and Theater*, no one can have the slightest doubt that the Asian American contribution is substantial, and, despite a comparatively small population base, incredibly rich and diversified. Moreover, since it is so new relatively, it is less researched and studied than other literary contributions. This historical dictionary is a particularly good place to learn more about Asian American literature and theater, starting with the chronology, which, while not reaching back that far, evidences a considerable and growing presence. The introduction tells us more about the ethnic background, the writers, and the themes. But it is the dictionary section that is a real treasure trove of information, with literally hundreds of entries on novelists, poets, and playwrights, telling us where they come from, something of their education and career, and especially what they have created. Meanwhile, other entries describe the historical background, cultural features, techniques, and major theaters and clubs. Nor should the bibliography be overlooked, since it is certainly the most up-to-date and in some ways also the most comprehensive one available, which points toward further reading of a general nature and also includes bibliographies on specific writers.

The author of this volume, Wenying Xu, is herself an Asian American with her roots in China, where she was born, grew up, and initially studied, before moving to the United States where she received an M.A. and a Ph.D. in English. She is a professor of English and, in addition, associate dean of the College of Arts and Letters at Florida Atlantic University. She has written numerous essays that were published in specialized journals, as well as two books on related topics. Equally relevant, and showing she is more than just an academic, she has published short fiction. She was president of the Society for the Study of Multi-Ethnic Literature of the United States (MELUS) from 2009 to 2012. This is certainly a good combination for the author of such a guide, and it is clear that she not only knows the field well but is also deeply engaged.

Jon Woronoff
Series Editor

Preface

This *Historical Dictionary of Asian American Literature and Theater* represents the culmination of nearly 120 years of literary achievement by the most diverse ethnic group in the United States. Diverse because this group of ethnic Americans includes those whose ancestral roots branch out to East Asia, Southeast Asia, South Asia, and Western Asia. Even within each of these regions, there exist vast differences in languages, cultures, religions, political systems, and colonial histories.

From the earliest publication in 1887 to the latest in 2011, this dictionary celebrates the incredibly rich body of fiction, poetry, memoirs, plays, and children's literature. This collection includes the editor's foreword, preface, acknowledgment, chronology, introduction, dictionary, bibliography, and information about the author.

Containing more than 600 entries, ranging from authors to genres, major terms, and subgroups, this dictionary applies the following criteria for inclusion: authors who came to the United States from Asia or who are descendants of Asian immigrants or who are of partly Asian descent; authors who have written in English; and authors who have published at least one book or produced multiple plays. Information on authors includes the person's name, date of birth and death if the person is deceased; an ethnic classification; place of birth; a brief biography of education and/or training; a list of publications and/or theatrical productions; a selection of awards, grants, fellowships, and other honors; and major themes. Of all the resource books on Asian American literature, this one offers the most comprehensive list of authors, the most extensive bibliography, and the most updated information, particularly on such emergent groups as Afghan, Cambodian, Hmong, Laotian, and Thai American writers. While I tried to make this collection as inclusive as possible, the omission of other important entries was unavoidable. For now, this edition leaves out authors whose ancestry traces back to Western Asia or the Middle East.

The dictionary represents the ongoing research and collection of materials from libraries, archives of major Asian American literary organizations, the World Wide Web, the MLA and Humanities databases, e-mails, interviews, and telephone calls. I hope that this book will be of value to librarians; teachers; high school, undergraduate, and graduate students; historians; scholars; literature lovers; Asian American community centers; and all others in need of information on Asian American literature and theater. It may hopefully lead to more detailed and specific studies by students and scholars of Asian American literary studies.

The entries in the dictionary appear alphabetically, and each entry appears in **boldface** the first time it is mentioned in an entry other than its own. Other cross-referencing is signaled by *See also*.

Acknowledgments

I am grateful to the editor, Jon Woronoff, for his guidance; my dean Dr. Coltman for her interest and support; the administrative assistant of the English Department at Florida Atlantic University, Rebecca Al-Hattab, for her assistance; my graduate research assistants in the past two years: Michael Buso, Jessica Pitts, and Tulasi Acharya for their studious work. I especially thank my family for their patience and love.

Chronology

1887 Lee Yan Phou publishes *When I Was a Boy in China*, the first Asian American autobiography in English.

1889 Sadakichi Hartmann publishes *Poems*, the first Asian American book of poetry in English.

1898 Jenichiro Oyabe publishes *A Japanese Robinson Crusoe*, the first autobiography in English by a Japanese American.

1899 Winnifred Eaton publishes the first Asian American novel *Miss Numé of Japan*, under her pseudonym, Onoto Watanna.

1902 Yone Noguchi publishes *The American Diary of a Japanese Girl*, the first Japanese American novel by a Japanese American.

1909 Edith Maude Eaton publishes "Leaves from the Mental Portfolio of a Eurasian," the first autobiography by a Chinese American woman.

1912 Edith Maude Eaton publishes "Tales of Chinese Children," the first Asian American children's stories.

1921 Philip Jaishn publishes *Hansu's Journey,* the first known fiction in English by a Korean American.

1924 Ling-Ai Li under the name of Gladys Li wrote the first Asian American play, *The Submission of Rose Moy.*

1928 Ilhan New publishes *When I Was a Boy in Korea*, the first Korean American autobiography in English. Dhan Gopal Mukerji publishes his children's book *Gay-Neck: The Story of a Pigeon,* which made him the first Asian American author to win a Newbery Medal.

1932 Kathleen Tamagawa publishes *Holy Prayers in a Horse's Ear*, the first autobiography in English by a Japanese American woman.

1933 José Garcia Villa publishes *Footnote to Youth* (1933), the first collection of short stories by a Filipino American.

1935 Lin Yutang publishes *My Country and My People*, the first Chinese American best seller.

1942 Helena Kuo publishes *I've Come a Long Way*, the first book-length autobiography by a Chinese American woman.

1945 Rama Santha Rau publishes *Home to India,* the first memoir written by a South Asian American.

1946 Carlos Bulosan publishes *America Is in the Heart*, the first Filipino American autobiography. Mine Okubo publishes *Citizen 13660*, the first picture book on the Japanese American internment experience.

1951 Shelley Ayame Nishimura Ota publishes the first Japanese American novel in English, *Upon Their Shoulders.*

1953 Monica Sone publishes *Nisei Daughter*, the first memoir on the experience of Japanese American internment.

1957 John Okada publishes *No-No Boy*, the first fiction on the experience of Japanese American internment.

1958 C. Y. Lee's novel *The Flower Drum Song* is adapted to a Broadway musical.

1964 Zulfikar Ghose publishes *The Loss of India*, the first collection of poetry by a South Asian American.

1965 The first Asian American theater group, the East West Players, is founded by Mako, et al.

1968 Bienvenido N. Santos won the American Book Award for his short story collection *The Scent of Apples*; he was the first Asian American writer to win this award.

1970 La Mama Chinatown, an Asian American theater, is funded by Ellen Stewart and led by Wu Jing-jyi and Ching Yeh.

1971 Frank Chin's *Chickencoop Chinaman* and Momoko Iko's *Gold Watch* receive the first prize in the East West Players' Playwriting Competition. Kumu Kahua (Original Stage) is founded in Honolulu, Hawaii, by a group of students at University of Hawaii and their professor, Dennis Carroll.

1973 Led by Frank Chin, the Asian American Theater Workshop is established as part of the American Conservatory Theater (ACT) in San Francisco.

1974 Frank Chin's *The Year of the Dragon* premieres at the American Place Theatre in New York City; it is the first Asian American play stage in a mainstream theater.

1975 Minfong Ho publishes *Sing to the Dawn*, the first novel by a Thai American.

1976 Maxine Hong Kingston publishes *The Woman Warrior: Memoirs of a Girlhood among Ghosts.*

1977 The Pan Asian Repertory Theatre is founded in New York City by Tisa Chang, et al.

1979 Aimee E. Liu publishes *Solitaire*, America's first memoir of anorexia.

1980 David Henry Hwang's *FOB* premieres at the Public Theater in New York City and wins an Obie Award.

1982 Quang Nhuong Huynh publishes *The Land I Lost*, the first Vietnamese American memoir.

1983 The Japan America Theatre (Los Angeles) has a grand opening. Wendy Law-Yone publishes *The Coffin Tree*, the first Burmese American novel. Ruthanne Lum McCunn publishes *Pie-Biter* and won an American Book Award, the first Asian American who wins this award for a children's book. A. K. Ramanujan wins the MacArthur Fellowship.

1987 The Northwest Asian American Theatre Company is established in Seattle. Haing S. Ngnor publishes *A Cambodian Odyssey*, the first memoir by a Cambodian American. The Association of Asian American Studies Book Award begins, and the first recipient is Wing Tek Lum for his book of poetry *Expounding the Doubtful Points*.

1988 **20 March:** David Henry Hwang's *M. Butterfly* debuts at the Eugene O'Neil Theater and wins a Tony Award for best play. The National Asian American Theatre Company in New York is founded by Richard Eng and Mia Katigbak.

1989 Phung Thi Le Ly Hayslip publishes *When Heaven and Earth Changed Places: A Vietnamese Woman's Journey from War to Peace*, the first Vietnamese American memoir by a woman. Ma-Yi Theater Company, a Filipino American theater, is founded in New York City. Teatro ng Tanan, a Filipino American theater, is founded in San Francisco. SAATh (South Asian American Theatre) is founded in Boston. Amy Tan publishes *The Joy Luck Club.* Wanwadee Larsen publishes *Confessions of a Mail Order Bride*, the first memoir by a Thai American.

1992 Theater Mu is founded in Minneapolis and St. Paul by Rick Shiomi, et al. The Pom Siab Hmoob Theatre (PSHT) is established by a group of Hmong American theater artists in Minneapolis; it later became the Center for Hmong Arts and Talent (CHAT).

1993 Cathy Song's *Picture Bride* won the Yale Younger Poet Series Award. The Club of O'Noodles, a Vietnamese American theater troupe, is founded in Los Angeles.

1995 The Asian American Repertory Theatre is founded in San Diego, California. The Society of Heritage Performers, the first Korean American performance group, is established in Los Angeles by Soon-Tek Oh.

1996 Dia Cha publishes *Dia's Story Cloth*, the first Hmong American book of memoir and stories.

1997 Lan Cao publishes *Monkey Bridge*, the first Vietnamese American novel. Han Ong wins a MacArthur fellowship, also known as the genius award. Asian American Literary Awards begin, and the first recipient is Lois-Ann Yamanaka for her novel *Blu's Hanging*. Maxine Hong Kingston receives from President Bill Clinton a National Humanities Medal from the National Endowment for the Humanities.

1998 The East West Players names its new main stage, the David Henry Hwang Theatre. Sam U Oeur publishes *Sacred Vows*, the first book of poetry by a Cambodian American. T. C. Huo publishes *A Thousand Wings*, the first novel by a Laotian American writer. Triplett Pimone publishes *Ruining the Picture*, the first book of poetry written by a Thai American. Prince Gomolvilas produces *Big Hunk O Burnin' Love*, the first play by a Thai American.

1999 Jhumpa Lahiri's short story collection *Interpreter of Maladies* wins the Pulitzer Prize for Fiction. Ha Jin wins the National Book Award for *Waiting*.

2000 Janice Mirikitani is named San Francisco's Poet Laureate.

2001 Khaled Hosseini publishes the first Afghan American novel *The Kite Runner*. The Grateful Crane Ensemble, a bilingual (English and Japanese) theater, is founded by Soji Kashiwagi in Los Angeles.

2002 Tsering Wangmo Dhompa publishes *Rules of the House,* the first Tibetan American book of poetry. Linda Sue Park wins the Newbery Medal for her children's book *A Single Shard.* Chang-rae Lee's first novel *Native Speaker* is chosen for "One Book, One New York."

2003 Bryan Thao Worra publishes *Touching Detonations*, the first book of poetry by a Laotian American. Shunya, an Indian American theater company is founded in Houston. Samrat Upadhyay publishes *The Guru of Love*, the first Nepalese American novel.

2004 Ishle Yi Park is named the third Poet Laureate of Queens, New York.

2005 Cynthia Kadohata wins the Newbery Medal for her children's book *Kira-Kira.*

2006 Gene Luen Yang publishes *American Born Chinese*, the first graphic novel to be nominated for a National Book Award. Lawson Fusao Inada is named the Poet Laureate of Oregon.

2008 Saymouka D. Vongsay publishes *No Regrets* (2008), the first collection of poetry by a Laotian American writer. Julie Shigekuni publishes *Unending Nora*, the first novel to expose the after effects of Japanese American internment on contemporary American life.

2010 Paolo Javier is named Queens' Poet Laureate, and Tina Chang is named Brooklyn's Poet Laureate. Yiyun Li wins the MacArthur Award.

Introduction

Asian Americans are a fast-growing group in the United States. According to the 2010 U.S. Census, 15.5 million Americans claim to be of Asian descent or multiracial Asians, and this figure constitutes 5 percent of the U.S. total population. Asian American literature is one of the most recent forms of ethnic literature and is already becoming one of the most prominent, given the large number of writers, the growing ethnic population from the region, the general receptivity of this body of work, and the quality of the authors. In recent decades, there has been an exponential growth in their output, and much Asian American literature has now achieved new levels of popular success and critical acclaim. Nurtured by rich and long literary traditions from the vast continent called Asia, this literature is poised between the ancient and the modern, between the East and the West, and between the oral and the written.

Asian America is a broad term covering many different strands, ranging from East Asia (China, Japan, and Korea) to Southeast Asia (Burma, Cambodia, Laos, the Philippines, Nepal, Thailand, and Vietnam), to South Asia (Afghanistan, Bangladesh, India, Pakistan, Nepal, and Sri Lanka), and to Western Asia or the Middle East (which is not included in this collection). Asian American authors may be immigrants, American born to immigrant parents, or adopted from these regions. Some authors are third, fourth, and, fifth generation Asian Americans while others are biracial or multiethnic.

Although the concept of Asian America seems clear, Asian American literature is not self-explanatory. Debates on what kinds of writing and what authors should be named Asian American have raised several important issues. The editors of the first anthology of Asian American literature *Aiiieeeee!* (1974) define Asian Americans as "Filipino–, Chinese–, and Japanese–Americans, American born and raised, who got their China and Japan from the radio, off the silver screen, from television, out of comic books . . ."[1] Elaine Kim tried to rid the concept of Asian Americans of their American birth by redefining Asian American literature as "published creative writings in English by Americans of Chinese, Japanese, Korean, and Filipino descent."[2] Her definition sparked further debate regarding the Asian American subject and media: Should Asian American literature depict only the American experience? Could it be written in other languages? For the fact remains that many

Asian immigrant writers have written about the "old" and "new" worlds in dual languages. In addition to these perplexing issues, contentions also have centered on who represents Asian America and what groups within it are underrepresented. With over 60 different Asian subgroups today in the United States, it is not an exaggeration to say that a Korean American is as different from a Filipino American as a French person from a Mexican. Given their different colonial pasts and religions, immigrants from Asia also speak from radically different memories and sensibilities.

Until the mid-1990s, Chinese, Japanese, and Filipino American writers and critics dominated Asian American literature and its studies, for they were the most established groups in America at that time. In response to protests by the underrepresented groups, *Position* published a special issue in the fall of 1997, edited by Elaine Kim and Lisa Lowe. It calls for "the creation and maintenance of solidarity across racial and national boundaries."[3] This issue of *Position* marked a shift from the dominance of a largely East Asian American literature to a Pan-Asian American literature, making space for a heterogeneous set of voices by recent emigrants from South and Southeast Asia. The new direction of Asian American literary studies not only attempts to include all ethnicities within Asian America but also to explode national boundaries to include diasporic writers in the Pacific Rim.

Asian American literature, beginning as a protest against socioeconomic discrimination and marginalization, political alienation, and cultural stereotypes, often draws its materials from the rich and troubled history that Asian Americans have lived—their participation in the construction of the transcontinental railroad and the building of an economy in California and Hawaii, their legalized exclusion and internment, their social and cultural marginalization in America, and their reflections on the colonial histories of their home countries. Cognizant of these histories, Asian American literature investigates some common questions, such as What does it mean to be an American? At what cost does one become an American? How does one recognize oneself as a racial minority? What does the hyphenated identity mean? Questions of this sort determine the shared themes in Asian American literature of ethnicity, Americanization, racialization, homeland, gender and class exploitation, sexuality, generation gap, the common misperception of Asian Americans as permanent aliens, etc. Some of these themes exercise some of the writers more than others.

The first known Asian American work was written by the Chinese American Lee Yan Phou, whose memoir *When I Was a Boy in China* (1887) attempted to present the rich and intricate Chinese culture, customs, and tradition. A student among the first group sent by the Chinese government to America, Lee graduated from Yale University. In his graduation address he remarked, "By passing a discriminating law against an already persecuted class, the Central Government [the U.S. government] yielded to the demands of the mob, and to that extent countenanced its violence and lawlessness."[4] The mainstream reading public knew little about Asian American writers, and it was not until 1976 when Maxine Hong Kingston published *The Woman Warrior*, which won multiple awards including the National Book Critic's Circle Award, that Asian American literature became prominent. Bill Moyer in his *A World of Ideas* remarks that Kingston's *Woman Warrior* and *China Men* were the most widely taught books by a living American author in the 1980s. However, it was David Henry Hwang's Tony Award–winning play *M. Butterfly* (1988) and Amy Tan's bestselling novel *Joy Luck Club* (1989) that thrust Asian American literature into the consciousness of the general public.

EAST ASIAN AMERICANS

The earliest Asian immigrants to America came from the Pacific coastline of China. Chinese sailors first came to Hawaii in 1778, the same year that Captain James Cook came upon the island. Many settled and married Hawaiian women. Some Island-born Chinese can claim to be seventh generation. Around 1785, individual Chinese are reported in Pennsylvania, and, by 1848, there were 325 Chinese in the United States. However, the Chinese began to arrive in significant numbers in response to the California gold rush of 1849 and to escape the Taiping Rebellion at home. Rather than becoming wealthy, most of the immigrants struggled to survive by building the transcontinental railroad and later by working in the crop fields and fisheries. The racism toward the Chinese from the settled European population culminated in massacres and forced relocations of Chinese migrants into what became known as Chinatowns. The anti-Chinese sentiment was so strong that the federal government passed on 6 May 1882 the first piece of legislation that singled out a nationality to bar from immigration, and this bill is known as the Chinese Exclusion Act, which ended the first wave of Chinese migration.

Between 1849 and 1882, nearly 300,000 Chinese entered the United States. Most of these early Chinese immigrants were men who practiced Confucianism, Buddhism and ancestral worship, spoke Cantonese, and answered to an imperial court. Their pigtail, an enforced custom in China of the ruling ethnic minority, the Manchurians, signified loyalty to the emperor, and a man would suffer death without it. After 1882, the Chinese population began to dwindle due to death, departures, and deportation. Chinatowns became aging bachelor societies with an increasingly conservative culture. Only one documented Chinese American writer published in English during this period—Lee Yan

Phou as mentioned above. However, some critics argue that Asian American literature began in the early 20th century with two Eurasian sisters—Edith Maude and Winnifred Eaton, who were born to a Chinese mother and a British father but took different literary paths. While Edith embraced her mother's ethnicity by using the pen name of Sui Sin Far and writing about the Chinese, the younger sister Winnifred chose to "pass" as half Japanese and half English, using the pen name of Onoto Watanna and focusing on the subject of biracial romance between Japanese women and Caucasian men. Sui Sin Far's *Mrs. Spring Fragrance* (1912) was a collection of linked short stories about Chinese Americans in California, and her sympathetic portrayal of the characters countered the prevalent stereotypes that dehumanized and caricaturized the Chinese immigrants. Following Sui Sin Far's work are Lin Yutang's memoir *My Country and My People* (1935), Chiang Yee's travelogue *The Silent Traveler: A Chinese Artist in Lakeland* (1937), and Helena Kuo's autobiography *I've Come a Long Way* (1942).

In 1943, the Chinese Exclusion Act was repealed because China became an American ally in World War II. The War Bride Act of 1945 further widened the door to emigration from Asia. The second wave of Chinese migration, consisting of a large number of women and children, changed the demographics of Chinatowns; families began to emerge and communities were forged. The Immigration and Nationality Act of 1965 abolished the National Origins Formula that had been in place in the United States since the Immigration Act of 1924, and this bill brought Chinese immigrants in even greater numbers. Hailing from China, Hong Kong, Indonesia, Malaysia, Singapore, and Taiwan, these new citizens-to-be were far from being homogeneous. Those who came from China carried traumatic memories of the Japanese occupation (1937–1941), the civil war (1941–1949), the Anti-Rightist Campaign (1957–1959), and the Cultural Revolution (1966–1976). The Chinese from Hong Kong, Malaysia, and Singapore, sharing a similar British colonial history, often speak fluent English in addition to such southern dialects as Hokkien, Haka, and Cantonese while the Chinese from Indonesia, a Dutch colony, speak these southern dialects as well as Indonesian. The Chinese from Indonesia came to the United States to escape anti-Chinese discrimination and violence. Those from Taiwan are of two distinct groups—the indigenous Taiwanese who often reject being labeled Chinese and consider themselves colonized by Chinese exiles from Mainland China and the Chinese who escaped to Taiwan because of the Chinese Communist takeover in 1949.

A great number of Chinese American writers broke onto the literary scene during these decades. Pardee Lowe and Alice Lin wrote autobiographies while others wrote fiction, such as Chin-Yang Lee and Monfoon Leong.

Most of their writing paints a portrait of Chinese Americans as hard working, disciplined, and law abiding, in other words, model minorities. The best example is Jade Snow Wong's *Fifth Chinese Daughter* (1945), a bestselling autobiography that focuses on the tension between Chinese and American values and expresses the author's admiration for American individualism and competitiveness.

The Civil Rights Movement in the 1960s nurtured a new generation of Chinese American authors who are politically conscious on matters of citizenship, race, and gender. Writers such as Frank Chin, Marilyn Chin, Maxine Hong Kingston, Amy Tan, Gish Jen, David Henry Wang, Eleanor Wong Telemaque, Shawn Wong, and Laurence Yep demonstrate ethnic pride as they recount and redefine the Chinese American experience.

In 1979, the U.S. government officially recognized the People's Republic of China, after which the third wave of migration began with a heavy exodus of graduate students, scholars, and professionals. Many of them benefited from the Chinese Student Protection Act of 1992, which granted permanent residency status to emigrants from China in response to the Tiananmen Events in June 1989.

The blossoming of Chinese American literature beginning in the late 1970s has produced a cornucopia of talented writers and fascinating works. Not only do they continue the investigation of enduring themes of ethnic identity, community, immigration, gender, and racism, but they also explore broad and universal themes of nature, memory, and language as practiced by such poets as Mei-mei Berssenbrugge, Alex Kuo, Li-Young Lee, and John Yau. The youngest group of Chinese American writers has become greatly diverse and individually oriented in terms of themes, genres, styles, and sensibilities. For the first time, genre fiction, such as detective fiction, science fiction, and fairytales, by authors like Henry Chang, Da Chen, Ted Chiang, Ed Lin, Xiaolong Qiu, Charles Yu, Kenneth Lin, and Aimee Liu, has become a part of Chinese American literature. Biracial or multiracial Chinese American writers, such as Sarah Shun Lien Bynum, Ruthanne Lum McCunn, Sigrid Nunez, Paisley Rekdal, and Thaddeus Rutkowski, explore themes of mixed-race identity, but often ethnicity is not their concern at all. Still others choose to transcend their own ethnicity by portraying characters of other ethnicities, such as Diana Chang, Eugenie Chan, and Kenneth Lin. One of the exciting phenomena in the recent development of Chinese American literature is the infusion of talents from Hong Kong, Taiwan, and Mainland China, persons who immigrated in the 1980s and 1990s. Such writers as Jean Kwok, Raymond K. Wong, Mingmei Yip, Victoria Chang, Justina Chen, Jeffrey Ethan Lee, Ha Jin, Yiyun Li, Anchee Min, Fan Wu, Wang Pin, and Geling Yan have diversified and strengthened Chinese American literature.

The history of Japanese immigration began in the early 19th century with survivors of shipwrecks brought to Hawaii and California. However, the actual current of immigration started in 1885 when 676 men, 159 women, and 108 children from Japan arrived in Honolulu on board the Pacific Mail passenger freighter *City of Tokio*. These immigrants, the first of many to Hawaii, came to work on the sugar plantations in response to an assisted passage program from the Hawaiian government. It is not surprising that as of 1900 the majority of the Japanese immigrants in the United States lived in Hawaii. Between 1885 and 1894, over 28,000 Japanese migrated to Hawaii, the vast majority of them being single men. Anticipating the legislation of American laws against contract labor to Hawaii in 1900, after the American takeover of the islands, Hawaiian plantation owners in 1899 brought more than 26,000 contract laborers from Japan in order to beat the ban—the largest number ever admitted in a single year. The contracts were then voided under American laws, however, leaving thousands of Japanese free to migrate to the West Coast of the U.S mainland.

After the Chinese Exclusion Act of 1882, American business owners sought the Japanese to replace the Chinese. In 1907, the "Gentlemen's Agreement" between the governments of Japan and the United States ended immigration of Japanese workers, but permitted the immigration of spouses of Japanese already in the United States. Japanese immigrants speak various dialects of Japanese, and the majority of them practiced Buddhism. Although Japanese immigrants during this period faced less racism and discrimination than the Chinese immigrants, they were subject to racist legislation such as the California Alien Land Law of 1913 that banned Japanese from purchasing land. The Immigration Act of 1924 banned the immigration of all but a token few Japanese. Significant Japanese immigration did not occur again until the Immigration and Nationality Act of 1965 ended 40 years of bans against emigration from Asia.

The ancestor of Japanese American literature is a Eurasian. Sadakichi Hartmann, born to a Japanese mother and a German father, published *Poems* in 1889, which was the first Asian American book of poetry in English. Following him are Jenichiro Oyabe, who authored the first Japanese American autobiography *A Japanese Robinson Crusoe* (1898), and Yone Noguchi, who published *The American Diary of a Japanese Girl* (1902), the first novel by a Japanese American. The earliest Japanese American women writers hail from Hawaii: Kathleen Tamagawa, a Eurasian, published *Holy Prayers in a Horse's Ear* (1932), the first Japanese American woman's autobiography, and Shelley Ayame Nishimura Ota, a second generation Japanese American, wrote *Upon Their Shoulders* (1951), the first novel by a Japanese American woman. Other than these two, all early women writers in English are first generation immigrants such as Jun Fujita, Ayako Tanaka Ishigaki, and Etsu Inagaki Sugimoto. This generation of Japanese American writers is credited with the introduction of such Japanese poetic forms as *haiku* and *tanka* into American literature. The strong presence of women in early Japanese American literature, which is not true in early Chinese and Filipino American writings, is largely due to the fact that the Page Act of 1875 prohibited the immigration of Chinese and Filipino women but allowed the entry of Japanese women. Today, Japanese Americans are the sixth largest group among Asian Americans at roughly 1.2 million, including those of mixed-race or mixed-ethnicity.

The single most important event in Japanese American history that has become a focal point for numerous writers is the Japanese American Internment. Responding to the Japanese airstrike at Pearl Harbor on 7 December 1941, President Franklin Delano Roosevelt signed Executive Order 9066 on 19 February 1942, which authorized the secretary of war and U.S. armed forces commanders to declare areas of the United States as military zones "from which any or all persons may be excluded." Although it did not specify a nationality or ethnic group, it was swiftly applied to one-third of the land area of the United States (mostly in the West) and was used against those with "foreign enemy ancestry"—Japanese and Koreans (since Korea was occupied by Japan during World War II). Thus began the internment program. Over the course of the war, approximately 110,000 Japanese Americans and Japanese who lived on the West Coast of the United States were uprooted from their homes and sent to concentration camps in such inland states as Arizona, Colorado, Texas, Idaho, North Dakota, New Mexico, and Montana. Between 1942 and 1945, about 120,000 Japanese and Japanese Americans on the mainland as well as Hawaii were interned on the grounds of national security.

The internment experience has been so traumatic to the Japanese American community that its writers maintained a near silence on the subject for over three decades. However, a few young artists refused to keep their silence. Mine Okubo, a practicing artist at the time she was sent to the camp, published her picture book *Citizen 13660* (1946) that documented with sketches and narratives her life in the camp. It took another seven years before Monica Sone published her memoir *Nisei Daughter* (1953) depicting her life before, during, and after the internment. John Okata wrote the first novel on this subject *No-No Boy* (1957), portraying the experience from a young man's point of view. This powerful novel, released in a small quantity by the Tokyo branch of Charles Tuttle, received little attention. Not until it was chanced upon by Jeffrey Chan in a second-hand bookstore in San Francisco and reprinted in 1976 with the donation of a group of Asian American writers (including Frank Chin, Shawn Wong, Jeffrey Chan, and Lawson Inada) that it became a classic in Asian American literature.

The internment experience has so dominated the literary imagination of Japanese Americans that it organizes their literature and theater into two groups—those who write about this experience and those who do not. The first group, mostly nisei and sansei writers, such as Hisaye Yamamoto, Monica Sone, Jeanne Wakatsuki Houston, Yoshiko Uchida, David Mura, Keiho Soga, and Julie Otsuka, portrayed the internment experiences in memoirs, fiction, poetry, and theater. Depicting its aftermath are numerous writers, including John Okada, Mitsuye Yamada, Momoko Iko, Lonny Kaneko, Toshio Mori, Garrett Hongo, Lawson Inada, and Janice Mirikitani. Contrary to their contemporaries on the mainland, nisei writers in Hawaii, however, found it easier to explore Japanese American history and identity in the immediate postwar years without the burden of the internment experience, such as Patsy Sumie Saiki, Milton Murayama, and Lois-Ann Yamanaka.

The past three decades have witnessed the emergence of new sensibilities and aesthetics in Japanese American literature, in which writers explore multiple themes unrelated to the internment experience. Writers like Cynthia Kadohata, Velina Hasu Houston, Karen Tei Yamashita, Ruth Ozeki, and Rick Noguchi portray Japanese American characters wrestling with issues ranging from gender and sexuality to environment. Many contemporary Japanese American writers, biracial or not, choose to transcend the concerns of race and ethnicity, such as Brian Komei Dempster, Kimiko Hahn, Maeshima Yukihide Hartman, Naomi Iizuka, Rahna Reiko Rizzuto, Lee Ann Roripaugh, and Brandon Shimoda. Still others, such as Dale Furutani, Naomi Hirahara, Dwight Okita, and Gail Tsukiyama, have gone on to write genre fiction like mysteries, science fiction, historical novels, etc.

Korean American history traces back to 1882 when the U.S. government signed a treaty of peace, friendship, and commerce with Korea, allowing each country to establish a diplomatic mission in the other's territory. Initially, a small number of Koreans began to arrive in the United States as diplomats, political exiles, merchants, or students. Korean immigration took off when the SS *Gaelic* landed in Honolulu on 13 January 1903, carrying 56 men, 21 women, and 25 children. Like the Japanese immigrants to Hawaii, the Koreans were brought as contract laborers to work on sugar plantations. This was a solution for the labor shortage that occurred after the Chinese and Japanese were banned from entry. Between 1904 and 1907, about 1,000 Koreans entered the mainland from Hawaii through San Francisco. Many Koreans dispersed along the Pacific coast as farm workers or as wage laborers in mining companies and as section hands on the railroads. This first wave of immigration saw roughly 7,500 people arrive from Korea, most of them being single males.

The Immigration Act of 1924 was part of a measured system excluding Asian immigrants into the United States. From 1924 to 1953, very few Koreans came to the United States. The second wave of migration began when the Korean War ended in 1953; a large group of immigrants consisting of wives of U.S. servicemen and Korean adoptees entered the United States. With the passage of the Immigration and Nationality Act of 1965, Koreans became one of the fastest growing Asian groups in the United States, surpassed only by Filipinos. Among them are about 100,000 Korean adoptees raised by White American families. The Korean American community boasts about 1.6 million people, comprising about 0.5 percent of the U.S. population and is the fifth largest Asian American subgroup. Korean Americans speak Korean and English and practice Christianity or Buddhism, with 70 to 80 percent of them identifying as Christians.

The first pioneer in Korean American literature is Philip Jaishn, whose novel *Hansu's Journey* (1921) marked the beginning of a rich literary tradition. Predictably, the majority of early Korean American writing is autobiographical done by the first generation of Korean immigrants, who were mostly male and Western-educated, writers such as Ilhan New and No-Young Park. Some of these autobiographers were either born in Hawaii like Peter Hyun or immigrated to Hawaii such as Easurk Emsen Charr. What makes early Korean American literature different from early Chinese American literature is the presence of women writers in this first generation. Writers such as Margaret K. Pai and Mary Paik Lee resided in Hawaii since the Gentleman's Agreement allowed Korean immigrants to bring their wives. Among the first generation of Korean American writers, Younghill Kang is the best known, whose autobiographical novel *The Grass Roof* (1931) received considerable publicity.

Among the second generation of Korean American writers, the best-known figure is a woman writer Theresa Hak Kyung Cha, whose only novel *Dictée* (1982), regarded as one of the most challenging texts in Asian American literature, sets the path for postmodern and postcolonial exploration of experiences of Koreans and Korean Americans. Other notable figures in this second generation include Ik Yong Kim, Gary Pak, Ty Pak, Sook Nyul Choi, Richard Kim, and Ronyoung Kim. The Japanese occupation and American colonization of Korea preoccupy many of these writers' imaginations. Wars continue to dominate the subjects of the third generation, many of whom are American born. While some writers tell stories about "comfort women" during World War II, such as Nora Okja Keller and the most celebrated Korean American writer Chang-rae Lee, many others such as Kwock Suji Kim, Heinz Insu Fenkle, and Walter Lew meditate on the divided state of Korea, children orphaned by the war, and biracial children because of the American military presence in South Korea.

At the turn of the 21st century, Korean American literature witnessed the emergence of numerous accomplished novelists, poets, and dramatists, and their works have reached a broad readership and audience and won mainstream awards. Most of these writers are American born such as Na An, Leonard Chang, Alexander Chee, Susan Choi, Patricia Jang, Susan Kim, Don Lee, Ed Park, and Youngsoo Park. Some of the best or most interesting poets in Asian American literature are Korean Americans like Myung Mi Kim, Cathy Song, Jason Koo, Ed Bok Lee, Juliette Sueyeun Lee, Walter K. Lew, Sun Yung Shin, and Mia Yun.

East Asian American theaters are less distinct from each other. The earliest theaters were organized by the joint effort of Chinese and Japanese American artists and playwrights, and they are the most established theaters in Asian American literature. The East West Players was the first Asian American theater, founded in Los Angeles in 1965 while the Asian Exclusion Act was founded by Garrett Hongo in 1975 in Seattle, which was renamed in 1981 as the Northwest Asian American Theatre Company. In 1975, Ping Chong launched Ping Chong & Company. The Pan Asian Repertory Theater was founded in 1999 in New York City and led by artistic director Tisa Chang. The Asian American Theater Company was established in 1979 in San Francisco. Its previous form was the Asian American Theater Workshop, under the artistic directorship of Frank Chin. David Henry Hwang Writers' Institute was created in 1991 by David Henry Hwang in collaboration with the East West Players. It provides writing classes to promote new Asian American work for the stage. Chinese American theaters together with other Asian American theaters have flourished in the past four decades. Korean American theater has been incorporated into these theaters mentioned above. The theater focusing on Korean American plays is the Lodestone Theatre Ensemble. The Young Jean Lee Theater Company, although founded by a Korean American playwright, does not regard its mission to be promoting Korean American theater alone. There are a few performance troupes that feature Korean music and dance such as Shinmyung Pae.

SOUTHEAST ASIAN AMERICANS

Among Southeast Asian Americans, the earliest immigrants came from the Philippines. In 1763, Filipino sailors who deserted Spanish ships began their settlement at Saint Malo in the bayous of Louisiana, as recorded by a journalist in *Harper's Weekly* in 1883. Significant Filipino immigration to the United States, however, did not begin until the 1900s, after the Spanish–American War when the Philippines became a U.S. colony, thus Filipinos became U.S.

nationals. Unlike other Asians barred from entry, Filipinos as U.S. nationals were free to migrate, and most of them went to Hawaii and California. They were engaged mainly in agricultural work. During this wave of migration, Filipino men outnumbered women by about 15 to 1.

The Tydings–McDuffie Act of 1934, also known as the Philippine Independence Act, in granting the Philippines independence, classified Filipinos as aliens. Accordingly, only 50 persons were allowed to enter the United States each year. However, this was offset by the U.S. Navy's recruitment of Filipinos. The War Brides Act of 1945 and the subsequent Alien Fiancées and Fiancés Act of 1946 allowed veterans to return home to bring back fiancées, wives, and children. In the years following the war, about 16,000 Filipinos entered the United States. These new immigrants enabled the formation of Filipino American communities around U.S. Navy bases, whose impact can still be seen today. Filipino American communities were also settled near Army and Air Force bases. In 1946, the Filipino Naturalization Act allowed for naturalization and citizenship for Filipinos who had arrived before March 1943.

After the passing of the Immigration and Nationality Act of 1965, Filipinos arrived in considerable numbers, and this continues to the present day. Roughly 20,000 immigrants come from the Philippines annually, and many of them are professionals such as doctors, lawyers, nurses, engineers, and the military. This is often referred to as "the brain drain." Filipino Americans speak multiple languages including Tagalog, Ilocano, Kapampangan, Pangasinan, Visayan languages, and Bicolano. In addition, an overwhelming majority of Filipino Americans are fluent in English, since it is one of the official languages in the Philippines. Because of 300 years of Spanish colonization, the majority of Filipino Americans are Roman Catholics.

Filipino American literature has been more transnational than other Asian American literatures, because the distinction between Filipino and Filipino American writers is blurred due to the effects of American colonization of the Philippines (1898–1946), which have made the use of English and nomadic life between the two countries common to many writers. This is true particularly with the first generation of writers, whose writings many critics prefer to call "Filipino English literature" rather than Filipino American literature. These pioneers include Jose Garcia Villa, Bienvenido Santos, Carlos A. Angeles, N. V. M. Gonzalez, and Alberto S. Florentino. Although writing at the same time period, Carlos Bulosan is an exception as all his writings were published in the United States. Jose Garcia Villa's short story collection *Footnote to Youth* (1933), the first publication among these pioneers, centers on the lives of young Filipinos in the rural Philippines. Bulosan's autobiographical novel *America Is in the Heart* (1946), however, is the best-known text from this period. It recounts Bulosan's aspirations, friendships, hardships, and success.

The second generation of Filipino American writers is better known to American readers, as several of them have been published by mainstream presses. Among them, Peter Bacho and Jessica Hagedorn are the most visible figures. Filipino American writers emerged in the 1970s, such as Ninotchta Rosca, Linda Ty-Casper, and Cecilia Manguerra Brainard, whose feminist historical fiction aligned Filipina American writing with other U.S. minority women writers such as Maxine Hong Kingston and Toni Morrison. These writers often explore the sensibilities of a nomadic existence, best captured by Jessica Hagedorn's line in her novel *Dogeaters* (1990) that she is "at home only in airports." Rosca's novel *Twice Blessed* (1992) won an American Book Award. The youngest generation of Filipino American writers is mostly born in the United States. Their works are highly diverse in genres and themes. This generation includes well-known novelists like Rick Barot and Zamora Linmark; poets such as Nick Carbo, Ferrer Vincente Gotera, Virginia Cerenio, and Sarah Gambito; and playwrights such as Jennie Baroga, Louella Dizon, Linda Faigao-Hall, Paul Stephen Lim, and Han Ong, who won the prestigious MacArthur Award. Several writers have pursued a multigenred career, such as Marisa De Los Santos and Eileen Tabios.

Filipino American theater did not emerge until the latter half of the 20th century. One of the first playwrights, Jeannie Baroga, has written more than 50 plays, including *Eye of the Coconut* and *Walls*. Jessica Hagedorn started creating multimedia theater pieces in experimental performance venues with her *Mango Tango* and *Tenement Lovers*. Other notable playwrights of Filipino descent include Alberto S. Florentino, Linda Faigao-Hall, Rey A. Pamatmat, Ralph B. Peña, and Han Ong. Ma-Yi Theater Company in New York established its reputation through producing Filipino American work. Other important Filipino American ensembles include San Francisco's Teatro Ng Tanan, Blindlestiff Studio, Tongue in a Mood, Kularts, Pintig Cultural Group in Chicago, Kinding Sindaw, and QBD Ink of Washington, D.C.

The history of Vietnamese immigration to the United States is very recent. Prior to 1975, most Vietnamese residing in the United States were spouses and children of American servicemen in Vietnam. The first wave of immigrants began with "the fall of Saigon" on 30 April 1975, which ended the Vietnam War. The year 1975 alone saw 125,000 Vietnamese leave their native country for U.S. military bases in Guam, Thailand, Wake Island, Hawaii, and the Philippines as part of "Operation New Life." Subsequently, they were transferred to four refugee centers in the United States: Camp Pendleton in California, Fort Chaffee in Arkansas, Eglin Air Force Base in Florida, and

Fort Indiantown Gap in Pennsylvania. The Indochina Migration and Refugee Act of 1975 established a program of domestic resettlement assistance for refugees who fled from Cambodia and Vietnam.

Beginning in 1977, more Vietnamese were fleeing their country because of the hardship and fear created by the country's Communist programs. Approximately two million Vietnamese fled their country in small, overcrowded boats, and they would come to be known as the "boat people." Most of them spent time in refugee camps in Thailand, Malaysia, Singapore, Indonesia, the Philippines, or Hong Kong while waiting to be accepted by foreign countries. To assist Vietnamese refugees, Congress passed the Refugee Act of 1980, which reduced restrictions on entry to the United States. The Refugee Act created the Office of Refugee Resettlement, set the number of refugee admissions at 50,000 per year (except in cases of emergency), and allowed a refugee to become a permanent resident after one year and a U.S. citizen after four more years. In addition, laws were also passed to allow children of American servicemen and former political prisoners to enter the United States. In total, the United States accepted 531,310 refugees and asylum seekers from Vietnam between 1981 and 2000.

Like other Asian American literary traditions, the earliest Vietnamese American writers wrote autobiographies or memoirs. Their works describe their experience of the war and the refugee camps. After the first memoirist Quang Nhuong Huynh published *The Land I Lost* (1982), a series of Vietnamese American memoirs followed, including Phung Thi Le Ly Hayslip's *When Heaven and Earth Changed Places*, Jade Ngoc Quang Huynh's *South Wind Changing*, Quang X. Pham's *A Sense of Duty: My Father, My American Journey*, Nguyen Thi Thu-Lam's *Fall Leaves*, and Nguyen Qui Duc's *Where the Ashes Are.* The younger generation of Vietnamese American writers were either born in the United States or came as young children. Most of them write fiction, poetry, and plays, and their common themes include war, memory, ethnicity, sexuality, and colonialism. Among them are the well known Lan Cao, Linh Dinh, Bich Minh Nguyen, Monique Truong, Hoa Nguyen, and Le Thi Diem Thuy. A number of Vietnamese American writers are biracial and explore themes of biraciality, mixed race, or universal themes like language, nature, and love. Among them are Maura Nguyen Donohue, Tina Brown Celona, and Kim-An Lieberman.

Vietnamese American theater is still in its budding stage. The Club O'Noodles is the only Vietnamese American troupe, featuring comedy, music, and dance. The Playwright Qui Nguyen directs the Obie Award–winning Vampire Cowboys Theatre Company, whose productions are penned and choreographed by him. However, Vampire Cowboys Theatre produces action drama that may or may not be related to Asian American themes. In Mixed

Company is a theater company founded by Vietnamese American playwright Maura Nguyen Donohue in New York City in 1995, which produces plays that portray identity issues and celebrate fluid identities.

Other than Vietnamese and Filipino Americans, Southeast Asian Americans also include those who trace their ancestral roots to Burma, Cambodia, Laos, Indonesia, Malaysia, Singapore, and Thailand. The most recent literary voices among Asian American literature are from this region. The Vietnam War impacted the neighboring countries of Cambodia and Laos, and a Communist takeover occurred simultaneously in all three countries when the United States withdrew in 1975. The consequence of this historical change was a significant number of refugees temporarily sheltered in other Southeast Asian countries and the eventual migration of many to the United States.

Between 1975 and 2000s, about 150,000 Cambodians settled in the United States under the Refugee Assistance Act of 1975 and the Refugee Act of 1980. Large communities of Cambodian Americans have taken root in cities such as Long Beach, Fresno, and Stockton in California, Providence, Rhode Island, as well as Lynn and Lowell in Massachusetts, and Seattle and Portland in the Pacific Northwest. The first Cambodian American who published a literary work is Sam U Oeur, whose book of poetry *Sacred Vows* (1998) recounts Cambodian history and his personal tribulations, drawing on Cambodian myths, folktales, and prophecies. Other writers to follow include memoirists such as Chanrithy Him, Haing S. Ngor, and Loung Ung, and authors of children's books such as Huy Voun Lee.

The writings by Laotian and Hmong Americans also reflect the history of the Vietnam War and the pain of transplantation, and they are among the most engaging literary voices in the 2000s. Bryan Thao Worra is the best-known Laotian American poet, whose poetry explores themes of transience, identity, memory, and home. T. C. Huo's novel *Land of Smiles* traces the life of a Laotian boy from swimming across the Mekong River to Thailand to arriving at San Francisco to returning to Laos. Young poets like Pos Moua, Mali Phonpadith, and Saymoukda D. Vongsay were children when they came to the United States, and their poetry depicts their voyages from war-torn Laos to America and expresses their longing for the homeland—its rivers, oceans, and mountains. Ova Saopeng is the cocreator of *Refugee Nation,* a play about the Laotian American experience, based on the stories of the Lao communities across the United States.

A subgroup of Laotian Americans is Hmong American. During the 1960s and 1970s, a Hmong secret army was formed and trained by the Central Intelligence Agency (CIA) to fight against the Communist army of Vietnam. In 1975 when the United States withdrew from Vietnam and the Communists took over Laos, a large number of Hmongs escaped to Thailand, and most of them gradually immigrated to the United States. They settled in California, Minnesota, and Wisconsin. Dia Cha is the first Hmong American memoirist, and her *Dia's Story Cloth* is a picture book that retells her life story, Hmong history, and a classic American immigration tale. Some of the Hmong American writers carry their traumatic memories of the war and refugee camps while others born in the refugee camps or in the United States, such as May Lee-Yang, Kao Kalia Yang, and Burlee Vang, inherited memories of the war, the escape, and the refugee camps, and these memories have been reorganized into memoirs, poetry, and drama. Ka Vang is a well-known journalist and playwright, whose plays, *Disconnect*, *Dead Calling*, and *From Shadows to Light*, influenced the younger playwrights, one of whom is May Lee-Yang, famous for her *Confessions of a Lazy Hmong Woman*.

The only Burmese American writer in this dictionary is Wendy Law-Yone, whose three novels, *The Coffin Tree*, *Irrawaddy Tango*, and *The Road to Wanting,* explore themes of alienation, exile, and madness. Writers tracing their root to Indonesia are small in number as well. The most prominent figure is Li-young Lee, who was born in Indonesia to Chinese parents. Most of the writers from Singapore and Malaysia are also Chinese or partly Chinese, for instance Shirley Geok-lin Lim, Chay Yew, Justin Chin, Wena Poon, and Tinling Choong.

Unlike the above groups, Thai Americans have experienced a different history that is not colonial or war-ridden. Thus, they focus on themes of cultural conflicts, assimilation, ethnic identity, gender, and sexuality. The first Thai American writer is Minfong Ho, and other prominent Thai American writers include Ira Sukrungruang, Pimone Triplett, Rattawut Lapcharoensap, Cherry Chevapravatdumrong, and Prince Gomolvilas.

SOUTH ASIAN AMERICANS

South Asian Americans are the fastest growing and the third largest subgroup of Asian Americans, following the Chinese and Filipino Americans. In this subgroup, 95 percent are immigrants from India and Pakistan, and the other 5 percent include people from Bangladesh, Sri Lanka, Nepal, and Afghanistan. Over 2.8 million Americans claimed Asian Indian descent according to the 2010 U.S. Census. As early as the 1790s, there is evidence of Indian sailors and adventurers settling in the United States. Between 1904 and 1911, 6,100 Indians immigrated to the United States, living almost exclusively on the West Coast. Many were Punjabi Sikhs who had first immigrated to western Canada but found work in lumber mills and railway construction in California and the Pacific Northwest. In 1834, when Great Britain abolished slavery in its empire, Indians became a major labor supply. Between 1834 and 1934, about 30 million Indians indentured themselves for terms of labor, creating an Indian diaspora in such countries as Mauritius, Malaysia, Singapore, South Africa, Suriname, Guyana, Fiji, Kenya, Tanzania, Uganda, Trinidad, and Jamaica. After the Luce–Celler Act of 1946, when Indian Americans were granted naturalization rights in the United States, a significant number of Indians arrived in America from this diaspora.

The largest flux of Indian immigrants came after the Immigration Act of 1965. Unlike the Punjabis, this wave of Indian immigrants included highly educated professionals, such as doctors and engineers, who came to pursue educational or occupational opportunities. Unlike other immigrant groups who were quickly marginalized from mainstream American society, the Indians arriving at this time were embraced because of their professional success. Since then, the Indian immigrants have steadily increased in number. According to the 2010 U.S. Census, the Indian population in the United States enjoys a growth of 69.37 percent, the highest for any Asian American community, and among the fastest growing ethnic group in the country.

The second largest subgroup of South Asian immigrants is Pakistanis. Between 1947 and 1965, only 2,500 Pakistani immigrants entered the United States; most of them were students who chose to settle in the United States after graduating from American universities. This marked the beginning of a distinct Pakistani community in America. After 1965, the number of Pakistanis immigrating to the United States increased dramatically. In 1990, the U.S. Census Bureau indicated that there were about 100,000 Pakistani Americans, and, by 2005, their population had grown to 210,000. The largest concentrations of Pakistani Americans are in New York City, Chicago, Philadelphia, and Los Angeles.

Bangladeshi Americans have a longer history than Pakistani Americans. As early as 1887, Bengali immigrants began arriving in the United States, though their numbers remained small due to discriminatory legislation. Some were Hindu and Muslim activists who fled following the British partition of the region into Hindu and Muslim zones in 1905. Almost all early immigrants were single men, and many of them married Mexican or mixed-race women. During the first wave of immigration following independence in 1971, most immigrants were well-educated professionals, fleeing the political turmoil of their country and frequently being granted refugee status. During the early 1990s, the number of Bangladeshi immigrants increased during the peak of 1991, with more than a 1,000 annually.

Significant Sri Lankan immigration to the United States did not occur until the 1950s and even then remained small. In 1980 the Sri Lankan American population was less than 200. As the civil war in Sri Lanka developed, however, almost 16,000 Sri Lankans immigrated to America, and in 2001–2002, Sri Lanka was second only to Afghanistan in the number of refugees admitted.

The two smallest subgroups are Afghan and Nepalese Americans. With Afghan Americans, their history began in the 1930s and 1940s when well-educated Afghans entered America. Between 1953 and early 1970, at least 230 migrated into the United States. Some of those who entered the United States were students who had won scholarships to study in American universities. The Soviet invasion of Afghanistan in 1979 drove five million Afghan citizens out of their country. Some sought refuge in neighboring Pakistan and Iran, and from there many made their way to Europe, North America, and Australia. According to the U.S. Census Bureau, there are approximately 65,972 Afghan Americans living in the country. The number of immigrants from Nepal, on the other hand, remained below 100 per year through 1996. The Nepalese community, however, experienced a significant growth in population during the 2000s.

The South Asian American population is the most diverse of all Asian Americans. They practice at least eight major religions and speak over 40 major languages and thousands of dialects. Their literary expressions coming from these deep and diverse traditions are among the most exciting writings in America today. The first generation of South Asian American writers, predictably, was mostly male, educated, and affluent. Unlike the earliest Chinese, Japanese, and Filipinos who came as laborers, the South Asians came as scholarship students in the early 1900s, and many of them lived diasporic lives among their home countries, Great Britain, and the United States, such as Raja Rao, A. K. Ramanujan, Govindas Desani, Zulfikar Ghose, Sharat G. S. Chandra, Dhan Gopal Mukerji, and Rama Santha Rau, who was the only woman among the first generation. Their themes and styles were often fashioned by British literary influences.

The large flux of immigrants from South Asia after 1965 yielded most of the well-known South Asian writers, many of whom are women. This second generation of writers does not shy away from politics and portrays the lives of immigrants in the postcolonial world, exploring the themes of home, memory, migration, gender, race/ethnicity, and colonialism. Among the most prominent writers in this generation are Meena Alexander, Agha Shahid Ali, Susham Bedi, Chitra Banerjee Divakaruni, Bharati Mukherjee, Bapsi Sidhaw, Sara Suleri, and Bina Sharif.

During the past decade or so, a group of U.S. or British-born South Asians has appeared on the literary scene, taking their immigrant parents' lives and their own experiences as materials. The best-known author in this third generation of South Asian American authors who has explored the themes of generational conflicts and alienation is the Pulitzer-winning Jhumpa Lahiri.

Other less known figures include Satyal Reddy, Srikanth Rakesh, Chandra Prasad, and Vikram Seth. Still, the majority of this third generation of writers consists of immigrants, and they write novels, poetry, stories, plays, children's books, and memoirs that vividly present the lives of nomadic characters, exploring the themes of belonging, memory, religion, and exile. Prominent writers in this youngest generation are Suketu Mehta, Srikanth Rakesh, Chandra Prasad, and Vikram Seth. Also, there are writers who have stayed away from these themes, such as Sujata Massey who has written detective stories, Shilpa Agarwal who has written ghost stories, and Mary Anne Mohanraj who has written erotic fantasies.

The newest voice among South Asian American writers belongs to Afghan Americans. Although their number is small, some of their writings have drawn great publicity. The best-known Afghan American writer is Khaled Hosseini, the first Afghan American novelist. His first novel *The Kite Runner* (2001), set in the final days of the monarchy to the present, explores themes of friendship, betrayal, and the price of loyalty. It describes the rich culture and beauty of a land in the process of being destroyed. His second novel *A Thousand Splendid Suns*, set against the volatile events of Afghanistan's last 30 years—from the Soviet invasion to the reign of the Taliban to the post-Taliban rebuilding—tells the story of two generations of characters brought jarringly together by the tragic sweep of war. Tamim Ansary is another well-known Afghan American novelist and memoirist, whose memoir *West of Kabul, East of New York* (2002) depicts what it was like to grow up straddling two vastly disparate cultures. Other Afghan writers include Awista Ayub and Donia Gobar.

The only Nepalese American writer in this collection is Samrat Upadhyay. His short story collections, *Arresting God in Kathmandu* (2001) and *The Royal Ghosts* (2006), and novels, *The Guru of Love* (2003) and *Buddha's Orphans* (2010), have drawn significant public attention.

South Asian American theaters began to emerge in the late 1980s. They feature drama, film, and dance to promote multicultural appreciation and religious tolerance. These theater groups include Desipina & Co., Krea, Naatak, Rasaka Theater Company, SAATh, SALAAM Theatre, Sruti, the Kathak Ensemble, Shunya, Rasaka Theatre Company, and the Post Natyam Collective.

CONCLUSION

By now it has become apparent that Asian American literature as a classification serves commercial purposes more than literary. While the concept renders a large and highly heterogeneous list of works easy to market and catalog, it cannot organize Asian American literature into a coherent literary tradition. It seems that the constant feelings of displacement and alienation, common to most immigrants and even their descendants, serve as a unifier of Asian American writers. Unlike some literary traditions, it is impossible for this literature to trace its influence to a few major figures since its aesthetics and sensibilities come from multiple sources. In addition to the influences of American and European literatures, ranging from realism, naturalism, magical realism, to postmodernism, many Asian American writers have nourished their imagination by absorbing the rich literary and oral traditions indigenous to their ethnic cultures. Living between worlds offers them unique resources for the fusion of literary horizons, voices, and strategies to produce a vibrant body of literature that mesmerizes the reader with its unpredictable movements.

NOTES

1. Frank Chin, et al., eds., *Aiiieeeee! An Anthology of Asian American Writers.* (Washington, D.C.: Howard University Press), 1974, p. vii.
2. Eliane H. Kim, *Asian American Literature: An Introduction to the Writings and Their Social Context.* (Philadelphia: Temple University Press, 1982), p. xi.
3. Elaine H. Kim and Lisa Lowe, eds., *Positions: New Formations, New Questions: Asian American Studies* 5.2 (1997), p. xi.
4. "Graduating Address of Yan Phou Lee, at Yale College," p. 5, online, accessed 27 September 2011, http://ebookbrowse.com/graduating-address-of-yan-phou-lee-at-yale-college-pdf-d87489881.

ABDULLAH, SHAILA (1971–). A **South Asian** fiction writer, Abdullah was born in Karachi, Pakistan, and immigrated to the United States in her twenties. She received a B.A. in English and diploma in graphic design from the University of Karachi. She lives in Austin, Texas, and works as a designer. Winner of Golden Quill Award, Reader Views Literary Award, and Kickstart Guy Book of the Year Award, her novel *Saffron Dreams* (2009) explores the tragedy of 9/11 from the perspective of a Muslim widow. Her short story collection *Beyond the Cayenne Wall* (2005) won Jury Prize for Outstanding Fiction in the Norumbega Fiction Awards, the ebook category of the DIY Book Festival. The stories portray Pakistani **women** who struggle to find their individualities despite the barriers imposed by society.

ADACHI, JIRO (1966–). A **Japanese American** novelist, Adachi was born in New York City to a Japanese father and a Hungarian mother. He received his B.A. in English from Columbia University and M.F.A. in creative writing from Colorado State University. He has taught at Lycée Français de New York, the Stern College for **Women**, Hunter College, and New York's New School. His novel *The Island of Bicycle Dancers* (2004) tells the coming-of-age story of a young woman (half Japanese and half Korean) from Japan, who comes to New York to find herself.

AGARWAL, SHILPA (1971–). A **South Asian American** novelist, Agarwal was born in Mumbai to a family uprooted by India's partition. She earned a B.A. in Asian and African literatures and Women's Studies at Duke University. She received her M.A. and Ph.D. in comparative literature at the University of California, Los Angeles. Agarwal's writing is informed by glimpses into moments of alienation and awakening, especially during geographic and metaphoric crossings: east meets west, centers meet the peripheries, the living meet the divine or the dead. Such themes are abundant in her debut novel *Haunting Bombay* (2009), a literary ghost story set in 1960s India, which received the First Words Literary Prize for South Asian writers and was a San Francisco Chronicle Bestseller.

AI (FLORENCE ANTHONY, 1947–2010). Ai is a well-known **Japanese American** poet. Multiethnic from her mother's side (part black, Choctaw, and Irish), Ai adopted her Japanese name after she learned that she was the product of her mother's affair with a Japanese man. Ai earned her B.A. in English and Japanese from the University of Arizona and her M.F.A. in creative writing from the University of California, Irvine. She devoted herself to a single form of **poetry**, the dramatic monologue, in the first person voice. However, her poetry centers not on herself; rather, she uses this form to give voice to a variety of personas—male, female, poor, rich, famous, infamous, unknown, and even dead—to explore themes of love, sex, violence, relationships, and death. She has authored *Cruelty* (1973), *Killing Floor* (1979), *Sin* (1986), *Fate* (1991), *Greed* (1993), *Vice: New and Selected Poems* (1999), and *Dread* (2003). *Killing Floor* was the 1978 **Lamont Poetry Selection** of the Academy of American Poets, and *Sin* received the **American Book Award** in 1987. *Vice* earned her the **National Book Award** in 1999. She was also the recipient of fellowships from the Guggenheim Foundation and the National Endowment for the Humanities.

ALEXANDER, MEENA (1951–). A prolific **South Asian American** poet and novelist, Alexander was born in India and raised in India and Sudan. She began graduate studies at the age of 18 at the University of Nottingham in England. After marrying an American she met in India, she moved to the United States. Her **poetry** often explores the themes of **exile**, displacement, self-(re)invention, and **identity negotiation** necessitated by migration. With lyrical beauty, her poetry depicts the painful realities of migration, of being female, and of being postcolonial in *The Bird's Bright Wing* (1976), *I Root My Name* (1977), *In the Middle Earth* (1977), *Without Place* (1978), *Stone Roots* (1980), *House of a Thousand Doors* (1988), *The Storm: A Poem in Five Parts* (1989), *Night-Scene, the Garden* (1992), *River and Bridge* (1996), *Illiterate Heart* (2002), *Raw Silk* (2004), *Indian Love Poems* (2005), and *Quickly Changing River* (2008). She also has written two novels: *Nampally Road* (1991) and *Manhattan Music* (1997), and two memoirs: *Fault Lines* (1993) and *The Shock of Arrival* (1996). She has received numerous honors including a PEN Open Book Award, fellowships from Guggenheim, Fulbright, and Rockefeller foundations, Arts Council of England, National Endowment for the Humanities, American Council of Learned Societies, National Council for Research on **Women**, New York State Council on the Arts, the New York Foundation for the Arts, etc.

ALI, AGHA SHAHID (1949–2001). A celebrated **South Asian American** poet, Ali was born in New Delhi, India, but identified himself as a Kashmiri

exile. He began writing **poetry** at the age of 10 and published his first book of poetry, *Bone-Sculpture*, in his early 20s. In 1984, Ali earned his Ph.D. in English at Pennsylvania State University. The publication of *The Half-Inch Himalayas* (1987) in the prestigious Wesleyan New Poets series launched his career in the United States. Ali's poetry centers on the loss of Kashmir as a **homeland** and explores themes of exile, loss, homeland, language, and family history. Though centering on the lost home, Ali's poetry is rooted in both the Urdu and Western poetic traditions. One finds in his poetry intertextuality with Emily Dickinson, Robert Frost, Virginia Woolf, and T. S. Eliot. A recipient of numerous awards such as Guggenheim, Ingram-Merrill fellowships, a Pushcart Prize, and grants from the Pennsylvania Council on the Arts and New York Foundation for the Arts, Ali authored *In Memory of Begum Akhtar and Other Poems* (1979), *A Walk through the Yellow Pages* (1987), *A Nostalgist's Map of America* (1991), *The Beloved Witness: Selected Poems* (1992), *The Country without a Post Office* (1997), *Rooms Are Never Finished* (2001), and *Call Me Ishmael Tonight: A Book of Ghazals* (2003). He is credited for popularizing **ghazals** in America through his poetry and his translation of the famous Urdu poet Faiz Ahmed Faiz.

ALI, KAZIM (1971–). A **South Asian American** poet and novelist, Ali was born in Great Britain to parents of Indian descent and raised in Canada and the United States. Ali received a B.A. and an M.A. in English from the State University of New York, Albany, and an M.F.A. in creative writing from New York University. He is the author of two books of **poetry**, *The Far Mosque* (2005), winner of Alice James Books' New England/New York Award, and *The Fortieth Day* (2008). He is also the author of two novels, *Quinn's Passage* (2005) and *The Disappearance of Seth* (2009). His other work *Bright Felon: Autobiography and Cities* (2009) is a transgenre work—part detective story, part literary memoir, part imagined history. His poetry centers on themes of religious mysticism, enlightenment, and language. His first novel portrays an artist's search for the sublime, and the second post-9/11 America. His work has been featured in *Best American Poetry 2007* and such journals as *American Poetry Review*, *Boston Review*, *Barrow Street*, *Jubilat*, and *Massachusetts Review*. He has taught at Oberlin College and the Stonecoast M.F.A. Program and is a founding editor of Nightboat Books.

ALI, SAMINA (1969–). A **South Asian American** novelist, Ali was born in India and came to the United States as an infant. She received her B.A. in English from the University of Minnesota and M.F.A. in creative writing from the University of Oregon. She is the author of a memoir *Madras on Rainy Days* (2004), which received the Prix du Premier Roman Etranger award from France and was also a finalist for the PEN/Hemingway Award in fiction. The novel centers on the themes of arranged marriage, gender roles, and religious boundaries.

ALUMIT, NÖEL (1970–). A **Filipino American** novelist and actor, Alumit was born in Baguio City, the Philippines, and raised in Los Angeles. He earned his B.F.A. in drama from the University of Southern California and studied playwriting at the **David Henry Hwang Writers' Institute**. He is the author of two novels, *Letters to Montgomery Clift* (2002), winner of the 2003 Stonewall Book Award for literature and the Violet Quill Award, and *Talking to the Moon* (2006). These novels explored the themes of **racism**, violence, and alienation. His play *Mr. and Mrs. La Questa Go Dancing* was produced by **Teatro Ng Tanan** in San Francisco and also in Los Angeles, Santa Barbara, Boston, and Philadelphia. His other plays have been showcased at the **East West Players** in Los Angeles and **Ma-Yi Theater Company** in New York. His one-man-show *The Rice Room: Scenes from a Bar* was voted one of the best solo shows of the year by the *San Francisco Bay Guardian*. He also wrote and performed another successful solo show *Master of the (Miss) Universe* at Highways Performance Art Space in Santa Monica, California. Among his other honors are a Global Filipino Literary Award and a James Duggins Award, a prize that recognizes talented midcareer gay writers.

AMERICAN BOOK AWARD. The Board of Directors of the Before Columbus Foundation established this book award in 1978 that would, for the first time, respect and honor excellence in American literature without restriction or bias with regard to race, sex, creed, cultural origin, size of press or ad budget, or even genre. The winners are not selected by any set quota for diversity (nor would "mainstream white male" authors be excluded). The only criteria would be outstanding contribution to American literature in the opinion of the judges. Many Asian American writers have received this award, such as **Ai** for her book of poems *Sin* (1986), **Peter Bacho** winning it twice for his novels *Cebu* (1991) and *Entrys* (2005), **Mei-mei Berssenbrugge** twice winning for her books of **poetry** *Random Possession* (1979) and *The Heat Bird* (1983), **Frank Chin** for his collection of short fiction *The Chinaman Pacific and Frisco R.R. Co.* (1988), **Chitra Banerjee Divakaruni** for her debut collection of short stories *Arranged Marriage* (1995), **Sesshu Foster** for his book of poetry *World Ball Notebook* (2008), **Kimiko Hahn** for her book of poems *Unbearable Heart* (1995), **Lawson Fusao Inada** for his book of poems *Legends from Camp* (1992), **Hiroshi Kashiwagi** for his memoir *Swimming in the American* (2004), **Nora Okja Keller** for her debut novel *Comfort Woman* (1997), **Alex Kuo** for his short story collection *Lipstick and Other Stories* (2001), **Alan Chong Lau** for his book of poetry *Songs for Jadina* (1980), **Carolyn Lau** for her book of poems *Wode Shuofa: My Way of Speaking* (1988), **Chang-rae Lee** for his first novel ***Native Speaker*** (1995), **Don Lee** for his novel *Country of Origin* (2004), **Li-Young Lee** for his lyrical memoir *The Winged Seed* (1995), **Russell Leong** for his short story collection *Phoenix Eyes and Other Stories* (2000), **Shirley Geok-lin Lim** twice winning for her memoire *Among the White Moon Faces* (1997) and co-edited anthology *The Forbidden Stitch: An Asian American Women's Anthology* (1989), **Wing Tek Lum** for his book of poetry *Expounding the Doubtful Points* (1987), **Ruthann Lum McCunn** for her **children**'s book *Pie-Biter* (1983), **Milton Murayama** for his novel *All I Asking for Is My Body* (1975), **Fae Myenne Ng** for her second novel *Steer toward Rock* (2008), **Ruth L. Ozeki** for her second novel *All Over Creation* (2003), **Rahna Reiko Rizzuto** for her debut novel *Why She Left Us* (1999), **Arthur Sze** for his book of poetry *Archipelago* (1995), **Hisaye Yamamoto** for her short story collection *Seventeen Syllables* (1988), **Bienvenido N. Santos** for his short story collection *The Scent of Apples* (1967), **Ninotchka Rosca** for her novel *Twice Blessed* (1992), and **Karen Tei Yamashita** for her novel *Through the Arc of the Rain Forest* (1990).

AMIRTHANAYAGAM, INDRAN (1960–). A **South Asian American** poet, Amirthanayagam was born in Sri Lanka. At age eight, he moved with his family to London and at 14 to Honolulu, Hawaii. He is the author of three books of **poetry**: *The Elephants of Reckoning* (1993), winner of a Paterson Poetry Prize, *Ceylon, R.I.P: Selected Poems* (2001), and *The Splintered Face: Tsunami Poems* (2007). His poems have appeared in several anthologies and literary journals, such as *Grand Street*, the *Kenyon Review*, the *Massachusetts Review*, *Exquisite Corpse*, *Hanging Loose*, *Bomb*, and elsewhere. He is a diplomat in the United States Foreign Service, based currently in Lima, Peru.

AN, NA (1972–). A **Korean American** novelist, An was born in Korea and immigrated to the United States as a child and grew up in San Diego. She received a B.A. in English from Amherst College and an M.F.A. in **children's literature** from Vermont College. She is the author of three teenage novels: *A Step from Heaven* (2003), winner of the American Library Association Printz Award and a **National Book Award** Finalist, *Wait for Me* (2006), and *The Fold* (2008). All three novels portray the lives of teenage Korean American girls living between the world of their immigrant parents and that of American teenagers.

ANGELES, CARLOS A. (1921–). A **Filipino American** poet, Angeles was born in Tocloban City, Leyte, Philippines. He studied at various universities, first in premedicine and next prelaw, but World War II interrupted his education. Angeles has been living in the United States since 1978. His first book of **poetry**, *A Stun of Jewels* (1963), was a sensation and received the Carlos Palancan Memorial Award for literature, the highest honor for a poet in the Philippines. It also won the Republic Cultural Heritage Award for literature. *A Bruise of Ashes: Collected Poems, 1940–1992* (1993) was his second book. His poetry explores themes of love, nature, memory, and home.

ANSARY, TAMIM (1948–). An Afghan American novelist and memoirist, Ansary was born in Kabul, Afghanistan, to an American mother and an Afghan father. The family moved to the United States in 1964. He attended Reed College in Portland, Oregon. He is the author of *West of Kabul, East of New York* (2002), a memoir that depicts how it was to grow up straddling two vastly disparate cultures. He is also the author of a historical novel set in Afghanistan in 1841, *The Widow's Husband* (2009). Ansary directs the San Francisco Writer's Workshop. *See also* SOUTH ASIAN AMERICAN LITERATURE AND THEATER.

ANTIMISCEGENATION LAWS. Also known as miscegenation laws, these laws banned interracial marriages. The term "miscegenation" came into existence in 1863 when slavery was abolished in the United States. The banning of intermarriage between whites and blacks, though, went as far back as the late 17th century in the 13 original colonies. These were state laws that defined miscegenation as a felony and criminalized marriage and cohabitation between whites and blacks, whites and Asians, and whites and Native Americans. In 1967, the U.S. Supreme Court unanimously ruled in *Loving v. Virginia* that antimiscegenation laws were unconstitutional, and with this ruling, the enforcement of these laws was ended in all states.

Asian immigrants suffered greatly from antimiscegenation laws as the **Page Act** and the **Chinese Exclusion Act** made it almost impossible for Asian **women** to enter the country. The consequence of these laws was the creation of aging **bachelor societies.** The banning of interracial relationships is one of the common subjects in Asian American literature. From depicting its consequences on Asian American men to decrying its inhumanity, many Asian American writers have attributed Asian immigrants' suffering and rage to this law. For instance, **Maxine Hong Kingston**, in *China Men*, depicts her male ancestors' painful longing for female companionship and their lonely deaths. **Ruthanne Lum McCunn** portrays the impossible affection between a white woman and a Chinese man in *Wooden Fish Songs*. *See also* BULOSAN, CARLOS; CHIN, FRANK; CHU, LOUIS; RACISM.

AOKI, BRENDA WONG (1953–). A **Chinese** and **Japanese American** dramatist and performer, Aoki was born in Salt Lake City, Utah, but grew up in Long Beach, California. A descendant of Japanese, Chinese, Spanish, and Scots ancestries, Aoki performs diversity and **liminality** in her solo acts of **theater**. She is most famous for having established the new artistic genre that combines Japanese **Noh and Kyogen** theater with modern dance and live jazz. Most of her performance explores the themes of history, mixed race, home, gender, and mythology. Her plays have received several Drama-Logue Awards, Critic's Circle Awards, and her recordings have received INDIE Awards for Best Spoken Word (1990 and 1999). She has been awarded fellowships from the National Endowment for the Arts; the Innovative Composition Award from the American Society for Composers, Authors and Publishers; a Golden Ring Award from the Asian American Arts Foundation; the U.S. Pan Asian Chamber of Commerce Excellence 2000 Award; the 1996 **Woman** Warrior Award (San Francisco); etc. Her monodramas have been commissioned by the National Endowment for the Arts, Japan Foundation, Asian Cultural Council, U.S. Congress, State of California and the City of San Francisco. She was selected by the Smithsonian to perform before the 1996 National Asian American Congressional Caucus. Her works include *The Legend of Morning Glory* (2008), *Uncle Gunjiro's Girlfriend* (2007), *Kuan-Yin: Our Lady of Compassion* (2002), *Ballad of Bones* (2000), *Mermaid* (1997), *Random Acts of Kindness* (1994), *The Queen's Garden* (1992), *Obake! Tales of Spirits of Past and Present* (1991), and *Tales of the Pacific Rim* (1990). Her recordings include *Legend of Morning Glory* (2009), *The Queen's Garden* (1999), *Tales of the Pacific Rim* (1990) Her published works include *The Queen's Garden* (1999), *Black Hair* (1998), *Tales of the Pacific Rim* (1990), *Living on Tokyo Time* (1987), *No Way Out* (1984), and *Layin' It on the Line* (1985). She was also featured in the film, *Living on Tokyo Time* (1987) by Steven Okazaki, and in Jefferson Starship's music videos for *No Way Out* (1984) and *Layin' It on the Line* (1985). Aoki has deep roots in San Francisco. Her grandfather was a founder of Japantown in the 1890s, and her grandmother was a leader of the first **Chinatown** garment union in the 1920s. She is married to her creative partner Asian Jazz pioneer composer, Mark Izu.

ARATANI/JAPAN AMERICA THEATRE. This **theater** in Los Angeles opened in 1983. It is an 880-seat, medium-sized theater with excellent acoustics and a warm, intimate ambience. More than $4.2 million of the $6.4 million cost of the theater was raised in Japan by a group headed by former ambassador to the United States, Nobuhiko Ushiba, and Shintaro Fukushima, chairman of the *Japan Times.* It specializes in performances by Japanese and Japanese American playwrights.

ASIAN AMERICAN LITERARY AWARDS. These are a set of annual awards that have been presented by the **Asian American Writers' Workshop** since 1998. The awards honor excellence in fiction, **poetry**, and nonfiction, chosen by a panel of literary and academic judges; a Members' Choice Award, voted on by the Workshop's members from the list of that year's entries; and a Lifetime Achievement Award. To be eligible, a book must be written by someone of Asian descent living in the United States and published first in English. Sonny Mehta, publisher and editor-in-chief of Alfred A. Knopf, **David Henry Hwang**, and **Maxine Hong Kingston** have been awarded the Lifetime Achievement Award.

Members' Choice Awards have been given to **Jason Koo** for his book of **poetry** *Man on Extremely Small Island* (2009), **Patrick Rosal** for his book of poetry *Uprock Headspin Scramble and Dive* (2003), **Ed Lin** twice for his novels *Waylaid* (2002) and *This Is a Bust* (2007), **Gene Luen Yang** for his graphic novel *American Born Chinese* (2006), **Ed Bok Lee** for the poetry book *Real Karaoke People* (2005), **Ishle Yi Park** for her book of poetry *The Temperature of This Water* (2004), **Don Lee** for the short story collection *Yellow* (2001), **Nick Carbó** for his poetry collection *Secret Asian Man* (2000), and **Bino Realuyo** for his novel *Umbrella Country* (1999).

The recipients of the Asian American Literary Awards include **Paul Yoon** for his collection of short stories *Once the Shore* (2009), **Jhumpa Lahiri** for the collection of short stories *Unaccustomed Earth* (2008), **Sesshu Foster** for his book of poetry *World Ball Notebook* (2008), **Mohsin Hamid** for his novel *The Reluctant Fundamentalist* (2007), **Linh Dinh** for his book of poetry *Borderless Bodies* (2006), **Amitav Ghosh** for his nonfiction *Incendiary Circumstances: A Chronicle of the Turmoil of Our Times* (2006), **Samrat Upadhyay** for his short story collection *The Royal Ghosts* (2007), **Sun Yung Shin** for her poetry collection *Skirt Full of Black* (2007), **Rattawut Lapcharoensap** for his short story collection *Sightseeing* (2005), **Shanxing Wang** for his book of poetry *Mad Science in Imperial City* (2005), **Brian Leung** for his story collection *World Famous Love Acts* (2004), **Suketu Mehta** for his nonfiction *Maximum City: Bombay Lost and Found* (2004), **Srikanth Reddy** for his book of poems *Facts for Visitors* (2004), **Mei-mei Berssenbrugge** twice for her poetry collections *Nest* (2003) and *Endocrinology* (1998), **Monique Truong** for her debut novel *The Book of Salt* (2003), **Walter Lew** for his poetry book *Treadwinds: Poems and Intermedia Texts* (2002), **Julie Otsuka** for her debut novel *When the Emperor Was Divine* (2002), **Alexander Chee** for his debut novel *Edinburgh* (2001), **Luis H. Francia** for his book of poetry *Eye of the Fish: A Personal Archipelago* (2001), **Christina Chiu** for her collection of linked stories *Troublemaker and Other Saints* (2001), **Ha Jin** for *The Bridegroom and Other Stories* (2000), **Eugene Gloria** for *Drivers at the Short Time Motel: Poems* (2000), **Akhil Sharma** for his debut novel *An*

Obedient Father (2000), **Eric Gamalinda** for his poetry *Zero Gravity* (2000), Chang-rae Lee for his second novel *A Gesture Life* (1999), **Susan Choi** for her first novel *The Foreign Student* (1998), **Arthur Sze** for his book of poetry *The Redshifting Web* (1998), and **Lois-Ann Yamanaka** for her novel *Blu's Hanging* (1997), the first award.

ASIAN AMERICAN THEATER COMPANY. This is one of the first four Asian American **theater** companies, established in 1979 in San Francisco. Its former form was the **Asian American Theater Workshop**, under the artistic directorship of **Frank Chin**. After Chin resigned his position in 1978, an artistic committee was formed to replace the artistic director position and renamed the workshop Asian American Theater Company.

ASIAN AMERICAN THEATER WORKSHOP. This was established in 1973 by the American Conservatory **Theater** in San Francisco to produce an Asian American production by the end of summer. ACT offered 10 tuition scholarships of $600 each to Asian American actors and actresses. **Frank Chin** led the evening workshops for Asian American writers, and Janis Chan, wife of **Jeffrey Paul Chan,** the acting workshops. By the spring of 1974, the Asian American Theater Workshop had produced nearly 30 trained Asian American theater artists. Janis Chan resigned in 1975 due to the pressure from students who felt that Chan, being white, did not understand the Asian American sensibility. The Asian American Theater Workshop under the leadership of Eric Hayashi left ACT and formed an advisory board of 16 members from the community. In the fall of 1976, the Asian American Theater Workshop received a $20,000 grant from the San Francisco Foundation, which enabled the Workshop to formally become the **Asian American Theater Company.**

ASIAN AMERICAN WRITERS' WORKSHOP. This is a literary arts organization founded in 1991 to support Asian American writers, literature, and community. Beginning in the basement below the Gap on St. Marks Place, New York City, the Workshop now is a publisher of books and its literary magazine, *Ten*. Each winter it holds the Annual **Asian American Literary Awards** Ceremony to recognize outstanding literary works by Americans of Asian descent.

ASIAN EXCLUSION ACT. An Asian American **theater** group that was founded by **Garrett Hongo** in 1975 in Seattle, its name parodied the Federal law, the **Chinese Exclusion Act**. Hongo served as its artistic director. This group was renamed in 1981 the **Northwest Asian American Theatre Company**.

ASIAN STORY THEATER. This is an Asian American **theater** group that dramatizes Asian and Pacific Island stories, arts, and themes. Founded in 1989, it began by dramatizing Chinese folk tales as a project sponsored by the San Diego Chinese Center. In 1995, the company became independent of the Center to diversify programming and expand touring operations to San Francisco and Los Angeles.

ASSIMILATION. This concept is often associated with the notion of America as a melting pot. Largely composed of immigrants from all over the world, America was famed for its ability to assimilate immigrants into the mainstream culture, characterized by the English language, Christianity, and Northern European cultures. In American history, assimilation efforts were accompanied by exclusion (**Asian Exclusion Act** and **Chinese Exclusion Act**) and **antimiscegenation laws** to safeguard the national ideal of Northern Europeans. Recent multiculturalism and race studies have challenged the assimilation and melting pot concepts, pointing out that assimilation requires nonwhite immigrants to abandon their heritages such as languages, religions, customs, rituals, and food practices in order to be absorbed into the mainstream and to access social and economic mobility. Such assimilation has been a coercive process to maintain whiteness as normative to American national identity. Many Asian American writers have written against this ideology. For instance, **David Wong Louie** satirizes his protagonist Sterling Lung in *The Barbarians Are Coming* for his assimilatory desires at the cost of losing his cultural inheritance, his relationship with his parents, and even his love for Chinese food. In **Frank Chin**'s *Donald Duk*, the desire to assimilate results in the protagonist's self-loathing and the recuperation of his eroded psyche lies in his re-acculturation into the Chinese American community. *See also* CHAO, EVELINA; CHIN, MARILYN; JEN, GISH; LAHIRI, JHUMPA; LEE, CHANG-RAE; YAU, JOHN.

AYUB, AWISTA (1979–). An Afghan American writer, Ayub was born in Kabul, Afghanistan. When she was two years old, her family fled the war with the Soviet Union and came to the United States. She earned her B.S. in chemistry from the University of Rochester and M.P.A. from the University of Delaware. Soon after the fall of the Taliban, Ayub founded the Afghan Youth Sports Exchange, an organization dedicated to nurturing Afghan girls through soccer. In 2004, she brought eight Afghan girls to the United States to learn soccer and represent their country in the International Children's Games. Her book *Kabul Girls Soccer Club* (2009) tells her story and the stories of the eight Afghan girls. The eight young women have created a small revolution in Afghanistan: 15 teams now compete in an organized league, with hundreds of girls participating through the Afghanistan Football Federation. *See also* SOUTH ASIAN AMERICAN LITERATURE AND THEATER.

B

BACHELOR SOCIETIES. This term refers to **Chinatowns** in the United States between the 1850s and 1970s. In the mid-1840s, the Chinese joined the Gold Rush in California, and the immigrants were predominantly male. This fact was compounded by the **Page Act** (1875), which barred Asian **women** from entering the country on the ground of immorality. In 1900, the ratio of Chinese male and female in the United States was 19:1. Further worsened by the **antimiscegenation laws**, which criminalized intermarriages and cohabitation between whites and Asians, blacks, and Native Americans, Chinese men lived and died in Chinatowns as bachelors. **Chinese American literature** often portrays the patriarchal and conservative culture fostered by this aging bachelor society. **Maxine Hong Kingston** presents a misogynist society in her portrayal of the Chinese American community in *The Woman Warrior*. In *Eat a Bowl of Tea*, **Louis Chu** depicts New York's Chinatown of the early 20th century as populated mostly by old men filled with anxiety about the community's regeneration. **Jeffery Paul Chan** depicts the last phase of the bachelor society in his novel *Eat Everything before You Die: A Chinaman in the Counterculture*. *See also* CHINESE EXCLUSION ACT; RACISM.

BACHO, PETER (1950–). A **Filipino American** fiction writer, Bacho was born and raised in Seattle. He attended Seattle University and earned his law degree from the University of Washington (UW). His first novel, *Cebu* (1991), won an **American Book Award**. His short story collection *Dark Blue Suit* (1996) won the Washington Governor's Writers Award. His second novel, *Nelson's Run* (2002), won his second American Book Award. He is also the author of *Entrys* (2005), a novel, and *Leaving Yesler* (2010), a **young adult novel**. Many of his books portray the Filipino American experience, and most of his characters are rough-hewn immigrants living in the darker quarters of Seattle. Bacho teaches in the Liberal Studies Program at the Evergreen State College, Tacoma Campus. He is also a lecturer in the Interdisciplinary Arts and Sciences program at UW, Tacoma.

BALGASSI, HAEMI (1967–). A **Korean American** author of **children's books**, Balgassi was born in Seoul, South Korea, and grew up in western Massachusetts, where she now resides with her family. Her stories, articles, essays, and **poetry** have been published in numerous publications, including *Cicada, Hopscotch, Liguorian, Complete Woman*, romance magazines, and literary journals. She is the author of *Peacebound Trains* (1996) and *Tae's Sonata* (1997), winner of the National Christian Schools Association with the 2000 Lamplighter Classic Award.

BAMBOO RIDGE. It is a Hawaii-based group that runs the literary journal *Bamboo Ridge* and the Bamboo Ridge Press. It was founded by **Eric Chock** and **Darrell Lum** in 1978 in order to give voice to Hawaiian writers. Since then, *Bamboo Ridge* has been devoted to publishing local literature. Writers who appeared within its pages have since become well-known literary figures from Hawaii—**Lois-Ann Yamanaka**, Rodney Morales, **Gary Pak**, **Nora Okja Keller**, Dana Naone Hall, **Wing Tek Lum**, Michael McPherson, Mari Kubo, **Cathy Song**, **Juliet Sanae Kono**, etc.

BANERJEE, ANJALI. A **South Asian American** novelist, Banerjee was born in India and raised in Canada and California. She received her B.S. in anthropology and psychology from the University of California, Berkeley, and did graduate studies at San Francisco State University. She has written three novels: *Imaginary Men* (2005), *Invisible Lives* (2006), and *Haunting Jasmine* (2011). Steeped in mysticism and magic, these novels center on **women**'s lives. She is also the author of five novels for youngsters: *Seaglass Summer* (2011), *Looking for Bapu* (2008), *Maya Running* (2006), *The Silver Spell: Knights of the Silver Dragon, Book 8* (2005), and *Rani and the Fashion Divas (Star Sisterz)* (2005). Recipient of the Barnes & Noble Star of Washington Award, she lives with her husband in the Pacific Northwest. *See also* CHILDREN'S LITERATURE.

BANTWAL, SHOBHAN (1970–). A **South Asian American** novelist, Bantwal was born and raised in a large, conservative Hindu family in Belgaum, India. An arranged marriage brought her to New Jersey. She earned her B.A. and M.A. in sociology from Karnatak University, Dharwar, India. After she came to the United States, she earned her second M.A. in Public Administration from Rider University. She worked for the State of New Jersey Department of Labor for 19 years. At the age of 50, she began writing and published *The Dowry Bride* (2007), *The Forbidden Daughter* (2008), *The Sari Shop Widow* (2009), *The Unexpected Son* (2010), and *The Full Moon*

Bride (2011). All these novels explore themes of religion, myths, legends, superstition, foods, history, and geography, centering on Indian **women**'s issues such as romance, arranged marriage, and search for agency. She has won the Golden Leaf Award for the Best Debut Book in 2008.

BAROGA, JENNIE (1949–). A Filipina American playwright, Baroga was born and raised in Milwaukee, Wisconsin. After she graduated from the University of Wisconsin at Milwaukee, she moved to Northern California to pursue the career of playwriting. She wrote over 50 plays, many of which have been featured on radio and cable television. In addition, she also produces and directs plays. Her plays portray the Filipino American experience and explore intergenerational conflicts. Baroga's accomplishment has garnered her numerous awards, including the Maverick Award from the Los Angeles **Women**'s Festival, the Joey Award from TeleTheatre, the Tino Award from TeleTheatre, Work of Excellence from Cupertino, and awards from the Bay Area Playwrights Festival, Ten-Minute Play Contest, and the Inner City Cultural Center Short Play Competition in Los Angeles. Her produced plays include *Banyan* (2005), *My Friend Morty* (2006), *Gadgets* (2000), *A Good Face* (1997), *Rita's Resources* (1995), *Walls* (1993), *Eye of the Coconut* (1991), *Talk-Story* (1992), and *Kenny Was a Shortstop* (1991). Her plays have been included in anthologies like *Unbroken Thread: An Anthology of Plays by Asian American Women*, *Bold Words: A Century of Asian American Writing*, and *But Still, Like Air, I'll Rise: New Asian American Plays*. *See also* THEATER.

BAROT, RICK (1969–). A **Filipino American** poet, Barot was born in the Philippines and grew up in the San Francisco Bay Area. He received his B.A. in English at Wesleyan University, M.F.A. from the Iowa Writers' Workshop, and was Wallace E. Stegner Fellow at Stanford University. He lives in Tacoma, Washington, and teaches both at Warren Wilson College and Pacific Lutheran University. His first book of **poetry**, *The Darker Fall* (2002), winner of the 2001 Kathryn A. Morton Prize in Poetry, depicts the sacred world of small things that create the self. His second book, *Want* (2008), explores the themes about the difficulty of knowing the self. He is the recipient of a grant from the National Endowment for the Arts. His poems and essays have appeared in numerous publications, including *New England Review*, *The New Republic*, *Poetry*, and *Virginia Quarterly Review*. His work has also appeared in many anthologies, including *The New Young American Poets*, *Asian American Poetry: The Next Generation*, and *Legitimate Dangers: American Poets of the New Century*.

BEDI, SUSHAM (1945–). A leading Indian author who lives in the United States and writes primarily in Hindi, Bedi teaches Hindi language and literature at Columbia University. Because of her long residence in the United States, she is considered a **South Asian American** novelist. She finds her **exile** enabling as it affords her freedom and objectivity in creative activities. She writes novels and short fiction, which portray the immigrant's condition in America from the point of view of a strong female protagonist. These **women** characters find themselves negotiating between the old and new while constructing new identities. Almost all her writings are accessible to American readers through translation. Her novels are *Havan* (*The Fire Sacrifice*) (1989), *Katra-Dar-Katra* (*Drop by Drop*) (1994), *Lautna* (*Returning*) (1993), *Itar* (*The Other*) (1997), *Gatha Amarbel Ki* (*Song of the Amarbel*) (1999), *Nava Bhum ki Rastha* (*Epic of the New Land*) (2002), *Portrait of Mira* (2006), *Morshe* (*Battlefronts*) (2006), *Shabdon Ki Khirkiyan* (*Words as Windows*) (2006), *Sarak ki Laya* (*Rhythm of the Road*) (2007), and *Chiriya aur Cheel* (*The Sparrow and the Kite*) (1995), a collection of short stories.

BERSSENBRUGGE, MEI-MEI (1947–). A **Chinese American** poet, Berssenbrugge was born in Beijing to a Chinese mother and a Dutch father. She grew up in Massachusetts and was educated at Reed College and Columbia University. She is a prolific poet, who writes mostly experimental, postmodern **poetry** that rejects lyricism and narrative structure. Her poetry does not deal with any of the common themes in Asian American literature, and her primary focus is language itself. Her early works, such as *Fish Souls* (1971), *Summits Move with the Tide* (1974), and *Random Possession* (1979), are more traditional than her later works in the sense that the personas express thoughts and emotions derived from events and images. Her fourth book, *The Heat Bird* (1983), marked her departure from lineal expressions and established her as an experimental poet and thus placed her among the language poets. Her unique style weaves abstract language, concrete images, and cultural and political meditation. She has received numerous awards, including two grants from the National Endowment for the Arts, two **American Book Awards**, and the Western States Art Foundation. She has been a contributing editor of *Conjunctions* magazine since 1978 and has taught poetry writing at Brown University. Her publications also include *Empathy* (1989), *Mizu* (1990), *Sphericity* (1993), *Endocrinology: Poetry, Art* (1997), *Four Year Old Girl* (1998), *Nest* (2003), *I Love Artists: New and Selected Poems* (2006), and *Concordance* (2006). She also wrote a play *One, Two Cups* (1994). *See also* POETRY.

BINDLESTIFF STUDIO. This is a **Filipino American theater** in San Francisco, established in 1989.

BRAINARD, CECILIA MANGUERRA (1947–). A **Filipina American** novelist, Brainard was born and raised in the Philippines. She immigrated to the United States in 1969 to flee the dictatorship of Ferdinand Marcos and to study film at the University of California, Los Angeles. In her short fiction and novels, she uses Filipino legends and folktales to create an element of **magical realism** in rewriting Philippine history of the Japanese occupation in World War II, in which she depicts how Japanese cruelty spoils the Edenic world of the Philippines. In some stories, gods and goddesses play significant roles, and food and rituals are rich motifs in her writings. She has published novels, such as *Song of Yvonne* (1991), *When the Rainbow Goddess Wept* (1995), and *Magdalena* (2002), and three short story collections: *Woman with Horns* (1987), *Seven Stories from Seven Sisters* (1992), and *Acapulco at Sunset and other Stories* (1995). Brainard is the recipient of awards such as the California Arts Council Artists' Fellowship in Fiction and the Fortner Prize.

BUDHOS, MARINA (1960–). A **South Asian American** novelist, Budhos was born in Queens, New York, to a Guyanese Indian father and a Russian Jewish mother. She teaches English and Asian Studies at William Paterson University. She has published two novels. *House of Waiting* (1995), based on actual historical events, depicts the stormy romance between an Orthodox **woman** and an Indian man from the Caribbean. *The Professor of Light* (1999) portrays the intense bond between a father and a daughter on a quest to understand light. Budhos has also written **young adult novels**. *Ask Me No Questions* (2006) is an American Library Association Notable and winner of the first James Cook Teen Book Award. It centers on a family of illegal immigrants from Bangladesh and the young girl's experience after 9/11. *Tell Us We're Home* (2010) is another young adult novel that tells the stories of three immigrant girls whose mothers work as maids and nannies to their classmates in the wealthy suburb of Meadowbrook, New Jersey. She has also written a nonfiction book *Remix: Conversations with Immigrant Teenagers* (2007) and coauthored with her husband, Marc Aronson, *Sugar Changed the World: A Story of Magic, Spice, Slavery, Freedom, and Science* (2010). Budhos' short stories, articles, essays, and book reviews have appeared in publications such as the *Kenyon Review*, *Ploughshares*, the *Literary Review*, *The Nation*, *Dissent*, *Marie Claire*, *Redbook*, *Travel & Leisure*, *Ms.*, *Los Angeles Times*, and in numerous anthologies. She has received an Exceptional Merit Media Award, a Rona Jaffe Award for Women Writers, a Fellowship from the New Jersey Council on the Arts, and a Fulbright Scholarship to India. *See also* CHILDREN'S LITERATURE.

BULOSAN, CARLOS (1911–1956). A pioneer **Filipino American** writer, Bulosan was born in the small village of Mangusmana in the Philippines. He came to Seattle in 1930 with the intention of becoming a student and a successful writer. Bulosan never enrolled in a university and worked sometimes as a dishwasher or bakery employee. His older brother and friends supported him while he devoted himself to reading and writing. Two years after he arrived in America, his **poetry** appeared in literary magazines. By 1940, his writings had appeared in such journals as *Poetry*, *Frontier and Midland*, and *Voices*. During World War II, he acquired a national reputation through his publications, such as *Letter from America* (1942), *The Voice of Bataan* (1943), and *The Laughter of My Father* (1944). One of his most famous essays was "Freedom from Want," commissioned by President Franklin D. Roosevelt as part of a series on the "Four Freedoms" and published on 26 March 1943 in the *Saturday Evening Post*. *The Laughter of My Father* was a collection of short stories, originally published in the *New Yorker* that was broadcast to American soldiers around the world during the war. He befriended Chris Mensalvas, founder of the United Cannery, Agricultural, Packing, and Allied Workers of America (UCAPAWA), and became involved in labor politics. He edited and wrote UCAPAWA publications until the end of his life.

It is no surprise that his union involvement occupies a significant place in his fictionalized autobiography *America Is in the Heart* (1946). Because of his labor politics, the Federal Bureau of Investigation blacklisted him as a Communist sympathizer after the war and almost succeeded in deporting him. Bulosan also met and befriended such writers as Richard Wright, William Carlos Williams, Louis Adamic, and William Saroyan. Today, Bulosan is best known for *America Is in the Heart*, which exposes **racism** through a personal account and dramatizes the pain and suffering of Filipino immigrants, their longing for home, and their disillusion with the American Dream. Bulosan's other works include *The Cry and the Dedication* (a novel posthumously published in 1995), *Chorus for America: Six Philippine Poets* (1942), and *Sound of Falling Light: Letters in Exile* (1960).

BYNUM, SARAH SHUN-LIEN (1972–). A **Chinese American** fiction writer, Bynum was born in Houston, Texas. She received her B.A. in English from Brown University and M.F.A. in creative writing from the University of Iowa. She is the author of a short story collection, *Ms. Hempel Chronicles* (2008), a finalist for the 2009 PEN/Faulkner Award, and a novel, *Madeleine Is Sleeping* (2004), a finalist for the 2004 **National Book Award** and winner of the Janet Heidinger Kafka Prize. *Ms. Hempel Chronicles* is a book of eight interconnected stories about a middle school English teacher while *Madeleine Is Sleeping*, part fairy tale and part coming-of-age story, follows a French girl as she leaves home, joins a gypsy circus, and falls into a triangle of desire and love. Bynum's fiction has appeared in several magazines and anthologies, including the *New Yorker, Tin House,* the *Georgia Review,* and the *Best American Short Stories 2004* and *2009.* Among the honors she has received are a Whiting Writers' Award and a National Endowment for the Arts Fellowship. She directs and teaches in the M.F.A. program at the University of California, San Diego.

C

CABICO, REGIE (1970–). A **Filipino American** poet, playwright, and performing artist, Cabico was born in Baltimore, Maryland. He received his B.F.A. in acting from New York University. He is the artistic director of Sol and Soul, a Washington, D.C., arts and activist organization. Although he does not have a collection of his own yet, his work has appeared in more than 30 anthologies including *Spoken Word Revolution*, *Aloud: Voices from the Nuyorican Poets Café*, and *Bullets and Butterflies*. A spoken word pioneer, he won the 1993 Nuyorican Poets Cafe Grand Slam Championship and has appeared on two seasons of HBO's Def **Poetry** Jam. His plays have been produced at the Humana **Theater** Festival, Kennedy Center Play Lab, Joe's Pub the Public Theater Festival, the Asian American Theater Festival, Living Word Festival, San Francisco, the Kitchen, Dixon Place, **La Mama**, the Philadelphia Fringe Festival, the New York Fringe Festival, Theater Offensive, among other venues. He received three New York Innovative Theater Award nominations for his work in the New York production of *Too Much Light Makes the Baby Go Blind* with a 2006 award for Best Performance Art Production. His latest solo play, *Unbuckled*, was presented in San Francisco at the Artaud Theater and developed with grants from National Performance Network and Mid-Atlantic Arts Foundation. He lives in Brooklyn, New York, and Columbia Heights.

CAO, LAN (1961–). A **Vietnamese American** novelist, Cao was born in Vietnam and experienced the Vietnam War (known to the Vietnamese as the American War) as a child. When she was 12, she immigrated to the United States. She received her B.A. in political science from Mount Holyoke College and her J.D. from the Yale University Law School. She now teaches law at College of William and Mary. *Monkey Bridge* (1997) is a semiautobiographical novel that tells the story of love, betrayal, and secrets in her family during and after the war. It is considered to be the first novel by a Vietnamese American.

CARBÓ, NICK (1964–). A **Filipino American** poet, Carbó was born in Legaspi, the Philippines. When he was two, he and his sister were adopted by a Spanish couple. He grew up in Manila and came to the United States for higher education. He studied at Bennington College in Vermont and received his M.F.A. in creative writing from Sarah Lawrence College. Carbó is the author of four books of **poetry**: *El Grupo McDonald's* (1995); *Secret Asian Man* (2000), winner of a Members' Choice Award of the **Asian American Literary Awards**; *Andalusian Dawn* (2004); and *Chinese, Japanese, What Are These?* (2009). Most of his poetry centers on the issues of colonialism, history of the Philippines, Filipino **diaspora**, identity, and **racism**. He has won numerous honors, including fellowships from National Endowment for the Arts and the New York Foundation for the Arts. Currently, he is a visiting poet in the M.F.A. program in poetry at Columbia College, Chicago.

CARLING, AMELIA LAU. A **Chinese American** writer and illustrator of **children's books**, Carling was born in Guatemala to Chinese parents. She attended the American School, where she learned English. After high school, she came to the United States to study art at Occidental College in California. She currently lives and works in New York City. Her debut book, *Mama and Papa Have a Store* (1998), tells the story of her childhood with her family's store in Guatemala City in the background. Her second book, *Sawdust Carpets* (2005), depicts a Spanish Holy Week celebration.

CEDAR GROVE ONSTAGE. This is an Asian Pacific American **theater** arts organization established in 2006, based in Los Angeles. It was cofounded by playwright **Tim Toyama** and Chris Tashima as artistic director. It has collaborated with the **East West Players** to produce the world premiere of **Dan Kwong's** *Be Like Water* at the **David Henry Hwang** Theatre.

CELONA, TINA BROWN (1974–). A **Vietnamese American** poet, Celona was born as Tina Brown to an American Foreign Service officer and his Vietnamese wife. She grew up in Tokyo, Paris, Kuala Lumpur, and Washington, D.C. She received her B.A. in English from Brown University and M.F.A. from the Iowa Writers' Workshop. Her husband is the poet Matt Celona. She is the author of two books of **poetry**: *The Real Moon of Poetry and Other Poems* (2002) and *Snip! Snip!* (2006). In the style of prose poetry, she explores themes of language, nature, and humor, among other things. Her works have also appeared in *Octopus*, *Shampoo*, *La Petite Zine*, *Puppyflowers*, *Explosive!*, *Epoch*, and *Fence*. She lives in Seattle, Washington.

CERENIO, VIRGINIA R. (1955–). A **Filipina American** poet, Cerenio was born in California. She received a B.A. in English and an M.A. in education from San Francisco State University. She has published two books of

poetry, *Without Names: A Collection of Poems* (1987) and *Trespassing Innocence* (1989). They center on the themes of identity, history, cultural legacy, and social justice. Her poetry is anthologized in *The Forbidden Stitches: An Asian American Women's Anthology*, *New Worlds of Literature: Writings from America's Many Cultures*, *Returning a Borrowed Tongue: An Anthology of Filipino and Filipino American Poetry*, and *Babaylan: An Anthology of Filipina and Filipina American Writers*. Her short fiction has appeared in *Berkeley Fiction Review* and anthologies like *Making Waves* and *Fiction by Filipinos in America*.

CHA, DIA (1962–). A Hmong American memoirist, Cha was born in Laos. After four years in a refugee camp in Thailand, she and the surviving members of her family came to the United States in 1979. She holds a B.A. in anthropology from Metropolitan State College, Denver, an M.A. in applied anthropology from Northern Arizona University in Flagstaff, and a Ph.D. in anthropology from the University of Colorado at Boulder. She is currently a professor of anthropology and ethic studies at St. Cloud State University in St. Cloud, Minnesota. Her memoir *Dia's Story Cloth* (1996) is a picture book that retells her life story, Hmong history, and a classic American immigration tale. *See also* SOUTHEAST ASIAN AMERICAN LITERATURE AND THEATER.

CHA, THERESA HAK KYUNG (1951–1982). A **Korean American** novelist and artist, Cha left Korea with her family for Hawaii and then San Francisco when she was a child. She received her education in comparative literature and art from the University of California, Berkeley, after which she went to Paris to study film theory. Cha is famed for her only novel, *Dictée* (1982), for its postmodern, experimental narrative structure. Regarded as one of the most challenging texts in Asian American literature, it presents a collage of fragmented narratives centering on female figures in Korea and America. These fragments include pictures, maps, ideographs, official documents, irregular spacing, language exercises, and broken tales. Two consistent themes throughout this novel are the histories and **diasporas** of Koreans. The title comes from the beginning scene of English and French dictation (*dictée*) exercises; Cha closely links language learning with national identity. The central character, Cha's mother, symbolizing mother tongue and motherland, bears the emotional burden of belonging and displacement because of colonization.

CHAI, MAY-LEE (1967–). A **Chinese American** novelist, short story writer, and memoirist, Chai was born in Redlands, California, to a Chinese

American father and an Irish American mother. She received her B.A. in French and Chinese Studies from Grinnell College, M.A. in East Asian Studies from Yale University, and a second M.A. in creative writing from the University of Colorado. She has taught at various universities including San Francisco State University, the University of Wyoming, and Amherst College in Massachusetts. Her novel *My Lucky Face* (1997) centers on cultural and personal alienation. Her short story collection *Glamorous Asian* (2004) tells stories of a diversity of Asian and Asian American **women** by exploring myths and **magical realism**. She is also the author of two memoirs: *The Girl from Purple Mountain* (2004), written in collaboration with her father, Winberg Chai, and *Hapa Girl: A Memoir* (2008), named a Kiriyama Prize Notable Book.

CHAN, EUGENIE (1962–). A **Chinese American** playwright, Chan is a fifth-generation Chinese American. Raised in San Mateo, California, she received her B.A. in literature from Yale University and M.F.A. in dramatic writing from New York University. Chan's plays are mostly set in the western or southwestern United States, featuring characters who are Chinese American, Latino, and Native American. Dominant themes include interracial relationships, female homoeroticism, and immigrant family dynamics. Chan has received commissions from the Magic Theatre/Sloan Science Initiative and Cutting Ball Theatre. She has received awards from Mixed Blood **Theater**, grants from the New Works Fund and Theatre Bay Area, and fellowships from the Berilla Kerr Foundation, the Affymax Foundation, the Tournesol Project/Z Space Studio, Film Arts Foundation, the Edward E. Ford Foundation, and the George Lucas Educational Foundation. Her plays include *Novell-Aah!* (1993), *Emil, a Chinese Play* (1994), *Willy Gee* (1994), *Paradise Plain* (1993), *Athena Adrift* (1997), *Esmerelda* (1997), and *Rancho Grande* (1997). Many of her plays have appeared in anthologies such as *Between Worlds: Contemporary Asian-American Plays*, *Contemporary Plays by Women of Color*, *Asian American Drama: 9 Plays from the Multiethnic Landscape*, and *Embodying Asian/American Sexualities*. *See also* THEATER.

CHAN, JEFFERY PAUL (1942–). A **Chinese American** novelist, Chan was a professor of Asian American studies and English at San Francisco State University (SFSU), where he also received his M.A. in creative writing. Chan was a cofounder of the Asian American Studies Department at SFSU. He was coeditor with **Frank Chin**, **Lawson Fusao Inada**, and **Shawn Wong**, of two editions of the famous anthology of Asian American literature *Aiiieeee!* He has written one novel, *Eat Everything before You Die: A Chinaman in the Counterculture* (2004), which tells the story of a Chinese orphan, Christopher

Columbus Wong, brought up in a Chinese **bachelor society** in California. Through the motifs of dream, food, sex, and family anecdotes, the novel dramatizes the life of Christopher Columbus Wong.

CHANDRA, G. S. SHARAT (1938–2000). A **South Asian American** poet and novelist, Chandra was born in India and received a law degree in India. He came to the United States at the age of 24 to become a writer. He received an M.S. in English from the State University of New York, Oswego, his L.L.M from the Osgoode Hall Law School in Toronto, and his M.F.A. in **poetry** writing from the University of Iowa. He taught English and creative writing at the University of Missouri, Kansas City. He is the author of seven poetry books. He is best known for *Family of Mirrors* (1993), which was nominated for a Pulitzer Prize for poetry. His other books include *April in Nanjangud* (1971), *Once or Twice* (1974), *The Ghost of Meaning* (1976), *Heirloom* (1982), *Immigrants of Loss* (1993–1994), and *Sari of the Gods* (1998), a story collection. His works explore themes of immigration, separation, otherness, death, and ethnicity. His works have also appeared in many journals, including *American Poetry Review*, *London Magazine*, the *Nation*, and *Partisan Review*. He was the recipient of a Fulbright Fellowship and a National Endowment for the Arts Literature Fellowship.

CHANDRA, VIKRAM (1961–). A **South Asian American** novelist, Chandra was born in New Delhi, India. He received part of his undergraduate education at Mayo College in Ajmer, Rajasthan, and St. Xavier's College in Mumbai. As a transferred student, he came to the United States and completed his B.A. in English at Pomona College. Chandra then attended film school at Columbia University, leaving the program to write his first novel. He attended writing programs at Johns Hopkins University and the University of Houston, and he finished his M.A. in creative writing at Johns Hopkins in 1987. He is now teaching at the University of California, Berkeley. His first novel, *Red Earth and Pouring Rain* (1995), inspired by the autobiography of James Skinner, a legendary 19th-century Anglo–Indian soldier, is an epic sweep of India's history, mythology, and magic interspersed with journeys across modern America. *Red Earth and Pouring Rain* received critical acclaim and won the Commonwealth Writers Prize (CWP) for Best First Book and the David Higham Prize for Fiction. His second work is a collection of short fiction, *Love and Longing in Bombay* (1997). The seven stories in this collection sport several genres ranging from a ghost story to a love story, a murder mystery, and a crime story, each tale connected to the others by the same narrator, Mr. Subramaniam, an old man drinking at a bar and regaling his audience with tales of love, secrets, jealousy, betrayal, and crime. *Love* *and Longing in Bombay* won the CWP for Best Book and was short-listed for the Guardian Fiction Prize. Sartaj Singh, a Sikh policeman in this collection becomes the central character of Chanadra's second novel, *Sacred Games* (2006). Set in Mumbai, this novel is a fantastic story of crime and punishment, with the central conflict between Inspector Sartaj Singh and Ganesh Gaitonde, the most wanted gangster in India. Chandra's major themes in this novel include the animosity of caste and religion, poverty, prostitution, and the criminal elite, who model themselves on corporations and even transnational corporations.

CHANG, DIANA (1934–). A **Chinese American** novelist and poet, Chang was born in New York City to a Chinese father and an American-born Eurasian mother. Her parents took her to China and raised her in various big cities in China, which greatly shaped her imagination. Shanghai is the background of her best-known novel, *Frontiers of Love* (1956). After high school, she returned to the United States for college and received her B.A. from Barnard College. Her early works explore the existential ambivalence of being biracial and bicultural. Her later works, however, feature only white characters and center on the conflicts of individuals versus social conventions, such as in *A Woman of Thirty* (1959), *A Passion for Life* (1961), *Eye to Eye* (1974), and *A Perfect Love* (1978). There was a major shift after her last novel, *The Gift of Love* (1978); she began to publish mostly **poetry** collections, such as *The Horizon Is Definitely Speaking* (1982), *What Matisse Is After* (1984), and *Earth Water Light* (1991). She is the recipient of a Fulbright and the John Hay Whitney Fellowship.

CHANG, HENRY (1951–). A **Chinese American** novelist, Chang was born and raised in **Chinatown**, New York. He received a B.A. in English, with a minor in Asian Studies, from City College of New York. He is the author of a trilogy of detective novels: *Chinatown Beat* (2007), *The Year of the Dog* (2008), and *Red Jade* (2010). This trilogy, set in Chinatown, New York, features Detective Jack Yu and the complex terrain of New York's Chinese American urban community. His poems and fiction have appeared in *Murdaland, Bridge Magazine,* and in anthologies such as *Yellow Pearl, Gangs in New York's Chinatown*, *On a Bed of Rice*, and *The NuyorAsian Anthology.* Chang has worked as a lighting consultant, and as a security director for major hotels, commercial properties, and retail businesses in Manhattan.

CHANG, JENNIFER (1976–). A **Chinese American** poet, Chang was born and raised in New Jersey. She received a B.A. in English from the University of Chicago, an M.F.A. in creative writing, and a Ph.D. in English from the

University of Virginia. Her debut book of **poetry**, *The History of Anonymity* (2008), explores diverse forms while focusing on the theme of search for self-knowledge in the natural world. Her other poems have appeared in *New England Review*, the *New Republic*, the *Virginia Quarterly Review*, and the anthologies *Best New Poets 2005* and *Asian American Poetry: The Next Generation.*

CHANG, LAN SAMANTHA (1965–). A **Chinese American** novelist, Chang was born and raised in Appleton, Wisconsin. She received her B.A. in East Asian Studies from Yale University, M.P.A. from Harvard University, and M.F.A. in creative writing from the University of Iowa. She has served as director of the Iowa Writers' Workshop since 2006. She is the author of a collection of short stories, *Hunger* (1998), and two novels: *Inheritance* (2004), winner of a Pen beyond Margins Award, and *All Is Forgotten, Nothing Is Lost* (2010). Her short stories center on themes of immigration, displacement, alienation, and hunger for belonging. While *Inheritance* traces three generations of **women** in China, *All Is Forgotten, Nothing Is Lost* portrays the lives of writers, exploring themes of love, betrayal, and loss. Among Chang's numerous honors are inclusions twice in the *Best American Short Stories*, Wallace Stegner and Truman Capote fellowships at Stanford University, a Henfield/Transatlantic Review Award, and a literature grant from the National Endowment for the Arts.

CHANG, LEONARD (1968–). A **Korean American** novelist, Chang was born in New York City. He received his B.A. in philosophy from Harvard University and M.F.A. in creative writing from the University of California, Irvine. He is a professor at Antioch University in Los Angeles. He is the author of six novels. *The Fruit 'n Food* (1996), winner of the Black Heron Press Award for Social Fiction, explores the tensions between African and Korean Americans. *The Dispatches from the Cold* (1998) won the Outstanding Local Discovery Award for Literature from *San Francisco Bay Guardian.* He is better known as the author of a popular and critically acclaimed noir trilogy: *Over the Shoulder* (2000), *Fade to Clear* (2001), and *Underkill* (2003). This trilogy centers on Allen Choice, a Korean American bodyguard, and his encounters with crimes and intrigues. *Crossing* (2009) is his most recent novel, which portrays the lives of Korean immigrants in the San Francisco Bay Area. His stories have appeared in literary journals such as ***Bamboo Ridge***, *Confluence*, *Crab Orchard Review*, *Crescent Review*, and *Prairie Schooner*.

CHANG, TINA (1969–). A **Chinese American** poet, Chang was raised in New York City. She is newly appointed Brooklyn Poet Laureate and currently teaches at Sarah Lawrence College and Hunter College. Her first book of **poetry**, *Half-Lit Houses* (2004), centers on the mystery of a missing father. Her second book of poetry, *Of Gods and Strangers* (2011), is a meditation on history and the imagination that bears witness to acts of genocide and to natural disasters in Ethiopia, Haiti, and Sri Lanka. Her work has appeared in *Ploughshares*, *Quarterly West*, the *Missouri Review*, the *Indiana Review*, *Sonora Review*, *Cream City Review*, and in anthologies, including *Identity Lessons*, *Poetry Nation*, *Asian American Literature*, *Asian American Poetry: The Next Generation*, *From the Fishouse: An Anthology of Poems*, and in *Poetry 30: Poets in Their Thirties.* She has received awards from the Association of American Publishers, the Barbara Deming Memorial Fund, the Ludwig Vogelstein Foundation, the New York Foundation for the Arts, Poets & Writers, and the Van Lier Foundation, among others.

CHANG, VICTORIA (1970–). A Taiwanese American poet, Chang was born to Taiwanese immigrants in Detroit, Michigan, and raised in the suburb of West Bloomfield. She graduated from the University of Michigan, Harvard University, and Stanford Business School. She earned her M.F.A. in **poetry** from the Warren Wilson M.F.A. Program for Writers. She lives in Southern California and works as a business researcher and writer. Her first book, *Circle* (2005), won the Crab Orchard Series in Poetry, the Association of Asian American Studies Book Award, and was the Finalist for the PEN Center West Book Award. Her most recent poetry collection *Salvinia Molesta* (2008) was the Finalist for the 2008 Commonwealth California Book Award. In both books of poetry, Chang mines Chinese history. While she focuses on **women** in the first book—concubines and traditional wives—of earlier periods, she takes on more recent political events and figures in her second book, such as the Japanese invasion of Nanking in 1937, the suicide of Mao Zedong's widow, recent financial shenanigans in the United States, etc. Chang's poetry has also appeared in many journals and magazines, including the *Paris Review*, the *Kenyon Review*, *Slate*, *New England Review*, the *Threepenny Review*, *Michigan Quarterly Review*, *Virginia Quarterly Review*, *The Nation*, and *Ploughshares.* She is also the editor of the anthology *Asian American Poetry: The Next Generation* (2004). Among her awards and honors are the Cohen Award, Breadloaf Writers' Conference Fellowship and Scholarship, and Sewanee Writers' Conference Fellowship. *See also* CHINESE AMERICAN LITERATURE AND THEATER.

CHAO, EVELINA (1949–). A **Chinese American** novelist and musician, Chao was born in Chicago to Chinese parents who immigrated to America from Mao's Communist China. She attended Oberlin College and Juilliard

School, became an accomplished viola musician, and joined the Amici Quartet, Indianapolis Symphony, and the Saint Paul Chamber Orchestra. Her novel *Gates of Grace* (1985) tells the story of a Chinese American family's journey of **assimilation**, which is fraught with experiences of discrimination and cultural clashes. Her memoir *Yeh Yeh's House* (2004) focuses on cultural identities and ancestral roots.

CHAO, PATRICIA (1955–). A **Chinese American** novelist, Chao was born in Monterey, California, and currently lives in New York City. She earned a B.A. and an M.A. in creative writing from New York University. Her first novel, *Monkey King* (1997), was a finalist for the Barnes and Noble Discover Great New Writers Award. It portrays the painful journey of recovery of a 28-year-old Chinese American artist from her haunting past of molestation. Chao's second novel, *Mambo Peligroso* (2005), departs from the themes of her first. This novel tells the story of Catalina Ortiz Midori—half Japanese, half Cuban, raised in New England—as she becomes a disciple of El Tuerto, a world-class dancer who teaches a class on the mambo peligroso. She is the recipient of a New York Foundation for the Arts Fellowship.

CHARI, SHEELA (1972–). A **South Asian American** author of **children's books**, Chari was born in Bangalore, India, and moved with her family to Iowa as a child. She holds a B.A. in economics from Stanford University, an M.A. in creative writing from Boston University, and an M.F.A. in creative writing from New York University. Her debut book, *Vanished* (2011), is a mystery for children.

CHARLIE CHAN. Charlie Chan is a fictional **Chinese American** detective in Earl Derr Biggers' novel *The House without a Key* (1925). Biggers was inspired during a vacation in Hawaii by two Chinese American detectives and conceived of Charlie Chan as an alternative to stereotypes of Asians as villains such as **Fu Manchu**. Chan is not only amiable, nonthreatening, and benevolent but also fat, awkward, and asexual. Even though Chan often experiences **racism**, he rarely speaks openly against it. Beginning in 1926, over four dozen films featuring Charlie Chan have been made. Asian actors played the character in early films, which met with little success. In 1931, Fox employed Warner Oland to portray Chan in *Charlie Chan Carries On*, and the film became a great hit. Fox went on to produce 15 more films with Oland as Chan. After Oland's death, Sidney Toler became Chan and appeared in 22 Chan films. After Toler's death, six more films were made, starring Roland Winters. Charlie Chan has also been featured in radio programs, television shows, and comics.

In Asian American literature and theater, Charlie Chan has become a short hand for many of the stereotypes in American popular culture of Asian American men as passive, subordinate, inscrutable, asexual, and compliant. Even though Charlie Chan is a "good" character on the side of the law, he inhabits the other extreme of the menacing and evil stereotype embodied by Fu Manchu. It is such polarizing representations of Asian men on the screen that have offended writers such as **Frank Chin** and **Jessica Hagedorn**, who have waged literary wars against Charlie Chan. For instance, Hagedorn edited *Charlie Chan Is Dead: An Anthology of Contemporary Asian American Fiction* (1993) and *Charlie Chan Is Dead 2: At Home in the World* (2004).

CHARR, EASURK EMSEN (1895–1986). A **Korean American** autobiographer, Charr was born in North Korea and came to Hawaii alone at the tender age of 10. *The Golden Mountain: The Autobiography of a Korean Immigrant 1895–1960* (1961) is Charr's story of his early years in Korea, his migration to Hawaii and the mainland, and the joys and pains of his life. He narrates how difficult it was for him to become a naturalized citizen, even after serving in the U.S. Army.

CHAT. CHAT stands for the Center for Hmong Arts and Talent. It evolved from **Pom Siab Hmoob Theatre (PSHT)**, which was established in 1992 by a group of Hmong American **theater** artists in Minnesota. CHAT is the first Hmong American arts organization. It nurtures, explores, and illuminates the Hmong American experience through artistic expressions. *See also* SOUTHEAST ASIAN AMERICAN LITERATURE AND THEATER.

CHAU, ANGIE (1974–). A **Vietnamese American** fiction writer, Chau was born in Vietnam and has lived in Vietnam, Malaysia, Italy, Spain, Kauai, and in Southern and Northern California. She earned a B.A. in **Southeast Asian** Culture and Political Economy from the University of California, Berkeley, and an M.A. in English with a Creative Writing emphasis from the University of California, Davis, where she also taught undergraduate fiction and was the fiction editor for the *Greenbelt Review*. Her debut story collection, *Quiet as They Come* (2010), explores the themes of immigration, **racism**, cultural alienation, displacement, and memory. She has been awarded a Hedgebrook Residency and a Macondo Foundation Fellowship. Her work has appeared in the *Indiana Review*, *Santa Clara Review*, *Slant*, and the anthology *Cheers to Muses*.

CHE, SUNNY (1929–). A **Korean American** memoirist, Che spent most of her early childhood in Japan, where she and her family were treated as outsiders. She returned to Korea, only to find herself a stranger in her **homeland**. Her memoir, *Forever Alien* (2000), recounts the trials of a young Korean girl growing up in Japan during its occupation of Korea, through liberation, and the beginning of the Korean War (1950–1953). Che was the 1996 recipient of the Democratic Achievement Award.

CHEE, ALEXANDER (1967–). A **Korean American** novelist, poet, and essayist, Chee was born in Rhode Island. He spent his first three years in South Korea before his family moved to Guam and then Maine. He attended Wesleyan University and the Iowa Writers' Workshop. He has taught creative writing at the New School University, Wesleyan University, and Amherst College. His short stories have appeared in several anthologies and numerous journals, such as *Blithe House Quarterly*, *Lodestar Quarterly*, *Northeast Magazine*, *Plume*, *Big*, the *James White Review*, etc. His **poetry** has appeared in *Barrow Street*, *LIT*, *Interview*, the *James White Review*, and *Fruit*. His creative nonfiction has appeared in *Granta.com*, *Guernica*, *LIT*, *Hope*, and several anthologies. His first novel, *Edinburgh* (2002), is a winner of the Michener Copernicus Prize, an **Asian American Literary Award**, and the **Lambda** Editor's Choice Prize. *Edinburgh* tells the story of the molestation of a Korean American boy and its aftermath. Chee has also received honors such as a residency from the MacDowell Colony and a National Endowment for the Arts Fellowship.

CHEN, CHING-IN (1978–). A **Chinese American** poet and novelist, Chen was born in Binghamton, New York, to Chinese immigrants. She received her B.A. in English and international relations from Tufts University and is currently working on her M.F.A. in creative writing at the University of California, Riverside. Her debut novel-in-poems, *The Heart's Traffic* (2009), portrays a single character in multi genres. Her work has appeared in such journals as *Iron Horse*, *Water-Stone Review*, *Poemeleon*, *CHO#17*, *Hyphen*, etc., and in anthologies, including *Yellow as Turmeric*, *Family Pictures*, *Growing Up Girl*, among others. *See also* POETRY.

CHEN, DA (1962–). A **Chinese American** memoirist and novelist, Chen was born in Southern China and came to the United States when he was 23. He received his B.A. in English from Beijing Languages and Culture University and J.D. from Columbia University School of Law. He is the author of two novels: *Brothers* (2007), a sprawling, dynamic family saga, and *Wandering Warrior* (2004), a Kong Fu story for **children**. He is also the author of three memoirs: *Colors of the Mountain* (2001), *China's Son* (2003), and *Sounds of the River* (2003), the sequel to his first memoir.

CHEN, JUSTINA (1968–). A Taiwanese American **young adult** novelist, Chen was born in Pennsylvania. She holds a B.A. in economics from Stanford University. Chen is the author of three novels: *Nothing but the Truth (and a few white lies)* (2007), *North of Beautiful* (2009), and *Girl Overboard* (2009). These novels explore the themes of teen **hapa** experience, beauty, class, and identity. Additionally, Chen cofounded readergirlz, a literacy-and-social media project for teens, which won a **National Book Award** for Innovations in Reading. She lives near Seattle, Washington. *See also* CHINESE AMERICAN LITERATURE AND THEATER.

CHEN, KEN (1979–). A **Chinese American** poet, Chen was born in San Diego, California, and lives in Brooklyn, New York. He earned his B.A. in English and a minor in creative writing from the University of California, Berkeley, and a J.D. from Yale Law School. His **poetry** and essays have appeared in *Art Asia Pacific*, *Boston Review of Books*, *Manoa*, *Field*, *Pleiades*, *Barrow Street*, *Bridge*, *Radical Society*, *5 Fingers Review*, and *Palimpsest*. He is the director of the **Asian American Writers' Workshop**. Yale University Press published his first book of poetry, *Juvenilia* (2010). He was previously an editor of *Arts & Letters Daily*.

CHENG, NIEN (1915–2009). A **Chinese American** autobiographer, Cheng was born in a wealthy family in Beijing, immigrated to the United States in 1980, and lived and died in Washington, D.C. While studying at the London School of Economics, she met and married her husband, Kang-chi Cheng, who became a prominent diplomatic officer of the Nationalist government. After the establishment of the Communist government, her husband began working for Shell International Petroleum Company in the Shanghai branch. After her husband passed away in 1957, Cheng became a special assistant to the general manager who succeeded her husband. She is well-known in America for her best-selling autobiography *Life and Death in Shanghai* (1986). This book gives a detailed account of her suffering and endurance during the Chinese Culture Revolution. For over six years, she was kept and tortured in a Chinese prison for her Western education and her work for the British company. She battled isolation and silence by reciting Chinese **poetry**, the Bible, and by studying Mao Zedong's writings. The latter she did in order to reason with her interrogators in their language. The great tragedy during her imprisonment was the mysterious death of her only daughter.

CHENG, TERRENCE (1972–). A **Chinese American** novelist, Cheng was born in Taiwan and came to New York with his parents when he was one. He received his B.A. in English from Binghamton University in New York and

M.F.A. in creative writing from the University of Miami. He is the author of two novels. *Sons of Heaven* (2002), inspired by the Tiananmen Event in 1989, fictionalizes the life of the young man who stood in front of a tank on the square. *Deep in the Mountain* (2007), a **young adult novel**, tells the story of a 15-year-old Chinese boy who is obsessed with graffiti culture. Cheng received a National Endowment for the Arts fellowship and teaches creative writing at Lehman College, New York.

CHEONG, FIONA. A Singapore **Chinese American** novelist, Cheong was born in Singapore. She received her B.A. in English and M.F.A. in creative writing from Cornell University. She is an associate professor of English at the University of Pittsburgh. She is the author of two novels: *The Scent of the Gods* (1991) centers on a teenage girl's life in her diasporic Chinese family and *Shadow Theater* (2002) draws on the tradition of belief in ghosts and vampires both benevolent and malevolent. Both novels explore the themes of gender, diaspora, and postcolonial conditions. Her short fiction has also appeared in Asian American literary anthologies. *See also* SOUTHEAST ASIAN AMERICAN LITERATURE AND THEATER.

CHERIAN, ANNE. A **South Asian American** novelist, Cherian was born and raised in Jamshedpur, India. She graduated from Bombay and Bangalore Universities and received graduate degrees in journalism and comparative literature from the University of California, Berkeley. She is the author of a novel, *A Good Indian Wife* (2008), which explores themes of gender, identity, and transculturation. *See also* WOMEN.

CHEVAPRAVATDUMRONG, CHERRY (CHERRY CHEVA). A Thai American novelist, Chevapravatdumrong was born in Columbus, Ohio, and raised in Ann Arbor, Michigan. She majored in psychology at Yale University and received a J.D. from New York University, after which she moved to Los Angeles to pursue writing. She is the author of two **young-adult novels**, *She's So Money* (2008) and *Duplikate* (2009). Both novels explore the issues of school, sex, and destination of college that teenagers face. Chevapravatdumrong currently serves as a writer/producer on the sitcom of *Family Guy*. She lives in Los Angeles. *See also* SOUTHEAST ASIAN AMERICAN LITERATURE AND THEATER.

CHIANG, FAY (1952–). A **Chinese American** poet, Chiang was born and raised in New York City. She majored in art at Hunter College. She is the author of three books of **poetry**: In *The City of Contradictions* (1979), *Miwa's Song* (1982), and *A Translocal Vision: 7 Continents 9 Lives* (2010). She has been awarded a New York State Commercialization Assistance Program grant in Poetry, a Columbia University Revson Fellowship, and grants from the New York State Council on the Arts.

CHIANG, TED (1967–). A **Chinese American** speculative fiction writer, Chiang was born in Port Jefferson, New York. He graduated from Brown University with a computer science degree and from Clarion Writers Workshop. He currently works as a technical writer in the software industry and lives in the Seattle area. Although most of his publications are short stories in literary magazines and anthologies, Chiang has already established himself as a notable speculative fiction writer, with numerous prestigious awards for his works: a Nebula Award for "Tower of Babylon" (1990); the John W. Campbell Award for Best New Writer in 1992, a Nebula Award, and the Theodore Sturgeon Memorial Award for "Story of Your Life" (1998); a Sidewise Award for "Seventy-Two Letters" (2000); a Nebula Award, Locus Award, and Hugo Award for his novelette "Hell Is the Absence of God" (2002); a Nebula and Hugo Award for his novelette "The Merchant and the Alchemist's Gate" (2007); and a British Science Fiction Association Award, a Locus Award, and the Hugo Award for Best Short Story for "Exhalation" (2009). His other stories include "Division by Zero" (*Full Spectrum* 3, 1991), "Understand" (*Asimov's*, 1991), "The Evolution of Human Science" (a.k.a. "Catching Crumbs from the Table") (*Nature*, 2000), "Liking What You See" (*Stories of Your Life and Others*, 2002), "What's Expected of Us" (*Nature,* 2006). He is also the author of a novella, *The Lifecycle of Software Objects* (2010), and a short story collection, *Stories of Your Life and Others* (2002).

CHIANG, YEE (1903–1977). A **Chinese American** autobiographer and travel writer, Chiang was born in Jiangxi Province, China. He received a B.S. from National Southeastern University in Nanjing. Chiang taught chemistry in middle schools, lectured at National Chi-Nan University, and then worked as an assistant editor of a daily newspaper in Hangzhou. Later, he was appointed magistrate of Jiujiang first, Dangtu second, and then Wuhu. Disappointed with the warlords' rule, Chiang resigned his post and left for England in 1933 where he taught Chinese at the University of London and worked in the Wellcome Museum of Medical Science in London.

In 1955, Chiang arrived in the United States and became a naturalized citizen in 1966. He taught at Columbia University and worked as a curator at the Peabody Museum. Chiang was a prose writer, a poet, a painter, and a calligrapher. He is mostly known for the "Silent Traveler" series, which recount his travel experiences in different cities and countries, such as *The Silent Traveler: A Chinese Artist in Lakeland* (1937), *The Silent Traveler in Dublin*

(1953), and *The Silent Traveler in Paris* (1959). Between 1937 and 1972, he wrote 12 such books. In addition, he also wrote autobiographies, *A Chinese Childhood* (1940) and *China Revised after Forty-two Years* (1977). His two novels are *Chin-Pao and the Giant Panda* (1939) and *The Men of the Burma Road* (1942). Chiang received such honors as honorary curator at Peabody Museum, Phi Beta Kappa orator at Harvard University, Emerson Fellow in Poetry, senior specialist awards from the East-West Center in Honolulu, etc.

CHIENG, CHIEH (1976–). A **Chinese American** novelist, Chieng was born in Hong Kong and moved to California when he was seven. His debut novel, *A Long Stay in a Distant Land* (2005), is told with a deadpan wit and sense of irony. The novel explores themes of history, memory, and family.

CHILDREN'S BOOK. *See* CHILDREN'S LITERATURE.

CHILDREN'S LITERATURE. This genre in Asian American literature began with one of the earliest Asian American writers, **Edith Maude Eaton**, whose "Tales of Chinese Children" first appeared in 1912. Following her was the **South Asian American** writer **Dhan Gopal Mukerji**, the first Asian American author to receive a Newbery Medal for his children's book *Gay-Neck: The Story of a Pigeon* (1928). However, it was not until the 1970s and 1980s that Asian American children's books and **young adult novels** became a force that drew the attention of the mainstream readership. One of the pioneers during these decades was the **Japanese American** writer **Yoshiko Uchida,** who has published more than 30 children's books and has been influential on the following generations of Japanese American children's book authors. Uchida's *The Journey to Topaz* (1971) led the way for a series of children's stories and young adult novels on the **Japanese American internment** experiences. Under Uchida's influence, Japanese American **Cynthia Kadohata** published *Kira-Kira,* which won the 2005 Newbery Medal. **Chinese American** author **Laurence Michael Yep** has written over 40 novels for children and young adults. His best-known novel, *Dragonwings* (1975), won the Newbery Honor, the Boston Globe–Horn Book Award, the International Reading Association Children's Book Award, and the Lewis Carroll Shelf Award. Yep's *Dragon's Gate* (1993) won him the second Newbery Honor.

The **Vietnamese American** author **Quang Nhuong Huynh** published his childhood memoir *The Land I Lost* (1982), winner of the Library of Congress Children's Books Award and the Blue Cobra Award, among other. Chinese American **Ruthanne Lum McCunn**'s *Pie-Biter* (1983) was the first Asian American children's book that won an **American Book Award**. **Korean American** writer **Marie Myung-Ok Lee** wrote the young adult novel

Finding My Voice in 1992, and Japanese American **Ken Mochizuki** published *Baseball Saved Us* in 1993, both of which center on ethnic identities. **Kyoko Mori**'s young adult novel *Shizuko's Daughter* (1993) was named a New York Times Best Young Children's Book.

In the 2000s, Asian American children's literature began to proliferate. Children's stories, young adult novels, and children's **poetry** have grown in quantity and popularity. The notable ones include *A Step from Heaven* (2003) by Korean American **Na An**; fantasies for children *The Conch Bearer* (2005), *The Mirror of Fire and Dreams* (2005), and *Shadowland* (2009) by the celebrated **South Asian American** novelist **Chitra Banerjee Divakaruni**; the historical novels by **Linda Sue Park**, *Seesaw Girl* (1999) and *A Single Shard* (2003), winner of the 2002 Newbery Medal, and the graphic novel *American Born Chinese* (2006) by **Gene Luen Yang**, which was the first graphic novel nominated for a **National Book Award**. Other notable authors include **Grace Lin**, **Jenny Han**, **Allen Say**, **Jyotsna Sreenivasan**, **Janet S. Wong**, **Lisa Yee**, **Laurence Yep**, **Uma Krishnaswami**, **Belle Yang**, **Lenore Look**, **Sook Nyul Choi**, and **Lensey Cho Namioka**. *See also* BACHO, PETER; BALGASSI, HAEMI; BANERJEE, ANJALI; BUDHOS, MARINA; CARLING, AMELIA LAU; CHARI, SHEELA; CHEN, JUSTINA; CHENG, TERRENCE; CHIN-LEE, CYNTHIA; CHOI, YANGSOOK; DASWANI, KAVITA; HALL, BRUCE EDWARD; HO, MINFONG; HONG, LILY TOY; JIANG, JI-LI; KAKUGAWA, FRANCES H.; KELTNER, KIM WONG; KIM, YONG IK; KONO, JULIET SANAE; LEE, HUY VOUN; LEE, MILLY; MAH, ADELINE YEN; MAK, KAM; PAK SOYUNG; PARK, FRANCES; PARK, GINGER; PERKINS, MITALI; SHETH, KASHMIRA; SHIN, SUN YUNG; SOENTPIED, CHRIS; TAN, AMY; TELEMAQUE, ELEANOR WONG; TUNG, ANGELA; WARTSKI, MAUREEN CRANE; YAMANAKA, LOIS-ANN; YAMATE, SANDRA S.; YANG, DORIS JONES; YIN; YOO, PAULA; YOUNG, ED.

CHIN, FRANK (1940–). One of the most famous **Chinese American** playwrights and novelists, Chin was born in Berkeley, California, to a Chinese immigrant father and a fourth-generation Chinese American mother. He received his B.A. in English from the University of California, Berkeley, and attended the Program in Creative Writing at the University of Iowa. Chin has written novels, short fiction, plays, and essays. He was the first Asian American playwright to stage his plays at the American Place Theatre in New York City. Chin is one of the pioneers in Asian American **theater** and founded the **Asian American Theater Workshop**, which became the **Asian American Theater Company** in 1973.

The Chickencoop Chinaman (1972) and *The Year of the Dragon* (1977) are two plays that earned his place in American theater. Both plays center on the challenges Asian American men face in a culture that has emasculated them through media stereotypes, socioeconomic exploitation, and legal discrimination. Asian American masculinity has preoccupied Chin's literary career. Writing against the **racist** media and culture with few male models among Asian American writers, he modeled his work upon African American writers, such as Ishmael Reed, and borrowed extensively from classic Chinese literature of warriors, such as *Water Margin* and *Romance of the Three Kingdoms*. In his novels and short stories, Chin makes voluminous allusion to Chinese mythology, classics, and American popular culture, such as in *Donald Duk* (1991), *Gunga Din Highway* (1994), and the short story collection *The Chinaman Pacific and Frisco R.R. Co.* (1988). Almost all his literary writings focus on the theme of the father–son relationship, exploring the generational tension due to the scarcity of positive Asian male images in American culture. **Charlie Chan**, the Chinese American detective on the screen, is a recurring figure in Chin's writing, serving as the epitome of racial and cultural stereotyping of Chinese American men in American popular culture.

Chin has also published *Bulletproof Buddhists and Other Essays* (1998) and *Born in the USA: A Story of Japanese America, 1889–1947* (2002). He received the **American Book Award** for his story collection *The Chinaman Pacific and Frisco R.R. Co.* and the Lannan Literary Award. He was the first editor of the first anthology of Asian American literature *Aiiieeeee!* (1974) and second editor of its revision entitled *The Big Aiiieeeee!* (1991). His work in these two anthologies has made him a controversial figure in Asian American literature and culture. There he accused other Asian American writers like **Maxine Hong Kingston**, **Amy Tan**, and **David Henry Hwang** of furthering negative stereotypes of Asians and misappropriating Chinese mythology.

CHIN, JUSTIN (1969–). A **Chinese** Malaysian American poet, performing artist, and memoirist, Chin was born in Malaysia and raised and educated in Singapore. He came to the United States at the age of 19. He earned a B.A. in journalism and an M.A. in interdisciplinary arts in the United States. He currently lives in San Francisco. He is the author of three books of **poetry**: *Bite Hard* (1997), *Harmless Medicine* (2001), and *Gutted* (2006), which received the 2007 Thom Gunn Award for Poetry by the Publishing Triangle. With humor and rage, Chin's poetry depicts what it means to be a queer Asian American in a country that valorizes Caucasian heterosexuality. He has also authored two books of nonfiction: *Mongrel: Essays, Diatribes and Pranks* (1999) and the ur-memoir *Burden of Ashes* (2002). These works explore themes of sexuality, desire, **hybridity**, belonging, **homelands**, and loss. *See also* SOUTHEAST ASIAN AMERICAN LITERATURE AND THEATER.

CHIN, MARILYN (1955–). A **Chinese American** poet and novelist, Chin was born in Hong Kong and raised in Portland, Oregon. She received her B.A. in Chinese language and literature from the University of Massachusetts at Amherst and her M.F.A. from the University of Iowa. Currently, she is a professor of creative writing at San Diego State University. Chin is primarily known as a poet and has written collections of **poetry**, such as *Dwarf Bamboo* (1987), *The Phoenix Gone, the Terrace Empty* (1994), and *Rhapsody in Yellow* (2002). Chin has won numerous awards for her poetry, including awards from the Radcliffe Institute at Harvard, the Rockefeller Foundation, and the National Endowment for the Arts. She has received a Stegner Fellowship, the PEN/Josephine Miles Award, four Pushcart Prizes, the Paterson Prize, and a Fulbright Fellowship to Taiwan. Her poetry has been included in the *Best American Poetry*.

Chin is unabashedly political in her poetry, which uses the "I" voice to explore themes of acculturation, **assimilation**, **racism**, **women**'s oppression, and the **model minority** syndrome among Asian Americans. Her frequent references to Chinese poetry and history demonstrate her deep concern about cultural and linguistic preservation in the face of assimilation. Her poetic voice is humorous, ironic, tender, subversive, and compassionate. Artistic **hybridity** is her signature in that she marries Chinese and Japanese poetics with the Western ones both in form and content. Her most recent publication *Revenge of the Mooncake Vixen* (2009) is an interrelated set of stories about two twin Chinese American sisters in Southern California. These stories, like Chin's poetry, interweaving Chinese mythology and folktales, make powerful political statements through humor, irony, and hyperboles.

CHIN-LEE, CYNTHIA (1958–). A **Chinese American** author of **children's books**, Chin-Lee was born and raised in Washington, D.C. She earned a B.A. in East Asian languages from Harvard University and an M.A. at the East-West Center at the University of Hawaii. Her first children's book, *Almond Cookies and Dragon Well Tea* (1993), is an autobiographical tale of friendship. She went on to write *A Is for Asia* (1997) and *A is for the Americas* (1999), which earned an award from the National Council for Social Studies and Children's Book Council as a Notable Children's Book in Social Studies; *Amelia to Zora: Twenty-six Women Who Changed the World* (2005), *Akira to Zoltan: Twenty-six Men Who Changed the World* (2008), and *Operational Marriage* (2011), which tells the story of two children arranging a wedding for their lesbian parents. Chin-Lee currently works as a technical writer and documentation manager at Sun Microsystems, Menlo Park, California.

CHINATOWN. The Chinese began to arrive in California in the mid-1800s to participate in the Gold Rush. The first Chinese neighborhood emerged in San Francisco's Portsmouth Square. By 1854 the Chinese Benevolent Association, also known as the Six Companies, was organized to help immigrants coming from their six respective provinces in China. Chinatown was thus formed, with the Kong Chow Temple (a Buddhist shrine) built in 1851, Old St. Mary's Church erected as a mission in 1854, and a Chinese hospital opened in 1900. After the 1906 San Francisco earthquake destroyed much of the neighborhood, Chinatown was rebuilt with distinctive Chinese architecture as a tourist attraction.

Due to the hardships from the increasing legislative discriminations against the Chinese and anti-Chinese violence along the West Coast, intensified by the **Page Act** and **Chinese Exclusion Act**, the **Chinese American** population began to move eastward and settled in big cities, such as Seattle, Chicago, Detroit, Boston, Philadelphia, and New York, and established Chinatowns in these cities. Today, modern Chinatowns have sprung up in many other cities, such as Washington, D.C., Houston, Los Angeles, San Gabriel Valley, and Miami. New York City now boasts multiple Chinatowns.

Chinatown is a familiar setting in Asian American literature. Its patriarchal culture serves not only as the *mise-en-scene* but also the source of conflicts in such novels as **Louis Chu**'s *Eat a Bowl of Tea*, **Jade Snow Wong**'s *Fifth Chinese Daughter*, **Maxine Hong Kingston**'s *The Woman Warrior*, and **Fae Myenne Ng**'s *Bone* and *Steer toward Rock*. Chinatown is also presented as a slum where violence and poverty rule the day, such as in **John Okada**'s ***No-No Boy***. Chinatown's history and culture engender the desperate search for paternal models in **Frank Chin**'s *Chickencoop Chinaman* and create the dysfunctional family relations in *The Year of the Dragon*. Chin's novel *Donald Duk*, however, celebrates a new Chinatown in which healthy families prosper and acculturate the young.

CHINESE AMERICAN LITERATURE AND THEATER. The earliest Chinese literary event in the United States is probably the first Chinese theatrical performance by Tong Hook Tong Dramatic Company in October 1852 at the American Theater on Sansome Street in San Francisco. It was followed by another Chinese **theater**, the Shanghai, that opened in an existing two-story building on Dupont Street (the present Grant Avenue) in San Francisco in the late fall of 1855. A more ambitious Chinese company, the Royal Chinese Theatre, opened on Jackson Street in San Francisco on 27 January 1868. It had an American-standard auditorium that could seat 1,100. These theaters provided ordinary Americans the first glimpse of Chinese dramatic and literary culture.

Aside from these theaters, the first generation of Chinese American writers were Western educated men, such as **Lee Yan Phou**, **Yee Chiang**, and **Yutang Lin**, who immigrated to the United States to attend college. Unlike their countrymen living in segregated ghettos and being treated with racial hostility by many Americans, these writers more or less succeeded in **assimilating** into the mainstream American cultural and intellectual life. Their genre was exclusively autobiography, a genre alien to the Chinese literary tradition before the 20th century. Their choice to write autobiographies could be attributed to two reasons: first, that they were Christian converts who found confessional writing more adapted for self-expression than other genres, and, second, that life writings were more effective in portraying themselves as equals to Americans—self-representations that would counter the degrading stereotypes of the Chinese. Despite these Chinese memoirists writing in the late 1800s and early 1900s, literary historians agree that Chinese American literature really began with **Edith Maude Eaton,** because she was the first one to write fiction. However different their choices of genre, the first generation of Chinese American writers shared two common objectives: serving as ambassadors of Chinese civilization and presenting Chinese immigrants with humanity and dignity.

Between the 1850s and 1940s, Chinese Americans endured much legislative discrimination at both local and federal levels, such as the **Page Act**, the Alien Land law, and the **Chinese Exclusion Act**. In addition, they were subjected to socioeconomic and cultural marginalization. Rampant **racism** against the Chinese sometimes escalated to lynching, beating, larceny, and robbing. The Naturalization Act of 1790 restricted naturalized U.S. citizenship to “free white persons.” As a result, the Chinese were unable to vote, and faced additional restrictions such as the inability to own land under many state laws.

It is against this historical background that the second generation of Chinese American writers was raised. Most of these writers were American born and ashamed of their ethnicity. Their writings explored common themes like generational and cultural conflicts, alienation from the Chinese community, and eagerness to assimilate into the mainstream America. Some of these writers are autobiographers, such as **Pardee Lowe** and **Alice Lin**, while others write fiction, such as **Chin-Yang Lee** and **Monfoon Leong**. Most of their writing paints a portrait of Chinese Americans as hard-working, disciplined, and law abiding, in other words, **model minorities**. The best example is *Fifth Chinese Daughter* (1945) by **Jade Snow Wong**, a bestselling autobiography that focuses on the tension between Chinese and American values and expresses the author’s admiration for American individualism and competitiveness.

The third generation of Chinese American writers came into political consciousness during the time of the civil rights movement and thus became radicalized on matters of citizenship, race, and gender. Writers such as **Frank Chin**, **Marilyn Chin, Maxine H. Kingston**, **Amy Tan**, **Gish Jen**, **David Henry Wang**, **Eleanor Wong Telemaque**, **Shawn Wong**, **David Wong Louie**, and **Laurence Yep** demonstrate ethnic pride as they recount and redefine the Chinese American experience. In doing so, they have contributed to the creation of a new Chinese American sensibility. Kingston's *Woman Warrior* (1976) served as a major landmark in Chinese American literature. In exposing mainstream's **racism** and **Chinatown**'s sexism, and in blurring the boundary between fiction and nonfiction, this book ushered in a new literary era that can be described as one of protest literature. However, there are also many poets who prefer broad and universal themes, rather than ethnic ones. Instead of probing the immigrant memory for Chinese American themes, poets such as **Mei-mei Berssenbrugge**, **Alex Kuo**, **Li-Young Lee**, and **John Yau** dedicate themselves to themes of nature, memory, and language.

The fourth generation, or the youngest, of Chinese American writers has become greatly diverse and individually oriented in terms of themes, genres, styles, and sensibilities. For the first time, genre fiction, such as detective fiction, science fiction, and fairytales by authors like **Henry Chang**, **Da Chen**, **Ted Chiang**, **Ed Lin**, **Xiaolong Qiu**, **Charles Yu**, **Kenneth Lin**, and **Aimee Liu**, becomes a part of Chinese American literature. Biracial or multiracial Chinese American writers, such as **Sarah Shun-Lien Bynum**, **Ruthanne Lum McCunn**, **Sigrid Nunez**, **Paisley Rekdal**, and **Thaddeus Rutkowski**, explore themes of mixed-race identity, but often ethnicity is not their concern at all. Still others choose to transcend their own ethnicity by portraying characters of other ethnicities, such as **Diana Chang, Eugenie Chan**, and **Kenneth Lin**. One of the exciting phenomena in the recent development of Chinese American literature is the infusion of talents from Hong Kong, Taiwan, and Mainland China, who immigrated to the United States in the 1980s and 1990s. Such writers as **Jean Kwok**, **Raymond K. Wong**, **Mingmei Yip**, **Victoria Chang**, **Justina Chen**, **Jeffrey Ethan Lee**, **Ha Jin**, **Yiyun Li**, **Anchee Min**, **Fan Wu**, **Ping Wang**, and **Geling Yan** have diversified and strengthened Chinese American literature.

The earliest Asian American theaters were organized by Chinese and Japanese Americans to produce predominantly Chinese and Japanese plays. The **East West Players** was the first Asian American theater, founded in Los Angeles in 1965, while the **Asian Exclusion Act** was founded by **Garrett Hongo** in 1975 in Seattle, which was renamed in 1981 to be the **Northwest Asian American Theatre Company**. In 1975, **Ping Chong** launched **Ping Chong & Company**. **Pan Asian Repertory Theatre** was founded in 1999 in New York City and led by artistic director Tisa Chang. **Asian American Theater Company** was established in 1979 in San Francisco. Its former form was the **Asian American Theater Workshop,** under the artistic directorship of Frank Chin. **David Henry Hwang Writers' Institute** was created in 1991 by David Henry Hwang in collaboration with the East West Players. It provides writing classes to promote new Asian American work for the stage. Chinese American theaters together with other Asian American theaters have flourished in the past four decades. The major playwrights include Frank Chin, David Henry Hwang, Eugenie Chan, **Cherylene Lee**, Kenneth Lin, **Elizabeth Wong**, **Chay Yew**, Ping Chong, etc. *See also* CARLING, AMELIA LAU; CHAI, MAY-LEE; CHAN, JEFFERY PAUL; CHANG, JENNIFER; CHANG, LAN SAMANTHA; CHANG, TINA; CHAO, EVELINA; CHAO, PATRICIA; CHEN, CHING-IN; CHEN, KEN; CHENG, NIEN; CHENG, TERRENCE; CHEONG, FIONA; CHIANG, FAY; CHIANG, YEE; CHIENG, CHIEH; CHIN-LEE, CYNTHIA; CHING, CARLA; CHIU, CHRISTINA; CHOCK, ERIC; CHOONG, TINLING; CHOU, CYNTHIA L.; CHUANG, HUA; CHUNG, FRANCES; DAVIES, PETER HO; FEI, DEANNA; FOO, LORA JO; FULBECK, KIP; HALL, BRUCE EDWARD; HAN, SUYING; HONG, LILY TOY; JIANG, JI-LI; KELTNER, KIM WONG; KUO, HELENA; LAU, CAROLYN; LEE, ANNETTE; LEE, C. Y.; LEE, GUS; LEE, MILLY; LEE, PRISCILLA; LEE, WENDY; LEONG, RUSSELL; LEUNG, BRIAN; LEYUNG-RYAN, TERESA; LI, LING-AI; LIM, GENNY; LIN, ADET; LIN, HAZEL AI CHUN; LIN, TAI-YI; LO, STEVEN C.; LOH, SANDRA TSING; LOOK, LENORE; LORD, BETTE BAO; LU, ALVIN; LU, CHI FA; LUM, DARRELL H.Y.; LUM, WING TEK; MAH, ADELINE YEN; MAK, KAM; MIN, ANCHEE; NAMIOKA, LENSEY CHO; NG, FAE MYENNE; NG, MEI; NIEH, HUALING; PEI, LOWRY; ROBERTS, DMAE; SAY, ALLEN; SEE, LISA LENINE; SHEPARD, KAREN; SU, ADRIENNE; SZE, ARTHUR; SZE, MAI MAI; TAO, LIN; TSENG, JENNIFER; TSIANG, H. T.; TSUI, KITTY; TUAN, ALICE; TUNG, ANGELA; TYAU, KATHLEEN; WANG, SHANXING; WEI, KATHERINE; WONG, MAY; WONG, NELLIE; WONG, SHAWN; WU, FAN; YANG, BELLE; YANG, DORIS JONES; YANG, GENE LUEN; YANG, JEFFREY; YANG, RAE; YEE, LISA; YEP, LAURENCE MICHAEL; YIN; YIP, WAI-LIM; YUNG, WING.

CHINESE EXCLUSION ACT. This was a federal act signed into law by President Chester A. Arthur on 8 May 1882. This act allowed the United States to suspend Chinese immigration for 10 years. This legislation was motivated by the anti-Chinese sentiment during the economic decline after the

Civil War and organized by politicians and labor unions on the West Coast. The 1888 Scott Act expanded upon the Chinese Exclusion Act, annulling the provision that allowed Chinese immigrants to leave and return. The Act was renewed for another 10 years by the 1892 Geary Act and again with no terminal date in 1902. The 1943 Magnuson Act repealed the Chinese Exclusion Act and allowed Chinese immigrants already residing in the country to become naturalized citizens. It also allowed a national quota of 105 Chinese immigrants per year. It was not until the Immigration Act of 1965 did the Chinese begin to be treated the same as Europeans.

The Chinese Exclusion Act is a significant reference in Chinese American literature. Many Chinese American writers have portrayed Chinese American men's lives without wives, without children, and without families. Many of these male characters marry before they leave China for the United States and never return to China for a visit due to the fear of being barred from reentry when returning to the United States. In *Eating a Bowl of Tea* by **Louis Chu**, the protagonist's father never visits home and his wife lives the life of a widow in China. To get around this legal ban of immigration, the Chinese created an identity known as **paper son**, who tried to enter the United States under a false identity as son to a Chinese already residing in the United States. Paper-son characters and their fear of deportation abound in Chinese American literature, such as in *Bone* and *Steer toward Rock* by **Fae Myenne Ng**, *The Woman Warrior* and *China Men* by **Maxine Hong Kingston**, and the short fiction by **Frank Chin**. The Chinese Exclusion Act had such an impact on the Asian American psyche that one of the early Asian American theatrical ensembles was named Asian Exclusion Act.

CHING, CARLA. A **Chinese American** dramatist, Ching was born and raised in Los Angeles. She received her B.A. from Vassar College and M.F.A. from New School for Drama. She is a playwright and teaching artist with the New Victory **Theater**, Lincoln Center Institute, and Young Playwrights. Her full-length plays include *TBA*, *Dirty*, *Found Objects*, *Big Blind/Little Blind*, and *The Sugar House at the Edge of the Wilderness*. Short plays include *Next Big Thing*, *The Further Adventures of Little Goth Girl*, *Dissipating Heat,* and *Closing Up Shop*. Her plays have been produced or workshopped by **Ma-Yi Theater Company**, the **Women's** Project, **Second Generation Productions**, Desipina & Company, the Hegira, and Vampire Cowboys, among others. She is a member of the Ma-Yi Writers Lab. She has received honors including an Urban Artists Initiative fellowship, a Teachers and Writers Collaborative Fellowship, and a Lark Play Development Center Playwrights Workshop Fellowship. *See also* THEATER.

CHIU, CHRISTINA. A **Chinese American** fiction writer, Chiu attended Bates College and earned her M.F.A. in creative writing from Columbia University. She published a collection of short stories, *Troublemakers and Other Saints* (2001), which is a collection of linked stories about generational conflict, ethnic identity, and gender roles. It won an **Asian American Literary Award**. One of the original founders of the **Asian American Writers' Workshop**, she has received its Van Lier Fellowship. She currently lives in New York. *See also* WOMEN.

CHOCK, ERIC (1950–). A **Chinese American** poet, Chock was born in Hawaii. He received his B.A. in sociology from the University of Pennsylvania and M.A. in creative writing from the University of Hawaii. He is widely known for the literary magazine *Bamboo Ridge* and the **Bamboo Ridge** Press, which he and his friend **Darrell Lum** founded in 1978. Since then, *Bamboo Ridge* has been devoted to publishing local literature. Writers who appeared within its pages have since become well-known literary figures—**Lois-Ann Yamanaka**, Rodney Morales, **Gary Pak**, **Nora Okja Keller**, Dana Naone Hall, **Wing Tek Lum**, Michael McPherson, Mari Kubo, **Cathy Song**, etc. Chock has received numerous awards and recognitions, such as the Pushcart Prize XVI, the 1996 Hawaii Award for Literature (HAL), the Cades Award for Literature, and the Hawaii Alliance for Arts Education's Arts Educator of the Year Award. Chock's **poetry** collection *Last Days Here* (1990) portrays the local culture in the Pidgin language to capture the rich imageries of fishing, tea drinking, food, religious ceremonies, the sugarcane field, and the lives of the immigrants. Chock's poetry has helped raise the profile of the writings by Pacific Islanders in Asian American literature, which has been dominated by writers from mainland America. Chock's other poetry has appeared in anthologies like *Breaking Silence: An Anthology of Contemporary Asian American Poets* and *Premonitions: The Kaya Anthology of New Asian North American Poetry*. Chock received the HAL for his work on *Bamboo Ridge*.

CHOI, ANNIE (1976–). A **Korean American** memoirist, Choi was born and raised in Los Angeles. She received a B.A. from the University of California, Berkeley, and an M.F.A. from Columbia University. Her memoir *Happy Birth or Whatever* (2007) explores the tensions between mothers and daughters and presents an uproariously funny account of growing up with her Korean American family in Los Angeles. *See also* WOMEN.

CHOI, DON MEE. A **Korean American** poet, Choi was born in South Korea and came to the United States as a student in 1981. She studied art at the

California Institute of the Arts. Her first book of poems, *The Morning News Is Exciting* (2010), explores the themes of colonialism, **homeland**, history, gender, and war. She lives in Seattle and translates contemporary Korean **women's poetry**.

CHOI, SOOK NYUL (1937–). A **Korean American** novelist, Choi was born in Pyongyang, North Korea, and lived through the Japanese occupation, Communism, and the Korean War (1950–1953). In 1958, she immigrated to the United States to attend Manhattanville College in New York. She has written three autobiographical novels that chronicle her family's experience in the wars, their escape to South Korea, and their lives in America. Her first novel, *Year of Impossible Goodbyes* (1991), depicts the challenge her family faced during the Japanese occupation to preserve their national and ethnic identity. Her second book, *Echoes of the White Giraffe* (1993), focuses on her family living the life of refugees in South Korea and the female protagonist's growing independence. *Gathering of Pearls* (1994) is her third book, which centers on the female protagonist's life in the United States and the tension between family's traditional expectations and American individualism. Choi won the Judy Lopez Book Award for the National **Women**'s Book Association in 1992 for her first novel. She has also published **children's books**, such as *Halmoni and the Picnic* (1993), *The Best Older Sister* (1997), and *Yummi and Halmoni's Trip* (1997).

CHOI, SUSAN (1969–). A **Korean American** novelist, Choi was born in South Bend, Indiana, to a Korean immigrant father and a first-generation Russian Jewish American mother. She received her B.A. in literature from Yale University and an M.F.A. in creative writing from Cornell University. In her first novel, *The Foreign Student* (1998), which won an **Asian American Literary Award**, Choi tells the story of a relationship between a Korean student and a young Southern **woman**, both of whom have dark pasts, and how their relationship blossoms into romance. *American Woman* (2003) was a finalist for the Pulitzer Prize in 2004. This novel fictionalizes the story of the Patty Hearst incident and centers on Jenny Shimada, a young Japanese American woman (based on a real-life person, Wendy Yoshimura) who agrees to help Patty/Pauline and her kidnappers. *A Personal Interest* (2008) was a finalist for the PEN/Faulkner Award in 2009. Inspired by the Wen Ho Lee accusations and the Unabomber Ted Kaczynski, this novel portrays Dr. Lee, a senior math professor in a Midwestern university and paints a powerful psychological landscape fraught with alienation and shame. Choi has also published many short stories in journals, such as the *Iowa Review*, *Epoch*, and *Shankpainter*.

CHOI, YANGSOOK (1967–). A **Korean American** author and illustrator of **children's books**, Choi was born and raised in Seoul, South Korea. She moved to New York to study art. She attended Kendall College of Arts and Design in Michigan before she went to the School of Visual Arts in New York City, from which she received an M.F.A. in illustration. In addition to illustrating many books, she is the author of several books of her own, including *The Name Jar* (2001), *New Cat* (1999), *Behind the Mask* (2006), *Peach Heaven* (2005), and *The Sun Girl and the Moon Boy: A Korean Folktale* (1997). Her works have received many honors, including Best of the Best by the Chicago Public Library, the Best Children's Books of the Year by Children's Book Council, the International Reading Association Children's Book Award, the American Library Association Notable Book, and the Skipping Stones Award.

CHONG, PING (1946–). An internationally acclaimed **Chinese American** director, playwright, and multidisciplinary artist, Chong was born in Toronto and grew up in New York City's **Chinatown**. A seminal figure in Asian American **theater** and the Asian American arts movement, Chong studied filmmaking and graphic design at Pratt Institute's School of Visual Arts. He began his career in 1966 at Meredith Monk's House Foundation. Later he collaborated with Monk on works like *The Travelogue Series* and *The Games*, for which they shared an Outstanding Achievement in Music Theatre Award in 1986. His first independent theater work was *Lazarus* (1972). Since then, he has created over 50 major works for the stage, including *Humboldt's Current* (**Obie Award**, 1977), *A.M./A.M.—The Articulated Man* (Villager Award, 1982), *Nosferatu* (Maharam Design Award, 1985), *Angels of Swedenborg* (1985), *Kind Ness* (USA Playwrights' Award, 1988), *Brightness*, which garnered two 1990 Bessie Awards, *Deshima* (1990), *Chinoiserie* (1995), and *After Sorrow* (1997). In addition, he is also the recipient of six National Endowment for the Arts fellowships, a Guggenheim Fellowship, a TCG/Pew Charitable Trust National Theatre Artist Residency Program Fellowship, a National Institute for Music Theatre Award, and the second Award for Sustained Achievement in 2000.

In 1975, Chong launched **Ping Chong & Company** (originally called the Fiji Theatre Company), which set as its mission the creation and performance of innovative multidisciplinary works of theater and art to explore the intersections of history, race, art, and technology in the contemporary world. The subjects of most of his works are **East-West relations** and cultural diversity. The company has created and toured works by Chong and his collaborators, presenting at major theaters, performing arts centers, and arts festivals in the world. Since 1992, Chong has created more than 30 works in the *Undesirable Elements* project, an ongoing series of oral-history theater works exploring issues of race, culture, and identity in the lives of individuals in specific communities. For this project, Chong and collaborators conduct interviews with potential participants from a local community. These interviews then inform the creation of a script, which is performed by the interviewees, that present life stories of individuals who live between cultures or worlds.

Chong's recent productions include several large-scale puppet theater works, *Cathay: Three Tales of China* (2005), *Obon: Tales of Rain and Moonlight* (2002), and *Kwaidan* (1998). *Cathay* told three interconnected stories to link three Chinese historical periods: the Tang Dynasty, the Japanese invasion during World War II, and contemporary China. *Cathay* was named one of the Top 10 Shows of the 2005–2006 Season by New York Theatre Wire and was awarded three Henry Hewes awards for achievement in theatrical design. In 2006, Chong received the prestigious USA Artist Fellowship by the U.S. Artists Foundation in recognition of his contribution to American arts. His published works include *Kind Ness* (1986), *Snow* (1988), *Nuit Blanche* (1990), *Undesirable Elements/New York* and *Gaijin* (1995), *Truth and Beauty* (2001), a video version of *Secret History*, a part of *Undesirable Elements* series (2000), and *East-West Quartet* (2005).

CHOONG, TINLING. A Malaysian **Chinese American** novelist, Choong was born and raised in Malaysia. She graduated from Wellesley College and is presently working toward a Ph.D. in Chinese literature at Yale University. She is the author of two novels. *Firewife: A Story of Fire and Water* (2007) draws on the ancient Chinese creation legend of Nuwa and the battle between fire and water to give a modern story of how **women** are connected throughout time. *Yuyu and the Banyan Tree* (2009) tells the coming-of-age story of an 11-year-old Malaysian Chinese girl who develops a deep relationship with the banyan tree across the street from her home. *See also* SOUTHEAST ASIAN AMERICAN LITERATURE AND THEATER.

CHOU, CYNTHIA L. (1926–). A **Chinese American** autobiographer, Chou was born in China and received a B.A. from a Chinese university. She and her husband immigrated to the United States in 1955. In 1957, she received an M.A. in education from the Teachers College of Columbia University. Although she pursued no profession, she has been frequently invited to speak to private organizations and clubs about her personal experiences. These speeches inspired her to write her autobiography *My Life in the United States* (1970). Organized chronologically, her autobiography recounts her experience as an immigrant living in New York and Michigan and her experience of cultural clashes, interspersed with anecdotes from her earlier life in China.

CHU, LOUIS HING (1915–1970). A **Chinese American** novelist, Chu was born in Guangdong, China, and immigrated to the United States with his family when he was nine. He attended Upsala College and majored in English and minored in sociology. Between 1943 and 1945, he served in the U.S. Army and was stationed in Kunming, a city in Southwestern China. He was able to bring a Chinese wife to **Chinatown**, New York, because of the War Brides Act of 1945. Chu is regarded as a very important figure in the Chinese American literary tradition even though he published only one novel, *Eat a Bowl of Tea* (1961). This is because his portrayal of the Chinese and Chinatown departed from the stereotypes that dominated then literary representations of the Chinese in American literature. Some of the early Chinese American writers, such as **Pardee Lowe**, **Jade Snow Wong**, and **Lin Yutang**, were participants in reaffirming the stereotypes.

Eat a Bowl of Tea depicts Chinatown, New York, in a way that neither exoticizes nor reviles it. Instead, it draws realistic pictures of its inhabitants as three-dimensional human beings who experience such problems in an aging **bachelor society** as patriarchal oppression, racial oppression, sexual deprivation, marriage crisis, etc. Chu attributes these problems to the U.S. legal exclusions of Chinese men and **women**, particularly the **Chinese Exclusion Act** and the **Page Act**. Symbolic of the aging community, the only young couple in the novel, Ben Loy and Mei Oi, is unable to conceive and regenerate despite the entire community's expectation and pressure. Only after they leave Chinatown, New York, are they able to become parents. Chu gives the novel an authentic Chinatown flavor by using creolized Cantonese English. *Eat a Bowl of Tea* was made into a film in 1989, directed by Wayne Wang.

CHUANG, HUA. A **Chinese American** novelist, Chuang was born in China to a wealthy family. To escape the Japanese occupation, her family left for England in 1937 and then to the United States. Chuang's education consisted of schooling in America and informal education by Chinese nursemaids, Scottish nannies, and Irish cooks. For a brief period, she worked in the investment business. To search for herself and some independence, she left New York for Paris. After a brief love affair there, she returned to New York, having crossed one threshold on her journey toward self-definition. We know only one publication by Chuang, *Crossings* (1968), which has been hailed by critics as Asian America's first modernist novel. *Crossings*, an autobiographical novel, represents several moments of cultural crossings in the life of Fourth Jane, who travels from China to Europe to America and back to Europe. Fraught with memories of small moments—dreams, fantasies, and Chinese mythology—the novel experiments with a formal fragmentation that seems to mirror the existential fragmentation of the protagonist.

CHUNG, FRANCES (1950–1990). A **Chinese American** poet, Chung was born and raised in **Chinatown**, New York. She received an undergraduate degree in mathematics from Smith College and taught at public schools at the Lower East Side of New York. She published her **poetry** in several anthologies and journals, including *The Portable Lower East Side* and *IKON*, and posthumously in *Premonitions: The Kaya Anthology of New Asian North American Poetry.* She left behind manuscripts of two books of poetry, which **Walter Lew** compiled and published as *Crazy Melon and Chinese Apple: The Poems of Frances Chung* (2000). She was awarded several poetry fellowships by the New York Times Company Foundation and New York State Council on the Arts.

CHUNG, PHILIP W. A **Korean American** playwright, film director, and producer, Chung is the author of several plays, such as *Yellow Face* (1997), *Home Is Where the Han Is* (1998), *Laughter Joy and Loneliness and Sex and Sex and Sex and Sex* (2000), *The Adventures of Byo Boy* (2001), *Aziatik Nation* (2004), *Dead of Night* (2000), *The Golden Hour* (2006), *One Nation under God* (2006), *My Man Kono* (2007), and *Grace Kim and the Spiders from Mars* (2009). He has also written scripts, including *A Ribbon of Dreams* (2002) and the ABC-TV series *Lois and Clark: The New Adventures of Superman* (1996). He is a cofounder of **Lodestone Theatre Ensemble** and serves as its coartistic director. *See also* THEATER.

CHUNG, SONYA. A **Korean American** novelist, Chung was born in the United States to Korean immigrants. She received her undergraduate education from Columbia University. She did not visit Korea until she was 29. Her debut novel, *Long for This World* (2010), explores themes of family, immigration, loss, and identity. Her stories and essays have appeared in such venues as the *Threepenny Review*, *Crab Orchard Review*, *Sonora Review*, and *Bomb Magazine*. She is a recipient of a Pushcart Prize nomination, the Charles Johnson Fiction Award, and the Bronx Council on the Arts Writers' Fellowship and Residency. She teaches creative writing at Columbia University.

CLUB O'NOODLES. This is a **Vietnamese American theater** troupe, established in 1993 in Los Angeles. Its mission is to provide socially conscious, alternative entertainment that engages Vietnamese American and other Asian American issues. Its repertoire includes comedy, serious drama, dance, and music.

COLD TOFU. This is an Asian American comedy improv and sketch group, located in Los Angeles, California. It is dedicated to promoting diverse images of Asian Pacific Americans through comedy and to developing multiethnic talent through education and performance. A nonprofit organization, Cold Tofu was founded in 1981 by Marilyn Tokuda, Denice Kumagai, Judy Momii, and Irma Escamilla.

CRASTA, RICHARD (AVATAR PRABHU, 1952–). A **South Asian American** novelist, essayist, and memoirist, Crasta was born in Bangalore, India, to Catholic parents. The church and the convent school occupied an important place in his development. He came to the United States to pursue graduate education at American University in Washington, D.C. Then, he attended Columbia University and received an M.F.A. in creative writing. In 1998, he began publishing under the name Avatar Prabhu but reverted to Richard Crasta in 2005. Crasta is best known for his first and only novel, *The Revised Kama Sutra: A Novel of Colonialism and Desire* (1993), which is a picaresque and comic first-person narrative about the young man Vijay Prabhu of Mangalore. It portrays the four stages of Vijay Prabhu's life from a young child steeped in a sensual environment that clashes with the convent school to an adolescent with awakening sexuality and austere parents, to a young man indulging in erotic adventures, and to an irreverent artist who wants to experience life to its fullest and to dream without hindrance. *Beauty Queens, Children, and the Death of Sex* (1997) is a collection of witty and political essays. In 2000, he published *Impressing the Whites: The New International Slavery*, a book of essays that demonstrates his usual humor and exuberance while reflecting the racial ramifications in **East-West relations**. Five years later, he published two other books, *What We All Need: An Anti-Terrorist Book of Incompletions, Unsafe Love and Writing While Brown* (2005), a humorous collection of stories and essays that comment on contemporary issues like terrorism, sex, and drugs, and *Fathers, Rebels and Dreamers*, a collaboration with two of his Mangalore friends, Arunachalam Kumar, conservationist, and Ralph Nazareth, poet and professor. *The Killing of an Author: Jackie Kennedy, Sonny Pfizer, Seven Little Ayatollahs and a Suicide Pact* (2008) is his most recent publication, a memoir.

DASWANI, KAVITA (1964–). A **South Asian American** novelist, Daswani was born in Hong Kong to Indian parents and lived there for 30 years. She worked as a journalist and fashion correspondent for CNN, CNBC Asia, and *Women's Wear Daily*. She moved to Los Angeles after marriage and began to write novels. *For Matrimonial Purposes* (2003), *The Village Bride of Beverly Hills* (2004), and *Salaam, Paris* (2007) are romantic comedies centering on first-generation Indian **women** immigrants' experience of love, marriage, work, and relationships. She is also the author of a **young adult novel** *Indie Girl* (2007).

DAVID HENRY HWANG WRITERS' INSTITUTE. It was created in 1991 by **David Henry Hwang** in collaboration with the **East West Players**. It provides writing classes to promote new Asian American work for the stage. Instructors have included playwrights such as Doris Baizley, Paula Cizmar, **Prince Gomolvilas**, **Amy Hill**, Silas Jones, **Annette Lee**, Peter Sagal, Rick Shiomi, Judy Soo Hoo, Kelly Stuart, **Alice Tuan**, **Elizabeth Wong**, **Chay Yew**, and Brian Nelson. Among guest lecturers were **Philip Kan Gotanda**, Desmond Nakano, **Wakako Yamauchi**, and David Henry Hwang himself.

DAVIES, PETER HO (1966–). A **Chinese American** fiction writer, Davies was born in Great Britain to a Chinese mother (raised in a Malaysian community) and a Welsh father. He studied physics at the University of Manchester and English at Cambridge University, England. He moved to the United States in 1992 to attend the graduate program in creative writing at Boston University. He has taught at the University of Oregon, Emory University, and is now director of the MFA Program in creative writing at the University of Michigan. His short fiction has been widely anthologized, such as in *Prize Stories: The O. Henry Awards 1998* and *Best American Short Stories* 1995, 1996, and 2001. In 2003, *Granta* magazine named him among its 20 "Best of Young British Novelists." His first collection of fiction, *The Ugliest House in the World* (1998), won the John Llewellyn Rhys and Pen/Macmillan Prizes in Great Britain and the 1998 H. L. Davis Award for Short Fiction. This collection, mostly set in a small Welsh village, explores with humor themes of travel, multiethnic identities, and human flaws. His second collection of fiction, *Equal Love* (2000), was a New York Times Notable Book of the Year. In this collection of 12 stories, Davies tells quiet stories about interracial marriages, class ambition, ambivalent emotions of disappointment and pleasure, alienation and belonging, longing and resentment. His first novel, *The Welsh Girl* (2008), explores the themes of displacement and cowardice through the stories about a World War II POW camp built by the British in the remote mountains of northern Wales, a perfect site to exhibit the conflicts between the British and the Germans, the British and the Welsh, and the Welsh and the Germans. Davies has received other honors like fellowships from the Guggenheim Foundation, the National Endowment for the Arts, and the Fine Arts Work Center in Provincetown, and a Pen/Malamud Award.

DAWESAR, ABHA (1974–). A **South Asian American** novelist, Dawesar was born in Delhi, India, and moved to the United States to study political philosophy at Harvard University. She has published four novels: *Miniplanner* (2000), *Babyji* (2005), winner of the American Library Association's Stonewall Award and **Lambda Literary Awards**, *That Summer in Paris* (2007), and *Family Value* (2009). All of them feature sensual, sexy, and adventurous cosmopolitan Indians. She currently lives in New York.

DE CRISTOFORO, VIOLET KAZUE (1917–2007). A **Japanese American** poet, De Cristoforo was born in Hawaii and educated in Japan between the age of eight and 13. She went to high school in Fresno, California. Her ***haiku*** reflect the time that she and her family spent in detention in **Japanese Internment camps** during World War II. Her best-known works are *Poetic Reflections of the Tule Lake Internment Camp, 1944* (1984) and *May Sky: There Is Always Tomorrow; an Anthology of Japanese American Concentration Camp Kaiko Haiku* (2000), which she edited. For her *haiku* in memory of the internment, she was the 2007 recipient of a National Endowment for the Arts with a National Heritage Fellowship Award for achievement in traditional and folk arts.

DE LA PAZ, OLIVER (1972–). A **Filipino American** poet, De la Paz was born in Manila, the Philippines, and raised in Ontario, Oregon. He received his B.S. in biology and B.A. in English from Loyola Marymount College, and M.F.A. from Arizona State University. He teaches creative writing at Western Washington University. He is the author of three collections of **poetry**.

While *Names above Houses* (2001), a novella in the form of a sequence of prose poems, portrays a Filipino boy with a great yearning to fly, *Furious Lullaby* (2007) centers on salvation and temptation in the 21st century. *Requiem for the Orchard* (2010), winner of the Akron Prize for poetry, is a love letter to memory. A recipient of a New York Foundation for the Arts Fellowship Award and a Grant for Artist Projects from Artist Trust, his work has appeared in numerous journals, including *Virginia Quarterly Review*, *North American Review*, *Tin House*, *Chattahoochee Review*, and in anthologies, such as *Asian American Poetry: The Next Generation*.

DE LOS SANTOS, MARISA (1966–). A **Filipina American** poet and novelist, De Los Santos was born in Baltimore to a Filipino American father and a Caucasian American mother and raised in Virginia. She teaches at the University of Delaware. She received a B.A. in English from the University of Virginia, an M.F.A. in **poetry** writing from Sarah Lawrence College, and a Ph.D. in English and creative writing from the University of Houston. Her first major publication is a collection of poetry, *From the Bones Out* (2000). She went on to write two novels: *Love Walked In* (2006) and *Belong to Me* (2010). Both center on **women**'s friendship. Her works also have appeared in *Poetry*, the *Southwest Review*, and *Prairie Schooner*.

DEMPSTER, BRIAN KOMEI (1969–). A **Japanese American** poet, Dempster was born in Seattle, Washington, to a Japanese American mother and a white American father. He received his B.A. in English and Ethnic Studies from the University of Washington and M.F.A. in creative writing from the University of Michigan. His poems have appeared in journals such as *The Asian Pacific American Journal*, *Bellingham Review*, *Beloit Poetry Journal*, *Crab Orchard Review*, *Fourteen Hills*, *Green Mountains Review*, *Gulf Coast*, *New England Review*, *North American Review*, *Ploughshares*, *Post Road*, *Prairie Schooner*, *River Styx*, *Quarterly West* as well as in anthologies, such as *Asian American Poetry: The Next Generation* and *Screaming Monkeys: Critiques of Asian American Images*. He is the editor of two books of nonfiction: *From Our Side of the Fence: Growing Up in America's Concentration Camps* (2001) and *Making Home from War: Stories of Japanese American Exile and Resettlement* (2010). Among the numerous honors he has received are two California Civil Liberties Public Education Program grants, **Nisei** Voices Award from the National Japanese American Historical Society, a Creative Artist Grant from the Arts Foundation of Michigan, and an Individual Artist Commission from the San Francisco Arts Commission. Currently, he teaches creative writing at the University of San Francisco.

DESAI, BOMAN (1950–). A **South Asian American** novelist, Desai was born in Bombay, India. He holds an M.A. in English from the University of Illinois, Chicago. He is the author of four novels. His debut novel, *The Memory of Elephants* (1988), is a science fiction of time travel through which the protagonist finds himself in the multigenerational saga of his own family, spanning three continents and a hundred years. *Asylum, USA* (2000) tells the story of a naive Indian immigrant. Facing deportation, he marries a lesbian and lives with her and her girlfriend in a one-bedroom apartment. *A Woman Madly in Love* (2004) depicts a betrayed **woman**'s love affair with a boy half her age. *Servant, Master, Mistress* (2005), set at the eve of World War II, tells the story of a spoiled son of a wealthy Parsi family, who marries an English woman. His short fiction, articles, and essays have been published in the United States, Great Britain, and India in such periodicals as *Another Chicago Magazine*, *Stand Magazine*, *Gay Chicago Magazine*, *Weber Studies*, *Sonora Review*, the *Atlantic Literary Review*, *Fezana Journal*, the *Times of India*, and the *Chicago Tribune*. His nonfiction novel in two volumes, *Trio* and *Trio 2* (2004/2006), is based on the lives of the German composers Robert Schumann and Johannes Brahms. His awards include an Illinois Arts Council Award, an American Songwriter Festival award, and the Stand Magazine Prize for fiction.

DESAI, KIRAN (1971–). A **South Asian American** novelist, Desai was born in India to the famous Indian novelist, Anita Desai. At the age of 14, her mother took her to England, and after one year there, they immigrated to the United States. She studied creative writing at Bennington College in Vermont and Columbia University. Her first novel, *Hullabaloo in the Guava Orchard* (1998), received the Betty Trask Award, a prize given by the Society of Authors for the best new novels by citizens of the Commonwealth of Nations under the age of 35. This debut novel tells a hilarious and ironic story from the point of view of a slow-witted boy named Sampath Chawla. Desai's second book, *The Inheritance of Loss* (2006), has received international accolades and won the 2006 Man Booker Prize as well as the 2006 National Book Critics Circle Fiction Award. Comical, delightful, and contemplative, this second novel, set in the mid-1980s, depicts the pain of **exile** and the ambivalence of postcolonial existence with a set of fascinating characters living along the border between India and Nepal and an exile's life in New York City.

DESANI, GOVINDAS (1909–2000). A **South Asian American** novelist and playwright, Desani was born in Nairobi, Kenya, to Indian parents. As a young man, he went to Great Britain and became a journalist who lived a **diasporic** life between Great Britain and India. He joined the philosophy faculty of the University of Texas, Austin, in 1969 and held his professorial position until his death. Although he wrote only one novel, one play, and several short stories, Desani's prominence is comparable to his more prolific contemporaries such as Mulk Raj Anand, R. K. Narayan, and **Raja Rao**. His novel *All about H. Hatterr* (1948) has been hailed as a comic masterpiece about a young man's picturesque adventures in search for Truth. What marks the novel as a pioneer of postcolonial literature is its **hybridization** of different Englishes—the queen's and babu's. Desani's hybrid English offers a model to Salman Rushdie, particularly in Rushdie's *Midnight's Children*. Desani's play *Hali* (1950) is a prose poem that tells the story of a man mourning the death of his beloved in solitude. The play is a series of monologues by Hali, his mother, and his adoptive mother, his beloved, and several mythic figures. The play received appraisal from T. S. Eliot and E. M. Forster, whose favorable words serve as the play's foreword in its first edition.

DESIPINA & CO. A **South Asian American** arts company in New York, it focuses on film and **theater** to promote social change. *Desipina* is a slang term describing a person of South Asian (desi) and Filipina (pina) descent. The company was founded soon after 9/11 by two sisters, Rehana Mirza and Rohi Mirza Pandya.

DHOMPA, TSERING WANGMO (1969–). The first Tibetan American poet, Dhompa was born to Tibetan refugees in India and was raised in India and Nepal. She came to the United States at 25 for graduate studies. She received her B.A. and M.A. in English from the University of Delhi. She also holds an M.A. in English from the University of Massachusetts, Amherst, and an M.F.A. in creative writing from San Francisco State University. Her first book of poems, *Rules of the House* (2002), was a finalist for an Asian American Literary Award. Other publications include *In the Absent Everyday* (2005) and two chapbooks: *In Writing the Names* (2000) and *Recurring Gestures* (2000). Her **poetry** explores the themes of loss, memory, **exile**, and mysticism. She works for a San Francisco based nonprofit foundation that provides humanitarian aid to people of the Himalayas.

DIASPORA. A word with Greek roots, it originally meant the scattering of seeds. In the English language, it means the migration of a population that shares a common ethnicity, such as the Jewish Diaspora, the Chinese Diaspora, and the African Diaspora. It refers to a permanently displaced and relocated community. This is a concept often evoked in Asian American literature, filled with emotional intensity. Indian Americans (classified as **South Asian American** in this dictionary) is one group that best exemplifies the term of diaspora. In 1834, when Great Britain abolished slavery in its empire, its colonies formerly dependent on slaves for their labor force turned to Indians. Between 1834 and 1934, about 30 million Indians indentured themselves for terms of labor, creating an Indian diaspora in such countries as Mauritius, Malaysia, Singapore, South Africa, Suriname, Guyana, Fiji, Kenya, Tanzania, Uganda, Trinidad, and Jamaica. After the Luce–Celler Act of 1946 granted Indian Americans naturalization rights in the United States, a significant number of Indians arrived in America from this diaspora. **Abraham Verghese**, for instance, is a novelist who was born to Indian parents in Ethiopia and educated in India and the United States. His bestselling autobiographical novel *My Own Country: A Doctor's Story* (1994) portrays his experiences in East Tennessee and explores the themes of diaspora, displacement, and the AIDS epidemic. **Jhumpa Lahiri**, a Pulizer-winning writer, was born in Great Britain to Indian parents and immigrated to the United States as a child. She portrays the diasporic Bengali community central to the first generation of immigrants and the dis-ease of the second-generation children with this community in her *Interpreter of Maladies*, *The Namesake*, and *Unaccustomed Earth.*

The **Chinese American** poet **Li-Young Lee** was born to Chinese parents exiled to Indonesia. As a child, he wandered with his family to several countries looking for safety until they came to the United States. In his poetry, the notions of diaspora and **exile** are prominent themes. His lyrical memoir is interestingly titled *The Winged Seed* and tells the stories of his parents' migration from China to Indonesia to the United States and his own sense of displacement. **Filipina American** poet **Barbara Jane Reyes** was born in Manila and raised in San Francisco. She is the author of **poetry** collections, *Diawata* (2010), *Gravities of Center* (2003), and *Poeta en San Francisco* (2005), and three chapbooks, *Easter Sunday* (2008), *Cherry* (2008), and *West Oakland Sutra for the AK-47 Shooter at 3:00 AM and other Oakland Poems* (2008). By incorporating English, Spanish, and Tagalog, Reyes consistently explores themes of diaspora, longing, postcoloniality, and memory. *See also* CARBÓ, NICK; CHA, THERESA HAK KYUNG; CHEONG, FIONA; EXILE; HOMELAND; IGLORIA, LUISA A.

DINH, LINH (1963–). A **Vietnamese American** poet and fiction writer, Dinh was born in Saigon, Vietnam, and came to the United States in 1975. He is the author of two story collections. While *Fake House* (2000) centers on the themes of race and sex as his characters negotiate their way in a post–Vietnam War world, *Blood and Soap* (2004) is a highly inventive collection of modern day fables and parables, depicting Vietnamese, American, and European characters. His most recent publication is a novel *Love like Hate*

(2010), a dysfunctional family saga in Vietnam. He is also the author of six books of **poetry**: *Drunkard Boxing* (1998), *All around What Empties Out* (2003), *American Tatts* (2005), *Borderless Bodies* (2006), *Jam Alerts* (2007), and *Some Kind of Cheese Orgy* (2009). *Borderless Bodies* won an **Asian American Literary Award**. His debut novel, *Love like Hate* (2010), portrays his native Vietnam from the war through the end of the twentieth century. His work has been anthologized in *Best American Poetry* in 2000, 2004, and 2007, and appeared in such journals as *Sulfur*, *American Poetry Review*, *Denver Quarterly*, and *Great American Prose Poems from Poe to the Present*. *The Village Voice* picked his *Blood and Soap* as one of the best books of 2004. He is the recipient of a Lannan Residency and a Pew Fellowship.

DIVAKARUNI, CHITRA BANERJEE (1956–). A prolific **South Asian American** poet and novelist, Divakaruni was born and raised in Calcutta, India. At the age of 19, she moved to the United States for graduate school. She obtained her Ph.D. in English from the University California, Berkeley. Divakaruni began her literary career as a poet writing about **women** and migration. In *Dark Like the River* (1987), *The Reason for Nasturtiums* (1990), *Black Candle: Poems about Women from India, Pakistan, and Bangladesh* (1991), and *Leaving Yuba City* (1997), Divakaruni writes narrative poems that mix rich, haunting, and vivid imageries of everyday life with stories of women's oppression, of domestic abuse, and of migrant women caught between worlds. Her latest collection *Leaving Yuba City* also pictures Punjabi men new to California and places their misery in the context of the Alien Land Laws that barred nonwhite immigrants from owning land in the United States. *Leaving Yuba City* won a Pushcart Prize, an Allen Ginsberg Prize, and a Gerbode Foundation award.

Divakaruni is more widely known for her fiction, which shares the same themes as her **poetry**. Her writing has been included in over 50 anthologies, including the *Best American Short Stories*, the *O. Henry Prize Stories*, and the *Pushcart Prize Anthology*. She also received the Distinguished Writer Award from the South Asian Literary Association in 2007. Her first collection of short stories, *Arranged Marriage* (1995), won an **American Book Award**. The stories in this collection portray South Asian women's powerlessness and fear. Her second novel, *Mistress of Spices* (1996), was a best seller, whose infusion of magic and mysticism has been compared to the **magical realism** in the works of Gabriel Garcia Marquez and Laura Esquivel. This novel has been adapted to the silver screen in 2005 under the direction of Paul Mayeda Berges. *Sister of My Heart* (1999) was Divakaruni's third novel, which tells the story of the twists and turns in the relationship between two cousins who grew up together in the same household as sisters. Divakaruni's charm in this novel is once again the juxtaposition of the magical with the realistic, the extraordinary with the ordinary. *Sister of My Heart* was made into a television series in Tamil and aired in India. Its sequel, *The Vine of Desires* (2002), takes the two sisters to the United States to explore the themes of love, betrayal, loss, jealousy, and forgiveness. Her second collection of short stories, *The Unknown Errors of Our Lives* (2001), depicts South Asian American women's lives shattered by violence and tortured by the conflicts between Indian traditions and American values. ***Queen of Dreams*** (2004) returns to magical realism and tells the stories of an Indian immigrant mother and an American born daughter. A dream reader trained by a secret sisterhood in India, the mother figure is a mystery for the daughter to understand, and by understanding her mother the daughter saves herself. *The Palace of Illusion* (2008) retells the Indian epic *Mahabharata* from the perspective of Princess Panchaali, a woman who occupies the very center of a world of warriors, gods, and bloodshed.

Divakaruni has also written fantasies for children. *The Conch Bearer* (2005), *The Mirror of Fire and Dreams* (2005), and *Shadowland* (2009) are the saga of the brotherhood of the conch, which centers on the fantastic adventures of the boy magician, Anand. Her most recent novel *One Amazing Thing* (2010) tells the stories of nine men and women of diverse ages and backgrounds as they are trapped in an Indian consulate when an earthquake hits. *See also* CHILDREN'S LITERATURE.

DIZON, LOUELLA (1966–). A **Filipina American** playwright, Dizon was born in Cebu City, the Philippines. In 1968, her family immigrated to the United States and settled in Detroit, Michigan. She earned a B.A. in English from Princeton University and then moved to New York City. Dizon wrote, produced, and directed her first play, *The Color Yellow: Memoirs of an Asian American* (1989), at Princeton as her thesis. Her play was under the influence of Samuel Beckett's use of language and inspired by **David Henry Hwang**'s *Sound of a Voice*, in which Dizon was a part of the Yale Drama Department production in 1987. *Till Voices Wake Us* (1992), included in *Contemporary Plays by Women of Color*, premiered in the Soho Rep in 1994. Dizon has written two other plays, *The Sweet Sound of Inner Light* (1994), which was staged as part of the New Works Festival at the Public **Theatre**, and *The Practical Heart* (1995). In her plays, Dizon blends present, past, and future into realities and evokes the power of spirituality in crossing time, borders, and spaces.

DODOITSU. A form of Japanese poetry developed in the 19th century. It consists of quatrains with the syllabic pattern of 7-7-7-5 without rhyme or meter. Usually comical, *dodoitsu* depicts work and love. This style has been used by Asian American poets such as **Sadakichi Hartmann**.

DONOHUE, MAURA NGUYEN (1970–). A **Vietnamese American** dancer, choreographer, and playwright, Donohue was born in Saigon, Vietnam, to a Vietnamese mother and an Irish American father. As an infant, she was brought to the United States and raised in Rhode Island. She majored in anthropology and dance at Smith College. Her family stories inspired her to write and choreograph many pieces exploring mix-race identity, also known as **hapa**. In 1995, she established the Donohue/**In Mixed Company**, which has performed theatrical, multimedia works that challenge static notions of identity and celebrate the fluid "self" situated in contexts of race, gender, sexuality, and nationality. Their athletic movement combines various traditional Asian and contemporary American dance/**theater** forms. Her works include *Islands: a happa wet dream* (1995), *When You're Old Enough* (1992), *Lotus Blossom Itch* (1997), *SKINning the surFACE* (1998), *Righteous Babes* (2000), *Enemy/Territory* (2004), *Rip it Open* (2002), *Jet Stream* (2009), etc. She and her company have won honors, such as Manhattan Community Arts Fund/New York City Department of Cultural Affairs, Fund for U.S. Artists–Arts International Travel Grant, and Rockefeller Foundation and Dance Theater Workshop/Suitcase Fund. Her works have been published in anthologies such as *Bold Words: A Century of Asian American Writing* and the *Best Plays of 1998–1999.*

D'SOUZA, TONY (1975–). A **South Asian American** novelist, D'Souza was born and raised in Chicago. He received his M.A. in writing from Hollins University and M.F.A. in creative writing from the University of Notre Dame. He served three years in the Peace Corps in West Africa. His short stories have appeared in the *New Yorker*, *Playboy*, *Salon*, *Esquire*, *Outside*, *Best American Fantasy*, *McSweeney's*, *Tin House*, etc. He is the recipient of a National Endowment for the Arts Fellowship, a National Endowment for the Arts Japan Friendship Fellowship, and a Guggenheim Fellowship. His first novel, *Whiteman* (2007), received the Sue Kaufman Prize from the American Academy of Arts and Letters. The novel, set in West Africa, tells the story of an American relief worker. His second novel, *The Konkans* (2008), portrays the lives of the Konkans, known as the Jews of India, when they were transplanted to Chicago.

DUC, NGUYEN QUI. A **Vietnamese American** memoirist and journalist, Duc was born in Vietnam and came to the United States in 1975. He authored *Where the Ashes Are: The Odyssey of a Vietnamese Family* (1994). Based on the short story by Le Minh Khue, he wrote the play *A Soldier Named Tony D*, which was produced in 1995 by EXIT Theatre at Knuth Hall, San Francisco. His essays, poems, and short stories have appeared in *City Lights Review*, *Salamander*, *Zyzzyva*, *Manoa Journal*, *Van, Van Hoc*, and *Hop Luu*, as well as in several anthologies, such as *Under Western Eyes*, *Watermark*, and *Veterans of War, Veterans of Peace.* In 2001, Nguyen was named one of 30 most notable Asian Americans by A-Media. His documentary on Chinese youths, *Shanghai Nights*, was part of the PBS Frontline/World series that was awarded the 2005 Edward R. Murrow Award of Excellence in Television Documentary from the Overseas Press Club of America, and, the same year, he also received a fellowship for outstanding achievements from the Alexander Gerbode Foundation. In October 2006, he received the Distinguished Service Award for his contributions to journalism from the Society of Professional Journalists.

DUEEAST THEATRE COMPANY. This is a Chicago-based Asian American **theater** company. Established in 2003, it is dedicated to performing arts that highlight the talents of Asian American playwrights and artists.

DUONG, UYEN NICOLE (1959–). A **Vietnamese American** novelist, Duong was born in Vietnam and arrived in the United States at the age of 16 as a political refugee. The family flew out of Vietnam five days before the fall of the city on 30 April 1975. She received a B.S. in communications and journalism from Southern Illinois University, a law degree from the University of Houston, and the advanced L.L.M. degree from Harvard. She was also trained at the American Academy of Dramatic Arts in Pasadena. She has been a journalist, public education administrator, attorney, law professor, and a self-taught painter. Now a professor at the Sturm School of Law, University of Denver, she is the author of three novels: *Daughters of the River Huong* (2005), *Mimi and Her Mirror* (2011), and *Postcards from Nam* (2011). These novels explore the themes of **women's** lives, family history, cultural conflict, traumatic memory, and redemption.

E

EAST WEST PLAYERS. This is the first Asian American **theater**, founded in Los Angeles in 1965 by Mako, Rae Creeby, James Hong, June K. Lu, Guy Lee, Pat Li, Yet Lock, Soon-Tek Oh, and Beulah Quo. It found a performance space at Bovard Auditorium at the University of Southern California with the help of its Asian Studies Program. Its first production was *Rashomon*, a Japanese crime mystery. Under the directorship of Mako, this group became the premier Asian American theater company. In 1998, the artistic director, Tim Dang, moved the company from a 99-seat theater to a new 240-seat venue at an Actors Equity Association contract level. In 1998, its main stage was named **David Henry Hwang** Theatre, housed within the historic Union Center for the Arts in downtown Los Angeles' Little Tokyo district.

EAST-WEST RELATIONS. This theme is most prevalent in Asian American literature and theater. The meditation on cross-cultural experience, transnational and **diasporic** life, Americanization, **hybrid** identity, and **homeland** inevitably entails a dialogue between East and West. Some Asian American writers attempt to educate the West of their ancestral cultures by rendering their customs, myths, and traditions accessible to the Western reader. Some of the Asian American literary pioneers did mostly this through autobiographies and fiction, such as **Edith Maude Eaton**, **Lee Yan Phou**, and **Lin Yutang** among the **Chinese American** writers, **Ilhan New** and **No-Young Park** among the **Korean American** writers, **Jun Fujita**, **Ayako Tanaka Ishigaki**, and **Etsu Inagaki Sugimoto** in **Japanese American** literary tradition, and **José Garcia Villa** and **Bienvenido Santos** among **Filipino American** writers.

During the era when the discourse of **assimilation** dominated American views on immigration, some Asian American writers examined their relationship to their home or ancestral cultures through a critical lens of Western democracy and individualism. While they assert their American citizenship and belonging, they express their discontent with their Asian cultures, such as **Pardee Lowe** in *Father and the Glorious Descendant* and **Jade Snow Wong** in *Fifth Chinese Daughter*. Awakened by the Western feminist discourse, many Asian American **women** writers critique arranged marriage, bride dowry, gender, and sexual exploitation even when they remain critical of certain Western values. Chinese American **Ling-Ai Li**, the first Asian American playwright, staged *The Submission of Rose Moy* (1924) that centers on a Chinese woman who refuses to comply with an arranged marriage. **Chitra Banerjee Divakaruni**'s debut collection of short stories, *Arranged Marriage*, presents from women's point of view vivid stories about **South Asian** women's domestic struggles.

Just as these women writers measure their Eastern cultures against Western ones, many writers probe into the social maladies of Western cultures through the critical lens of Asian values in family, community, and nature. **Frank Chin** in *Donald Duk* portrays the San Francisco **Chinatown** as a strong community that thrives upon the values of caring, collaboration, and security, and in contrast the mainstream American culture is depicted to be ruthless, self-centered, and insecure. **Li-Young Lee**'s poetry reflects Asian aesthetics in its approach to nature, nature not only as a refuge but also as the primary mirror of the human psyche. **David Henry Hwang**'s play ***M. Butterfly*** is an ironic allegory of the orientalist fantasy that the West has entertained about the East. Other well-known authors who explore themes related to the meeting between East and West through immigrant experiences and/or postcolonial legacy include **Bharati Mukherjee**, **Ping Chong**, **Richard Crasta**, **Jessica Hagedorn**, **Monique Truong**, and **Bich Minh Nguyen**. *See also* HOMELAND.

EATON, EDITH MAUDE (SUI SIN FAR, 1865–1914). A **Chinese American** fiction writer, Edith Eaton was born in Macclesfield, England, to a Chinese mother and a white English father. She was the older sister of **Winnifred Eaton**, who used the pseudonym Onoto Watanna to pen her novels. The Eatons moved to Hudson, New York, for a brief while before they relocated to Montreal, Canada. Eaton, as a young girl, published articles on the Chinese people in Montreal's English-language newspapers, the *Montreal Star* and the *Daily Witness*. She moved to San Francisco first and then Seattle before she went to Boston. Although she could easily pass as an English **woman**, she embraced her mother's culture by adopting the pseudonym Sui Sin Far, narcissus flower in Chinese, and writing articles about what it was like to be a Chinese woman in North America.

Eaton was the first writer of Chinese ancestry to defend Chinese Americans and to challenge the prejudice against the Chinese at the time. Her autobiographical essay "Leaves from the Mental Portfolio of a Eurasian" (1909) centers on the education in race relations of a Eurasian in white societies and the pain endured by a person socially ostracized on two counts: her race and her single state. Here she shares her experiences of **racism** from both whites and Chinese. Despite the pain, Eaton shows her courage to address the injustices done to the Chinese and to serve as a bridge between the Asians and the Caucasians. *Mrs. Spring Fragrance* (1912) is her collection of linked short stories, set in Seattle and San Francisco, depicting the lives of Chinese Americans in a way that counters the prevailing racist stereotypes and critiques the legislative discriminations against the Chinese in America. For instance, in the ironically titled story "In the Land of the Free," Eaton portrays the suffering caused by the discriminatory immigration laws. Her other works include "Chan Hen Yen, Chinese Student" (1912), "A Love Story from the Rice Fields of China" (1911), "The Bird of Love" (1910), "An Autumn Fan" (1910), and "A Chinese Ishmael" (1899).

EATON, WINNIFRED (ONOTO WATANNA, 1875–1954). Although a **Chinese American**, Eaton has been known as a **Japanese American** writer because of her subject matters. Regarded as the first Asian American novelist, she enjoyed fame and popularity in the early part of the 20th century. Eaton was the eighth child of 16 born to a Chinese mother and a white English father and raised in Montreal, Canada. Later she moved to Chicago. She and some of her siblings were able to pass as white. Her older sister **Edith Maude Eaton** was also a writer, but they chose two distinctively different paths. While Edith chose to identify herself as Chinese by adopting the Chinese name Sui Sin Far, Winnifred took on a Japanese identity and the pseudonym, Onoto Watanna. She built her fame on writing interracial romances between Japanese or half-Japanese ladies and white men. She cultivated the media's misrepresentation of her as a Japanese noblewoman from Nagasaki and showed photos of herself in kimonos.

Eaton published at least 10 such interracial romances, several of which became best sellers, and one of which, *A Japanese Nightingale* (1901), was made into a Broadway play as well as a film. For a while she was living in New York City and writing a novel a year naming her heroines after flowers, such as *The Wooing of Wisteria* (1902), *The Heart of Hyacinth* (1903), *The Love of Azalea* (1904), and *A Japanese Blossom* (1906). Departing from her successful formula, she wrote a novel from the perspective of an Irish immigrant cook, *The Diary of Delia* (1907). Her other works include *Miss Numé of Japan* (1899), *Tama* (1910), *The Honorable Miss Moonlight* (1912), *Sunny-San* (1922), *Cattle* (1923), and *His Royal Nibs* (1925). Between 1924 and 1931, Eaton worked in Hollywood, writing and editing screenplays like *Mississippi Gambler* (1929) and *Shanghai Lady* (1930), but many of the films she worked on did not credit her. Near the end of her life, Eaton acknowledged and regretted her reliance on clichés and racial prejudice for her success.

18 MIGHTY MOUNTAIN WARRIORS. This is an Asian American comedy ensemble based in San Francisco. Since its premiere production in 1994, the group has written and produced a dozen feature shows, performed numerous workshop productions and benefit one-night stands around the greater Bay Area, and toured nationally and internationally at colleges, universities, arts festivals, and theatrical venues. The group seeks to explore and articulate images of Asian Pacific Islander Americans alternative to what has been perpetuated in the mainstream media. One of the group's strategies is to push the envelope as comedic performers in both style and content, as well as to break down prevailing stereotypes and promote more positive images. Much of the group's impact lies in its lack of hesitation in lambasting the Asian American community itself as well.

ELLIOTT, DUONG VAN MAI (1941–). A **Vietnamese American** memoirist, Elliot was born and raised in Vietnam. She is a graduate of Georgetown University. Her memoir *The Sacred Willow: Four Generations in the Life of a Vietnamese Family* (2000) was nominated for a Pulitzer Prize. It tells the stories of a family involved in every thread of the war against French colonial rule and the Vietnam War.

ETERAZ, ALI (1980–). A **South Asian American** writer, Eteraz was born in Lahore and raised in the Dominican Republic, Pakistan, and the United States. He received his B.A. in philosophy from Emory University and J.D. from Temple University. His memoir, *Children of Dusk* (2009), won a Nautilus Book Award. His memoir depicts Islamic fundamentalism, life in rural Pakistan, the culture shock of moving to the United States, and a journey of reconciliation to the modern Middle East.

EXILE. A frequently evoked concept in Asian American literature and **theater**, it denotes forceful removal from one's **homeland**. Western colonialism and neocolonialism have played significant roles in forcing peoples out of their homelands and in attracting them to the West. Migration in search for safety and economic and educational betterment is by no means a voluntary act. Due to the colonial history of Asia, an exodus from that continent to the West began over 200 years ago and is still going strong. In Asian American literature and theater, exile carries a deep sense of woe and pining for home, often mingling feelings of nostalgia and alienation. For instance, **Agha Shahid Ali**'s *The Half-Inch Himalaya* (1987) begins with an epigraph from Virginia Woolf, "I die in exile" and laments the loss of homeland by evoking the rich Urdu poetic tradition. In **Theresa Hak Kyung Cha**'s *Dictée*, exile is a major motif that generates most of the emotional resonance. **Li Young-Li**'s poetry explores his life and his father's life as exiles in the United States. Not only does he feel perpetually haunted by traumatic memories of their escape from persecution in Indonesia and their wandering in Asia before arriving in the United States, he also regards his condition of exile as an ontological one. This condition has proved to be immensely productive of emotional intensity and imagination. *See also* DESAI, KIRAN; FUJITA, JUN; LAW-YONE, WENDY; LEONG, RUSSELL; YAU, JOHN.

F

FAIGAO-HALL, LINDA (1948–). A **Filipina American** playwright, Faigao-Hall was born in the Philippines. She received her undergraduate education in English at Silliman University, the Philippines, and graduate degrees in English and Educational Theater from New York University. She also studied Medieval Theater at Bretton Hall College, Wakefield, England. Faigao-Hall has written 14 plays, 11 of which have been produced in **theaters** on both east and west coasts such as **Ma-Yi Theater Ensemble** in New York, **Pan Asian Repertory Theatre** in New York, **Asian American Theater Company** in San Francisco, Philippine Performing Company in New York, and a tour to Arlington, Virginia, Washington, D.C., Tufts University, Rutgers University, Syracuse University, and Cornell University. In her plays, Faigao-Hall weaves Filipino mythology and folklore into contemporary life to achieve the stylistic effects of **magical realism** and to offer an alternative worldview that values dreams, myth, and the occult. Her plays explore the subjects of American imperialism, third-world poverty, hate crimes, sexism, homophobia, religious alienation, and domestic abuse, all the challenges Filipino Americans face. Her plays include *State without Grace* (1984), *Requiem* (1986), *Men Come and Go* (1987), *Sparrow* (1990), *Burning Out* (1991), *Manila Drive* (1992), *Pidgin' Hole* (1996), *The Interview* (1997), *Duet* (1998), *Woman from the Other Side of the World* (1996), *God, Sex, and Blue Water* (1998), *He and She* (1998), *The 7th of October* (1999), *Heart of a Woman* (2000), *Walking Iron* (2002), *The A-Word* (2005), *Dying in Boulder* (2006), etc. *Woman from the Other Side of the World* is published, and other plays appear in anthologies, such as *Savage Stage: Plays By Ma-Yi Theater Company*, *Brown River, White Ocean: An Anthology of Twentieth-Century Philippine Literature in English*, *The Best Plays of 2000–2001: The Otis Guernsey/Burns Mantle Theatre Yearbook*, *Asian American Drama: 9 Plays from the Multiethnic Landscape*, and *Contemporary Plays by Women of Color.*

FEI, DEANNA (1978–). A **Chinese American** novelist, Fei was born in Flushing, New York, and has lived in Beijing and Shanghai, China. She received her B.A. in English and sociology from Amherst College and M.F.A. from the Iowa Writers' Workshop. She has received a Fulbright grant, a New

York Foundation for the Arts fellowship, and a Chinese Cultural Scholarship, among other awards. She currently teaches in public schools in Brooklyn, New York. She is the author of *A Thread of Sky* (2010), a novel that explores the relationships among three generations of Chinese American **women** upon their visit to their ancestral home—China. It was a New York Times Editor's Choice and Indie Next Notable Book.

FENKLE, HEINZ INSU (1960–). A **Korean American** novelist, translator, and folklorist, Fenkle was born in Inchon, Korea, to a Korean mother and a white American father. Raised in Korea, Germany, and the United States, he often explores issues of biraciality and cross-cultural transformation in his writings. He received his B.A. in English from Vassar College and M.F.A. in creative writing from the University of California, Davis. He was a Fulbright Scholar to Korea to study folklore and shamanism. Currently, he teaches at the State University of New York, New Paltz. He is best known for his autobiographical novel *Memories of My Ghost Brother* (1996) about his growing up in Korea as a biracial child in the 1960s, for which he was named a Barnes and Noble "Great New Writer" and a PEN/Hemingway finalist. His second novel, *Shadows Bend* (2000) (a collaborative work, published under the pseudonym of Richard Raleigh), was an innovative, dark "road novel" about H. P. Lovecraft, Robert E. Howard, and Clark Ashton Smith. His translations of classic Chinese **poetry** and stories appeared in his collection *Cathay* (2007). He is also coeditor of two collections of Korean American fiction: *Kŏri: The Beacon Anthology of Korean American Literature* (2002) and *Century of the Tiger: 100 Years of Korean–American Immigration* (2003).

FERIA, BENNY F. (1911–1978). A **Filipino American** writer, Feria was born in the Philippines. At age 10, he began keeping the diary, which would eventually become materials for his autobiography. At age 15, he came to the United States and worked in Fresno, California, in a farm labor camp. Several months later, he moved to Chicago and worked as a dishwasher. With the earnings from a variety of low-paying jobs, he paid for his college education at Lewis Institute, DePaul University, and the University of Chicago. While still a student, Feria published **poetry** in a Manila weekly newspaper. As a poet and foreign correspondent, he began to contribute to several Philippine-based publications. Later he began publishing the first Filipino American newspaper in Chicago, known as the *Commonwealth Press*, then as *The United Filipino Press*. His first collection of poetry, *Never Tomorrow* (1947), explores the themes of the tenacity of the human spirit in the face of challenges as experienced by Filipino immigrants. Although a poet, Feria is better known for his autobiography *Filipino Son* (1954), which recounts his struggles as an immigrant to overcome poverty and homesickness to achieve his goals. He firmly believes in America's promise of equal opportunity for all. While **Carlos Bulosan** in *America Is in the Heart* depicts the brutality and hostility Filipino immigrants faced in the American West, Feria largely ignores in *Filipino Son* the **racism** or discrimination Filipino immigrants experienced.

FERRELL, MONICA (1975–). A **South Asian American** poet and novelist, Ferrell was born in New Delhi, India, to an Indian mother and a Caucasian American father. She received a B.A. in social studies from Harvard College and an M.F.A. in **poetry** writing from Columbia University. A former "Discovery"/The Nation prize winner and Wallace Stegner Fellow at Stanford University, she has authored a novel, *The Answer Is Always Yes* (2008), and a book of poetry, *Beasts for the Chase* (2008). Ferrell was also a winner of the Kathryn A. Morton Prize in Poetry. While *The Answer Is Always Yes* portrays a college freshman's obsessive pursuit of being cool, *Beasts for Chase* presents various speakers undergoing metamorphoses, from human to animal, girl to **woman**, powerful to powerless, etc. Her writing has appeared in the *New York Review of Books*, *Paris Review*, *Tin House*, and other magazines and anthologies. She currently lives in Brooklyn, New York.

FILIPINO AMERICAN LITERATURE AND THEATER. Filipino American Literature is a problematic label. Unlike the case of East Asian American writers, for whom the use of the English language and time spent in the United States often determine one's classification as an Asian American writer, the distinction between Filipino and Filipino American writers is blurred due to the effects of American colonization of the Philippines (1898–1946), which have made the use of English and nomadic life between the two countries common to many writers. This is true particularly with the first generation. Many critics prefer to classify the writings of the first generation "Filipino English Literature." These pioneers include **Jose Garcia Villa**, **Bienvenido Santos**, **Carlos A. Angeles**, **N. V. M. Gonzalez**, and **Alberto S. Florentino**. Although writing at the same time period, **Carlos Bulosan** is an exception as all his writings were published in the United States. Jose Garcia Villa's short story collection *Footnote to Youth* (1933), the first publication among these pioneers, centers on the lives of young Filipinos in the rural Philippines. Bulosan's autobiographical novel *America Is in the Heart* (1946), however, is the best-known text from this period. It recounts Bulosan's aspirations, friendships, hardships, and success.

Significant immigration began in 1903 when 103 Filipino students arrived at American universities, and soon other Filipinos came to Hawaii to work on sugarcane plantations and to the West Coast to seek a better life. They worked many long hours on farms and in the agricultural fields picking produce, and in Alaska they worked in the fish canneries. Because the **Page Act** (1875) barred the entrance of Asian **women**, including Filipinas, on the ground of morality, the ratio of Filipino men to women was severely imbalanced. In addition, the anti-miscegenation laws illegalized any marriage between a Filipino and a white woman. Soon the bar of women's immigration extended to men, with the Tydings–Mcduffie Act of 1934 that limited Filipino immigration to 50 per year. It is against this background that the first generation of writers expressed their longing for home, disappointment with America, and experience of racial and economic discrimination.

The second generation of Filipino American writers is better known to American readers as several of them have been published by mainstream presses. Among them, **Peter Bacho** and **Jessica Hagedorn** are the most visible figures. Filipina American writers emerged at this point, such as **Ninotchka Rosca**, **Linda Ty-Casper**, and **Cecilia Manguerra Brainard**, whose feminist historical fiction aligned Filipina American writing with other U.S. minority women writers such as **Maxine Hong Kingston** and Toni Morrison. These writers often explore the sensibilities of a nomadic existence, best captured by Jessica Hagedorn's line in *Dogeaters* (1990) that she is "at home only in airports." The youngest generation of Filipino American writers is mostly born in the United States. Their works are highly diverse in genres and themes. This generation includes well-known novelists like **Rick Barot** and **Zamora Linmark**, and poets such as **Nick Carbó**, **Vincente Ferrer Gotera**, **Virginia Cerenio**, **Sabina Murray**, and **Sarah Gambito**. Several writers have pursued a multigenred career, such as **Marisa De Los Santos** and **Eileen Tabios**.

Filipino American **Theater** did not emerge until the latter half of the 20th century. One of the first playwrights, **Jennie Baroga**, has written more than 50 plays, including *Eye of the Coconut* and *Walls*. Jessica Hagedorn started creating multimedia theater pieces in experimental performance venues with her *Mango Tango* and *Tenement Lovers*. Other notable playwrights of Filipino descent include Alberto S. Florentino, **Linda Faigao-Hall**, **Rey A. Pamatmat**, **Ralph B. Peña**, and **Han Ong,** who won the prestigious MacArthur Award. **Ma-Yi Theater Company** in New York established its reputation through producing Filipino American work. Other important Filipino American ensembles include San Francisco's **Teatro Ng Tanan**, **Bindlestiff Studio**, **Tongue in a Mood**, **Kularts**, **Pintig Cultural Group** in Chicago, **Kinding Sindaw**, and **QBd Ink** of Washington, D.C. *See also* ALUMIT, NÖEL; CABICO, REGIE; DE LA PAZ, OLIVER; FERIA, BENNY F.; FRANCIA, LUIS H.; GAMALINDA, ERIC; JAVELLANA, STEVEN;

JAVIER, PAOLO; LEGASPI, JOSEPH O.; LIM, PAUL STEPHEN; LIM, PAULINO; PEÑARANDA, OSCAR; PINEDA, JON; REALUYO, BINO A.; ROSAL, PATRICK; STARNES, SOFIA M.; STICKMON, JANET; TAGAMI, JEFF; TAGATAC, GERONIMO; TAN, JOËL BARRAQUIEL; VILLA, JOSÉ GARCIA.

FLORENTINO, ALBERTO S. (1931–). A **Filipino American** playwright, Florentino spent his first 52 years in the Philippines before he and his family moved to the United States. He was already an established playwright before he came to this country. Heavily influenced by American writers like Theodore Dreiser, Eugene O'Neill, John Steinbeck, Erskine Caldwell, William Saroyan, and Clifford Odets, Florentino regards himself as a socially conscious writer. His first major play, *The World Is an Apple* (1954), won the first prize in the first annual postwar Carlos Palanca Memorial Awards for Drama. This play remains the most performed play in the Philippines. After this play, he went on to write more than 50 plays for the stage and more than 100 for television both in English and Tagalog, including *Oil impan* (1959), *Wedding Dance* (1968), *Memento Mori* (1971), etc. In the Philippines, Florentino is a cultural and literary celebrity. Representing the dispossessed, the poor, and the disadvantaged, he is regarded as Philippines' social conscience. In 2008, he was awarded a Presidential Medal of Merit for being a distinguished literary figure by President Gloria Macapagal-Arroyo. His name, however, is little known in the United States because of the limited distribution of his works by Philippines publishers. For the past 20 some years, he has lived in New York City and continues to publish chapbooks by Philippine, Filipino American, Asian American, and mainstream American writers.

FONG-TORRES, BEN (1945–). A **Chinese American** rock journalist and memoirist, Fong-Torres was born and raised in Alameda, California. He majored in radio–television–film in San Francisco State College. He worked for *Rolling Stone* magazine between 1969 and 1981 and has written for numerous magazines and radio programs. He has published a memoir *The Rice Room: From Number Two Son to Rock and Roll* (1994), detailing his and his brother's lives.

FOO, LORA JO (1951–). A **Chinese American** photographer and writer, Foo was born and raised in San Francisco. She holds a B.A. in psychology from San Francisco State University, a J.D. from Golden Gate University School of Law, and an M.P.A. in public administration from Harvard University. She is the author of a memoir *Earth Passages: Journeys through Childhood* (2008), which consists of 28 vignettes and 53 color nature photographs.

It tells her story of growing up in poverty, working in a garment sweatshop at age 11, and finding sanctuary in the woods. She works as an attorney and advocates for workers' rights.

FOSTER, SESSHU (1957–). A **Japanese American** poet, Foster was born to a white father and **nisei** mother and grew up in a Chicano barrio in Los Angeles. He has taught composition and literature in East L.A. since 1985, and has also taught at the University of Iowa, the California Institute of the Arts, the University of California, Santa Cruz, and the Jack Kerouac School's Summer Writing Program. He was in residence at California State University, Los Angeles. He is the author of several books of **poetry**, including *World Ball Notebook* (2008); *Atomik Aztex* (2005), winner of a Believer Book Award; *American Loneliness: Selected Poems* (2006); and *City Terrace Field Manual* (1996). *World Ball Notebook* won both the **American Book Award** and **Asian American Literary Award**.

FOUR SEAS PLAYERS. This is a **Chinese American theater** group, founded in 1970 in New York's **Chinatown** as a community outreach program for young people and recent immigrants. Its purpose is to promote a spirit of harmony and cooperation through artistic involvement and to nurture an interest in and appreciation for the dramatic arts, especially in the tradition of Chinese culture and its relationship with the Western art form as seen in New York. The Company has been able to produce two to three full-length theatrical productions each year in Cantonese Chinese, Mandarin Chinese, and English. The theater group is under the artistic direction of Mr. Jackie Huang (1999–2003, 2006–present), Ms. Liang-Tee Tu (1993–1998, 2004–2006), Mr. Yeh Yung-Ching (1973–1983), and Dr. Joanna Chan (1970–1972, 1984–1992). It has presented more than 100 productions, ranging from Chinese to Western classics, such as *The Monkey King*, *The True Story of Ah Q*, *Thunderstorm*, *A Midsummer Night's Dream*, *Inherit the Wind*, *The Odd Couple*, and *Murder*.

FRANCIA, LUIS H. (1945–). A **Filipino American** poet, Francia was born in Manila, the Philippines, and moved to New York in the early 1970s. He received his B.A. in the humanities from Ateneo de Manila University, with a major in philosophy and a minor in English. He is the author of four books of **poetry**: *The Beauty of Ghosts* (2010), *Museum of Absences* (2004), *Her Beauty Likes Me Well* (1979), and *The Arctic Archipelago and Other Poems* (1992). His poetry explores themes of love, loss, and redemption while portraying people living between worlds. He is also the author of a book of nonfiction, *Eye of the Fish* (2001), winner of the PEN Open Book and an **Asian American Literary Award**.

FU MANCHU. This is a character in a series of novels by British writer Sax Rohmer during the first half of the 20th century. The character, featured in films, TV shows, radio programs, comic strips, and comic books, became the archetype of a criminal genius in both British and American popular cultures. Fu Manchu first appeared in the 1923 British film *The Mystery of Dr. Fu Manchu* starring Harry Agar Lyons, who also played the character in *The Further Mysteries of Fu Manchu* the following year. The best-known Fu Manchu film was made in Great Britain in 1932, *The Mask of Fu Manchu,* staring Boris Karloff and Myrna Loy. In 1940, Republic Pictures made *Dreams of Fu Manchu,* a 15-episode serial. *The Mysteries of Dr. Fu Manchu* (1929) was the first American rendition, starring Warner Oland, best known for his role as **Charlie Chan**. Oland played Fu in a series of films, such as *The Return of Dr. Fu Manchu, Daughter of the Dragon, Paramount on Parade, Philo Vance,* and *Sherlock Holmes.* The most recent adaptation is by Nicolas Cage in *Werewolf Women of the SS* (2007).

Fu Manchu has dominated the imagination of generations of viewers and readers about China and the Chinese people. As a stereotype, it is often associated with the **Yellow Peril** and inspired many other villains in subsequent "Yellow Peril" thrillers such as Ming the Merciless from *Flash Gordon,* Chang Yen from *The Big Four,* Dr. No from *James Bond,* The Celestial Toymaker from *Doctor Who,* Dr. Yen-Lo from *The Manchurian Candidate,* etc. Many Asian American writers and critics are deeply offended by this stereotype. For instance, In *Aiiieeeee!* **Frank Chin** attacks both Fu Man Chu and Charlie Chan as **racist**, anti-Asian, and emasculating stereotypes. To challenge and subvert these flat Asian characters popular in Hollywood is one of the chief items on the agenda in Asian American literature and **theater**.

FUJITA, JUN (1888–1963). A **Japanese American** poet, Fujita was born in a village near Hiroshima, Japan. He came to the United States as a young man and settled in Chicago. He finished his interrupted high school education in Chicago and studied mathematics at the old Armour Institute of Technology (now the Illinois Institute of Technology) to become an engineer. To pay his way through college, he took a job at the old *Chicago Evening Post,* later the *Chicago Daily News,* as the *Chicago Evening Post*'s first and only photojournalist. Fujita published a book of **poetry** *TANKA: Poems in Exile* (1923), which was the first American ***tanka*** collection.

FULBECK, KIP (1965–). A **Chinese American** filmmaker and memoirist, Fulbeck was born in Fontana, California, to a Chinese mother and a Caucasian father. He received an M.F.A. in visual arts from the University of California (UC), San Diego, and currently teaches art at UC, Santa Barbara. He became famous after his short film *Banana Split* (1991), which explores mixed race identity. Following it are other films, including *Asian Studs Nightmare* (1994), *Sex, Love and Kung Fu* (2000), and *Lilo and Me* (2003). *Paper Bullets: A Fictional Autobiography* (2001) is Fulbeck's memoir about growing up half Chinese in a white community.

FURUTANI, DALE (1941–). A **Japanese American** novelist and poet, Furutani was born in Hilo, Hawaii, and grew up in California. He received a B.A. in creative writing from California State University, Long Beach, and an M.B.A. from the University of California, Los Angeles. He has published fiction, nonfiction, and **poetry**. His first mystery novel, *Death in Little Tokyo: A Ken Tanaka Mystery* (1997), received the Macavity Award for Best First Mystery Novel, the Anthony Award for the Best First Novel, and an Agatha Award nomination. This novel is followed by four other mystery novels: *The Toyotomi Blades* (1997), *Death at the Crossroads* (1998), *Jade Palace Vendetta* (1000), and *Kill the Shogun* (2000), with the last three being a historical trilogy centering on a samurai named Kaze Matsuyama living in 1603.

G

GALANG, M. EVELINA (1961–). A **Filipina American** fiction writer, Galang was born in Harrisburg, Pennsylvania. She obtained her B.A. in radio–television–film from the University of Wisconsin, Madison, and M.F.A. in creative writing from Colorado State University. She has authored a collection of short stories, *Her Wild American Self* (1996), and a novel, *One Tribe* (2006). She is the recipient of numerous awards, including the 2004 Gustavus Myers Outstanding Book Awards Advancing Human Rights and the 2004 Association of Writers and Writing Programs Prize in the Novel for *One Tribe.* She is currently a professor of creative writing at the University of Miami.

GAMALINDA, ERIC. A **Filipino American** novelist and poet, Gamalinda was born in Manila, Philippines. His novel *My Sad Republic* (2000) won a Philippine Centennial Literary Prize in 1998 for Best Work written in Philippine English. His other novels are *Confessions of a Volcano* (1990) and *Planet Waves* (1990). He has also published a book of fiction, *People Are Strange* (2011). His books of **poetry** include *Fire Poem/Rain Poem* (1976), *Lyrics from a Dead Language* (1991), *The Empire of Memory* (1992), *Peripheral Vision* (2002), *Amigo Warfare* (2007), and *Zero Gravity* (2000), which won an **Asian American Literary Award.** His literary works appeared on the pages of *Harper's Magazine, Frank*, *Hootenanny*, and other international literary journals.

GAMBITO, SARAH (1973–). A **Filipina American** poet, Gambito was born in Portsmouth, Virginia. She holds a B.A. in English from the University of Virginia and an M.F.A. in creative writing from Brown University. She is the author of two collections of **poetry**: *Delivered* (2009) and *Matadora* (2004), winner of a New England/New York Award and a Global Filipino Literary Award for Poetry. Her poetry explores the themes of ethnicity, gender, sex, immigration, nationality, and memory. Her honors include a Barnes & Noble Writers for Writers Award from *Poets & Writers*, and grants and fellowships from the New York Foundation for the Arts, Urban Artists Initiative, and MacDowell Colony. Her poems have been published in literary journals and magazines, including the *Iowa Review*, the *Antioch Review*, the *New Republic*, *Quarterly West*, *Fence*, and in anthologies including *From the Fishouse*. She is also cofounder, with **Joseph O. Legaspi**, of **Kundiman**, a nonprofit organization that serves emerging Asian American poets. Gambito lives in New York City and teaches creative writing at Fordham University.

GANESAN, INDIRA (1960–). A **South Asian American** novelist, Ganesan was born in Southern India and came to the United States at five. She received her B.A. in English from Vassar College and her M.F.A. from the Iowa Writers' Workshop. She has taught at the University of Missouri, the University of California (UC), San Diego, UC, Santa Cruz, the Bunting Institute, Radcliff College, Southampton College, and Lesley University. She is also the fiction editor of *Many Mountains Moving* literary magazine. Ganesan acknowledges her influences in masters such as Shakespeare, James Joyce, Virginia Woolf, Isaac Babel, Vladimir Nabokov, Gabriel Garcia Marquez, Toni Morrison, Zora Neale Hurston, and **Maxine Hong Kingston**. Her first novel, *The Journey* (1990), tells the story of Indian Americans' return to their **homeland**. In exploring the theme of the mutual prejudice between Westerners and Indians, the novel satirizes the irrational allegiance to one's own culture. Her second novel, *Inheritance* (1998), is a coming-of-age story told by a 15-year-old girl who is half Indian and half American. Ganesan has received fellowships at the Paden Institute for Writers of Color in Essex, New York, the Mary Ingraham Bunting Institute at Radcliffe College, the MacDowell Colony, and the Fine Arts Work Center in Provincetown.

GANESHANANTHAN, VASUGI V. (1980–). A **South Asian American** novelist, Ganeshananthan was born in Hartford, Connecticut. She earned her B.A. at Harvard College and M.A. in journalism from Columbia University. She was a graduate of the Iowa Writers' Workshop. Her first novel, *Love Marriage* (2008), depicts one extended Sri Lankan family in North America and how it copes with dislocation, violations of tradition, political conflicts, and guilt after the beginnings of Sri Lanka's dissolution in 1983. She now teaches creative writing at the University of Michigan.

GHAZALS. A poetic form popular in Iran, India, and Pakistan, it is composed of rhyming couplets and a refrain, ranging from five couplets to 15. Each line of the poem shares the same meter; this rule is not imposed in English though. This form traditionally gives expression to love, beauty, separation, longing, and pain. Originating in sixth century pre-Islamic Arabic verse, ghazals are often sung by Iranian, Indian, and Pakistani musicians. This style has been used by South Asian poets like **Agha Shahid Ali**.

GHOSE, ZULFIKAR (1935–). An internationally known **South Asian American** novelist and poet, Ghose was born and raised in Sialkot, India (now Pakistan). After the partition of British India into Pakistan and India, his family moved to England. He graduated from Keele University and taught at Ealing Mead School in London. During this phase of his life, he published two collections of **poetry**, *The Loss of India* (1964) and *Jets from Orange* (1967), an autobiography *Confessions of a Native-Alien* (1965), and his first two novels, *The Contradictions* (1966) and *The Murder of Aziz Khan* (1969). In 1969, he moved to the United States to teach at the University of Texas, Austin, and has lived there ever since. During this second phase, he published his trilogy *The Incredible Brazilian* (1972, 1975, and 1978), a picaresque prose epic of Brazilian history. This trilogy established his international reputation. Ghose went on to publish three more books of poetry: *The Violent West* (1972), *A Memory of Asia* (1984), and *Selected Poems* (1991), and many a novel: *Crump's Terms* (1975), *Hulme's Investigations Into the Bogart Script* (1981), *A New History of Torments* (1982), *Don Bueno* (1983), *Figures of Enchantment* (1986), *The Triple Mirror of the Self* (1992), and *Veronica and the Góngora Passion: Stories, Fictions, Tales and One Fable* (1998).

GHOSH, AMITAV (1956–). A **South Asian American** novelist, Ghosh was born in Calcutta, India, and was educated at St. Stephen's College, Delhi, Delhi University, Alexandria, and St. Edmund Hall, Oxford, where he earned a Ph.D. in social anthropology. In 1999, he joined the faculty at Queens College, City University of New York, as Distinguished Professor in Comparative Literature. He has also been a visiting professor at Harvard University since 2005. Ghosh lives in New York with his writer and editor wife, Deborah Baker. He is the author of seven novels, *The Circle of Reason* (1986), *The Shadow Lines* (1988), *The Calcutta Chromosome* (1995), *The Glass Palace* (2000), *The Hungry Tide* (2004), and *Sea of Poppies* (2008), the first volume of *The Ibis* trilogy, set in the 1830s, just before the Opium War, which encapsulates the colonial history of the East. His latest work of fiction is *River of Smoke* (2011), the second volume of *The Ibis* trilogy. *The Circle of Reason* won the Prix Médicis étranger; *The Shadow Lines* won the Sahitya Akademi Award and the Ananda Puraskar; and *The Calcutta Chromosome* won the Arthur C. Clarke Award. *Sea of Poppies* was shortlisted for the 2008 Man Booker Prize. It was the cowinner of the Vodafone Crossword Book Award in 2009, as well as cowinner of the 2010 Dan David Prize. Ghosh's most notable nonfiction writings are *In an Antique Land* (1992), *Dancing in Cambodia and At Large in Burma* (1998), *Countdown* (1999), *The Imam and the Indian* (2002), and *Incendiary Circumstances: A Chronicle of the Turmoil of Our Times* (2007), which won an **Asian American Literary Award**.

GLORIA, EUGENE (1957–). A **Filipina American** poet, Gloria was born in Manila and grew up in San Francisco. She earned her B.A. from San Francisco State University, her M.A. from Miami University of Ohio, and her M.F.A. in creative writing from the University of Oregon. She is the author of two books of poems: *Hoodlum Birds* (2006) and *Drivers at the Short-Time Motel* (2000), which was selected for the 1999 National Poetry Series and the 2001 **Asian American Literary Award**. Her **poetry** has also appeared in *Shenandoah*, the *North American Review,* and the *Greensboro Review*. Her poetry depicts ephemeral lives, souls lost to war, feelings of dislocation, ruined love, redemption, and the common man's search for connection to the self and to the world. She has received a Fulbright Research Grant, a grant from the San Francisco Arts Council, a Poetry Society of America award, and a Pushcart Prize. She teaches creative writing and English literature at DePauw University in Greencastle, Indiana.

GOBAR, DONIA. An Afghan American poet, artist, physician, and educator, Gobar was born in Kabul, Afghanistan. She earned her M.D. from Kabul University Medical School and specialized in obstetrics and gynecology and earned a master's in public health from University of Michigan. She is a Pittsburgh Art Council Board member and founder of the True Humanity club. She won the International Poet of Merit Award 2000–2001, Editor's Choice Award, and **Poetry**'s Elite: The Best Poets of Year 2000 (International Society of Poets). *The Invisibles* (2003) is her first collection of poetry and artwork, which explores the themes of home, memory, personal journeys, war, and violence. *See also* SOUTH ASIAN AMERICAN LITERATURE AND THEATER.

GOLD MOUNTAIN. This is a term the Chinese used for San Francisco during the Gold Rush. Many Chinese American writers use this term in their writings, such as **Maxine Hong Kingston**, **Frank Chin**, **Fae Myenne Ng**, **Lisa Lenine See**, and **Cherylene Lee**.

GOMOLVILAS, PRINCE (1972–). A Thai American playwright, Gomolvilas was born in Indianapolis, Indiana, and grew up in Monrovia, California. He received a B.A. in film and screenwriting and an M.F.A. in creative writing and playwriting from San Francisco State University. He now lives and writes in Los Angeles and is the author of eight plays that have been produced around the United States and in Singapore: *Big Hunk O Burnin' Love* (1998), *Seat Belts and Big Fat Buddhas* (1999), *The Theory Of Everything* (2000), *Debunking Love* (2000), *Bee* (2001), *Boyz of All Nationz: The Rise and Fall of a Multi-Ethnic Boy Band* (2002), *Mysterious Skin*

(2003), *The Fabulous Adventures of Captain Queer* (2006), and *Jukebox Stories* (2006). These plays have been produced in such cities as Arlington, Virginia, Chicago, Los Angeles, New York, San Francisco, Santa Ana, Seattle, Singapore, and Washington, D.C., by such companies as **Asian Story Theater**, **dueEast Theatre Company**, the **East West Players**, Lorraine Hansberry Theatre, New Conservatory Theatre Center, **Pork Filled Players**, Rude Guerrilla **Theater** Company, Singapore Repertory Theatre, and SIS Productions. His one-act play *Donut Holes in Orbit* was also produced at Ensemble Studio Theatre and the Smithsonian Institution. Gomolvilas is the recipient of the PEN Center USA Literary Award for Drama, Julie Harris/Janet and Maxwell Salter Playwright Award, International Herald Tribune/SRT Playwriting Award, and East West Players' Made in America Award for Outstanding Artistic Achievement for the Asian Pacific Islander Community. He has received grants from the National Endowment for the Arts, Theatre Communications Group's Residency Program for Playwrights, and the Wallace Alexander Gerbode Foundation's New Play Production Program. *See also* SOUTHEAST ASIAN AMERICAN LITERATURE AND THEATER.

GONZALEZ, N.V.M. (1915–1999). A **Filipino American** writer, Gonzalez was born in Romblon, the Philippines, and raised in Mansalay. He attended National University without finishing his undergraduate degree. He studied creative writing at Stanford University and returned to the Philippines and taught at various universities. Later he taught at the University California (UC), Santa Barbara, California State University, Hayward, University of Washington, UC, Los Angeles, and UC, Berkeley. He is the author of three novels: *The Winds of April* (1941), *A Season of Grace* (1956), and *The Bamboo Dancers* (1988). He has also published many short stories collections, including *A Grammar of Dreams and Other Stories* (1997), *The Bread of Salt and Other Stories (*1993), *Mindoro and Beyond: Twenty-One Stories* (1981), *Selected Stories* (1964), *Look, Stranger, on This Island Now* (1963), *Children of the Ash-Covered Loam and Other Stories* (1954), and *Seven Hills Away* (1947). Most of his works explore the themes of home, memory, land, and inner strength. Among his honors are Philippines Centennial Award for Literature, National Artist Award for Literature, Republic Cultural Heritage Award, and Rockefeller Foundation fellowships.

GOTANDA, PHILIP KAN (1951–). One of the most prolific and well-known **Japanese American** playwrights, Gotanda was born in Stockton, California. He enrolled at the University of California, Santa Cruz, with the intention of becoming a psychiatrist. After one year, he left for Japan to study ceramic art. Upon his return, he resumed his studies at the University of

California, Santa Cruz, and completed his B.A. in Japanese arts. Fond of music and writing lyrics, Gotanda's initiation to playwriting was "Ballad of the Issei" and "All-American Asian Punk," both of which were lyrics to songs. Unsure of what he wanted to do, he enrolled in Hastings School of Law and completed a law degree in 1978. His first theatrical piece was a musical inspired by the well-known Japanese folktale "Momotaro the Peach Boy." He caught the attention of Mako, a veteran actor and founder of the **East West Players**, who invited Gotanda to Los Angeles to develop *The Avocado Kid, or Zen and the Art of Guacamole* (1979) for the East West Players. He went on to write *A Song for Nesei Father* (1980) telling the story of his father from childhood in Hawaii to **Japanese Internment** during World War II to old age as husband and father. It was performed at the **Asian American Theater Company** where **David Henry Hwang** directed its world premiere, the **Pan Asian Repertory Theatre** (1983), the East West Players (1984), and the **Northwest Asian American Theatre** (1911).

In his *Bullet Headed Birds* (1981), *Dream of Kitamura* (1982), and *Day Standing on Its Head* (1994), Gotanda experimented with surrealism. His reputation as a playwright was firmly established by his play *The Wash* (1985), portraying the death of a **nisei** marriage. *The Wash* was premiered at Eureka Theatre in San Francisco in 1987 and was filmed for American Playhouse in 1990. His next play *Yankee Dawg You Die* (1986) was an unrelenting ironic examination of **racist** treatments of two Asian American actors. He wrote, produced, directed, and starred in his first short film *The Kiss* (1992), shown at several film festivals including the Sundance, Berlin, and Edinburg film festivals. This was the beginning of a series of short films, including *Drinking Tea* (1996) and *Life Tastes Good* (1999). His play *Ballad of Yachiyo* (1996) was produced at London's Gate Theatre in coproduction with the Royal National Theatre. His most recent work, *After the War*, premiered at the American Conservatory Theatre in March 2007. It is a play about the postwar period in San Francisco's Japantown sharing the neighborhood with a vibrant African American jazz scene. Gotanda has been a recipient of numerous honors, including Guggenheim, Pew Trust, three Rockefeller fellowships, Lila Wallace, the National Endowment for the Arts/**Theater** Communications Playwriting Award, PEN Center West, LA Music Center Award, and **Asian American Theater Company** Life Time Achievement.

GOTERA, VINCENTE FERRER (1952–). A **Filipino American** poet, Gotera was born to immigrant parents from the Philippines and raised in San Francisco, California. His education at Stanford University was interrupted by the Vietnam War. After serving in the army between 1972 and 1975, he returned to college and earned an A.A. in General Studies from City College of

San Francisco, a B.A. in English from Stanford University, and then an M.A. in English from San Francisco State University. Gotera then entered Indiana University, where he earned an M.F.A. in **poetry** and a Ph.D. in English and in American Studies. He has been teaching since 1995 at the University of Northern Iowa, and, in 2000, he was appointed editor of the *North American Review*. Gotera is the author of three books of poetry: *Fighting Kite* (2007); *Ghost Wars* (2003), winner of the Global Filipino Literary Award for Poetry in 2004; and *Dragonfly* (1994). Most of his poetry pertains to his experience during the Vietnam War. His work has appeared in such literary magazines as *Ploughshares*, *Caliban*, *Amerasia*, the *Kenyon Review*, the *Asian Pacific American Journal*, *Zone 3*, and others, as well as in anthologies like *Contemporary Fiction by Filipinos in America, Tilting the Continent:* ***Southeast Asian*** *American Writing*, and *From Totems to Hip-Hop: A Multicultural Anthology of Poetry across the Americas, 1900–2002*. Among the honors he has received are an international award sponsored by the journal *Our Own Voice,* a Creative Writing Fellowship in Poetry from the Nation Endowment for the Arts, the Felix Pollak Prize in Poetry from the *Madison Review*, the Mary Roberts Rinehart Award in poetry, and an Academy of American Poets Prize. He has been nominated for the Pushcart Prize three times.

GOWDA, SHILPI SOMAYA (1970–). A **South Asian American** novelist, Gowda was born and raised in Toronto, Canada, to parents who migrated there from Mumbai, India. She holds a bachelor's degree from the University of North Carolina at Chapel Hill and an M.B.A. from Stanford University. She now makes her home in California with her husband and children. Gowda spent a summer in college as a volunteer in an Indian orphanage, which seeded the idea for *Secret Daughter* (2010), her debut novel. Gowda explores the themes of cultural identities and adoption.

GRATEFUL CRANE ENSEMBLE (THE). This is a **Japanese American theater** group in Los Angeles, founded in 2001. Its mission is to present educational and theatrical programs in appreciation for the unique hardships and inspiring contributions of Japanese Americans in U.S. history.

GREAT LEAP INC. This is a multiethnic performance company in Los Angeles. It was founded in 1978 by Nobuko Miyamoto as an Asian American group, creating original musicals such as *Chop Suey* and *Talk Story*. *A Slice of Rice,* a festival, presented a host of Asian American artists. The cultural conflicts, which led to the Los Angeles uprisings in 1992, transformed Great Leap into a multicultural organization with a new show, *A Slice of Rice, Frijoles, and Greens*, featuring stories of Asian, Latino, and African American artists, which continues to tour today. Responding to the religious divides created by 9/11, Great Leap presented workshops to bring communities of different faiths together. It produced *Leaps of Faith*, a **theater** piece, created from personal stories of artists of diverse spiritual paths. In 2009, *Leaps of Faith* was performed at the Parliament of World's Religions in Melbourne, Australia. In 2009, Great Leap began to address the environmental crisis in its COLLABORATORY workshop process, and in 2010 it created its first music video, "B.Y.O. CHOPSTIX," a humorous look at the perils of disposable chopsticks on the environment. *See also* THEATER.

HAGEDORN, JESSICA (1949–). One of the best-known **Filipina American** writers and performing artists, Hagedorn was born in Manila, the Philippines. She and her family moved to San Francisco when she was 14 years old. She studied **theater** at the American Conservatory Theatre in San Francisco. In 1978, she moved to New York and began her professional career of writing and performing plays. In almost all her writings, she demonstrates her political engagement in the critique of imperialism. She wrote and performed plays such as *Chiquita Banana* (1972), *Mango Tango* (1977), *Tenement Lover* (1981), *Teenytown* (1990), and *Airport Music* (1993). The common themes in these plays are colonialism, violence, and the **liminal** space that immigrants occupy. These plays are anthologized in *Third World Women, Out from Under: Texts by Women Performance Artists*, and *Between Worlds: Contemporary Asian American Plays*. Hagedorn also wrote **poetry** and short fiction, which are collected in *Dangerous Music* (1975) and *Pet Food and Tropical Apparitions* (1981), both of which are assembled in *Danger and Beauty* (1993). Crossing the borders between music and writing, Hagedorn's poetry exudes the energy and spontaneity of performance whose aesthetics are affiliated with oral traditions, music, and dance. The themes of her poetry range from the personal to the political, condemning American neocolonialism in the Philippines, distaining empty intellectualism, affirming the spirituality of art, and meditating on romantic and filial love.

Hagedorn is best known for her novels *Dogeaters* (1990), *The Gangster of Love* (1996), and *Dream Jungle* (2004). She is also widely known for her edited anthologies, ***Charlie Chan** Is Dead: An Anthology of Contemporary Asian–American Fiction* (1993) and *Charlie Chan Is Dead 2: At Home in the World* (2004). *Dogeaters* was a finalist for the **National Book Award**. Set in Manila between 1950s and 1980s, the novel presents a postmodernist collage of characters experiencing discordant, displaced, alienating, and alienated lives. *The Gangster of Love* follows an immigrant family from Manila to San Francisco, centering on the female protagonist Rocky. Rocky's passion for music leads her into encounters with other struggling musicians and artists in New York's milieu of drugs and sex. The central themes of this novel project spiritual emptiness, a profound sense of homelessness, **East-West relations**.

Dream Jungle centers on the famous event of the alleged discovery of a lost Stone Age tribe in the Philippines. Through the eyes of a young female protagonist, Hagedorn exposes corruptions at various levels in the Philippines and the domination of America.

HAHN, KIMIKO (1955–). A **Japanese American** poet, Hahn was born in Mt. Kisco, New York, to a Japanese American mother from Hawaii and a German American father from Wisconsin. As a teenager, she became highly interested in her Asian half and eagerly participated in the Asian American movement in New York City. Hahn attended the University of Iowa and majored in English and East Asian studies. She earned an M.A. in Japanese literature from Columbia University. This graduate education provided her with a rich literary tradition that inspired her **poetry**. She went back to Iowa and earned her M.F.A. in poetry writing. She is a distinguished professor at Queens College.

Her first collection, *Air Pocket* (1989), explores cross-cultural, interlingual, and intertextual poetics that invoke Japanese myth, culture, and language. Sharing with the first book of poetry the themes of race, class, power, and **women**'s sexuality and subjectivity, her second volume, *Earshot* (1992), reaches into classic Japanese literary tradition, such as *The Tale of Genji*, to articulate women's creative power and aesthetics. Women's sexual passion and autonomy of the body become dominant themes in her third book of poetry, *The Unbearable Heart* (1995), which won the **American Book Award**. Here she also expresses her deep grief over her mother's passing. In several poems of this collection, Hahn delves into theoretical language of feminism and psychoanalysis. Hahn becomes increasingly interested in weaving the theoretical into the poetic in her more recent volumes of poetry like *Volatile* (1999), *Mosquito and Ant* (1999), *The Artist's Daughter* (2002), *The Narrow Road to the Interior* (2006), collection of ***tanka*** and *zuihitsu*. In these poems, she tightens the relationship between poetry and social criticism, particularly on issues of gender and race. In her most recent collection, *Toxic Flora* (2010), inspired by articles from the weekly "Science Times" section of the *New York Times*, Hahn experiments with the imagery of science to explore identity, extinction, and survival. Hahn is the recipient of numerous honors, including the PEN/Voelcker Award, an Association of Asian American Studies Literature Award, a Lila Wallace–Reader's Digest Award, a Theodore Roethke Memorial Poetry Prize, and the Shelley Memorial Prize from the Poetry Society of America. Her fellowships include those from National Endowment for the Arts and the New York Foundation for the Arts.

HAIKU. A form of Japanese poetry whose English format consists of three lines, distributed 5, 7, and 5 syllables respectively. *Haiku* typically contain a seasonal reference, and a verbal caesura. In Japanese, *haiku* are traditionally printed in a single vertical line. Many Asian American poets employ this style, such as **Violet Kazue De Cristoforo** and **Sadakichi Hartmann.** *See also* NOGUCHI, YONE; SAIJO, ALBERT; VONGSAY, SAYMOUKDA D.

HAJI, NAFISA (1969–). A **South Asian American** novelist, Haji was born to parents from Karachi, Pakistan, and was raised in Los Angeles, Chicago, Karachi, and London. She studied American history at the University of California (UC), Berkeley, taught elementary school in downtown Los Angeles for seven years in a bilingual Spanish program, and earned a doctorate in education from UC, Los Angeles. She is the author of two novels: *The Writing on My Forehead* (2009) and *The Sweetness of Tears* (2001). Her novels explore the themes of family history, family secrets, religious conflicts, and forbidden love. Nafisa now lives in Northern California with her husband and son.

HALL, BRUCE EDWARD (1954–2003). A **Chinese American** memoirist, Hall was born to third-generation Chinese American parents in New York City. He studied **theater** at Syracuse University and worked as a puppeteer, who performed periodically with the Muppets between 1983 and 1990. His most notable Henson project was *Muppets Take Manhattan*, performing Beth Bear and Masterson Rat. He is the author of a memoir, *Tea That Burns: A Family Memoir of Chinatown* (1998), and a book of nonfiction, *Diamond Street: The Story of the Little Town with the Big Red Light District* (1994). His **children's book**, *Henry and the Kite Dragon* (2001), won Jane Addams Children's Book Awards.

HAMID, MOHSIN (1971–). A **South Asian American** novelist, Hamid was born in Lahore, Pakistan, and moved to the United States for higher education. After receiving degrees from Princeton's Woodrow Wilson School of Public and International Affairs and Harvard Law School, he worked in New York and London as a management consultant and then as managing director. He now lives and writes in Lahore. Hamid is the author of two novels: *Smoke Moth* (2000) and *The Reluctant Fundamentalist* (2007). *Smoke Moth* depicts themes of sex, drugs, and class conflicts in the 1990s urban Pakistan. The novel won a Betty Trask Award and was a finalist for the PEN/Hemingway Award. *The Reluctant Fundamentalist*, set in New York City, explores the fear and suspicion after the 9/11 terrorist attacks. It won numerous awards, including the Ambassador Book Award, Anisfield–Wolf Book Award, and an **Asian American Literary Award**, and was short-listed for the Man Booker.

HAN, JENNY. A **Korean American** writer of **young adult novels** and **children's books**, Han was born and raised in Richmond, Virginia. She graduated from the University of North Carolina at Chapel Hill and earned an M.F.A. in writing for children at New School University. She lives in New York City. She's the author of three young adult novels: *The Summer I Turned Pretty* (2010), *It's Not Summer without You* (2011), *We Will Always Have Summer* (2011). She has also written two children's books: *Shug* (2007) and *Clara Lee and the Apple Pie Dream* (2011).

HAN, SUYING (ROSALIE CHOU, 1917–). A **Chinese American** memoirist and novelist, Han was born to a Chinese father and a Belgian mother in Beijing. She attended Yenching University in Beijing and then moved to Brussels to study medicine but returned to her parents when Japan invaded China. Eventually, she completed her medical studies at London University and moved to Hong Kong to work as a doctor. In 1963, Han ended her 16-year medical practice for full time writing. Han is known for her numerous autobiographies and autobiographical novels, such as *Destination Chungking* (1942), *A Many-Splendored Thing* (1952), *. . . And the Rain My Drink* (1956), *The Mountain Is Young* (1958), *Two Loves* (1962), *The Four Faces* (1964), *The Crippled Tree: China, Biography, History, Autobiography* (1965), *A Mortal Flower: China, Autobiography, History* (1966), *China in the Year 2001* (1967), *Birdless Summer: China, Autobiography, History* (1968), and *My House Has Two Doors: China, Autobiography, History* (1980), *Till Morning Comes: A Novel* (1982), etc.

HAPA. A Hawaiian term used to describe a person of mixed racial or ethnic heritage. It originated from the English word *half.* In Hawaiian Pidgin, it has an extended meaning of "half-caste" or "of mixed descent," often taken to mean "part white."

HARTMAN, YUKIHIDE MAESHIMA (1939–). A **Japanese American** poet, Hartman was born in Tokyo and raised by a Japanese mother and an American stepfather. At age 19, he moved with his family to Pearl River, New York. He was enlisted in the U.S. Army for two years, before, during, and after which he attended Fairleigh Dickinson University, the University of South Carolina, and the New School for Social Research. Although he has worked in computer programming and system analysis, Hartman has always been passionate about writing **poetry**. During his time at the New School, he studied poetry writing with **José Garcia Villa** and later published his first chapbook, *A One of Me* (1970). He began to study more seriously at the St. Mark's Poetry Project in 1977. Subsequently, he published *Hot Footsteps* (1976), *Red Rice* (1980), *Ping* (1984), *New Poems* (1991), *A Coloring Book* (1996), and *Triangle* (1997). Hartman is most keen on exploring his interior world and giving it expression through images of quiet and subtle beauty in nature, love, friendship, and food. He has received a number of awards, including a Pushcart Prize, the Fund for Poetry Prize, and a three-time fellow at the MacDowell Colony.

HARTMANN, SADAKICHI (1867–1944). A **Japanese American** poet, fiction writer, and playwright, Hartmann was born in Japan to a German father and a Japanese mother. Hartmann was raised by his paternal grandmother and an uncle in Hamburg, Germany. Facilitated by his wealthy uncle, Hartmann was initiated into the world of arts. Later he wrote *A History of American Art* (1902), which became a popular textbook. When Hartmann was 15, his father sent him to live with poor relatives in Philadelphia. Two years later, he met and befriended Walt Whitman, with whom he discussed literature and arts. *Conversations with Walt Whitman* (1895) is the fruit of that friendship. Under the elderly poet's influence and encouragement, young Hartmann wrote his first poems imitating Whitman's style. However, this phase did not last. Soon Hartmann became interested in French symbolism and published his first collection of symbolist poetry, *Poems* (1889), which is the first book of poetry by an Asian American. At age 24, Hartmann accepted the position with the McClure's Syndicate as a foreign correspondent in Europe, where he met Stéphane Mallarmé and became even more inspired by French symbolism. This experience resulted in the publication of *Naked Ghosts* (1898), which he dedicated to Mallarmé. Four years later, he revised this collection to include two earlier poems to pay homage to his first mentor, Whitman.

His third collection, *Drifting Flowers of the Sea and Other Poems* (1904), presents six adaptations of ***tanka***. His interest in Japanese poetic forms continued in his later work *My Rubaiyat* (1913), a collection of unrhymed poetry written in quatrains. His Japanese poems were revised and edited several times and were published in *Japanese Rhythms* (1926), which included ***haiku***, *tanka*, and ***dodoitsu***. In addition, Hartmann wrote short stories and plays. The stories are collected in *Schopenhauer in the Air* (1899), and he also wrote a novella, *The Last Thirty Days of Christ* (1920). His plays include *A Tragedy in a New York Flat* (1986), *Christ* (1893), *Buddha* (1897), and *Confucius* (1923). Other than *A Tragedy*, a realist play, all the others are best described as symbolist. Hartmann received critical acclaims from Gertrude Stein and Ezra Pound. *See also* POETRY; THEATER.

HAYSLIP, PHUNG THI LE LY (1949–). A **Vietnamese American** memoirist, Hayslip was born in Vietnam. Hayslip is Le Ly's married name after her second American husband. Le Ly was 12 years old when the war invaded her village in central Vietnam. By the time she was 15, she had fought in the war, been imprisoned, starved, tortured, and raped. She immigrated to the United States in 1970 through marriage to an American man. *When Heaven and Earth Changed Places: A Vietnamese Woman's Journey from War to Peace* (1989) was her first memoir, which weaves three lines of story: her life in Vietnam, her life in the United States, and her return to Vietnam as a wealthy Vietnamese American in 1986. Oliver Stone adapted this memoir to a film, *Heaven and Earth,* in 1993. *Child of War, Woman of Peace* (1993) continues the story of her life in the United States, the cultural clashes she experienced, and her travel between her home country and her adopted country. It narrates how she became wealthy and how she built East Meets West Foundation, a charitable group dedicated to improving the health and welfare of Vietnamese.

HEREANDNOW. This is an Asian American **theater** company that tours across the nation. Founded in 1989 by John Miyasaki in Occidental College in Los Angeles, the company has had over 200 cast members over the years.

HILL, AMY (1953–). A **Japanese American** dramatist and actress, Hill was born in Deadwood, South Dakota, to a Japanese mother and a Finish American father. At age 18, she went to Japan, and her experience during her four years of living and working in Japan became the material for her first solo piece *Tokyo Bound*, which was first staged in the **East West Players** in Los Angeles in 1991 and later became anthologized in *Asian American Drama: 9 Plays from the Multiethnic Landscape*. While working on her B.A. in Japanese art at the University of Washington, she met **Garrett Hongo**, a founder of the **Asian Exclusion Act**, now known as the **Northwest Asian American Theatre**. This led her to the job of stage-managing **Frank Chin**'s *Year of the Dragon*. She later wrote and performed *Beside Myself* (1992), *Reunion* (1995), *Out of the Light/Into the Fire* (1997), and *Deadwood to Hollywood* (1999). These plays explore the common themes of biraciality, cultural clashes, and intercultural negotiation. Hill also appeared in films and TV programs, including *Dim Sum*, *Singles*, *Rising Sun*, *Seinfeld*, *All American Girl*, *Six Feet Under*, *Desperate Housewives*, *Curb Your Enthusiasm*, etc. *See also* THEATER.

HIM, CHANRITHY (1965–). A Cambodian American memoirist, Him was born in Takeo Province, Cambodia, and moved to the countryside when the Khmer Rouge entered Phnom Penh in 1975. Her family fled to the refugee camps at the Thai border when Vietnam invaded Cambodia in 1979. Him and her family moved to the United States when she was 16. She received her B.S. in biochemistry from the University of Oregon. She is the author of a memoir *When Broken Glass Floats: Growing up under the Khmer Rouge* (2000), which won an Oregon Book Award and was Finalist for the Kiriyama Pacific Rim Book Prize. *See also* SOUTHEAST ASIAN AMERICAN LITERATURE AND THEATER.

HIRAHARA, NAOMI (1962–). A **Japanese American** mystery writer, Hirahara was born in Pasadena, California, to **issei** parents. She received her B.A. in international relations from Stanford University and studied at the Inter-University Center for advanced Japanese language studies in Tokyo. She also spent three months as a volunteer work camper in Ghana, West Africa. She has written four mysteries, known as the Mas Arai Mysteries, that center on a Japanese American gardener living in Pasadena, California, named Mas Arai, who is haunted by powerful secrets from World War II and the bombing of Hiroshima in August 1945, with the exception of the second book that focuses on Mas Arai's daughter Mari—a gasa gasa girl (never sitting still, always on the go, getting into everything). *Summer of the Big Bachi* (2004) is her first mystery, a finalist for Barbara Kingsolver's Bellwether Prize and nominated for a Macavity mystery award. She went on to publish *Gasa-Gasa Girl* (2005), *Snakeskin Shamisen* (2006), winner of an Edgar Allan Poe award in the category of Best Paperback Original, and *Blood Hina* (2010). Her short stories have been published in a number of anthologies, including *Los Angeles Noir* (2007), *A Hell of a Woman: An Anthology of Female Noir* (2007), and *The Darker Mask* (2008). She has also published her first middle-grade book, *1001 Cranes* (2008).

HMONG AMERICAN WRITERS' CIRCLE (HAWC). This was founded in 2004 by Hmong American poet **Burlee Vang**. It is a forum to nurture creative writing within the Hmong community, and its members have partaken in writing residencies and conferences at Hedgebrook, **Kundiman**, Tinhouse, and Napa Valley. Through the years, HAWC's efforts and achievements have been geared toward the creation of a visible body of Hmong American literature and the establishment of a Hmong literary culture. *See also* SOUTHEAST ASIAN AMERICAN LITERATURE AND THEATER.

HO, MINFONG (1951–). A **Chinese** and Thai **American** author of fiction for **young adults**, Ho is considered the first Thai American author. Born in Rangoon, Burma, to Chinese–Thai parents, Ho attended Tunghai University in Taichung, Taiwan. In the late 1960s, she immigrated to the United States to attend Cornell University and earned her B.A. in history and economics and M.F.A. in creative writing. She has written four novels: *Sing to the Dawn* (1975), *Rice without Rain* (1986), *The Clay Marble* (1991), and *Gathering* *the Dew* (2003). She has also published a short story collection, *Tanjong Rhu and Other Stories* (1986). She also wrote *Maples in the Mis: Children's Poems from the Tang Dynasty* (1996). Her novels portray the lives of young girls from Southeast Asia. She has received numerous honors, including the first prize from the National Book Development council of Singapore, a Best Books for Young Adults citation from American Library Association, and Commonwealth Book Awards from the Commonwealth Book Council. *See also* SOUTHEAST ASIAN AMERICAN LITERATURE AND THEATER.

HOLTHE, TESS URIZA (1966–). A **Filipina American** fiction writer, Holthe was born in and raised in San Francisco. She received her undergraduate degree in accounting from Golden Gate University. Her debut novel, *When the Elephants Dance* (2002), is a national best seller. The novel retells supernatural tales inspired by indigenous Filipino mythology. Her short story collection, *The Five-Forty-Five to Cannes* (2007), received American Library Association's 2008 Notable Book award, as well as being named a 2007 notable book by the *San Francisco Chronicle*. She is also published in the *Louisville Review* and *Filipinas Magazine*.

HOMELAND. This is a frequently evoked concept in Asian American literature and **theater**. Fraught with nostalgia, homeland is often idealized as a romantic place that one has lost due to migration. As the past is often remembered via the mediation of memory, narrative, fantasy, and myth, physical displacement from homelands and social and cultural alienation in the United States inevitably engender the need to create fictions and imaginary homelands. Homeland as an imagined place of beauty, belonging, and meaning, however, is also associated with poverty, oppression, inequality, war, and violence that have compelled one to leave home in search for a better future. Even as many Asian American writers conjure up the magic of home, they cannot forget or ignore the reasons for their self-exile. **Agha Shahid Ali**'s book of **poetry** *The Country without a Post Office* is a nostalgic evocation of Kashmir, his homeland, at a time when Kashmir rebelled against Indian rule and the subsequent violence destroyed villages and towns. In his fictional autobiography *America Is in the Heart*, **Carlos Bulosan** depicts the idyllic beauty of his village as well as the abject poverty of his family. **Theresa Hak Kyung Cha** in *Dictée* employs the trope of mother tongue to evoke a motherland prior to Japanese colonization. Despite Korea's devastation, motherland continues via the memories and rituals that **women** maintain. **Li-Young Lee**'s poetry imagines a homeland, which he hardly remembers or has never known. In *The City in Which I Love You*, Lee melts his own love for his wife and sons into his father's memory and vision as he escapes Indonesia with his family. In *Rose*, Lee pictures China as a homeland through his mother's songs and stories. The Laotian American poet **Pos Moua** learned to read in a refugee camp in Thailand and arrived in the United States in time to enter the fifth grade. His poetry book *Where the Torches Are Burning* pictures the homeland he hardly remembers through idyllic depictions of the rivers, oceans, and mountains. *See also* EXILE.

HONG, CATHY PARK (1976–). A **Korean American** poet, Hong was born and raised in Los Angeles. She received her B.A. in English from Oberlin College and M.F.A. from the Iowa Writers' Workshop. Much of her work involves the mixing of languages. Her first book of **poetry**, *Translating Mo'um* (2002), winner of a Pushcart Prize, presents linguistic jokes that speak to the dislocation of transnational experience. Her second collection, *Dance Dance Revolution* (2007), winner of the Barnard Women Poets Prize, is part poetic sequence, part science fiction about a future city called the Desert—a Vegas-like manmade tourist trap. Hong is the recipient of a Fulbright Fellowship, a National Endowment for the Arts, a New York Foundation for the Arts Fellowship, and a Village Voice Fellowship for Minority Reporters. Her poems have been published in *A Public Space*, *Paris Review*, *Poetry*, *American Letters & Commentary*, *Denver Quarterly*, *Jubilat*, and other journals, and she has reported for the *Village Voice*, the *Guardian*, *Salon*, and *Christian Science Monitor*. She now lives in New York City and teaches at Sarah Lawrence College.

HONG, LILY TOY (1958–). A **Chinese American** author of **children's books**, Hong was born in Salt Lake City, Utah. She holds a B.F.A. in illustration from Utah State University. She is the author of five books: *Two Chinese Tales* (2010); *Two of Everything* (1995), winner of Utah Children's Picture Book Award; *The Empress and the Silkworm* (1995); *How the Ox Star Fell from the Heaven* (1991), named Parenting Magazine Ten Best Books of 1991; and *Marco Polo and Kublai Khan: A Great Friendship* (1995).

HONGO, GARRETT (1951–). A **Japanese American** poet, Hongo was born in Hawaii and moved to Los Angeles with his family when he was six years old. He received his B.A. in English from Pomona College and then went to Japan to live and study at Kyoto Temple for one year. Upon returning to the United States, Hongo enrolled in the master's program in Japanese language and literature at the University of Michigan, but after a year he left the program and settled in Seattle. Hongo educated himself in several literary traditions, such as Chinese and Japanese **poetry** and European modernism. His friendship with **Wakako Yamauchi**, **Alan Chong Lau**, and **Lawson Inada**

made a great impact on his life and poetry. Hongo was the founder of the **theater** group the **Asian Exclusion Act.** In 1978, he entered the M.F.A. program at the University of California, Irvine, and finished the program in 1980. A professor of creative writing at the University of Oregon, he directed the Program in Creative Writing from 1989 to 1993. Hongo has published two books of poetry: *Yellow Light* (1982) and *The River of Heaven* (1988), with the latter a **Lamont Poetry** Selection and a finalist for the Pulitzer Prize for Poetry. His latest book, *Volcano: A Memoir of Hawaii* (1995), was awarded the 2006 Oregon Book Award for Literary Nonfiction. Hongo has also worked as an editor on *Songs My Mother Taught Me: Stories, Plays and Memoir by Wakako Yamauchi* (1994), *The Open Boat: Poems from Asian America* (1993), and *Under Western Eyes: Personal Essays from Asian America* (1995). Hongo has received fellowships from the Guggenheim Foundation, the National Endowment for the Arts, and the Rockefeller Foundation.

HOSOKAWA, BILL (1915–2007). A **Japanese American** autobiographer and journalist, Hosokawa was born in Seattle, Washington. He studied journalism at the University of Washington. During World War II, his family (wife and infant son) was interned in the Heart Mountain Relocation Center in Wyoming. There, he helped to establish the *Heart Mountain Sentinel*, a newspaper to serve the inmates of the camp. After he was released in 1943, he joined the staff of the *Register* in Des Moines, Iowa, as a copyeditor. Then, he changed his job to the *Denver Post*, where he held various positions until he retired, including executive news editor and assistant managing editor. Most of his writings were heavily influenced by his camp experience. His first book, ***Nisei****: The Quiet Americans* (1969), explored this experience and became a national best seller. He wrote two other autobiographies: *Thirty-five Years in the Frying Pan* (1978) and *Out of the Frying Pan: Reflections of a Japanese American* (1989). Both are Hosokawa's meditation on the predicaments and rewards of being Japanese and American and his memory of the **internment**.

HOSSEINI, KHALED (1965–). The first Afghan American novelist, Hosseini was born in Kabul, Afghanistan. His father was a diplomat with the Afghan Foreign Ministry and his mother taught Farsi and history at a large high school in Kabul. The Hosseinis moved to Paris when he was 11, and in 1980, the family moved to San Jose, California. Hosseini earned his B.S. in biology from Santa Clara University and M.D. from the University of California, San Diego. Hosseini was a practicing internist between 1996 and 2004. He is the author of two novels: *The Kite Runner* (2001) and *A Thousand Splendid Suns* (2007). *The Kite Runner,* set in the final days of the monarchy to the present, explores themes of friendship, betrayal, and the price of loyalty. It describes the rich culture and beauty of a land in the process of being destroyed. *A Thousand Splendid Suns*, set against the volatile events of Afghanistan's last thirty years—from the Soviet invasion to the reign of the Taliban to the post-Taliban rebuilding—tells the story of two generations of characters brought jarringly together by the tragic sweep of war. Hosseini was named in 2006 a goodwill envoy to the United Nations Refugee Agency. He has been working to provide humanitarian assistance in Afghanistan through the Khaled Hosseini Foundation. Currently, he lives in Northern California. *See also* SOUTH ASIAN AMERICAN LITERATURE AND THEATER.

HOUSTON, JEANNE WAKATSUKI (1934–). A **Japanese American** writer, Houston was born in Inglewood, California. She studied sociology and journalism at San Jose State University. She is best known for her autobiographical novel, *Farewell to Manzanar* (1973), which is based on her family experiences at the Manzanar Camp during World War II in California's Owens Valley. It begins by describing the Wakatsukis as a peaceful and close-knit family before World War II. The bombing of Pearl Harbor (7 December 1941) marks the beginning of a terrible and frightening time in their life. After their release from the camp, the Wakatsukis can never return to their prewar peace and closeness. Ridden with fear, guilt, and shame, the family quietly copes with **racism** and alienation from each other.

HOUSTON, VELINA HASU (1957–). An internationally acclaimed **Japanese American** author of 20 plays as well as **poetry**, essays, and film scripts, Houston was born in Tokyo, Japan, to an African American and Native American father and a Japanese mother. When she was two years old, her family moved to the United States. Because of the interracial union between her parents, both of their families cut their ties with the couple. With her father's early death, Houston was raised by her mother in near isolation from American culture. She attended Kansas State University and earned a B.A. in journalism, communication, and **theater**. She earned her M.F.A. in theater arts with a minor in screenwriting from the University of California School of Theater, Film, and Television in Los Angeles. Currently, she is a professor of English and playwright in residence, director of the playwriting program at the University of Southern California School of Theatre. Houston solidified her playwriting career in 1987 when her play *Tea* was staged at Manhattan Theatre Club.

Most of her plays center on interracial and multicultural conflicts in identity formations. Her earlier plays focused on her family stories, often referred to as the trilogy: *Asa Ga Kimashita* (1980), *American Dreams* (1983), and

Tea (1983). *Waiting for Tadashi* (1999), though published much later, actually belongs to the group of her earlier plays in continuing the family stories. It fictionalizes her brother's life—an Amerasian orphan, abandoned by his single mother, taken in by an orphanage in Tokyo, adopted by an African American GI who marries a Japanese **woman**, and brought to the United States by his new family. Her second group of plays includes *The Matsuyama Mirror* (1979), *Kokoro* (1989), *Christmas Cake* (1990), *Cultivated Lives* (1994), *Hula Heart* (1994), *Ikebana* (1999), *Shedding the Tiger* (2001), *The Eyes of Bones* (2006), etc.

Houston is the recipient of 15 playwriting commissions from distinguished institutions, such as Manhattan Theatre Club, Los Angeles Opera, Asia Society, Lila Wallace–Reader's Digest Foundation, Mark Taper Forum, State of Hawaii Foundation on Culture and the Arts, Jewish Women's Theatre Project, Sacramento Theatre Company, Cornerstone Theatre Company, Mixed Blood Theatre Company, Honolulu Theatre for Youth, and Silk Road Theatre Project, Chicago. She has been a fellow of Rockefeller Foundation (twice), the California Arts Council, Los Angeles Endowment for the Arts, James Zumberge (trice), Japan Foundation, the McKnight Foundation, Sidney F. Brody. Among her numerous awards and honors are the Made in America Visionary Award, Pinter Review Prize for Drama Silver Medal, Women in Theatre Red Carpet Award, Twin Cities Ivey Award, Remy Martin New Vision Screenwriting Award from Sidney Poitier and the American Film Institute, Lorraine Hansberry Playwriting Award, David Library of American Freedom Playwriting Award, Japanese American Woman of Merit 1890–1990 by the National Japanese American Historical Society, East West Players Made in America Award, and others.

HUO, T. C. A **Chinese** Laotian American novelist, Huo was born in Laos and immigrated to the United States in 1980 and now lives in Santa Clara, California. He received his M.F.A. in creative writing from the University of California, Irvine. His first novel, *A Thousand Wings* (1998), tells the tale of one man's courtship of another through the food and stories of their shared heritage. His second novel, *Land of Smiles* (2000), traces the life of a Laotian boy from swimming across the Mekong River to Thailand to arriving at San Francisco to returning to Laos. In 2001, he received the award for adult fiction from the Asian/Pacific American Librarians Association. *See also* SOUTHEAST ASIAN AMERICAN LITERATURE AND THEATER.

HUYNH, JADE NGOC QUANG (1957–). A **Vietnamese American** memoirist, Huynh was born in South Vietnam. He was attending Saigon University when the capital fell in 1975. The Viet Cong sent him to a reeducation camp for hard labor. In 1977, he escaped by boat to Thailand and lived in a refugee camp before he came to Corinth, Tennessee. He received a B.A. in English from Bennington College, Vermont, an M.F.A. in creative writing from Brown University, and a Ph.D. from Cardiff University in the United Kingdom. He is the author of a memoir *South Wind Changing* (1994), which details his family's life during wartime, his survival of prison camp, his escape attempts, and his struggle to resettle in the United States. It was short-listed for the **National Book Award** and was a Time Magazine Non-Fiction Book of the Year for 1994.

HUYNH, QUANG NHUONG (1946–2001). A **Vietnamese American** author of **children's books**, Huynh was born in My Tho, Vietnam. He earned a B.S. in chemistry from Saigon University. After the outbreak of the Vietnam War, Huynh was drafted into the South Vietnamese army and was shot and paralyzed. He came to the United States in 1963. He then earned an M.A. in comparative literature from Long Island University and an M.A. in French from the University of Missouri. His first book, *The Land I Lost* (1982), which received the America Library Association Booklist Editors' Choice award, the Notable Children's Trade Book in the Field of Social Studies, the Library of Congress Children's Book award, the William Allen White Children's Book Award, the Friends of American Writers Award, and the Blue Cobra Award. His second book was *Water Buffalo Days* (1997). Both books focus on his childhood. He was also the recipient of a National Endowment for the Arts.

HWANG, CAROLINE. A **Korean American** novelist and magazine editor, Hwang earned her B.A. from the University of Pennsylvania and M.F.A. from New York University. Her debut novel, *In Full Bloom* (2004), packs the fun of a chic **woman**'s quest for love and fulfillment into a poignant immigrant's tale. Her work has appeared in *Glamour*, *Redbook*, *Self*, *Newsweek*, *Mademoiselle*, *CosmoGirl*, and *YM*. She lives in New York.

HWANG, DAVID HENRY (1957–). One of the best-known **Chinese American** playwrights, Hwang was born in Los Angeles. He majored in English at Stanford University and began writing plays in his junior year. He attended the first Padua Hills Playwrights Festival where he learned playwriting from Sam Shepard and Maria Irene Fornes. The first play that earned him public attention is *FOB*, which was staged at the Public **Theater** in New York City in 1980. *FOB* won an **Obie Ward** in 1981. Hwang worked briefly at the **Asian American Theater Company** in San Francisco as a director. In 1980, Hwang entered the Yale University School of

Drama but left the program after one year. In 1981, his *The Dance and the Railroad* and *Family Devotions* were produced at the Public Theater. He is best known for ***M. Butterfly***, which premiered at the National Theatre in Washington, D.C., and opened on Broadway the following month. *M. Butterfly* was the most publicized Asian American play, which won the Outer Critics Circle Award, the Drama Desk Award, and the Tony Award for the best play of 1988. Hwang wrote other plays, such as *Face Value* (1992); *Bondage* (1992); *Golden Child* (1996), which won him the second Obie Award; and *Yellow Face* (2007), a revision of *Face Value* that won him the third Obie Award. He also collaborated with music composer Bright Sheng and choreographer Muna Tseng to create *The Silver River* (2000), a music drama based on Chinese folklore, and wrote an adaptation of *Flower Drum Song* (2001) and the film adaptation of *M. Butterfly*.

Hwang has received numerous grants, including fellowships from the National Endowment for the Arts, the Guggenheim and Rockefeller Foundations, New York State Council on the Arts, and the Pew Charitable Trusts. He has also received honors from the Asian American Legal Defense and Education Fund, the Lifetime Achievement Award from the **Asian American Literary Awards**, the Association for Asian Pacific American Artists, the Museum of Chinese in the Americas, the **East West Players**, the Organization of Chinese Americans, the Media Action Network for Asian Americans, the Center for Migration Studies, the Asian American Resource Workshop, the China Institute, and the New York Foundation for the Arts. In 1998, the nation's oldest Asian American theater company, the East West Players, named its new main stage the David Henry Hwang Theatre.

HYBRIDITY. Frequently used in Ethnic Studies and Postcolonial Theory, the term refers to the emergence of a new cross- or transcultural consciousness brought about by migration, **diaspora**, colonialism, and **assimilation**. The cultural identities of Asian Americans often come from the **liminal** space in which contradiction and ambivalence inform **identity negotiation** and construction, which is never a movement from one identity to another. Rather, it is a movement of perpetual shifting of constellations of cultural, religious, political, and linguistic affinities. Many Asian American writers take advantage of their hybrid identities by exploring their richly multicultural and polyvocal existence. Their diverse backgrounds have informed their aesthetic choices in literary forms. For instance, **Ping Chong**'s **theater** works often combine Chinese and Japanese techniques with the Western ones. **Marilyn Chin** marries Chinese and Japanese poetics with British and American poetic tradition. **Brenda Wong Aoki** created a hybrid form of theater in which Jazz works its way into Japanese **Noh and Kyogen**. **Govindas Vishnudas Desani**

creates a unique blend of Englishes in his novel *All about H. Hatterr.* The hybrid queen's and babu's Englishes create much of the comedy in the novel. *See also* LIMINALITY.

HYUN, PETER (1906–1993). A **Korean American** autobiographer, Hyun was born in Hawaii and was taken to Korea by his parents when he was an infant. The family escaped to Shanghai from the Japanese occupation when he was a teenager and then returned to Hawaii. Hyun majored in religion at DePauw University in Indiana but soon changed to **theater**. Without completing his college education, he began to work in the theater in New York, Hawaii, California, and Quebec both as an actor and a director. Experiencing blatant **racism** in the theater, he left it for good in 1937. In 1944, he joined the army and became a major in the Asian Languages Intelligence Section because of his proficiency in Korean, Japanese, Chinese, and Tagalog. He published his first autobiography, *Man Sei! The Making of a Korean American* (1986), which tells the story of his family's flight from Japanese-occupied Korea and their **exile** to China. His second autobiography, *In the New World: The Making of a Korean American*, was published posthumously (1995). It centers on the discriminatory and racist treatment he had encountered in the United States.

I

IDENTITY NEGOTIATION. This is a concept frequently used by Asian American scholars to describe the identity struggles of characters in Asian American literature and **theater**. Often torn between two different and at times even opposing linguistic, cultural, and religious loyalties, Asian American characters must constantly work at their identities strategically to achieve their goals. In **John Okada**'s *No-No Boy*, Ichiro the protagonist is tormented by the question—Who am I? At a time when he can neither be Japanese nor American, his daily life is filled with painful decisions. Many characters have to reinvent themselves to survive, to succeed, and to form new relations in America. There is a kind of violence in this act of constant self-reinvention, as such an act requires the severing of the past, of old allegiance and loyalty, even though it may be momentary. For instance, in **Bharati Mukherjee**'s novel *Jasmine*, to survive in the United States, the protagonist moves rapidly from locale to locale, and each time she assumes a different name and a different persona. Immigrant **women** often practice identity negotiation due to the clash between the old culture's gender expectation and the American one. The female characters in **Chitra Banerjee Divakaruni**'s short stories face conflicts with their husbands when they begin to reassess their abilities and expectations, and many of them emerge with newly constructed identities that allow them to straddle two worlds. *See also* ALEXANDER, MEENA; KIRCHNER, BHARTI.

IGLORIA, LUISA A. (MARIA LOUISA AGUILAR-CARIÑO, 1961–). A **Filipina American** poet, Igloria was born in the Philippines. She earned her B.A. from the University of the Philippines College Baguio, M.A. from Ateneo de Manila University, and Ph.D. from the University of Illinois, Chicago. She currently teaches English at Old Dominion University. She is the author of seven books of **poetry**: *Juan Luna's Revolver* (2008), winner of the Ernest Sandeen Prize, *Trill and Mordent* (2005), *Blood Sacrifice* (1998), *Songs for the Beginning of the Millennium* (1997), *In the Garden of the Three Islands* (1995), *Encanto* (1994), and *Cartography* (1992). She also wrote a book of essays, *Not Home, But Here: Writing from the Filipino Diaspora*

(2003), which explores the enigma and the complexity of the Filipino **diaspora**. Her work has appeared in numerous anthologies and journals, including *Poetry*, *Crab Orchard Review*, the *Missouri Review*, *Indiana Review*, *Poetry East*, *Sweet*, *Smartish Pace*, *Natural Bridge*, *Rattle*, the *North American Review*, *Bellingham Review*, *Shearsman*, *PRISM International*, *Poetry Salzburg Review*, the *Asian Pacific American Journal*, and *TriQuarterly*. She is the recipient of numerous honors, including the 49th Parallel Poetry Prize, James Hearst Poetry Prize, the National Writers Union Poetry Prize, the Richard Peterson Poetry Prize, Stephen Dunn Award for Poetry, Fugue Poetry Prize, three Pushcart Prize nominations, and 11 Carlos Palanca Memorial Awards for Literature in poetry, short fiction, and nonfiction, and the Palanca "Hall of Fame" distinction (the Palanca Awards are the Philippine equivalent of the Pulitzer).

IIZUKA, NAOMI (1965–). A **Japanese American** playwright, Iizuka was born in Tokyo to a Japanese father and a Hispanic American mother and grew up in Indonesia, the Netherlands, and Washington, D.C. She received her B.A. in classical literature from Yale University and M.F.A. from the University of California (UC), San Diego. Drawing from her training in classical literature, she brings classic and mythological characters to life in contemporary America. For instance, *Polaroid Stories* (1997) sets the Greek myth of Eurydice and Orpheus among contemporary Americans in Minnesota. *Anon(ymous)* (2006) modernizes Homer's *Odyssey* by depicting a young South Asian refugee's journey to America. One of the most commissioned playwrights in the United States, she has authored numerous plays, including *Tattoo Girl* (1994), *Skin* (1995), *War of the Worlds* (2000), *36 Views* (2003), *Aloha Say All the Pretty Girls* (1999), *Language of Angels* (2000), *17 Reasons Why!* (2002), *At the Vanishing Point* (2004), *Hamlet, Blood in the Brain* (2006), *Concerning Strange Devices from the Distant West* (2010), *Ghostwritten* (2009), *Strike-Slip* (2006), etc. She has received numerous honors, including a Joyce Award, Whiting Writers' Award, McKnight Advancement Grant, NEA/TCG Artist-in-Residence Fellowship, Princeton University's Hodder Fellowship, Alpert Award in the Arts, Stavis Award from the National **Theatre** Conference, Rockefeller Foundation MAP grant, Gerobe Foundation Fellowship, Jerome Fellowship, and PEN Center USA West Award for Drama. Currently, she is a professor of dramatic arts at UC, San Diego, and serves as the director of its M.F.A. Program in Playwriting.

IKEDA, STEWART DAVID. A **Japanese American** novelist, Ikeda earned an M.F.A. in creative writing from the University of Michigan and has lectured, given workshops, and taught at the University of Michigan, University of Wisconsin, and Boston College. He is the author of a novel *What the Scarecrow Said* (1997), winner of an Avery and Jule Hopwood Award for Major Fiction. This novel, set at the end of World War II, portrays the Japanese American character William Fujita's life in the **internment** camp and relocation in New England. Ikeda's short fiction, **poetry**, commentaries, and creative nonfiction have also appeared in such venues as *Story*, *Ploughshares*, *Glimmer Train*, *Pacific Citizen*, the *Minetta Review*, the *Gallatin Review*, *A Different Drummer*, and *New America Media*.

IKO, MOMOKO (1940–). A **Japanese American** playwright, Iko was born in Wapato, Washington. When she was eight, her family was interned in the Heart Mountain Concentration Camp in Wyoming. She received her B.A. in English at the University of Illinois, Urbana–Champaign, and her M.F.A. at the University of Iowa. Her first play, *Gold Watch* (1972), remains her best work, which has been produced at various theaters including **Northwest Asian American Theatre** and aired on television by PBS in 1975. *Gold Watch*, loosely based on her parents' experience, tells the story of a Japanese American family's travails in an **internment camp**. Iko has received awards from the **East West Players**, the Rockefeller Foundation, the National Endowment for the Arts, and the Zellerbach Foundation.

IN MIXED COMPANY. This is a **theater** company founded by **Vietnamese American** playwright **Maura Nguyen Donohue** in New York City in 1995. Its highly theatrical, multimedia, performance works challenge static notions of identity, often exploring the fluid experience of "self" against the highly charged backdrops of gender, race, and national alliance. Its athletic movement style draws on various traditional Asian and contemporary American dance/theater forms.

INADA, LAWSON FUSAO (1938–). A prominent **Japanese American** poet, Inada is a **sansei** born in Fresno, California. He was named in 2006 the poet laureate of Oregon. During World War II, his family was sent to three different **internment camps**, when Inada was four years old. After the war, he became a jazz musician. He received his undergraduate education at California State University, Fresno, and his graduate at the University of Iowa, the University of California, Berkeley, and eventually earned his M.F.A. from the University of Oregon. His **poetry** is never far from Fresno and "Camp." He has written *Before the War: Poems as They Happen* (1971), *Legends from Camp* (1992), which won a 1994 **American Book Award**, *Drawing the Line* (1997), which received the Hazel Hill Award for Poetry in 2000, *Just Intonations* (1996), and two coauthored collections, *3 Northwest*

Poets: Drake, Inada, and Lawder (1970) and *The Buddha Bandits down Highway 99* (1978). Almost all his poetry pursues the common themes of home, displacement, and beauty in the midst of victimization and practices the aesthetics from two traditions significant in Inada's background: Japanese folk art and American jazz. He has received several poetry fellowships from the National Endowment for the Arts. He also won the 1997 Stafford/Hall Award for Poetry. Inada's essays on the internment experience appear in many anthologies, such as *In This Great Land of Freedom: The Japanese Pioneers of Oregon, Touching the Stones: Tracing One Hundred Years of Japanese American History, Only What We Could Carry: The Japanese American Internment Experience, A Matter of Conscience: Essays on the World War II Heart Mountain Draft Resistance Movement.*

INOUYE, DANIEL K. (1924–). A **Japanese American** politician and autobiographer, Inouye was born in Honolulu, Hawaii, and grew up in a poor neighborhood. He spoke Japanese at home and English in school. When he was 17, the Japanese bombed Pearl Harbor. The following year, he enlisted to prove his loyalty to the United States. He and the rest of all the Japanese American 442 Infantry fought Germans in Italy. After he lost his right arm, he came home with honors. Inouye returned to the University of Hawaii to complete his degree. He received his J.D. from the George Washington University Law School. He participated in local politics and became the first Hawaiian congressman in 1959 when Hawaii became a state. He won a seat for the U.S. Senate in 1962 and has remained in the Senate ever since. His autobiography, *Journey to Washington* (1967), recounts his life from childhood to his service in the U.S. Army and his prominence in national politics. The book explores themes of cultural clashes, national loyalty, and war.

INTERNMENT CAMPS. *See* JAPANESE AMERICAN INTERNMENT.

ISHIGAKI, AYAKO TANAKA (HARU MATSUI, 1903–1996). A **Japanese American** writer, Ishigaki was born in Tokyo, Japan. As a young **woman**, she rebelled against tradition and asserted herself as a "new woman." She came to the United States at the age of 23. She was vocal against Japan's aggression toward China and wrote under various pseudonyms for New York–based radical publications. *Restless Wave* (1940) is her only English-language book, published under the name of Haru Matsui. Part fiction, part autobiography, and part reportage, it tells the story of Haru's coming-of-age as a feminist and antiwar activist. Because of their radical ideas and friendship with the left-wing activist Agnes Smedley, the U.S. government constantly harassed her and her husband, and in 1951 her husband was deported.

Following her husband, Ishigaki returned to Japan and became one of the first feminists in Japan.

ISSEI. This is a Japanese term used in North America, South America, and Australia to specify the first generation of Japanese immigrants. *See also* NISEI; SANSEI.

J

JAISOHN, PHILIP (1864–1951). A **Korean American** novelist, Jaisohn was born Jae-pil Suh in North Ju-la Province of Korea. He came to the United States at the age of 21 and adopted the name of Philip Jaisohn by rearranging the letters from his Korean name. In 1890, he became the first Korean to become a naturalized U.S. citizen. Two years later, he became the first Korean to receive a medical degree from George Washington's Medical School. He is the author of *Hansu's Journey* (1921), a novella published under the pseudonym of N. H. Osia. *Hansu's Journey* is the first known fiction in English by a Korean American. It portrays a young man's life in Korea during the Japanese occupation and his journey to China and then to the United States.

JAMES LAUGHLIN AWARD. *See* LAMONT POETRY PRIZE.

JAMES, TANIA (1980–). A **South Asian American** novelist, James was born in Chicago and raised in Louisville, Kentucky. She received her B.A. in visual and environmental studies from Harvard University and M.F.A. in fiction writing from Columbia University. Her debut novel *Atlas of Unknowns* (2009) was a Barnes & Noble Discover Great New Writers pick and an Editor's Choice for the *San Francisco Chronicle* and the *New York Times*. The novel tells the story of two Indian sisters separated by immigration. Her recent work has appeared in literary magazines, including *One Story*, *Guernica*, and *Elle India*.

JANG, PATRICIA (1976–). A **Korean American** playwright, Jang was born in West Long Branch, New Jersey. She holds a B.A. in English from Smith College and an M.F.A. from New York University (NYU). She is a member of the **Ma-Yi** Writers' Lab. Her plays include *The Kimono Project*, ***Yellow Peril*** *3.0*, *Regarding the Sloth*, *Artifact*, *An Atomic Life*, *Westward*, *Aboveboard*, *Counterspace*, *The Fix*, and *Next Paris*. Her plays have been read or staged by Ma-Yi **Theater**, New York Theatre Workshop, NYU, Ensemble Studio Theatre, Kennedy Center American College Theater Festival, Speaking Ring Theatre, Chicago Dramatists, Women's Theatre Alliance, and

Theatre Limina. *Mood Indigo*, Jang's first screenplay, won the Best Graduate Screenplay award at the Fusion Film Festival. She was awarded the New York Theatre Workshop Playwriting Fellowship, a Donahue Tremaine Residuary grant, the Harry Kondoleon Graduate Award in Playwriting, and an Illinois Arts Council fellowship in playwriting and was a finalist for the Yale Drama Series Prize.

JAPANESE AMERICAN INTERNMENT. This was the forcible relocation and internment of people of Japanese ancestry by the U.S. government in 1942–1945. In the wake of Japan's bombing of Pearl Harbor, President Franklin D. Roosevelt authorized Executive Order 9066 on 19 February 1942, which allowed approximately 120,000 Japanese Americans and Japanese residing in the United States to be interned in "War Relocation Camps." Not until 1988 did the U.S. government redress this injustice when Congress passed and President Ronald Reagan signed legislation that apologized for the internment. Over $1.6 billion in reparations were later made by the U.S. government to Japanese Americans who had either suffered internment or were heirs of those who had suffered internment. This historical event powerfully informed the writings of many Japanese American writers, such as **John Okada**, **Lawson Fusao Inada**, **Monica Sone**, **Lonny Kaneko**, etc. Monica Sone's memoir ***Nisei** Daughter* (1953) was among the first to depict the lives in the internment camps, vividly evoking the American hysteria after the bombing of Pearl Harbor, the forced relocation of everyone who had Japanese blood, and the harsh treatment of the internees in the camps. *See also* DE CRISTOFORO, VIOLET KAZUE; IKEDA, STEWART DAVID; IKO, MOMOKO; KADOHATA, CYNTHIA; MORI, TOSHIO; RORIPAUGH, LEE ANN; SATO, KIYO; SUYEMOTO, TOYO; TAKEI, GEORGE; TOYAMA, TIM; UCHIDA, YOSHIKO; YAMAUCHI, WAKAKO.

JAPANESE AMERICAN LITERATURE AND THEATER. Along with Chinese and **Filipino Americans**, Japanese American writers were the pioneers of Asian American literature and **theater**. Many **issei** published poems in Japanese-language newspapers in Hawaii and California, but very few of them wrote and published in English. The first Japanese American publishing in English is **Sadakichi Hartmann**, a Eurasian. His *Poems* (1889) is the earliest Asian American book of **poetry** that we know. Following him is the first Japanese American autobiographer **Jenichiro Oyabe**, author of *A Japanese Robinson Crusoe* (1898) and the first Japanese American novelist **Yone Noguchi**, who published his novel *The American Diary of a Japanese Girl* in 1902. The earliest Japanese American **women** writers hailed from Hawaii: **Kathleen Tamagawa**, a Eurasian, published *Holy Prayers in a*

Horse's Ear (1932), the first Japanese American woman's autobiography, and **Shelley Ayame Nishimura Ota**, a **nisei**, wrote *Upon Their Shoulders* (1951), the first novel by a Japanese American woman writer. Other than these two, all early women writers in English are issei such as **Jun Fujita**, **Ayako Tanaka Ishigaki**, and **Etsu Inagaki Sugimoto.** This generation of Japanese American writers is credited with the introduction of such Japanese poetic forms into the United States as ***haiku*** and ***tanka***. Among this group are two **women** writers, Ishigaki and Sugimoto. The strong presence of women in early Japanese American literature, which is not true in early Chinese and Filipino American writings, is largely due to the fact that the **Page Act** prohibited the immigration of Chinese and Filipino women but allowed the entry of Japanese women.

Japanese began to immigrate in significant numbers after 1868. After the **Chinese Exclusion Act** of 1882, Japanese immigrants were sought by business owners to replace the Chinese immigrants. In 1907, the "Gentlemen's Agreement" between the governments of Japan and the United States ended immigration of Japanese workers, but permitted the immigration of spouses of Japanese immigrants already in the United States. The Immigration Act of 1924 banned the immigration of all but a token few Japanese. Significant Japanese immigration did not occur until the Immigration Act of 1965 ended 40 years of bans against immigration from Asia. The Naturalization Act of 1790 restricted naturalized U.S. citizenship to "free white persons," which excluded the issei from citizenship. As a result, the issei were unable to vote, and faced additional restrictions, such as the inability to own land under many state laws.

Between 1942 and 1945, about 120,000 Japanese and Japanese Americans were interned on the grounds of national security, and the first book documenting the experience was **Mine Okubo**'s picture book, *Citizen 13660* (1946). The **Japanese American internment** so dominated the literary imagination of Japanese Americans that it organizes their literature and theater into two groups—those who write about this experience and those who do not. The first group, mostly nisei writers, such as **Hisaye Yamamoto**, **Monica Sone**, **Jeanne Wakatsuki Houston**, **Yoshiko Uchida**, **David Mura**, **Keiho Soga**, and **Julie Otsuka**, portrayed the internment experiences in memoirs, fiction, poetry, and theater. Depicting its aftermath are numerous writers, including **John Okada**, **Mitsuye Yamada**, **Momoko Iko**, **Lonny Kaneko**, **Toshio Mori**, **Garrett Hongo**, **Lawson Inada**, and **Janice Mirikitani**. Contrary to their contemporaries in the mainland, nisei writers in Hawaii, however, found it easier to explore Japanese American history and identity in the immediate postwar years without the burden of the internment experience, such as **Patsy Sumie Saiki, Milton Murayama**, and **Lois-Ann Yamanaka**.

The past three decades have witnessed the emergence of new sensibilities and aesthetics in Japanese American literature and theater in which writers explore multiple themes unrelated to the internment experience. Writers like **Cynthia Kadohata**, **Velina Hasu Houston**, **Karen Tei Yamashita**, **Ruth Ozeki**, and **Rick Noguchi** portray Japanese American characters wrestling with issues ranging from gender and sexuality to environment. Many contemporary Japanese American writers are biracial and sometimes choose to transcend the concerns of race and ethnicity, such as **Brian Komei Dempster**, **Kimiko Hahn**, **Maeshima Yukihide Hartman**, **Naomi Iizuka**, **Rahna Reiko Rizzuto**, **Lee Ann Roripaugh**, and **Brandon Shimoda**. Still others have gone on to write genre fiction like mysteries, science fiction, historical novels, etc., such as **Dale Furutani**, **Naomi Hirahara**, **Dwight Okita**, and **Gail Tsukiyama**.

The earliest Asian American theaters were organized by Chinese and Japanese Americans to produce predominantly Chinese and Japanese plays. The **East West Players** was the first Asian American theater, founded in Los Angeles in 1965. The **Asian Exclusion Act** was founded by **Garrett Hongo** in 1975 in Seattle. This group was renamed in 1981 to be the **Northwest Asian American Theatre Company**. **Pan Asian Repertory Theatre** was founded in 1999 in New York City and led by artistic director Tisa Chang. **Asian American Theater Company** was established in 1979 in San Francisco. Its former form was the **Asian American Theater Workshop**, under the artistic directorship of the Chinese American playwright **Frank Chin**. Japanese American theaters have flourished in the past four decades. A few groups produce only Japanese and/or Japanese American performances, such as **Theatre of Yugen** and the **Grateful Crane Ensemble**. In Los Angeles, **Aratani/Japan America Theatre** opened in 1983 and provided the space for the production of many Asian American plays. Major Japanese American playwrights include **Philip Kan Gotanda**, **Amy Hill**, Velina Hasu Houston, Naomi Iisuka, **Jude Narita**, **Denise Uyehara**, **Brenda Wong Aoki**, and **Wakako Yamauchi**. *See also* ADACHI, JIRO; AI; DE CRISTOFORO, VIOLET KAZUE; FOSTER, SESSHU; HARTMAN, YUKIHIDE MAESHIMA; IKEDA, STEWART DAVID; KAGEYAMA-RAMAKRISHNAN, CLAIRE; KAKUGAWA, FRANCES H.; KASHIWAGI, HIROSHI; KITAMURA, KATIE; KONO, JULIET SANAE; MATSUEDA, PAT; MATSUOKA, TAKASHI; MCKINNEY, CHRIS; MIYAMOTO, KAZUO; MORI, KYOKO; NARASAKI, KEN; NGAI, SIANNE; NOGUCHI, RICK; SAIJO, ALBERT; SAKAMOTO, EDWARD; SASAKI, R. A.; SHIGEKUNI, JULIE; SHIMODA, TODD; SUYEMOTO, TOYO; TOYAMA, TIM; UCHIDA, YOSHIKO; UYEMOTO, HOLLY; WATKINS, YOKO KAWASHIMA; YAMADA, MITSUYE.

JAVELLANA, STEVEN (ESTEBAN JAVELLANA, 1918–1977). A **Filipino American** novelist, Javellana was born in San Mateo, Rizal, Philippines. He fought against the Japanese invasion of the Philippines. After World War II, he graduated from the University of the Philippines College of Law and then came to the United States. He was the author of the best-selling war novel *Without Seeing the Dawn* (1947), also known as *The Lost Ones*. The same novel was made into a film by the Filipino film maker and director Lino Brocka under the title *Santiago!* His short stories were published in the *Manila Times* magazine in the 1950s, among which are "Two Tickets to Manila," "The Sin of Father Anselmo," "Sleeping Tablets," "The Fifth Man," and "The Tree of Peace and Transition."

JAVIER, PAOLO (1974–). A **Filipino American** poet, Javier was born in Quezon City, the Philippines. His family immigrated to the United States when he was 12 years old. He received his B.A. in fine arts and creative writing from the University of British Columbia and M.F.A. in creative writing from Bard College. In June 2010, he became the fifth Queens Poet Laureate. Javier is the author of five books of poetry: *The Time at the End of This Writing* (2004), which received a Small Press Traffic Book of the Year Award, *60 Lv Bo(e)ms* (2005), *LMFAO* (2008), *Goldfish Kisses* (2007), *The Feeling Is Actual* (2010), and *Megton Gasgan Krakoom* (2010). His **poetry** explores a range of themes from colonialism, race, and sexuality to memory, history, and language. He has been described as one of the most aurally and visually perceptive poets writing today. He is the editor and publisher of *2nd Avenue Poetry*. Among his other awards and fellowships are the 2010 Millay Colony for the Arts Writer-in-Residence and Lower Manhattan Cultural Council Writer-in-Residence.

JEN, GISH (1956–). One of the best-known **Chinese American** novelists, Jen was born as Lillian Jen to Chinese immigrant parents in Long Island and grew up in Yonkers and Scarsdale, New York. After receiving a B.A. in English from Harvard University, she attended the Stanford Business School for one year and then went to China to teach English. After her return to the United States, she enrolled at the University of Iowa and earned her M.F.A. in creative writing. She is the author of four novels: *Typical American* (1991), a New York Times Notable Book of the Year and a finalist for the National Book Critics' Circle Award; *Mona in the Promised Land* (1996), also a finalist for the National Book Critics' Circle Award; *The Love Wife* (2005); and *World and Town* (2010). She has also written a short story collection, *Who's Irish* (1999). Her other works have appeared in *Iowa Review*, *Fiction International*, *Yale Review*, *Southern Review*, *Nimrod*, *Atlantic Monthly*, *New Yorker*, the

Best American Short Stories of the Century, the *Best American Short Stories* of 1988 and 1995, etc. Most of her works explore the themes of **assimilation**, the American Dream, identity, displacement, interracial relationships, and generational conflicts. Among the numerous honors she has received are a Mildred and Harold Strauss Living Award from the American Academy of Arts and Letters, Lannan Literary Award, and fellowships from Fulbright, Radcliffe Institute for Advanced Study, Guggenheim Foundation, the National Endowment for the Arts, and Radcliffe College Bunting Institute.

JIANG, JI-LI (1954–). A **Chinese American** memoirist, Jiang was born and raised in Shanghai, China. During the Chinese Cultural Revolution, Jiang's father was falsely accused of listening to foreign radio and was detained and forced to do hard labor by the government. She graduated from Shanghai Teachers' College and Shanghai University and was a science teacher before she came to the United States in 1984. She also graduated from the University of Hawaii. In 1992, Jiang cofounded East West Exchange, promoting cultural exchange between western countries and China. In 2003, she started a nonprofit organization, Cultural Exchange International to continue and expand the cultural exchanges between the United States, and Western countries. She now lives in San Francisco. Her memoir *Red Scarf Girl* (1998) recounts her and her family's experience of the Chinese Cultural Revolution. She is also the author of the **children's book** *The Magical Monkey King* (2004), a retelling of the traditional Chinese tale about the trickster Monkey King.

JIN, HA (1956–). One of the most prolific **Chinese American** writers, Jin has written short stories, novels, **poetry**, and essays. He was born as Xuefei in Liaoning Province, China, into a military family. His formative years coincided with the Chinese Cultural Revolution (1966–1976). He served in the Chinese Army between the ages of 14 and 20. He received his B.A. and M.A. in English from Shandong University, China. He immigrated to the United States in 1985 and earned his Ph.D. from Brandeis University. He currently teaches English and creative writing at Boston University. Jin is the author of six novels: *In the Pond* (1998); *Waiting* (1999), winner of **National Book Award** and the PEN/Faulkner Award; *The Crazed* (2002), a New York Times Notable Book and a Washington Post and Los Angeles Times Best Book of the Year; *War Trash* (2004), winner of the PEN/Faulkner Award and a finalist for the Pulitzer Prize; *A Free Life* (2007); and *Nanjing Requiem* (2011), a historical novel. He has also written four books of short fiction: *Ocean of Words* (1996), winner of the PEN/Hemingway Award; *Under the Red Flag* (1997), winner of the Flannery O'Connor Award for Short Fiction; *The Bridegroom* (2000), winner of an **Asian American Literary Award**;

and *A Good Fall* (2009). In addition, he is the author of three books of poetry: *Between Silences* (1990), *Facing Shadows* (1996), and *Wreckage* (2001). *The Writer as Migrant* (2008) is his book of essays.

Many of Jin's stories and novels are set in the fictional Muji City, centering on survival, conflict between tradition and Communist ideology, and the pain of modernization. Some of his stories and novels portray the lives of Chinese immigrants, such as *A Free Life* and *A Good Fall.* Other honors he has received include three Pushcart Prizes for fiction and a *Kenyon Review* Prize, Guggenheim Fellowship, Asian Fellowship (2000–2002), Townsend Prize for Fiction (2002), and inclusion in *Best American Short Stories* of 1997 and 1999.

KADOHATA, CYNTHIA (1956–). A **Japanese American** novelist, Kadohata was born in Chicago to **nisei** parents. She spent most of her early childhood on the road with her family to Arkansas, Georgia, Michigan, and back to Chicago before finally settling down in Los Angeles. She earned her degree in journalism from the University of Southern California. After an auto accident, Kadohata moved to Boston where she began to write. She attended the writing programs at the University of Pittsburgh and Columbia University. Her first novel, *The Floating World* (1989), is a coming-of-age story about a 12-year-old Japanese American girl, Olivia, who is always on the move with her family in order to find jobs after they were released from an **internment camp**. Her second novel, *The Heart of the Valley of Love* (1992), is set in Los Angeles in the year 2052. In an episodic style, this dystopia presents a 19-year-old orphan of Asian and African descent in a search for meaning in a violent and chaotic city. *The Glass Mountains* (1996) was her third novel, a fantasy. She has also written **children's books**, such as *Kira-Kira* (2004), *Weedflower* (2009), and *Cracker, the Best Dog in Vietnam* (2007), *Outside Beauty* (2008), and *A Million Shades of Gray* (2010). She has received grants from the National Endowment for the Arts and a Whiting Award. *Kira-Kira* won the 2005 Newbery Medal.

KAGEYAMA-RAMAKRISHNAN, CLAIRE (1969–). A **Japanese American** poet, Kageyama-Ramakrishnan was born in Santa Monica and raised in Los Angeles. She holds a B.A. in English from Loyola Marymount University in Los Angeles, an M.F.A. in creative writing from the University of Virginia, an M.A. in English from the University of California, Berkeley, and a Ph.D. in English and creative writing from the University of Houston. Her debut book of **poetry**, *Shadow Mountain* (2008), was the winner of the Four Way Books Intro Prize in Poetry. She draws on the stories of Japanese Americans **interned** at Manzanar Relocation Center, California, and on her own childhood and memories of her grandparents. Her most recent publication is another book of poetry, *Bear, Diamonds and Crane* (2011). She teaches at Houston Community College, Central Campus, and lives in Houston.

KAIPA, SUMMI (1957–). A **South Asian American** poet, Kaipa was born in Detroit and raised in Arkansas. She received a B.A. in interdisciplinary studies from the University of California, Berkeley, and an M.F.A. in poetry from the Iowa Writers' Workshop. She is the author of three chapbooks of **poetry** and stories: *The Language Parable* (2006), *One: I Beg You Be Still* (2003), and *The Epics* (1999). She was the founder and editor of *Interlope*, a magazine featuring innovative writing by Asian Americans (1998–2003), and she coedited *Indivisible: An Anthology of Contemporary South Asian American Poetry*, which won the Northern California Book Award and the PEN Oakland Award. Her work has been published in *Chain*, *XCP: Cross Cultural Poetics*, the *Literary Review*, and the anthology *Bay Poetics*. She received the Holmes Award from the *Fourteen Hills Review* and the Portrero Nuevo Fund Prize in 2002.

KAKUGAWA, FRANCES H. (1936–). A **Japanese American** poet, Kakugawa was born and raised on the Big Island of Hawaii in Kapoho. She received her B.A. in education from the University of Hawaii. The author of one book of poetry, *Mosaic Moon* (2002), which meditates on care-giving, she has also written two **children's books** of **poetry**: *Wordsworth the Poet* (2004), winner of Best Children's Book from Hawaii Publishers Association, and *Wordsworth Dances the Waltz* (2007), winner of Best Illustrated Children's Book from Northern California Publishers & Authors and Mom's Choice Award. She has taught for many years in the Michigan and Hawaii public school systems and now lives in Sacramento, California.

KANEKO, LONNY (1939–). A **Japanese American** poet and fiction writer, Kaneko was born to **nisei** parents. Like other Japanese American families, he was relocated to Camp Harmony in Puyallup, Washington, and then moved to Minidoka, Idaho, during World War II. Kaneko spent his preschool years in the camp, which has cast an indelible impact on him. He began writing **poetry** in 1960 in Theodore Roethke's writing classes. He has published poetry in many magazines and anthologies, but it is his chapbook, *Coming Home from Camp* (1986), that established him as a poet. His poetry in this collection reiterates the thesis that the idea of home for Japanese Americans is shattered by the **internment**. Kaneko's most famous short story, anthologized in *The Big Aiiieeeee!*, is "The Shoyu Kid," a dark and haunting story about a teenager in the camp. He has won several awards, including the Coeur D'Alene Festival of Arts poetry contest (1973), *Amerasia Journal*'s short-story contest (1975), the Pacific Northwest Writer Conference award, and a National Endowment for the Arts fellowship.

KANG, CONNIE K. (1943–). A **Korean American** memoirist, Kang was born in North Korea and grew up in Korea and Japan. She came to the United States to study journalism. *Home Was the Land of the Morning Calm* (1995) is a historical memoir covering the end of the Japanese occupation of Korea until the 1990s, including the Korean War (1950–1953) and its aftermath.

KANG, YOUNGHILL (1903–1972). A **Korean American** novelist, Kang was born in a small village north of Seoul, Korea, under Japanese occupation. At a young age, he left home to study in Seoul, and this early **exile** dominated his sensibility and aesthetics for the rest of his life. At age 11, Kang went to Japan to study science. In 1921, Kang immigrated to the United States and attended Harvard University but received his B.S. from Boston University in 1924. He returned to Harvard and completed his M.A. in English education. While teaching in the Comparative Literature Department at New York University, Kang befriended a fellow teacher, Thomas Wolfe, who made a major impact on Kang's career as a writer. His first autobiographical novel, *The Grass Roof* (1931), received considerable publicity. The novel appealed to American readers then with its picturesque portrayal of a boy growing up in a small Korean village and his efforts to escape the primitive nation of grass-roofed huts. His second book, *The Happy Grove* (1933), is a **children**'s version of *The Grass Roof*. In 1937, Kang published *East Goes West: The Making of an Oriental Yankee*, a novel loosely based on his life. A bildungsroman, *East Goes West* explores the American Dream as a major theme to depict the journey of an immigrant from rags to riches. Despite the success, the protagonist Han remains alone and exiled at the end of the novel. Kang received numerous honors, such as a Guggenheim Foundation Fellowship, the Halperine Kaminsky Prize in France for the translation of *The Grass Roof*, the Louis S. Weiss Memorial Prize, and an honorary doctorate from Koryo University.

KAPIL, BHANU (1969–). A **South Asian American** author, Kapil was born in Hillingdon, Great Britain, to Indian parents and came to the United States in 1990. She holds a B.A. in English from Loughborough University, Great Britain, and an M.A. in English from the State University of New York, Brockport. Writing at the intersection of **poetry**, prose, and nonfiction, she has authored three books: *The Vertical Interrogation of Strangers* (2001), *Incubation: A Space for Monsters* (2006), and *Humanimal: A Project for Future Children* (2009). Her works explore the themes of belonging, identity, memory, history, and postcolonial legacy. Kapil lives in Colorado, where she teaches in the Jack Kerouac School of Disembodied Poetics at Naropa University.

KASHIWAGI, HIROSHI (1922–?). A **Japanese American** poet, playwright, and actor, Kashiwagi was born in Sacramento, California, and grew up in Loomis, California. During World War II, he and his family were **interned** in the Tule Lake War Relocation Center. When the U.S. government forced detainees to fill out the "loyalty questionnaire," Kashiwagi refused to answer the infamous questions 27 and 28 and was thus branded a **no-no boy**. He and his family were segregated as "disloyals" and ostracized by the Japanese American community. Through government coercion, he renounced his U.S. citizenship. After the end of World War II, Kashiwagi attended the University of California (UC), Los Angeles, and received a B.A. in Asian languages. He wrote his first play in 1949 for the **Nisei** Experimental Group, a **theater** group formed in Los Angeles. His one-act play, *The Plums Can Wait*, was first performed in Los Angeles in 1950, and in San Francisco and Berkeley the following year. In 1959, Kashiwagi won the legal battle and had his U.S. citizenship restored. He later received his M.A. in library science from UC, Berkeley. His memoir, *Swimming in the American: A Memoir and Selected Writings*, won the **American Book Award** in 2005. He has also published a book of **poetry**, *Ocean Beach* (2009), and a collection of plays, *Shoe Box Plays* (2008), which chronicle the experiences of Japanese Americans from the hardships of the Depression of the 1930s to the bitterness and dislocation of the internment during World War II and the rise of Asian American consciousness and pride in the late 1960s and 1970s to today. Kashiwagi appeared in several films, including *Black Rain* and *Hito Hata: Raise the Banner*.

KATHAK ENSEMBLE (THE). This is a **South Asian American** performance group that showcases the classical North Indian dance style Kathak, its storytelling techniques (*katha*), and its accompanying Hindustani music. The Ensemble also creates its own innovative repertoire, in which *Kathak* interacts with familiar American arts forms. Founded in 1978 as an informal performance collective by four young American-born artists, the Kathak Ensemble is located in New York and is under the artistic direction of Janaki Patrik.

KELLER, NORA OKJA (1965–). A **Korean American** novelist, Keller was born in Seoul, Korea, to a German father and a Korean mother and grew up in Hawaii. She attended the University of Hawaii and earned her Ph.D. in American literature from the University of California, Santa Cruz. She received the Pushcart Prize for her short story "Mother Tongue," which was the seed for her first novel, *Comfort Woman* (1997). This novel, winner of the 1998 **American Book Award**, portrays the lives of the Korean **women**

forced into sexual slavery by the Japanese Army during World War II. Her second novel, *Fox Girl* (2003), depicts unflinchingly the lives of mixed-raced teenagers in Korea in the 1960s. These children, born to American GIs and Korean prostitutes and known as "throwaway children," exist at the edge of society enduring daily poverty, prejudice, and despair.

KELTNER, KIM WONG (1969–). A **Chinese American** novelist, Keltner was born to second-generation Chinese parents in San Francisco. She received a B.A. in English and a B.A. in arts from the University of California, Berkeley. She is the author of three novels: *The Dim Sum of All Things* (2004), *Buddha Baby* (2005), and *I Want Candy* (2008), a **young adult novel**. Keltner's books belong to the emergent genre of "chick lit" and are graced with humor and honesty. The first two novels center on a young Chinese American professional **woman**'s relationship with her family history and cultural roots. *I Want Candy* portrays a 14-year-old Chinese American girl who works in her parents' restaurant while dreaming to be "normal."

KHANNA, VANDANA (1972–). A **South Asian American** poet, Khanna was born in New Delhi, India, and arrived in the United States when she was a child. She received her B.A. in English from the University of Virginia and M.F.A. from Indiana University. Her **poetry** collection, *Train to Agra* (2000), won the Crab Orchard Review First Book Prize. Her work has been nominated for a Pushcart Prize and has appeared in *Crazyhorse*, *Callaloo*, the *Indiana Review*, and the *Atlanta Review*, among others.

KIM, ELIZABETH. A **Korean American** journalist memoirist, Kim was born in Korea to a Korean mother and an American father who had deserted her mother. *Ten Thousand Sorrows* (2002) depicts her memory of a horrific childhood and her struggle for identity and belonging.

KIM, EUGENIA (1953–). A **Korean American** novelist, Kim was born in White Plains, New York, to Korean immigrants. She received a B.A. in studio art (painting) from the University of Maryland and an M.F.A. in creative writing from Bennington College. Her debut novel, *The Calligrapher's Daughter* (2010), follows the journey of a headstrong girl in turn-of-the-century Korea. The novel, winner of the 2009 Borders Original Voices award, is a Washington Post Critic's Pick, Best Book for 2009, and a Publishers Weekly First Fiction Pick.

KIM, MYUNG MI (1957–). A prolific **Korean American** poet, Kim was born in Seoul, Korea, and immigrated with her family to the United States at the age of nine. Her family moved several times from Oklahoma to South Dakota and then to Ohio. She attended Oberlin College with the intention of following in her father's footsteps to become a physician. Instead, she found love in writing **poetry** and received a graduate degree in creative writing from Johns Hopkins University. In 1986, she received an M.F.A. from the Iowa Writers' Workshop. Her friendship with poet Kathleen Fraser led to the publication of her poetry in the avant-garde journal *How(ever)*, which she coedited in the early 1990s. Her first book of poetry, *Under Flag* (1991), received critical acclaim and the Multicultural Publishers Exchange Award of Merit in 1992. She went on to publish more collections of poetry: *The Bounty* (1996), *Dura* (1998), *Spelt* (1999), *Commons* (2002), *River Antes* (2006), and *Penury* (2009). A language poet, Kim investigates a third language informed by the collision between English and Korean. Her poetry explores language as the very site where identities, power relations, and resistance take place. Kim has received honors, including two Fund for Poetry Awards, two Gertrude Stein Awards for Innovative North American Poetry from Sun & Moon Press, a writing residency at the Djerassi Resident Artists Program, the Edelstein–Keller Writer in Residence at University of Minnesota, and an artist in residence at her alma mater, Oberlin College.

KIM, PATTI (1970–). A **Korean American** novelist, Kim was born in Pusan, Korea, and immigrated with her family to the United States when she was four. She was the Diane Cleaver Fellow at Ledwig House, the New York writers' colony. Her debut novel, *A Cab Called Reliable* (1998), won the 1997 Towson University Prize for Literature and was a nominee for the Book-of-the-Month Club's Stephen Crane Award for First Fiction. She lives in Potomac, Maryland.

KIM, RICHARD E. (1932–). A **Korean American** novelist, Kim was born in northern Korea while the country was under Japanese occupation. His family had to live in Manchuria for a few years to escape Japanese persecution. The year (1950) he entered Seoul National University to study economics, the Korean War (1950–1953) broke out. He was a reserve officer in the Marine Corps and later became a liaison officer between the United States and South Korean forces. He came to the United States in 1955 to study at Middlebury College in Vermont, majoring in political science and philosophy of history. He earned an M.A. in creative writing at Johns Hopkins University in 1960 and an M.F.A. in creative writing at the Iowa Writers' Workshop in 1962. The following year, he received his M.A. in Far Eastern Studies at Harvard University. He has written three novels: *The Martyred* (1964), *The Innocent* (1968), and *Lost Names* (1970). They all deal with the historical events occurring in 20th-century Korea, and none includes the Korean American experience. They explore the common themes of war, good and evil, religion, human suffering, and death. Kim has received fellowships from Guggenheim, Fulbright, the National Endowment for the Arts, and Ford Foundation.

KIM, RONYOUNG (GLORIA HAHN, 1926–1987). A **Korean American** novelist, Kim was born Gloria Jane Kim in Koreatown of Los Angeles. Most of her life, she was wife to her husband and mother to her three daughters. The discovery of breast cancer at age 50 prompted her to work toward fulfilling her dream of writing a book, and the fruit of her labor is *Clay Walls* (1986), which was nominated for a Pulitzer Prize. The novel is loosely based on the life of her mother in Los Angeles between the 1920s and 1940s and explores the themes of gender, class, and race relations.

KIM, SUJI KWOCK (1969–). A **Korean American** poet and playwright, Kim received her B.A. from Yale College and M.F.A. in creative writing from the Iowa Writers' Workshop. She was a Stegner Fellow at Stanford University and a Fulbright Scholar at Seoul National University. Her debut book of **poetry**, *Notes from the Divided Country* (2003), won the 2002 Walt Whitman Award of the Academy of American Poets, the 2003 California Book Award for Best Book of Poetry, and the Kiriyama Prize Notable Book. Her poems have also appeared in *The Nation*, the *New Republic*, the *Paris Review*, *Poetry*, the *Yale Review*, *DoubleTake*, *Threepenny Review*, *Tin House*, the *New England Review*, *Salmagundi*, the *Southwest Review*, *Ploughshares*, the *Harvard Review*, *Columbia*, the *Michigan Quarterly Review*, etc. She is coauthor of *Private Property*, a multimedia play showcased at Playwrights Horizons, produced at the Edinburgh Festival Fringe, and featured on BBC-TV. She is the recipient of numerous awards, including a National Endowment for the Arts, Addison Metcalf Award, Whiting Writers' Award, the Discovery/the Nation Award, and grants from the New York Foundation for the Arts, the California Arts Council, and the Washington State Artist Trust.

KIM, SUKI. A **Korean American** novelist, Kim was born in Seoul, South Korea. Her family immigrated to New York City when she was 13. She majored in English and minored in East Asian Literature at Barnard College and studied at the School of Oriental and African Studies in London. Her debut novel, *Interpreter* (2003), a murder mystery, won the PEN beyond the Margins Award and Gusnavus Myers Outstanding Book Award. Debunking the myth of the **model minority**, *The Interpreter* traverses the distance between old worlds and new, poverty and privilege, language and understanding. Her nonfiction has appeared in the *New York Times*, the *New York Review of*

Books, the *Wall Street Journal*, *Harper's*, etc. She is the recipient of a Fulbright research grant and a Guggenheim fellowship.

KIM, SUSAN (1958–). A **Korean American** playwright, Kim was born in New York City to Korean parents who immigrated to the United States in the 1950s. She received her B.A. from Wesleyan University and began working as a television producer for Public Television in New York. Unsatisfied with her work, she began to take playwriting classes in her spare time. Her first play, *Open Spaces* (1988), won a Drama League Award. She went on to write *Rapid Eye Movement* (1991), *Seventh Word, Four Syllables* (1993), *Dreaming for Alice* (1999), and *Where It Came From* (2000). She was commissioned by **Amy Tan** to write the script of *The Joy Luck Club*. *See also* THEATER.

KIM, TAE HUN (1970–). A **Korean American** novelist, Kim was born in Inchon, South Korea, and immigrated to the United States in 1971. He spent most of his childhood growing up in Brooklyn, New York. He earned his B.A. in history from Haverford College in Pennsylvania and J.D. from New York University School of Law. Following graduation from law school, Kim worked as a securitization attorney for several years, a legal analyst, and then a senior credit officer. He is currently a senior vice president in the Structured Products Group at HSBC Bank USA. His debut novel, *War with Pigeons* (2010), was honored as an Award-Winning Finalist in the Fiction & Literature: Multicultural Fiction and Fiction & Literature: Romance categories of the 2010 Best Books Awards sponsored by *USA Book News*. *War with Pigeons* is a story of love, loss, and hope, exploring themes of race, gender, immigration, displacement, and memory. Kim resides in New Jersey with his family.

KIM, YONG IK (1920–1995). A **Korean American** novelist, Kim was born in South Korea and studied English literature at Aoyama Gabuin College in Tokyo. At the age of 28, he came to the United States to study English literature at Florida Southern College and then went on to study creative writing at the Iowa Writers' Workshop. He taught at the University of California, Berkeley, and Duquesne University. He returned to Korea in spring of 1995 and died the same year. He was a prolific writer of novels, short stories, plays, and essays. He was mostly known for novels like *Moons of Korea* (1959), *The Happy Days* (1960), *The Diving Gourd* (1962), *Blue in the Seed* (1964), *Love in Winter* (1963), and *The Shoes from Yang San Valley* (1970). *The Happy Days* was selected by the American Library Association as Notable **Children's Book** for 1960. It was also selected as an outstanding juvenile book of 1960 by the *New York Times*. His short stories have been published in *Atlantic Monthly*, the *Hudson Review*, *Harper's Bazaar*, and the *New Yorker*. Two of his stories were included in *Best American Short Stories*, and his short story, "Crown Dick," was made into a PBS film, after winning the PEN Syndicated Short Fiction Project in 1984.

KINDING SINDAW. This is a **Filipino American** dance **theater** ensemble resident at **La Mama** Theater since 2000. It is based in New York City.

KINGSTON, MAXINE HONG (1940–). The most celebrated and widely read **Chinese American** writer, Kingston was born in Stockton, California, and grew up listening to her mother's stories and her father's recitation of Chinese **poetry**. She attended the University of California (UC), Berkeley, to study engineering initially and then English. She has taught English and mathematics in high schools in California and Hawaii, and creative writing at the University of Hawaii and UC, Berkeley. Kingston became instantly famous upon the publication of her first book of nonfiction *The Woman Warrior* (1976), which won the National Book Critics' Circle Award and the *Mademoiselle* magazine award. Though labeled nonfiction by the press, *The Woman Warrior* is a highly creative book rich in imagination, fantasy, and lyricism. In the tradition of **talk-story**, the book deals with themes of cultural clashes, gender injustice, family history, and self-identity. It tells the stories mostly of the **women** in her family, such as her paternal aunt, her mother, her maternal aunt, and herself. *China Men* (1980) is her second nonfiction that focuses on the male members of her family and a recipient of the **National Book Award**, the Stockton, the California Arts Council Award, and a PEN West award for fiction. In the same year, she was named "Living Treasure of Hawaii." Rich in mythology and family history, *China Men* presents the Chinese American contributions to America, such as the Chinese labor that grew sugarcane in Hawaii, built the transcontinental railroad, cultivated an agricultural economy in California, and fought in the Vietnam War.

Her first novel, *Tripmaster Monkey: His Fake Book* (1989), alludes to the Chinese classic *Journey to the West*, which centers on the most memorable and magic character, Monkey King, a rebellious and restless immortal who is assigned by Buddha to accompany Tripitaka on the perilous quest to India for the Sutra. Its ability to transform into 72 different forms saves its master repeatedly from danger, harm, and death. Kingston's protagonist Whitman Ah Sing, evocative of Walt Whitman and "Song of Myself," is a self-transformer of sort, living in the turbulent 1960s in the San Francisco Bay Area. He shares with Monkey King more than anything else the rebellious and restless spirit. Kingston went on to publish *To Be the Poet* (2002), a fusion of prose and poetry, *The Fifth Book of Peace* (2003), an autobiography, *Veterans of War, Veterans of Peace* (2006), a collection of personal stories by veterans, and *I Love a Broad Margin to My Life* (2011), a collection of essays. Kingston has also received honors, such as the Lifetime Achievement Award from the **Asian American Literary Awards**, Medal for Distinguished Contribution to American Letters: National Book Foundation, the National Endowment for the Arts Writers Award, and the Anisfield–Wolf Race Relations Award.

KIRCHNER, BHARTI (1940–). A **South Asian American** novelist, Bharti was born in Calcutta, India. After she received her undergraduate and graduate degrees in mathematics at Presidency College in Calcutta, she came to Seattle to study. She worked as a computer programmer and systems analyst in Chicago, the Middle East, and Europe. She left her IBM position to become a full-time student in the writing program at the University of Washington. She is widely known for her cookbooks and essays on food, travel, and fitness. She has authored four novels and four cookbooks. Her first novel, *Shiva Dancing* (1998), reflects her knowledge of the software industry, world cuisines, and health. Her protagonist, a software engineer, distance runner, and connoisseur of food, takes on a journey from San Francisco to India. The novel explores themes of search for roots, **identity negotiation**, and **diaspora**. Her second novel, *Sharmila's Book* (1999), repeats the plot of return to India by an Indian American **woman**, who goes to India for an arranged marriage. This novel further explores an Indian American woman's existence between two worlds. *Darjeeling* (2003) is a family saga ranging from New York City to India, fraught with forbidden love, sibling rivalry, and family honor. *Pastries: A Novel of Desserts and Discoveries* (2004) tells the story a South Asian American bakery owner in Seattle, exploring such themes as family, friendship, romance, and self-renewal. Bharti has won two Seattle Arts Commission literature grants and an Artist Trust Grants for Artist Projects grant.

KITAMURA, KATIE (1979–). A **Japanese American** novelist, Kitamura was born in California to Japanese parents. She received her B.A. from Princeton University and Ph.D. from London University. She is the author of a novel, *The Longshot* (2008), a story about a mixed martial arts fighter, and a memoir, *Japanese for Travellers* (2006). She has written for the *New York Times*, the *Guardian*, and *Wired and Frieze*.

KONO, JULIET SANAE (1943–). A **Japanese American** poet, Kono was born in Hawaii to **nisei** parents. While an undergraduate student at the University of Hawaii, she became involved with the **Bamboo Ridge** study group, whose press published her books of **poetry** *Hilo Rains* (1988) and *Tsunami Years* (1995). Using Hawaii Creole English, her first book of poems describes the difficult lives of Japanese American plantation workers in the sugarcane fields, and her second volume centers on a middle-aged **woman** mourning for the loss of her older son, caring for her mother-in-law, and depicting the devastation caused by the 1946 and 1960 tsunamis. She has also authored a collaborative work of linked poems with three other poets: *No Choice but to Follow* (2010), a short story collection *Ho'olulu Park and the Pepsodent Smile* (2004), and a **children's book,** *The Bravest 'Opihi* (2005). Her most recent publication is a novel, *Anshu: Dark Sorrow* (2010), which tells the story of a pregnant, unmarried Hilo teenager, spanning the cane fields of Hawaii and the devastation in Hiroshima. Kono is the recipient of the Japan–United States Friendship Commission Fellowship (1998), the Elliot Cades Award for Literature (1991), the James Clavell Award (1991), the Palapala Po'okela for Excellence in Writing Literature (1996), and the Hawaii Award for Literature in 2006.

KOO, JASON (1976–). A **Korean American** poet, Koo was born in New York City and grew up in Cleveland, Ohio. He earned his B.A. in English from Yale, his M.F.A. in creative writing from the University of Houston, and his Ph.D. in English and creative writing from the University of Missouri, Columbia. He is the author of a book of **poetry**, *Man on Extremely Small Island* (2009), winner of the 2008 De Novo Poetry Prize and the Members' Choice Award from the **Asian American Literary Awards.** His poetry explores themes of desire, anger, betrayal, and compromises of young love. His poetry and prose have also appeared in journals, including the *Yale Review, North American Review*, and the *Missouri Review*. He is the recipient of fellowships from the National Endowment for the Arts and the Vermont Studio Center. He teaches at New York University and Lehman College and serves as Poetry Editor of *Low Rent.*

KOREAN AMERICAN LITERATURE AND THEATER. Although early Korean American literature began with a novel, *Hansu's Journey* (1921), by **Philip Jaisohn**, it predictably presents mostly autobiographies by the first generation of Korean immigrants, who were mostly male and Western-educated, such as **Ilhan New** and **No-Young Park**. Some of these autobiographers were either born in Hawaii like **Peter Hyun** or immigrated to Hawaii, such as **Easurk Emsen Charr.** What makes early Korean American literature different from early **Chinese American literature** is the presence of Korean American **women** writers in this first generation, and they all hailed from Hawaii such as **Margaret K. Pai** and **Mary Paik Lee**.

The first wave of Koreans began to arrive after 1903 when a boat of 120 men, women, and children landed in Hawaii. The majority of them found work on sugar plantations. Over the next few years, over 7,000 Korean immigrants—mostly men—arrived in Hawaii to meet growing labor needs. Unlike the case of the Chinese barred from entrance by the 1882 **Chinese Exclusion Act**, the Gentlemen's Agreement between U.S. and Japanese governments allowed Japanese and Korean wives to join their husbands in the United States (Korea was under Japan's occupation then). Many of the Korean male laborers married "picture brides," and about 1,000 Korean women immigrated this way. However, this flow of immigration halted with the Immigration Act of 1924, one of a series of anti-Asian exclusion laws. The second wave of Korean immigration began during the Korean War (1950–1953) when the War Brides Act of 1946 enabled the brides of U.S. servicemen to enter the United States. The years from 1951 to 1964 saw the arrival of war brides, war orphans, professional workers, and students from Korea. The largest wave of immigration from Korea began with the passing of the Immigration Act of 1965.

Among the first generation of Korean American writers, **Younghill Kang** is the best known, whose autobiographical novel, *The Grass Roof* (1931), received considerable publicity. Among the second generation of Korean American writers, the best-known figure is a woman writer, **Theresa Hak Kyung Cha**, whose only novel, *Dictée* (1982), regarded as one of the most challenging texts in Asian American literature, sets the path for postmodern and postcolonial exploration of experiences of Koreans and Korean Americans. Other notable figures in this second generation include **Yong Ik Kim**, **Gary Pak**, **Ty Pak**, **Sook Nyul Choi**, **Richard Kim**, and **Ronyoung Kim**, etc. Japanese occupation and American colonization of Korea preoccupy many of these writers' imaginations. Wars continue to dominate the subjects of the third generation, many of whom are American born. While some writers tell stories about comfort women, such as **Nora Okja Keller** and the most celebrated Korean American writer **Chang-rae Lee**, many others, such as **Suji Kwock Kim**, **Heinz Insu Fenkle**, and **Walter Lew**, meditate on the divided state of Korea, orphaned children by the war, and biracial children because of the American military presence in South Korea. In the past 10 years, Korean American literature has witnessed the emergence of numerous accomplished novelists, poets, and dramatists, and their works have reached a broad readership and won mainstream awards. Most of these writers are American born, such as **Na An**, **Leonard Chang**, **Alexander Chee**, **Susan Choi**, **Patricia Jang**, **Susan Kim**, **Don Lee**, **Ed Park**, and **Youngsoo Park**. Some of the best or most interesting poets in Asian American literature are Korean Americans like **Myung Mi Kim**, **Cathy Song**, **Jason Koo**, **Ed Bok Lee**, **Sueyeun Juliette Lee**, **Walter K. Lew**, **Sun Yung Shin**, and **Mia Yun**.

Korean American **theater** is incorporated into many Pan Asian American theaters, such as the **Northwest Asian American Theatre Company**, **Ping Chong & Company**, **Pan Asian Repertory Theatre**, **Asian American Theater Company**, the **Asian American Theater Workshop**, **David Henry Hwang Writers' Institute**, and the **East West Players**. The major theater focusing on Korean American plays is **Lodestone Theatre Ensemble**. **Young Jean Lee's Theater Company**, founded by a Korean American playwright, does not regard its mission to be promoting Korean American theater alone. There are a few performance troupes that feature Korean music and dance, such as **Shinmyung Pae**. Major playwrights include **Philip W. Chung**, Patricia Jang, **Susan Kim, Diana Son, Lloyd Suh**, etc. *See also* BALGASSI, HAEMI; CHE, SUNNY; CHOI, ANNIE; CHOI, DON MEE; CHOI, YANGSOOK; CHUNG, SONYA; HAN, JENNY; HONG, CATHY PARK; HWANG, CAROLINE; HYUN, PETER; KANG, CONNIE K.; KIM, ELIZABETH; KIM, PATTI; KIM, SUKI; LEE, JANICE Y. K.; LEE, MARIE MYUNG-OK; LEE, MARY PAIK; LEE, MIN JIN; MCKINNEY, CHRIS; MIN, KATHERINE; MUN, NAMIE; PAHK, INDUK; PAK, SOYUNG; PARK, FRANCES; PARK, GINGER; PARK, ISHLE YI; PARK, LINDA SUE; PARK, THERESE S.; RNO, SUNG JUNG; ROH-SPAULDING, CAROL; SOENTPIED, CHRIS; SUNÉE, KIM; TRENKA, JANE JEONG; WOO, SUNG J.; YOO, DAVID; YOO, PAULA; YOON, PAUL; YOUN, MONICA.

KREA. It is a U.S.-based Indian **theater**, founded in 2001 by Dheepa Ramanujam, her husband Ramanujam, and their friends Naveen Kumar Nathan and Venu Subramaniam. It is located in Fremont, California, and its mission is to bring the richness of the Indian theatrical heritage to the North American audience.

KRISHNASWAMI, UMA (1956–). A **South Asian American** author of **children's books**, Krishnaswami was born in New Delhi and immigrated to the United States as an adult. She holds a B.A. in political science from Lady Shri Ram College, New Delhi, India, an M.A. in social work from Delhi School of Social Work, and an M.A. in rehabilitation counseling from the University of Maryland, College Park. She has published over a dozen children's books and **young adult novels**, including *The Grand Plan to Fix Everything* (2011), *Out of the Way, Out of the Way* (2010), *Many Windows* (2008), *Naming Maya* (2004), *Remembering Grandpa* (2007), *The Closet Ghosts* (2006), *The Happiest Tree* (2005), and *Monsoon* (2003). Her books have been picked for a number of awards: Parents' Choice, Internal Reading Association Notable Books for a Global Society, Scientific American Young

Readers' Book Awards, Bank Street Best Books of the Year, and the Paterson Prize. Her picture book, *Chachaji's Cup* (2003), has been adapted into an off-Broadway musical. She is on the editorial board of *Kahani*, an award-winning South Asian children's magazine, and a founding member of the Bisti Writing Project, a northwest New Mexico site of the National Writing Project. She lives in New Mexico.

KULARTS. Founded in 1985 by Robert L. Henry, Marcella Pabros, and Alleluia Panis, Kularts is a **Filipino American** music and dance company based in San Francisco. Its mission is to inform and expand the understanding of Filipino American culture and preserve the spirit and integrity of ancient Pilipino art forms.

KUMAR, AMITAVA (1963–). A **South Asian American** writer, Kumar was born in Ara Bihar, India, and grew up in Patna, India. He immigrated to the United States when he was 23. He received his B.A. in political science from Hindu College, Delhi University, India, M.A. in linguistics from Delhi University, M.A. in English literature from Syracuse University, and Ph.D. in cultural studies and comparative literature from the University of Minnesota. Currently, he is Professor of English at Vassar College. He is the author of four books of creative nonfiction: *A Foreigner Carrying in the Crook of His Arm a Small Bomb* (2010), *Husband of a Fanatic* (2005), which was an Editors' Choice book at the *New York Times*, *Bombay–London–New York* (2002), and *Passport Photos* (2000). His novel *Home Products* (2007) was a finalist for India's premier literary award, Vodafone Crossword Prize, and was published in the United States under the title *Nobody Does the Right Thing* (2009). He has also written a book of **poetry**, *No Tears for the N.R.I.* (1996). Most of Kumar's writings center on fundamentalism and the global war on terror. His other nonfiction and poetry have been published in the *Nation*, *Harper's*, *Kenyon Review*, *New Statesman*, *Boston Review*, *Transition*, *American Prospect*, the *Chronicle of Higher Education*, *Toronto Review*, *Colorlines*, *Biblio*, *Outlook*, *Frontline*, *India Today*, the *Hindu*, *Himal*, the *Friday Times*, the *Times of India*, and a variety of other venues. He is the script writer and narrator of the prize-winning documentary films *Pure Chutney* (1997) and *Dirty Laundry* (2005).

KUMU KAHUA THEATRE. This is a community **theater** in Honolulu, Hawaii. Founded in 1971 by Dennis Carroll, a theater professor at the University of Hawaii, Manoa, Kumu Kahua Theatre produces plays written by local playwrights, especially plays featuring themes and stories of the people of Hawaii. Many plays have incorporated or are solely written in Hawaii

Creole English. Appropriately, the Hawaiian words *kumu kahua* translate to "original stage." In 1994, the Hawaii State Legislature awarded the group its current 100-seat playhouse located in downtown Honolulu at 46 Merchant Street. After Dennis Carroll stepped down as its artistic director, Harry Wong III took over the role.

KUNDIMAN. This is a nonprofit organization that sponsors writing retreats, a reading series, and a **poetry** prize. Its mission is to provide a "safe yet rigorous space where Asian American poets can explore, through art, the unique challenges that face the new and ever changing **diaspora**." Cofounded in 2002 by Asian American poets **Sarah Gambito** and **Joseph O. Legaspi**, it has received support from National Endowment for the Arts, the Geraldine R. Dodge Foundation, the University of Virginia, Asian American Arts Alliance's (SOAR) Program, Philippine American Writers, and individual patrons.

KUO, ALEX (1939–). A **Chinese American** poet and fiction writer, Kuo was born in Boston and taken back to China by his parents between the ages of three and five before they moved to Hong Kong. He completed elementary and secondary schooling in Hong Kong and received a General Certificate of Education from London University at 16. In 1955, his family moved to Windsor, Connecticut. He received his B.A. in writing at Knox College in Illinois and went on to study creative writing with famous Asian American writers like **Frank Chin** and **Lawson Inada** at the University of Iowa's M.F.A. program. He has published numerous books of **poetry** and novels as well as a large number of short stories in literary journals, such as *Ploughshare*, *Chicago Review*, *Green Mountains Review*, etc. Kuo's novels are *Chinese Opera* (1998) and *Panda Diaries* (2006). His short story collections include *Lipstick and Other Stories* (2001), which received the **American Book Award**, and *White Jade and Other Stories* (2008). His poetry collections include *The Window Tree* (1971), *New Letters from Hiroshima and Other Poems* (1974), *Changing the River* (1986), and *This Fierce Geography* (1999). He has received three National Endowment for the Arts awards, grants from the United Nations, and grants from the Idaho Commission on the Arts.

KUO, HELENA (1911–1999). A **Chinese American** writer and journalist, Kuo was born in Macao. One of the few **women** in China of her generation who received higher education, she graduated from Shanghai University. In the 1930s, she worked as a reporter for the *Shanghai Evening News* and other Chinese newspapers. She fled to England from the Japanese invasion in 1937 and became a columnist for the *Daily Mail* of London. In 1939, she came to the United States at Eleanor Roosevelt's invitation. In addition to books of nonfiction, she wrote a novel and an autobiography. *Westward to Chungking* (1944) is a novel about a Chinese family uprooted by the Japanese invasion and occupation. Her autobiography, *I've Come a Long Way* (1942), recounts her journeys as a journalist in China, Hong Kong, Europe, and the United States.

KWOK, JEAN (1968–). A **Chinese American** novelist, Kwok was born in Hong Kong and moved to Brooklyn, New York, when she was five. She received her B.A. in English from Harvard University and M.F.A. from Columbia University. She is the author of the novel *The Girl in Translation* (2010), which tells the story of a young immigrant from Hong Kong, who lives a double life between school and sweatshop. The novel hit the extended New York Times Best Seller List, was a Discover Great New Writers pick for Barnes and Noble, and selected as an Indie Next List pick for May 2010. Her work has been published in *Story* magazine, *Prairie Schooner*, *Elements of Literature: Third Course*, and the *Nuyorasian Anthology.*

KWONG, DAN (1954–). A Chinese **Japanese American** playwright and performance artist, Kwong was born in Los Angeles to a Japanese American mother and a **Chinese American** father. He spent two years at the University of Southern California before transferring to the School of the Art Institute of Chicago. Accustomed to negotiating cultural conflicts, he chooses the competing cultures in his background as the subject of his performance and writing. His successful debut as a performer in *Secrets of the Samurai Centerfielder* in 1989 encouraged him to embark on a career of writing and performing. In 1994, he began a performance group "Everything You Ever Want to Know about Asian Men in Los Angeles." His solo performances explore identity issues of Asian Americans and HIV/AIDS, utilizing storytelling, **poetry**, martial arts, dance, slide projection, video, sculptural installation, and music. They are humorous, honest, and political. Kwong's other works include *Tales from the Fractured Tao with Master Nice Guy* (1991), *Monkhood in Three Easy Lessons* (1993), *The Dodo Vaccine* (1994), *The Night the Moon Landed on 39th Street* (1999), *Correspondence of a Dangerous Enemy Alien* (1995), and *It's Great 2B American* (2008). These performances have been staged at venues in the United States, Great Britain, Mexico, Thailand, Indonesia, and Canada. Kwong's plays have been published in *From Inner Worlds to Outer Space: The Multimedia Performances of Dan Kwong*, *The Journal of American Drama and Theatre*, *Getting Your Solo Act Together*, *High Performance* magazine, and various anthologies, including *On a Bed of*

Rice: A Feast of Asian American Erotica and *Yellow Light: The Flowering of Asian American Arts*. He is the recipient of numerous fellowships, including from the National Endowment for the Arts, Rockefeller Foundation, Asian Cultural Council, Art Matters Inc., Los Angeles Cultural Affairs Department, and California Community Foundation. In June 2004, he received an award for Mid-Career Artists from the California Arts Council Artists. *See also* THEATER.

L

LA MAMA CHINATOWN. This is an Asian American **theater**, established in 1970 and funded by Ellen Stewart and led by Wu Jing-jyi and Ching Yeh. It became the **Pan Asian Repertory Theatre** in 1977 and was led by artistic director Tisa Chang.

LAHIRI, JHUMPA (1967–). A **South Asian American** novelist, Lahiri was born in London to Bengali Indian immigrants and immigrated to the United States when she was two. She grew up in South Kingston, Rhode Island. She received her B.A. in English from Barnard College and M.F.A. in creative writing from Boston University. Believing that an academic career would be more secure than creative writing, she went on to earn an M.A. in English, an M.A. in comparative literature, and a Ph.D. in Renaissance Studies from Boston University. She is the author of two collections of short stories and one novel: *Interpreter of Maladies* (1999), winner of a Pulitzer Prize for Fiction and a PEN/Hemingway Award; *Unaccustomed Earth* (2008), winner of an **Asian American Literary Award**; and her novel *The Namesake* (2003), adapted into the popular film of the same name. Her writings center on the themes of immigration, alienation, generational conflicts, **assimilation**, and identity. She is the recipient of numerous honors, including the O. Henry Award, TransAtlantic Award from the Henfield Foundation, Addison Metcalf Award from the American Academy of Arts and Letters, Guggenheim Fellowship, James Beard Foundations' M.F.K. Fisher Distinguished Writing Award, and inclusion in *Best American Short Stories* of 1999, 2000, and 2002. Appointed by President Barack Obama, Lahiri serves on the President's Committee on the Arts and Humanities. Since 2005, she has been a vice president of the PEN American Center.

LAMBDA LITERARY AWARDS. This award began in 1989 by the Lambda Literary Foundation. The purpose of the Awards in the early years was to identify and celebrate the best of lesbian and gay books in the year of their publication. Since their inception, the Lambda Literary Awards have been presented in conjunction with the nation's premier book convention, Book Expo America (previously the American Booksellers Association), traveling each year to a different host city. The Awards have ranged over many categories, and from the very first year they have made the statement that lesbian, gay, bisexual, and transgender stories are part of the literature of the nation. Asian American writers who have won this award include **Abha Dawesar** for her novel *Babyji* (2005) and **Brenda Shaughnessy** for her book of poems *Interior with Sudden Joy* (1999).

LAMONT POETRY PRIZE. This was first established in 1954 by a bequest from Mrs. Thomas W. Lamont. Between 1954 and 1975, it was the annual award given by the Academy of American Poets to a poet's first published volume. Between 1976 and 1995, it was given annually for a poet's second published book; it is the only major **poetry** award that honors excellent second books. Known as the **James Laughlin Award** since 1996, it is noted as one of the major prizes awarded to younger poets in the United States. Asian American poets winning this award include **Ai** for *Killing Floor* (1979), **Li-Young Lee** for *The City in Which I Love You* (1990), **Garrett Hongo** for *The River of Heaven* (1988), and **Vijay Seshadri** for *The Long Meadow* (2003).

LOUIE, DAVID WONG (1954–). A **Chinese American** novelist, Louie was born in Rockville Center, New York. He received a B.A. from Vassar College and an M.F.A. in creative writing from the University of Iowa. He is the author of the novel, *The Barbarians Are Coming* (2000), a winner of the Shirley Collier Prize, and the short story collection *Pangs of Love* (1991), which won the *Los Angeles Times* Book Review First Fiction Award, the *Ploughshares* First Fiction Award, was a *New York Times Book Review* Notable Book of 1991, and a Voice Literary Supplement Favorite of 1991. His writings explore themes of alienation, masculinity, class, displacement, interethnic relationships, fatherhood, and so on. Among his other honors are fellowships from the Lannan Writing and the National Foundation for the Arts. Louie currently teaches at University of California, Los Angeles.

LAPCHAROENSAP, RATTAWUT (1979–). A Thai American fiction writer, Lapcharoensap was born in Chicago and raised in Bangkok. He currently lives in Brooklyn and teaches high-school English. "Farangs," his first published story, appeared in *Granta* 84. Since then, his work has been published in several literary magazines, as well as in *Best New American Voices 2005* and *Best American Nonrequired Reading 2005*. His debut short-story collection, *Sightseeing* (2005), was selected for the National Book Foundation's '5 Under 35' program and won the **Asian American Literary Award**. His stories explore the themes of family, relationships, displacement, and human frailty. *See also* SOUTHEAST ASIAN AMERICAN LITERATURE AND THEATER.

LARSEN, WANWADEE. A Thai American memoirist, Larsen was born in Thailand and came to the United States as a mail order bride. She received her B.A. in art from Francis Marion University and M.A. in art from California State University. She is the author of *Confessions of a Mail Order Bride* (1989). *See also* SOUTHEAST ASIAN AMERICAN LITERATURE AND THEATER.

LAU, ALAN CHONG (1948–). A **Chinese American** poet, Lau was born in Oroville and raised in Paradise, California. He received his B.A. in art from the University of California, Santa Cruz. *The Buddha Bandits Down Highway 99* (1978) was his first book of **poetry** in collaboration with **Lawson Fusao Inada** and **Garrett Hongo**. He then published his own book of poems, *Songs for Jadina* (1980), which won the 1981 **American Book Award**. Both books of poems explore his family history and ethnic identity. After a 20-year gap, Lau published *Blues and Greens: A Produce Worker's Journal* (2000), which portrays his years spent working in an Asian grocery store. In 2007, he published *no hurry*, a hand-produced chapbook of poetry about his travel in Japan. His poems have also appeared in numerous anthologies, including *From Totems to Hip-Hop: A Multicultural Anthology of Poetry across the Americas 1900–2002* and *What Book!? Buddha Poems from Beat to Hiphop.* He is the recipient of fellowships from the Japan–United States Friendship Commission, the National Endowment for the Arts, and the Agency for Cultural Affairs of the Japanese Government. He has also received grants from Seattle Arts Commission, King County Arts Commission, and the California Arts Council.

LAU, CAROLYN (1946–). A **Chinese American** poet, Lau was born in Hawaii and educated at San Francisco State University. In addition to being widely published and anthologized, Lau has published two collections of poetry, *Wode Shuofa: My Way of Speaking* (1988) and *Ono Ono Girl's Hula* (1997). *Wode Shuofa*, which investigates themes such as Chinese philosophies, gender, sexuality, and the craft of writing, won an **American Book Award** and a California Arts Council Fellowship. *Ono Ono Girl's Hula* is a book of prose poetry that stays close to her personal life. Her poems also appeared in *The Best American Poetry of 1996.*

LAW-YONE, WENDY (1947–). A Burmese American novelist, Law-Yone was born in Mandalay and grew up in Rangoon. She states that she is "half Burman, a quarter Chinese, and a quarter English." Her family endured political persecution by the military regime, and she was imprisoned after attempting escape to Thailand. She came to the United States in 1973, settling in Washington, D.C., after attending college in Florida. She is the author of three novels: *The Coffin Tree* (1983), *Irrawaddy Tango* (1993), and *The Road to Wanting* (2010). She explores themes of alienation, **exile**, and madness. She was the recipient of a National Endowment for the Arts Literature Award for Creative Writing and a David T. K. Wong Creative Writing Fellowship from the University of East Anglia. *See also* SOUTHEAST ASIAN AMERICAN LITERATURE AND THEATER.

LÊ THI DIEM THÚY (1972–). A **Vietnamese American** poet, playwright, and performer, Lê was born in Vietnam. When she was six, she and her father became refugees in Singapore before they immigrated to San Diego. She received her B.A. in cultural studies from Hampshire College, Massachusetts. For her graduating thesis, she wrote her first play, *Red Fiery Summer*, which she put on as a solo performance between 1995 and 1997 at a variety of venues across the country. She was then commissioned by the New World **Theater** and the New England Foundation for the Arts to write her second play, which became *The Bodies between Us* (1996). Her first novel, *The Gangster We Are All Looking For* (2001), received raving reviews for its poetical prose and psychological poignancy. Structured in vignettes that each features one unforgettable image, it relates a devastating story of a family torn by war, displacement, alienation, and hopelessness. Her work has also appeared in the *Massachusetts Review*, *Harper's Magazine*, and the *Very Inside* anthology, and she has received honors, such as fellowships from the Radcliffe and Guggenheim Foundations.

LEE, ANNETTE (1968–). A **Chinese American** dramatist, Lee was born and raised in Los Angeles. She received her B.S. in marketing from New York University and M.F.A. in playwriting from the University of California, Los Angeles. Her social comedy, *A Dirty Secret between the Toes* (2001), was a finalist in the **East West Players**. Her comedic fantasy, *Happy Talk*, was the winner at the 2008 *Last Play Standing* Competition at Another Chicago **Theater** Company. Her other plays include *Hacienda Heights* (2009), *English Only* (2008), *Higher Up* (2008), *Negation Delirium on Toast Points* (2007), *Holiday Lamplights* (2002), *One Cold Dark Night* (2001), *Walk the Mountain* (2000), and *From the Corner of My Eye* (1999). They have been produced by Wells Fargo Radio Theater, Aspen's Theater Masters, Another Chicago Theater Company, **Lodestone Theatre Ensemble**, the East West Players, Upper Reaches Theater, etc.

LEE, CHANG-RAE (1965–). One of the best-known **Korean American** novelists, Lee was born in Korea and came to the United States with his parents at the age of three. Lee received a B.A. in English from Yale University and an M.F.A. in creative writing from the University of Oregon. He currently teaches creative writing at Princeton University. His first novel, ***Native Speaker*** (1995), was an instant success, for which he received the PEN/Hemingway Award for Best First Fiction, the Discover Award, and the **American Book Award**. The novel, richly lyrical and deeply psychological, laces two mutually illuminating plots to drive home its major themes of **assimilation**, alienation, language, political representation, and identity. The protagonist's occupation as an industrial spy allegorizes the double life almost all immigrants lead. Lee's second novel, *A Gesture Life* (1999), winner of an **Asian American Literary Award**, centers on an unreliable narrator, Doc Hata, who was a Korean Japanese medic during World War II. Hata's meandering memory reveals startling secrets about his past. For this novel, Lee was named one of the 20 best American writers under 40 by the *New Yorker* magazine. His third novel, *Aloft* (2004), has nothing to do with Asian Americans or immigrants. However, it continues the same themes of alienation, cultural dissonance, and emotional distance that one finds in his writings about immigrants. His most recent novel, *Surrendered* (2010), returns to the subjects of Korea and the War.

LEE, CHERYLENE (1953–). A **Chinese American** actress and playwright, Lee was born in Los Angeles to third-generation Chinese American parents. Because her mother was an extra in Hollywood, Lee began to act at age three and has appeared in TV sitcoms and films. She earned her B.S. in paleontology at the University of California, Berkeley, and M.S. in geology from the University of California, Los Angeles. In her 30s, she began writing plays. Her earlier plays center on themes of immigration, race, interracial marriage, and identities. Reflecting the context of the **Page Act**, Lee's first two plays, *Wang Bow Rides Again* (1985) and *Yin Chin Bow* (1986), dramatize the first generation of Chinese immigrants who came to America as young men to fulfill the dream of the **Gold Mountain**, but, instead, they found an alien and hostile culture where they could neither find Chinese nor be allowed to marry white **women**. These male characters either die lonely deaths or become destitute old men. *Arthur and Leila* (1991) is Lee's third play that pairs an old alcoholic gambler with his younger successful sister in an uneasy but comical relationship that eventually leads to the revelation of family secrets. This play was her first major success; it was selected for the O'Neill National Playwrights Conference, and because of it Lee received a significant Fund for New American Plays Grant from the John F. Kennedy Center for the Performing Arts and a Rockefeller MAP Grant.

Her later plays often choose current political events as their subjects. For instance, *Carry the Tiger to the Mountain* (1998) is about Vincent Chen's murder, *Knock off Balance* (2000) about the return of Hong Kong to China, and *Legacy Codes* (2001) on the Wen Ho Lee incident. Lee went on to write *Antigone Falun Gong* (2004), *Mixed Messages* (2006), *American Bamboo* (2010), etc. Lee has received a Playwright in Residence grant with the **East West Players**, a California Arts Council Playwriting Fellowship, a Wallace A. Gerbode Play Commission, and two San Francisco Individual Artists Grants (one in literature and one in performing arts). She was honored with the 2003 Made in America Award for playwrights at the East West Players and was honored as the 2003 Anthony J. Haney Fellow at Theatreworks for artistic excellence. Lee has also published **poetry** and short fiction. *See also* THEATER.

LEE, CHIN-YANG (1917–?). Chin-Yang Lee is a **Chinese American** novelist, born in Hunan Province, China. He attended Shandong University, and when Japan invaded China, he went to Southwest Associated University in Kunming. Lee immigrated to the United States in 1942 and entered the graduate comparative literature program at Columbia University. Without finishing at Columbia, Lee transferred to Yale to study drama. In 1947, he received an M.F.A. from Yale's Drama School. His first novel, *The Flower Drum Song* (1957), was made into a Broadway musical and later into a film. He went on to write nine more novels: *Lover's Point* (1958), *The Sawbwa and His Secretary* (1959), *Madame Goldenflower* (1960), *Cripple Mah and the New Order* (1961), *The Virgin Market* (1964), *The Land of the Golden Mountain* (1967), *China Saga* (1987), *The Second Son of Heaven* (1990), and *Gate of Rage* (1991). Most of Lee's novels center on China and its historical events. *The Second Son of Heaven*, for instance, dramatizes the Taiping Rebellion in the mid-19th century, and *Gate of Rage* the Tiananmen Square incident in 1989. Recently, he has written plays, including *The Body and Soul of a Chinese Woman* (2006) and *The Fan Tan King* (2006), produced at Stella Adler Theatre and **Pan Asian Repertory Theatre**.

LEE, DON (1959–). A **Korean American** novelist, Lee was born in Tokyo, Japan. Son of a career State Department officer, he spent most of his childhood in Tokyo and Seoul. He received his B.A. in English from the University of California, Los Angeles, and M.F.A. in creative writing from Emerson College. Between 1988 and 2007, he served as the principal editor of *Ploughshares*. He has taught creative writing at Emerson College, Macalester College, Western Michigan University, and Temple University. He is the author of two novels: *Wrack and Ruin* (2008) and *Country of Origin* (2004), which won an **American Book Award**, the Edgar Award for Best First Novel, and a Mixed Media Watch Image Award for Outstanding Fiction. Both novels humorously explore the themes of family and identity. He has also written a collection of short stories, *Yellow* (2001), which won the Sue Kaufman Prize for First Fiction from the American Academy of Arts and Letters and the Members Choice Award from the **Asian American Writers' Workshop**. He has received numerous honors, including the inaugural Fred R. Brown Literary Award for emerging novelists from the University of Pittsburgh's creative writing program, an O. Henry Award, and a Pushcart Prize, and fellowships from the Massachusetts Cultural Council, the St. Botolph Club Foundation, and residencies from Yaddo and the Lannan Foundation. His stories have been published in the *Southern Review*, the *Kenyon Review*, *GQ*, the *North American Review*, the *Gettysburg Review*, *Manoa*, *American Short Fiction*, *Glimmer Train*, *Charlie Chan Is Dead 2*, *Screaming Monkeys*, *Narrative*, and elsewhere.

LEE, ED BOK (1974–). A **Korean American** poet, Lee was born and raised in North Dakota and Minnesota. He studied Russian and Central Asian languages and literatures at the University of Minnesota, Kazakh State University in Almaty, Kazakhstan, and the University of California, Berkeley. He received his M.F.A. from Brown University. Lee is the author of *Real Karaoke People: Poems and Prose* (2005), winner of a PEN/Beyond Margins Award, a Members' Choice Award from the **Asian American Literary Awards**, an Urban Griots Best Book Award, and a 2007 national **poetry** best seller. The poems and stories are exhilarating and cosmopolitan, exploring themes of politics, sex, loss, memory, and dislocation. His plays, including *Passage*, *El Santo Americano*, and *St. Petersburg* have been staged at **theaters** like Guthrie Theater, New York Theatre Workshop, Joseph Papp Public Theatre, **Theater Mu**, Taipei Theatre, Trinity Repertory Company, and the Walker Art Center. Among the honors he has received are grants from the Jerome Foundation, Minnesota State Arts Board, Loft Literary Center, and the National Endowment for the Arts.

LEE, GUS (1946–). A **Chinese American** novelist, Lee was born in San Francisco. He attended the Military Academy at West Point without graduating and finished his bachelor's degree and a J.D. from the University of California, Davis. His novels are largely based on his life at various stages. *China Boy* (1991) tells the story of his boyhood in a predominantly African American neighborhood in San Francisco. *Honor and Duty* (1994) depicts his experience at West Point. *Tiger's Tail* (1996) covers his years as an army attorney in postwar Korea. *No Physical Evidence* (1998) fictionalizes one of his cases when working in the Sacramento County District Attorney's office. Two major themes preoccupy Lee in his novels: an ethnic minority's struggle for recognition and Asian American masculinity. He has also authored a book of nonfiction, *Chasing Hepburn* (2004).

LEE, HELIE (1964–). A **Korean American** memoirist, Lee was born in Seoul, South Korea. She was four when her parents brought her to Montreal, Canada, and then to California a year later. She grew up in San Fernando Valley of Southern California. She received a B.A. in political science from the University of California, Los Angeles. She is the author of two memoirs about her family's traumatic past in the war-torn Korea from the 1930s to 1997. She has written two memoirs. *Still Life with Rice* (1996), a national best seller, details her maternal grandmother's life in North Korean until she came to the United States. *In the Absence of Sun* (2002) depicts her family's desperate attempts to make contact with and rescue her grandmother's lost son in North Korea.

LEE, HUY VOUN (1970–). A Cambodian American writer and illustrator of **children's books**, Lee was born in Phnom Penh, Cambodia, and came with her family to the United States in 1975 as refugees. She holds a B.F.A. in illustration from the School of Visual Arts in New York City. She is the author of five books: *At the Beach* (1994), *In the Snow* (2000), *In the Leaves* (2005), *In the Park* (1998), and *1. 2. 3. Go* (2001). *See also* SOUTHEAST ASIAN AMERICAN LITERATURE AND THEATER.

LEE, JANICE Y. K. (1972–). A **Korean American** novelist, Lee was born in Hong Kong to Korean parents and lived there until she was 15 when she came for boarding school in New Hampshire. She received her B.A. in English from Harvard University and M.F.A. in creative writing from Hunter College. Her debut novel, *The Piano Teacher* (2009), set in Hong Kong, is a love story and a mystery, exploring themes of race, class, cultural divides, loss, betrayal, regret, and finding oneself.

LEE, JEFFREY ETHAN (1962–). A Taiwanese American poet, Lee was born in Philadelphia to immigrant parents who are native Taiwanese. He rejects being classified as a **Chinese American**. He holds a B.A. from Moravian College, an M.F.A. in creative writing, and a Ph.D. in English from New York University. He is the author of two books of **poetry**: *Identity Papers* (2006), a finalist for the Colorado Book Award for poetry, and *Invisible Sister* (2004). He also published two chapbooks of poetry: *The Sylf* (2003), winner of the Sow's Ear Poetry Review Chapbook prize, and *Strangers in a Homeland* (2001). His poetry explores the themes of race, family, cultural identity, memory, and home. He also won the first Tupelo Press award for literary fiction in 2001 for a novel, *The Autobiography of Somebody Else*. He has published numerous poems, stories, and essays in *Many Mountains Moving, CrossConnect, North American Review, African American Review, Xconnect, Crazyhorse, Crab Orchard Review, Washington Square, Green Mountain Review, American Poetry Review*, etc. He is the senior poetry editor for *Many Mountains Moving*, a journal and small poetry press.

LEE, LI-YOUNG (1957–). One of the most celebrated **Chinese American** poets, Lee was born in Indonesia to Chinese parents and grew up in East Vandergrift, Pennsylvania, where his father was the minister of an all-white Presbyterian congregation. He went to the University of Pittsburgh to major in biochemistry but fell in love with **poetry** in Gerald Stern's class. Lee went on to study in the M.F.A. programs at the University of Arizona and the State University of New York at Brockport. Although he never finished his degree, the State University of New York at Brockport awarded him an honorary doctorate. Lee has published several books of poetry, including *Rose* (1986), *The City in Which I Love You* (1990), *Book of My Nights* (2001), *From Blossoms* (2007), *Behind My Eyes* (2009), and a lyrical memoir, *The Winged Seed* (1995). Lee's poetry portrays two stages of his life—a lonely child who was tenderly loved by his father and a searching young man whose memory of his father intensifies his love for his family. The figure of the father, larger than life, dominates his poetic meditation on themes such as inheritance, love, memory, and loss. Lee has received almost all the prestigious honors for a poet, such as Fellowship of the Academy of American Poets, William Carlos Williams Award, **Lamont Poetry** Selection, Delmore Schwartz Memorial Award from New York University, **American Book Award**, Whiting Writers' Award, Lannan Literary Award, Fellowship of the National Endowment for the Arts, Fellowship of Guggenheim Memorial Foundation, and Grants from Illinois Arts Council, Commonwealth of Pennsylvania, and Pennsylvania Council on the Arts. *See also* SOUTHEAST ASIAN AMERICAN LITERATURE AND THEATER.

LEE, MARIE MYUNG-OK (1964–). A **Korean American** novelist, Lee was born in Hibbing, Minnesota, and hers was the only Korean family in town. She earned a B.A. in economics from Brown University. Lee has lectured at Yale University and was a founder of the **Asian American Writers' Workshop**. She has written novels for **children** and **young adults**. *Finding My Voice* (1992), *Saying Goodbye* (1994), and *Necessary Roughness* (1997) are for young adult readers, which all depict young Asian American protagonists dealing with their differences from the cultures of small-town America. *If It Hadn't Been for You, Yoon Jun* (1993) and *F is for Fabuloso* (1999) were written for younger readers and center on what it is like growing up as immigrants in America. *Night of the Chupacabras* (1998) is a mystery about Mexican vampires. Her adult novel, *Someone's Daughter* (2006), tells the story of a Korean adoptee returning to Korea to find her biological mother. She has received many honors, including an O. Henry honorable mention for an adaptation of a chapter from *Somebody's Daughter*, a MacDowell Colony fellow, and served as a **National Book Award** judge. She is currently a Visiting Lecturer at the Center for the Study of Race and Ethnicity in the Americas at Brown University. *See also* CHILDREN'S LITERATURE.

LEE, MARY PAIK (1900–1995). A **Korean American** autobiographer, Lee was born in Pyongyang, Korea, and immigrated to Hawaii with her parents when she was five. A year later, her family moved to San Francisco. Three years after high school, she married and worked in rice farming with her husband until 1950. Lee published her autobiography, *Quiet Odyssey: A Pioneer Korean Woman in America*, in 1990 at the age of 90.

LEE, MILLY (1933–). A **Chinese American children's book** author, Lee was born and raised in San Francisco's **Chinatown.** She studied at the University of California at Berkeley and the University of San Francisco and became a school librarian. She is the author of three children's books: *Nim and the War Effort* (2002), *Earthquake* (2001), and *Landed* (2006). All of these depict historical events and explore themes of ethnicity, immigration, and Americanization.

LEE, MIN JIN (1969–). A **Korean American** novelist, Lee was born in South Korea and came to the United States when she was seven years old. She grew up in Elmhurst, Queens, New York. She studied history at Yale College and law at Georgetown University Law Center. She became a writer after working as a corporate lawyer in New York for several years. Lee currently lives in Tokyo with her husband and son. Her debut novel, *Free Food for Millionaires* (2007), depicts the ambivalences of a 22-year-old Korean American woman, who is caught between struggling immigrant parents and expensive habits and tastes she has acquired from an ivy league education. The novel explores themes of love, money, race, and belief systems. Lee has also published short stories in literary magazines, including *Narrative* magazine and the *Missouri Review.* She has received the New York Foundation for the Arts Fellowship for Fiction, the Peden Prize from the *Missouri Review* for Best Story, and the Narrative Prize for New and Emerging Writer. Her fiction has been featured on NPR's Selected Shorts.

LEE, PRISCILLA (1966–). A **Chinese American** poet, Lee was born and raised in San Francisco's **Chinatown**. She studied at the University of

California, Berkeley, and San Francisco State University. She is the author of a book of **poetry**, *Wishbone* (2000), which explores family history and identity issues. Recipient of the Emily Chamberlain Poetry Prize, the James D. Phelan Literary Award, and the Association of Asian American Studies Book Award, she has published poetry in *Ploughshares*, the *Kenyon Review*, *Zyzzyva*, and so on.

LEE, SUEYEUN JULIETTE (1977–). A **Korean American** poet, Lee was born in Washington, D.C. She holds a B.A. in English and an M.F.A. in **poetry** from the University of Massachusetts, Amherst. She is the author of a book of poetry, *That Gorgeous Feeling* (2008), and four chapbooks of poetry: *Underground National* (2010), *Mental Commitment Robots* (2007), *Perfect Villagers* (2006), and *Trespass Slightly In* (2005). Her poetry explores the themes of identity, history, memory, and language, among others. She edits *Corollary Press* and is working toward her Ph.D. at Temple University.

LEE, WENDY (1976–). A **Chinese American** novelist, Lee was born in Princeton, New Jersey, to Chinese immigrants. She received her B.A. in English from Stanford University and M.F.A. in creative writing from New York University. Her debut novel, *Happy Family* (2008), offers an unflinching look at international adoption. Lee has been named a MacDowell Colony fellow and has also received a writing residency from the Corporation of Yaddo. She lives in New York City.

LEE, YAN PHOU (1861–1938?). A **Chinese American** memoirist, Lee was born in Guang Zhou, China, and came to the United States in 1873 as a member of the first government sponsored group of Chinese students. He chose to attend Yale University. The Chinese government, however, changed its mind a year later and recalled the students. Several years later, Lee returned to his studies at Yale and graduated in 1887. *When I Was a Boy in China* (1887) was his memoir that focused on his school days in China.

LEE, YOUNG JEAN (1974–). A **Korean American** playwright and producer, Lee was born in Korea and moved to the United States when she was two years old. She grew up in Pullman, Washington, and earned a B.A. in English from the University of California, Berkeley, and studied Shakespeare in the Ph.D. program of the same university for six years. She moved to New York to become a playwright in 2002 and earned an M.F.A. from Mac Wellman's playwriting program at Brooklyn College. In 2003, she founded **Young Jean Lee's Theater Company** and has remained its artistic director. A 2011 Guggenheim Fellow, Lee was named by *American Theatre* magazine as one of the 25 artists who will shape the American **theater** over the next

25 years. Since then, she has directed her plays at such theaters as Soho Rep, the Kitchen, the Public Theater, HERE Arts Center, and the Ontological-Hysteric Theater. Her plays have been published in *New Downtown Now* (2006); *Three Plays by Young Jean Lee* (2007); *Songs of the Dragons Flying to Heaven and Other Plays* (2009), a collection of all her plays; and *The Shipment and Lear* (2010). Her plays shift dramatically from comedy to exaggerated violence, to subtle irony, and moments that are unsettling and often difficult for an audience. She has won numerous honors, including an Emerging Playwright **Obie Award**, a Prize in Literature from the American Academy of Arts and Letters, and residencies from Yaddo, the MacDowell Colony, the Ucross Foundation, and Hedgebrook.

LEE-YANG, MAY (1979–). A Hmong American playwright and performance artist, Lee-Yang was born in Ban Vinai, a refugee camp in Thailand. Nine months after her birth, her family resettled in St. Paul, Minnesota, where she lives to this day. She received her B.A. in English from the University of Minnesota. Her theater-based works include *Confessions of a Lazy Hmong Woman*, *Sia(b)*, *Ten Reasons Why I'd Be a Bad Porn Star*, *Stir-Fried Pop Culture*, and *The Child's House*. Her work has been produced through Mu Performing Arts, the Center for Hmong Art and Talent (**CHAT**), Out North Theater, Kaotic Good Productions, Intermedia Arts, the MN Fringe Festival, etc. Her work often explores the lives of Hmong **women** and what it is like to live in a bicultural world. She is the recipient of several honors including a Midwestern Voices and Visions Residency Award, Minnesota State Arts Board Artist Initiative Grant for Theater and Literature, a National Performance Network Creation Fund Grant for Theater, and a Bush Leadership Fellowship. She is a cofounder of the Unit, a collective of emerging playwrights of color. *See also* SOUTHEAST ASIAN AMERICAN LITERATURE AND THEATER.

LEGASPI, JOSEPH O. (1971–). A **Filipino American poet**, Legaspi was born in the Philippines and immigrated to Los Angeles with his family at age 12. He holds a B.A. in English from Loyola Marymount University and an M.F.A. in creative writing from New York University. He is the author of a **poetry** collection *Imago* (2007), which portrays an immigrant boy's painful and poignant rites of passage. His poems have appeared in numerous journals, including *North American Review*, *Gulf Coast, Crab Orchard Review*, *Bloomsbury Review*, *Puerto Del Sol*, *Seneca Review*, the *Literary Review*, *Gay & Lesbian Review*, *Hayden's Ferry Review*, ***Bamboo Ridge***, and the anthologies, *Contemporary Voices of the Eastern World*, *PinoyPoetics*, and *Titling the Continent*. A recipient of a poetry fellowship from the New York

Foundation for the Arts, he and **Sarah Gambito** cofounded **Kundiman**, a nonprofit organization serving Asian American poets. Currently, he lives in Manhattan and works at Columbia University.

LEONG, MONFOON (1916–1964). A **Chinese American** fiction writer, Leong was born in San Diego's **Chinatown**. He was the first Chinese to be employed by Convair Aircraft and Naval Air Station in North Island as a patternmaker and draftsman. He worked for the U.S. Army Air Force during World War II. He received his B.A. in English from Stanford University and an M.A. in American Studies from the University of Minnesota. His collection of short stories, *Number One Son* (1974), portrays the cultural and generational conflicts between the first generation Chinese Americans and their American-born children.

LEONG, RUSSELL (1950–). A **Chinese American** poet, Leong was born and raised in San Francisco's **Chinatown**. He received his B.A. in English from San Francisco State University, took graduate courses at National Taiwan University, and obtained his M.F.A. in film from the University of California, Los Angeles. He is the author of one collection of **poetry**, *The Country of Dreams and Dust* (1993), which won the PEN Josephine Miles Literature Award. The poems are written in the form of letters exchanged between a Chinese American man and his relatives in China. *Phoenix Eyes and Other Stories* (2000), winner of the **American Book Award**, is his collection of short fiction that portrays a range of characters from Taiwanese, Asian Americans, and American sinologists to a French Algerian. His writings explore common themes of cultural **exile**, displacement, identity, love, and sexuality. His works have also appeared in anthologies, including *Charlie Chan Is Dead* and *Aiiieeeee!* He has served as the poetry editor for *Amerasia Journal* as well as head of the Asian American Studies Center Press. He is also a professor at the University of California, Los Angeles.

LEUNG, BRIAN (1967–). A **Chinese American** novelist, Leung was born in San Diego County to an American mother and a Chinese father. He earned his B.A. and M.A. from California State University, Los Angeles, and an M.F.A from Indiana University. Currently, he is director of creative writing at the University of Louisville. His debut novel, *Lost Men* (2007), tells the story of an estranged American–Chinese father and son traveling through China, and his second novel, *Take Me Home* (2010), is a historical fiction set in 1885 Wyoming against the background of the anti-Chinese riot in which 28 Chinese coal miners were massacred in Rock Springs. His short story collection *The World Famous Love Acts* (2004) won the Mary McCarthy Award in short fiction and the **Asian American Literary Award**. Leung's fiction is noted for its use of telling stories from a wide range of racial, political, and religious points of view. He frequently writes about the conflicts that occur when an American is multiracial and at the same time expected to reflect each of those internal racial perspectives. His fiction, creative nonfiction, and **poetry** have also appeared in *Story*, *Crazyhorse*, *Grain*, *Gulf Coast*, *Kinesis*, the *Barcelona Review*, *Mid-American Review*, *Salt Hill*, *Gulf Stream*, *River City*, *Runes*, the *Bellingham Review*, *Hyphen*, *Velocity*, the *Connecticut Review*, *Blithe House Quarterly*, *Indiana Review*, *Crab Orchard Review*, and *Crowd.*

LEW, WALTER K. (1955–). A **Korean American** poet, Lew was born in Baltimore, Maryland. He received his B.S. in cognitive science and premedicine from Hampshire College, M.A. in English from Brown University, M.A. in Korean Studies from the University of California, Los Angeles, and took doctorate courses in East Asian Cultural Studies at the University of California, Los Angeles. He is the author of four books of **poetry**: *Excerpts from: IKTH DIKTE for DICTEE* (1982), *Treadwinds: Poems and Intermedia Texts* (2002), winner of an **Asian American Literary Award** and Finalist for the PEN Center USA Literary Award in Poetry 2003. He edited *Premonitions: The Kaya Anthology of New Asian North American Poetry* (1995), *Muae 1* (1995), and *Crazy Melon and Chinese Apple: The Poems of Frances Chung* (2000), and was coeditor of *Kôri: The Beacon Anthology of Korean American Fiction* (2001). Among the numerous honors he has received are fellowships and grants from National Endowment for the Arts, New York State Council on the Arts, and Association for Asian Studies. He is a professor of English at the University of Miami.

LEYUNG-RYAN, TERESA (1958–). A **Chinese American** novelist, LeYung-Ryan was born in Hong Kong and grew up in San Francisco. Her debut novel, *Love Made of Heart* (2002), was a story about self-forgiveness, based on her relationship with her mother suffering from domestic abuse and mental illness. She lives in Oakland, California, and works as a writing career coach, among other things.

LI, LING-AI (GLADYS LI, 1910–?). A **Chinese American** playwright and director, Li was born in Hawaii to the first two Chinese doctors in Hawaii. When she was a student at the University of Hawaii, she published the first Asian American play, *The Submission of Rose Moy* (1924), in the school journal. The play centers around a Chinese **woman** who refuses to comply with an arranged marriage. She went on to publish two more plays, *The Law* *of Wu Wei* and *The White Serpent*. These plays were later anthologized in *Paké: Writings by Chinese in Hawaii*. Between 1932 and 1936, she studied music and **theater** in China and worked as a director of theater in the Beijing Institute of Fine Arts. She became political after the Japanese invaded China in 1937 and directed a documentary, *Kukan* (1941), about China's resistance to the Japanese military occupation, for which she received an Academy Award and the honor of meeting President and Mrs. Franklin D. Roosevelt in the White House in 1941. Her novel, *Children of the Sun in Hawaii* (1944), tells the story of a boy's friendships with children of different ethnicities. She also wrote an autobiography, *Life Is for a Long Time: A Chinese Hawaiian Memoir* (1972). This book chronicles her parents' immigration to and life in Hawaii more than her own life.

LI, YIYUN (1972–). A **Chinese American** novelist, Li was born and raised in Beijing and came to the United States in 1996. She received a B.S. from Beijing University, an M.S. in immunology from the University of Iowa (UI), and an M.F.A. in creative writing from UI. Her collection of short stories, *A Thousand Years of Good Prayers* (2005), won the Frank O'Connor International Short Story Award, Guardian First Book Award, and California Book Award for first fiction. Her debut novel, *The Vagrant* (2009), set in China in the late 1970s, follows a group of people in a small town after the execution of a young woman. Her stories and essays have been published in the *New Yorker*, *Best American Short Stories*, *O. Henry Prize Stories*, the *Paris Review*, and elsewhere. She is the recipient of a Whiting Writers Award, a Lannan Foundation residency, and a 2010 MacArthur fellow. She teaches at the University of California, Davis, and serves as an editor of the Brooklyn-based literary magazine *A Public Space*.

LIEBERMAN, KIM-AN (1974–). A **Vietnamese American** poet, Lieberman was born in Rhode Island to a Vietnamese mother and a Jewish father and raised in the Pacific Northwest. She holds a B.A. in interdisciplinary humanities from the University of Washington and a Ph.D. in English from the University of California, Berkeley. Her debut collection of **poetry**, *Breaking the Map* (2008), is a journey through mythical Vietnam and contemporary America. Her poems and essays have also appeared in *Poetry Northwest*, *Prairie Schooner*, *Quarterly West*, *ZYZZYVAZyzzyva*, *Calyx*, *Threepenny Review*, and anthologies such as *Asian America.Net: Ethnicity, Nationalism, and Cyberspace*, *Poets of the American West, and Jack Straw Writers Anthology.* She is the recipient of awards from the Jack Straw Writers Program and the Mellon Foundation for the Humanities.

LIM, GENNY (1946–). A **Chinese American** poet, performance artist, and playwright, Lim was born in San Francisco. She received a certificate in broadcast journalism from Columbia University. Then she studied **theater** arts at San Francisco State University and earned a B.A. and M.A. in English. Her better-known plays are *Paper Angels* (1978), which portrays seven Chinese immigrants detained at Angel Island waiting and hoping to be allowed into the United States, and *Bitter Cane* (1989), which, against the backdrop of the 1882 **Chinese Exclusion Act**, dramatizes the life of Chinese laborers at Hawaii's sugarcane plantations. *The Only Language She Knows* (1984) depicts the generational and cultural gap between mother and daughter. Her plays have been staged at **Asian American Theater Company**, Asian Pacific Theater Project (Sacramento), Asian Theater Group (Seattle), **Theater Mu** (Minneapolis), Zellerbach Playhouse (Berkeley), etc. Lim has published two books of **poetry**, *Winter Place* (1989) and *Child of War* (2003). She is widely known as the coeditor of *Island: Poetry and History of Chinese Immigrants on Angel Island, 1910–1940* (1980). This collection won the **American Book Award**. She has received other honors, including the Robert Frost Award for Poetry, the Lee and Lawrence First Prize Playwriting Award, the Bay Guardian Goldie Award for Outstanding Performance, the Distinguished Award for Culture from the San Francisco Chinese Culture Center Foundation, and the James Wong How Award.

LIM, PAUL STEPHEN (1944–). A Chinese **Filipino American** playwright, Lim was born in Manila, the Philippines. He received his education in English from Jesuits and Catholics. Moving to the United States at the age of 24 to pursue further education, he earned his B.A. and M.A. in English from Kansas University (KU). His first play, *Conpersonas* (1976), was performed in the Eisenhower **Theater** at the John F. Kennedy Center for the Performing Arts. His initial success launched him into a serious career of playwriting. He went on to write numerous plays, including *Points of Departure* (1977), *Chambers* (1979), *Flesh, Flash and Frank Harris* (1985), *Hatchet Club* (1985), *Homerica* (1985), *Woeman* (1985), *Figures in Clay* (1992), *Mother Tongue* (1992), *Report to the River* (1997), and *Zooks* (1980). Biblical allusions, verbal sparring, cinematic references are common to his plays, whose themes stay close to his personal life, such as sexuality, gender, racial identity, and colonialism, **exile**, and homelessness. Lim is the founder of the English Alternative Theatre (EAT) in 1989 on KU campus. Lim has also published **poetry** and short stories in journals as well as a book of fiction, *Some Arrivals, But Mostly Departures* (1982). He is the recipient of numerous honors, including the Palanca Memorial Award for Literature (the most prestigious in the Philippines), the Shubert

Playwriting Fellowship, the Midwest Playwrights Laboratory Fellowship, and a Kansas Arts Commission Fellowship in Playwriting.

LIM, PAULINO (1935–). A **Filipino American** novelist, Lim was born in the Philippines. He is a professor emeritus of English at California State University, Long Beach. He earned his M.A. at the University of Santo Tomas in Manila and his Ph.D. at University of California, Los Angeles. He was a Fulbright lecturer in Taiwan, a recipient of a grant from the National Endowment for the Humanities, and visiting professor at De La Salle University in Manila for more than a decade. He won first prize in the *Asiaweek* short story competition in 1985 with his fiction "Homecoming." He is the author of two short story collections: *Passion Summer and Other Stories* (1988) and *Curaao Cure and Other Stories* (2005), a three-act play, *Ménage Filipinescas* (2008), and five novels: *Tiger Orchids on Mount Mayon* (1990), *Sparrows Don't Sing in the Philippines* (1994), *Requiem for a Rebel Priest* (1996), *Ka Gaby, Nom de Guerre* (2001), and *Death of the English Zen Professor* (2011). Most of his writings portray how the Marcos regime changed people's lives.

LIM, SHIRLEY GEOK-LIN (1944–). A versatile and prolific **Chinese** Malaysian American poet, novelist, and memoirist, Lim was born in Malacca, Malaysia. She received British colonial educations at a Catholic convent school and the University of Malaya. She entered Brandeis University on scholarships she won and completed her M.A. and Ph.D. in English and American literature. One of the few Asian American writers who have achieved great success in almost all genres, Lim has written **poetry**, autobiography, novel, short stories, and literary criticism. Her books of poetry include *Walking Backwards: New Poems* (2010), *Listening to the Singer: New and Selected Malaysian Poems* (2007), *A Gathering of Poems from Pok Fu Lam* (2002), *What the Fortune Teller Didn't Say* (1998), *Monsoon History* (1994), *Modern Secrets* (1989), *No Man's Grove and Other Poems* (1985), and *Crossing the Peninsula and Other Poems* (1980). She has published three novels: *Princess Shawl* (2008), a **children**'s novel, *Sister Swing* (2006), and *Joss and Gold* (2001); three collections of short stories: *Two Dreams* (1997), *Life's Mysteries* (1995), *Another Country and Other Stories* (1982); and one autobiography, *Among the White Moon Faces* (1996). Her poetry is precise, lyrical, personal, and political, centering on major themes of race, gender, class, home, homelessness, and colonialism. She has received numerous honors, including the Commonwealth Poetry Prize, two **American Book awards**, National Endowment for the Humanities fellowships, a Mellon Fellowship, and a Fulbright Scholarship. She is a professor at the University of California, Santa Barbara. *See also* SOUTHEAST ASIAN AMERICAN LITERATURE AND THEATER.

LIMINALITY. This term comes from the Latin word *limen*, meaning "threshold," to describe a psychological, subjective, conscious state of being between two different existential planes. This term has become significant in recent theoretical movements, such as Critical Race Studies, Cultural Studies, and Postcolonial Theory. Pertinent in Asian American Literary Studies, the liminal is useful in describing the "in-between" space in one's cultural, religious, political, and linguistic identities. One can think of this as the transcultural space in which constant adaptation, negotiation, resistance, appropriation, and contestation take place in consciousness and action. For many Asian Americans, there is no monolithic place from which to think and speak, and the liminal produces **hybridity** or hybrid identities. The same can be said about their aesthetic choices; because of multiple influences, they often choose hybrid literary forms.

LIM-WILSON, FATIMA (1961–). A **Filipina American** poet, Lim-Wilson was born in Manila. After she completed her B.A. in English literature at the Ateneo de Manila University, she traveled to Japan to study Japanese literature and language for one year. She came to the United States and earned an M.A. in English with an emphasis in creative writing from State University of New York at Buffalo. Between 1986 and 1989, she worked in the Philippines as the confidential assistant to a politician, after which she returned to the United States for further studies. In 1992, she completed her Ph.D. in creative writing from the University of Denver. Her first book of **poetry**, *Wandering Roots/From the Hothouse* (1991), won both the Philippine National Book Award and the Colorado Book Award. She went on to publish *Crossing the Snow Bridge* (1995), which won the Ohio State University Press/The Journal Award in Poetry. Her poetry ranges from traditional English poetic forms to free verse, visiting a wide range of subjects including politics, imperialism, colonialism, family, love, the body, and sex. She has received honors including scholarships and grants from Breadloaf Writers' Conference, Duke University Writers' Workshop, Seattle Arts Commission, etc.

LIN, ADET (1923–1971). A **Chinese American** writer, Lin was the daughter of **Lin Yutang**. Born in Xiamen, China, she immigrated to the United States at the age of 13. After attending Columbia University between 1941 and 1943, she chose to work for the American Bureau for Medical Aid to China until 1946. Upon return, she began to work for the U. S. Information Service and the Voice of America. Her first novel, *Flame from the Rock* (1943), is a love story at the time of the war between China and Japan (1937–1945). She collaborated with her sisters **Lin Tai-yi** and Mei Mei Lin and published two autobiographies: *Our Family* (1939) and *Dawn over Chungking* (1941).

LIN, ALICE P. (1942–). A **Chinese American** autobiographer, Lin was born in Chengdu, China, and was taken to Taiwan by her parents when the Communists took over China. She attended Donghai University, a small Christian college, and then went to the University of Michigan to study social work. She eventually received her Ph.D. in social policy and planning from Columbia University. She currently teaches at the Fuqua School of Business at Duke University. She is the author of one autobiography, *Grandmother Had No Name* (1988). The book focuses on the social conditions and gender restrictions of **women** in pre-Communist China.

LIN, ED. A **Chinese American** novelist, Lin was born in New York City. He received a B.S. in mining engineering and M.S. in journalism from Columbia University. His debut novel, *Waylaid* (2002), depicts the life of a 12-year-old boy, son of Taiwanese immigrants. He is also the author of two detective novels, *This Is a Bust* (2007), and its sequel, *Snakes Can't Run* (2010). Both novels are set in NYC involving violence against Asians. He won the Members' Choice Awards from the **Asian American Literary Awards** for *Waylaid* and *This Is a Bust.*

LIN, GRACE. A Taiwanese American writer of **children**'s stories and illustrator, Lin was born to immigrant parents and raised in Upstate New York. A graduate of the Rhode Island School of Design, she has authored over a dozen books, including *Year of the Dog* (2005), *The Ugly Vegetables* (1999), *Dim Sum for Everyone!* (2001), and *Year of the Rat* (2007). Her most recent novel, *Where the Mountain Meets the Moon* (2009), was awarded the 2010 Newbery Honor. She lives in Somerville, Massachusetts.

LIN, HAZEL AI CHUN (1913–1986). A **Chinese American** surgeon and novelist, Lin was born in Foochow, China. She earned a B.S. from Yenjing University, an M.D. from the Beijing Union Medical College, and an M.S. from the University of Michigan. She served as an endocrinologist and surgeon at Jersey City Medical Center until her death. Lin authored four novels. Her first book, *The Physicians* (1951), is an autobiographical novel about an orphaned Chinese girl, granddaughter of a famous Beijing surgeon, who studies Western medicine. Lin's other three novels, *The Moon Vow* (1958), *House of Orchids*, and *Rachel Weeping for Her Children Uncomforted* (1976), center on **women**, marriage, love, and gender injustices.

LIN, KENNETH (1978–). A **Chinese American** playwright, Lin was born in the Bronx and raised in Long Island, New York. He attended Cornell University and the Yale School of Drama. He researches extensively for his plays and bases some of them on real stories, such as *Intelligence-Slave* (2010), the story of a concentration prisoner kept alive by the Nazis because he was believed to have invented the first hand-held calculator, which the Nazis wanted to present as a gift to Hitler, and *The Lynching of a Black Man in Rural, CA* (2010), telling the story of a woman from New England who arrives in rural California to meet the murderer of her son. Lin also writes plays that are science fiction. *Agency* (2005) is a story of a Catholic priest, turned assassin, who is on a mission to terminate a computer that has become conscious, and *Genius in Love* (2008), a verse play about Isaac Newton and Gottfried Leibniz coming together at the end of their lives to create a love potion. His other plays are *said Saïd* (2006), about the meeting of an Algerian political prisoner and his French torturer years later to decipher a message in a dying language only they understand, and *Po Boy Tango* (2008), about a Taiwanese immigrant and an African American chef cooking a banquet together as they investigate an incident 10 years ago. Lin's plays have been premiered, commissioned, and developed at **theaters** throughout the country, including the Alliance Theatre, Northlight Theatre Company, Alley Theatre, South Coast Rep, Manhattan Theatre Club, the Wilma Theatre, Arena Stage, and P73 Productions. Among the honors he has received are the Princess Grace Award, the Alliance Theatre's Kendeda Graduate Playwriting Competition, the Williamstown Theatre's L. Arnold Weissberger Award, and the TCG Edgerton New Play Prize. Recently, he was recognized by the Dramatists Guild as one of the 50 top playwrights to be watched.

LIN, TAI-YI (ANOR LIN or LIN WU-SHUANG, 1926–2003). A **Chinese American** novelist, Lin was born in Beijing, China. She was the daughter of the famous writer **Lin Yutang** and sister to the novelist **Adet Lin**. Lin Tai-yi immigrated to the United States with her family when she was a young child. She attended Columbia University from 1946 to 1949. Having married a Hong Kong government official, she lived in Hong Kong for many years and was well-known as the general editor of Hong Kong's *Reader's Digest* from 1965 to 1988. She and her family moved back to the United States and settled in Washington, D.C. At age 17, Lin wrote her first novel, *War Tide* (1943), and it was followed by *The Golden Coin* (1946). Both novels depict Chinese characters' struggles during the Sino–Japanese war (1937–1945). She went on to write three more novels: *The Eavesdropper* (1959), *The Lilacs Overgrow* (1960), and *Kampoon Street* (1964). *The Eavesdropper* is her only novel that is set in China and America that portrays a Chinese immigrant's life on both shores. Lin has collaborated with her sisters, Adet Lin and Mei Mei Lin, in writing their autobiographies, *Our Family* (1926) and *Dawn over Chungking* (1941).

LIN, YUTANG (1895–1976). A well-known **Chinese American** writer, Lin was born in Fujian, China, and died in Hong Kong. Lin earned his bachelor's degree at Saint John's University in Shanghai and then came to the United States to study for a doctoral degree at Harvard University. He left Harvard without completing his degree, moving to France first and then to Germany, where he earned a doctoral degree in Chinese at the University of Leipzig. From 1923 to 1926, he taught English literature at Peking University and returned to the United States in 1928. In addition to authoring more than 35 books in both Chinese and English, Lin is also known as the inventor of a Chinese typewriter. His friendship with Pearl Buck led him to write his first book in English, *My Country and My People* (1935), the first Chinese American best seller in the United States. His novels include *Looking Beyond* (1955), *Moment in Peking* (1939), *Chinatown Family* (1948), *The Flight of the Innocents* (1965), *The Vermillion Gate* (1953), etc. He was nominated for the Nobel Prize in 1975.

LINMARK, R. ZAMORA (1968–). A **Filipino American** novelist, poet, and playwright, Linmark was born in Manila, the Philippines, and moved to Hawaii at the age of nine. He is of Filipino, Spanish, and Swedish descent. He earned his B.A. and M.A. in literature from the University of Hawaii at Manoa. He is the author of two novels, *Rolling the R's* (1997) and *Leche* (2011). Both novels are a carnival of linguistic contortion, uproarious, irreverent, and satirical in their descriptions of transcultural experiences. He has also authored two books of **poetry**, *Prime Time Apparitions* (2005) and *The Evolution of a Sigh* (2008), which continues his novels' carnivalesque language. His plays include the one-acts *Bino and Rowena Make a Litany to Our Lady of the Mount*, *PM Talking with Kris Aquino*, and the full-length *Rolling the R's* (2008). Among the honors he has received are fellowships from National Endowment for the Arts, the Fulbright Foundation, and the Japan–United States Friendship Commission. He currently divides his home between Manila, Honolulu, and San Francisco.

LIU, AIMEE, E. (1953–). A **Chinese American** writer, Liu was born in Connecticut and is one-quarter Chinese. She majored in art at Yale University. She currently teaches creative writing at Goddard College. Working as a fashion model and flight attendant, she developed anorexia. Her first publication is an autobiography, *Solitaire* (1979), about her girlhood, the pressure of gender expectations, and her struggles with eating disorder. *Solitaire* was America's first memoir of anorexia. She went on to publish numerous self-help books. Her first novel, *Face* (1994), is the story of an Amerasian heroine coming to terms with her own mix-race identity and her family secrets. *Cloud Mountain* (1998) is based on her grandparents' romance, one between a white woman and a Chinese man, at the time of antimiscegenation in the United States. *Flash House* (2003) is part love story and part tale of espionage.

LIU, TIMOTHY (1965–). A **Chinese American** poet, Liu was born in San Jose, California, to Chinese immigrants. He received an M.A. from the University of Houston. He is the author of several books of **poetry**: *Bending the Mind around the Dream's Blown Fuse* (2009), *For Dust Thou Art* (2005), *E Pluribus Unum a.k.a. Kamikaze Pilots in Paradise* (2005), *Of Thee I Sing* (2004), a Public Weekly's Book-of-the-Year, *Hard Evidence* (2001), *Say Goodnight* (1998), *Burnt Offerings* (1995), and *Vox Angelica* (1992), a winner of the Poetry Society of America's Norma Farber First Book Award. He has also edited *Word of Mouth: An Anthology of Gay American Poetry* (2000). His poems have been included in many anthologies and have appeared in such magazines and journals as *American Letters & Commentary*, *Bomb*, *Grand Street*, *Kenyon Review*, *The Nation*, *New American Writing*, *Paris Review*, *Ploughshares*, *Poetry*, and *Virginia Quarterly Review*. He teaches at William Paterson University.

LO, STEVEN C. (1949–). A **Chinese American** novelist, Lo was born in Taiwan and moved to the United States in 1972 to pursue graduate studies at Texas Technologies University but completed his M.S. at Northwestern University. Since 1979, Lo has represented major U.S. and Asian companies in doing business with China. His novel, *The Incorporation of Eric Chung* (1989), drew upon his life and business experience and centered on themes of immigrants' alienation, cultural commodification, and corporal manipulation.

LODESTONE THEATRE ENSEMBLE. This is a **Korean American theater** in Los Angeles, established in 1999. Its mission is to develop, create, promote, and present edgy, compelling, and impassioned works that bridge communities through truthful and entertaining artistry. Tracing its origin to the **Society of Heritage Performers**, which veteran actor Soon Tek Oh organized in 1995. **Philip W. Chung** and Chil Kong are currently coartistic directors of Lodestone.

LOH, SANDRA TSING (1962–). A **Chinese American** artist and writer, Loh was born to a German mother and a Chinese father. Although she received training in classical piano, she studied physics and literature at the California Institute of Technology. She received her M.A. in English from the University of Southern California. Her first national fame came from a piano concert above a major freeway in downtown Los Angeles in 1987. Her short story "My Father's Chinese Wives" won the Pushcart Prize for literature in 1995, and her novel *If You Lived Here, You'd Be Home by Now* was voted one of the best books of 1997 by the *Los Angeles Times*. She has written plays, such as *Aliens in America* (1997) and *Mother on Fire* (2008); a collection of personal essays, such as *Depth Takes a Holiday: Essays from Lesser Los Angeles* (1996) and *A Year in Van Nuys* (2001). She currently produces an NPR segment entitled *The Loh-Down on Science*. She is a regular commentator on NPR's *Morning Edition*, PRI's *This American Life*, and other public radio programs.

LOOK, LENORE. A **Chinese American** writer of **children's books**, Look is a graduate of Princeton University and lives in Randolph, New Jersey, with her husband and children. She is the author of numerous children's books, including *Ruby Lu, Empress of Everything* (2006), *Ruby Lu, Brave and True* (2004), *Love as Strong as Ginger* (1999), *Henry's First-Moon Birthday* (2001), and *Uncle Peter's Amazing Chinese Wedding* (2006). All her stories depict the lives of Chinese American families and children. Her books have received numerous awards, such as the American Library Association Notable Book, Cooperative Children's Book Center Choices, and National Council of Teachers of English Notable Children's Books in the Language Arts.

LORD, BETTE BAO (1938–). A **Chinese American** writer, Lord was born in Shanghai, China. She immigrated to the United States with her family at the age of eight. After she received her undergraduate education from Tufts University, she enrolled in and received her M.A. from the Fletcher School of Law and Diplomacy. Accompanying her husband, the U.S. ambassador to China, Lord lived in Beijing between 1985 and 1989. Her first publication is nonfiction *Eighth Moon* (1964), based on the narrative of San San, Lord's sister who was left behind in China and separated from her family for 17 years. Her first novel, *Spring Moon* (1981), was a best seller. Set in prerevolutionary China, it tells the stories of Lord's family members. Her second novel, *The Middle Heart* (1996), portrays the friendship among three people whose loyalty to each other is repeatedly tested by private as well as public turmoil.

LOWE, PARDEE (1904–1996). A **Chinese American** autobiographer, Lowe was born in San Francisco. He received a B.A. from Stanford University and an M.A. from Harvard Business School. In the 1930s, he worked for a research organization, the International Secretariat of the Institute of Pacific Relations, particularly in the relationship between the United States and Asia. During World War II, Lowe enlisted in the U.S. Army. He published his autobiography, *Father and the Glorious Descendant* (1943), at a time when the political climate was favorable to Chinese Americans, as China and the United States were allies against Japan. The autobiography offers a window into traditional Chinese culture as well as the adaptation of Lowe's family to American culture. Lowe expresses in his autobiography his disapproval and rejection of his ancestral culture and his desire to conform to American culture.

LU, ALVIN. A **Chinese American** novelist, Lu earned his M.F.A. from Brown University. He is also the vice president of Publishing at Viz Media. His debut novel, *The Hell Screens* (2000), examines the relationship between a Chinese American ex-patriot living in Taipei and the supernatural fixation therein.

LU, CHI FA (1949–). A **Chinese American** memoirist, Lu was born in China and became an orphan at the age of three. He spent the rest of his childhood being shuffled among relatives. His sister-in-law sold him to a Communist couple for the price of five bags of rice. He was treated as a slave by the couple. He escaped to Hong Kong with his sister-in-law and nephew, where he begged to support his family. At 20, he came to the United States and realized his American Dream. His memoir, *Double Luck: Memoirs of a Chinese Orphan* (2000), recounts his life in China. He is a restaurateur in Morro Bary, California.

LUM, DARRELL H. Y. (1950–). A **Chinese American** writer, Lum was born and raised in Hawaii. He studied engineering at Case Institute of Technology in Cleveland, but after one year he transferred to the University of Hawaii (UH) and began taking creative writing classes. He received his B.A. in liberal studies, creative writing, and graphic design from UH. He then received an M.A. in educational communications and technology and a doctorate in educational foundation from UH. He has been an academic adviser at UH since 1974. Lum is widely known as the cofounder of **Bamboo Ridge Press** with **Eric Chock**. He has authored fiction, plays, essays, and **children's books**. He received the Elliot Cades Award for literature, the outstanding Book Award in Fiction from Association of Asian American Studies, and the Hawaii Award for Literature for his work on Bamboo Ridge. His trilogy of one-act plays portrays three generations of a Chinese family. *Orange Are Lucky* (1976) tells the story of the grandmother; *Fight Fire*

(1995) is the father's story; and *My Home Is down the Street* (1986) is the story of the son's conflict with his aging father. *A Little Bit Like You* (1991) centers on the theme of mixed blood identities. Lum's collections of fiction are *Sun, Short Stories and Drama* (1980) and *Pass On, No Pass Back* (1990). *See also* THEATER.

LUM, WING TEK (1946–). A **Chinese American** poet, Lum was born in Hawaii to second-generation Chinese American parents. While studying engineering at Brown University, he took some creative writing classes and developed his interest in **poetry** writing. This new interest led him to the editorship of the University's literary magazine. After graduation, Lum went to New York City and attended the Union Theological Seminary. During this time, he received the Poetry Center Award (now known as the Discovery/The Nation Award). In NYC, he met **Frank Chin**, whose views on Asian American literature greatly influenced Lum's work. In 1973, he moved to Hong Kong to learn Cantonese and returned to Hawaii in 1976. His sole book of poems, *Expounding the Doubtful Points* (1987), received an **American Book Award** and an Outstanding Book Award from Association of Asian American Studies. Lum also published numerous poems in journals, particularly in **Bamboo Ridge**.

M. BUTTERFLY. This is the best-known play in Asian American literature. Written by the **Chinese American** playwright **David Henry Hwang**, *M. Butterfly* won several awards, including the Tony Award for the Best Play of 1988. This is based on the true story that the French diplomat Bernard Boursicot carried on a 20-year love affair with the Peking opera singer Shi Pei Pu without knowing she was a man and a spy for Communist China. Boursicot was tried for treason by the French government, and only then did he realize his beautiful Chinese lady was a man. Hwang's play, named after Giacomo Puccini's opera *Madama Butterfly* and staged with significant parallels with, and ultimately ironic reversals of, Puccini's opera, brings into relief the orientalist fantasies the West has entertained about the East. With *M. Butterfly* standing for Monsieur Butterfly, Hwang explores the stereotypes that underlie and distort relations between **Eastern and Western** cultures (*See* EAST-WEST RELATIONS), and between men and **women**.

The play begins in a Paris prison cell where the Frenchman Rene Gallimard recalls his time as a clerk in the French Embassy in Beijing between 1960 and 1970. The flashback is set against the backdrop of the Vietnam War during which the French Embassy is privy to American military actions. Gallimard meets and falls in love with the Peking opera singer Song Liling at a performance of *Madama Butterfly*, in which she plays Cio-Cio San, the Japanese woman who commits suicide at the end when her faithless American husband Pinkerton abandons her. Gallimard imagines himself to be Pinkerton having the fate of a beautiful Asian woman in his hand. He remarks, "We, who are not handsome, nor brave, nor powerful, yet somehow believe, like Pinkerston, that we deserve a Butterfly. She arrives with all her possessions in the folds of her sleeves, lays them all out, for her man to do with as he pleases" (I.v.10). It is this fantasy about Western masculine power versus the Eastern feminine submission that blinds Gallimard from truths. Song Liling plays to a tee the beautiful, submissive, shy, vulnerable, and self-effacing "oriental" woman as she obtains and passes to the Chinese government French intelligence on the U.S. military deployment in Vietnam. When she is in danger of losing him, she invents the story of her pregnancy and produces a baby months later. After Gallimard returns to Paris, Song follows him and resumes their relationship and continues to supply the Chinese government with French intelligence. It is in 1986 that Gallimard is tried in court. Hwang's sharp critique of the West's self-image constructed against and over the East is made vivid by Song's ironic statement in the courtroom; "The West thinks of itself as masculine—big guns, big industry, big money—so the East is feminine—weak, delicate, poor . . . but good at art, and full of inscrutable wisdom—the feminine mystique" (III, I, 83). At the end of the play, Gallimard transforms himself into a Japanese woman, the Butterfly, and commits suicide.

MA-YI THEATER COMPANY. This group began in 1989 in New York City to showcase plays by **Filipino American** playwrights. The founders chose "Ma-Yi" because it was used by ancient Chinese traders, prior to Spanish colonization, to refer to a group of islands known today as the Philippines. The company has produced a number of original Filipino American plays, including the **Obie Award**–winning play *Flipzoids* by **Ralph B. Peña**. The company in recent years has broadened its mission to pan-Asian American **theater** and to develop new plays and performance works that represent Asian American experiences.

MAGICAL REALISM. This is a literary genre that is often associated with Latin American writers, such as Jorge Luis Borges, Pedro Paramo, Juan Rulfo, Isabel Allende, and Gabriel Garcia Marquez. In their writings, magical elements, miraculous happenings, or illogical scenarios appear in an otherwise realistic or even "normal" setting. Many Asian American writers, particularly South Asian and **Filipino American** writers, have employed magical realist elements in their writings. In **Cecilia Manguerra Brainard**'s novels, for instance, such as *Song of Yvonne*, *When the Rainbow Goddess Wept*, and *Magdalena*, gods and goddesses play significant roles in the lives of humans. **Chitra Banerjee Divakaruni** gives her female protagonists mystic vision and magic power. In her *Mistress of Spices*, the central character possesses the power of spices and uses this knowledge to heal, to predict the future, and to change the course of events. In *Queen of Dreams*, Mrs. Gupta, trained by a secret sisterhood, can enter into people's dreams and reveal to them what fortunes or misfortunes will befall them. **Linda Faigao-Hall** weaves Filipino mythology and folklore into contemporary life in her plays to offer an alternative worldview that values dreams, myth, and the occult, such as in *Woman from the Other Side of the World* and *God, Sex, and Blue Water*. **Vikram Chandra** in his novel *Red Earth and Pouring Rain* portrays a typing monkey who is the reincarnation of a 19th century poet. *See also* BA-

NERJEE, ANJALI; CHAI, MAY-LEE; DHOMPA, TSERING WANGMO; NIGAM, SANJAY; YAMASHITA, KAREN.

MAH, ADELINE YEN (1937–). A **Chinese American** autobiographer, Mah was born in Tianjin, China, and grew up in Tianjing, Shanghai, and Hong Kong. After she earned her medical degree from Britain, she moved to California to practice medicine. Her memoir, *Falling Leaves: The True Story of an Unwanted Chinese Daughter* (1997), recounts the abusive family environment in which she grew up and her overcoming of all obstacles to gain independence. It was adapted to a **children's novel** *Chinese Cinderella* (1999).

MAHAJAN, KARAN (1984–). A **South Asian American** novelist, Mahajan was born in Stamford, Connecticut, and grew up in New Delhi, India. He received his B.A. in English and economics from Stanford University. His debut novel, *Family Planning* (2008), chronicles a middle-class couple in contemporary, urban India, with 13 children and another on the way. His writing has appeared in the *Believer*, NPR's *All Things Considered*, the *Daily Beast*, the *San Francisco Chronicle*, *Granta*, *Bookforum*, *Tehelka*, the *New York Sun*, and the anthology *Stumbling and Raging: More Politically Inspired Fiction*. He is the recipient of several honors, including the Joseph Henry Jackson Award and fellowships from the Elizabeth George Foundation, the Camargo Foundation, the Ucross Foundation, and the Corporation of Yaddo.

MAK, KAM (1961–). A **Chinese American** author of **children's books** and artist, Mak was born in Hong Kong, and his family moved to the United States in 1971 and settled in New York City. He holds a B.F.A. from the School of Visual Arts in New York City. Mak is the author of an illustrated book, *My Chinatown One Year in Poems* (2011), a Parent's Choice 2002 Recommended Award Winner by the Parents' Choice Foundation. He has received numerous honors for illustration, including the Oppenheim Platinum Medal, the National Parenting Publication Gold Metal, and the Stevan Dohanos Award from the Society of the Illustrators. Mak is an assistant professor at the Fashion Institute of Technology. He lives in Brooklyn with his family.

MAKI, JOHN MCGILVRY (1909–2006). A **Japanese American** memoirist, Maki was born Hiroo Sugiyama in Tacoma, Washington. His **issei** parents, unable to support him, gave him up to Mr. and Mrs. Alexander McGilvry to raise. Later they officially adopted him. He received his B.A. in English and M.A. in Oriental Studies from the University of Washington. After spending two years studying in Tokyo on a Japanese government fellowship, he adopted the Japanese surname "Maki." He and his wife were interned with the rest of Japanese Americans in Seattle. However, soon he was recruited as a Japan specialist by the Federal Communications Commission and joined the Office of War Information in Washington, D.C. After the war, he enrolled at Harvard University and received his Ph.D. in Asian Studies. He privately published his memoir, *A Voyage through the Twentieth Century*.

MALLADI, AMULYA (1974–). A **South Asian American** novelist, Malladi was born in the small town of Sagar in central India. She arrived in the United States at the age of 20. She earned her B.A. in electronic engineering from Osmania University, Hyderabad, India, and her M.A. in journalism from the University of Memphis (UM), Tennessee. After graduating from UM, she worked as an online editor for a high-tech publishing house in San Francisco and then as a marketing manager for a software company in Silicon Valley. She is the author of five novels: *A Breath of Fresh Air* (2002), *The Mango Season* (2003), *Serving Crazy with Curry* (2004), *Song of the Cuckoo Bird* (2005), *The Sound of Language* (2007). These novels portray South Asian **women**'s lives in the West and explore the themes of gender, arranged marriage, mother–daughter relationship, and memory. Malladi currently resides in Copenhagen, Denmark, with her husband and two sons.

MASSEY, SUJATA (1963–). A **South Asian American** novelist, Massey was born in Sussex, Great Britain, of a German mother and an Indian father. Her family immigrated to the United States when she was five. She received her B.A. in creative writing from Johns Hopkins University. Her marriage to a navy man took her to Japan for two years. She is the author of nine detective novels, in which the main protagonist is Rei Shimura, a half Japanese and half Caucasian young woman. All nine novels center on her adventures in solving murder cases. *The Salaryman's Wife* (1997), winner of the Agatha Award for the best first novel; *Zen Attitude* (1998); *The Flower Master* (1999), the Macavity Award for the best novel; and *The Floating Girl* (2000) are all set in Japan. *The Bride's Kimono* (2001), *The Samurai's Daughter* (2003), *The Pearl Diver* (2004), *The Typhoon Lover* (2005), *Girl in a Box* (2006), and *Shimura Trouble* (2008) are mainly set in the United States.

MATSUEDA, PAT (1952–). A **Japanese American** poet, Matsueda was born in Fukuoka, Japan, to a Japanese American serviceman and Japanese national. She came to the United States at the age of seven and settled with her father's extended family in Honolulu, Hawaii. She studied English literature at the University of Hawaii. She was the editor of the *Hawaii Literary Arts*

Council Newsletter between 1977 and 1980 and founder and editor-in-chief of the *Paper*, one of Hawaii's early literary periodicals. *X* (1983) was her first volume of **poetry**, and two years later she published her second, *Fish Catcher* (1985). She is the winner of the Hawaii Elliot Cades Award for an emerging writer in 1988. Her poetry is described to be quiet and apolitical.

MATSUOKA, TAKASHI (1947–). A **Japanese American** novelist, Matsuoka was born in Japan and raised in Hawaii. He worked in a Zen Buddhist temple in Hawaii before he became a full-time writer. He is the author of two novels, *Clouds of Sparrows* (2005) and its sequel *Autumn Bridge* (2004). Both novels, set in 19th-century Japan, tell stories of love, adventure, and violence involving Western missionaries in Japan.

MCCUNN, RUTHANNE LUM (1947–). A **Chinese American** novelist, McCunn was born in San Francisco to a Chinese mother and a Scottish American father. She has lived in Hong Kong. She attended Diablo Valley College and the University of California, Berkeley. She is the author of six novels: *Thousand Pieces of Gold* (1981); *Pie-Biter* (1983), a **children's book** and winner of **American Book Award**; *Sole Survivor* (1985); *Wooden Fish Songs* (1995), winner of Jeanne Farr McDonnell Best Fiction Award from Women's Heritage Museum; *The Moon Pearl* (2000); and *God of Luck* (2008), winner of the Best Adult Fiction from the Chinese American Librarians Association and the Kiriyama Prize Notable Book. All these novels are historical, portraying the lives of Chinese and Chinese Americans, with the exception of *God of Luck*, which depicts the lives of Chinese coolies in Peru.

MCKINNEY, CHRIS. An Asian American novelist of mixed ancestry (**Korean**, **Japanese**, and Scottish), McKinney was born in Honolulu and grew up in Kahaluu on the island of Oahu. He holds a B.A. in English from the University of Hawaii. He is the author of four novels: *The Tattoo* (1999), *The Queen of Tears* (2001), *Bolohead Row* (2005), and *Mililani Mauka* (2009). Most of his works depict the dark underbelly of Hawaii, exploring themes of violence, drugs, poverty, and mixed race. He has also written a screen script, *Broke* (2011). He has won numerous honors, including the Ka Palapala Po'okela Award for Excellence in Literature and the Elliot Cades Award for Literature. He is a professor of creative writing at Honolulu Community College. *See also* JAPANESE AMERICAN LITERATURE AND THEATER; KOREAN AMERICAN LITERATURE AND THEATER.

MEER, AMEENA (1965–). A **South Asian American** novelist, Meer was born in Boston to Indian parents. Moving around the world with her diplomat father, she received her education in Great Britain, the United States, and India. Meer has published short stories in *Flaming Spirit* and *New Writing*, among others. She was managing editor of the New York–based art literary magazine *Bomb*. In her debut novel, *Bombay Talkie* (1994), Sabah, a second-generation adolescent immigrant, visits India and is drawn into the unraveling lives of her movie-star uncle and family, and her American-born friend Rani.

MEHTA, SUKETU (1963–). A **South Asian American** writer, Mehta was born in Calcutta and raised in Bombay and New York. He is a graduate of New York University (NYU) and the Iowa Writers' Workshop. He is the author of *Maximum City: Bombay Lost and Found* (2004), which won the Kiriyama Prize and the Hutch Crossword Award, an **Asian American Literary Award**, and was a Pulitzer Prize finalist. This book of nonfiction chronicles the uneasy return of a native son, who tells fascinating stories about Bombay—mafia dons, hired killers, gang members, and billionaires turning to an ascetic life as wandering Jain monks. His work has been published in the *New York Times Magazine*, *National Geographic*, *Granta*, *Harper's Magazine*, *Time*, and *Condé Nast Traveler*. Among his honors are a Whiting Writers Award, an O. Henry Prize, a New York Foundation for the Arts fellowship, and a Guggenheim fellowship. Mehta teaches Journalism at NYU.

MEHTA, VED PARKASH (1934–). A **South Asian American** writer, Mehta was born in Lahore, Pakistan. At age three, he suffered an attack of cerebrospinal meningitis and became totally blind. At 15 he came to the United States to attend the Arkansas School for the Blind in Little Rock, after which he went to Ponoma College and received his B.A. He then attended Oxford University to study modern history. Returning to the United States, he enrolled in Harvard on a fellowship and received his M.A. in 1961. He began contributing to the *New Yorker* in 1959, and two years later he became a staff writer and remained in this position until 1994. Mehta has published 17 books, some of which are memoirs and others are on Indian history, culture, and politics. He wrote his autobiography, *Face to Face* (1957), at the age of 22, recounting his life as a blind child and student. *Daddyji* (1972) and *Mamaji* (1979) describe his parents' lives before his birth. *The Ledge between the Streams* (1984) covers his life between nine and 15, with observations about the partition of India. *Sound-Shadows of the New World* (1986), *The Stolen Light* (1989), and *Up at Oxford* (1993) are three memoirs depicting his lives as a student at Arkansas, Poloma, and Oxford.

MEYER, MARLANE (1951–). A Polynesian American playwright with a multiethnic heritage, Meyer was born in San Pedro, California. She received a B.A. in **theater** from California State University, Long Beach. Her professional career began with *Etta Jenks* (1988), which premiered at the Los Angeles Theatre Center and won the Kesselring Award and the Dramalogue Award. *Kingfish* (1986) won the Dramalogue Award and the PEN Center West Award. *The Geography of Luck* (1989) also won the Dramalogue Award, and *Moe's Lucky Seven* received the Susan Smith Blackburn Prize. Meyer frequently presents fringe characters like prostitutes, pimps, gamblers, alcoholics, bartenders, homosexuals, and ex-cons. However, her plays are not exactly realistic. Incorporating certain mythical elements, her plays demonstrate the power of transformation and the ambiguity of identities. Many of her plays have been staged in Los Angeles, New York City, Chicago, and Great Britain. She has also written TV plays, such as *Sirens* for ABC, *Better off Dead* for Lifetime, *Life Stories* for NBC, and *Out of the Sixties* for HBO. In addition, she has taught playwriting at the Yale School of Drama. She is also the recipient of other honors, including the Brody Foundation Grant for Literature, the Creative Artists Public Service Grant, and a National Endowment for the Arts.

MIN, ANCHEE (1957–). A **Chinese American** memoirist and novelist, Min was born in Shanghai, China. She lived her formative years during the decade of the Chinese Cultural Revolution (1966–1976). Like many young people of her generation, she was sent to the farm to receive reeducation. When the Shanghai Film Studio came looking for talents, she was chosen and later given the lead role in *Red Azalea*, a film about Madam Mao. But with Mao's death, the political scene was dramatically changed. So was Min's fate, demoted from actress to a clerk. She came to the United States in 1984 and earned a B.F.A and M.F.A. from the Art Institute of Chicago. Her memoir, *Red Azalea* (1994), won the Quality Paperback Club's nonfiction award. Her novel *Katherine* (1995) depicts the first encounter between Chinese students and an American teacher after the Cultural Revolution. She went on to write more novels: *Becoming Madame Mao* (2001), a historical novel based on the life of Mrs. Mao, Jiang Qing; *Wild Ginger* (2002), set in the Chinese Cultural Revolution, depicting the lives of the young; *Empress Orchid* (2004), a first-person account of the life of Empress Dowager Cixi, from her humble beginnings to her rise as the Empress Dowager. *The Last Empress* (2007) is its sequel. *Pearl of China* (2010) fictionalizes Pearl Buck's girlhood in China and her friendship with a Chinese girl.

MIN, KATHERINE (1959–). A **Korean American** novelist, Min was born in Champaign–Urbana, Illinois. She received a B.A. in English from Amherst College and an M.S. from the Columbia School of Journalism. She currently teaches at the University of North Carolina, Asheville, and the Iowa Summer Writing Festival. Her debut novel, *Second Hand World* (2008), portrays a Korean American teenage girl trapped between two cultures, whose actions lead to her family's demise. The novel was a finalist for the PEN/Bingham Award, selected one of the best books of 2006 by *School Library Journal.* Min's short stories have appeared in numerous publications, including *TriQuarterly*, *Ploughshares*, the *Threepenny Review*, and *Prairie Schooner*, and have been widely anthologized, most recently in the *Pushcart Book of Stories: The Best Short Stories from a Quarter-Century of the Pushcart Prize.* "Eyelids" was listed as one of 100 distinguished stories in the *Best American Short Stories of 1997.* "The Brick" was read on National Public Radio's *Selected Shorts* program in 1999. "Courting a Monk" won a Pushcart Prize. Among the honors she has received are New Hampshire Arts Council fellowships and a grant from the National Endowment for the Arts.

MIRIKITANI, JANICE (1941–). A **Japanese American** poet, Mirikitani was born in Stockton, California, to **nisei** Japanese American parents. Her family was interned in Rohwer, Arkansas, when she was an infant. Although she was too young to remember the **internment** experience, it nevertheless is a chief subject in her **poetry**. She earned a B.A. in arts from the University of California (UC), Los Angeles, her teaching credential from UC, Berkeley, and took graduate courses in creative writing at San Francisco State University. She was the editor of the first Asian American literary magazine *Aion* (1970–1971). Mirikitani has published four books of poetry: *Awake in the River* (1978), *Shedding Silence* (1987), *We, the Dangerous* (1995), and *Love Works* (2003). In 2000, she was named San Francisco's second Poet Laureate. She is also the recipient of numerous awards and honors, including the American Book Lifetime Achievement Award for Literature, the Woman Warrior in Arts and Culture Award from the Pacific Asian–American Bay area **Women**'s Coalition, and the first Woman of Words Award from the Women's Foundation.

MIYAMOTO, KAZUO. A **Japanese American** autobiographer, Miyamoto was born in Hawaii to Japanese immigrants. He attended Stanford University and graduated from Washington University. Despite the fact that he served in the U.S. Army in World War I, he was interned during World War II. He authored two autobiographies. *Hawaii: End of the Rainbow* (1964), although written in the third person, is an illuminating autobiography. *One Man's Journey: A Spiritual Autobiography* (1981) recounts his Buddhist journey.

MIYAMOTO, NOBUKO (1939–). A **Japanese American** dancer, actress, and playwright, Miyamoto was born in Los Angeles and interned with her parents in Montana and later to Utah. She was one of the first Asian American dancers to draw the attention of respected American choreographers. At the age of 15, she debuted in the film *The King and I* and was a principal dancer in Broadway and film classics, such as *Flower Drum Song* and *Kismet*. She was a singer and dancer in *West Side Story*. In the 1960s, she became a political activist and collaborated with other Asian American activists on writing and performing music. In 1978, Miyamoto founded **Great Leap Inc.**, one of the oldest Asian American arts organizations, and remains as its artistic director. She coauthored and produced with Benny Yee the musical *Chop Suey* in 1980–1981. She wrote and performed her solo performance *A Grain of Sand* (1994). She was also the codirector and creator of *Laughter from the Children of War* (1996), which inaugurated **Club O'Noodles**, the first **Vietnamese American theater** company. Her other works include *Talk Story I and II* (1987), *Joanne Is My Middle Name* (1990), *To All Relations* (1998).

MOCHIZUKI, KEN (1954–). A **Japanese American** writer of books for **children** and young adults, Mochizuki was born in Seattle to **nisei** parents. He received his B.A. in communication from the University of Washington. He worked as an actor and journalist for a number of years before he turned to writing. His **children's books** include *Baseball Saved Us* (1993), *Heroes* (1995), and *Passage to Freedom: The Sugihara Story* (1997). *Beacon Hill Boys* (2002) is his **young adult fiction**. These stories explore the common themes of race, identity, and violence.

MODEL MINORITY. The term was coined by sociologist William Peterson in his article "Success Story: **Japanese American** Style" published in the *New York Times Magazine* in January 1966. Peterson reasoned that because of their family values and work ethics Japanese Americans were able to overcome prejudice and to avoid becoming a "problem minority." A second article similarly describing Chinese Americans was printed in *U.S. News and World Report* on 26 December 1966, titled "Success Story of One Minority Group in U.S." The article pointed out that **Chinese Americans** in **Chinatowns** were disciplined and self-reliant, and thus became a model of self-respect and achievement. These two articles appeared at the height of the Civil Rights Movement. "Problem minority," "family values," and "work ethics" were coded words insinuating criticisms of African Americans. This term was evoked again by Jason Richwine in "Indian Americans: The New Model Minority," published in *Forbes* on 24 February 2009. The concept of "model minority" has been regarded as a racial stereotype by many Asian Americans, one that handicaps and neutralizes them culturally and politically. Asian American writers have investigated and critiqued this concept. **Mei-mei Berssenbrugge** lampoons the notion in her **poetry**. In his story collection, *The Pang*, and the novel, *The Barbarians Are Coming*, **Davie Wong Louie** portrays Chinese American men successful in their professions but suffering from cultural and social impotence because of their anxiety over their model minority identity. **Suki Kim** critiques the myth of the model minority in her novel *The Interpreter*.

MOHANRAJ, MARY ANNE (1971–). A **South Asian American** novelist, Mohanraj was born in Sri Lanka and moved to the United States when she was two. She earned a B.A. in English from the University of Chicago, an M.F.A. in creative writing from Mills College, and a Ph.D. in creative writing from the University of Utah. She is a professor of English at Roosevelt University. She is the author of the collection of related stories *Bodies in Motion* (2005), which depicts the lives of two generations of a Sri Lankan family. *Silence and the Word* (2004) is a multigenre book of stories, poems, and essays exploring themes of sexuality and ethnicity. *Torn Shapes of Desire* (1997) is a collection of erotic fiction and **poetry**. She has also published two create-your-own erotic fantasy books: *Kathryn in the City* (2003) and *The Classic Professor* (2003).

MONG-LAN (1970–). A **Vietnamese American** poet, painter, photographer, and tango dancer, Mong-Lan was born in Saigon, Vietnam, and left the country on the last day of evacuation of Saigon. She received her B.A. in English and psychology from Excelsior College, her M.F.A. in creative writing from the University of Arizona, and was a Wallace E. Stegner Fellow in **poetry** for two years at Stanford University. She has authored four books of poetry. Her debut collection, *Song of the Cicadas* (2001), won the Juniper Prize, the Great Lakes Colleges Association's New Writers Awards for Poetry, and was a finalist for the Poetry Society of America's Norma Farber First Book Award. Her other collections of poetry include *Why Is the Edge Always Windy?* (2005), *Love Poem to Tofu and Other Poems* (2007), and *Tango, Tangoing: Poems and Art* (2008). Her poems often deal with the struggle of constructing one's identity through language, using language to sift through and sculpt the layers of being and consciousness. Among her numerous honors are a Fulbright Fellowship in Vietnam; inclusion in *Pushcart Book of Poetry: Best Poems from 30 Years of the Pushcart Prize*, 2006; Inaugural Visual Artist and Poet in Resident at the Dallas Museum of Art; and a National Endowment for the Arts grant. Her poetry has been anthologized in *Best American Poetry*, *Making More Waves*, *Watermark*, and *Asian American Poetry: The Next Generation.* Her poetry has also appeared in numerous literary journals, such as the *Kenyon Review*, the *Antioch Review*, and the *North American Review.* Her paintings and photographs have been exhibited in such venues as the Capital House in Washington, D.C., the Dallas Museum of Art, the Museum of Fine Arts in Houston, in galleries in the San Francisco Bay Area, and in public exhibitions in Tokyo, Seoul, Bangkok, Buenos Aires, and Bali.

MORI, KYOKO (1957–). A **Japanese American** novelist, Mori was born in Kobe, Japan. Her mother's suicide when she was 12 and a difficult stepmother heavily influenced her writings. She came to Arizona as an exchange student during her junior year and permanently immigrated to the United States when she was a college student. Mori received her B.A. at Rockford College and M.A. and Ph.D. from the University of Wisconsin, Milwaukee. Her **young adult novel** *Shizuko's Daughter* (1993) was a New York Times Best Young **Children's Book**, and it was followed by a book of **poetry**, *Fallout* (1994). Mori's memoir, *The Dream of Water* (1995), details her travels back to Kobe to make peace with her mother's suicide and to visit the family she left behind. Her second young adult novel, *One Bird*, was published in 1995. *Polite Lies* (1998), a book of essays, offers meditation on her life as a Japanese American woman in the Midwest. *Stone Field, True Arrow* (2000) is her first book of adult fiction that tells the story of a Japanese American **woman**'s emotional struggles after her father dies in Japan.

MORI, TOSHIO (1910–1980). A **Japanese American** novelist, Mori was born in San Leandro, California. Mori received high school education and continued his education by frequenting local bookstores and libraries after a day of work in a plant nursery. He and his family were relocated to an **internment camp** in Utah while his brother was serving in the U.S. Army. His best-known book of short stories, *Yokohama, California* (1949), was accepted for publication in 1941, but due to anti-Japanese sentiment during the war, Caxton Printers postponed it until after the war. This intervention altered the book's nature as well as the author's intention. Before the book was finally published, Mori added two stories set in the Topaz Camp, Utah (where he and his family were incarcerated) to an already complete collection of stories set exclusively in his California hometown, fictionalized as Yokohama. These two camp stories changed the tones of what would have been funny, hopeful, and uplifting stories about Japanese immigrants' Americanization. Critics have noted the influence of Sherwood Anderson's *Winesburg, Ohio* on Mori's *Yokohama, California* as it centers on a fictional community and its inhabitants. Mori also wrote a novel, *Woman from Hiroshima* (1979).

MOUA, POS. A Laotian American poet, Moua was born in Laos. He learned to read in a refugee camp in Thailand. Upon his family's arrival in the United

States, he entered the fifth grade in Spokane, Washington. He earned his M.A. in English from the University of California, Davis. His debut book of **poetry**, *Where the Torches Are Burning* (2002), expresses his love for rivers, oceans, and mountains and explores the themes of home, memory, and eternal return. Currently, Moua teaches at Merced Junior College and Merced High School in California. *See also* SOUTHEAST ASIAN AMERICAN LITERATURE AND THEATER.

MUEENUDDIN, DANIYAL. A **South Asian American** fiction writer, Mueenuddin is the son of a Pakistani father and an American mother and was brought up in Lahore, Pakistan, and Elroy, Wisconsin. He received his B.A. from Dartmouth College and J.D. from Yale Law School. He is the author of the fiction collection *In Other Rooms, Other Wonders* (2009), eight interconnected stories that picture a place and people plagued by class and ancestral tension and caught between the past and an uncertain future. His stories have appeared in the *New Yorker*, *Granta*, *Zoetrope*, the *Best American Short Stories 2008*, and *the PEN/O. Henry Prize Stories 2010*.

MUKERJI, DHAN GOPAL (1890–1936). A multigenred **South Asian American** writer, Mukerji was born in India and died by his own hands in New York. He immigrated to the United States at the age of 20 to attend the University of California, Berkeley. He earned a graduate degree from Stanford University in comparative literature and remained at Stanford as a lecturer. He is best known for his numerous **children's books**. He also wrote an adult novel, two books of **poetry**, three plays, and an autobiography. For his children's book *Gay-Neck: The Story of a Pigeon* (1928), Mukerji was the first Asian American author to receive the Newbery Medal. His children's novels also include *Kari, the Elephant* (1922), *Jungle Beasts and Men* (1923), *The Master Monkey* (1932), etc. His single adult novel is *The Secret Listeners of the East* (1926), and his poetry books are *Rajani: Songs of the Night* (1916) and *Sandhya: Songs of Twilight* (1917). His plays include *Chintamini: A Symbolic Play* (1914), *Layla-Majnu: A Musical Play in Three Acts* (1916), and *The Judgment of India* (1922). *Caste and Outcast* (1923), written when Mukerji was 35, gives an autobiographical account of his life as a Hindu and his adaptation to America.

MUKHERJEE, BHARATI (1940–). One of the best-known **South Asian American** novelists, Mukherjee was born and raised in Calcutta, India. She earned her B.A. from the University of Calcutta and M.A. in English and Ancient Indian Culture from the University of Baroda, India. She came to the United States to attend the Iowa Writers' Workshop and earned her M.F.A.

from it. Then she went on to earn her Ph.D. in English and comparative literature from the University of Iowa. Married to a Canadian writer, she moved to Canada, took Canadian citizenship, and returned to the United States in 1980. Currently, she is a professor at the University of California, Berkeley. Mukherjee has authored seven novels: *The Tiger's Daughter* (1971), *Wife* (1975), *Jasmine* (1989), *The Holder of the World* (1993), *Leave It to Me* (1997), *Desirable Daughters* (2002), and *The Tree Bride* (2004); two collections of short stories: *Darkness* (1985) and *The Middleman* (1988). She has coauthored with her husband two books of nonfiction: *Days and Nights in Calcutta* (1977) and *The Sorrow and the Terror* (1987). She is the recipient of the National Book Critics Circle Award for Best Fiction for *The Middle Man*. Most of her writings explore themes related to the meeting between **East and West** through immigrant experiences. It has been noted that Mukherjee often rejects the traditional society of the East in preference to the empowering and individualistic society of the West. Many of her female characters live between these two cultures, and these characters' transformation necessitates as well as is made necessary by violent collisions between these two cultures.

MUN, NAMIE (1968–). A **Korean American** novelist, Mun was born in Seoul, South Korea, came to the United States when she was eight, and grew up in Bronx, New York. She received her B.A. in English from the University of California, Berkeley, and M.F.A. in creative writing from University of Michigan. Her debut novel, *Miles from Nowhere* (2009), was shortlisted for the Orange Award and selected for *Booklist*'s Editors' Choice as well as Top Ten First Novels and Amazon's Best Fiction of 2009. The novel is a heartbreaking story of a Korean American teenage runaway on the streets of 1980s New York. Mun is the recipient of a Pushcart Prize and a Whiting Award. Her stories have been published or are forthcoming in *Granta*, *Pushcart Prize Anthology*, the *Iowa Review*, *Evergreen Review*, *Witness*, *Bat City Review*, *Tin House*, and elsewhere. She currently lives and teaches in Chicago.

MURA, DAVID (1952–). A **Japanese American** poet, memoirist, novelist, and performer, Mura was born in Illinois to **nisei** parents and raised in the suburbs of Chicago. Mura received his B.A. from Grinnell College and M.F.A from Vermont College. His first book, *A Male Grief: Notes on Pornography and Addiction* (1987), won the Milkweed Prize for Creative Nonfiction. His first book of **poetry**, *After We Lost Our Way* (1989), won the National Poetry Series Contest in 1989, and his second, *The Colors of Desire* (1995), is the winner of the Carl Sandburg Literary Award from the Friends of the Chicago Public Library. *Angels for the Burning* (2004) is his third book of poetry. Mura has written two memoirs: *Turning Japanese: Memoirs* *of a* ***Sansei*** (1991), which won a 1991 Josephine Miles Book Award from the Oakland PEN and was listed in the New York Times Notable Books of Year, and *Where the Body Meets Memory: An Odyssey of Race, Sexuality and Identity* (1996). His debut novel, *Famous Suicides of the Japanese Empire* (2008), depicts a Japanese American man's search for his lost family. Although Mura's parents were silent about their camp experience, the **Japanese internment** dominates his meditations on history, race, gender, and sexuality.

As a performer, Mura collaborated with African American writer Alexs Pate on a multimedia performance piece, *Secret Colors*, about their lives as men of color, which premiered for the Walker Art Center, Minneapolis, (1994) and has been presented at various venues throughout the country. This piece was adapted to a TV film *Slowly, This*, broadcast in the PBS series *Alive TV*. His other performance pieces and plays include *Relocations: Images from a Sansei* (1990), *Silence and Desires* (1994), and *After Hours* (1995). Mura's stage adaptation of **Li-Young Lee**'s memoir *The Winged Seed* premiered at Pangea World **Theater**. His play *Internment Voices*, cowritten with Esther Suzuki, received a Civil Liberty Public Education Fund grant and premiered with **Theater Mu**. Mura has received numerous awards, such as a Lila Wallace–Reader's Digest Writers' Award, a United States–Japan Creative Artist Fellowship, two National Endowment for the Arts Literature Fellowships, two Bush Foundation Fellowships, four Loft–McKnight Awards, several Minnesota State Arts Board grants, and a Discovery/The Nation Award.

MURAYAMA, MILTON (1923–?). A **Japanese American** novelist, Murayama was born and raised in Hawaii. Murayama was attending the University of Hawaii (UH) when Japan bombed Pearl Harbor. As a volunteer in the army, he served as an interpreter in India, China, and Taiwan during the second half of World War II. After the war, he returned to school and earned his B.A. in English from UH and M.A. in Chinese and Japanese from Columbia University. He is well known for the trilogy of the Oyama family in Hawaii: *All I Asking for Is My Body* (1975), *Five Years on a Rock* (1994), and *Plantation Boy* (1998). *All I Asking for Is My Body*, a recipient of the **American Book Award**, focuses on the themes of class and ethnicity in the life of the sugar plantation, and it's narrated by the son, Kiyoshi. *Five Years on a Rock* presents the voice of his mother, Sawa, and *Plantation Boy* tells the story of the older brother of Kiyoshi, Toshio. His most recent novel is *Dying in a Strange Land* (2008). Murayama has also written plays, such as *Yoshitsune* (1977), *Althea* (1982), and *All I Asking for Is My Body* (1989). *See also* THEATER.

MURRAY, SABINA (1968–). A **Filipina American** novelist and screenwriter, Murray was born in Lancaster, Pennsylvania, to a Filipina mother and a white father. She has lived in Australia and the Philippines, and she now lives in Amherst, Massachusetts, where she directs and teaches in the Creative Writing Program at the University of Massachusetts. She received her B.A. in art history from Mount Holyoke College and her M.A. in literature and M.F.A. in creative writing from the University of Texas (UT) at Austin. Murray's novel *Slow Burn* (1990) was published when she was only 21. She went on to publish another two novels, *A Carnivore's Inquiry* (2004) and *Forgery* (2007), and two collections of short stories, *The Caprices* (2002), which won the PEN Faulkner Award, and *Tales of the New World* (2011). Her novels and fiction explore themes of war, power, hunger, and authenticity. Murray is also a screenwriter and wrote the script for the film *Beautiful Country* (2005). Murray has received numerous honors, including a Michener Fellow at UT, Austin, a Bunting fellow at Radcliffe, a Guggenheim Fellow, a Massachusetts Cultural Council Grant, and a Fred Brown Award for the Novel from the University of Pittsburgh.

NAATAK. This is a group of Indian **theater** enthusiasts in the San Francisco Bay area, founded in 1995 by students at the University of California, Berkeley, and Stanford University. It is dedicated to staging thought-provoking plays and producing independent films.

NAMIOKA, LENSEY CHO (1929–). A **Chinese American** author of **children's books**, Namioka was born in China and came to the United States when she was nine. Her husband is a Japanese American. She studied mathematics at the University of California, Berkeley. She is the author of over 20 books, including *The Samurai and the Long-Nosed Devils* (1976), *White Serpent Castle* (1976), *Yang the Youngest and His Terrible Ear* (1992), *Yang the Third and Her Impossible Family* (1995); *The Loyal Cat* (1995), *Ties that Bind, Ties that Break* (1999), *The Hungriest Boy in the World* (2001), *An Ocean Apart, a World Away* (2002), *Half and Half* (2003), and *Mismatch* (2006). She won the Washington State Governor's Writers Award twice for *Island of Ogres* (1989) and *April and the Dragon Lady* (1945).

NAQVI, H. M. (1974–). A **South Asian American** novelist, Naqvi was born in Karachi, Pakistan, and grew up in Karachi, Islamabad, Algiers, and New York. He majored in English and economics at Georgetown University and received his M.F.A. in creative writing from Boston University. He is the author of *Home Boy* (2009), a story of three Pakistani boys who embark upon a journey to find their missing friend and are forced to question their identities, both as Pakistanis and Americans, in the rapidly changing world after 9/11. He is the recipient of a Lannan Fellowship and Phelam Prize.

NAQVI, TAHIRA (1945–). A **South Asian American** fiction writer, Naqvi was born and raised in Lahore, Pakistan. She received her education from Lahore College and Government College in Karachi. She moved to the United States with her husband and completed her M.A. in English from Western Connecticut State University. Her short story collections *Attar of Roses* (1998) and *Dying in a Strange Country* (2001) portray Pakistani **women**'s lives in the United States and Pakistan. Naqvi has also translated from Urdu several works of renowned writer Ismat Chughtai and a collection of stories by the well-known Pakistani writer Khadija Mastur.

NARASAKI, KEN (1958–). A **Japanese American** playwright and actor, Narasaki was born to **nisei** parents in Seattle, Washington. He studied **theater** at the Cornish School of the Arts. He is the former literary manager of the **East West Players**. Narasaki has written *Ghosts and Baggage*, *Innocent When You Dream*, co-authored with Doris Baizley, *The Mikado Project*, and he has adapted **John Okada**'s ***No-No Boy*** to the stage. These plays were produced at the Los Angeles Theater Center, the Electric Lodge in Venice, California, the Smithsonian Institution, **Lodestone Theatre Ensemble**, and the Miles Memorial Playhouse. He has received such honors as the **Kumu Kahua Theatre** Pacific Rim Playwrights Award and Pacific Rim Playwriting Award.

NARAYAN, KIRIN (1959–). A **South Asian American** novelist and memoirist, Narayan was born in Bombay, India, to a German American mother and an Indian father. She earned her Ph.D. in anthropology from the University of California, Berkeley, and currently teaches at the University of Wisconsin, Madison. Her novel *Love, Stars, and All That* (1995) is a coming-of-age story about an Indian woman in America and centers on the question of cultural, national, and racial identity. *Mondays on the Dark Side of the Moon* (1997) is a book of folktales, ethnography, and personal narrative. It was the fruit of Narayan's collaboration with a woman from the Himalayan foothills village. Her most recent work, *My Family and Other Saints* (2007), is a memoir about her youth in Bombay, India.

NARITA, JUDE (1952–). A **Japanese American** playwright, performer, and producer, Narita was born in Long Beach, California. Frustrated with the stereotypical roles available to Asian American actresses, she turned to writing and performing solo pieces that center on Asian American culture and history. Narita is best known for her one-woman play, *Coming into Passion/Song for a **Sansei*** (1985), which received the Los Angeles Drama Critics' Circle Award, a Drama-Logue Award for Creation and Performance, a James Wong Howe "JIMMIE" from the Association of Asian Pacific American Artists, and a VESTA Award from the Woman's Building of Los Angeles. Almost all her plays examine and celebrate the lives of Asian and Asian American **women**, such as in *Stories Waiting to Be Told* (1992), which depicts the lives of 10 very different Asian American women characters; *Celebrate Me Home* (1996); *Walk the Mountain* (1997), a play that dramatizes the continuing effects of the Vietnam War on Vietnamese and Cambodians;

With Darkness behind Us, Daylight Has Come (2000), a multi-media play on the **Japanese internment** experience.

NATIONAL ASIAN AMERICAN THEATRE COMPANY. This group produces European and American classics and new plays that are not written by or about Asians or Asian Americans. Yet, these plays are realized by an all-Asian American cast. Formed in 1988 by Richard Eng and Mia Katigbak in New York City, this company appeals to the kinship among disparate cultures by superimposing Asian faces on a non-Asian repertory.

NATIONAL BOOK AWARD, (THE). This is a prestigious book award by book publishers. On 15 March 1950, a consortium of book publishers sponsored the first annual National Book Award (NBA) Ceremony and Dinner at the Waldorf Astoria Hotel in New York City. With the mission to enhance the public's awareness of exceptional books written by Americans and to promote reading in general, NBA has become one of the nation's preeminent literary prizes. Today, the Awards recognize achievements in four genres: Fiction, Nonfiction, **Poetry**, and Young People's Literature. The winners, selected by five-member, independent judging panels for each genre, receive a $10,000 cash award and a crystal sculpture. Several Asian American authors have received this honor, including **Ai** for her poetry collection *Vice* (1999), **Ha Jin** for the novel *Waiting* (1999), and **Maxine Hong Kingston** for the nonfiction *China Men* (1980).

***NATIVE SPEAKER*.** This is the first novel by the best-known **Korean American** writer, **Chang-rae Lee**. Upon its publication, *Native Speaker* (1995) won numerous awards, including the **American Book Award**, PEN/Hemingway Award for First Best Novel, Barnes and Noble Discover Great New Writers Award, Quality Paperback Book Club New Visions Award, and Oregon Book Award. It was chosen for "One Book, One New York" in 2002. It is not surprising that the selection committee recognized in this novel the quintessential New York City with its hugely diverse population, legal and illegal, its political machinery, ethnic enclaves, its hustle and bustle, and its crime and violence.

The novel's protagonist is a Korean American man, Henry Park, who immigrated to the United States as a child. Driven by the desire to assimilate, to be a true American (meaning a member of the white middle class), or a native speaker, so to speak, Henry has acquired a good education, married a white woman, and become estranged from his immigrant father, a successful grocer. However, Henry perpetually feels like a stranger, belonging neither to the white American nor Korean American community. He is beginning to fear that he has betrayed both. In the first chapter, Lee opens a window to Henry's identity crisis through his wife Lelia's note to him upon leaving him. She describes him to be "surreptitious, B+ student of life, illegal alien, emotional alien, Yellow peril: neo-American, stranger, follower, traitor, spy . . ." Lee gives Henry a perfect profession—espionage, for what a spy does well is "passing." A spy is in constant disguise, masquerading as someone else; a spy is a stranger peeping into other people's lives; and a spy cannot make any emotional connections. Henry thinks of espionage as "the perfect vocation for the person I was, someone who could reside in one place and take half steps out whenever he wished . . . I thought I had finally found my truest place in the culture." Espionage, serving as the guiding metaphor of the novel, powerfully encapsulates an immigrant's alienated and alienating existence in America.

Henry's assignment to spy on a Filipino American doctor goes badly, and he almost blows his cover by sharing his real life stories with his victim. The story begins to pick up pace when Henry receives his new assignment to spy on the Korean American politician, John Kwang, who is in the race for mayor of New York City. John Kwang's charisma, confidence, elegant speech, and comfort in his own skin so deeply touch Henry that he unwittingly begins to identify John as a surrogate father. Against his professional instinct, Henry begins to get dangerously close to his victim, thus failing his assignment. At the end of the novel when John Kwang is disgraced and returns to Korea, Henry's world becomes dismantled, and out of it emerges a new Henry Park who finally takes "half-steps" in and recognizes his pattern of thought and behavior as cultural inheritances from his Korean parents.

Linked to this plot line is Henry's strained marriage after the accidental death of their son Mitt. His professional habit of hiding his emotions stands in the way of his relationship with his wife and his coming to terms with his son's death. Suffocated by the weight of his playmates, literally squashed, their son serves as another metaphor: the beautiful hybrid between two ethnicities and cultures cannot exist in this world of racial strife, and the dream of fusion has been squashed.

Writing in a precise yet lush prose that leads the reader deep into Henry's psyche, Lee packs this story with compelling metaphors, allegories, and intrigues. *Native Speaker* offers insights into the multiethnic metropolis of America as well as universal themes of love, belonging, father–son relationship, identity, and the alien in us all. *See also* EAST-WEST RELATIONS.

NAZARETH, PETER (1940–). A **South Asian American** novelist, dramatist, and literary critic, Nazareth was born in Uganda of Goan and Malaysian ancestry and was educated at Makerere University (Uganda) and at the Universities of London and Leeds in Great Britain. In 1973, he accepted a fellowship at Yale University and has remained in the United States ever since. He currently teaches at the University of Iowa. He is the author of two novels, *The General Is Up* (1984) and *In a Brown Mantle* (1972). He has also written two radio plays, "The Hospital" (1963) and "X" (1965), both broadcast by the BBC. *See also* SOUTHEAST ASIAN AMERICAN LITERATURE AND THEATER.

NEW, ILHAN (1895–1971). A **Korean American** autobiographer, New was born in Korea. His father, who was converted to Christianity by American missionaries, believed that it was best to educate his son in the United States. New came to Nebraska at the age of nine and lived in a Presbyterian household. He earned a B.A. from the University of Michigan in 1919. In 1926, he returned to Korea and ran a successful import business but came back to California 10 years later. He enrolled in the University of Southern California and earned an M.B.A. He wrote *When I Was a Boy in Korea* (1928), which offers little information about the author's life despite its classification as an autobiography. Instead, it introduces Korean culture.

NEZHUKUMATATHIL, AIMEE (1974–). A **Filipina**–Malayali Indian American poet, Nezhukumatathil was born in Chicago to a Filipina mother and a Malayali Indian father. She received her B.A. in English and M.F.A. in **poetry** and creative nonfiction from Ohio State University. She now teaches poetry writing and literature at State University of New York, Fredonia. She is the author of three books of poetry: *At the Drive-In Volcano* (2007), winner of the Balcones Prize; *Miracle Fruit* (2003), which won *Foreword Magazine*'s Poetry Book of the Year Award and was chosen for the Tupelo Press First Book Prize, was named cowinner of the Global Filipino Literary Award and was a finalist for the Asian American Literary Award in poetry; and *Fishbone* (2000), winner of the Snail's Pace Press Prize. Nezhukumatathil, informed by her Filipina and Malayali Indian backgrounds, writes lush poetry about love, loss, food, nature, and the land. She has received numerous awards, including a fellowship from the National Endowment for the Arts, the Pushcart Prize, the Angoff Award from the *Literary Review*, the Boatwright Prize from *Shenandoah*, the Richard Hugo Prize from *Poetry Northwest*, an Association of Writers and Writing Programs Intro Award in creative nonfiction, and fellowships to the MacDowell Arts Colony. Her other poems and essays are published in *American Poetry Review*, *FIELD*, *the Antioch Review*, *New England Review*, *Black Warrior Review*, *Poetry Northwest*, *Prairie Schooner*, *Tin House*, *Shenandoah*, *the Southern Review*, *Chelsea*, *Mid-American Review*, *the Southeast Review*, *River Styx*, *Beloit Poetry Journal*, *Quarterly West*, *Crab Orchard Review*, *Virginia Quarterly*,

Slate, and *North American Review*. *See also* FILIPINO AMERICAN LITERATURE AND THEATER.

NG, FAE MYENNE (1957–). A **Chinese American** novelist, Ng was born in San Francisco. She attended the University of California, Berkeley, and received her M.F.A. from Columbia University. Her first novel, *Bone* (1993), is the story of a Chinese immigrant family in San Francisco's **Chinatown** and explores the themes of identity, alienation, and the **paper son**. *Bone* was nominated for the PEN/Faulkner Award and became a national best seller. Her second novel, *Steer toward Rock* (2008), winner of an **American Book Award**, continues the theme of the paper son. Again set in San Francisco's Chinatown, the novel portrays a Chinese man who purchases his identity at the price of two years of labor and a fake marriage. Ng has also authored numerous short stories published in literary magazines like *Harpers*, the *New Republic*, *Granta*, and *City Lights Review*. She has also received a grant from National Endowment for the Arts and a Guggenheim Fellowship.

NG, MEI (1967–). A **Chinese American** novelist, Ng was born and raised in New York to Chinese immigrant parents. She earned a B.A. in **women**'s studies from Columbia University. She is the author of one widely reviewed novel, *Eating Chinese Food Naked* (1998). The novel tells the story of Ruby Lee, a graduate of women's studies from Columbia, and her summer stay at her parents' in Queens. It centers on sexuality, the mother–daughter relationship, and personal freedom.

NGAI, SIANNE (1971–). A **Japanese American** poet, Ngai was born in Washington, D.C., and raised in Hawaii. She received her B.A. in English and M.F.A. in creative writing from Brown University and Ph.D. from Harvard University. Currently, she teaches English at University of Los Angeles. She is the author of two books of **poetry**, *Criteria* (1998) and *Discredit* (1997), which explore themes of language, objects, and representation.

NGOR, HAING S. (1941–1996). A Cambodian American autobiographer, Ngor was born in Cambodia and earned his medical degree from the University of Phnom Penh. In 1979, Ngor escaped from the Khumer Rouge to Thailand and arrived in the United States in 1980. Ngor appeared in the films *The Killing Fields* (1984) and *Heaven and Earth* (1993), and for the former he won an Academy Award for his performance. He was robbed and murdered in Los Angeles by Asian American gangs. Ngor authored an autobiography, *A Cambodian Odyssey* (1987), which recounts his imprisonment and torture by the Khmer regime and his life as a refugee. *See also* SOUTHEAST ASIAN AMERICAN LITERATURE AND THEATER.

NGUYEN, BICH MINH (1974–). A **Vietnamese American** writer, Nguyen was born in Saigon, Vietnam. The night before the city fell, her family fled Vietnam by ship. After staying in refugee camps in Guam and at Fort Chaffee in Arkansas, they settled in Grand Rapids, Michigan. She received an M.F.A. in creative writing from the University of Michigan and teaches creative writing at Purdue University. Her memoir, ***Stealing Buddha's Dinner*** (2007), received the PEN/Jerard Award from the PEN American Center, in which she writes about growing up in a Vietnamese household in an "All-American" city in the 1980s. Her novel, *Short Girls* (2009), portrays the relationship of two Vietnamese American sisters and their reconciliation with their father. Common themes in her work include generational conflicts, **assimilation**, alienation, and **East-West relations**. She is married to novelist Porter Shreve.

NGUYEN, HOA (1967–). A **Vietnamese American** poet, Nguyen was born near Saigon and grew up in the Washington, D.C., area. She studied **poetry** at New College in San Francisco. She is the author of five books of poems: *Dark* (1998), *Parrot Drum* (2000), *Your Ancient See Through* (2001), *Red Juice* (2005), and *Hecate Lochia* (2009). Her poems often explore themes of domesticity, motherhood, marriage, art, and work. She currently lives in Austin, Texas, where she teaches creative writing.

NGUYEN, KIEN (1967–). A **Vietnamese American** novelist and memoirist, Nguyen was born in South Vietnam to a Vietnamese mother and an American father. He came to the United States in 1985 after spending time at a refugee camp in the Philippines. He is a dentist in New York City and the author of *The Unwanted: A Memoir of Childhood* (2001) and two novels: *The Tapestries* (2002), an epic tale of family, greed, revenge, and love set in Vietnam during the early decades of the 20th century; and *Le Colonial* (2004) about three French missionaries in Vietnam in 1773.

NGUYEN, QUI (1976–). A **Vietnamese American** playwright, Nguyen was born in El Dorado, Arkansas. He holds a B.A. in **theater** from Louisiana Tech University and an M.F.A. in playwriting from Ohio University. He is an artistic director of the **Obie Award** and Caffe Cino Award winning Vampire Cowboys Theatre Company, whose productions, penned and choreographed by Nguyen, have performed to sold-out audiences at the New York International Fringe Festival and been published nationally in *Place and Playwrights 2005*. His plays include *Soul Samurai*, *Alice in Slasherland*, *Fight Girl Battle World*, *Trial by Water*, *Living Dead in Denmark*, *Stained Glass Ugly*, *A Beginner's Guide to Deicide*, *Men of Steel*, *Bike Wreck*, and *Vampire Cowboy Trilogy*. He is a member of New Dramatists, Ensemble Studio Theatre, and the codirector of **Ma-Yi Theater Company**'s Writers Lab. His plays have been produced at Metropolitan Playhouse, Vital Theatre, Ma-Yi Theater, Noho Studios, Fourth Wall Productions, Channel Z, Theater Wit, Mark Taper Forum, the Goodman, the Lark, New Dramatists, the New Group, **Pan Asian Repertory Theatre**, and the Immigrant's Theatre Project. He has received numerous honors, including the New Dramatists Playwriting Fellowship, nomination for Best Production in 2006 and Best Choreographer by the 2005 and 2007 New York Innovative Theatre Awards.

NIEH, HUALING (1925–?). A **Chinese American** novelist, Nieh was born in China. She received her B.A. in English from National Central University, China. In 1949, she went to Taiwan and became an editor of *Free China*, a popular magazine. During her residence in Taiwan, she wrote several novels and translated American literature to Chinese. In 1964, she came to the United States as a writer-in-residence in the Iowa Writers' Workshop and received an M.F.A. In 1967, Nieh cofounded the Iowa International Writing Program with Paul Engle, who became her husband in 1971. Her best-known novel is *Mulberry and Peach: Two Women of China* (1988), which centers on the female character Mulberry's psychological turmoil brought about by political oppression. Her other novels and story collections include *The Lost Golden Bell* (1960), *Far Away, a River* (1984), *The Purse: A Collection of Short Stories Written in English* (1959), and *Tales from the Deer Garden* (1996).

NIGAM, SANJAY (1959–). A **South Asian American** novelist, Nigam was born in Delhi, India, and brought by his parents to the United States as an infant and raised in Arizona. He is a physician, researcher, and professor of pediatrics and medicine at the University of California, San Diego. Influenced by Russian novelists and Latin American **magical realists**, Nigam's novels are allegorical, witty, fantastic, and filled with medical lore. His first novel, *The Snake Charmer* (1998), tells the story of madness and redemption of a snake charmer. His second novel, *Translation Man* (2003), is told from the perspective of a resident at a hospital in New York's Little India, who meets a man, Translation Man, who harbors seven transplanted organs from people of different religions. Nigam has also published short stories in *Grand Street* and the *Kenyon Review*.

NISEI. This is a Japanese term used in North America, South America, and Australia to specify the children born in the new country to the first generation of Japanese immigrants. *See also* ISSEI; SANSEI.

NISHIKAWA, LANE (1956–). A **Japanese American** playwright, filmmaker, and performer, Nishikawa was born in Hawaii. He moved with his family as a child to San Diego. He is best known for his trilogy: *Life in the Fast Lane* (1981), *I am on a Mission from Buddha* (1989), and *Mifune and Me* (1994), which examines the ironies of being an Asian American actor. *I am on a Mission from Buddha* was adapted to a TV show and aired across the United States in 1994. He went on to coauthor and perform *The Gate of Heaven* (1994), a story of the unlikely friendship sustained for half a century between a **nisei** soldier and the Jewish prisoner he liberates. Between 1986 and 1994, Nishikawa served as the artistic director of the **Asian American Theater Company**. In 2005, he directed and starred in the independent feature film *Only the Brave*, a fictional account of the rescue of the Lost Battalion by the 100th Infantry Battalion/442nd Regimental Combat Team, a segregated Japanese American fighting unit during World War II. He has written and directed two short films about World War II veterans, *Forgotten Valor* (2001) and *When We Were Warriors* (2000).

NO-NO BOY. This is one of the best-known **Japanese American** novels. Published by **John Okada** in 1957, it was the first novel to depict the aftermath of the **Japanese American internment**. The book was released by the Tokyo branch of Charles Tuttle but received little public reception. It was not until 1970 when **Jeffrey Chan** chanced upon it in a J-Town San Francisco second-hand bookstore that it became discovered. In 1976, a group of Asian American writers (including **Frank Chin**, Jeffrey Chan, **Lawson Inada**, and **Shawn Wong**) pooled their resources to form the Combined Asian–American Resources Project (CARP) and reprinted the novel. Upon its republication, *No-No Boy* gained immediate public attention and has since become a classic in Asian American literature.

No-No Boy centers on a Japanese American young man, Ichiro Yamada, who is interned during World War II for two years and then imprisoned in a federal prison for another two for answering negatively both loyalty questions put to all men of Japanese descent. At the opening of the novel, Ichiro is released from the prison and returns to Seattle, to a home that is both broken and divided, with his mother clinging to the belief that Japan is victorious in the war, his father dominated by his wife painfully and bitterly keeping her belief intact, and his brother Taro dropping out of high school and joining the army to spite his parents. Shame, anger, guilt, and confusion dominate Ichiro's life while he searches for answers about who he is. Living in an America that demands **assimilation**, he finds no way to articulate his **hybrid** identity. Instead, he is torn between his mother's culture and his own. Ichiro screams at his mother, "I don't understand you who were the half of me that is no more and because I don't understand what it was about that half that made me destroy the half of me that was American" (16).

Readers of *No-No Boy* generally experience feelings of urgency and frantic depression. The sentences move at such a tempo that one's heartbeat quickens as though catching the end of a sentence were paramount to the successful rescue of the suffering protagonist. Born out of rage, fear, ambivalence, and revulsion, *No-No Boy* is a breathless narration about Ichiro's identity crisis and his inability to choose an identity. Okada offers four scenarios concerning the possible fate of Japanese American men during that era. Kenji, a Yes-Yes Boy, has fought for the United States but dies a gradual death from a war wound. Fred, another No-No Boy, loathes himself so much he actively and successfully seeks self-destruction. Bull, another Yes-Yes Boy, displaces self-loathing in his contempt for his fellow Japanese Americans but collapses under the weight of hollowness. Ichiro never finds a resolution, and the best the novelist can offer is a "faint and elusive insinuation of promise" for a community at the end of the novel (251).

NO-NO BOYS. This term refers to the **Japanese Americans** who answered negatively to loyalty question 27 and 28 while **interned** during World War II. On 8 February 1943, the War Relocation Authority and the Army gave out applications called "Statement of U.S. Citizenship of Japanese American Ancestry." All Japanese men who were 17 and older had to answer a questionnaire. Question 27: "Are you willing to serve in the armed forces of the United States on combat duty wherever ordered?" Question 28: "Will you swear unqualified allegiance to the United States of America and faithfully defend the United States from any or all attack by foreign or domestic forces, and forswear any form of allegiance or obedience to the Japanese emperor, or any other foreign government, power, or organization?" Both questions posed dilemmas. Question 27 presented a contradiction between being interned as dangerous aliens and being drafted by the U.S. Amy. Question 28 presupposed allegiance to the Japanese emperor, and to answer "yes" meant the admission of this allegiance. Many Japanese American men answered "no" to both questions, and the consequence was two years in a federal prison. *See also* KASHIWAGI, HIROSHI; OKADA, JOHN.

NOGUCHI, RICK (1967–). A **Japanese American** poet, Noguchi was born in Los Angeles. He received his B.A. in English from California State University, Long Beach, an M.F.A. in creative writing from Arizona State University, and an M.B.A. from Pepperdine University. He is the author of two books of **poetry**: *The Wave He Caught* (1995), winner of the Pearl Editions Prize, and *The Ocean inside Kenji Takezo* (1996), winner of the Association of Writers and Writing Programs (AWP) Award in Poetry. Both books of poetry exploit the riches of water metaphors, such as wave and surfing, for the journey of life. Noguchi also coauthored with Deneen Jenks a **children**'s book, *Flowers from Mariko* (2001). His work has been published in a variety of journals and anthologies, including *Asian American Poetry: The Next Generation, Place as Purpose: Poetry from the Western States, Motion: American Sports Poems, American Poetry: The Next Generation, The New Young American Poets: An Anthology*, and *Fever Dreams: Contemporary Arizona Poets.*

NOGUCHI, YONE (1875–1947). A **Japanese American** poet, Noguchi was born in Japan and came to the United States in 1893. In San Francisco, he worked as a Japanese-language newspaper delivery boy, a domestic servant, and a dishwasher. After he gained English proficiency, he worked as a translator of the Japanese-language newspaper, the *Soko Shimbun* (San Francisco News). Noguchi began writing English **poetry** in the 1890s and published initially in literary journals, such as the *Lark* (San Francisco), *Chap-Book* (Chicago), and *Philistine* (New York). In 1900, he traveled to the East Coast and settled down in New York. In 1904, he took a professorship in American literature at now Keio University, Japan, which he kept for 40 years. During World War II, Noguchi wrote propagandistic poetry in Japanese to advance the cause of Japan's imperialism. His English poetry consists of seven collections, including *Seen and Unseen, or Monologues of Homeless Snail* (1897), *The Voice of the Valley* (1897), *From the Eastern Sea* (1903), and *The Pilgrimage* (1909). He is also the author of two novels, *The American Diary of a Japanese Girl* (1902) and *The American Letters of a Japanese Parlor-Maid* (1905), and an autobiography, *The Story of Yone Noguchi* (1915). Noguchi played a significant role in promoting ***haiku*** and **Noh** drama in the West and modern British and American literature in Japan.

NOH AND KYOGEN THEATRE. Traditional Japanese forms of performing arts that originated in the eighth century (Noh) and the 14th century (Kyogen). Today, they are a combined form of **theater**. Noh is a musical drama evoking quiet elegance and conveys symbolic messages about human destiny on a simple stage. In the highly stylized and refined performance, the main actor wears a mask that represents female or nonhuman (divine, demonic, and animal) characters. Kyogen is a comic drama whose intention is to arouse laughter. Accompanied by music of the flute, drum, and gong, actors perform folktales and stories of the common people. All roles in Noh and Kyogen theater are played by men. Several Asian American dramatists borrow from these forms, such as **Brenda Wong Aoki** and **Yone Noguchi**.

NORTHWEST ASIAN AMERICAN THEATRE COMPANY. One of the four Asian American **theater** groups, it was founded in 1981 in Seattle, whose preincarnation was **Asian Exclusion Act**. Bea Kiyohara was its artistic director. This theater group established itself as the major Asian American theater company in the Northwest region and community-based theater in Seattle's International District.

NUNEZ, SIGRID (1951–). A **Chinese American** novelist, Nunez was born in New York City to a Chinese–Panamanian father and a German mother. She received her B.A. from Barnard College and her M.F.A. from Columbia University. She is the author of six novels: *A Feather on the Breath of God* (1995), winner of the Association of Asian American Studies Award for best novel of the year; *Naked Sleeper* (1996); *Mitz: The Marmoset of Bloomsbury* (1998), winner of the Richard and Hinda Rosenthal Foundation Award from the American Academy of Arts and Letters; *For Rouenna* (2001); *The Last of Her Kind* (2006); and *Salvation City* (2010). She has also written a memoir about Susan Sontag, *Sempre Susan* (2011). Among the journals she has contributed to are the *New York Times*, *Harper's*, *McSweeney's*, the *Believer*, the *Threepenny Review*, *Tin House*, and *O: The Oprah Magazine.* Nunez's writings center on language, memory, identity, class, and writing itself. She has received numerous honors, including a Whiting Writer's Award, a fellowship from the New York Foundation for the Arts, a residency from the Lannan Foundation, a Rome Prize Fellow in Literature at the American Academy in Rome, and a Berlin Prize Fellow at the American Academy in Berlin. In 2003, she was elected as a Literature Fellow to the American Academy of Arts and Sciences.

OBIE AWARDS. These Off-Broadway **Theater** Awards are annual awards presented by the *Village Voice* to theater artists and groups in New York City. The awards were launched in 1956 by Edwin Fancher, publisher of the *Village Voice,* under the direction of theater critic Jerry Tallmer. Initially, only off-Broadway productions were eligible; in 1964 off-off-Broadway productions were made eligible. Except for Lifetime Achievement and Best New American Play awards, there are no fixed categories and the winning actors and actresses are in a single category titled performance. There are no announced nominations. Awards in the past have included performance, direction, best production, design, special citations, and sustained achievement. Not every category is awarded every year. The *Village Voice* also awards annual Obie grants to selected companies, totaling $10,000. Asian American playwrights who have won this award include **David Henry Hwang** for *FOB* (1980), *Golden Child* (1996), and *Yellow Face* (2007); **Qui Nguyen** as artistic director of Vampire Cowboys Theatre Company; **Ping Chong** for *Humboldt's Current* (1977); **Young Jean Lee** as an emerging playwright; **Chay Yew** for direction; and **Ralph B. Peña** for *Flipzoids* (1996).

OEUR, U SAM (1936–). A Cambodian American poet, Oeur was born in Cambodia. After finishing his studies at the School of Arts and Trades in Phnom Penh, he came to California to study industrial arts at California State University, Los Angeles. Discovering his talent for **poetry**, the Iowa Writers' Workshop admitted him, from which he earned an M.F.A. There he met and formed a life-long friendship with poet Kenneth McCullough, who became Oeur's translator. He returned to Cambodia in 1968, and in the 1970s he served in Lon Nol's internal security army, in the National Assembly, as a delegate to the United Nations, and was appointed secretary general of the Khmer League for Freedom. However, when the Khmer Rouge became the ruling power, Oeur and his family were sent to labor camps, where he lost his twin daughters. With McCullough's help, Oeur was allowed to immigrate to the United States as a fellow of the International Writing Program at the University of Iowa. His book of poetry, *Sacred Vows* (1998), a 1999 finalist for the Minnesota Book Award in poetry, recounts Cambodian history and his personal tribulations, drawing on Cambodian myths, folktales, and prophecies. He has also written a memoir, *Crossing Three Wildernesses* (2005). *See also* SOUTHEAST ASIAN AMERICAN LITERATURE AND THEATER.

OKADA, JOHN (1923–1971). A **Japanese American** novelist, Okada was born in Seattle to Japanese immigrant parents and died of a heart attack in Los Angeles. He received his B.A. in English from the University of Washington and M.A. in English from Columbia University. During World War II, he and his family were incarcerated in a **Japanese internment** camp in Idaho. He took the only exit allowed by volunteering for military duty and served as a sergeant in the U.S. Air Force until 1946. After the war, he worked as a librarian in Seattle and then in Detroit, during which time he began writing his novel, ***No-No Boy*** (1957). At the time of his death, he left behind the draft of a second novel about the experience of the first generation of Japanese Americans. His wife burned it along with other manuscripts. Although *No-No Boy* is Okada's only published work of fiction, it has become a classic in Asian American literature and is regarded as the first fiction on the experience of Japanese American internment. The novel centers on a young Japanese American's painful quest for identity after his release from a two-year term in a Federal prison for answering "no-no" to the loyalty questions posed by the U.S. government.

OKITA, DWIGHT (1958–). A **Japanese American** poet and playwright, Okita was born and raised in Chicago to **nisei** Japanese Americans. During World War II, his parents were interned as enemy aliens. Okita majored in **theater** at the University of Illinois, Chicago, and graduated with a B.A. in creative writing. He has written several plays, including *Dream/Fast* (1987), *Richard Speck* (1991), *The Salad Bowl Dance* (1993), *The Rainy Season* (1993), and *The Spirit Guide* (1994). He wrote in collaboration with three other playwrights *The Radiance of a Thousand Suns: The Hiroshima Project* (1995). He also wrote a film script, *My Last Week on Earth* (1998). *Crossing with the Light* (1992) is Okita's first book of poems. His most recent publication is a futuristic science fiction, *The Prospect of My Arrival* (2009), about the choices of an unborn child named Prospect. He is the recipient of an Illinois Arts Council Fellowship for achievement in **poetry**. *See also* THEATER.

OKUBO, MINE (1912–2001). A **Japanese American** artist and writer, Okubo was born in Riverside, California, to Japanese immigrant parents. She received her M.F.A. from the University of California at Berkeley. A recipient of the Bertha Taussig Memorial Traveling Fellowship in 1938, Okubo spent two years traveling in France and Italy, where she continued her development as an artist. After the bombing of Pearl Harbor (7 December 1941), she and her family were sent to the **Japanese Internment** camp. After her release, she relocated to New York and published a book of her experiences, *Citizen 13660* (1946), which documented the indignities, struggle, and sparse humor of daily life at the camps. Named for the number assigned to her family unit, the book contains over two hundred of her pen and ink sketches accompanied by brief explanatory text. It was the first book on the Japanese internment experience. In 1981, Okubo testified before the Commission on Wartime Relocation and Internment of Civilians.

ONG, HAN (1968–). A Chinese **Filipino American** playwright, Ong was born to Chinese parents in Manila, the Philippines. His family immigrated to the United States in 1984 and settled in Los Angeles. Ong was a high school dropout but fell in love with the **theater**. His work caught the attention of Robert Brustein, the artistic director of the American Repertory Theater. When he was 29, Ong won one of the prestigious MacArthur fellowships, also known as genius awards. He has written a large number of plays, including *Symposium in Manila* (1991), *Cornerstone Geography* (1992), *Bachelor Rat* (1992), and *Reasons to Live. Reason to Live. Half. No Reason* (1991). In 1993, Ong collaborated with **Jessica Hagedorn** on *Airport Music*. Then, he went on to write *The L.A. Plays* (1993), *The Chang Fragments* (1996), and *Swooney Planet* (1999). His most recent writings are two novels, *Fixer Chao* (2002) and *The Disinherited* (2005). His major themes include ethnicity, cultural clash, class conflicts, and same-sex love. He is the recipient of the Guggenheim Fellowship for Fiction and the TCG/NEA Playwriting Award.

OPM. This stands for "Opening People's Minds," and is an Asian American sketch comedy troupe in Los Angeles, headed by Charles Kim, artistic director, and fellow producer Ewan Chung. Founded in Seattle in 1996, it moved to Los Angeles in 2002. Its mission is to create and present original, comedic entertainment based on Asian American experiences by uniting committed artists in a nurturing and collaborative environment.

OTA, SHELLEY AYAME NISHIMURA (1911–?). A **Japanese American** novelist, Ota was born to Japanese immigrants in Hawaii. She holds a B.A. in English from the University of Hawaii. She is the author of the novel *Upon Their Shoulders* (1951), a family saga of the Japanese American experience in Hawaii. It is considered to be the first published novel in English based on the Japanese American immigration experience.

OTSUKA, JULIE (1962–). A **Japanese American** novelist, Otsuka was born in Palo Alto, California, to an **issei** father and **nisei** mother. She earned her B.A. in arts from Yale University and attended the M.F.A. program at the University of Indiana before moving to New York to take classes at the New York Studio School of Drawing, Painting and Sculpture. In her early 30s, she turned to fiction and earned her M.F.A. in creative writing from Columbia University. Her first novel, *When the Emperor Was Divine* (2002), won American Library Association's Alex Award and an **Asian American Literary Award**. It tells the story of one Japanese American family's experience during World War II and the **internment**. Her second novel, *The Buddha in the Attic* (2011), is a lyrical novel about Japanese **women** immigrants before and during the internment.

OYABE, JENICHIRO (1867–1940). A **Japanese American** autobiographer, Oyabe was born in Tokyo. His mother died early in his life, and abandoned by his father, he was raised by relatives. Inspired by American missionaries, he became a Christian and sailed to the United States as a cabin boy in 1888. He studied at Hampton Institute, a school for blacks and Native Americans, before he enrolled at Howard University to study theology. He completed his doctorate in divinity from Yale University, after which he worked as a missionary in Hawaii for two years. His autobiography, *A Japanese Robinson Crusoe* (1898), is arguably the earliest book by a Japanese American. After the book, he returned to Japan and never returned to the United States.

OZEKI, RUTH L. (1956–). A **Japanese American** novelist, Ozeki was born and raised in New Haven, Connecticut, by an American father and a Japanese mother. She studied English and Asian Studies at Smith College and traveled extensively in Asia. She received a Japanese Ministry of Education Fellowship to do graduate work in classical Japanese literature at Nara University. During her years in Japan, she worked in Kyoto's entertainment district, founded a language school, and taught in the English Department at Kyoto Sangyo University. She is the author of two novels. *My Year of Meats* (1998) won the Kiriyama Pacific Rim Award, the Imus/Barnes and Noble American Book Award, and a Special Jury Prize of the World Cookbook Awards in Versailles. It tells parallel stories of a Japanese woman and the U.S. meat industry. *All Over Creation* (2003) is a New York Times Notable Book, the recipient of a 2004 **American Book Award**, as well as the Willa Literary Award for Contemporary Fiction. In this novel, Ozeki centers on potatoes in a story of a farmer, his daughter, environmental activists, and a New Age corporate spin doctor, whose lives and interests collide in Liberty Falls, Idaho.

P

PAGE ACT. Passed in 1857, it was the first federal law in the United States to prohibit immigration based on race or nationality. This act identified undesirable immigrants as any individual from China, Japan, or any "Oriental" country who was coming to America to be a contract laborer as well as any Asian woman who would engage in prostitution. The law was named after Horace F. Page, a Republican Congressman in the House of Representatives, who introduced the bill. The Page Act imposed a fine of up to $2,000 and a maximum jail sentence of one year upon any individual who tried to bring a person from China, Japan, or any Asian country to the United States. While the prohibition of Asian laborers was not strictly carried out until the **Chinese Exclusion Act** in 1882, the bar on female Asian immigrants was heavily reinforced. Since it was nearly impossible for any Asian woman to prove that she was not coming to America to engage in prostitution and since the interrogation and physical examination were so humiliating, Asian **women** simply stopped coming. The devastating consequence was the fast shrinking of the male to female ratio in the Chinese American population and thus the halt of community regeneration. In 1900, the ratio was one Chinese woman to every 19 Chinese men in **Chinatowns**.

This piece of legislature is a significant reference in Asian American literature and theater. The dysfunctional family relationships and the conservative cultures in Chinatowns, dramatized in Asian American novels and dramas, are partial results of the severe imbalance between Asian men and women between the 1850s and 1960s. For example, in **Louis Chu**'s novel *Eat a Bowl of Tea*, the drama centers on the scarcity of women in Chinatown, New York, and the community's pressure on Mei and Ben, the only young couple in the novel, to reproduce a new generation. This pressure results in Ben's impotence and Mei's infidelity. The short stories by the **Filipino American** writer **Bienvenido Santos** portray the loneliness of Filipino men in America and their longing for women. Discriminatory laws are so important to Asian American writers that **Maxine Hong Kingston** devotes an entire chapter of *China Men* to the narrative of California State and Federal laws barring the entry of Asian immigrants and discriminating against Asians already in the United States. *See also* LEE, CHERYLENE.

PAHK, INDUK (1896–1980). A **Korean American** autobiographer, Pahk was born in Pyongyang, Korea, and received her early education from Methodist missionaries. She came to the United States to study at Wesleyan College but graduated with an M.A. from Columbia University. She traveled back and forth between Korea and America to raise money and promote education of Korean children. She wrote three autobiographies: *September Monkey* (1954), *The Hour of the Tiger* (1965), and *The Cock Still Crows* (1977). *September Monkey* chronicles her life from birth to the beginning of her extensive lecture tours in America. *The Hour of Tiger* covers the details of her fund-raising efforts in America to the opening of her vocational school for Korean boys, and *The Cock Still Crows* combines early memories with her activities in raising funds, building a school and its curriculum, and collecting Korean legends and proverbs. All three autobiographies convey a deep religious belief in Christianity.

PAI, MARGARET K. (1914–?). A **Korean American** memoirist, Pai was born in Hawaii to Korean immigrants. *The Dreams of Two Yi-Min* (1989) was a memoir about her mother, a picture bride from Korea, married to a man who builds upholstery/furniture/custom drapery businesses in Hawaii during the 1920s to the 1940s.

PAK, GARY (1952–). A third-generation **Korean American** writer, Pak was born and raised in Hawaii. He received his B.A. from Boston University and his M.A. and Ph.D. from the University of Hawaii. He is the author of two books of fiction: *The Watcher of Waipuna and Other Stories* (1992) and *Language of the Geckos and Other Stories* (2005). He has also written two novels: *A Ricepaper Airplane* (1998) and *Children of a Fireland* (2004). His most recent work is a book of creative nonfiction, *Chon-go Ma-bi / High Sky and Horse Fattening: Essays on Contemporary Korean Culture* (2005). He has published a **children**'s play, *Beyond the Falls*, which was produced by the Honolulu **Theater** for Youth in 2001. Almost all his stories are set in Hawaii and dramatize the hopes and despairs of characters with diverse backgrounds. Pak received multiple honors, including a Ludwig Vogelstein Foundation Fellowship, the Elliot Cades Literary Prize, and a Fulbright Fellowship.

PAK, SOYUNG. A **Korean American** writer of **children's books**, Pak was born in Seoul, South Korea, but spent her childhood in the suburbs of southern New Jersey. She holds a B.F.A. from New York University's Tisch School of the Arts and an M.B.A. from the University of Chicago. She is the author of two books, *Dear Juno* (1999), winner of the Ezra Jack Keats Award, and *A Place to Grow* (2002). She now resides in Chicago.

PAK, TY (1938–). A **Korean American** novelist, Pak was born in Korea and experienced the ending of Japanese occupation and the Korean War (1950–1953). He received a degree in law from Seoul National University and worked as a journalist for five years. He came to the United States at the age of 27 to study at Bowling Green State University, where he received his Ph.D. in English. Between 1970 and 1987, he taught at the University of Hawaii. He is the author of two short story collections, *Guilt Payment* (1983) and *Moonbay* (1999), and one novel, *Cry, Korea, Cry* (1999). His short stories portray Korean immigrant men in Hawaii carrying traumatic memories of their past. His novel tells the story of a mixed-blood Korean War orphan.

PAMATMAT, A. REY. A **Filipino American** playwright, Pamatmat received his B.F.A. in drama from New York University and M.F.A. in playwriting from Yale School of Drama. He is the 2010 Princess Grace Fellow for Playwriting. He has authored many plays, including *Edith Can Shoot Things and Hit Them*, *This Is How It Ends*, *Thunder Above, Deeps Below*, *DEVIANT*, *Ain't Meat*, *1260 Minute Life*, *Red Rover*, *High/Limbo/High*, *Beautiful Day*, *New*, *Picture 24*, *Pure*, and *Unstick the* ***Woman***. His work has been featured in HX Magazine's Top Ten Plays of 2005 and nominated for two 2006 New York Innovative Theater Awards, including Outstanding New Script. His work has been developed at the Eugene O'Neill Playwrights Conference, New Work Now!, the Public **Theater**, Victory Gardens' Ignition Festival, Playwrights' Horizons, Ars Nova, **Ma-Yi Theater Company**, Rattlestick, E.S.T., the Lark, New Dramatists, the National New Play Network, and the National Asian American Theater Conference. A member of the Ma-Yi Writer's Lab, he has been a New York Foundation for the Arts Playwriting Fellow, an artist–delegate to the first U.S. Social Forum, and a Truman Capote Literary Fellow.

PAN ASIAN REPERTORY THEATRE. This is one of the four Asian American **theater** groups. Founded in 1977 in New York City and led by artistic director Tisa Chang, it aims to provide professional opportunities to Asian American artists and to specialize in intercultural productions of Asian American plays.

PAPER SON. This is a term used by Chinese immigrants before 1944 to refer to those who claimed to be sons of U.S. citizens while in actuality theirs was a purchased identity. The **Chinese Exclusion Act** of 1882 prohibited the immigration of most Chinese except for merchants, students, diplomats, and children of citizens.

The 1906 earthquake and fire in San Francisco destroyed all public records. As a result, thousands of Chinese men claimed American births in San Francisco, and the U.S. government had no choice but to accept their claims. With this citizenship, a Chinese man could claim citizenship for his offspring born in China. In subsequent trips to China, the father would report the birth of one or two sons upon his return. While some of the births were legitimate, others were created as slots so that they could be bartered, bought, or reserved to bring other male relatives to the United States. Aware of this practice among the Chinese immigrants, U.S. immigration officials often subjected Chinese young men attempting immigration to rigorous interrogations in order to determine if they were true sons of citizens. Only after the Exclusion Act was repealed in 1944 did such interrogations stop.

PARK, ED (1970–). A **Korean American** novelist, Park was born in Buffalo, New York. He graduated from Yale University and received his M.F.A. in creative writing from Columbia University, where he currently teaches. He is a founding editor of *the Believer* and the former editor of the *Voice Literary Supplement*, and has worked as an editor at the **Poetry** Foundation. His articles, essays, and reviews have appeared in the *New York Times*, *Salon*, *Modern Painters*, and elsewhere. His debut novel, *Personal Days* (2008), was a finalist for the PEN Hemingway Award, the John Sargent Sr. First Novel Prize, and the Asian American Literary Award. It was named one of *Time*'s Top 10 Fiction Books of the year. *Personal Days* captures perfectly the culture of the modern corporate office and is described as "a layoff narrative for our times." His short fiction and nonfiction have appeared in anthologies and journals, such as *Trampoline*, *Turn This Book*, and *Read Hard, the Believer* anthology.

PARK, FRANCES (1955–) and PARK, GINGER (1962–). They are **Korean American** sisters who collaborate in writing books for **children** and young adults. Frances was born in Cambridge, Massachusetts, while Ginger was born in Washington, D.C., and both grew up in D.C. Frances received a B.S. in psychology from Virginia Polytechnic Institute. Their books, inspired by their family's experiences, explore themes of love, loss, and war. *When My Sister Was a Cleopatra Moon* (2001) is a **young adult novel** about two Korean American sisters. *To Swim across the World* (2002) is a novel based on the love story of their parents, set in Korea before, during, and after the Korean War (1950–1953). *The Royal Bee* (2000), a winner of the Sugarman Award for Children's Literature, is a picture book based on their grandfather's determination to obtain an education despite poverty. *Good-bye 382 Shin Dang Dong* (2002) tells the story of a young girl's reluctance to leave

Korea for America. Other **children's books** include *The Have a Good Day Café* (2005), *Where on Earth Is My Bagel?* (2001), and *My Freedom Trip* (2010). They have also written a joint memoir, *Chocolate Chocolate: The True Story of Two Sisters, Tons of Treats, and the Little Shop That Could* (2011).

PARK, ISHLE YI (1977–). A **Korean American** poet and performer, Park was born and raised in Queens, New York. She received a B.A. in creative writing from Sarah Lawrence College and an M.F.A. in creative writing from New York University. She was a Poet Laureate of Queens, New York. Her first book of **poetry**, *The Temperature of This Water* (2004), won a Pen America Award for Outstanding Writers of Color and a Members' Choice Award of the **Asian American Literary Awards**. Her work has appeared in over 30 anthologies, including the *Best American Poetry of 2003* and *Century of the Tiger: One Hundred Years of Korean Culture in America*. Most of her poetry explores themes of gender, race, identity, violence, and sexuality, portraying the lives of the underrepresented with wit and honesty. She was a touring cast member of the Tony Award winning Def Poetry Jam show and is a regular on the HBO series. A featured performer at over 300 venues and festivals in the United States, Cuba, Korea, Singapore, and New Zealand, Park has received numerous grants including those from the New York Foundation for the Arts, the San Francisco Arts Council, and the *Korea Times*.

PARK, LINDA SUE (1960–). A **Korean American** writer of **children's books**, Park was born in Urbana, Illinois, to Korean immigrant parents. She received her B.A. in English from Stanford University and worked as a food journalist and teacher before turning to writing books for children. Her stories are often set in historical Korea. For instance, her first book, *Seesaw Girl* (1999), tells the story of a little girl in 17th-century Korea who is not allowed outside the walls of her home, and *A Single Shard* (2003) is set in 12th-century Korea. This book is the winner of 2002 Newbery Medal and 2002 American Library Association Best Book for **Young Adults**. Her other books include *The Kite Fighters* (2000); *When My Name Was Keoko* (2002), winner of a 2002 Publishers Weekly Best Books of the Year award and a 2002 School Library Journal Best Books of the Year award; *Archer's Quest* (2006); *Project Mulberry* (2005); *Keeping Score* (2008); and *A Long Walk to Water* (2010).

PARK, NO-YOUNG (1899–1976). A Korean **Chinese American** autobiographer, Park was born and raised in Manchuria, China, where his parents took refuge after escaping the Japanese colonization of Korea. Fleeing from an arranged marriage, Park left home and joined a Buddhist monastery. After the end of World War I, he went to Europe in search of knowledge and enlightenment. Disappointed with Europe, Park came to America in 1921. With the help of some American benefactors, he attended Evansville College in Indiana and learned English and transferred to Northwestern University to study history and political science. Without finishing his degree, he transferred again to the University of Minnesota where he earned his B.A. in political science. It was at this time he began his lifelong career as a paid speaker on Far Eastern affairs. Park then entered Harvard and earned his Ph.D. in international relations. In his life, he lectured and taught in several American universities. His autobiography, *A Chinaman's Chance* (1929), details his search for Western learning, his faith in American ideals, and his repeated encounters with **racist** treatment.

PARK, THERESE S. (1941–). A **Korean American** novelist, Park was born and raised in South Korea. She received a bachelor degree in music from Seoul National University and a master's degree in cello performance from Ecole Normale de Musique de Paris, France. She came to the United States to play cello with the Kansas City Philharmonic in 1966. Her debut novel, *A Gift of the Emperor* (1997), tells the story of a 17-year-old girl who is kidnapped to become a comfort woman. Her second novel, *When a Rooster Crows at Night* (2004), is based on what she witnessed during the Korean War (1950–1953). Her essays and articles have been published in such publications as the *Kansas City Star*, the *Sun Publication*, the *Best Times*, *Our Family* (Canada), the *Beat Magazine*, *Korea Bridge* (South Korea), and others.

PARK, YOUNGSOO (1972–). A **Korean American** novelist, playwright, and a filmmaker, Park was born in South Korea and currently lives in Harlem, New York. He received his B.A. in English from Swarthmore College and M.F.A. in playwriting from New York University. His debut novel, *Boy Genius* (2002), was selected for the Notable Title for the 2002 Kiriyama Book Prize and a finalist for the 2003 Asian American Literary Award. It is a fantastic tale about a brilliant boy avenging the wrongs perpetrated on his parents by the governments of South Korea and the United States. His second novel, *La Cucarachas* (2004), paints a painfully honest and often wickedly funny portrait of a Korean American boy growing up in a crumbling, multiethnic New York City housing project in the 1980s. He also wrote and directed the film *Free Country* (1996) and cowrote *Mojo Tango* (2010). *See also* THEATER.

PEI, LOWRY (1946–). A **Chinese American** novelist, Pei was born to a Chinese father and a white American mother in Chicago and was raised in

St. Louis. He holds a B.A. in English from Harvard University and a Ph.D. in English from Stanford University. Currently, he teaches writing at Simmons College. Pei is the author of a coming-of-age novel *Family Resemblances* (1986) and numerous short stories in such journals as the *Ohio Review*, *Imagine*, *Writer's Bar-B-Q*, etc. His stories have been selected to appear in the *Best American Short Stories in 1984* and the *Best of Story Quarterly* (1990).

PEÑA, RALPH B. (1963–). A **Filipino American** playwright and actor, Peña was born in Manila, the Philippines. His family moved to the United States when he was 10 years old. He then returned to the Philippines for high school and became involved with the Philippine Educational **Theater** Association. In 1984, he returned to California and enrolled in the University of California, Los Angeles. He helped to establish the New York–based **Ma-Yi Theater Ensemble** to showcase Filipino American theater artists and later became its artistic director. Peña wrote several plays, including *Cinema Verite* (1991) and *Flipzoids* (1996). The latter was staged across the country and won an **Obie Award**. Peña has been commissioned by many, including the Rockefeller Foundation, South Coast Repertory, Joseph Papp Public Theatre, New York Ethical Society, the Henry Street Settlement, and Theatre for the New City.

PEÑARANDA, OSCAR. A **Filipino American** poet and fiction writer, Peñaranda was born in the Philippines. When he was 12 years old, his family moved to Vancouver, Canada, where he lived until age 17. In his senior year of high school, his family moved to San Francisco. He earned his B.A. in literature and M.A. in creative writing at San Francisco State University. He is the author of a **poetry** collection, *Full Deck (Jokers Playing)* (2004), and a collection of stories, *Seasons by the Bay* (2004), which was awarded Global Filipino Literary Award for best fiction and the award for fiction from Philippine American Writers and Artists.

PEREZ, CRAIG SANTOS (1980–). A Chamoru poet, Perez was born and raised on the Pacific Island of Guam and has lived in California since 1995. He received a B.A. in art history and literature from the University of Redlands and an M.F.A. in creative writing from the University of San Francisco. He is currently a Ph.D. candidate in Comparative Ethnic Studies at the University of California, Berkeley, where he studies Native American and Native Oceanic literature and theory. He is the cofounder of Achiote Press and author of several chapbooks, including *Constellations Gathered along the Ecliptic* (2007), *All with Ocean Views* (2007), and *Preterrain* (2008). He is the author of two books of **poetry**, *From Unincorporated Territory*

[*Hacha*] (2008) and *From Unincorporated Territory* [*Saina*] (2010). In his poetry, Perez incorporates Guam's histories of colonial domination by the Spanish, the Japanese, and the United States, intimate stories of his childhood experiences, his family's migration to the United States, and the myths of his ancestors. His poetry, essays, fiction, reviews, and translations have also appeared in *New American Writing*, *Pleiades*, the *Denver Quarterly*, the *Colorado Review*, *Sentence*, and *Rain Taxi*, among others. He is the recipient of a 2010 Poets & Writers California Writers Exchange Award.

PERKINS, MITALI. A **South Asian American** author of **young adult novels**, Perkins was born Mitali Bose in Calcutta, India. Her family moved to California just in time for her to start middle school. She earned her B.A. in political science at Stanford University and her M.A. in public policy at the University of California, Berkeley. She is the author of several young adult novels, including *Bamboo People* (2010), *The Not-So-Star-Spangled-Life of Sunita Sen* (2005), *Monsoon Summer* (2006), *First Daughter* (2007), *Rickshaw Girl* (2008), and *Secret Keeper* (2010). Her protagonists are often strong female characters trying to bridge different cultures. Her books have received numerous honors, such as International Reading Association Notable Book for a Global Society, American Library Association Amelia Bloomer Project Award, and Christian Schools Association's Lamplight Award, etc.

"PERSIMMONS." This is one of the best-known poems in Asian American Literature. It was written by **Li-Young Lee**, who was born in Indonesia to **Chinese** parents and came to the United States as a child. Widely anthologized and studied, "Persimmons" is richly imagistic and beautifully lyrical. The poem, centering on this fruit popular among East Asians, employs simple and ordinary images to convey important themes of cross-cultural communication, **racism**, and family. Persimmon is the unifying imagery in this poem and serves as the locus from which Lee articulates an immigrant's analysis of his own experience between two cultures and his critique of the intolerance of the mainstream culture. The adult speaker returns to his childhood memory keyed up by two words, "persimmon" and "precision." The young Lee, speaking Bahasa Indonesia and Mandarin Chinese, encounters the difficulty of reproducing the sequence of sounds that distinguishes the first syllable of "persimmon" from that of "precision." The poem begins by picturing a classroom situation where the immigrant child is punished for making this phonetic error. "In six grade Mrs. Walker/ slapped the back of my head/ and made me stand in the corner/ for not knowing the difference/ between *persimmon* and *precision*." Lee makes it apparent that the child knows the difference in meaning between these two words—"How to choose/ persimmons. This is precision." He then describes precisely how to choose, peel, and eat the perfect persimmon. "Ripe ones are soft and brown-spotted./ Sniff the bottoms. The sweet one/ will be fragrant. How to eat:/ put the knife away, lay down newspaper./ Peel the skin tenderly, not to tear the meat./ Chew the skin, suck it,/ and swallow. Now, eat/ the meat of the fruit,/ so sweet,/ all of it, to the heart." The speaker's sophisticated knowledge in the selection and consumption of the fruit counters the common, racist assumption that broken or accented speech signifies underdeveloped intellect.

The sharp irony in "Persimmons" points to two situations. First, Mrs. Walker humiliates the child for "not knowing the difference" between two English words. Second, Mrs. Walker demonstrates her ignorance by committing the errors of selecting a green persimmon, calling it a "Chinese apple," and cutting it up with a knife. Through the reference of this fruit, Lee contrasts the cruelty of the American society, whose microcosm is Mrs. Walker's classroom, with the love and comfort inside the immigrant home. The image of a persimmon round as the moon and warm as the sun, central to the aesthetics and ethics of this poem, counters the earlier scene of punishment and humiliation in the classroom. In the sixth stanza, the centerpiece, Lee de-exoticizes the fruit by giving it a private value. "My mother said every persimmon has a sun/ inside, something golden, glowing,/ warm as my face." These three lines evoke an intimate image of a mother cupping her son's face in her hands and trying to heal his injured psyche. Persimmons capture all that is golden, warm, sweet, tender, and gratifying in such a moment.

PHAM, ANDREW X. (1967–). A **Vietnamese American** memoirist, Pham was born in Vietnam and came to the United States as a child. He studied engineering at the University of California, Los Angeles. His travel memoir, *Catfish and Mandala: A Two-Wheeled Voyage through the Landscape and Memory of Vietnam* (1999), won the 1999 Kiriyama Pacific Rim Book Prize. His second memoir, *The Eaves of Heaven: A Life in Three Wars* (2008), is about his father. He has received numerous honors, including a Whiting Writer Award, Quality Paperback Book Prize, the Oregon Literature Prize, and a Guggenheim Fellowship.

PHAM, QUANG X. (1964–). A Vietnamese American memoirist, Pham was born in Saigon, fled Vietnam in 1975 when Saigon fell, and resettled in California. Quang graduated from the University of California, Los Angeles, and went on to complete Marine Corps Officer Candidate School. He was the first Vietnamese American to earn naval aviator's wings in the U.S. Marine Corps and flew CH-46 helicopter missions in the Persian Gulf War. His memoir, *A Sense of Duty: My Father, My American Journey* (2005), traces his journey from the Vietnam War to the Gulf War, from his experiences as a refugee to his becoming a combat aviator, and his many incarnations in between.

PHAN, AIMEE (1977–). A **Vietnamese American** fiction writer, Phan was born and raised in Orange County, California. She received her B.A. in English from the University of California, Los Angeles, and M.F.A. from the Iowa Writers' Workshop. She currently teaches at California College of the Arts. Her debut book of fiction, *We Should Never Meet* (2005), was named a Kiriyama Prize Notable Book in fiction and was a winner of the 2004 Association of Asian American Studies Book Award. The collection weaves the lives of eight characters surrounding the events of Operation Babylift, the emergency evacuation of 2,000 Vietnamese and Amerasian orphans from Vietnam in April 1975. Phan's other writing has appeared in the *New York Times*, *Virginia Quarterly Review*, *USA Today*, and the *Oregonian*.

PHONPADITH, MALI (1975–). A Laotian American poet, Phonpadith was born in Laos during the Vietnam War. Her family fled across the Mekong River on a boat and made it safely to the refugee camps of Ubon Rachatani, Thailand. She and her family arrived in the United States when she was five years old. She earned a B.S. in international business, a B.S. in marketing, and a B.A. in Spanish from the University of Maryland, College Park. At 17, she published her first poem, and her debut book of **poetry**, *A Million Fireflies* (2011), is a memoir about her voyage from war-torn Laos to America. She was nominated Best Poet of the Year by the International Society of Poets in 2007. *See also* SOUTHEAST ASIAN AMERICAN LITERATURE AND THEATER.

PINEDA, JON (1971–). A **Filipino American** poet, Pineda was born in Charleston, South Carolina. He received his B.A. in English from James Madison University and an M.F.A. in creative writing from Virginia Commonwealth University. His first collection of **poetry**, *Birthmark* (2004), winner of the 2003 Crab Orchard Award Series Open Competition, explores the father–son relationship in a mixed race context. *The Translator's Diary* (2008), winner of the 2007 Green Rose Prize, is a long elegy that studies loss, memory, and absence. His poetry has also appeared in literary journals, such as *Crab Orchard Review*, *Poetry Northwest*, and *Prairie Schooner*. He is the recipient of a Virginia Commission for the Arts Individual Artist Fellowship and teaches creative writing at Queens University of Charlotte.

PING CHONG & COMPANY. Originally the Fiji Theatre Company, it was founded in 1975 by the **Chinese American** playwright **Ping Chong**. Located in New York, the company's mission is to explore the intersections of race, culture, history, art, media, and technology in the modern world. Today, the company creates innovative works of **theater** and art for modern, multicultural audiences.

PINTIG CULTURAL GROUP. Founded in April 1991, Pintig, meaning "pulse" in Filipino, is a **Filipino American** performing company based in Chicago.

POETRY. Asian American literature boasts a rich tradition of poetry. Other than autobiography, poetry was the earliest genre in this literary tradition, and the earliest Asian American poets were **Japanese Americans. Sadakichi Hartmann** published his collection *Poems* in 1889, which was the first Asian American book of poetry in English. It is this first generation of Japanese American poets who introduced and promoted poetic forms new to American literature, such as ***tanka***, ***haiku***, and ***dodoitsu***. While *tanka* first appeared in Sadakichi Hartmann's *Drifting Flowers of the Sea and Other Poems* (1904), it was **Jun Fujita** who wrote the first American *tanka* collection, *TANKA: Poems in Exile* (1923). About the same time, **Yone Noguchi** played a significant role in promoting *haiku*, and his article "A Proposal to American Poets" in *Reader* 3:3 (1904) introduced the form in a sophisticated fashion. Sadakichi Harman's collection *Japanese Rhythms* (1926) also made a significant contribution to American poetry by adapting *haiku*, *tanka*, and *dodoitsu* to English. *Haiku* has become the most popular Japanese poetic form practiced in the West. Other Asian American poets who have written *haiku* include **Violet Kazue De Cristoforo**, **Albert Saijo**, and **Saymoukda D. Vongsay**. In addition, Sadakichi Harman's collection *Japanese Rhythms* (1926) made a significant contribution to American poetry by adapting *haiku*, *tanka*, and *dodoitsu* to English. The year 1959 saw the publication of what may be the earliest English-language anthology containing *tanka* poetry, *Japan: Theme and Variations: A Collection of Poems by Americans*, edited by Charles E. Tuttle, founder of the publishing house that bears his name.

Asian American poetry has been a significant venue for social protest. In the early 20th century, the **Chinese** immigrants detained in the immigration center on Angel Island left behind anonymous poetry, which they carved in Chinese on the wooden walls of their barracks to express their sorrow, longing, dream of prosperity, and anger toward the discriminatory immigration laws. These poems have been translated into English and published in a volume titled *Island: Poetry and History of Chinese Immigrants on Angel Island 1910–1940.* Under the influence of the civil rights movement, many Asian American poets have been writing since the 1970s powerful poetry that challenges **racism** and injustice, raises political consciousness, and affirms ethnic identities. Some of the best-known poets of this generation include **Ai**, **Marilyn Chin**, **Lawson Fusao Inada**, **Garrett Hongo**, **Myung Mi Kim**, **Regie Cabico**, **Rick Barot**, **Meena Alexander**, **Walter Lew**, **Arthur Sze**, **Wing Tek Lum**, **Eric Gamalinda**, **Shirley Geok-lin Lim**, **Timothy Liu**, and others.

Since the 1990s, Asian American poetry has blossomed in forms, content, as well as literary reputation. Some of the high profile poets include **Mei-mei Berssenbrugge**, **Kimiko Hahn**, **Li-Young Lee**, **Shahid Agha Ali**, **Jason Koo**, **Sun Yung Shin**, **Ed Bok Lee**, **Ishle Yi Park**, **Srikanth Reddy**, **Eugene Gloria**, **John Yau**, Lawson Fusao Inada, Garrett Hongo, etc. *See also* ALI, KAZIM; AMIRTHANAYAGAM, INDRAN; ANGELES, CARLOS A.; CELONA, TINA BROWN; CERENIO, VIRGINIA R.; CHANDRA, G. S. SHARAT; CHANG, DIANA; CHANG, JENNIFER; CHANG, TINA; CHANG, VICTORIA; CHEN, CHING-IN; CHEN, KEN; CHIANG, FAY; CHIN, JUSTIN; CHOCK, ERIC; CHOI, DON MEE; CHUNG, FRANCES; DE LA PAZ, OLIVER; DE LOS SANTOS, MARISA; DEMPSTER, BRIAN KOMEI; DHOMPA, TSERING WANGMO; FERRELL, MONICA; FURUTANI, DALE; GAMBITO, SARAH; GHOSE, ZULFIKAR; GOTERA, VINCENTE FERRER; HARTMAN, YUKIHIDE MAESHIMA; HONG, CATHY PARK; IGLORIA, LUISA A.; JAVIER, PAOLO; KAGEYAMA-RAMAKRISHNAN, CLAIRE; KAIPA, SUMMI; KAKUGAWA, FRANCES H.; KANEKO, LONNY; KASHIWAGI, HIROSHI; KHANNA, VANDANA; KIM, SUJI KWOCK; KONO, JULIET SANAE; KUO, ALEX; LAU, ALAN CHONG; LAU, CAROLYN; LÊ THI DIEM THÚY; LEE, JEFFREY ETHAN; LEE, PRISCILLA; LEE, SUEY-EUN JULIETTE; LEGASPI, JOSEPH O.; LEONG, RUSSELL; LIEBERMAN, KIM-AN; LIM, GENNY; LIM-WILSON, FATIMA; LINMARK, R. ZAMORA; LUM, WING TEK; MATSUEDA, PAT; MIRIKITANI, JANICE; MONG-LAN; MOUA, POS; MUKERJI, DHAN GOPAL; MURA, DAVID; NEZHUKUMATATHIL, AIMEE; NGAI, SIANNE; NGUYEN, HOA; NOGUCHI, RICK; OEUR, U SAM; OKITA, DWIGHT; PEÑARANDA, OSCAR; PEREZ, CRAIG SANTOS; PHONPADITH, MALI; PINEDA, JON; RAMANUJAN, A. K.; REALUYO, BINO A.; REDDY, SRIKANTH; REHMAN, BUSHRA; REKDAL, PAISLEY; REYES, BARBARA JANE; RNO, SUNG JUNG; RORIPAUGH, LEE ANN; SESHADRI, VIJAY; SETH, VIKRAM; SHAH, PURVI; SHANKAR, RAVI; SHAUGHNESSY, BRENDA; SHIMODA, BRANDON; SOGA, KEIHO; STARNES, SOFIA M.; SU, ADRIENNE; SUYEMOTO, TOYO; TABIOS, EILEEN; TAGAMI, JEFF; TAN, JOËL BARRAQUIEL; TAO, LIN; THAM, HILARY; TRAN, BARBARA; TRIPLETT, PIMONE; TSENG, JENNIFER; TSENG, SANDY;

TSUI, KITTY; VANG, BURLEE; VAZIRANI, REETIKA; WANG, PING; WOO, MERLE; WORRA, BRYAN THAO; YAMADA, MITSUYE; YAMANAKA, LOIS-ANN; YANG, JEFFREY; YIP, WAI-LIM; YOUN, MONICA; YOUNG, C. DALE.

POM SIAB HMOOB THEATRE (PSHT). This theater was established in 1992 by a group of Hmong American **theater** artists in Minnesota. It became the Center for Hmong Arts and Talent (**CHAT**). *See also* SOUTHEAST ASIAN AMERICAN LITERATURE AND THEATER.

POON, WENA (1974–). A Singapore American novelist, Poon was born in Singapore and moved to the United States at age 17. She received her B.A. in English and J.D. from Harvard University. Her first book, *Lions in Winter* (2007), nominated for the Frank O'Connor Award, the Singapore Literature Prize, and the Malaysia Popular Readers' Choice Awards, depicts self-exiled Singaporeans in the West. Her four volume science-fiction series, *The Biophilia Omnibus* (2009), was voted Best Book Gift of the Year (CNN Singapore). Set in 2015, *Biophilia* portrays an America at the brink of ruin. She is also the author of *The Proper Care of Foxes* (2009), a collection of short stories about transatlantic characters, also nominated for the Frank O'Connor Award. Her most recent novel, *Alex y Robert* (2010), portrays an American teenage girl training to be a matador in Spain and was selected by the BBC for radio serialization. Poon won the British Willesden Short Story Award in 2010. She still practices corporate law and lives in Austin, Texas. *See also* SOUTHEAST ASIAN AMERICAN LITERATURE AND THEATER.

PORK FILLED PLAYERS. This is an Asian American sketch comedy group, founded in 1997 and based in Seattle. It got its name from a local Japanese supermarket lunch menu. Its mission is to produce comedies that intimately reflect Asian American topics and issues.

POST *NATYAM* COLLECTIVE. This is a multinational community of dance artists, scholars, and organizers critically and creatively engaging with South Asian dance forms and aesthetic concepts. It emerged from ongoing collaborations among its founding members: Anjali Tata, Sandra Chatterjee, and Shyamala Moorty.

PRABHU, AVATAR. *See* CRASTA, RICHARD.

PRADHAN, MONICA. A **South Asian American** novelist, Pradhan was born to Indian immigrants in Pittsburgh and grew up in Washington, D.C.

She received a B.S. in managerial law and public policy from Syracuse University and an M.B.A. in finance from the University of Cincinnati. Her debut novel, *The Hindi-Bindi Club* (2007), has been compared to **Amy Tan**'s *Joy Luck Club* as it centers on the first-generation immigrant mothers and their American-born daughters.

PRASAD, CHANDRA (1975–). A prolific **South Asian American** writer of fiction and nonfiction, Prasad was born in New Haven, Connecticut, to an Indian father and a mother of Swedish, English, and Italian ancestries. She received her B.A. in English and **Women**'s Studies from Yale University. Fascinated with history, Prasad has authored three novels, all set in past eras. *Breathe the Sky* (2009) is based on the life of Amelia Earhart. *On Borrowed Wings* (2008), set in Depression-era Connecticut, tells the story about a quarryman's daughter who attends a prestigious university in the guise of a boy. *Death of a Circus* (2006) chronicles the Bringlebright Circus, a small fictional troupe traveling the United States in the early 20th century. Prasad's works have appeared in the *New York Times*, the *New York Times Magazine*, the *Week*, *Teen Voices*, and the *Wall Street Journal*, among others. She has also edited and contributed to *Mixed: An Anthology of Short Fiction on the Multiracial Experience*.

Q

QAZI, JAVAID (1947–). A **South Asian American** fiction writer, Qazi was born in Pakistan and came to the United States in 1968 to study English literature. He now lives in San Jose, California. He is the author of a novel, *Well Met in Cyprus* (2011), and a collection of stories, *Unlikely Stories* (1998). His work has appeared in the *Kansas Quarterly*, *Sequoia*, *Chelsea*, the *Toronto South Asian Review*, *Massachusetts Review*, and the *Anaïs Nin: International Journal*. Qazi refused to write immigrant stories; rather, he has chosen to explore such universal themes as meaning, fulfillment, and redemption.

QBD INK. This is a **Filipino American theater** group based in Washington, D.C. Founded by Remy Cabacungan in 1994, with Remé Grefalda as the artistic director, QBd began as a facilitator for performing groups.

QIU, XIAOLONG (1953–). A **Chinese American** novelist and poet, Qiu was born in Shanghai, China. He received a B.A. in English from the Chinese Academy of Social Sciences and a Ph.D. in comparative literature from Washington University in St. Louis. He is the author of a detective series featuring Inspector Chen: *The Death of a Red Heroine* (2000); *A Loyal Character Dancer* (2002), winner of Anthony Award; *When Red is Black* (2004); *A Case of Two Cities* (2006); *Red Mandarin Dress* (2007); *The Mao Case* (2009); and *Year of Red Dust* (2010). In each novel, Inspector Chen solves a case that is as much political as criminal. He has also published a collection of poems, *Lines around China* (2003).

QUEEN OF DREAMS. This is a recent novel by one of the best-known **South Asian American** writers, **Chitra Banerjee Divakaruni**. Published in 2004, *Queen of Dreams* follows the success of Divakaruni's other novels, such as *The Mistress of Spices*, *Sister of My Heart*, and *The Vine of Desire*. As in her earlier novels, she unfolds the plot of *Queen of Dreams* through the inexplicable, the enigmatic, and the magical. The novel travels along two story lines: the one of Mrs. Gupta, told through her dream journals, and the other of her daughter, Rakhi, who is a divorced mother, an artist, a coffee shop owner, and an Americanized Indian. While the story of Mrs. Gupta centers on her relationship to herself, the story of Rakhi deals primarily with her relationships with others—ex-husband, father, and diseased mother. Implicit in these relationships, however, is Rakhi's lack of relationship to her cultural heritage. The mother's story, told through her dream journals, and the daughter's story are interspersed.

Queen of Dreams opens with Mrs. Gupta's premonition of her own impending death. This hook ushers the reader into a fascinating world in which some of Mrs. Gupta's choices illuminate a radical departure from the Western patriarchal tradition. One particular choice central to her story is celibacy, a choice she makes against her passion after she discovers that her power as a dream reader is gradually sapped by her sexual relationship with her husband. Soon into the novel, Mrs. Gupta dies in a car crash and leaves behind her dream journals that finally introduce her story to her daughter.

The dream journals begin with the caves, introducing Rakhi in an ancient tongue to the women's society in the caves, of which her mother was a member. The condition of its membership is the exclusion of men in their lives. The **women** dream readers take a field trip to Calcutta to test their abilities, and it is in Calcutta that Mrs. Gupta breaks her vow of virginity. She chances upon Mr. Gupta in a garden, who mesmerizes her with love songs. The two meet in secret and consummate their love. Unlike a secret male society that is most likely to exact physical punishment or death for a member's violation of rules, the mothers in the caves offer the culprit three penalties to choose from. One, she may remain in the caves with the elders for the rest of her life and be a teacher. The elder would dream walk into her memory and remove the man's image. Two, she may give up her talent and live out her life as that of most ordinary of women, as a wife. The elders would adjust her memory so that she wouldn't remember anything about the caves. The third is that she be allowed to keep her powers, the lesser ones, so that she might help others in the world. In return, she could live with the man, but she must promise not to marry him. Choosing the third option, Mrs. Gupta believes, "The door for my return to the sisterhood would thus not be closed completely in case I saw the folly of my choice and wished to come back" (196). Upon her departure, her aunt gives her a small pouch that contains a handful of red earth from the walkway in front of the caves, literally "grounds that centuries of dream tellers have stepped on" (197). The red dirt not only represents the pathway between the outside world and the secret sisterhood inside the caves, but also materially represents the lives of women whose bodies have returned to the red earth after spending their lives among other women. Mrs. Gupta takes the red dirt with her to America without a clear idea what she is to do with it, but she deeply trusts its power.

In California, Mrs. Gupta feels increasingly alienated from her talent. Dreams do not come to her. She begins to experiment with the red dirt. At first, she scatters a little in her garden. It makes her flowers bloom but does not help her dream. Then she mixes it in her food, but it gives her cramps. Finally, she places the pouch of red dirt under her pillow, and her sleep "was filled with the colors and scents of home" (198), but her husband wakes up with a headache, complaining that "his sleep had been filled with terrible images, blood and rubble and dying animals" (198). She realizes that in order to have her dreams, she will have to stop sharing her husband's bed. To her dismay, however, the red earth in the pouch becomes less each time she uses it. By now she recognizes her mistake and realizes that she must break off all ties with her husband and find a way back to the caves. She welcomes death because it returns her to the caves.

Through reading (via her father's translation) her mother's dream journals, Rakhi reconciles with her father and becomes initiated into her ancestral culture. Mrs. Gupta's spirit casts mysterious influences upon her daughter's life, guiding her through difficult moments. 9/11 that occurs at the end of the novel both escalates Rakhi's inner conflict and steers her toward a stronger connection with the multiethnic community of Northern California.

RACISM. Asian Americans have experienced racism in myriad ways, ranging from lynching to exclusionary legislation to such racial framing as **model minorities**. Racial violence against them began almost as soon as they landed on American soil and continued in such recent events as the murder of Vincent Chin in 1982 and the Los Angeles riots of 1992. In 1852, a California Assembly Committee issued a report critical of Chinese labor and argued that the Chinese were inassimilable and, therefore, a threat to American democracy. The anti-Chinese platform was thus set for many Californian politicians and political entities, such as the Know-Nothing Party, the Workingmen Party, and "anti-Coolie" clubs. Their nativist rhetoric inflamed racial hostility against the Chinese. In the late 19th century, the anti-Chinese sentiment accelerated into riots that burned down **Chinatowns** and killed many Chinese on the West Coast and in the Northwest and Mountain states. For instance, the earliest urban anti-Chinese riots took place in 1871 in Los Angeles, in which 21 Chinese were shot, hanged, or burned to death. Between 1866 and 1867, over 100 Chinese were killed in Idaho. In Wyoming, the violence occurred in 1885, in which 28 Chinese died and 15 were wounded.

Racist legislation traces back to the original Nationality Act of 1790, which dictated that only a free white person who had resided in the United States for two years was eligible for naturalization, effectively barring Asians, blacks, and Native Americans from citizenship. In 1868, the enactment of the 14th Amendment extended citizenship to anyone born in the United States as well as to aliens of African nativity and persons of African descent. However, racial exclusion continued to apply to Asians. Racial discrimination in nationality laws persisted for 162 years; it was not until 1952 that the U.S. Congress lifted the racial bar on naturalization.

In addition to the racist nationality laws, other federal, state, and municipal laws prevented the Asians from gaining the full rights of U.S. citizenship. These laws were not only motivated by racial prejudice but also class and gender discrimination. The U.S. Congress passed the **Page Act** in 1875, which was the first federal immigration legislation that excluded a group based on its race and gender. It was made to stop the immigration of Asian

women for the purpose of prostitution, and the immigration officers effectively barred the entry of nearly all Chinese women by classifying them as prostitutes. The 1882 **Chinese Exclusion Act**, the first piece of federal legislation that singled out a group based on nationality and class to bar from immigration, specifically prohibited Chinese laborers from entering the United States for 10 years. The Chinese Exclusion Act was extended until 1943 when China became an American ally during World War II. The California Alien Land Law of 1913, prohibiting aliens ineligible for citizenship from owning land or property, affected all Asians, and the law remained valid until 1952.

Another major event in Asian American history is the **Japanese American internment** during World War II. This was the forcible relocation and internment of people of Japanese ancestry by the U.S. government in 1942–1945. In the wake of Japan's bombing of Pearl Harbor (7 December 1941), President Franklin D. Roosevelt authorized Executive Order 9066 on 19 February 1942, which allowed approximately 120,000 **Japanese Americans** and Japanese residing in the United States to be interned in "War Relocation Camps." It was not until 1988 that the U.S. government redressed this injustice when Congress passed and President Ronald Reagan signed legislation that apologized for the internment.

In the past 60 years or so, Asian Americans have undergone the racial framing of model minority. This identity is a racial stereotype that handicaps and neutralizes them culturally and politically. On the one hand, Asian Americans have been regarded as so self-sufficient and community centered that they do not need any government assistance. On the other, Asian Americans have so internalized this stereotype that they suffer quietly injustices and discrimination they encounter.

Cultural, social, and legal racism against Asian Americans has powerfully informed their literary and artistic expression. Earlier writers, such as **Edith Maude Eaton** and **Carlos Bulosan**, attempted to restore full humanity in their writings to **Chinese Americans** and **Filipino Americans**. However, some writers' defense against racism ironically reinforces racial discrimination, as they are eager to show their valorization of American individualism over Chinese communalism. Chinese American writers, such as **Jade Snow Wong**, **Pardee Lowe**, and **Monfoon Leong**, told their life stories in which they were disadvantaged by being Chinese and by being raised in a Chinese family. A large number of Asian American writers came into their political consciousness during the civil rights movement, and their literary expressions offer a scathing critique of racial discrimination and injustices against Asian Americans. These writers include **Frank Chin**, **Marilyn Chin**, **Maxine H. Kingston**, **Amy Tan**, **Gish Jen**, **David Henry Wang**, **Eleanor**

Wong Telemaque, Shawn Hsu Wong, Laurence Yep, Hisaye Yamamoto, Monica Sone, Jeanne Wakatsuki Houston, Yoshiko Uchida, David Mura, Keiho Soga, John Okada, Mitsuye Yamada, Momoko Iko, Lonny Kaneko, Toshio Mori, Garrett Hongo, Lawson Inada, and **Janice Mirikitani.** *See also* FERIA, BENNY F.; HYUN, PETER; PARK, NO-YOUNG; SEE, LISA LENINE; WOO, MERLE.

RAHMAN, IMAD (1970–). A **South Asian American** short story writer, Rahman was born in Karachi, Pakistan, and moved to the United States at age 18. He received his B.A. in English from Ohio Wesleyan University, M.A. in English from Ohio State University, and M.F.A. in creative writing from the University of Florida. His collection of interlinked stories, *I Dream of Microwaves* (2004), features a Pakistani American actor who laments that he cannot even get work in the United States portraying criminals. Rahman teaches at Cleveland State University.

RAMANUJAN, A. K. (1929–1993). A **South Asian American** poet, Ramanujan was born in Mysore City, India. After receiving his B.A. and M.A. in English from the University of Mysore, he came to the United States as a Fulbright Scholar and earned his Ph.D. in linguistics from Indiana University. He taught at the University of Chicago and passed away in Chicago. He is the author of numerous books of **poetry**, including *The Striders* (1966), *Hokkulalli Huvilla, No Lotus in the Navel* (1969), *Relations* (1971), *Selected Poems* (1976), *Mattu Itara Padyagalu and Other Poems* (1977), *Poems of Love and War* (1985), and *Second Sight* (1986). His poetry explores the themes of **hybridity**, transculturation, home, memory, and **exile**. He was the recipient of a MacArthur Fellowship.

RAO, RAJA (1908–2006). A **South Asian American** novelist, Rao was born in Hassan, Karnataka, India. After he completed his B.A. in English and history from Madras University, India, he received a government scholarship to study abroad. He went to France and studied French language and literature at the University of Montpellier and later at the Sorbonne. He returned to India for a period of time and came to the United States to teach at the University of Texas, Austin, where he worked between 1966 and 1983 until he retired. He is the author of numerous novels, including *Kanthapura* (1938), *The Serpent and the Rope* (1960), *The Cat and Shakespeare: A Tale of India* (1965), *Comrade Kirilov* (1976), *The Chessmaster and His Moves* (1988), and *On the Ganga Ghat* (1989). He also wrote two collections of short stories: *The Cow of the Barricades, and Other Stories* (1947) and *The Policeman and the Rose: Stories* (1978). In addition, he authored *Great Indian Way: A*

Life of Mahatma Gandhi (1998). In 1988, he received the prestigious International Neustadt Prize for Literature.

RASAKA THEATRE COMPANY. This group is based in Chicago and is the first **South Asian American** ensemble in the Midwest. It was established in 2003, with the goal to increase diversity among artists and audience by engaging and illuminating the South Asian American experience. It is particularly dedicated to providing a platform for the artistic expression of South Asian artists.

RAU, SANTHA RAMA (1923–2009). A **South Asian American** travel writer, novelist, and playwright, Rau was born in Madras, India, and died in New York. Rau attended St. Paul's Girls' School in London and spent time in South Africa, where her father was a diplomat. In 1941, she came to the United States to study and earned a B.A. from Wellesley College in 1944. She is well known for her travel writings: *East of Home* (1951), *This Is India* (1954), *View to the Southeast* (1957), and *My Russian Journey* (1959). She is the author of two novels: *Remember the House* (1956) and *The Adventuress* (1970), and two memoirs: *Home to India* (1945) and *Gifts of Passage* (1961). Rau is well remembered for her dramatic adaptation of E. M. Foster's novel *A Passage to India*, which opened in Oxford in 1960.

REALUYO, BINO A. A **Filipino American** novelist and poet, Realuyo was born and raised in Manila, the Philippines. As a teenager he came to the United States with his parents and has lived most of his adult life in New York City. He received his B.A. in International Studies from the American University and Universidad Argentina de la Empresa, and his M.A. in Education from Harvard. He has been an adjunct professor of creative writing at Fairleigh Dickinson University. His novel *The Umbrella Country* (1999) was a recipient of the first Members' Choice Award from the **Asian American Literary Awards**. This novel explores the themes of poverty, violence, colonialism, human tenacity, and redemption. His **poetry** collection, *The Gods We Worship Live Next Door* (2006), won the 2005 **Agha Shahid Ali** Prize in Poetry and received a 2009 Philippine National Book Award. He is a regular contributor to the *Literary Review* and guest edited its special issue, *Am Here: Contemporary Filipino Writings in English* (2000). He is also the editor of *The NuyorAsian Anthology: Asian American Writings about NYC* (2000), commemorating 100 years of Asian American presence in New York City, which was awarded a Pen Open Book Award. Among his numerous literary awards and fellowships are a Van Lier Foundation Fellowship for poetry, the Lucille Medwick Memorial Award from the Poetry Society of America, a New York Foundation for the Arts Fellowship for fiction, an Urban Artist Initiative Grant for fiction, a Valparaiso Literary Fellowship for fiction, and a Yaddo Fellowship for poetry. A cofounder of the **Asian American Writers' Workshop**, Realuyo has published stories, essays, and poetry in the *Nation, Manoa, Mid-American Review*, *Puerto del Sol, New Letters*, and *Kenyon Review*. His work is widely anthologized and reviewed internationally, and his poetry is included in the *Norton Anthology, Language for a New Century* and *Fire in the Soul: 100 Poems for Human Rights.*

REDDY, SRIKANTH (1973–). A **South Asian American** poet, Reddy was born to Indian immigrants and grew up in Chicago's western suburbs. He received his B.A. and Ph.D. in English from Harvard University and M.F.A. in creative writing from University of Iowa. His **poetry** collection, *Facts for Visitors* (2004), winner of an **Asian American Literary Award**, explores themes of war, prejudice, and oppression as well as the transcendence of love and awe. He wrote most of these poems during the summers he spent doing literacy work in rural Andhre Pradesh, India. His most recent publication is another book of poems, *Voyager* (2011). His poetry has also appeared in *American Poetry Review*, *Grand Street*, *Fence*, and the *Harvard Review*.

REHMAN, BUSHRA (1974–). A **South Asian American** poet, essayist, and fiction writer, Rehman was born in Brooklyn, New York, to Pakistani immigrants and grew up in Queens. She was educated at the College of New Rochelle, New York, Dominican University of California, and she earned her M.F.A. in creative writing from Brooklyn College. She is the author of a book of **poetry**, *Marianna's Beauty Salon* (2001), which tells the stories of runaway desi girls leaving Queens. Her work has appeared in *ColorLines*, *Mizna*, *Curve*, *SAMAR*, *Voices of Resistance: Muslim Women on War*, *Faith and Sexuality*, and *Stories of Illness and Healing:* ***Women*** *Write Their Bodies*. She performs her work around the country.

REKDAL, PAISLEY (1970–). A **Chinese American** poet, Rekdal was born in Seattle, Washington, to a Chinese American mother and a Norwegian American father. She received her B.A. in English from University of Washington, M.A. in medieval studies from University of Toronto, and M.F.A. in creative writing from University of Michigan. She is the author of a book of essays, *The Night My Mother Met Bruce Lee* (2000), and three books of **poetry**: *A Crash of Rhinos* (2000), *Six Girls without Pants* (2002), and *The Invention of the Kaleidoscope* (2007). She has also authored a **hybrid** photo-text memoir, *Intimate: A Family Photo Album* (2011), which combines poems, nonfiction, and fiction with photography. Her poetry explores the themes of love, family, desire, artistic transformation, and political unrest. Her work has received a Village Voice Writers on the Verge Award, a National Endowment for the Arts Fellowship, Utah Arts Council Poetry Fellowship, the University of Georgia Press' Contemporary Poetry Series Award, a Fulbright Fellowship, a Pushcart Prize, and the Laurence Goldstein Poetry Prize from *Michigan Quarterly Review*. Her poems and essays have appeared in the *New York Times Magazine*, NPR, *Nerve*, *Ploughshares*, *Poetry*, *Tin House*, *Michigan Quarterly Review*, *Denver Quarterly*, *Black Warrior Review*, *New England Review*, *Virginia Quarterly Review*, *Kenyon Review*, and *American Poetry Review*, among others. She teaches creative writing at the University of Utah.

REYES, BARBARA JANE (1971–). A **Filipina American** poet, Reyes was born in Manila, the Philippines, and raised in the San Francisco Bay Area. She received her B.A. in Ethnic Studies at the University of California, Berkeley, and her M.F.A. at San Francisco State University. She is the author of *Diawata* (2010), *Gravities of Center* (2003), and *Poeta en San Francisco* (2005), which received the James Laughlin Award. She has also authored three chapbooks: *Easter Sunday* (2008), *Cherry* (2008), and *West Oakland Sutra for the AK-47 Shooter at 3:00 AM and other Oakland Poems* (2008). Incorporating English, Spanish, and Tagalog, Reyes consistently explores themes of longing, desire, gender, **diaspora**, postcoloniality, memory, and death. Her works have also appeared in *Asian Pacific American Journal*, *Chain*, *Filipinas Magazine*, *Hyphen*, *Interlope*, *Kartika Review*, *Lantern Review*, *Latino Poetry Review*, *New American Writing*, *North American Review*, *Notre Dame Review*, *XCP: Cross Cultural Poetics,* among others. She has taught at Mills College and at University of San Francisco's Philippine Studies Program. She lives with her husband, poet Oscar Bermeo, in Oakland, where she is coeditor of Doveglion Press.

RIZZUTO, RAHNA REIKO (1963–). A **Japanese American** novelist and memoirist, Rizzuto was born in Honolulu, Hawaii, to a **nisei** mother and a half Italian and half Irish father. She was the first woman to receive a degree in astrophysics from Columbia University. Her debut novel, *Why She Left Us* (1999), winner of an **American Book Award**, depicts a Japanese American family living in the aftermath of World War II. She has also published a memoir, *Hiroshima in the Morning* (2010). Rizzuto is a professor at Goddard College in Vermont.

RNO, SUNG JUNG (1967–). A **Korean American** playwright, Rno was born in Minnesota. He received his B.A. in physics from Harvard University but decided to study **poetry** at Brown University and received an M.F.A. His first play, *Cleveland Raining*, a piece he wrote in a workshop, received a staged reading at the **Pan Asian Repertory Theatre**, won first prize at the Seattle Multicultural Playwrights' Festival in 1992, and premiered at the **East West Players** in 1995. The play centers on a dysfunctional Korean American family. Rno then adapted short stories by the Korean writer Hwang Sun-won into three plays: *In a Small Village*, *Drizzle*, and *Masks* (1992), all of which explore the themes of pain and loss. He went on to write more plays: *Konishini, Mon Amour* (1993), *New World* (1994), and *Gravity Falls from Trees* (1994). His most recent plays *Principia* (1996), *wAve* (1999), and *Yi Sang Counts to 13* (1999) explore the world of science, futuristic worlds, and surrealism. He is the recipient of several honors, including Van Lier Playwriting Fellowship at New Dramatists, a fellowship at New York **Theater** Workshop, and residency at Millay Colony for the Arts and at Mabou Mines.

ROBERTS, DMAE (1957–). A **Chinese American** playwright and radio artist, Roberts was born in Taiwan to a Chinese mother and an American father and raised in Junction City, Oregon. She earned a B.A. in journalism from the University of Oregon. She produced the radio program *Legacies: Tales from America*, which was broadcast nationwide on NPR. She has written and produced more than 400 audio art pieces and documentaries for NPR and PRI programs. Informed by her biracial background, her work often centers on cross-cultural peoples. Roberts won the prestigious George Foster Peabody Award for her autobiographical radio docuplay, *Mei Mei, a Daughter's Song* (1990), based on her mother's life in Taiwan. She went on to write *Breaking Glass* (1995) and *Picasso in the Back Seat* (1995), with the latter receiving the Portland Drama Critics Circle Award for Best Original Play and the Oregon Book Award for Best Play. Among her other plays are *Lady Buddha* (1997), *Tell me, Janie Bigo* (1998), and *Volcano Embrace* (1999). Her most recent work is *Crossing East*, a radio series on Asian American history, which won her a second Peabody Award. She is the recipient of multiple honors, such as the Dr. Suzanne Award for Civil Rights and Social Justice and was one of the 50 artists around the country to be selected recently for the 2007 U.S. Artists Fellowship. She has also received grants from the Corporation for Public Broadcasting and the National Endowment for the Arts, the Oregon Arts Commission Fellowship, the United Nations Silver Award, the Robert F. Kennedy Journalism Award, the Oregon Playwrights Award, the Casey medal, and the New Langton Arts Fellowship.

ROH-SPAULDING, CAROL (1962–). A **Korean American** writer, Roh-Spaulding is half Korean and half Caucasian, born in Oakland, California.

She holds a Ph.D. in English from the University of Iowa. She is the author of the fiction chapbook *The Brides of Valencia* (2000), which won the A. E. Coppard Prize for Long Fiction. Her stories explore issues of biraciality and gender. Her fiction has won other awards, including the Heathcote Award from the National Society of Arts and Letters, a Cohen Award for Best Story of the Year in *Ploughshares*, a Pushcart Prize for fiction, a Katherine Anne Porter Prize for Fiction, and most recently a David Nathan Meyerson Prize from the *Southwest Review*. She is a professor of English at Drake University.

ROOM TO IMPROV. An Asian American performance group, it was founded by Elvin Lubrin. It seeks to create a space for Asian Americans to tell stories and to examine issues that are humorous to a diverse audience. Since 2000, it has performed across the country at colleges and festivals as well as local hospitals and community events.

RORIPAUGH, LEE ANN (1965–). A **Japanese American** poet, Roripaugh was born in Laramie, Wyoming, to a Japanese mother and a white American father. Daughter of poet Robert Roripaugh, she began writing early. Her degrees include an M.M. in music history, a B.M. in piano performance, and an M.F.A. in creative writing, all from Indiana University. She is the author of three books of **poetry**, all of which are informed by Japanese myths and fairy tales. *Beyond Heart Mountain* (1999) was selected for the National Poetry Series and was also a finalist for the 2000 Asian American Literary Awards. It portrays experiences of wars and the **Japanese American internment**. *Year of the Snake* (2004), the winner of the Association of Asian American Studies Book Award in Poetry, explores themes of mixed-race female identities, evoking snakes and insects as an ongoing metaphor for transformation of self. *On the Cusp of a Dangerous Year* (2009) is a **hybrid** book of poems and images that examines the tumultuous life of the modern **woman**. The recipient of a 2003 Archibald Bush Foundation Individual Artist Fellowship, she was also named the 2004 winner of the Prairie Schooner Strousse Award, the 2001 winner of the Frederick Manfred Award for Best Creative Writing, and the 1995 winner of the Randall Jarrell International Poetry Prize. Her poetry and short stories have appeared in numerous journals and anthologies. Her other honors include the Association of American Publishers (AAP) Prize, the Association of Writers and Writing Programs (AWP) Intro Award, and the 1995 Randall Jarrell International Poetry Prize. Her poetry has appeared in numerous journals and anthologies, including *Black Warrior Review*, *Cream City Review*, *Crab Orchard Review*, *New England Review*, *Parnassus: Poetry in Review*, *Phoebe*, *Seneca Review*, *American Identities: Contemporary Multicultural Voices*, *American Poetry: The Next*

Generation, and *Waltzing on Water: Poetry by Women*. She teaches creative writing at the University of South Dakota.

ROSAL, PATRICK (1969–). A **Filipino American** poet, Rosal was born in New Jersey to Filipino immigrants. He received his B.A. in English from Bloomfield College (1996) and M.F.A. in creative writing from Sarah Lawrence College. He is the author of two books of **poetry**. *Uprock Headspin Scramble and Dive* (2003), winner of the Members' Choice Award from the **Asian American Writers' Workshop**, centers on immigration, rite-of-passage, family history, and love. *My American Kundiman* (2006), winner of the Association of Asian American Studies Book Award in Poetry and a Global Filipino Literary Award, delineates his ambivalence about America and celebration of his heritage. His poems and essays have been published widely in journals and anthologies, including *American Poetry Review*, *New Orleans Review*, *Harvard Review*, *Crab Orchard Review*, *Indiana Review*, *North American Review*, the *Literary Review*, *Pindledyboz*, *Black Renaissance Noire*, and *Brevity*. A recipient of a Fulbright grant, he has taught at Pennsylvania State University at Altoona, Centre College, University of Texas at Austin, and Drew University. He serves on the advisory board of CavanKerry Press, the Editorial Board of Cypher Books, and as a contributing editor of *Black Renaissance Noire*.

ROSCA, NINOTCHKA (1948–). A **Filipina American** novelist, Rosca was born in Manila, the Philippines. She received a B.A. in comparative literature from the University of the Philippines. In 1976, she came to the United States to study in the University of Iowa's International Writing Program. Rosca has published two novels, *State of War* (1988) and *Twice Blessed* (1992), with the latter receiving an **American Book Award**. Both novels center on characters living under the martial rule of Marcos (1972–1981) in the Philippines. She has also written two books of short fiction: *Bitter Country* (1970) and *The Monsoon Collection* (1983), and three books of nonfiction: *Endgame: The Fall of Marcos* (1987), *Jose Maria Sison: At Home in the World—Portrait of a Revolutionary* (2004), and *Sugar and Salt* (2006). She serves on the Board of Directors of PEN International Women's Committee and PEN American Center.

ROWLAND, LAURA JOH (1954–). A **Korean** and **Chinese American** mystery writer, Rowland was born and raised in Harper Woods, Michigan, to Korean and Chinese parents. She received a B.A. in microbiology and a M.A. in public health from the University of Michigan. She worked as a microbiologist and chemist for public and private agencies for many years before becoming a full-time writer. She is best known for her Sano Ichiro mystery series, which are set in the 1600s Edo (later known as Tokyo), Japan, and center around Sano—a teacher, samurai, and reluctant police officer. The series are *Shinju* (1994), *Bundori* (1996), *The Way of the Traitor* (1997), *The Concubine's Tattoo* (1998), *The Samurai's Wife* (2000), *Black Lotus* (2001), *The Pillow Book of Lady Wisteria* (2002), *The Dragon King's Palace* (2003), *The Perfumed Sleeve* (2004), *The Assassin's Touch* (2005), *The Red Chrysanthemum* (2006), *The Snow Empress* (2007), and *The Fire Kimono* (2008).

RUTKOWSKI, THADDEUS (1954–). A **Chinese American** novelist, Rutkowski was born in Kingston, Pennsylvania, of a Chinese mother and Polish father. He received his B.A. in English and B.F.A. in fine arts from Cornell University, and M.A. in creative writing from Johns Hopkins University. He is the author of three novels: *Tetched* (2005), *Roughhouse* (1999), and *Haywire* (2010). The first two were finalists for an **Asian American Literary Award**. All three novels, experimental and dark humored, are autobiographical and coming-of-age stories of the biracial narrator growing up in a dysfunctional family and escaping it to find self. His stories and poems have been nominated five times for a Pushcart Prize. He has been the fiction and nonfiction editor of the literary journal *Many Mountains Moving* since 2007. His stories have appeared in *Asia Literary Review*, *American Letters and Commentary*, *Crowd*, *CutBank*, *Faultline*, *Fiction*, *Fiction International*, *Global City Review*, *Hawai'i Pacific Review*, *Hayden's Ferry Review*, the *Laurel Review*, *Pleiades*, *Potomac Review*, and other magazines. He teaches fiction writing at New York's West Side YMCA and lives in Manhattan.

S

SAATh. This acronym stands for **South Asian American Theater**, based in Boston. Founded by its Managing Trustee, Rajendra Joshi in 1989, it is dedicated to raising awareness and appreciation of the South Asian community by showcasing themes, plays, and **theater** artists of South Asia and its **diaspora**. It collaborates with North America's various theatrical, cultural, and religious communities in confronting all forms of fundamentalism dividing the world by race, religion, gender, class, or nation.

SAIJO, ALBERT (1926–?). A **Japanese American** poet, Saijo was born in Los Angeles. His family was **interned** in Wyoming during World War II. While still interned, he was drafted into the U.S. Army. He received a B.A. in international politics from the University of Southern California. In the late 1950s, he met and befriended Jack Kerouac and other Beat poets. Saijo was the blueprint of George Baso in Keroac's novel *Big Sur*. His cross-country drive with Kerouac and Lew Welch inspired the collaboration on *Trip Trap* (1973), a book of road-trip ***haiku***. *Outspeaks: A Rhapsody* (1997) is his only book of **poetry**. Written all in capital letters and slang and punctuated only with dashes, Saijo's poetry is an exuberant and ranting stream of consciousness.

SAIKI, PATSY SUMIE (1915–). A **Japanese American** fiction writer, Saiki was born in Hawaii to Japanese immigrants. She received her B.A. and M.A. in education from the University of Hawaii (UH), and her Ph.D. in education from Columbia University. She taught at UH and worked in the Hawaii State Department of Education. Saiki has published a novel, *Sachie: A Daughter of Hawaii* (1978), which details the life the Himeno family experiencing racial discrimination and alienation, told from a 12-year-old girl's point of view. Saiki is also the author of three books of short stories: *Ganbare: An Example of Japanese Spirit* (1982), *Japanese Women in Hawaii*, and *Early Japanese Immigrants in Hawaii* (1993). She has also written plays, such as *The Return* (1959), *The Second Choice* (1959), and *The Return of Sam Patch* (1966). All of her works center on the lives of Japanese Americans in Hawaii. *See also* THEATER.

SAKAMOTO, EDWARD (1940–). A **Japanese American** playwright, Sakamoto was born in Honolulu, Hawaii. He wrote his first play, *In the Alley*, while he was an undergraduate student at the University of Hawaii, and it was produced on campus. After college, he moved to Los Angeles. He broke into the scene of Asian American **theater** with *Yellow Is My Favorite Color* (1972), which was staged by the **East West Players**. Sakamoto has written over 15 plays, and many of them are included in *Hawai'i No Ka Oi: The Kamiya Family Trilogy* (1995) and *Aloha Las Vegas and Other Plays* (2000). Most of his plays are set in Hawaii, featuring Japanese American characters and exploring with humor themes of home, race, and class. Sakamoto has received various awards, including two Hollywood Dramalogue Critic's awards for his writing for *Chikamatsu's Forest* and *Stew Rice*, the Po'okela Award for Excellence in Original Script for *Aloha Las Vegas*, and the 1997 Hawaii Award for Literature. He is also the recipient of grants from National Endowment for the Arts and the Rockefeller Foundation.

SALAAM THEATRE. This is a **South Asian American** multidisciplinary **theater** company, founded in 2000 by Geeta Citygirl, its artistic director, and located in New York. Its mission is to promote South Asian American artistic excellence.

SAMARASAN, PREETA. A **South Asian American** novelist, Samarasan was born in Malaysia to Indian immigrants and moved to the United States to finish high school. She received her B.A. from Hamilton College and M.F.A. in creative writing from the University of Michigan. She did doctoral work in musicology at the University of Rochester, but decided to abandon her dissertation to complete her novel. *Evening Is the Whole Day* (2008), her debut novel, won the Avery and Jule Hopwood Novel Award. The novel, set in Malaysia, depicts an Indian immigrant family's secrets and lies. Her short fiction and nonfiction have appeared in the *Asian Literary Review*, *Five Chapters*, *Hyphen*, *the Michigan Quarterly Review*, *EGO Magazine*, *A Public Space*, etc. She currently lives in France.

SAN DIEGO ASIAN AMERICAN REPERTORY THEATER. This is San Diego's premier contemporary Asian American **theater** company, established in 1995 by five local Asian/Pacific American artists: Vince Soberano, Andy Lowe, Jennifer Wong, Jyl Kaneshiro, and Donna Maglalang. It has produced Asian American plays, such as *Letters to a Student Revolutionary* by **Elizabeth Wong**, *FOB* by **David Henry Hwang**, *Masks* and *Cleveland Raining* by **Sung Jung Rno**, and *Tea* by **Velina Hasu Houston**.

SANSEI. This is a Japanese term used in North America, South America, and Australia to specify the grandchildren born in the new country to the first generation of Japanese immigrants. *See also* ISSEI; NISEI.

SANTOS, BIENVENIDO N. (1911–1996). A **Filipino American** novelist, Santos was born and died in the Philippines. He received his B.A. from the University of the Philippines and came to the United States in 1941 on a government scholarship to study at Columbia University and Harvard University. He earned his M.A. in English from the University of Illinois. He moved back and forth between the United States and the Philippines, holding professorship at the University of Nueva Caceres, the Philippines, Ohio State University, Wichita State University, etc. The majority of his writings were published in the Philippines, such as his five novels: *Villa Magdalena* (1965), *The Volcano* (1965), *The Praying Man* (1982), *The Man Who (Thought He) Looked like Robert Taylor* (1983), and *What the Hell for You Left Your Heart in San Francisco* (1987). His collections of short stories include *You Lovely People* (1955), *Brother, My Brother* (1960), *The Day the Dancers Came* (1967), *Toledo Is the Love* (1969), *Dwell in the Wilderness* (1985), and *The Scent of Apples* (1967), which was the only book published in the United States and won the **American Book Award**. Santos also published an autobiography, *Memory's Fictions* (1993), and two books of **poetry**: *The Wounded Stag* (1956) and *Distances: In Time* (1983). Almost all his writings deal with Filipino American experiences and their nostalgia for the Philippines when they were in the United States and for the United States when they were in the Philippines. Santos received many honors, including a Rockefeller Fellowship at the Iowa Writers' Workshop, a Fulbright lectureship, a Guggenheim Foundation Fellowship, and a Republic Cultural Heritage Award in Literature.

SAOPENG, OVA (1973–). A Laotian American actor and playwright, Saopeng was born in Savannakhet, Laos, and raised in Honolulu, Hawaii. He received his B.A. in **Theater** from the University of Southern California and since then has performed nationally with theater companies, including the Children's Theater Company in Minneapolis, Mark Taper Forum/P.L.A.Y., the **East West Players**, and **hereandnow**. A member of We Tell Stories and Water's Edge Theater, he is a TeAda Productions Company Artist and cocreator of *Refugee Nation*, a play about the Laotian American experience, based on the stories of the Lao communities across the United States. His one-man show "Welcome to Lao as a Second Language" explores the American identity, cultural and generational conflicts, and the universal struggle to find oneself in this world. He also acted in the film *Pirates of the Caribbean: At World's End. See also* SOUTHEAST ASIAN AMERICAN LITERATURE AND THEATER.

SASAKI, R. A. (1952–). A **Japanese American** fiction writer, Sasaki is a **sansei**, born in San Franciscan. She attended the University of Kent in Canterbury, has a B.A. from the University of California at Berkeley, and an M.A. in creative writing from San Francisco State University. She has authored a book of nine stories, *The Loom and Other Stories* (1991), which investigates themes of family, generational conflicts, and history. Winner of the 1983 American Japanese National Literary Award, she has had stories published in the *Short Story Review* and *Making Waves: An Anthology of Writing by Asian–American Women.* She lives in California.

SATO, KIYO (1923–). A **Japanese American** memoirist, Sato was born and raised in Sacramento, California, to **issei** parents. The bombing of Pearl Harbor (7 December 1941) and **Japanese American internment** occurred when she was attending Sacramento Junior College. After her release from the camp, she joined the U.S. Air Force, completing her college education in nursing and achieving the rank of captain. She is the author of the memoire *Dandelion through the Crack* (2007), winner of the William Saroyan Prize for International Writing. It was reprinted in 2009 as *Kiyo's Story: A Japanese–American Family's Quest for the American Dream*. Her memoir recounts her family's experience, coping with the Depression, being interned in concentration camps, and ultimately surviving and succeeding despite terrible odds and oppressive prejudice.

SATYAL, RAKESH (1980–). A **South Asian American** novelist, Satyal was born and raised in Cincinnati, Ohio. He received his B.A. in comparative literature and creative writing from Princeton University. He is the author of the novel *Blue Boy* (2009), a gender-bending comedy about a young Indian American boy's fascination with the Hindu god Krishna. He has been published in several anthologies, including the **Lambda** Award–winning *The Man I Might Become: Gay Men Write about Their Fathers* and the second volume of the *Fresh Men* series. Satyal is an editor at HarperCollins and lives in Brooklyn, New York.

SAY, ALLEN (1937–). A **Japanese American** author of **children's books**, Say was born in Yokohama, Japan, to a Japanese American mother and a Korean father who was adopted by British parents and raised in Shanghai. As a boy, he apprenticed himself for many years to his favorite cartoonist, Noro

Shinpei. His father brought him to the United States. Say served in the U.S. Army for a time, stationed in Germany. Upon returning to the United States, he pursued photography as a career choice and was encouraged to explore his illustrations. He is the author and illustrator of numerous children's books. The best known was *Grandfather's Journey* (1993), a picture book detailing Say's grandfather's voyage from Japan to the United States and back again, which won the 1994 Caldecott Medal. Other books include *The Ink-Keeper's Apprentice* (1975), *The Bicycle Man* (1989), *Tree of Cranes* (1991), *Tea with Milk* (1999), *Emma's Rug* (1996), *The Sign Painter* (2000), *El Chino* (1990), *Music for Alice* (2004), *The Lost Lake* (1992), *Erika-san* (2009), *Kamishibai Man* (2005), *Drawing from Memory* (2011), *Under the Cherry Blossom Tree: An old Japanese Tale* (2005), *Allison* (1997), and *Home of the Brave* (2002).

SECOND GENERATION PRODUCTIONS. This is an Asian American **theater**, founded in 1997 in New York City. Cultivating the next generation of Asian American dramatic arts, the group nurtures a vibrant community of actors, directors, and writers from the established and emerging preprofessionals. It connects with new and underserved audiences, especially young Asian Americans, toward the establishment of a vital and effective platform for Asian American voices to be heard on the world's stage.

SEE, LISA LENINE (1955–). A prolific **Chinese American** novelist, born in Paris, France, to an American mother (novelist Carolyn Laws) and a father with one-quarter Chinese blood. See spent her first six years in Europe. Although her parents were divorced when she was four, she spent much time with her father's relations in **Chinatown**, Los Angeles. After she graduated with a B.A. from Loyola Marymount University, See began her career as a journalist and a writer. She was West Coast correspondent for *Publishers Weekly* (1983–1996) and has written articles for the *Washington Post*, *Sporting Times*, *Los Angeles Times*, *Vogue*, *Self*, etc. She is the author of the critically acclaimed memoir *On Gold Mountain: The One-Hundred-Year Odyssey of My Chinese American Family* (1995). She then went on to publish novels, *Flower Net* (1997), *The Interior* (1999), *Dragon Bones* (2003), *Snow Flower and the Secret Fan* (2005), *Peony in Love* (2007), and *Shanghai Girls* (2009). All these novels feature Chinese and/or Chinese American characters, who engage in cross-cultural struggles and demonstrate courage and tenacity in overcoming **racism**. See has written the libretto for the opera based on *On* ***Gold Mountain*** and has helped develop the Family Discovery Gallery for the Autry Museum, which portrays Los Angeles in the 1930s from the perspective of her father as a seven-year-old boy. Among her awards and recognitions are the Organization of Chinese American Women's 2001 award as National Woman of the Year and the 2003 History Makers Award presented by the Chinese American Museum. See served as a Los Angeles city commissioner.

SEKARAN, SHANTHI. A **South Asian American** novelist, Sekaran was born in Sacramento, California, and now divides her time between Berkeley and London. She was first published in *Best New American Voices 2004* (Harcourt) and attended the Writing Seminars at Johns Hopkins University. *The Prayer Room* (2009), her debut novel, deals with the themes of love, betrayal, sexuality, displacement, and religion.

SESHADRI, VIJAY (1954–). A **South Asian American** poet, essayist, and literary critic, Seshadri was born in India and came to the United States at the age of five. He grew up in Columbus, Ohio. He holds an A.B. degree from Oberlin College, an M.F.A. in creative writing, and a Ph.D. in Middle Eastern Languages and Literature from Columbia University. He is the author of three collections of **poetry**. *Wild Kingdom* (1996) depicts street scenes and seascapes in search of the primordial face behind the civilized mask. *The Long Meadow* (2003), winner of the **James Laughlin Award**, explores the themes of history, fable, fairytale, and fantasy. *The Disappearances* (2007) investigates history, loss, and nightmare. Seshadri's poems, essays, and reviews have appeared in *AGNI*, *Antaeus*, *Boulevard*, *Epiphany*, the *Nation*, the *New Yorker*, the *New York Times*, the *Paris Review*, *Shenandoah*, *Southwest Review*, the *Threepenny Review*, *Verse*, and *Western Humanities Review*. He has received grants from the New York Foundation for the Arts and the National Endowment for the Arts. He has been awarded the *Paris Review*'s Bernard F. Conners Long Poem Prize, the MacDowell Colony's Fellowship for Distinguished Poetic Achievement, and a Guggenheim fellowship. He currently teaches poetry and is the director of the graduate nonfiction writing program at Sarah Lawrence College.

SETH, VIKRAM (1952–). A prolific **South Asian American** poet and novelist, Seth was born in Calcutta, India. He has studied at Oxford, Stanford, and Nanjing Universities. He abandoned his Ph.D. studies in economics at Stanford University after he published his first verse novel, *The Golden Gate* (1986). The novel describes the experiences of a group of friends living in California. His acclaimed epic of Indian life, *A Suitable Boy* (1993), won the WH Smith Literary Award and the Commonwealth Writers Prize. Set in India in the early 1950s, it is the story of a young girl and her search for a husband. *An Equal Music* (1999) is the story of a violinist haunted by the memory of a former lover. He is also the author of a travel book, *From Heaven Lake:*

Travels through Sinkiang and Tibet (1983), an account of a journey through Tibet, China, and Nepal that won the Thomas Cook Travel Book Award. His **poetry** books include *Mappings* (1980), *The Humble Administrator's Garden* (1985), winner of the Commonwealth Poetry Prize (Asia), *All You Who Sleep Tonight: Poems* (1990), and *Three Chinese Poets* (1992). His **children's book**, *Beastly Tales from Here and There* (1992), consists of 10 stories about animals told in verse. His most recent publication is a memoir, *Two Lives* (2005), about the marriage of his great uncle and aunt.

SHAH, PURVI (1972–). A **South Asian American** poet, Shah was born in Ahmadabad, India, and came to the United States with her family when she was two. She grew up in various states including Georgia, Florida, Indiana, and Virginia. She currently lives in New York City. She received her B.A. in comparative literature from the University of Michigan and M.A. in American literature from Rutgers University. She is the author of a book of **poetry**, *Terrain Track* (2006), which won a Many Voices Project prize. Her poems explore themes of nature, family, travel, cultural heritage, and immigration. Her works have been published in various journals, including *Descant*, *Drunken Boat*, the *Literary Review*, the *Massachusetts Review*, *Black Water Review*, *Natural Bridge*, *Crab Orchard Review*, and *South Asian Review*, as well as in anthologies. She serves as executive director of Sakhi for South Asian Women, an organization based in New York City that works to end violence against **women**, and is a board member of the New York Women's Foundation, a cross-cultural alliance of women helping women fund change.

SHANKAR, RAVI (1975–). A **South Asian American** poet, Shankar was born in Washington, D.C., to Indian immigrants and raised in Manassas, Virginia. He received his B.A. in English from University of Virginia and M.F.A. in **poetry** from Columbia University. He has published two books of poems: *Instrumentality* (2004), a finalist for the 2005 Connecticut Book Awards, and *Voluptuous Bristle* (2010). He has also coauthored with Reb Livingston a chapbook, *Wanton Textiles* (2006). He is the founding editor of the online journal *Drunken Boat*. His work has appeared in such places as the *Paris Review*, *Poets & Writers*, *Time Out New York*, *Gulf Coast*, the *Massachusetts Review*, *Descant*, *LIT*, *Crowd*, the *Cortland Review*, *Catamaran*, the *Indiana Review*, *Western Humanities Review*, the *Iowa Review*, and the *AWP Writer's Chronicle*, among other publications. Shankar's poetry does not dwell on themes of ethnicity and immigration; rather it plays with language, sound, and abstraction. He is a recipient of a Connecticut Commission on Culture & Tourism Fellowship in Poetry.

SHANKAR, S. (1962–). A **South Asian American** novelist, Shankar was born in India. Son of a diplomat, he grew up in different countries. He received his B.A. in English from Loyola College and M.A. in English from Madras Christian College. In 1987, Shankar came to the United States to pursue a Ph.D. degree in English and completed it at the University of Texas, Austin. His dissertation on Jonathan Swift's *Gulliver's Travels* cast a strong influence on his first novel, *A Map of Where I Live* (1997), in which an Indian historian discovers that Lilliput (as in Swift's *Gulliver's Travels*) really exists. His most recent novel, *No End to the Journey* (2005), weaves a father–son story with the threads and colors of the ancient epic of Ramayana. Shankar has also written **poetry** and short stories. Currently, he is a professor of English at the University of Hawaii, Manoa.

SHARIF, BINA (1940–). A **South Asian American** playwright, actress, director, and visual artist, Sharif was born in Pakistan and came to the United States as an adult, having already earned an M.D. degree. She then enrolled in Johns Hopkins University and received a master's degree in public health but did not pursue a medical career in order to focus on writing and acting. Sharif has authored more than 20 plays, including the highly acclaimed post-9/11 play *Afghan Woman* (2002), *Closet Full of Juicy Plums* (1997), *A Decent Job* (1997), *Love Is a Stranger in a Windowless Room* (1994), *Here Comes the Change* (2000), *My Ancestor's Home* (2000), *Republic of Iraq* (2006), *Think of Ben Brantley and Write a Happy Play* (2006), *Why* (2004), *Stream of Consciousness of Singing Birds* (2010), *One Thousand Hours of Love* (1992), and *Watchman* (1989). She has received several awards, including 10 from the Jerome Foundation, two from the New York State Council on the Arts, and a Franklin Furnace award. *See also* THEATER.

SHARMA, AKHIL (1971–). A **South Asian American** novelist, Sharma was born in Delhi, India, and immigrated to the United States when he was eight. While he was studying for his B.A. in public policy at the Woodrow Wilson School at Princeton, he also studied creative writing with famous writers like Toni Morrison, Joyce Carol Oates, and Russell Banks. He was a Stegner Fellow at Stanford and won several O. Henry Prizes. Disappointed with his prospect as a screenwriter, he left Stanford to attend Harvard Law School. He is the author of one novel, *An Obedient Father* (2000), for which he won the 2000 PEN/Hemingway Award, the 2001 Whiting Writers' Award, and the 2001 **Asian American Literary Award**. The novel tells dark family secrets of a corrupt official in the New Delhi school system. Sharma has also published stories in the *New Yorker*, the *Atlantic Monthly*, the *Quarterly*, *Fiction*, the *Best American Short Stories*, and the *O. Henry Award Winners* anthology. His short story "Cosmopolitan" was anthologized in the *Best American Short Stories 1998* and was also made into an acclaimed 2003 film of the same name, which has appeared on the PBS series *Independent Lens*.

SHARMA, POONAM (1977–). A **South Asian American** novelist, Sharma was born and raised on Long Island, New York. She received her bachelor's degree in economics from Harvard College and M.B.A. from the Wharton School of Business at the University of Pennsylvania. She is the author of two books on business entrepreneurship, and two novels that fall into the category of romantic comedy. *Girl Most Likely To* (2007) draws heavily on her experience as an Indian American **woman** balancing the worlds of cultural conservatism, interracial romance, and high finance in Manhattan. *All Eyes on Her* (2008) takes the reader into the world of a Hollywood celebrity divorce attorney, who is maneuvering the jealousy of a professional rival, dodging the pitfalls of her emotionally bereft mother, and coming to terms with the romantic mess she has made of her own life.

SHAUGHNESSY, BRENDA (1970–). A **Japanese American** poet, Shaughnessy was born in Okinawa, Japan, and grew up in Southern California. She received her B.A. in literature and **women**'s studies at the University of California, Santa Cruz, and she earned an M.F.A. in creative writing at Columbia University. She is the author of two books of **poetry**. *Human Dark with Sugar* (2008), winner of the James Laughlin Award, explores with contagious humor themes of love, sex, and pain. *Interior with Sudden Joy* (1999), winner of a **Lambda Literary Award** and the Norma Farber First Book Award, is a celebration of erotic life. Her poems have appeared in *Best American Poetry*, *Bomb*, *Boston Review*, *Conjunctions*, *McSweeney's*, the *New Yorker*, the *Paris Review*, the *Yale Review*, and elsewhere. Shaughnessy is the recipient of a Bunting Fellowship and a Japan/U.S. Friendship Commission Artist Fellowship. She is the poetry editor at *Tin House* magazine and currently teaches creative writing at Princeton University and Eugene Lang College at the New School.

SHEIKH, MOAZZAM (1962–). A **South Asian American** fiction writer, Sheikh was born and raised in Lahore and migrated to the San Francisco Bay Area in 1985. He holds a B.A. in commerce from Pakistan, a B.A. in film from San Francisco State University, and an M.A. in library science from San Jose State University. He is the author of one collection of short stories, *The Idol Lover and Other Stories of Pakistan* (2008). His short fiction has been anthologized widely. The major themes in his writing are the interplay of power and desire, miscommunication, class struggle, colonialism, **exile,**

and postcolonial tensions, codependence of sexism and patriarchy, and postmodernity in literature and art. He won the Katha Translation Award for the Urdu category by translating noted Urdu writer Naiyer Masud. He is currently an art and music librarian at the San Francisco Public Library.

SHEPARD, KAREN (1965–). A **Chinese American** novelist, Shepard was born and raised in New York City. She received her B.A. in English from Williams College and M.F.A. in creative writing from the University of Houston. She is the author of three novels. Her debut novel, *An Empire of Women* (2001), captures the reunion of a famous French–Chinese photographer with her Asian American daughter and granddaughter. *The Bad Boy's Wife* (2005) is the story of a relationship and marriage told in reverse, from its fateful end to its magical beginnings. Her most recent publication, *Don't I Know You?* (2007), is a psychological drama centering on a murder case. Her short fiction has been published in the *Atlantic Monthly*, *Bomb*, *Failbetter*, *Glimmertrain*, *Mississippi Review*, and *Southwest Review*, among others. Her nonfiction has appeared in *Self*, *USA Today*, and the *Columbia Companion to the 20th Century American Short Story*, as well as other anthologies. Her honors include a William Goyen–Doris Roberts Fellowship for Fiction from the Christopher Isherwood Foundation, a National Magazine Award Finalist in 2002, and a recipient of a Massachusetts Cultural Council Artist Grant. She teaches writing and literature at Williams College in Williamstown, Massachusetts, where she lives with her husband, novelist Jim Shepard.

SHETH, KASHMIRA (1952–). A **South Asian American** children's storywriter and young adult novelist, Sheth was born in Bhavangar, India, and moved to Iowa for college at age 17. She received a B.S. in microbiology and zoology from Iowa State University and an M.S. in microbiology from University of Wisconsin, Madison. She is the author of six **children's books**, all of which are set in India. *Blue Jasmine* (2004), a **young adult novel**, won a Paul Zindel First Novel Award and Oppenheim Toy Portfolio Platinum Award. *Boys without Names* (2010) is a coming-of-age story. *Keeping Corner* (2009), a historical young adult novel, won a Parents' Choice Gold Award and a Friends of American Writers Award, and *Koyal Dark, Mango Sweet* (2006) is a love story for young adult readers. *Monsoon Afternoon* (2007) and *My Dadima Wears a Sari* (2008) are illustrated children's stories. Her works explore the themes of immigration, social justice, family, and coming of age. She lives in Madison, Wisconsin.

SHIGEKUNI, JULIE (1962–). A **Japanese American** novelist and documentary filmmaker, Shigekuni was born in Panorama, California. She holds a B.A. from Hunter College and an M.F.A. from Sarah Lawrence College.

She is the author of three novels: *A Bridge between Us* (1995), *Invisible Garden* (2003), and *Unending Nora* (2008). *Unending Nora* is the first work of literature to expose the after effects of **Japanese American internment** on contemporary American life. She has won several awards for her writing, including the PEN Josephine Miles Award for Excellence in Literature, the Henfield Award, and the Japanese American National Literary Award. She is a professor of creative writing at University of New Mexico. Shigekuni is coproducer and director of a video documentary, *Manju Mammas and the An-Pan Brigade*, the story of three **nisei** Christian **women** and their nontraditional offspring set amidst the local Buddhist Obon festival.

SHIMODA, BRANDON (1978–). A **Japanese American** poet, Shimoda was born in Tarzana, California, to a Japanese American father and a white American mother. He has received degrees from Sarah Lawrence College and the University of Montana, where he also taught English composition and creative writing. Shimoda has published drawings, collaborations and writings in numerous publications in print and online, and is the author of *The Alps* (2008), *The Inland Sea* (2008), *Lake M* (2010), *The Girl without Arms* (2011), and *O Bon* (2011), as well as collaborations with the poets Phil Cordelli (*The Pines*, Volumes 1–6, 2005–2009), Sommer Browning (*The Bowling*, 2010), and Julia Cohen (*Samaritan*, 2011). Shimoda has helped edit numerous literary magazines, including *CutBank*, *Octopus Books & Magazine*, and *Slope*. From 2005 through 2008, he curated the New Lakes Reading Series in Missoula, Montana, and was cohost of the New Lakes Poetry radio show. From 2008 through 2010, he was the director of marketing of Wave Books, an independent **poetry** press based in Seattle.

SHIMODA, TODD (1955–). A **Japanese American** novelist, Shimoda was born and raised in Colorado. He received his B.S. in engineering, M.S. in communication from Colorado State University, and Ph.D. in science and mathematics education from the University of California, Berkeley. He is the author of three novels. *Oh! A Mystery of Mono No Aware* (2009), a **hybrid** novel mixing nonfiction and artwork, tells the story of a young Japanese American man searching for an aesthetic and emotional life while traveling in Japan. *The Fourth Treasure* (2002) is a mystery and a love story spanning three decades involving characters living on both shores of the Pacific Ocean. *365 Views of Mt. Fuji* (1998), set in Japan, tells the story of a disenchanted salaryman, an outsider from Japan's corporate cliques.

SHIN, SUN YUNG (1974–). A **Korean American** poet, Shin was born in Seoul, Korea, and raised in Chicago as the adopted child of a Polish–Irish–German American family. She received her B.A. in English from Macalester

College and M.A.T. from University of St. Thomas. Her book of poems, *Skirt Full of Black* (2007), winner of an **Asian American Literary Award**, explores themes of immigration, transcultural adoption, and language. She has also published a **children's book**, *Cooper's Lesson* (2004). Her poems have appeared in journals, such as *Indiana Review*, *Swerve*, *Court Green*, *Mid-American Review*, *Sonora Review*, *Capilano Review*, and elsewhere. She is the recent recipient of grants and awards from the Bush Foundation, Minnesota State Arts Board, and the Jerome Foundation.

SHINMYUNG PAE. This is a New York–based **Korean American** performance troupe, founded in 1990. Its mission is to promote a progressive awareness of Korean American culture, to engender pride in one's roots, and to build bridges between diverse communities through its music and dance. It showcases and teaches the traditional music and dance of Korea.

SHUNYA. This is a **South Asian American** troupe established in 2003 and based in Houston, Texas. Shunya literally means "zero, nothing, or emptiness" in Sanskrit. The name comes from the Buddhist concept of "nothing" as the ultimate goal of realization. In India, **theater** traditions have always been intertwined with spiritual pursuits. Shunya provides a voice to the South Asian American experience through the visual and performing arts.

SIDHWA, BAPSI (1938–). A **South Asian American** novelist, Sidhwa was born in Karachi before the partition and grew up in Lahore. She received her B.A. from Kinnaird College for **Women** in Lahore in 1957. An activist, she represented Pakistan at the 1975 Asian Women's Conference. She is the recipient of a Bunting fellow at Radcliffe/Harvard and a National Endowment for the Arts grant. She has taught at the University of Houston, Rice University, Columbia University, Mount Holyoke College, and Brandeis University. Her first novel, *The Bride* (1983), depicts a young woman's honor killing because she tries to escape from an arranged marriage. *The Crow Eaters* (1980) is her second novel though published before the first; it is a comic treatment of several generations of a Parsi family in Lahore. Her third novel, *Cracking India* (1991), made Sidhwa famous in the United States and Great Britain. It is a story about the violent partition of India and Pakistan in 1947. She went on to write *An American Brat* (1993), a sequel to *The Crow Eaters*; *Bapsi Sidhwa Omnibus* (2001); *City of Sin and Splendor* (2006); and *Water* (2006). In collaboration with the filmmaker Deepa Mehta, Sidhwa adapted *Cracking India* and *Water* to the well-known partition films: *Earth* (1998) and *Water* (2005). She has received multiple honors, including visiting scholar at the Rockefeller Foundation, Bellagio

Center, Italy; Sitara-i-Imtiaz (Pakistan's highest national honor in the arts); Lila Wallace–Reader's Digest Writer's Award; and Italy's Premio Mondello for Foreign Authors for *Water*.

SKINNER, MICHELLE CRUZ (1965–). A **Filipina American** fiction writer, Cruz was born and raised in the Philippines to a Caucasian American father and a Filipina mother. She earned her B.A. from the University of Hawaii and her M.F.A. in creative writing from Arizona State University. She currently teaches at Punahou School in Honolulu. She is the author of three collections of short stories: *Mango Seasons* (1996), *Balikbayan* (2008), and *In the Company of Strangers* (2009). All her stories explore the themes of alienation, dislocation, homesickness, and Filipino American struggles.

SOCIETY OF HERITAGE PERFORMERS (THE). This group was established by veteran actor Soon-Tek Oh in 1995. It evolved into **Lodestone Theatre Ensemble** in 1999.

SOENTPIET, CHRIS (1970–). A **Korean American** author and illustrator of **children's books**, Soentpiet was born in South Korea. At the age of eight, he moved to Hawaii to live with his adoptive family. He studied fine arts and education at Pratt Institute in New York City. A year later, the Soentpiets relocated to Portland, Oregon. He currently lives and works in New York City. He is the author and illustrator of *Around Town* (1994). He is recognized as an award-winning illustrator in the children's book industry and has received numerous honors, including the International Reading Association Teachers' Choice Award, National Association for the Advancement of Colored People Image Award, Parents' Choice Gold Award, Parents Magazine Best Children's Book of the Year, North Carolina Children's Book Award, Georgia Children's Picture Book Award, and International Reading Association Notable Children's Book.

SOGA, KEIHO (1873–1957). A **Japanese American** poet and memoirist, Soga was born in Japan and immigrated to Hawaii in 1896. He worked as a reporter for *Hawaii Shimpo*. He was interned at Oahu, then Lordsburg, and Santa Fe during World War II. He is most known for his memoir *Life behind Barbed Wire: The World War II* ***Internment*** *Memoirs of a Hawaii* ***Issei*** (2007). He coauthored *Poets behind Barbed Wire:* ***Tanka*** *Poems* (1983), which received an **American Book Award**. His **poetry** has appeared in several anthologies, including the *New Anthology of American Poetry*, *Quiet fire*, and *The Best of* ***Bamboo Ridge***.

SON, DIANA (1965–). A **Korean American** playwright, Son was born in Philadelphia and raised in Dover, Delaware. She majored in dramatic literature at New York University between 1983 and 1987 and studied directing composition between 1991 and 1992 with Anne Bogard at Playwrights Horizons Theatre School in New York City. In 1993, she attended the Iowa Playwrights' Workshop but left without finishing her degree. At Iowa she participated in the Asian American Playwrights Lab at the Public **Theater** and wrote *R.A.W. ('Cause I'm a Woman)*, her first piece to address Asian American themes. She went on to write *Boy* (1996), *Stop Kiss* (1998), *Stealing Fire* (1992), *The Joyless Bad Luck Club* (1993), *2000 Miles* (1993), *Fishes* (1995), *Satellites* (2006). Common themes in these plays include identity, transformation, sexuality, and human connection. She is also a writer and coexecutive producer of the TV show *Law & Order: Criminal Intent*. Son has won awards, such as the Gay & Lesbian Alliance against Defamation Media Award for Outstanding New York Production and the Berilla Kerr Award for Playwriting. She was the 2000–2001 NEA/TCG playwright-in-residence at the Mark Taper Forum in Los Angeles and a visiting lecturer in playwriting at the Yale School of Drama.

SONE, MONICA (1919–2011). A **Japanese American** memoirist, Sone was born in Seattle to **issei** parents. After the bombing of Pearl Harbor (7 December 1941), her family was interned in Camp Minidoka in Idaho. After one year in camp, she was allowed to attend Wendell College on a scholarship obtained through the help of church friends and went on to finish her undergraduate degree from Hanover College and graduate degree in clinical psychology from Western Reserve University. Her only book, *Nisei Daughter* (1953), is the first memoir about the experience of **Japanese American internment**.

SONG, CATHY (1955–). A well-known **Chinese–Korean American** poet, Song was born in Hawaii to a second-generation Chinese mother and a second-generation Korean father. She received her B.A. in English from Wellesley College and M.F.A. from Boston College. She was only 27 when she won the Yale Series of Young Poets Award for her book of **poetry**, *Picture Bride* (1983). In addition to a large number of poems published in literary journals, Song has published books of poetry: *Frameless Windows, Squares of Light* (1988), *School Figures* (1994), and *The Land of Bliss* (2001). Song's poetry is primarily autobiographical and family centered. Song has taught creative writing at the University of Hawaii, Manoa, since 1987. She received the Shelly Memorial Award from the Poetry Society of America and the Hawaii Award for Literature in 1993 as the youngest recipient in the award's history.

SOUTH ASIAN AMERICAN LITERATURE AND THEATER. South Asia—a term coined by the U.S. Department of State in the 1960s—refers to Afghanistan, Bangladesh, India, Nepal, Pakistan, and Sri Lanka. However, these countries (their statehood itself was a result of colonization) are far from being a monolithic whole, as they have diverse cultures, languages, religions, and ethnicities. South Asian American writers are one of the newest voices in Asian American literature and **theater**. They are first, second, or third generation immigrants from South Asia, or via stopovers by their families in places like Africa, East Asia, and the Caribbean. Having been colonized by Great Britain, these countries, with the exception of Afghanistan, have adopted English as their official language. Thus, South Asian immigrants came to the United States, speaking/writing English and versed in British literature.

The first generation of South Asian American writers was mostly male, educated, and affluent. Unlike the earliest Chinese, Japanese, and Filipinos who came as laborers, the South Asians came as scholarship students in the early 1900s, and many of them lived **diasporic** lives among their home countries, Great Britain, and the United States, such as **Raja Rao**, **A. K. Ramanujan**, **Govindas Desani**, **Zulfikar Ghose**, **G. S. Sharat Chandra**, **Dhan Gopal Mukerji**, and **Rama Santha Rau**, who was the only woman among the first generation. Their themes and styles were often fashioned by British literary influences.

Facilitated by a more liberal immigration policy in the United States in the 1960s, a large number of South Asian professionals arrived in America. Out of these middle- and upper-class immigrants emerged most of the well-known South Asian writers, many of whom are **women**. This second generation of writers does not shy away from politics and portrays the lives of immigrants in the postcolonial world, exploring the themes of home, memory, migration, gender, race/ethnicity, and colonialism. Some of the most prominent writers in this generation are **Meena Alexander**, **Agha Shahid Ali**, **Susham Bedi**, **Chitra Banerjee Divakaruni**, **Bharati Mukherjee**, **Bapsi Sidhwa**, **Sara Suleri**, and **Bina Sharif**.

During the past decade or so, a group of U.S. or British-born South Asians has appeared in the literary scene, taking their immigrant parents' lives and their own experiences as materials. The best-known author in this third generation of South Asian American authors who has explored the themes of generational conflicts and alienation is **Jhumpa Lahiri**. Other less known figures include **Srikanth Reddy**, **Rakesh Satyal**, **Chandra Prasad**, and **Vikram Seth**. Still, the majority of this third generation of writers consists of immigrants, and they write novels, **poetry**, stories, plays, **children's books**, and memoirs that vividly present the lives of nomadic characters, exploring the themes of belonging, memory, religion, and **exile**. Prominent writers in this youngest generation are **Suketu Mehta**, **Srikanth Rakesh**, **Chandra Prasad**, and **Vikram Seth**. Then, there are writers who have stayed away from these themes, such as **Sujata Massey** who has written detective stories, **Shilpa Agarwal** who has written ghost stories, and **Mary Anne Mohanraj** who has written erotic fantasies.

The newest voice among South Asian American writers belongs to Afghan Americans. Although their number is small, some of their writings have drawn great publicity. The best-known Afghan American writer is **Khaled Hosseini**, the first Afghan American novelist. His first novel, *The Kite Runner* (2001), set in the final days of the monarchy to the present, explores themes of friendship, betrayal, and the price of loyalty. It describes the rich culture and beauty of a land in the process of being destroyed. His second novel, *A Thousand Splendid Suns*, set against the volatile events of Afghanistan's last 30 years—from the Soviet invasion to the reign of the Taliban to the post-Taliban rebuilding—tells the story of two generations of characters brought jarringly together by the tragic sweep of war. **Tamim Ansary** is another well-known Afghan American novelist and memoirist, whose memoir, *West of Kabul, East of New York* (2002), depicts what it was like to grow up straddling two vastly disparate cultures. Other Alfghan writers include **Awista Ayub** and **Donia Gobar**.

South Asian American theaters began to emerge in the late 1980s. They feature drama, film, and dance to promote multicultural appreciation and religious tolerance. These theater groups include **Desipina & Co.**, **Krea**, **Naatak**, **Rasaka Theatre Company**, **SAATh**, **SALAAM Theatre**, **Sruti**, the **Kathak Esemble**, **Shunya**, and the **Post *Natyam* Collective.** *See also* ALI, SAMINA; AMIRTHANAYAGAM, INDRAN; BANERJEE, ANJALI; BANTWAL, SHOBHAN; BUDHOS, MARINA; CHANDRA, VIKRAM; CHARI, SHEELA; CHERIAN, ANNE; CRASTA, RICHARD; DASWANI, KAVITA; DAWESAR, ABHA; DESAI, BOMAN; DESAI, KIRAN; D'SOUZA, TONY; ETERAZ, ALI; FERRELL, MONICA; GANESAN, INDIRA; GANESHANANTHAN, VASUGI V.; GHOSH, AMITAV; GOWDA, SHILPI SOMAYA; HAJI, NAFISA; HAMID, MOHSIN; JAMES, TANIA; KAIPA, SUMMI; KAPIL, BHANU; KHANNA, VANDANA; KIRCHNER, BHARTI; KRISHNASWAMI, UMA; KUMAR, AMITAVA; MAHAJAN, KARAN; MALLADI, AMULYA; MASSEY, SUJATA; MEER, AMEENA; MEHTA, SUKETU; MEHTA, VED PARKASH; MUEENUDDIN, DANIYAL; NAQVI, H. M.; NAQVI, TAHIRA; NARAYAN, KIRIN; NAZARETH, PETER; NIGAM, SANJAY; PERKINS, MITALI; PRADHAN, MONICA; QAZI, JAVAID; RAHMAN, IMAD; RAMANUJAN, A. K.; REDDY, SRIKANTH; REHMAN, BUSHRA; SEKARAN, SHANTHI;

SESHADRI, VIJAY; SHAH, PURVI; SHANKAR, RAVI; SHANKAR, S.; SHARMA, AKHIL; SHARMA, POONAM; SHEIKH, MOAZZAM; SHETH, KASHMIRA; SREENIVASAN, JYOTSNA; SUNDARESAN, INDU; SURI, MANIL; UMRIGAR, THRITY; VAZIRANI, REETIKA; VERGHESE, ABRAHAM.

SOUTHEAST ASIAN AMERICAN LITERATURE AND THEATER. Other than **Vietnamese** and **Filipino Americans**, Southeast Asian Americans also include those who trace their ancestral roots to Burma, Cambodia, Laos, Indonesia, Malaysia, Singapore, and Thailand. The most recent literary voices among Asian American literature are from this region. The Vietnam War impacted the neighboring countries of Cambodia and Laos, and a Communist takeover occurred simultaneously in all three countries when the United States withdrew in 1975. The consequence of this historical change was a significant number of refugees temporarily sheltered in refugee camps of other Southeast countries and the eventual migration of many to the United States.

Between 1975 and 2000s, about 150,000 Cambodians settled in the United States under the Refugee Assistance Act of 1975 and the Refugee Act of 1980. Large communities of Cambodian Americans have taken root in cities such as Long Beach, Fresno, and Stockton in California, Providence, Rhode Island, as well as Lynn and Lowell in Massachusetts, and in the Pacific Northwest, Seattle and Portland. The first Cambodian American who published a book of literary work is **Sam U Oeur**, whose book of **poetry**, *Sacred Vows* (1998), recounts Cambodian history and his personal tribulations, drawing on Cambodian myths, folktales, and prophecies. Other writers to follow include memoirists such as **Chanrithy Him**, **Haing S. Ngor**, and **Loung Ung**, and authors of **children's books**, such as **Huy Voun Lee**.

The writings by Laotian and Hmong Americans also reflect the history of the Vietnam War and the pain of transplantation, and they are among the most engaging literary voices in the 2000s. **Bryan Thao Worra** is the best-known Laotian American poet, whose poetry explores themes of transience, identity, memory, and home. **T. C. Huo**'s novel, *Land of Smiles*, traces the life of a Laotian boy from swimming across the Mekong River to Thailand to arriving in San Francisco to returning to Laos. Young poets like **Pos Moua**, **Mali Phonpadith**, and **Saymoukda D. Vongsay** were children when they came to the United States, and their poetry depicts their voyages from the war-torn Laos to America and expresses their longing for the **homeland**—its rivers, oceans, and mountains. **Ova Saopeng** is the cocreator of *Refugee Nation*, a play about the Laotian American experience, based on the stories of the Lao communities across the United States.

A subgroup of Laotian Americans is Hmong American. During the 1960s and 1970s, a Hmong secret army was formed and trained by the Central Intelligence Agency to fight against the Communist army of Vietnam. In 1975, when the United States withdrew from Vietnam and the Communists took over Laos, a vast number of Hmongs escaped to Thailand, and most of them gradually migrated to the United States. They settled in California, Minnesota, and Wisconsin. **Dia Cha** is the first Hmong American memoirist, and her *Dia's Story Cloth* is a picture book that retells her life story, Hmong history, and a classic American immigration tale. Some of the Hmong American writers carry their traumatic memories of the war and refugee camps while others born in the refugee camps or in the United States, such as **May Lee-Yang**, **Kao Kalia Yang**, and **Burlee Vang**, inherited memories of the war, the escape, and the refugee camps, and these memories have been reorganized into memoirs, poetry, and drama. **Ka Vang** is a well-known journalist and playwright, whose plays, *Disconnect*, *Dead Calling*, and *From Shadows to Light*, influenced the younger playwrights, one of whom is May Lee-Yang, famous for her *Confessions of a Lazy Hmong Woman*.

The only Burmese American writer in this dictionary is **Wendy Law-Yone**, whose three novels, *The Coffin Tree*, *Irrawaddy Tango*, and *The Road to Wanting,* explore themes of alienation, **exile**, and madness. Writers tracing their root to Indonesia are small in number as well. The most prominent figure is **Li-young Lee**, who was born in Indonesia to **Chinese** parents. Most of the writers from Singapore and Malaysia are also Chinese or partly Chinese, for instance, **Shirley Geok-lin Lim**, **Chay Yew, Justin Chin**, **Wena Poon**, and **Tinling Choong**.

Unlike the above groups, Thai Americans have experienced a different history that is not colonial or war-ridden. Thus, they focus on themes of cultural conflicts, **assimilation**, ethnic identity, gender, and sexuality. The first Thai American writer is **Minfong Ho**, and other prominent Thai American writers include **Ira Sukrungruang**, **Pimone Triplett**, **Rattawut Lapcharoensap**, **Cherry Chevapravatdumrong**, and **Prince Gomolvilas**. *See also* EAST-WEST RELATIONS; LARSEN, WANWADEE; NAZARETH, PETER.

SREENIVASAN, JYOTSNA (1964–). A **South Asian American** writer of **children's books**, Sreenivasan was born to immigrant parents from India and raised in northeastern Ohio. She earned her B.A. in English from Kent State University and M.A. in English from the University of Michigan. She has written three novels for ages eight to 12: *The Moon over Crete* (1996), a time-travel adventure story with a feminist theme; *Aruna's Journeys* (1997), about an Indian American girl's search for identity; and *And Laughter Fell from the Sky* (2012). *Aruna's Journeys* won a Skipping Stone Magazine award for multicultural fiction. Her short fiction (for adults) has been published in numerous literary magazines and anthologies. She lives in Moscow, Idaho, and works as a science writer at the University of Idaho.

SRUTI. This is an Indian Music and Dance Society based in the Philadelphia region. Founded in 1986, Sruti's principal mission is to promote and present Indian classical music and dance. In addition, the society seeks to educate the Philadelphia community at large about Indian arts. Sruti publishes an annual magazine, *Sruti Ranjani*, and a periodical, *Sruti Notes*.

STAPLETON, LARA (1967–). A **Filipina American** writer, Stapleton was born to a Filipina mother and an Irish American father in East Lansing, Michigan, and raised in both East Lansing and Manila, the Philippines. She earned her B.A. in English from the University of Michigan and M.A. in English from New York University. Her collection of short stories, *The Lowest Blue Flame before Nothing* (1997), portrays the lives of young **women** experiencing racial ambivalence. This collection won the 1998 Columbia Journal fiction prize, the PEN Open Book Award, and was an Independent Booksellers' selection. She is also an editor of *Juncture: 25 Very Good Stories and 12 Excellent Drawings* (2005) and *The Thirdest World: The Stories and Essays by Three Filipino Writers* (2007). She lives in New York City where she teaches writing.

STARNES, SOFIA M. (1952–). A **Filipina American** poet, Starnes was born in Manila and was educated at Saint Pedro Poveda College. She moved to Spain, where she received an advanced degree in English philology from the University of Madrid, after which she moved to the United States. A recipient of a Poetry Fellowship from the Virginia Commission for the Arts, Starnes has won several other awards for her **poetry**. Her chapbook, *The Soul's Landscape* (2002), was selected by the U.S. Poet Laureate Billy Collins as one of two cowinners of the 2001 Aldrich Poetry Prize. Her poetry book, *A Commerce of Moments* (2001), won the Editor's Prize in the 2001 Transcontinental Poetry Award competition and was named Honor Book in the 2004 Virginia Literary Awards Competition. Her collection, *Corpus Homini: A Poem for Single Flesh* (2008), was awarded the Whitebird Poetry Series Prize. Her most recent poetry collection is *Fully into Ashes* (2011). Her poetry explores themes of religion, memory, spirituality, and language. Her other recognitions include the Rainer Maria Rilke Poetry Prize, a Pushcart nomination, Editor's Prize in the 2002 Marlboro Prize in Poetry competition, the 2004 Conference on Christianity and Literature Poetry Prize, the 2005 Superior Achievement Award (Virginia Writer's Club), and designation as a

Distinguished Scholar by Union College, Kentucky. Her work has appeared or is forthcoming in numerous journals, including the *Southern Poetry Review*, the *Notre Dame Review*, *Hayden's Ferry Review*, the *Laurel Review*, *Hubbub*, *Pleiades*, *Gulf Coast*, the *Madison Review*, *Hotel Amerika*, the *Hawaii Pacific Review*, the *Marlboro Review*, and *War, Literature, and the Arts*. Starnes currently lives in Williamsburg, Virginia.

STEALING BUDDHA'S DINNER. This is a well-known memoir written by the **Vietnamese American** writer **Bich Minh Nguyen**. Published in 2007, *Stealing Buddha's Dinner* received multiple honors, including a PEN/Jerard Award, a Chicago Tribune Best Book of 2007, a Kiriyama Prize Notable Book, an Asian American Literature Award finalist, and the all-state Great Michigan Read.

Stealing Buddha's Dinner dramatizes a Vietnamese girl's coming-of-age journey in America. Nguyen arrived in Grand Rapids, Michigan, as a toddler with her grandmother, father, older sister, and uncles soon after the Vietnam War ended. As the title suggests, food and eating are major motives. The first thing the reader notices is the chapter titles, all of which are food items such as "Pringles," "Dairy Cone," and "Bread and Honey." In fact, in this memoir, food is the most dominant language to delineate an ethnic and female bildungsroman that portrays the young protagonist's harrowing experience in Americanization. The culinary differences between her family and her peers, from the refugee child's point of view, represent the ontological distance between her and other Americans, a distance so vast that it can never be fully bridged. The child protagonist experiences heightened sensitivity toward her culinary difference over other race-related markers of difference, such as skin color, hair color and texture, or facial features. To assimilate into the culture of Grand Rapids and to gain acceptance of neighbors and schoolmates, Bich chooses food as a means to her end.

The opening chapter of *Stealing Buddha's Dinner*, titled "Pringles," juxtaposes the longing for this uniquely American snack to the mysterious absence of the mother figure in the life of the child protagonist. By such juxtaposition, Nguyen invites the reader to consider food longing in the context of the primordial trauma over her mother's absence. What makes *Stealing Buddha's Dinner* a fascinating text is the fact that alimentary desires clearly gesture toward their ontological significance. Nguyen's account of her childhood obsession with food makes a powerful statement that, whereas physical hunger can be satisfied by candies, chips, and plenty of rice and beef in America, the other kind of hunger, that for belonging, for acceptance, and for love is nearly impossible to appease. Bich, our young protagonist, cannot change the fact that she looks visibly other, and being an Asian in America, particularly in the Midwest, she will always be perceived as a foreigner. But in appetite and consumption she believes she is able to transform herself, identifying the ingestion of American foods as the most accessible path to belonging. To her disappointment, however, the more she consumes them, the hungrier she becomes. As if they conspired against her plan of self-reinvention, neither her grandmother nor her stepmother cooks "real" American food. Her Hispanic stepmother Rosa does things differently from mothers of her white schoolmates. Rosa "sprinkled wheat germ on grapefruit and bought maple sugar oatmeal over peaches and cream. These small differences accumulated within my growing stockpile of shame and resentment, as if Rosa herself were preventing me from fitting in and being like everyone else" (52). The author's choice of the word "shame" clearly attaches moral value to foodways. Not only are culinary differences from the mainstream/Midwestern fare experienced by her as alienating and shameful but also as outside one's own control, for one is dependent on others in supplying food. Because of the impossibility of placating this ontological hunger, Bich's relationship to the foodways of her culture deteriorates to that of disavowal and repugnance. "No one at school knew how I really ate" (56). She hides her ethnic foodways as if they signified filth and immorality.

Located at the heartland of America, the Nguyen family always occupies the position of the Other despite their aspiration to and practice of American middle-class values. Owning properties, listening to American music, and joining a Brownie troop cannot change their physical appearance, religious faith, foodways, and linguistic habits, all that which set them apart from the white citizens of Grand Rapids. No matter how hard Nguyen tries, she and her family are always different from "how *real* people lived" (139). This discourse of "real" Americans defined against the *others* racializes the child refugee and inculcates in her a melancholic identification with the national ideal. Her melancholia finds expression in fantasies like "I became convinced that I had once been a sad and lonely blond girl who lived in a cold mansion isolated on a moor in England" (183).

Implied in the title, Buddhism plays a significant role, as it is instrumental to Nguyen's journey toward a **hybrid** identity that recuperates the immigrant's past, for the young protagonist does arrive at a moment of enlightenment. At the end of Chapter 13, Bich steals a plum from the Buddha statue and eats it. She stares at the plum's pit. "It was an eye. I realized. A wrinkled, wizened eye. . . . I left the plum's eye in the plum tree. It was gone the next time I climbed up there. I imagined it carried off by the wind, or by my ancestors' spirits, coming to collect the meager offering I had left behind" (196). Bich associates Buddha with ancestral spirits as his statue stands side by side with the portraits of her deceased ancestors who share the offerings of fruits.

In this image of the eye is a subtle epiphany of wisdom beyond description. It is as though by stealing and eating Buddha's plum she had eaten the spirit of Buddha, whose eye stares back at her. It is from this point on the memoir turns to Bich's journey home, to accepting her grandmother's food, and thus her cultural heritage.

Nguyen's rite of passage is a culinary text that gestures toward a greater parameter of identity formation. She observes insightfully that in school, "a student was measured by the contents of her lunch bag, which displayed status, class, and parental love" (75). The foods she longs for—Pringles, Toll House Cookies, Chef Boyardee—symbolize various self-expressions and modes of being that are inaccessible to her, a refugee child. The hunger for American food and fast food serves in this memoir as a central metaphor for the tyranny as well as the impossibility of being American normal. It is through the table narrative that Nguyen succeeds in concretizing the protagonist's ambivalent relationship to American culture and to her self.

STICKMON, JANET (1973–). A **Filipina American** memoirist, Stickmon was born in Yuba City, California, to a Filipina mother and an African American father. She holds a B.A. in civil engineering from the University of California, Irvine, and an M.A. in religion and society from the Graduate Theological Union in Berkeley. Her memoir, *Crushing Soft Rubies* (2003), recounts her story of growing up poor and colored. Her most recent work is *Midnight Peaches, Two O'Clock Patience* (2012), a collection of fiction, **poetry**, and essays. She is also a spoken-word artist.

STROM, DAO (1973–). A **Vietnamese American** fiction writer, Strom was born in Saigon, Vietnam. She and her mother fled Vietnam in 1975 when Saigon fell; her father stayed behind and was imprisoned for the next 10 years. These events—the aftermath of war, separation, exodus, and the interplay of art and personal experience—inform her writing. Strom grew up in Northern California and received her B.A. in film production from San Francisco State University and M.F.A. from the Iowa Writers' Workshop. She is the author of a fiction collection and a novel. *The Gentle Order of Girls and Boys* (2006) contains four loosely linked novellas about young Vietnamese **women** living in present-day California and Texas, and *Grass Roof, Tin Roof* (2003) is her debut novel that tells the story of a woman journalist in Vietnam and her exodus and life in the United States. Strom has been the recipient of a National Endowment for the Arts, a James Michener fellowship, and the *Chicago Tribune*'s Nelson Algren award. She is also a songwriter and released her debut album, *Send Me Home*, in 2004.

SU, ADRIENNE (1967–). A **Chinese American** poet, Su was born to Chinese immigrants and raised in Atlanta, Georgia. She received her B.A. in English from Harvard University and her M.F.A. in creative writing from the University of Virginia. She is the author of three books of poems: *Middle Kingdom* (1997), which explores themes of culture, language, and identity; *Sanctuary* (2006) on maternity, parenting, and career; and *Having None of It* (2009) on displacement and migration. She is the recipient of a fellowship in **poetry** from National Endowment for the Arts and a Pushcart Prize. Her poems have appeared in such journals as *Antioch Review*, *Crazyhorse*, *New Letters*, *Poet Lore*, *Prairie Schooner*, *Southwest Review*, and *Oxford American*, and in anthologies.

SU, LAC (1974–). A **Vietnamese American** memoirist, Su was born in Vietnam. He escaped Vietnam under gunfire and began his life in Los Angeles at age five. He received his bachelor's in social psychology from the University of California, Irvine, and his master's and Ph.D. in Industrial-Organizational Psychology from the California School of Professional Psychology. His memoir, *I Love Yous Are for White People* (2009), tells the story of his search for a sense of worth and belonging from a violent father and local gangs.

SUGIMOTO, ETSU INAGAKI (1874–1950). A **Japanese American** novelist and autobiographer, Sugimoto was born in Japan and died in Tokyo. Raised in an aristocratic class, she received a thorough education in English and Western culture. She came to the United States at age 18 to marry her husband, a Japanese merchant. She is the author of three novels: A *Daughter of the Narikin* (1932), *A Daughter of the Nohfu* (1935), and *Grandmother O Kyo* (1940). She is best known for her autobiography, *The Daughter of the Samurai* (1925), which narrates her childhood in Japan in a large, wealthy household, her education, and her adaptation to American culture. Sugimoto's autobiography, more than the author's life, introduces Japanese culture and customs to the American reader in the style of a cultural anthropologist.

SUH, LLOYD. A **Korean American** playwright, Suh was born to Korean immigrant parents in southern Indiana and currently lives in Brooklyn, New York. Winner of both the Dasha Epstein Next Step Fellowship and the Dramatists Guild of America Playwriting Fellowship, his work has been produced and workshopped with **Second Generation Productions** and the Ensemble Studio Theatre, at venues including the New York Shakespeare Festival/ Joseph Papp Public **Theater**, the **Asian American Writers' Workshop**,

Expanded Arts, and the New York International Fringe Festival. He is the author of *American Hwangap* (2009), *The Children of Vonderly* (2007), *Masha No Home* (2002), *The Garden Variety* (2006), *Great Wall Story, Happy End of the World* (2001), among others. His plays have been presented across the country, including the Lark Play Development Center, Ojai Playwrights Conference, New York Stage & Film, McCarter Theatre Center's IN-Festival, Stamford Center for the Arts, and others. He has been the recipient of grants and commissions from the NEA/Arena Stage New Play Development Project, the Jerome Foundation, South Coast Repertory, Theatre Communications Group, the New York Foundation for the Arts, and New York State Council on the Arts, and was honored by the **National Asian American Theatre Company** and **Pan Asian Rep**. He currently serves as artistic director for Second Generation and codirector of the **Ma-Yi** Writers Lab, the largest resident company of Asian American playwrights ever assembled.

SUKRUNGRUANG, IRA (1976–). A Thai American writer, Sukrungruang was born in Chicago to Thai immigrant parents. He received his B.A. in English from Southern Illinois University and M.F.A. in creative nonfiction from the Ohio State University. He is the author of a memoir, *Talk Thai: The Adventures of Buddhist Boy* (2010), which tells hilarious stories of his growing up between the world of Thailand at home and the world of America outside home. He coedited, with Donna Jarrell, *What Are You Looking At?: the First Fat Fiction Anthology* (2004) and *Scoot Over, Skinny: The Fat Nonfiction Anthology* (2005). He now edits *The Clever Title* and *Sweet: A Literary Confection*. He teaches in the M.F.A. program of University of South Florida. *See also* SOUTHEAST ASIAN AMERICAN LITERATURE AND THEATER.

SULERI, SARA (1953–). A **South Asian American** writer, Suleri was born in Karachi, Pakistan, to a Pakistani father and a Welsh mother. She immigrated to the United States to attend graduate school at Indiana University, where she earned her Ph.D. in 1980. Upon the completion of her degree, Suleri became a professor at Yale University. She has written two memoirs: *Meatless Days* (1989) and *Boys Will Be Boys* (2003). *Meatless Days* won the 1989 Pushcart Prize. A classic of postcolonial literature, *Meatless Days* recounts her girlhood in Pakistan after the 1947 partition. It intertwines the violent history of Pakistan's independence with her intimate memories of her grandmother, mother, and sisters. In *Boys Will Be Boys*, she returns to her childhood and early adulthood to pay tribute to her father, the political journalist Z. A. Suleri.

SUNDARESAN, INDU. A **South Asian American** novelist, Sundaresan was born and brought up in India. She came to the United States for graduate school at the University of Delaware and earned an M.S. in operations research and an M.A. in economics. She is the author of four novels. The Taj Mahal trilogy—*The Twentieth Wife* (2002), *The Feast of Roses* (2003), and *Shadow Princess* (2010)—is an epic tale centering on the family history and stories of Mehrunnisa, Empress Nur Jahan, one of India's most powerful **women**. *The Splendor of Silence* (2006), set in 1942 in India, tells the story of the unlikely romance between an American army captain and an Indian woman. Sundaresan has also published a collection of stories, *In the Convent of Little Flowers* (2008).

SUNÉE, KIM (1970–). A **Korean American** memoirist, Sunée was born in South Korea, adopted, and raised in New Orleans. She traveled and lived in Europe for 10 years. She is the author of a memoir, *Trail of Crumbs: Hunger, Love, and the Search for Home* (2008). The memoir depicts the horrendous death of her mother, her adoption by an American couple, and her search for home via travel and food. Sunée began working as a food editor at *Southern Living* and then worked as the founding food editor of *Cottage Living* magazine. Her writing has appeared in *Entree*, *The Oxford American*, *Cooking Light*, and *Asian American Poetry and Writing*. Sunée has also appeared several times as a guest judge on the Food Network's *Iron Chef America.*

SURI, MANIL (1959–). A **South Asian American** novelist, Suri was born and raised in Bombay, India. He came to the United States as a student at age 20 and obtained his Ph.D. in applied mathematics from Carnegie Mellon University and is a professor of mathematics and statistics at the University of Maryland, Baltimore County. His debut novel, *The Death of Vishnu* (2001), blends comedy with Hindu mythology. His second novel, *The Age of Shiva* (2009), is set in modern India and explores themes of mythology, love, and motherhood. He received a Guggenheim Fellowship for fiction in 2004.

SUYEMOTO, TOYO (1916–2003). A **Japanese American** poet, Suyemoto was born in California to Japanese immigrants and died in Columbus, Ohio. She received her B.A. in English and Latin from University of California, Berkeley. In the fall of 1942, she and her family were relocated to an internment camp in Utah. She worked in the library of the University of Cincinnati for over 10 years after the camp, during which time she took writing workshops at the University. In 1964, she received an M.L.S from the University of Michigan, after which she took the position at the library of Ohio State University and retired from it in 1985. Suyemoto's **poetry** has appeared in literary journals and collections. Her best-known poems center on the **Japanese American internment** experience. Her last publication is a memoir, *I Call to Remembrance* (2007), primarily recounting her experience in the camp.

SZE, ARTHUR (1950–). A **Chinese American** poet, Sze was born in New York City. He attended the Massachusetts Institute of Technology for two years before transferring to the University of California, Berkeley, to study **poetry** writing, Chinese poetry and language, and philosophy. His translation of classic Chinese poetry appears with his own poetry in the early collections *Willow Wind* (1972) and *Two Ravens* (1976). His recent translation of Chinese poetry appears in *The Silk Dragon* (2001). After Berkeley, Sze moved to New Mexico and married a Native American woman. Native American culture has since then become significant in his life and writing. Often Native American rituals, dances, and artifacts commingle with Chinese philosophy, historical figures, and events. Since 1984, Sze has been a professor at the Institute of Indian American Arts in Santa Fe. His other collections of poetry are *Dazzled* (1982), *River River* (1987), *Archipelago* (1995), *The Redshifting Web* (1998), and *Quipu* (2005). While *Redshfting Web* won an **Asian American Literary Award,** *Archipelago* won the 1995 Lannan Award and the 1996 **American Book Award**. Sze's poetry has become increasingly experimental both in form and content and explores subjects of science, philosophy, nature, and history.

SZE, MAI MAI (1910–1992). A **Chinese American** writer and artist, Sze was born in Beijing, China, and died in New York. Daughter of a Chinese ambassador to Great Britain and the United States, Sze lived in England, France, and the United States. She attended British boarding schools, a private American high school, and Wellesley College. She published her autobiography, *Echo of a Cry* (1945), recounting her experiences living and traveling between the West and China. Her allegorical novel, *Silent Children* (1948), depicts the lives of dispossessed children in an imaginary country. She also wrote about the philosophy of Chinese painting in *The Tao of Painting* (1946).

T

TABIOS, EILEEN (1960–). A **Filipina American** poet, fiction writer, artist, and publisher, Tabios was born in the Philippines. She moved to the United States at the age of 10. She earned a B.A. in political science from Barnard College and an M.B.A. in economics and international business from New York University. She has released 16 print, four electronic, one CD **poetry** collections, an art essay collection, a poetry essay/interview anthology, a novel, and a short story book. Among her best-known works are *Reproductions of the Empty Flagpole* (2002), a book of prose and poetry balancing on the much-contested border between "prose" and "poetry"; *I Take Thee, English, for My Beloved* (2005), a multigenre collection fusing the forms of poem, memoir, art monograph, play, novel, and questionnaire; and *The Thorn Rosary* (2010), another book of multigenre tapestry. Tabios invented a poetic form called hay(na)ku, a tercet with a total of six words—1 in the first line, 2 in the second line, and 3 in the third line. In the 'reverse' haynaku, the longest line is placed first and the shortest last. The total is still 6 words: 3 in the first line, 2 in the second line, and 1 in the third line. Multiple hay(na)ku can be chained to form a longer poem. She is the recipient of the Philippines' **National Book Award** for Poetry, and her poetry and editing projects have also received numerous awards, including the PEN Oakland/Josephine Miles Literary Award, the Potrero Nuevo Fund Prize, the Gustavus Meyers Outstanding Book Award in the Advancement of Human Rights, Foreword Magazine Anthology of the Year Award, *Poet Magazine*'s Iva Mary Williams Poetry Award, Judds Hill's Annual Poetry Prize, and the Philippine American Writers & Artists' Catalagan Award, as well as grants from the Witter Bynner Foundation, the National Endowment for the Arts, the New York State Council on the Humanities, the California Council for the Humanities, and the New York City Downtown Cultural Council.

TAGAMI, JEFF (1954–). A **Filipino American** poet, Tagami was born in Watsonville, California. He received a B.A. in English from the University of California, Santa Clara, and an M.A. in English and creative writing from San Francisco State University. Tagami authored *October Light* (1987), a book of **poetry** that depicts the rural life of Filipino Americans. His work has appeared in numerous literary magazines and anthologies, including *Breaking Silence* and the *Open Boat*.

TAGATAC, GERONIMO (1941–). A **Filipino American** fiction writer, Tagatac was born to a Filipino father and a Jewish Russian mother. During the Vietnam War, he was a member of the U.S. Special Forces. He was a modern and ballet dancer, a folk-singer, and a civil servant in the Oregon state government. Tagatac is the author of a collection of interrelated stories, *The Weight of the Sun* (2006), which conjures a fictional Guerrero family of people who are broken, homeless, and lost.

TAKEI, GEORGE (1937–). A **Japanese American** actor and writer, Takei was born in Los Angeles. At age four, he and his family were incarcerated in a **Japanese internment** camp in Arkansas and then in Tule Lake Camp, California. After release from the camp at age nine, Takei and his family returned to Los Angeles. He received his B.A. and M.A. in **theater** from the University of California, Los Angeles. He also attended the Shakespeare Institute at Stratford-Upon-Avon in England, and Sophia University in Tokyo, Japan. He is famous for his role as Sulu in the series *Star Trek*. He has served on the board of governors of the **East West Players** and is one of the founders of the Japanese American National Museum. Takei currently serves as a spokesperson for the Human Rights Campaign "Coming Out Project." His autobiography, *To the Stars* (1994), recounts his childhood in the internment camps and his acting and political careers. He also coauthored with Robert Asprin a science fiction, *Mirror Friend, Mirror Foe* (1985).

TALK-STORY. This is a Hawaiian expression, used as a noun or verb, meaning "an informal chat" or "to chat informally." This style of narrative has influenced such Asian American writers as **Maxine Hong Kingston**, **Milton Murayama**, **Gary Pak**, **Patsy Sumie Saiki**, and **Lois-Ann Yamanaka**.

TAMAGAWA, KATHLEEN (1893–1979). A **Japanese American** writer, Tamagawa was born in Cape May, New Jersey, to her Japanese father and Irish mother and died in New York. Between 1907 and 1915, she lived in Japan where her father worked for an American company. She published her autobiography, *Holy Prayers in a Horse's Ear* (1932), in which she discusses her confusion with her biracial and dual cultural identities and her global travels. This is the first autobiography by a Japanese American **woman**, and its title is a Japanese proverb, meaning supplications to the powerless.

TAN, AMY (1952–). One of the best-known **Chinese American** novelists, Tan was born in Oakland, California, to Chinese immigrants. She received her B.A. in English and linguistics and M.A. in linguistics from San Jose State University. Her first novel, *The Joy Luck Club* (1989), was an instant best seller and was adapted to the screen, directed by Wayne Wang. It tells the story of four Chinese American mothers and their relationships with their American-born daughters. Tan went on to publish four more novels: *The Kitchen God's Wife* (1991), *The Hundred Secret Senses* (1995), *The Bonesetter's Daughter* (2001), *Saving Fish from Drowning* (2005). Most of her novels continue the themes of her first, centering on mother–daughter relationships and the conflicts between the immigrant parents and their Americanized children. The trope of journey as discovery and reconciliation structures many of her stories. Her latest novel, *Saving Fish from Drowning*, unlike the previous ones, is set mostly in Burma, about a group of American tourists' adventures. She has also written a book of nonfiction, *The Opposite of Fate: A Book of Musings* (2003). Tan and her works have received numerous honors, including the Bay Area Book Reviewers Award, Commonwealth Gold Award, American Library Association's Notable Books, American Library Association Best Book for **Young Adults**, selected for the National Endowment for the Arts' Big Read, New York Times Notable Book, Booklist Editors Choice, Audie Award: Best Non-fiction, Parents' Choice Award, etc.

TAN, JOËL BARRAQUIEL (1968–). A **Filipino American** poet, Tan was born in the Philippines and came to the United States with his family as a child. He received his B.A. in ethnic studies at the University of California, Berkeley, and his M.F.A. in creative writing from Antioch University. He is the author of two **poetry** collections: *Monster* (2002) and *Type O Negative* (2008), which mines childhood traumas as well as traumatic loss of friends and lovers to AIDS. His essays, short fiction, and poetry have appeared in various anthologies, including *Fresh Men: New Gay Men's Fiction*, *Pinoy Poetics*, and *Asian American Sexualities*. He is the editor of *Queer Papi Porn: Gay Asian Erotica* (1998), *Best Gay Asian Erotica* (2004), and *Inside Him: New Gay Asian Erotica* (2006). He currently lives in San Francisco's Bay Area.

TANKA. One of the most ancient and popular forms of poetry in Japan, it is short and lyrical. Structured in 31 syllables, it is arranged in groups of 5, 7, 5, 7 and 7, in a two-part form with the first part in 5, 7, 5, and the second part in 7 and 7. A *tanka* often evokes a moment or marks an occasion about nature, seasons, love, or sadness. This style is common among **Japanese American**

poets such as **Sadakichi Hartmann** and **Jun Fujita**. *See also* HAHN, KIMIKO; SOGA, KEIHO.

TAO, LIN (1983–). A **Chinese American** novelist and poet, Tao was born in Virginia to Taiwanese immigrant parents and grew up in Orlando, Florida. He currently lives in Brooklyn, New York. Tao received his B.A. in journalism from New York University. He is the author of five books of fiction and **poetry**: two novels, *Richard Yates* (2010) and *Eeeee Eee Eeee* (2007); a novella, *Shoplifting from American Apparel* (2009); a short story collection, *Bed* (2007); and two poetry collections, *You Are a Little Bit Happier Than I Am* (2006), which won Action Books' December Prize, and *Cognitive-Behavioral Therapy* (2008). His work has appeared in literary journals, newspapers, and magazines, such as *Noon*, *Vice*, *Esquire*, the *Stranger*, *3:AM Magazine*, the *Mississippi Review*, the *Poetry Foundation*, *Nerve*, *Bear Parade*, the *Cincinnati Review*, *Other Voices*, and *Fourteen Hills*.

TEATRO NG TANAN. This is the San Francisco/Bay Area's only community-based **Filipino American theater** and cultural arts organization. Founded in 1989, Teatro ng Tanan carries the mission to promote a greater understanding of the Filipino community, its arts and its contributions to the cultural diversity of the United States. The name means "Theater for Everyone" in Tagalog.

TELEMAQUE, ELEANOR WONG (1930–). A **Chinese American** writer, Telemaque was born in Albert Lea, Minnesota. She attended the University of Chicago and graduated from University of Minnesota. She was hauled before the U.S. Department of State Loyalty Board for questioning during the McCarthy era and absolved by the office of John F. Kennedy (senator at the time). She is best known for her **young adult novel**, *It's Crazy to Stay Chinese in Minnesota* (1978). In 2007, she published a memoir, *The Sammy Wong Files Confessions of a Chinese American Terrorist*, for which she was tied with **Jessica Hagedorn** for first Manhattan Borough President Award for Excellence in Literature. Both works are based on her memories of her Midwest girlhood, of her parents, and her struggle with identity in a multiracial world. Her 1980 book, *Haiti through Its Holidays*, was written to honor her Haitian-born husband Maurice Telemaque and their daughter.

THAM, HILARY (1946–). A Chinese Malaysian American poet, autobiographer, and artist, Tham was born in Kelang, Malaysia, to Chinese Malaysian parents. She studied English literature at the University of Malaya. After marrying her American husband, she moved to the United States. She has authored six books of **poetry**: *No Gods Today* (1969), *Paper Boats* (1987), *Bad Names for Women* (1989), *Tigerbone Wine* (1992), *Men and Other Strange Myths* (1994), and *Counting* (2000). She published an autobiography, *Lane with No Name: Memoirs and Poems of a Malaysian–Chinese Girlhood* (1997). In her poetry, Tham explores private relations as well as social issues of gender, race, and culture. Uniting several of her books of poetry is a character Mrs. Wei, whose dramatic monologue critiques cultural values in both Malaysia and the United States as well as reveals her limited perspective. *See also* SOUTHEAST ASIAN AMERICAN LITERATURE AND THEATER.

THEATER. The first Asian theater, Tong Hook Tong Dramatic Company, a **Chinese** theater from China, opened its doors in October 1852 in San Francisco. It was not until more than a century later that the first Asian American theater appeared; **East West Players** was established in 1965 in Los Angeles by Chinese and **Japanese American** playwrights and actors. Three generations of Asian American playwrights have been born through the growing array of educational programs sponsored by the East West Players, such as the Actors Conservatory; **David Henry Hwang Writers' Institute**; the career program; Alliance of Creative Talent Services; and the touring Theatre for Youth. The East West Players paved the way for subsequent Asian American theater groups. On the East Coast, **La Mama Chinatown** was founded in 1970 by Ellen Stewart and led by Ching Yeh, which evolved into **Pan Asian Repertory Theatre** in 1999 in New York City, led by artistic director Tisa Chang. Another Chinese theater group was formed in New York's Chinatown in 1970 called **Four Seas Player** as a community outreach program for young people and recent immigrants. In Hawaii, **Kumu Kahua Theatre** was founded in 1971 in Honolulu. The **Asian Exclusion Act** was founded by **Garrett Hongo** in 1975 in Seattle, which was renamed in 1981 to be the **Northwest Asian American Theatre Company**. In 1975, **Ping Chong** launched **Ping Chong & Company**, and in 1979 the **Asian American Theater Company** was established in San Francisco. Its previous form was the **Asian American Theater Workshop,** under the artistic directorship of **Frank Chin**.

In the 1970s and 1980s, several other Asian American theaters emerged. Among the **South Asian American** theaters are the **Kathak Ensemble** established in 1978 in New York and **SAATh**, standing for South Asian American Theater, founded by its managing trustee, Rajendra Joshi in 1989 and based in Boston. The year 1989 saw the establishment of **Asian Story Theater** in San Diego. In the 1990s, Asian American theaters and performance groups mushroomed both in number and in ethnicities. The first Hmong American theater, **Pom Siab Hmoob Theatre** (PSHT), was established in Minneapolis.

Korean American groups include New York's **Shinmyung Pae** and **Lodestone Theatre Ensemble** in Los Angeles. **Filipino Americans** established several theater groups: **Teatro ng Tanan**, **Bindlestiff Studio**, and **Tongue in a Mood** in San Francisco; **QBd Ink** in Washington, D.C.; and **Ma-Yi Theater** in New York City. **Vietnamese American** artists established **Club O'Noodles** in Los Angeles. Several pan-Asia American theaters were founded as well, such as **Pork Filled Players** in Seattle, **San Diego Asian American Repertory Theater**, **Second Generation Productions** in New York City, **Theater Mu** in Minnesota, **Theatre Rice** at the University of California, Berkeley, and comedy ensembles, such as the **18 Mighty Mountain Warriors** in San Francisco and **Cold Tofu** in Los Angeles. **Vietnamese American** playwright **Maura Nguyen Donohue** founded **In Mixed Company** in New York City that showcases multiethnic performances. The youngest theaters established in the 2000s are the Chicago-based **DueEast Theater Company**, the Japanese American theater group the **Grateful Crane Ensemble**, **Cedar Grove OnStage**, and South Asian American theater **Shunya** in Houston, Texas.

Asian American playwrights were late in emerging. It was not until 1924 that the first Asian American play was written, and very few people know that it was written by a **woman. Ling-Ai Li** under the name of Gladys Li published in the University of Hawaii (UH) school journal *The Submission of Rose Moy*, which tells the story of a Chinese woman who refuses to comply with an arranged marriage. It was premiered in 1928 at the Arthur Andrews Theatre at UH. The first Asian American theater, the East West Player, nurtured the pioneers and provided the venue for their works, such as **Momoko Iko**'s *Gold Watch* (1972), **Frank Chin**'s *The Chickencoop Chinaman* (1972) and *The Year of the Dragon* (1977), **Wakako Yamauchi**'s *And the Soul Shall Dance* (1976), **Philip Kan Gotanda**'s *The Avocado Kid, or Zen and the Art of Guacamole* (1979) and *A Song for Nesei Father* (1980). Almost all of the early playwrights deal with themes of ethnic identity, **racism**, **Japanese American internment**, and generational conflicts. As Asian American theaters began to proliferate in the 1980s and 1990s, Asian American playwrights increased their visibility in the mainstream theaters. Several of them won **Obie Awards**, including **Ping Chong** for *Humboldt's Current* (1977), **Ralph B. Peña** for *Flipzoids* (1996), and **David Henry Hwang** three times for *FOB* (1981), *Golden Child* (1996), and *Yellow Face* (2007). Hwang also won a Tony Award for ***M. Butterfly*** (1988). Unlike the earlier generations who found the West Coast fertile ground for their artistic development, the most recent generation of playwrights has identified New York City to be their playground, such as **Young Jean Lee**, **Qui Nguyen**, **Han Ong**, and **Rey A. Pamatmat**, to name a few. Other well-known Asian

American playwrights include **Jennie Baroga**, **Philip W. Chung**, **Eugenie Chan**, **Linda Faigao-Hall**, **Ralph B. Peña**, **Velina Hasu Houston**, **Jessica Hagedorn**, **Chay Yew**, etc. *See also* CABICO, REGIE; CHING, CARLA; DIZON, LOUELLA; DONOHUE, MAURA NGUYEN; FLORENTINO, ALBERTO S.; GOMOLVILAS, PRINCE; IIZUKA, NAOMI; JANG, PATRICIA; KASHIWAGI, HIROSHI; KIM, SUJI KWOCK; KIM, SUSAN; LÊ THI DIEM THÚY; LEE, CHERYLENE; LIM, GENNY; LIM, PAUL STEPHEN; LIN, KENNETH; LINMARK, R. ZAMORA; LUM, DARRELL H. Y.; MEYER, MARLANE; MIYAMOTO, NOBUKO; NARASAKI, KEN; NARITA, JUDE; NISHIKAWA, LANE; OKITA, DWIGHT; PARK, YOUNGSOO; RAU, SANTHA RAMA; RNO, SUNG JUNG; ROBERTS, DMAE; SAKAMOTO, EDWARD; SAOPENG, OVA; SHARIF, BINA; SON, DIANA; SUH, LLOYD; TOYAMA, TIM; TSIANG, H. T.; TUAN, ALICE; UYEHARA, DENISE; VANG, KA; VINLUAN, ERMENA MARLENE; VONGSAY, SAYMOUKDA D.; WONG, ELIZABETH; WOO, MERLE.

THEATER MU. This is a pan-Asian performing arts group in Minneapolis, founded in 1992. It presents four shows a year, blending Asian and Western artistic forms to tell Asian and Asian American stories. *See also* THEATER.

THEATRE OF YUGEN. Founded in 1978, Theatre of Yugen is a **Japanese American** experimental ensemble in San Francisco dedicated to the pursuit of the intangible essence called *Yuen* through its exploration of dramatic and literary classics and the crafting of new works of world **theater**. It follows the discipline of Japanese theatrical aesthetics—primarily the classical forms of **Noh** drama and **Kyogen** comedy. Through training, creating, presenting, collaborating, and performing, it aims to foster intercultural understanding and keep theatrical discipline vital.

THEATRE RICE. This is the first modern Asian American **theater** group at the University of California, Berkeley. Founded in 1998, Theatre Rice provides people (particularly, but not exclusively, Asian Americans), who might not otherwise have a chance to participate in theatrical arts, with the opportunity to act, write, sing, direct, dance, and learn stage techniques. Its mission is combating the misrepresentation, as well as the lack of representation, of the Asian American community in popular culture.

THU-LÂM, NGUYÈN THI (1940–). A **Vietnamese American** autobiographer, Thu-Lâm was born in Vietnam and immigrated to the United States in 1969 when she married an American. Her autobiography, *Fallen Leaves*

(1989), recounts her childhood during the Vietnamese national movement for independence from the French and her adulthood struggles for financial independence from husbands.

TONGUE IN A MOOD. This is a **Filipino American** performance group, first established in 1992 by comedians Allan Manalo, Kennedy Kabasares, Ron Muriera, and Rex Navarette, and it was re-established in 1996 by Allan Manalo, who brought in performance artist Patty Cachapero and comedian Kevin Camia.

TOYAMA, TIM (1952–). A **Japanese American** playwright and producer, Toyama is a **sansei** living in Los Angeles, California. He is cofounder of the Asian American media company Cedar Grove Productions and its sister Asian American **theater** company, **Cedar Grove OnStage**. He studied English at California State University, Northridge. He is best known for his play *Visas and Virtue*, which portrays Holocaust rescuer Chiune "Sempo" Sugihara—known as "The Japanese Schindler." Adapted into a short film, the 26-minute drama received the Academy Award for Live Action Short Film in 1998. Toyama partnered with Aaron Woolfolk to write the play *Bronzeville* about Little Tokyo during World War II, when African Americans became the primary residents after Japanese Americans were relocated to **internment camps**. His play *Independence Day* was also adapted to the screen by Cedar Grove Productions, as a half-hour television special for PBS.

TRAN, BARBARA (1968–). A **Vietnamese American** poet, Tran was born in New York City and received her B.A. from New York University and her M.F.A. from Columbia University. Her first **poetry** collection, *In the Mynah Bird's Own Words* (2002), was selected as a PEN Open Book Award finalist. This collection is composed of lined poems and prose poems and explores memories of Vietnam and America. She coedited the anthology *Watermark: Vietnamese American Poetry and Prose* (1998) and guest edited *Viet Nam: Beyond the Frame*, a special issue of *Michigan Quarterly Review* (Fall 2004). She is the recipient of a Lannan Foundation Writing Residency, Breadloaf Writers' Conference Scholarship, MacDowell Colony Gerald Freund Fellowship, and Pushcart Prize.

TRENKA, JANE JEONG (1970–). A **Korean American** memoirist, Trenka is a Korean adoptee raised by white parents in Minnesota. As an adult, she went to Korea and found her biological mother. She is the author of two memoirs, *The Language of Blood* (2003) and *Fugitive Vision: An Adoptee's Return to Korea* (2009).

TRIPLETT, PIMONE (1965–). A Thai American poet, Triplett was born in Oakland, California. She received her B.A. in English from Sarah Lawrence College and M.F.A. from the Iowa Writers' Workshop. She is the author of three books of poems: *Rumor* (2009); *The Price of Light* (2005), winner of the Levis Poetry Prize; and *Ruining the Picture* (1998). Most of her **poetry** employs **Eastern and Western** myths to illuminate contemporary issues. Her poems have appeared in many literary journals, including *Poetry*, *Paris Review*, *Ploughshares*, *Agni*, *Yale Review*, *Triquarterly*, and *New England Review*, and in such anthologies as *Legitimate Dangers*, *Contemporary Voices from the East*, and *New American Poets: A Bread Loaf Anthology*. She teaches creative writing at the University of Washington. *See also* SOUTHEAST ASIAN AMERICAN LITERATURE AND THEATER.

TRUONG, MONIQUE (1968–). A **Vietnamese American** novelist, Truong was born in Saigon, Vietnam, and immigrated to the United States as a refugee at the age of six. She received her B.A. in English from Yale University and J.D. from the Columbia University School of Law. Truong practiced intellectual property law before she began to pursue her writing career. Her debut novel, *The Book of Salt* (2003), won American Library Association's Barbara Gittings Book Award in Literature, an **Asian American Literary Award**, and the 2003 Bard Fiction Prize. The novel centers on a Vietnamese cook in the household of Gertrude Stein and Alice B. Toklas in Paris, exploring themes of sexuality, **East-West relations**, and race. Her second novel, *Bitter in the Mouth* (2010), received the Rosenthal Family Foundation Award from the American Academy of Arts and Letters. It is a coming-of-age tale about the search for identity, family, and human connection.

TSENG, JENNIFER (1969–). A **Chinese American** poet, Tseng was born in Indiana to a German mother and a Taiwanese father and raised in California. She began writing poetry seriously after graduation from Colorado College. She received her M.A. in Asian American Studies from the University of California, Los Angeles, and her M.F.A. from the University of Houston. She was twice a fellow at the Fine Arts Work Center in Provincetown. Her first book of **poetry**, *The Man with My Face* (2005), traces her immigrant father's journey while exploring timeless questions of language, displacement, foreignness, and desire. Her poetry and prose have also appeared in *Ploughshares*, *Green Mountains Review*, *Indian Review*, *Hawai'i Review*, *Grand Street, Barrow Street*, *APA Journal*, *Massachusetts Review*, and *Zyzzyva*. She lives in California and Massachusetts. Tseng was the first recipient of the Gift of Freedom Award from a Room of Her Own Foundation in 2002.

TSENG, SANDY (1974–). A **Chinese American** poet, Tseng was born in Taipei, Taiwan, and immigrated with her parents to the United States as a child. She received her B.A. in English from Dickinson College and her M.F.A. in creative writing from the University of Pittsburgh. Her debut book of **poetry**, *Sediment* (2009), explores themes of memory, ancestry, and displacement. Her poems have appeared in *Crab Orchard Review*, *Crazyhorse*, *Fugue*, *Hunger Mountain*, the *Nation*, *Third Coast*, and other magazines. Among the awards she has received are the *Nation*'s Discovery Award and scholarships from Breadloaf Writers' Conference and the Vira I. Heinz Foundation.

TSIANG, H. T. (JIAN XIZENG, 1899–1971). A **Chinese American** poet, playwright, novelist, and actor, Tsiang was born in Jiangsu, China. He received his B.A. in political economy from Southeastern University in Nanjing. He came to study at Stanford University and became the founder of the bilingual periodical *Chinese Guide in America.* After one year at Stanford, he moved to New York and enrolled at Columbia University, where he began writing seriously. He self-published a book of **poetry**, *Poems of the Chinese Revolution* (1929), and went on to publish three novels: *China Red* (1931), *Hanging on Union Square* (1935), and *And China Has Hands* (1937). These novels portrayed patriotic characters resisting Japanese occupation of China. In 1938, he turned to the stage and wrote and acted in the play *China Marches On*. He acted in films such as *Behind the Rising Sun* (1943), *The Keys of the Kingdom* (1944), *Tokyo Rose* (1946), *The Babe Ruth Story* (1948), *Panic in the Streets* (1950), and *Ocean's Eleven* (1960). *See also* THEATER.

TSUI, KITTY (1952–). A **Chinese American** poet, Tsui was born in Hong Kong. Her family moved to San Francisco in 1968. She studies Chinese and creative writing at San Francisco State University. She is the author of four books of **poetry**: *The Sparks Fly* (1997); *Breathless: Erotica* (1996), winner of Firecracker Alternative Books Award; *Nightvision* (1984); and *The Words of a Woman Who Breathes Fire* (1983). All her poetry explores lesbian sexuality and **women**'s silence.

TSUKIYAMA, GAIL (1957–). A **Japanese American** novelist, Tsukiyama was born in San Francisco to a **nisei** father from Hawaii and a Chinese mother from Hong Kong. She earned a B.A. and M.A. in English from San Francisco State University. She is the author of six novels. Some of them are historical novels set in Japan, China, or Hong Kong, such as *Women of Silk* (1991) and its sequel *The Language of Threads* (1999), *The Samurai's Garden* (1995), and *Night of Many Dreams* (1998). Her other novels are *Dreaming Water*

(2002) and *The Street of a Thousand Blossoms* (2007). She is the recipient of an Academy of American Poets Award.

TUAN, ALICE (1963–). A **Chinese American** playwright, Tuan was born in Seattle. She received her B.A. in economics from the University of California, Los Angeles, and her M.A. in English as a second language from California State University, Los Angeles. Tuan became interested in playwriting and earned an M.F.A. from Brown University in 1997. Her plays explore issues of immigration, generational conflicts, gender, and sexuality. They include *Last of the Sun* (1995), *Ikebana* (1996), *Some Asians* (1997), *Asians in Los Angeles,* (1999), *Ajax* (1998), *4 Days in Red Gulch* (2002), *Heaven and Hell, A Divine Comedy* (2001), *Hit* (2000), *The Roaring Girle* (2002). More recent works include the Virtual Hypertext Play *Coastline* (2005) and *BATCH: An American Bachelor/ette Party Spectacle* (2007). Tuan is a recipient of the Richard E. Sherwood Award from Los Angeles' Mark Taper Forum, the Colbert Award for Excellence, the New Voices Playwriting Award from the **East West Players**, and the Drama-Logue Award for Best Play. *See also* THEATER.

TUNG, ANGELA. A **Chinese American** children's book writer, Tung holds a B.A. in English from Barnard College, an M.A. in creative writing from Boston University, and an M.S. in library science from the Pratt Institute. She is the author of a **children's book**, *Balto the Hero!* (1995) and two **young adult novels**, *Song of the Stranger* (1999) and *Trane and Me* (2000). Her latest book, *Black Fish: Memoir of a Bad Luck Girl* (2010), chronicles the failed marriage between a Chinese woman and Korean man, both American-born but still bound by old world traditions. She currently lives in San Francisco.

TY-CASPER, LINDA (1931–). A **Filipina American** novelist, Ty-Casper was born in Manila, the Philippines. She earned a law degree from the University of the Philippines in 1956 and moved to Boston the following year. She then studied international law at Harvard University. She is the author of over 15 books ranging from historical novels such as *DreamEden* (1997), *The Peninsulares* (1964), *The Three-Cornered Sun* (1974), and *Ten Thousand Seeds* (1987) to political novels including *Awaiting Trespass* (1985), *Wings of Stone* (1986), *A Small Party in a Garden* (1988), *Dread Empire* (1980), and *Fortress in the Plaza* (1985). She has also published three collections of short fiction: *The Transparent Sun* (1963), *The Secret Runners* (1974), and *Common Continent* (1991). All her writings center on Philippine history and describe the lives of historical figures as well as ordinary people. She has received numerous awards, such as Djerassi, Filipino–American **Women**

Network Award for Literature; fellowships from the Massachusetts Artists Foundation and Wheatland Foundation; a UNESCO/PEN Short Story award; Southeast Asian Writers Award; SEA Write Award (Bangkok); a Rockefeller Foundation Bellagio residency, etc.

TYAU, KATHLEEN (1947–). A **Chinese American** novelist, Tyau was born in California and grew up in Hawaii. She went to Oregon to attend Clark College, where she earned a B.A. in English and has lived there ever since. She is the author of two novels: *A Little Too Much Is Enough* (1995), winner of the Pacific Northwest Booksellers' Award and a finalist for the Oregon Book Award; and *Makai* (1999), also a finalist for the Oregon Book Award. Her stories portray the lives of working-class Chinese **women** in Hawaii.

U

UCHIDA, YOSHIKO (1921–1992). A **Japanese American** novelist and autobiographer, Uchida was born in Alameda, California. During her senior year at the University of California, Berkeley, she and her family were relocated to a **Japanese internment camp** in Utah. After release from the camp, Uchida attended Smith College and earned an M.A. in education and thereafter began teaching at a Quaker School outside Philadelphia. She wrote over 30 **children's books**, one adult novel, *Picture Bride* (1987), and one autobiography, *Desert Exile* (1982). Uchida is best known for her children and **young adult** books, such as *The Journey to Topaz* (1971), *Samurai of Gold Hill* (1972), and *A Jar of Dreams* (1981), for which she received an American Library Association Notable Book citation and a Commonwealth Club of California medal for the best juvenile book twice.

UMRIGAR, THRITY (1961–). A **South Asian American** novelist, Umrigar was born in Bombay, India. She moved to the United States for graduate school in 1981. She received her B.S. from Bombay University and Ph.D. from Kent State University. She is the author of three novels. *Bombay Time* (2001) depicts the lives of Parsis, a small ethnic minority in India while *The Space between Us* (2006) centers on the lives of two **women** separated by class. *The Weight of Heaven* (2009) portrays an American couple in India. She has also published a memoir, *First Darling of the Morning* (2004).

UNG, LOUNG (1970–). A Cambodian American memoirist, Ung was born in Phnom Penh, Cambodia. She was five years old when the Communist Khmer Rouge took power. When she was 10, her family fled the country to the refugee camp in Thailand, and five months later came to Essex Junction, Vermont. She received a B.A. in political science from St. Michael's College in Vermont. In 1995, she returned to Cambodia for the first time. She has written two memoirs: *First They Killed My Father: A Daughter of Cambodia Remembers* (2000), which received an Asian Pacific American Award for Literature and a Books for a Better World Literary Award, and *Lucky Child: A Daughter of Cambodia Reunites with the Sister She Left Behind* (2005). *See also* SOUTHEAST ASIAN AMERICAN LITERATURE AND THEATER.

UPADHYAY, SAMRAT (1964–). The first Nepalese American fiction writer, Upadhyay was born in Kathmandu, Nepal, and came to the United States at age 21. He received his Ph.D. in English from the University of Hawaii and now teaches in and directs the Creative Writing Program at Indiana University. *Arresting God in Kathmandu* (2001) is his first collection of short stories and won the Whiting Writers' Award. *The Guru of Love* (2003) is Upadhyay's first novel, a New York Times Notable Book of the Year 2003 and a San Francisco Chronicle Best Book. Both novels explore the common themes of money, sex, and family. *The Royal Ghosts* (2006), which won an **Asian American Literary Award**, is a collection of nine short stories that turn to politics and sex in Nepal. His most recent novel, *Buddha's Orphans* (2010), tells the love story between an orphan boy and a girl from a wealthy family against Nepal's political upheavals of the past century.

UYEHARA, DENISE (1966–). A **Japanese American** playwright and a performer, Uyehara was born in Tustin, California. She attended the University of California, Irvine, and began as a biology major but changed to comparative literature. During the college years, she took courses in fiction writing and playwriting. She received an M.F.A. in arts from the University of California, Los Angeles. She continued studying playwriting at the Mark Taper Forum's Mentor Playwright Program and at the **David Henry Hwang Writers' Institute**. She has published many plays, including *Hobbies* (1989), *Hiro* (1993), *Headless Turtleneck Relatives* (1993), *Hello (Sex) Kitty: Mad Asian Bitch on Wheels* (1994), and *Maps of City and Body* (1999). Uyehara's works explore identity issues of gender, race, and sexuality. She has won numerous awards, including a Langton Arts/National Endowment for the Arts grant, the mid-career C.O.L.A. Award from the Los Angeles Department of Cultural Affairs, the Brody Arts Fund, the James Irvine Fellowship, and the James Clavell Japanese American Literary Award. *See also* THEATER.

UYEMOTO, HOLLY (1970–). A **Japanese American** novelist, Uyemoto was born in Ithaca, New York, to **sansei** parents. She dropped out of high school to devote herself to the writing of her first novel, *Rebel without a Clue* (1989). She went on to publish her second novel, *Go* (1995). Both novels explore the lives and perspectives of teenagers and their rites of passage, exploring themes of idealism, drugs, AIDS, and dysfunctional families. Uyemoto continued her education at Wellesley College.

V

VANG, BURLEE (1982–). A Hmong American poet, Vang was born in Santa Ana, California. He holds a B.A. in English and Art Studio from the University of California, Davis, and an M.F.A. in fiction from California State University, Fresno. The founder of the **Hmong American Writers' Circle**, Vang is the author of a book of **poetry**, *The Dead I Know: Incantation for Rebirth* (2010), winner of the Swan Scythe Press 2010 Poetry Chapbook Contest. He is also coeditor of *How Do I Begin? A Hmong American Literary Anthology* (2011). His prose and poetry have appeared in *Ploughshares*, *North American Review*, *Alaska Quarterly Review*, *Massachusetts Review*, and *Asia Literary Review*, among other literary journals. *See also* SOUTHEAST ASIAN AMERICAN LITERATURE AND THEATER.

VANG, KA (1975–). A Hmong American playwright and a fiction writer, Vang was born in Long Cheng, Laos. She spent her early years in Thai refugee camps and resettled in Minnesota when she was five. She earned her B.A. in political science from the University of Minnesota, Twin Cities. She worked as a journalist for the *Minnesota Daily*, the *Chicago Tribune*, and the *Pioneer Press*. Her plays include *Disconnect* (2001), *Dead Calling* (2001), and *From Shadows to Light* (2004), which have been performed at the Playwrights' Center, **Theater Mu**, and Mixed Blood Theater in Minnesota. Her short stories have appeared in Asian American literary anthologies. Vang's work confronts with dark humor issues of gender, sexuality, race, and culture. She is a recipient of the Archibald Bush Artist Fellowship and an Asian American Renaissance/Jerome Foundation Artist's Career Development Grant. *See also* SOUTHEAST ASIAN AMERICAN LITERATURE AND THEATER.

VAZIRANI, REETIKA (1962–2003). A **South Asian American** poet, Vazirani was born in India, immigrated to the United States with her family as a child, and grew up in Maryland. She received her B.A. in English from Wellesley College and M.F.A. in creative writing from the University of Virginia. Her first collection of poetry, *White Elephants* (1996), won the Barnard New **Women** Poets Prize. Her second collection, *World Hotel* (2002), won the 2003 Anisfield–Wolf Book Award. While *White Elephants* centers on the theme of immigration, showing how much the old world insinuates itself into the new, *World Hotel* relives/reinvents her mother's life. Her last book of **poetry**, *Radha Says* (2009), was posthumously published. Vazirani received numerous honors, including a Pushcart Prize, a Poets & Writers Exchange Program Award, the Glenna Luchei Award from *Prairie Schooner*, and a Discovery/The Nation award. She was writer-in-residence at Sweet Briar College and later at the College of William and Mary in 2002. Vazirani took her own life and that of her two-year old son on 16 July 2003.

VERGHESE, ABRAHAM (1955–). A **South Asian American** novelist and physician, Verghese was born in Ethiopia to parents from Kerala, India. He is the professor for the Theory and Practice of Medicine at Stanford University Medical School and senior associate chair of the Department of Internal Medicine. He also earned his M.F.A in creative writing from Iowa Writers' Workshop. Dr. Verghese began his medical training in Ethiopia, but his education was interrupted by a military coup. He came to America with his parents and two brothers and worked as an orderly for a year before going to India where he completed his medical studies at Madras Medical College in Madras, after which he returned to the United States. He wrote the best seller *My Own Country: A Doctor's Story* (1994) about his experiences in East Tennessee and explores the themes of displacement, **diaspora**, and the AIDS epidemic. His second book, *The Tennis Partner* (1999), is a memoir describing his experience moving to El Paso in the midst of an unraveling marriage and his love for tennis. His first novel, *Cutting for Stone* (2009), is an epic autobiographical novel of twin brothers, orphaned by their mother and forsaken by their father. Verghese's writing has also appeared in the *New Yorker*, *Texas Monthly*, *Atlantic*, the *New York Times*, the *New York Times Magazine*, *Granta*, *Forbes.com*, the *Daily Beast*, and the *Wall Street Journal.*

VIETNAMESE AMERICAN LITERATURE AND THEATER. This is one of the newest voices in Asian American literature. Prior to the fall of Saigon in 1975, the end of the Vietnam War, the number of Vietnamese Americans was so small that their lives were rarely documented. A large number of Vietnamese refugees began to arrive in the United States in 1979 through the Orderly Departure Program. The earliest Vietnamese American writers are memoirists describing their experience of the war. After **Quang Nhuong Huynh** published *The Land I Lost* (1982), the first Vietnamese American book, a series of Vietnamese American memoirs followed, including **Phung Thi Le Ly Hayslip**'s *When Heaven and Earth Changed Places*, **Jade Ngoc Quang Huynh**'s *South Wind Changing*, **Quang X. Pham**'s *A*

Sense of Duty: My Father, My American Journey, **Nguyen Thi Thu-Lâm**'s *Fall Leaves*, and **Nguyen Qui Duc**'s *Where the Ashes Are*. The younger generation of Vietnamese American writers has either been born in the United States or came as young children. Most of them write fiction, **poetry**, and plays. Their common themes include war, memory, ethnicity, sexuality, and colonialism. Among them are the well known **Lan Cao**, **Linh Dinh**, **Bich Minh Nguyen**, **Monique Truong**, **Hoa Nguyen**, and **Lê Thi Diem Thúy**. A number of Vietnamese American writers are biracial and explore themes of biraciality, mixed race, or universal themes like language, nature, and love. Among them are **Maura Nguyen Donohue**, **Tina Brown Celona**, and **Kim-An Lieberman**.

Vietnamese American **theater** is still at its budding stage. **Club O'Noodles** is the only Vietnamese American troupe, featuring comedy, music, and dance. The Playwright **Qui Nguyen** directs the **Obie Award**–winning Vampire Cowboys Theatre Company, whose productions are penned and choreographed by him. However, Vampire Cowboys Theatre produces action drama that may or may not be related to Asian American themes. Vietnamese American playwright Maura Nguyen Donohue founded **In Mixed Company** in New York City in 1995. The theater company produces plays that portray identity issues and celebrates fluid identities. *See also* CHAU, ANGIE; DUONG, UYEN NICOLE; ELLIOTT, DUONG VAN MAI; MONG-LAN; NGUYEN, KIEN; PHAM, ANDREW X.; PHAN, AIMEE; STROM, DAO; SU, LAC; TRAN, BARBARA.

VILLA, JOSÉ GARCIA (1908–1997). A **Filipino American poet**, Villa was born in Manila, the Philippines, and died in New York. He published his first story in the *Manila Times* at 15. He attended the University of the Philippines first to study medicine and then law. All the while, his real passion lay in the arts: painting and creative writing. He immigrated to the United States in 1929, earned his B.A. at the University of New Mexico in 1933, and began his graduate studies in Columbia University. Villa's first book was a collection of short stories, *Footnote to Youth* (1933), after which he wrote only **poetry**. For his poetry, he adopted the pen name Doveglion (Dove, Eager, and Lion). His poetry publications include *Many Voices* (1939), *Poems by Doveglion* (1941), *Have Come, Am Here* (1942), *Volume Two* (1949), *Selected Poems and New York* (1958), and *A Doveglion Book of Philippine Poetry* (1962). He introduced a new rhyming scheme called "reversed consonance," wherein the last sounded consonants of the last syllable, or the last principal consonant of a word, are reversed for the corresponding rhyme. He also introduced a poetic style he called "comma poems," wherein each word is followed by a comma. Villa received the Poetry Award of the

American Academy of Arts and Letters, a Guggenheim Fellowship in Poetry, a fellowship from Bollingen Foundation, the Shelley Memorial Award of the Poetry Society of America, and a Rockefeller Fellowship for poetry. He also received some of the highest awards in the Philippines, including a Rizal Pro-Patria Award, the Republic Cultural Heritage Award, and was named Philippine National Artist in literature in 1973.

VILLANUEVA, MARIANNE. A **Filipina American** fiction writer, Villanueva was born and raised in Manila, the Philippines. She came to the United States at age 25 to study creative writing at Stanford University. Her first collection of short fiction, *Ginseng and Other Tales from Manila* (1991), is mostly set in Manila. The collection was short-listed for the Philippines' National Book Award. Her second book of stories, *Mayor of the Roses* (2005), is set mostly in the United States. She has edited an anthology of Filipina **women**'s writings, *Going Home to a Landscape*. She currently lives in the San Francisco Bay Area.

VINLUAN, ERMENA MARLENE (1949–). A **Filipina American** playwright, Vinluan was born in Berkeley, California. She attended the University of California, Berkeley, for one semester before leaving to study in the Philippines for a year and a half, after which she returned to the University of California, Berkeley. Vinluan became interested in playwriting at a very young age and became a part of the Sining Bayan, a group that aims to train youth in various forms of arts and to serve the socially marginalized. She wrote plays, such as *Isuda Ti Imuna* (*Those Who Were First*, 1973), *Mindanao* (1974), *Tagatupad* (1976), *The Frame-Up of Narciso and Perez* (1979), *Visions of a Warbride* (1979), *Ti Mangyuna* (*Those Who Led the Way*, 1981). *See also* THEATER.

VONGSAY, SAYMOUKDA D. (1981–). A Laotian American poet, playwright, and performance artist, Vongsay was born in a refugee camp in Thailand. She received her B.A. in English from the University of Minnesota (UM), Morris, and is currently working for her M.L.S. from UM, Morris. She is the author of *No Regrets* (2008), a collection of **poetry** and ***haikus***. Her work has been published by *Altra Magazine*, the *Journal of* ***Southeast Asian*** *American Education and Advancement*, *Hmong Today*, *Lao American Magazine*, and *Bakka Literary Journal*, to name a few. She is the inaugural winner of the Alfred C. Carey Prize in Spoken Word Poetry in August 2010. *See also* SOUTHEAST ASIAN AMERICAN LITERATURE AND THEATER.

WANG, PING (1957–). A **Chinese American** fiction writer and poet, Wang was born in Shanghai, China, and grew up in a naval base on an island in the East China Sea. She came to the United States in 1985. She received her B.A. in English from Beijing University, M.A. in English from Long Island University, and Ph.D. in comparative literature from New York University. *American Visa* (1994) was her first book of short stories that center on lives of young **women** on a Chinese navy base. *Foreign Devil* (1996) is a novel that portrays a young woman whose desire for a free life earns her the disparagement of her family and friends. *Of Flesh and Spirit* (1998) is a book of poems, and *The Magic Whip* (2003) is a **hybrid** book of verse and prose, winner of the Bush Artist Fellowship for **Poetry**. Her nonfiction *Aching for Beauty* (2000), winner of the Eugene M. Kayden Book Award in 2001 for the Best Book in the Humanities, studies the Chinese history of foot binding. Her most recent novel, *The Last Communist Virgin* (2007), is about love in a fast-changing world. She currently teaches at Macalester College.

WANG, SHANXING (1965–). A **Chinese American** poet, Wang was born in Shanxi Province of China. He holds an M.S. in mechanical engineering from Xi'an Jiaotong University. As a faculty member at Beijing University of Chemical Technology, he was an active participant in the Tiananmen Square demonstrations during the spring of 1989. He moved to the United States in 1991 and earned a Ph.D. in mechanical engineering from the University of California, Berkeley. He is the author of *Mad Science in Imperial City* (2005), winner of the 2006 **Asian American Literary Award** for **Poetry**. The work operates at multiple levels, including math, mechanics, fantasy, music, film, and dreams.

WARTSKI, MAUREEN CRANE. A **Japanese American** young adult novelist, Wartski was born in Ashiya, Japan. She attended Redlands University in California and holds a B.A. in literature from Sophia University, Tokyo, Japan. She lives in Raleigh, North Carolina. She has authored many midgrade and **young adult novels**, among them the award-winning *A Boat To Nowhere* (1981) and the critically acclaimed *Candle in the Wind (1995).*

Her other books include *A Long Way from Home* (1982), *My Brother Is Special* (1981), and *Yuri's Brush with Magic* (2011). Although her focus is on writing for young people, Maureen Wartski has also authored Regency novels for Fawcett Crest and Avon; historical romances for Pageant Books, Tapestry Historical Romances, and Charter/Diamond; contemporary romances for Berkley, Harlequin, and New American Library. *See also* CHILDREN'S LITERATURE.

WATANABE, SYLVIA A. (1953–). A **Japanese American** short story writer, Watanabe was born and raised in Hawaii. She earned a B.A. in English and an M.A. in English and creative writing from State University of New York, Binghamton. She teaches English and creative writing at Oberlin College. Her first collection of short stories, *Talking to the Dead* (1992), was a finalist for the 1993 PEN Faulkner Award and a recipient of the PEN Josephine Miles Literature Award for fiction. She has received a National Endowment for the Arts Creative Writing Fellowship in fiction and an Ohio Arts Council Individual Artist Grant in nonfiction. Her stories and personal essays have been widely anthologized and have been included in the O. Henry and Pushcart Prize collections.

WATKINS, YOKO KAWASHIMA (1933–). A **Japanese American** autobiographer, Watkins was born in Japan. Her family lived in Manchuria, China, where her father was stationed as a Japanese government official, and later the family moved to Nanam in northern Korea, where her father was overseeing Japanese political interests. They returned to Japan when it became clear that Japan was losing World War II. She studied English at Kyoto University and worked at the U.S. Air Force Base as a translator, where she met her future husband, Donald Watkins, an American pilot. Her husband brought her to the United States in 1955. Her first book, *So Far from the Bamboo Grove* (1986), centers on her childhood in Korea, and her second book, *My Brother, My Sister, and I* (1994), centers on the years they lived as refugees in Japan.

WEI, KATHERINE (1930–). A **Chinese American** autobiographer, Wei was born in Beijing, China, and immigrated to the United States in 1945. She earned her degree in nursing from Columbia University and worked as a nurse and an administrator at JFK Airport medical facility from 1951 to 1971. She wrote in collaboration with the novelist Terry Quinn her autobiography, *Second Daughter: Growing Up in China, 1930–1949* (1984). The autobiography offers a picture of an upper class Chinese family in the contexts of the Japanese invasion, the Chinese Civil War, and the immigration to the United States.

WOMEN. When Asian immigration to California began in significant numbers in the 1850s, few women took the arduous journey across the Pacific to seek their fortune in the United States. The women who did immigrate were mostly wives and daughters of Asian men already in the United States. Some Asian women were tricked, kidnapped, or smuggled into the country to engage in the sex trade. The impression that *all* Asian women were prostitutes, which emerged at that time, shaped the public attitude toward and action against Asian women for almost a century. The **Page Act** of 1875 barred the entry of Asian women on the ground of immorality. The 1882 **Chinese Exclusion Law** further prevented Chinese women from entering the country, and this law was not lifted until the 1940s. According to the 1900 Census, only 410 of 24,326 Japanese were female, and a study of the **Chinese American** population indicates that in 1920 women numbered fewer than 10 percent of the Chinese American population. It is not until 1965 when immigration and nationality laws were liberalized that Asian women began to arrive in large numbers. This is why most of the Asian American women writers emerged only after the 1970s.

Asian American literature in the 1900s rarely portrays women. This is not only because of the near absence of women in Asian American communities but also because male writers were mainly writing autobiographies. It was not until the early 1900s that some women writers began to depict the lives of Asian American women. Chinese American writer **Edith Maude Eaton** published her autobiography, "Leaves from the Mental Portfolio of a Eurasian" (1909), and a collection of interlinked stories, *Mrs. Spring Fragrance* (1912). Her sister, **Winnifred Eaton**, inventing an identity of white and Japanese noble blood, taking the pseudonym Onoto Watanna, was the first Asian American novelist and published 10 interracial romances between 1899 and 1930. **Japanese American** writer **Etsu Inagaki Sugimoto** published an autobiography, *Daughter of the Samurai* (1925), and three novels: *A Daughter of the Narikin* (1932), *A Daughter of the Nohfu* (1935), and *Grandmother O Kyo* (1940). In the mid-1900s, more Asian American women appeared on the literary scene. The first Asian American play was written by Chinese American **Ling-Ai Li**, whose *The Submission of Rose Moy* was staged in Hawaii in 1924.

The first Chinese American woman writer to excite significant public readership was **Jade Snow Wong**, whose autobiography, *Fifth Chinese Daughter* (1945), became the first Asian American best seller. **Monica Sone**'s *Nisei Daughter* (1953) was a significant moment in Asian American literature, for it is the first piece of protest literature by a woman against the injustice of the **Japanese American internment. Rama Santha Rau**, a **South Asian American**, was among this early generation of women writers. She is well known for her travel writings: *East of Home* (1951), *This Is India* (1954), *View to the*

Southeast (1957), and *My Russian Journey* (1959). She is the author of two novels: *Remember the House* (1956) and *The Adventuress* (1970), and two memoirs: *Home to India* (1945) and *Gifts of Passage* (1961).

The real blossoming of Asian American women's writing would have to wait until after the civil rights movement, which inspired many Asian American women. In addition, the Asian American population became larger and more diverse after the 1965 immigration reform, with a rapid increase of the Chinese, Filipinos, and South Asians.

Maxine Hong Kingston's *The Woman Warrior* (1976) was a major feminist voice that critiques both Chinese and American patriarchy. One may say that Kingston's book opened the floodgate of Asian American women's writings, for, during the subsequent years, we have witnessed a rich and diverse body of literature written by Asian American women. Among the Chinese American women writers, the best-known figures are Maxine Hong Kingston, **Marilyn Chin**, **Gish Jen**, **Amy Tan**, **Eleanor Wong Telemaque**, **Mei-mei Berssenbrugge**, **Lisa Lenine See**, **Fae Myenne Ng**, etc. Among the Japanese American women writers are **Ai, Hisaye Yamamoto, Brenda Wong Aoki, Cynthia Kadohata, Velina Hasu Houston**, **Karen Tei Yamashita**, **Ruth Ozeki**, **Julie Otsuka**, **Lois-Ann Yamanaka**, **Yoshiko Uchida**, **Janice Mirikitani, Kimiko Hahn**, **Jeanne Wakatsuki Houston**, etc. **Korean American** women writers include **Sook Nyul Choi**, **Nora Okja Keller**, **Theresa Hak Kyung Cha**, **Myung Mi Kim**, **Susan Choi**, **Patricia Jang**, **Susan Kim**, **Cathy Song**, **Margaret K. Pai, Young Jean Lee** and so on. **Filipina American** women writers include **Jessica Hagedorn**, **Ninotchka Rosca**, **Linda Ty-Casper**, **Cecilia Manguerra Brainard**, **Linda Faigao-Hall**, etc. Among the South Asian American women writers are **Meena Alexander**, **Chitra Banerjee Divakaruni**, **Jhumpa Lahiri**, **Bharati Mukherjee**, **Sara Suleri**, etc. The most recent women writers in this group are Alfghan Americans, such as **Awosta Ayub** and **Donia Gobar**.

The **Vietnamese American** women writers include **Phung Thi Le Ly Hayslip, Lan Cao, Bich Minh Nguyen**, **Monique Truong**, **Lê Thi Diem Thúy, Maura Nguyen Donohue, Dao Strom, Tina Brown Celona**, **Kim-An Lieberman, Mong-Lan,** etc. These women writers explore as many common themes as male writers, such as identity, history, **racism**, class, love, **assimilation**, generation gap, memory, colonial and postcolonial legacy, among others. Closely related to Vietnamese American literature is **Southeast Asian American** writers, for they share not only geographical proximity but also historical and political affinity. The Vietnam War impacted several other countries in this region, including Cambodia and Laos. Women writers like Laotian American **Mali Phonpadith** and **Saymoukda D. Vongsay**, Burmese American **Wendy Law-Yone**, and Hmong American **May Lee-Yang** and

Kao Kalia Yang courageously faced their or their parents' traumatic memories in literature and **theater**. Other Southeast Asian American writers hail from Indonesia, Malaysia, Singapore, and Thailand, and the most prominent women writers from this group include **Shirley Geok-lin Lim**, **Wena Poon**, and **Minfong Ho**.

Asian American women writers have explored a wide range of themes. Two of the common themes are gender and sexism, as demonstrated in **Shaila Abdullah**'s *Beyond the Cayenne Wall*, **Samina Ali**'s *Madras on Rainy Days*, **Susham Bedi**'s *Katra-Dar-Katra* (*Drop by Drop*), **May-Lee Chai**'s *Glamorous Asian*, **Lan Samantha Chang**'s *Inheritance*, **Fiona Cheong**'s *The Scent of the Gods*, **Anne Cherian**'s *A Good Indian Wife*, **Christina Chiu**'s *Troublemakers and Other Saints*, **Don Mee Choi**'s *The Morning News Is Exciting*, Maura Nguyen Donohue's *Islands: A happa wet dream*, **Sarah Gambito**'s *Matadora*, **Carolyn Lau**'s *Ono Ono Girl's Hula*, **Hazel Ai Chun Lin**'s *House of Orchids*, **Anchee Min**'s *Red Azalea*, Bharati Mukherjee's *Jasmine*, **Tahira Naqvi**'s *Dying in a Strange Country*, **Jude Narita**'s *Stories Waiting to Be Told*, **Purvi Shah**'s *Terrain Trac*, **Julie Shigekuni**'s *Bridge between Us*, Dao Strom's *Grass Roof, Tin Roof*, **Alice Tuan**'s *The Roaring Girle*, **Kathleen Tyau**'s *A Little Too Much Is Enough*, **Denise Uyehara**'s *Hello (Sex) Kitty: Mad Asian Bitch on Wheels*, **Merle Woo**'s *Yellow Woman Speaks*, **Mia Yun**'s *House of the Winds*, among many others.

Other popular themes are mother–daughter relationship and female friendship, such as in the works by **Mei Ng**—*Eating Chinese Food Naked*, **Amulya Malladi**—*Serving Crazy with Curry*, Maxine Hong Kingston—*The Woman Warrior*, Amy Tan—*The Joy Luck Club*, **Deanna Fei**—*A Thread of Sky*, **Jennie Baroga**—*A Good Face*, Chitra Banerjee Divakaruni—*Sister of My Heart*, **Marisa De Los Santo**—*Love Walked In*, **Thrity Umrigar**—*The Space between Us*, **Genny Lim**—*Paper Angels*, among many others. Sexuality, love, and marriage are also favorite themes that are well presented by many Asian American women writers including **Kavita Daswani**, Kimiko Hahn, **Kitty Tsui**, **Gail Tsukiyama**, and **Uyen Nicole Duong.** Many South Asian American women writers explore the theme of arranged marriage, such as **Shobhan Bantwal** in *The Dowry Bride*, Chitra Banerjee Divakaruni in *Arranged Marriage*, **Bharti Kirchner** in *Sharmila's Book*, Amulya Malladi in *The Mango Season*, and **Bapsi Sidhwa** in *The Bride*. Interracial marriage or romance is also a significant theme with women writers, such as in **Aimee E. Liu**'s *Cloud Mountain* and Winnifred Eaton's *The Wooing of Wisteria.* In addition, they study many issues common to their male counterparts, such as alienation, racism, memory, history, immigration, colonialism, postcolonialism, language, etc. *See also* AGARWAL, SHILPA; AN, NA; AYUB, AWISTA; BANERJEE, ANJALI; BUDHOS, MARINA; BYNUM, SARAH

SHUN-LIEN; CERENIO, VIRGINIA R; CHAN, EUGENIE; CHANG, DIANA; CHANG, JENNIFER; CHANG, TINA; CHANG, VICTORIA; CHAO, EVELINA; CHAO, PATRICIA; CHARI, SHEELA; CHAU, ANGIE; CHE, SUNNY; CHEN, CHING-IN; CHEN, JUSTINA; CHENG, NIEN; CHEVAPRAVATDUMRONG, CHERRY; CHIANG, FAY; CHIN-LEE, CYNTHIA; CHING, CARLA; CHOI, ANNIE; CHOONG, TINLING; CHOU, CYNTHIA L.; CHUANG, HUA; CHUNG, FRANCES; CHUNG, SONYA; DAWESAR, ABHA; DE CRISTOFORO, VIOLET KAZUE; DESAI, KIRAN; DIZON, LOUELLA; ELLIOTT, DUONG VAN MAI; FERRELL, MONICA; FOO, LORA JO; GALANG, M. EVELINA; GANESAN, INDIRA; GANESHANANTHAN, VASUGI V.; GLORIA, EUGENE; GOWDA, SHILPI SOMAYA; HAJI, NAFISA; HAN, JENNY; HAN, SUYING; HILL, AMY; HIM, CHANRITHY; HIRAHARA, NAOMI; HOLTHE, TESS URIZA; HONG, CATHY PARK; HONG, LILY TOY; HWANG, CAROLINE; IGLORIA, LUISA A.; IIZUKA, NAOMI; IKO, MOMOKO; ISHIGAKI, AYAKO TANAKA; JAMES, TANIA; JANG, PATRICIA; JIANG, JI-LI; KAGEYAMA-RAMAKRISHNAN, CLAIRE; KAIPA, SUMMI; KAKUGAWA, FRANCES H.; KANG, CONNIE K.; KAPIL, BHANU; KELTNER, KIM WONG; KHANNA, VANDANA; KIM, ELIZABETH; KIM, EUGENIA; KIM, PATTI; KIM, SUJI KWOCK; KIM, SUKI; KITAMURA, KATIE; KONO, JULIET SANAE; KUO, HELENA; KWOK, JEAN; LEE, ANNETTE; LEE, CHERYLENE; LEE, HELIE; LEE, JANICE Y. K.; LEE, MARIE MYUNG-OK; LEE, MARY PAIK; LEE, PRISCILLA; LEE, SUEYEUN JULIETTE; LEE, WENDY; LEYUNG-RYAN, TERESA; LI, YIYUN; LIM-WILSON, FATIMA; LIN, ADET; LIN, ALICE P.; LIN, GRACE; LIN, TAI-YI; LOH, SANDRA TSING; LORD, BETTE BAO; MAH, ADELINE YEN; MAHAJAN, KARAN; MASSEY, SUJATA; MATSUEDA, PAT; MCCUNN, RUTHANNE LUM; MEER, AMEENA; MEYER, MARLANE; MIN, KATHERINE; MIYAMOTO, NOBUKO; MOHANRAJ, MARY ANNE; MORI, KYOKO; MUN, NAMIE; NARAYAN, KIRIN; NEZHUKUMATATHIL, AIMEE; NGAI, SIANNE; NGUYEN, HOA; NIEH, HUALING; NUNEZ, SIGRID; OKUBO, MINE; OTA, SHELLEY AYAME NISHIMURA; PAHK, INDUK; PARK, FRANCES; PARK, GINGER; PARK, ISHLE YI; PARK, LINDA SUE; PARK, THERESE S.; PHAN, AIMEE; PRASAD, CHANDRA; REHMAN, BUSHRA; REKDAL, PAISLEY; REYES, BARBARA JANE; RIZZUTO, RAHNA REIKO; ROBERTS, DMAE; ROH-SPAULDING, CAROL; RORIPAUGH, LEE ANN; ROWLAND, LAURA JOH; SAIKI, PATSY SUMIE; SASAKI, R.A.; SEKARAN, SHANTHI; SHARIF, BINA; SHARMA, POONAM; SHAUGHNESSY, BRENDA; SHEPARD, KAREN; SHETH, KASHMIRA; SHIN, SUN YUNG; SKINNER, MICHELLE CRUZ; SON, DIANA;

SREENIVASAN, JYOTSNA; STAPLETON, LARA; STARNES, SOFIA M.; STICKMON, JANET; SU, ADRIENNE; SULERI, SARA; SUNDARESAN, INDU; SUNÉE, KIM; SUYEMOTO, TOYO; SZE, MAI MAI; TABIOS, EILEEN; TAMAGAWA, KATHLEEN; THAM, HILARY; TRAN, BARBARA; TRENKA, JANE JEONG; TRIPLETT, PIMONE; TSENG, JENNIFER; TSENG, SANDY; TYAU, KATHLEEN; UNG, LOUNG; UYEMOTO, HOLLY; VANG, KA; VAZIRANI, REETIKA; VILLANUEVA, MARIANNE; VINLUAN, ERMENA MARLENE; WANG, PING; WATANABE, SYLVIA A.; WEI, KATHERINE; WONG, ELIZABETH; WONG, JANET S.; WONG, MAY; WONG, NELLIE; WU, FAN; YAMADA, MITSUYE; YAMATE, SANDRA S.; YAMAUCHI, WAKAKO; YAN, GELING; YANG, RAE; YEE, LISA; YIP, MINGMEI; YOO, PAULA; YOUN, MONICA.

WONG, ELIZABETH (1958–). A **Chinese American** playwright, Wong was born in South Gate, California, to Chinese immigrant parents. She received her B.A. in journalism from the University of Southern California. After eight years of news reporting, she became disillusioned with journalism and came to recognize her desire to act and write plays about Asian American people. She went to the Yale School of Drama and then moved to New York University's Tisch School of the Arts and earned an M.F.A. Her most popular and oft-produced plays include *Letters to a Student Revolutionary* (1989), about the Tiananmen Square incident, and *Kimchee and Chitlins* (1990), about conflicts between African Americans and Korean immigrants in Brooklyn. She joined Touchstone Television and was a staff writer for the ABC sitcom *All-American Girl* (1994–1995). In addition, she also wrote other plays, such as *China Doll* (1996), *The Concubine Spy* (1992), *Let the Big Dog Eat* (1998), *Punk Girls* (2000), *Dating and Mating in Modern Times* (2003), and *The Love Life of a Eunuch* (1992). *The Happy Prince* (1997) and *The Play Formerly Known as the Happy Prince* (1996) are adaptations of a short story by Oscar Wilde. Wong is the recipient of numerous honors, including the Playwright Forum Award from **Theatre** Works in Colorado Springs, a Margo Jones New Play Citation for *Letters to a Student Revolutionary*, the Jane Chambers Award for *China Doll*, the David Mark Cohen National Playwriting Award, and the Petersen Emerging Playwright Award.

WONG, JADE SNOW (1922–2006). A **Chinese American** autobiographer, Wong was born in San Francisco, California, to Chinese immigrants from Hong Kong. Wong earned an A.A. from San Francisco Junior College and a B.A. from Mills College. At the age of 24, she published her famous autobiography *Fifth Chinese Daughter* (1945), and its revised version was printed in 1950. In this autobiography, Wong offers Americans a guided tour of Chinese American society and articulates how she negotiates between two cultures. For this book, she received an honorary doctorate from Mills College and a Silver medal from the Commonwealth Club of San Francisco. In 1976, she was featured as the best representative of Asian Americans for a PBS documentary about racial minorities. Wong also published a travel book, *No Chinese Stranger* (1975).

WONG, JANET S. (1962–). A prolific **Chinese–Korean American** writer of **children's books**. Wong was born in Los Angeles to a Chinese father and a Korean mother. She received her B.A. in history from the University of California, Los Angeles, and J.D. from Yale Law School. She is the author of 21 books for children, mainly picture books and **poetry** collections, including *Me and Rolly Maloo* (2010), *The Dumpster Diver* (2007), *TWIST: Yoga Poems* (2007), *Minn and Jake's Almost Terrible Summer* (2008), and *Behind the Wheels: Driving Poems* (2010). Wong's poems and stories have been featured in many textbooks and anthologies. Her books have received numerous awards and honors, such as the International Reading Association's "Celebrate Literacy Award" for exemplary service in the promotion of literacy, and the prestigious Stone Center Recognition of Merit, given by the Claremont Graduate School. She currently resides near Princeton, New Jersey.

WONG, MAY (1944–). A **Chinese American** poet, Wong was born in Chongqing, China. She moved to Singapore with her mother in 1950. She received her B.A. in English literature from the University of Singapore and her M.F.A. in creative writing from the University of Iowa. Her first book of **poetry**, *A Bad Girl's Book of Animals* (1969), uses animals to convey human sensibilities. She then published two more books of poetry: *Reports* (1974) and *Superstitions* (1978). She is married to an Irish professor of physics and lives in Dublin.

WONG, NELLIE (1934–). A **Chinese American** poet, Wong was born in Oakland, California, to Chinese immigrant parents. Because of economic hardship, she had to work to help support the family of eight and was not able to go to college until she was in her mid-30s. At San Francisco State University, Wong began to realize her passion for and talent in writing **poetry**. She has published three volumes of poetry: *Dreams in Harrison Railroad Park* (1977), *The Death of a Long Steam Lady* (1986), and *Stolen Moments* (1997). Her poetry comes from her life in **Chinatown**, her working life, and her family's stories. In the late 1970s and early 1980s, Wong cofounded Unbound Feet, an Asian American feminist literary and performance group.

It consisted of six Asian American women, including **Merle Woo** and **Kitty Tsui.** The group performed at colleges, universities, and community centers.

WONG, RAYMOND K. (1966–). A **Chinese American** novelist and actor, Wong was born and raised in Hong Kong. He came to the United States at the age of 18 to attend college and graduated from the University of Pittsburgh with honor. Later, he studied creative writing at the University of California, Los Angeles. His debut novel, *The Pacific Between* (2006), won an Independent Publishers Book Award. It centers on themes of love, betrayal, and self-discovery. He has also published a collection of short stories, *A Bunch of Stories* (2008).

WONG, SHAWN HSU (1949–). A **Chinese American** novelist, Wong was born in Oakland, California, and raised in Berkeley. He began college as a premed but fell in love with creative writing and graduated with a B.A. in English from the University of California, Berkeley. He received his M.F.A. from San Francisco State University. He is currently an English professor at the University of Washington. His first novel, *Homebase* (1979), is autobiographical and explores an Asian American young man's pursuit for self-knowledge. This novel won both the 1980 Pacific Northwest Booksellers' Award and Washington State Governor's Writers Day Award. Wong's second novel, *American Knees* (1995), presents a set of mature Asian American characters and explores with irony themes of love, sexuality, ethnicity, and interracial relations. *American Knees* was made into an independent feature film entitled *Americanese* (2009), written and directed by Eric Byler. Wong has been awarded a National Endowment for the Arts Creative Writing Fellowship and a Rockefeller Foundation residency in Italy.

WOO, MERLE (1941–). A **Chinese–Korean American** poet, playwright, and performer, Woo was born in San Francisco, California, to a Chinese father and Korean mother. She received her B.A. and M.A. in English from San Francisco State University. Currently, she is a lecturer at the University of California, Berkeley. She is the author of a collection of poems, *Yellow Woman Speaks* (1986), which focuses on topics such as **racism**, sexism, love, and sex. She has also written plays, including *Home Movies* (1979) and *Balancing* (1980).

WOO, SUNG J. (1971–). A **Korean American** novelist, Woo was born in Seoul, South Korea, arrived at the United States when he was 10, and grew up in Ocean Township, New Jersey. He received his B.A. in English from Cornell University and M.F.A. in creative writing from New York University.

He currently lives in Washington, New Jersey. His debut novel, *Everything Asian* (2009), winner of the 2010 Asian/Pacific American Award for Literature, is a story of a Korean immigrant family's first year in the United States as it struggles to make a living by running a gift shop in a strip mall. Woo's short stories and essays have appeared in the *New York Times*, *McSweeney's*, and *KoreAm Journal*. His short story, "Limits," was an Editor's Choice winner in *Carve Magazine*'s 2008 Raymond Carver Short Story Contest.

WORRA, BRYAN THAO (1973–). A Laotian American poet, Worra was born Thao Somnouk Silosoth in Bientiane, Laos. Adopted by an American pilot when he was three days old, he was brought to the United States as an infant. He attended Otterbein College in Ohio. He is the author of five books of **poetry**: *The Tuk-Tuk Diaries: My Dinner with Clusterbombs* (2003), *Touching Detonations* (2003), *On the Other Side of the Eye* (2007), *Winter Ink* (2008), and *Barrow* (2009). His poems have appeared in the literary anthology *Bamboo among the Oaks* and periodicals including the *Paj Ntaub Voice Hmong Literary Journal*, *Defenestration*, *Speakeasy*, *Whistling Shade*, *Urban Pioneer*, *Unarmed*, the *Asian Pacific Journal*, and the *Journal of the Asian American Renaissance*. Worra's writing explores many themes including transience, identity, and home. In 2009, he became the first Laotian American writer to receive a fellowship in literature from the National Endowment for the Arts. In addition, he has received a Minnesota Playwrights' Center Many Voices Award and a Minnesota State Arts Board Cultural Collaboration Award. *See also* SOUTHEAST ASIAN AMERICAN LITERATURE AND THEATER.

WU, FAN (1973–). A **Chinese American** novelist, Wu was born in Jiangxi Province, China. In 1997, she came to the United States to attend Stanford University. After she earned her M.A. in mass media studies, she joined Yahoo!, a Silicon Valley–based Internet company. She has published two novels: *February Flowers* (2007), chosen by Picador Asia as its inaugural book, and *Beautiful as Yesterday* (2009). Both novels tell stories about Chinese **women** trapped between two nations, two cultures, and tradition and modernity. Her short fiction, besides being anthologized and nominated for the Pushcart Prize, has appeared in *Granta*, the *Missouri Review*, *Ploughshares*, and elsewhere. She currently lives in Northern California.

YAMADA, MITSUYE (MAY) (1923–). A **Japanese American** poet, Yamada was born in Fukuoka, Japan, and moved with her family to Seattle when she was three. At age 11 her parents sent her back to Japan for schooling, and she returned to the United States for high school, which was interrupted by the **Japanese internment**. Most of her writings dwell on this period of her life and her feeling of being an outsider both in America and in Japan. After release from the camp, she studied at New York University and earned her B.A. in English and an M.A. in English literature from the University of Chicago. She is the author of two books of **poetry**: *Camp Notes and Other Poems* (1976) and *Desert Run: Poems and Stories* (1988).

YAMAMOTO, HISAYE (1921–). A **Japanese American** fiction writer, Yamamoto was born in Redondo Beach, California, to Japanese immigrants. She attended Campton Junior College, which was interrupted when the bombing of Pearl Harbor (7 December 1941) occurred. At age 21, she, along with her family, was **interned** in the Poston Relocation Center in Arizona. Her camp experience profoundly shaped her life and writings. After the camp, she worked for the *Los Angeles Tribune.* Her collection of short stories, *Seventeen Syllables: 5 Stories of Japanese American Life*, was first published in Japan in 1985 and in the United States in 1988. The title story has become a classic piece in Asian American literature, influential to the following generations of writers. Most of her stories portray the Japanese American **women**'s struggle against the strict gender role for free expression. For her achievement and influence, she received in 1986 the **American Book Award** for Lifetime Achievement. Her stories have appeared in major literary magazines, such as *Partisan Review*, *Kenyon Review*, *Carleton Miscellany*, and *Harper's Bazaar*.

YAMANAKA, LOIS-ANN (1961–). A **Japanese American** poet and novelist, Yamanaka was born in Hawaii to **nisei** parents. She earned her B.Ed. and M.Ed. from the University of Hawaii, Manoa. She published one collection of a verse novella, *Saturday Night and the Pahala* ***Theater*** (1993), which won the Pushcart Prize. She is better known for her six novels: *Wild*

Meat and the Bully Burgers (1996), *Blu's Hanging* (1997), *Heads by Harry* (1999), *Name Me Nobody* (1999), *Father of the Four Passages* (2001), and *Behold the Many* (2006). In these novels, Yamanaka tells the stories of the Asian American working class people in Hawaii and explores themes of ethnicity, family history, poverty, violence, and **racism**, and she achieves her unique voice by using Pidgin dialect. She has also written a **children's story**, *The Heart's Language* (2005). She has received multiple honors, including a Nation Endowment for the Humanities grant, the Elliot Cades Award for Literature, a Carnegie Foundation grant, a National Endowment for the Arts fellowship, the Rona Jaffe Award for Women Writers, the Lannan Literary Award, and an **American Book Award** for *Blu's Hanging*, etc.

YAMASHITA, KAREN TEI (1951–). A **Japanese American** novelist, Yamashita was born in Oakland, California, and raised in Los Angeles. She studied English and Japanese literatures at Carleton College. After graduation, she studied Portuguese in an intensive program. Awarded a Thomas J. Watson Fellowship, she went to Brazil in 1974 to research Japanese immigration to Brazil. This trip became 10 years of stay and a marriage to a Brazilian architect. Her life in Brazil deeply influenced her novels, such as *Through the Arc of the Rain Forest* (1990), *Brazil-Maru* (1992), *Tropic of Orange* (1997), and her short story collection, *Circle K Cycles* (2001). In these stories, Yamashita employs **magical realism** to depict the lives of the Japanese in Brazil. Yamashita has also written plays, including *Hannah Kusoh* (1989), *Tokyo Carmen vs. L.A. Carmen* (1990), a musical *Godzilla Gomes to Little Tokyo* (1991), and *Noh Bozos* (1993). Her plays have been produced by the **East West Players**. *I Hotel* (2010) is her most recent work in collaboration with two others. It is a collage of prose, playwriting, graphic art, and philosophy that tells an epic tale of the struggle for civil rights in San Francisco's **Chinatown**. Yamashita now teaches literature and creative writing at the University of California, Santa Cruz. She is the recipient of an **American Book Award** and Janet Heidinger Kafka Award. *See also* THEATER.

YAMATE, SANDRA S. (1959–). A **Japanese American** writer of **children's books**, Yamate is a fourth-generation Japanese American. She received her B.A. from University of Illinois and J.D. from Harvard Law School. After practicing law for 10 years, she established in Chicago a children's press called Polychrome Publishing. She is the author of two children's books, *Ashok, by Any Other Name* (1992) and *Char Siu Bao Boy* (2000). Both portray Asian American boys' struggles to accept their ethnic identities.

YAMAUCHI, WAKAKO (1924–). A **Japanese American** playwright, Yamauchi was born in Westmorland, California, to Japanese immigrant parents.

During World War II, she, a high school senior, and her family were interned in Poston, Arizona. After her release, she went to Chicago and took painting classes at the Otis Art Center. Her first play, *And the Soul Shall Dance* (1976), based on a short story, portrays the lives of two Japanese American farm families during the Depression era when Japanese immigrants were forbidden to own land by California State law. This play was first performed at the **East West Players** theater in Los Angeles and won the Los Angeles Drama Critic Circle Award for best new play of 1977. "*12-1-A*" (1982) dramatizes the **Japanese American internment** experience. Its title refers to her family's address in an internment camp. She went on to write *The Music Lesson* (1980), *Face Box* (1984), *The Chairman's Wife* (1990), *Not a Through Street* (1991), *Shirley Hot-Cha-Cha* (1991), etc. A collection of her plays and stories has been published under the title *Songs My Mother Taught Me* (1994). *See also* THEATER.

YAN, GELING (1958–). A **Chinese American** novelist and screen writer, Yan was born in Shanghai and came to the United States in 1989. She holds a B.A. in literature from Wuhan University and an M.F.A. in fiction writing from Columbia College, Chicago. To date, she has published over 20 books in various editions in China, Taiwan, Hong Kong, the United States, Great Britain, and elsewhere. She is the recipient of more than 30 literary and film awards. After publishing her first novel in 1985, she has produced ever since a steady stream of novels, short stories, novellas, essays, and scripts. Her best-known novels in English are *The Lost Daughter of Happiness* (2001), a novella and short story collection called *White Snake and Other Stories* (1999), *The Banquet Bug* (2006), *The Sojourner* (2009), *A Woman's Epic* (2007), etc. Her novels explore themes of class, gender, sexuality, history, etc. Some of Yan's works have been adapted for film, including internationally distributed films *Xiu Xiu: The Sent-Down Girl*, directed by Joan Chen, and *Siao Yu*, directed by Sylvia Chang. Yan has also written numerous scripts based on her own and other authors' work, both in English and Chinese.

YANG, BELLE. A **Chinese American** author and artist of **children's books** and **young adult novels**, Yang was born in Taiwan but spent part of her childhood in Japan. At age seven, she immigrated to the United States with her family. She attended Stirling University in Scotland, graduated from the University of California, Santa Cruz, in biology but went on to study art at Pasadena Art Center College of Design and the Beijing Institute of Traditional Chinese Painting. She is the author of children's picture books, such as *Foo the Flying Frog of Washtub Pond* (2008), *Always Come Home to Me* (2007), winner of a Chinese American Librarian Association Best Picture Book of 2008 award, *Hannah Is My Name* (2004), *Forget Sorrow* (2011),

Archie's War (2007), and *Chili-Chili-Chin-Chin* (1999). She has also authored two illustrated books of nonfiction: *Baba: A Return to China upon My Father's Shoulders* (1994) and *The Odyssey of a Manchurian* (1996), based on her father's life. Her major themes include immigration, cultural identity, and family.

YANG, DORIS JONES. A **Chinese American young adult novelist**, Yang was born in Youngstown, Ohio, to a Chinese American father and white American mother. She received her education at Princeton University and Johns Hopkins University. She worked for many years as a journalist stationed in China for *Business Week* and *U.S. News & World Report.* She is the author of *Daughter of Xanachu* (2011), *The Secret Voice of Gina Zhang* (2000), *The Brother Who Gave Rice* (2007), and *Bring Me Three Gifts* (2007). Her novels depict strong female characters.

YANG, GENE LUEN (1973–). A **Chinese American** comics artist and graphic novelist, Yang was born in Alameda, California. He holds a B.S. in computer science from the University of California, Berkeley, with a minor in creative writing and an M.A. in education from California State University, East Bay. Yang began publishing comic books under the name Humble Comics in 1996. His graphic novel, *American Born Chinese* (2006), won the 2007 Members' Choice Award from the **Asian American Literary Workshop**, the 2007 Michael L. Printz Award for young-adult literature, and an Eisner Award. It became the first graphic novel to be nominated for a **National Book Award**. Yang also wrote in collaboration with Derek Kirk Kim, *The Eternal Smile* (2009), a collection of three short stories in comics, which also won an Eisner Award. His third book is a graphic novella, *Prime Baby* (2010), which was originally serialized in the *New York Times Magazine*. Yang's most recent work is a graphic novel, *Level Up* (2011), with art by Thien Pham. His books center on the themes of ethnic identity, youth, geek culture, aliens, fantasy, and Chinese mythology. Yang currently lives with his family in the San Francisco Bay Area, where he teaches computer science at Bishop O'Dowd High School and will soon begin teaching at Hamline University in its M.F.A. program in Writing for Children and Young Adults.

YANG, JEFFREY (1974–). A **Chinese American** poet, Yang was born in Escondido, California, to Chinese immigrants. He received his B.A. in English and B.S. in animal physiology/neuroscience from the University of California, San Diego, and M.F.A. in creative writing from New York University. His debut book of poems, *An Aquarium* (2008), is a finalist of the Asian American Literary Award for **poetry**. Through the language of aquatic life, his poetry meditates on war, environmental degradation, language, and history. His most recent publication is another book of poetry, *Vanishing-Line* (2011). He has also edited an anthology *Birds, Beasts, and Seas: Nature Poems from New Directions* (2011), and coedited another *Two Lines: Some Kind of Beautiful Signal* (2010). He works as an editor at New Directions Publishing. His poetry has appeared in the *Nation* and the *Paris Review*, and he lives in Beacon, New York.

YANG, KAO KALIA (1980–). A Hmong American memoirist, Yang was born in a Hmong refugee camp in Thailand and moved with her family to Minnesota at age six. She received her B.A. in English from Carleton College and M.F.A. in creative writing from Columbia University. She has published a memoir, *The Latehomecomer: A Hmong Family Memoir* (2008). Together with her sister, she founded Words Wanted, a company dedicated to helping immigrants with writing, translating, and business services. She lives in Andover, Minnesota. *See also* SOUTHEAST ASIAN AMERICAN LITERATURE AND THEATER.

YANG, RAE (1950–). A **Chinese American** autobiographer, Yang was born in Beijing, China. She came to the United States in 1981 to study at the University of Massachusetts and received a Ph.D. in comparative literature. She is now a professor at Dickinson College. Her autobiography, *Spider Eater* (1997), tells the story of her experience in the Chinese Cultural Revolution.

YAU, JOHN (1950–). A prolific **Chinese American** poet and fiction writer, Yau was born in Lynn, Massachusetts, to a Chinese mother and a Eurasian father. He received his B.A. from Bard College and M.F.A. from Brooklyn College. Yau's **poetry** is rich, challenging, and political, investigating issues of race, **assimilation**, **exile**, cultural dislocation, and mixed race identity. Critics often classify him as a postmodern poet keen on the relationship between language and identity. His numerous books of poetry include *Paradiso Diaspora* (2006), *Ing Grish* (2005), *Borrowed Love Poems* (2002), *I was a Poet in the House of Frankenstein* (1999), *Forbidden Entries* (1996), *Postcards from Trakl* (1994), *Edificio Sayonara* (1992), *Big City Primer* (1991), *Radiant Silhouette* (1989), *Dragon's Blood* (1989), *Corpse and Mirror* (1983), *Notarikon* (1981), *The Sleepless Night of Eugene Delacroix* (1980), *Sometimes* (1979), *The Reading of an Ever-Changing Tale* (1977), and *Crossing Canal Street* (1976). He has also written two books of short stories: *Hawaiian Cowboys* (1994) and *My Symptoms* (1998). He has been the arts editor of the *Brooklyn Rail* since March 2004, and he currently is a professor of art criticism at Rutgers University. He has received many honors, including the Lavan Award from the Academy of American Poets, the Jerome Shestack Prize from the *American Poetry Review*, Brenda Gill Award, and grants from the National Endowment for the Arts, the New York Foundation for the Arts, the General Electric Foundation, and the Guggenheim Foundation.

YEE, LISA (1959–). A **Chinese American** writer of **children's books**, Yee was born and raised near Los Angeles. She studied English and humanities at the University of Southern California. Her books include *Millicent Min, Girl Genius* (2003), *Stanford Wong Flunks Big-Time* (2005), *So Totally, Emily Ebers* (2007), *Good Luck, Ivy* (2007), *Absolutely Maybe* (2009), *Bobby vs. Girls (Accidentally)* (2009), *Bobby the Brave (Sometimes)* (2010), *Aloha, Kanani* (2011), *Good Job, Kanani* (2011), and *Warp Speed* (2011). Some of Yee's stories share the same characters, and all of her books explore common themes of friendship, trust, family, and belonging. She is the recipient of numerous honors, such as the Sid Fleischman Humor Award, Chinese American Librarians Association Best Book of the Year award, Family Choice Award, Washington Post Book of the Week award, and Bank Street College of Education Best Book of the Year award.

YELLOW PERIL. This was a racial epithet directed against people of Asian descent, popular in the United States in the late-19th to 20th centuries. It signified the fear of white Americans who perceived Asian immigration as a threat to Christendom and Western civilization. This fear has been depicted by many Asian American writers, such as **Frank Chin**, **Marilyn Chin**, **Patricia Jang**, **Shawn Hsu Wong**, **Lawson Fusao Inada**, **Garrett Hongo**, and **Jessica Hagedorn**.

YEP, LAURENCE MICHAEL (1948–). A **Chinese American** novelist for **children** and **young adults**, Yep was born in San Francisco. He majored in journalism at Marquette University but transferred to the University of California, San Cruz. He earned a Ph.D. in English from the State University of New York, Buffalo. Yep has written over 40 novels. His best-known novel, *Dragonwings* (1975), won the Newbery Honor, the Boston Globe–Horn Book Award, the International Reading Association Children's Book Award, and the Lewis Carroll Shelf Award. He won the Newbery Honor again for *Dragon's Gate* (1993). *Child of the Owl* (1977) won the Boston Globe–Horn Book Award and the Jane Addams Children's Book Award. He has also written an autobiography, *The Lost Garden* (1991).

YEW, CHAY (1966–). A **Chinese American** playwright and director, Yew was born in Singapore to Chinese parents. He came to the United States at the age of 16 to study **theater** at Pepperdine University. After two years, he returned to Singapore and wrote his first play, *As If He Hears* (1989), which was banned by the government for its sympathetic portrayal of gay men. He returned to the United States in 1988 to continue studying theater at Boston University. *Porcelain* (1992) was his graduating thesis, whose production in England won him the London Fringe Award for Best Playwright and Best Play. He went on to write *A Language of Their Own* (1995), *Half Lives* (1996), *Red* (1998), *Wonderland* (1999), *A Beautiful Country* (1998), *White* (2001), *Here and Now* (2002), *Snapshot* (2002), *A Winter People* (2002), *Question 27, Question 28* (2003), *Malaya* (2003), *Second Skin* (2004), *A Distant Shore* (2005), *The Long Season* (2005), *Neon Mirage* (2006), etc. Most of his plays explore themes of race, sexuality, global capitalism, immigration, etc. Yew's plays have been produced by many theaters, including the New York Shakespeare Festival/Public Theater in New York City, Royal Court in London, Mark Taper Forum, the **East West Players**, Manhattan Theatre Club, La Jolla Playhouse, Wilma Theatre, Long Wharf Theatre, Intiman Theatre, Portland Center Stage, Cornerstone Theatre Company, Perseverance Theatre, Singapore Repertory Theatre, etc. He has served as artistic director at the **Northwest Asian American Theatre** and the Mark Taper Forum's Asian Theatre Workshop in Los Angeles. Among his numerous honors are an **Obie Award** for direction, George and Elisabeth Marton Playwriting Award, the Gay and Lesbian Alliance against Defamation Media Award, Asian/Pacific Gays and Friends Community Visibility Award, Made in America Award, and Robert Chesley Award, and grants from the Rockefeller MAP, McKnight Foundation, and the TCG/Pew National Residency Program. *See also* SOUTHEAST ASIAN AMERICAN LITERATURE AND THEATER.

YIN. A **Chinese American** writer of **children's books**, Yin was born in Brooklyn, New York. She graduated from college with a finance degree and worked on Wall Street as a financial writer until she decided to manage her husband, award-winning illustrator, **Chris Soentpiet**'s career. She is the author of *Coolies* (2001), winner of the Parents' Choice Foundation's Gold Award for Best Picture Book in 2001, an American Library Association Notable Book award, and she was an International Reading Association Book Award Winner in 2002. *Brothers* (2006) is the sequel of *Coolies*, an International Reading Association (IRA) Teachers' Choice in 2007. *Dear Santa, Please Come to the 19th Floor* (2011) is her most recent book based on her childhood dream of Santa's visit.

YIP, MINGMEI (1951–). A **Chinese American** novelist, musician, and painter, Yip was born and raised in Hong Kong. She immigrated to the United

States in 1992. She holds a B.A. in English language and literature from Hong Kong Baptist College, an M.A. in Chinese literature from Hong Kong New Asia Research Institute, and a Ph.D. in musicology from the University of Paris, Sorbonne. She is the author of three novels. Her debut novel, *Peach Blossom Pavilion* (2008), portrays the last Chinese poet–musician–courtesan. *Petals from the Sky* (2010) tells the story of a young Chinese **woman** who escapes her dysfunctional family to become a Buddhist nun, only to realize she had run away from her own heart. *Song of Silk Road* (2011) tells the adventure of a young Chinese American woman on the ancient Silk Road in search of a fortune. She has also published *Chinese Children's Favorite Stories* (2004), which she illustrated. In addition, she has numerous Chinese publications in Hong Kong and Taiwan.

YIP, WAI-LIM (1937–). A **Chinese American** poet, Yip was born in Guangdong, China, and moved to Hong Kong at the age of 12. He holds a B.A. in literature from National Taiwan University and M.A. in English literature from National Taiwan Normal University. Yip came to the United States to attend the Iowa Writers' Workshop, from which he received an M.F.A. He then went to Princeton University and received his Ph.D. in comparative literature. He is the author of two **poetry** collections: *Between Landscapes* (1994) and *Between/Entre* (2008). He has taught at the University of California, San Diego, Chinese University of Hong Kong, Beijing University, and Qinghua University. Yip is better known for his poetic theory, relating modernist poetry to Taoist aesthetics.

YOO, DAVID (1974–). A **Korean American** novelist, Yoo was born in Manchester, Connecticut. He received a B.A. in government and English literature from Skidmore College and M.A. in creative writing from the University of Colorado, Boulder. He is the author of three **young adult novels**: *Girls for Breakfast* (2005), *Stop Me If You've Heard This One Before* (2008), and *A Fistful of Feathers: A Short Story from Guys Read; Funny Business* (2010). They all explore themes of ethnicity, love, and sex. He currently teaches in the M.F.A. program at Pine Manor College and at the Gotham Writers' Workshop.

YOO, PAULA. A **Korean American** novelist, **children's book** author, TV writer, and violinist, Yoo was born in New York City. She holds a B.A. in English from Yale University, an M.S. in journalism from Columbia University, and an M.F.A. in creative writing from Warren Wilson College. Before becoming a full-time author and screenwriter, she was a journalist for the *Seattle Times*, the *Detroit News*, and *People Magazine*'s Los Angeles bureau. Her debut novel, *Good Enough* (2009), chronicles the journey of an over-achieving, Ivy-bound teen itching to rebel. She is also the author of two children's nonfiction picture books, *Sixteen Years in Sixteen Seconds: The Sammy Lee Story* (2003) and *Shooting Star: The Anna May Wong Story* (2009). She is currently coproducer for the *Eureka* series on the SyFy Channel. Her other TV writing credits include NBC's *The West Wing*, FOX's *Tru Calling*, the N's (Paramount/MTV cable network) *Beyond the Break*, the CW's *Hidden Palms*, and Lifetime's *Side Order of Life*.

YOON, PAUL (1980–). A **Korean American** fiction writer, Yoon was born in New York City. He received his B.A. in English from Wesleyan University. His debut collection of short stories, *Once the Shore* (2009), winner of the John C. Zacharis First Book Award and the **Asian American Literary Award**, explores the themes of family, lost love, silence, alienation, and the effects of the Japanese occupation and the Korean War (1950–1953) on the poor communities of a small, imaginary South Korean island. His work has appeared in *One Story*, *Ploughshares*, *TriQuarterly*, *Glimmer Train*, *American Short Fiction*, etc. Among his honors are an O. Henry award and inclusion in the *Best American Short Stories 2006* and the *PEN/O. Henry Prize Stories 2009*. He lives in Boston.

YOSHIDA, JIM (1921–?). A **Japanese American** autobiographer, Yoshida was born in Seattle to Japanese immigrant parents. During his visit to Japan in the summer of 1940, he was detained when all traffic between Japan and the United States was suspended because of World War II. He was drafted into the Japanese army and did not succeed in returning to the United States until 10 years later. It was through his successful legal suit against the U.S. government that he re-obtained his American citizenship and was allowed to return to the States. His autobiography collaborated with Bill Hosokawa, *The Two Worlds of Jim Yoshida* (1972), tells his experience of being trapped between the two cultures.

YOUN, MONICA. A **Korean American** poet, Youn was born and raised in Houston, Texas. She received her B.A. from Princeton University, a J.D. from Yale Law School, and a Master of Philosophy from Oxford University where she was a Rhodes Scholar. She was a Stegner Fellow at Stanford University. She is the author of two books of poems: *Barter* (2003) and *Ignatz* (2010). The latter, exploring the theme of unrequited desire, is a series of poems loosely based on the mouse character from George Herriman's Krazy Kat comic strip. Her **poetry** has appeared in *Agni*, *American Letters & Commentary*, the *Denver Quarterly*, *Fence*, *LIT*, *Poetry Review*, *Tin House*, and

Cue: A Journal of Prose Poetry. She is the recipient of the Witter Bynner Poetry Fellowship. She works as a media and entertainment lawyer in Manhattan. For her work on *Ignatz*, she has been awarded the Witter Bynner Fellowship from the Library of Congress, and residencies from the MacDowell Colony, the Corporation of Yaddo, and the Rockefeller Foundation.

YOUNG ADULT NOVEL. *See* CHILDREN'S LITERATURE.

YOUNG JEAN LEE'S THEATER COMPANY. This is an **Obie Award**–winning New York–based experimental **theater** company that has been creating and presenting shows written and directed by **Young Jean Lee**, who founded the company in 2003. Although a **Korean American**, Lee writes and produces plays that cross ethnic boundaries. Her work deals with major issues in unpredictable and complicated ways that stick in people's minds and challenge them to think rather than reaffirming their pre-existing beliefs.

YOUNG, C. DALE. An Asian American poet who traces his ancestry to China, India, Europe, and Latin America, Young was born in the Caribbean and educated in Florida with both an M.F.A. and an M.D. from the University of Florida. He practices medicine in the San Francisco Bay Area and serves as the **poetry** editor of the *New England Review*. He is the author of three books of poems: *Torn* (2011), *The Second Person* (2007), and *The Day underneath the Day* (2001). His poetry explores the themes of memories, death, nature, love, and sexuality. He has received numerous awards, including a Poetry Fellowship from the National Endowment for the Arts, a **Lambda Literary Award** in Poetry, and the Grolier Prize. His poems and fiction have appeared in many anthologies and magazines, including the *Best American Poetry*, the *Atlantic Monthly*, the *Paris Review*, the *New Republic*, *Poetry*, *Guernica*, and *Yale Review*.

YOUNG, ED (1931–). A **Chinese American** illustrator and author of **children's books**, Young was born in Tianjing, China, grew up in Shanghai, and later moved to Hong Kong. As a young man, he came to the United States to study architecture but turned instead to his love of art. A graduate of the Art Center College of Design in Pasadena, Young has since taught at the Pratt Institute, Yale University, Naropa Institute, and the University of California at Santa Cruz. In 1990, his book *Lon Po Po* was awarded the Caldecott Medal. He has also received two Caldecott Honors—for illustrating *The Emperor and the Kite* and *Seven Blind Mice* (2002)—and was twice nominated for the Hans Christian Andersen Medal. His other books include *Cat and Rat* (1998), *The Lost Horse: A Chinese Folktale* (2004), *Mouse Match: A Chinese*

Folktale (1997), and *Beyond the Great Mountains* (2005). Young lives in Westchester County, New York.

YU, CHARLES (1976–). A **Chinese American** novelist, Yu was born and raised in Los Angeles, where he now lives and practices law. He graduated from the University of California, Berkeley, and Columbia Law School. His debut novel, *How to Live Safely in a Science Fictional Universe* (2010), portrays a universe where people get into time machines and try to do the one thing they should never do: change the past. His story collection, *Third Class Superhero* (2006), treats issues of identity, insecurity, envy, and ambition with humor. Yu received the National Book Foundation's 5 Under 35 Award for *Third Class Superhero* and the Sherwood Anderson Fiction Award. His work has been published in the *Harvard Review*, the *Gettysburg Review,* the *Alaska Quarterly Review*, the *Mississippi Review*, and the *Mid-American Review*, among other journals.

YUN, MIA. A **Korean American** novelist, Yun was born and raised in South Korea. She received her M.F.A. in creative writing from City College of New York. She has worked as a reporter, translator, and freelance writer, and is currently the Korean correspondent for the *Evergreen Review.* She is the author of two novels: *House of the Winds* (1998) and *Translations of Beauty* (2004). Her first novel, set in the 1960s and 1970s of Korea, portrays a Korean family and especially its **women** whose lives have been deeply affected by its tumultuous history: the 36 years of Japanese rule and the Korean War (1950–1953). *Translations of Beauty* depicts the immigrant experience and the corroding American dream while closely examining one Korean family's struggle to remain whole in white America. Yun now makes her home in New York City.

YUNG, WING (RONG HONG, 1828–1912). A **Chinese American** autobiographer, Yung was born in a village in Guangdong, China. He attended missionary schools in Macao and Hong Kong, and in 1847 he came to America to continue his education, first at Monson Academy in Massachusetts and then at Yale College, from which he received a B.A., becoming the first Chinese person to earn a bachelor's degree in the United States. Even though he became a U.S. citizen, he returned to China in 1855, determined to reform China through education. Yung brought over 100 Chinese boys to Hartford, Connecticut, for education. He wrote his autobiography at age 74, *My Life in China and America* (1909). He died in Connecticut.

Z

ZUIHITSU. A Japanese literary genre consisting of informal personal essays and fragmented ideas that typically respond to the author's surroundings and the change of seasons. The name is derived from two Kanji meanings "to follow" and "brush," suggestive of casual or random jottings down of thought. Traditionally, *zuihitsu* is strongly rooted in Buddhist thought, typically containing the author's musings on the impermanence of the material world. **Kimiko Hahn** is well known for her *zuihitsu.*

Bibliography

There is an abundance of books, journals, and articles devoted to Asian American literature and theater, and more are published all the time on a large number of topics, genres, and subgroups. This extensive bibliography attests to a growing and deepening scholarly attention. Employing a wide range of literary theories and critical methodologies, Asian American literary criticism became mature and sophisticated in the 1990s. The past three decades have witnessed an exponential growth in this field, with publications focusing on themes, histories, genres, genders, and subgroups of Asian America.

However, despite this, the area of Asian American children's literature is little researched and investigated. Rocío G. Davis guest-edited the special issue of the *Lion and the Unicorn* (April 2006), which was the first book-length study devoted to the interpretation and criticism of Asian American children's literature. The following year, Davis published his book *Begin Here: Reading Asian North American Autobiographies of Childhood* (2007) that incorporates children's literature in its last chapter. This is an area that will experience rapid growth in the next decade.

Although this bibliography is not exhaustive, it represents the most comprehensive bodies of anthologies, interpretation, criticism, and source books thus far. The section of "Anthologies" offers an almost exhaustive list that demonstrates the concerted effort to organize anthologies by communities, genres, genders, generations, and other useful rubrics. *Aiiieeeee!* (1974) opened the floodgate of Asian American literary anthologies. Most early anthologies are chiefly Pan-Asian American, including mostly Chinese, Japanese, and Filipino American writings, such as Jessica Hagedorn's *Charlie Chan Is Dead* (1993) and its second edition in 2004, *The Forbidden Stitch: An Asian American Women's Anthology* (1993) by Shirley Geok-lin Lim et al., which won an American Book Award, Shawn Wong's *Asian American Literature: A Brief Introduction and Anthology* (1996), and Shirley Geok-lin Lim's *Asian American Literature* (1999).

Following the trajectory of Asian American literary tradition, the Chinese, Japanese, and Filipinos led the way of anthology production. The earlier Chinese American collections include Eric Choc's *Pakė: Writings by Chinese in Hawaii* (1989), *Island: Poetry and History of Chinese Immigrants on Angel Island, 1910 to 1940* (1999) by Him Mark Lai et al., also an American Book Award winner, and *Chinese American Poetry: An Anthology* (1992) by L. Ling-chi Wang et al. Among the Japanese American anthologies, the most significant ones are *Ayumi: A Japanese American Anthology* (1980) by Janice Mirikitani et al. and Violet Kazue De Cristoforo's *May Sky: There Is Always Tomorrow; An Anthology of Japanese American Concentration Camp Kaiko Haiku* (2000). The 1990s and 2000s have seen several anthologies of Korean American literature, such as *Echoes upon Echoes: New Korean American Writings* (2003) edited by Elaine H. Kim et al., *Kori: The Beacon Anthology of Korean American Fiction* (2002) by Heinz Fenkle et al., and the collection of Korean adoptees, *Seeds from a Silent Tree: An Anthology by Korean Adoptees* (1997), edited by Jo Rankin et al.

South Asian American writers are equally active in organizing their anthologies. *Our Feet Walk the Sky: Women of the South Asian Diaspora* (1993) by the Women of South Asian Descent Collective is one of the earliest anthologies that showcases women writers exploring themes of gender, sexuality, class, home, and memory. Roshni Rustomji-Kerns's *Living in America: Poetry and Fiction by South Asian American Writers* (1995) raised the visibility of South Asian American literature before several South Asian American novelists broke into the mainstream reading public. Shyam Selvadurai's *Story-Wallah: Short Fiction from South Asian Writers* (2005) focuses on the genre of short fiction from a South Asian diaspora—India, Sri Lanka, the United States, Great Britain, Guyana, Malaysia, Trinidad, Fiji, etc.

South East Asian Americans brought out their own anthologies in the 1990s and 2000s. Shirley Geok-lin Lim and Cheng Lok Chua's *Tilting the Continent: Southeast Asian American Writing* (2000) is the only one of its kind, encompassing fiction, poetry, and nonfiction by South East Asian American writers from Burma, Cambodia, Indonesia, Laos, Malaysia, the Philippines, Thailand, and Vietnam. In this group, the Filipino American writers enjoy a deeper history than the rest. Nick Carbo's *Returning a Borrowed Tongue: An Anthology of Filipino and Filipino American Poetry* (1995) is one of the earliest in this subgroup. Cecilia Manguerra Brainard's *Contemporary Fiction by Filipinos in America* (1997) showcases fiction written by prominent Filipino American authors. *Babaylan: An Anthology of Filipina and Filipina American Writers* (2000), edited by Nick Carbo et al., provides us with the choice of a transnational generation of women writers on both sides of the pacific. The most recent and complete anthology of Vietnamese American literature is Michele Janette's *My Viet: Vietnamese American Literature in English, 1962-Present* (2011).

The most recent South East Asian American anthologies come from the newly arrived immigrants from Afghanistan, Cambodia, and Laos. For the Afghan Americans, there are *Snapshots: This Afghan American Life* (2008) by Tamim Ansary et al. and *One Story, Thirty Stories: An Anthology of Afghan* (2010) by Zohra Saed et al. While *Snapshots* offers personal narratives and poetry on the experiences of being exiles, refugees, and immigrants in the United States, *One Story* features fiction, poetry, and essays describing Afghan American experiences post 9/11. Hmong American literature has born rich fruit, as the refugee children arriving between 1975 and 1990 have begun speaking about their memory and their families' experiences of the traumatic exile and relocation, and the second generation has reached adulthood. The earliest anthology is Pos Moua's *Where the Torches Are Burning* (2002), focusing on Hmong poets living in California's central valley. It was immediately followed by Mai Neng Moua's *Bamboo among the Oaks: Contemporary Writing by Hmong Americans* (2002), representing fiction, poetry, drama, and nonfiction written by first and second generations of Hmong American writers. The most recent one is *How Do I Begin? A Hmong American Literary Anthology* (2011), preserving the rich oral, textile, and literary tradition of the Hmong people.

Anthologies on a specific genre of Asian American literature abound as well. Several significant anthologies exemplify the fast developing and vibrant Asian American theater. The first anthology is Misha Berson's *Between Worlds: Contemporary Asian-American Plays* (1990), and it is followed by Roberta Uno's *Unbroken Thread: An Anthology of Plays by Asian American Women* (1993), Velina Hasu Houston's *But Still, Like Air, I'll Rise: New Asian American Plays* (1997), Brian Nelson's *Asian American Drama; Nine Plays from the Multiethnic Landscape* (1997), *Asian American Plays for a New Generation* (2011) edited by Josephine Lee et al., and Chay Yew's *Version 3.0: Contemporary Asian American Plays* (2011).

Asian American poetry has given rise to a large number of anthologies, with some being Pan-Asian and others concentrating on one subgroup. *American Born and Foreign: An Anthology of Asian American Poetry* (1979) is one of the earliest and has ushered in numerous poetry anthologies, such as Garret Hongo's *The Open Boat: Poems from Asian America* (1993), Walter K. Lew's *Premonitions: The Kaya Anthology of New Asian North American Poetry* (1995), Victoria M. Chang's *Asian American Poetry: The Next Generation* (2004), Anne Marie Fowler's *Yellow as Turmeric, Fragrant as Cloves: A Contemporary Anthology of Asian American Women's Poetry* (2008), and *Indivisible: An Anthology of Contemporary South Asian American Poetry* (2010) edited by Neelanjana Banerjee et al.

But there are many more anthologies. A significant number represents other groups than those mentioned above, such as gay and lesbian Asian American literature, graphic novels, comics, literature by Pacific Islanders and multiracial Asian Americans, etc. What follows is a comprehensive list of Asian American literary anthologies.

"Interpretation and Criticism" is considerably larger in quantity than "Anthologies." A search at amazon.com or the MLA International Bibliography database will yield a daunting number of books, whose topics range from such popular themes as ethnicity and race, gender, sexuality, language, hybridity, diaspora, and transnationalism to eclectic themes of food, law, disease, filth, and death. These interpretations and criticisms have been published not only by American presses but also by international ones. Clearly, Asian American literary studies have become an area of rapidly growing interest in the world.

Providing an extensive list of book-length studies of Asian American literature and theater, this section features over 100 books, which attests to the exponential growth of Asian American literary scholarship in the past three decades, during which time we also see the expansion of theoretical approaches and an increasing interest in interethnic studies. The influential studies in the 1990s, which helped to shape the directions of Asian American literary studies, include *Reading the Literatures of Asian America* (1992) edited by Shirley Geok-lin Lim and Amy Ling, Sau-ling C. Wong's *Reading Asian American Literature: From Necessity to Extravagance* (1993), and Lisa Lowe's *Immigrant Acts: On Asian American Cultural Politics* (1996).

The majority of the book-length interpretation and criticism tends to be Pan-Asian American. Despite this general tendency, most of the subgroups enjoy some representation. On Chinese American literature, Amy Ling's *Between Worlds: Chinese American Women Writers of Chinese Ancestry* (1990) has been one of the most influential works. Steven G. Yao's *Foreign Accents: Chinese American Verse from Exclusion to Postethnicity* (2010) offers sophisticated analysis of Chinese American poetry. While there is not a single book exclusively devoted to Korean American literature, Min Hyoung Song's *Strange Future: Pessimism and the 1992 Los Angeles Riots* (2005) is an excellent meditation on Korean American experiences, and interethnic conflicts, with an interpretation of Chang-rae Lee's *Native Speaker*. On the Japanese American literary tradition, two significant books have helped to shape this field: *Reading Japanese American Literature: The Legacy of Three Generations* (1999), edited by Teruyo Ueki and Gayle K. Sato, and Traise Yamamoto's *Masking Selves, Making Subjects: Japanese American Women, Identity, and the Body* (1999). South Asian American literature has also enjoyed critical attention, such as Deepika Bahri's *Between the Lines: South Asians and Postcoloniality* (1996), and Rajini Srikanth's *The World Next Door: South Asian American Literature and the Idea of America* (2004). Isabelle Thuy Pelaud's *This Is All I Choose to Tell: History and Hybridity in Vietnamese American Literature* (2010) is the only one in this subgroup so far. Two of the studies of Filipino American literature are Martin Ponce's *Beyond the Nation: Diasporic Filipino Literature and Queer Reading* (2012) and Allan Punzalan Isaac's *American Tropics: Articulating Filipino America* (2006).

Other notable books offer models for useful critical methodologies. Psychoanalysis, for instance, has been one of the frequently used methodologies in U.S. ethnic literary studies, and many Asian American critics have written illuminating books, such as Anne Anlin Cheng's *The Melancholy of Race* (2000) and David L. Eng's *Racial Castration: Managing Masculinity in Asian America* (2001). Among the frequently discussed themes are nationalism and citizenship, such as David Leiwei Li's *Imagining the Nation: Asian American Literature and Cultural Consent* (1998), and Jinqi Ling's *Narrating Nationalism: Ideology and Form in Asian American Literature* (1998). An increasing number of scholars are paying attention to Asian American literature's relationship to other U.S. ethnic literatures, such as Daniel Kim's *Writing Manhood in Black and Yellow: Ralph Ellison, Frank Chin, and the Literary Politics of Identity* (2005), and Judith Oster's *Crossing Cultures: Creating Identity in Chinese and Jewish American Literature* (2003).

The past decade or so has witnessed serious attention paid to aesthetics, particularly that of poetry, and this is exemplified by Josephine Park's *Apparitions of Asia: Modernist Form and Asian American Poetics* (2008) and Timothy Yu's *Race and the Avant-Garde: Experimental and Asian American Poetry Since 1965* (2009). Significant work on theater includes Karen Shimakawa's *National Abjection: The Asian American Body Onstage* (2002) and Esther Kim Lee's *A History of Asian American Theatre* (2006).

The largest segment of the bibliography, however, is "Selective Bibliography of Specific Writers," whose principle of inclusion is three or more major critical studies.

In addition to authors who have become classics, the list also includes several young burgeoning authors who are just beginning to catch the eyes of critics. Most of the young authors publishing in the late 2000s have not drawn much scholarly attention, and one can expect many of them to become subjects of books, articles, master's theses, and doctoral dissertations in the near future.

The most studied authors are Chinese and Japanese Americans. The Chinese American writers include Mei-mei Berssenbrugge, Frank Chin, Marilyn Chin, Edith Maude Eaton, David Henry Hwang, Ha Jin, Gish Jen, Maxine Hong Kingston, Li-Young Lee, Chong Ping, Amy Tan, and Jade Snow Wong. Among the Japanese American writers, the most studied are Ai, Winnifred Eaton, Philip Kan Gotanda, Garrett Hongo, Velina Hasu Houston, Lawson Fusao Inada, Janice Mirikitani, Toshio Mori, John Okada, Monica Sone, Hisaye Yamamoto, and Lois-Ann Yamanaka. Like Chinese and Japanese American authors, Filipino American authors have a deeper history than other subgroups, and the most notable authors are Carlos Bulosan, Jessica Hagedorn, Ninotchka Rosca, Jose Garcia Villa, and Jose Garcia Villa. In the group of Korean American authors, the following boast most critical attention: Theresa Hak Kyung Cha, Younghill Kang, Nora Okja Keller, Myung Mi Kim, and Chang-rae Lee. Though late comers, numerous South Asian American writers have received extensive attention from critics, and the most studied authors include Agha Shahid Ali, Vikram Chandra, G. V. Desani, Chitra Bannerjee Divakaruni, Jhumpa Lahiri, Bharati Mukherjee, Bapsi Sidhwa, and Sara Suleri. However, despite the fact there is a large number of Southeast Asian American writers, many of them have not attracted attention from scholars, except for Malaysian Chinese American Shirley Geok-lin Lim and Vietnamese American Lan Cao.

One way to gage the maturity of a field is to see the number of source books devoted to it, and without doubt, Asian American literature and theater has gained a solid place in American literature and enjoys a wealth of source books, as displayed in the section titled "Source Books." Several source books are most comprehensive and recent, such as Gale's *Asian American Writers* (2005), Facts on File's *Encyclopedia of Asian-American Literature* (2007), and *The Greenwood Encyclopedia of Asian American Literature* (2008). Joining forces with the above sections of the bibliography, this portion further demonstrates the irrefutable significance of this U.S. ethnic literature. The publishing industry has continued to bring out more source books in this field since 1979 when the first resource book, *Asian American Literature of Hawaii: An Annotated Bibliography*, was published. The official recognition of this literature as a vital facet of American literature came in 1988 when Modern Language Association Press published its *Asian American Literature: An Annotated Bibliography*.

The Internet has made research easier than ever, and the recent years have seen the emergence of many useful sites, among which the good ones include the official site of Asian American Writers' Workshop and the site maintained by Dr. Noelle Brada-Williams of San José State University. These sites provide bibliographies of literary writings as well as anthologies and criticisms. Some of them also offer links to other useful sites.

ANTHOLOGIES

Ansary, Mir Tamim, and Yalda Asmatey, eds. *Snapshots: This Afghan American Life*. San Francisco: Kajakai Press, 2008.

Banerjee, Neelanjana, Summi Kaipa, and Pireeni Sundaralingam, eds. *Indivisible: An Anthology of Contemporary South Asian American Poetry*. Fayetteville: University of Arkansas Press, 2010.

Berson, Misha, ed. *Between Worlds: Contemporary Asian-American Plays*. New York: Theatre Communications, 1990.

Brainard, Cecilia Manguerra, ed. *Contemporary Fiction by Filipinos in America*. Pasig City, Philippines: Anvil, 1997.

Bruchac, Joseph, ed. *Breaking Silence: An Anthology of Contemporary Asian American Poets*. New York: Greenfield Review Press, 1983.

Carbo, Nick, ed. *Returning a Borrowed Tongue: An Anthology of Filipino and Filipino American Poetry*. Minn: Coffee House, 1995.

Carbo, Nick, and Eileen Tabios, ed. *Babaylan: An Anthology of Filipina and Filipina American Writers*. San Francisco: Aunt Lute Books, 2000.

Chang, Victoria M., ed. *Asian American Poetry: The Next Generation*. Chicago: University of Illinois Press, 2004.

Chiang, Fay et al., eds. *American Born and Foreign: An Anthology of Asian American Poetry*. New York: Sunbury Press Books, 1979.

Chin, Frank, Jeffrey Paul Chan, and Lawson Fusao Inada, eds. *Aiiieeeee! An Anthology of Asian-American Writers*. Washington, D.C.: Howard University Press, 1974.

Chin, Frank, Jeffrey Paul Chan, Lawson Fusao Inada, and Shawn Hsu Wong, eds. *The Big Aiiieeeee! An Anthology of Chinese American and Japanese American Literature*. New York: Meridian, 1991.

Chin, Marilyn, David Wong Louie, and Ken Weisner, eds. *Dissident Song: A Contemporary Asian American Anthology*. Special issue of *Quarry West* 29–30 (1991).

Choc, Eric, ed. *Small Kid Time Hawaii*. Honolulu: Bamboo Ridge Press, 1981.

———, ed. *Talk Story: An Anthology of Hawaii's Local Writers*. Honolulu: Petronium Press, 1978.

———, ed. *Ten Thousand Wishes*. Honolulu: Bamboo Ridge Press, 1978.

Choc, Eric, James R. Harsatad, Darrell Lum, and Bill Teter, eds. *Growing Up Local: An Anthology of Prose and Poetry from Hawai'i*. Honolulu: Bamboo Ridge Press, 1998.

Choc, Eric, and Darrell Lum, eds. *The Best Bamboo Ridge*. Honolulu: Bamboo Ridge Press, 1986.

———, eds. *Best of Honolulu Fiction*. Honolulu: Bamboo Ridge Press, 1999.

———, eds. *Paké: Writings by Chinese in Hawaii*. Honolulu: Bamboo Ridge Press, 1989.

Ch'oe, Yon-hong, and Haeng-ja Kim, eds. *Surfacing Sadness: A Centennial of Korean American Literature, 1903–2003*. Dumont, N.J.: Homa & Sekey Books, 2003.

Choi, Yearn Hong, ed. *An Empty House: Korean-American Poetry*. Dumont N.J.: Homa & Sekey Books, 2008.

———, ed. *Fragrance of Poetry: Korean-American Literature*. Dumont, N.J.: Homa & Seka Books, 2005.

Chung, Cristy, Alison Kim, and A. Kaweah Lemeshewsky, eds. *Between the Lines: An Anthology by Pacific-Asian Lesbians of Santa Cruz, California*. Santa Cruz: Dancing Bird, 1987.

Dabydeen, Cyril, ed. *Another Way to Dance: Contemporary Asian Poetry from Canada and the United States.* Toronto: TSAR, 1996.

De Cristoforo, Violet Kazue, ed. *May Sky: There Is Always Tomorrow; An Anthology of Japanese American Concentration Camp Kaiko Haiku*. Los Angeles: Sun and Moon Press, 2000.

Desai, Jigna, and Khyati Joshi, eds. *Asian Americans and the U.S. South: An Anthology*. Athens: University of Georgia Press, 2010.

Eng, Alvin, ed. *Tokens? The NYC Asian American Experience on Stage*. Philadelphia: Temple University Press, 2000.

Fenkl, Heinz Insu, and Walter K. Lew, eds. *Kori: The Beacon Anthology of Korean American Fiction.* Boston: Beacon Press, 2002.

Fisher, Dexter, ed. *The Third Woman: Minority Women Writers of the United States*. Boston: Houghton Mifflin, 1980.

Fowler, Anne Marie, ed. *Yellow as Turmeric, Fragrant as Cloves: A Contemporary Anthology of Asian American Women's Poetry.* O'Fallon, Ill.: Deep Bowl Press, 2008.

Gee, Emma, ed. *Counterpoint: Asian American Perspectives*. Los Angeles: Asian American Studies Center, University of California, 1976.

Hagedorn, Jessica, ed. *Charlie Chan Is Dead: An Anthology of Contemporary Asian American Fiction.* New York: Penguin, 1993.

Hagedorn, Jessica, and Elaine Kim, eds. *Charlie Chan Is Dead 2: At Home in the World.* New York: Penguin, 2004.

Hamasaki, Richard, ed. *Seaweeds and Constructions: Anthology of Hawaii*. Honolulu, Elepaio Press, 1979.

Hiura, Jerrold Asao, ed. *The Hawk's Well: A Collection of Japanese American Art and Literature.* San Jose, Calif.: Asian American Art Project, 1986.

Hmong American Writers Circle (The). *How Do I Begin? A Hmong American Literary Anthology.* Berkeley, Calif.: Heyday, 2011.

Hom, Marlon K., ed. and trans. *Songs of Gold Mountain: Cantonese Rhymes from San Francisco Chinatown.* Berkeley: University of California Press, 1987.

Hong, Maria, ed. *Growing Up Asian American: An Anthology*. New York: William Morrow & Co, 1993.

Hong, Maria, and David D. Kim, eds. *Voices Stirring: An Anthology of Korean American Writing*. Special issue of *Asian Pacific American Journal* 1.2 (1992): 1–53.

Hongo, Garrett, ed. *The Open Boat: Poems from Asian America*. New York: Anchor-Doubleday, 1993.

———, ed. *Under Western Eyes: Personal Essays from Asian America*. New York: Anchor-Doubleday, 1995.

Houston, Velina Hasu, ed. *But Still, Like Air, I'll Rise: New Asian American Plays*. Philadelphia: Temple University Press, 1997.

———, ed. *The Politics of Life: Four Plays by Asian American Women*. Philadelphia: Temple University Press, 1993.

Houston, Velina Hasu, and Teresa K. Williams, eds. *No Passing Zone: The Artistic and Discursive Voices of Asian-Descent Multiracials*. Special issue of *Amerasia Journal* 23.1 (1997).

Hsu, Kai-yu, and Helen Palubinskas, eds. *Asian-American Authors*. Boston: Houghton, 1972.

Huang, Su-Ching. *Mobile Homes: Spatial and Cultural Negotiation in Asian American Literature*. New York: Routledge, 2006.

Hune, Shirley, and Gail Nomura, eds. *Asian/Pacific Islander American Women: A Historical Anthology*. New York: New York University Press, 2003.

Janette, Michele, ed. *My Viet: Vietnamese American Literature in English, 1962–Present*. Honolulu: University of Hawaii Press, 2011.

Kardux, Johanna, and Doris Einsiedel. *Moving Migration: Narrative Transformations in Asian American Literature*. Berlin: Lit Verlag, 2011.

Karlin, Wayne, Le Minh Khue, and Truong Vu, eds. *The Other Side of Heaven: Postwar Fiction by Vietnamese and American Writers*. Willimantic, Conn.: Curbstone, 1995.

Kim, Elaine H., and Laura Kang, eds. *Echoes upon Echoes: New Korean American Writings*. Philadelphia: Temple University Press, 2003.

Kim, Elaine H., and Lilia V. Villanueva, eds. *Making More Waves: New Writing by Asian American Women*. Boston: Beacon, 1997.

Kim, Elaine H., and Eui-Young Yu, eds. *East to America: Korean American Life Stories*. New York: New Press, 1996.

Kudaka, Geraldine, ed. *On a Bed of Rice: An Asian American Erotic Feast*. New York: Anchor-Doubleday, 1995.

Lai, Him Mark, Genny Lim, and Judy Young, eds. *Island: Poetry and History of Chinese Immigrants on Angel Island, 1910 to 1940*. Seattle: University of Washington Press, 1999.

Lee, Josephine, Donald Eitel, and Rick Shiomi, eds. *Asian American Plays for a New Generation*. Philadelphia: Temple University Press, 2011.

Lew, Walter K., ed. *Premonitions: The Kaya Anthology of New Asian North American Poetry*. New York: Kaya, 1995.

Lim-Hing, Sharon, ed. *The Very Inside: An Anthology of Writing by Asian and Pacific Islander Lesbian and Bisexual Women*. Toronto: Sister Vision, 1994.

Lim, Shirley Geok-lin, ed. *Asian American Literature: An Anthology*. New York: McGraw-Hill Companies, 1999.

Lim, Shirley Geok-lin, and Cheng Lok Chua, eds. *Tilting the Continent: Southeast Asian American Writing*. Moorhead, Minn.: New Rivers Press, 2000.

Lim, Shirley Geok-lin, Mayumi Tsutakawa, and Margarita Donnelly, eds. *The Forbidden Stitch: An Asian American Women's Anthology*. Corvallis, Ore.: CALYX Books, 1993.

Maira, Sunaina, and Rjini Srikanth, eds. *Contours of the Heart: South Asians Map North America*. New York: Asian American Writers' Workshop, 1996.

Mandal, Somdatta, ed. *The Diasporic Imagination: Asian-American Writing*. New Delhi: Prestige Books, 2000.

Mirikitani et al., eds. *Ayumi: A Japanese American Anthology*. San Francisco: Japanese American Anthology Committee, 1980.

Moua, Mai Neng, ed. *Bamboo among the Oaks: Contemporary Writing by Hmong Americans*. Minneapolis: Minnesota Historical Society Press, 2002.

Moua, Pos, ed. *Where the Torches Are Burning*. Sacramento, Calif.: Swan Scythe Press, 2002.

Nakano, Jiro, and Kay Nakano, eds. *Poets behind Barbed Wire*. Honolulu: Bamboo Ridge, 1983.

Nelson, Brian, ed. *Asian American Drama: Nine Plays from the Multiethnic Landscape*. New York: Applause, 1997.

Nixon, Lucille M., and Tomoe Tana, trans. *Sounds from the Unknown: A Collection of Japanese-American Tanka*. Denver, Colo.: Alan Swallow, 1963.

Perkins, Kathy A., and Roberta Uno, eds. *Contemporary Plays by Women of Color*. New York: Routledge, 1996.

Rankin, Jo, and Tonya Bishoff, eds. *Seeds from a Silent Tree: An Anthology by Korean Adoptees*. Glendale, Calif.: Pandal Press, 1997.

Realuyo, Bino A., ed. *The NuyorAsian Anthology: Asian American Writing in New York City*. Philadelphia: Temple University Press, 1993.

Rustomji-Kerns, Roshni, ed. *Living in America: Poetry and Fiction by South Asian American Writers*. Boulder, Colo.: Westview, 1995.

Saed, Zohra, and Sahar Muradi, eds. *One Story, Thirty Stories: An Anthology of Afghan American Literature.* Fayetteville: University of Arkansas Press, 2010.

Selvadurai, Shyam, ed. *Story-Wallah: Short Fiction from South Asian Writers*. New York: Mariner Books, 2005.

Srikanth, Rajini. *Bold Words: A Century of Asian American Writing*. Brunswick, N.J.: Rutgers University Press, 2001.

Stewart, Frank, and John Unterecker, eds. *Poetry Hawaii: A Contemporary Anthology.* Honolulu: University of Hawaii Press, 1979.

Sunoo, Brenda Paik, ed. *Korean American Writings*. New York: Insight, 1975.

Tachiki, Amy, Eddie Wong, Franklin Odo, and Buck Wong, eds. *Roots: An Asian American Reader*. Los Angeles: University of California Asian American Studies Center, 1971.

Tran, Barbara, Monique T. D. Truong, and Luu Truong Khoi, eds. *Watermark: Vietnamese American Poetry and Prose*. New York: Asian American Writers Workshop, 1998.

Uno, Roberta, ed. *Unbroken Thread: An Anthology of Plays by Asian American Women*. Amherst: University of Massachusetts Press, 1993.

Wand, David Hsin-Fu, ed. *Asian-American Heritage: An Anthology of Prose and Poetry*. New York: Pocket-Washington Square, 1974.

Wang, L. Ling-chi, and H. Y. Zhao, eds. *Chinese American Poetry: An Anthology*. Seattle: University of Washington Press, 1992.

Watanabe, Sylvia, and Carol Bruchac, eds. *Home to Stay: Asian American Women's Fiction.* New York: Greenfield Review Press, 1990.

———, eds. *Into the Fire: Asian American Prose*. New York: Greenfield Review Press, 1996.

Witness Aloud: Lesbian, Gay, and Bisexual Asian Pacific American Writings. Special issue of *Asian Pacific American Journal* 2.1 (1993): 1–140.

Women of South Asian Descent Collective, ed. *Our Feet Walk the Sky: Women of the South Asian Diaspora*. San Francisco: Aunt Lute, 1993.

Wong, Shawn, ed. *Asian American Literature: A Brief Introduction and Anthology*. New York: Harper, 1996.

Wu, Jean Yu-wen Sheng, and Min Song, eds. *Asian American Studies: A Reader*. New Brunswick, N.J.: Rutgers University Press, 2000.

Yang, Jeff, Parry Shen, Keith Chow, and Jerry Ma, eds. *Secret Identities: The Asian American Superhero Anthology*. New York: the New Press, 2009.

Yep, Laurence, ed. *American Dragons: Twenty-Five Asian American Voices*. New York: Harper, 1993.

Yew, Chay, ed. *Version 3.0: Contemporary Asian American Plays*. New York: Theatre Communications Group, 2011.

INTERPRETATION AND CRITICISM

Amirthanayagam, Guy, ed. *Asian and Western Writers in Dialogue*. London: Macmillan, 1982.

Bahri, Deepika. *Between the Lines: South Asians and Postcoloniality*. Philadelphia: Temple University Press, 1996.

Bloom, Harold, ed. *Asian-American Women Writers*. Philadelphia: Chelsea House, 1997.

———, ed. *Asian-American Writers*. Philadelphia: Chelsea House, 1999.

Bow, Leslie. *Betrayal and Other Acts of Subversion: Feminism, Sexual Politics, Asian American Women's Literature*. Princeton, N.J.: Princeton University Press, 2001.

Chae, Youngsuk. *Politicizing Asian American Literature: Towards a Critical Multiculturalism*. New York: Routledge, 2007.

Chan, Jachinson. *Chinese American Masculinities: From Fu Manchu to Bruce Lee*. New York: Routledge, 2001.

Chang, Joan Chiung-huei. *Transforming Chinese American Literature: A Study of History, Sexuality, and Ethnicity*. New York: Peter Lang Publishing, 2000.

Chang, Yoonmee. *Writing the Ghetto: Class, Authorship, and the Asian American Ethnic Enclave*. Brunswick, N.J.: Rutgers University Press, 2010.

Chen, Tina. *Double Agency: Acts of Impersonation in Asian American Literature and Culture*. Stanford, Calif.: Stanford University Press, 2005.

Cheng, Anne Anlin. *The Melancholy of Race*. New York: Oxford University Press, 2000.

Cheung, King-Kok. *Articulate Silences: Hisaye Yamamoto, Maxine Hong Kingston, Joy Kogawa*. Ithaca, N.Y.: Cornell University Press, 1993.

———, ed. *Words Matter: Conversations with Asian American Writers*. Honolulu: University of Hawaii Press, 2000.

Chiu, Monica. *Filthy Fiction: Asian American Literature by Women*. New York: Altamira Press, 2004.

Christopher, Renny. *The Viet Nam War / The American War: Images and Representations in Euro-American and Vietnamese Exile Narratives*. Amherst: University of Massachusetts Press, 1995.

Chu, Patricia P. Assimilating Asians: Gendered Strategies of Authorship in Asian America. Durham, N.C.: Duke University Press, 2000.

Chuh, Kandice. *Imagine Otherwise: On Asian Americanist Critique*. Durham, N.C.: Duke University Press, 2003.

Davis, Rocío G.*Begin Here: Reading Asian North American Autobiographies of Childhood.* Honolulu: University of Hawaii Press, 2007.

———. *Relative Histories: Mediating History in Asian American Family Memoirs*. Honolulu: University of Hawaii Press, 2011.

———, ed. *The Lion and the Unicorn Special Issue: Asian American Children's Literature* 30:2 (April 2006).

Davis, Rocío G., and Sue-Im Lee. *Literary Gestures: The Aesthetic in Asian American Writing*. Philadelphia: Temple University Press, 2006.

Davis, Rocío G., and Sämi Ludwig, eds. *Asian American Literature in the International Context: Readings on Fiction, Poetry, and Performance.* Hamburg, Germany: Lit, 2002.

Duncan, Patti. *Tell This Silence: Asian American Women Writers and the Politics of Speech.* Iowa City: University of Iowa Press, 2004.

Eaton, Allen Hendershott. *Beauty behind Barbed Wire: The Arts of the Japanese in Our War Relocation Camps.* New York: Harper, 1952.

Eng, David L. *Racial Castration: Managing Masculinity in Asian America*. Durham, N.C.: Duke University Press, 2001.

Eng, David L., and Alice Y. Hom, eds. *Q & A: Queer in Asian America*. Philadelphia: Temple University Press, 1998.

Feng, Peter X. *Identities in Motion: Asian American Film and Video.* Durham, N.C.: Duke University Press Books, 2002.

Feng, Pin-chia. *Diasporic Representations: Reading Chinese American Women's Fiction*. Berlin: Lit Verlag, 2011.

Ghymn, Esther Mikyun, ed. *Asian American Studies: Identities, Images, Issues Past and Present*. New York: Peter Lang, 2000.

———. *Images of Asian American Women by Asian American Women Writers*. New York: Peter Lang, 1997.

———. *The Shapes and Styles of Asian American Prose Fiction*. New York: Peter Lang, 1993.

Grice, Helena. *Asian American Fiction, History and Life Writing: International Encounters.* New York: Routledge, 2009.

———. *Negotiating Identities: An Introduction to Asian American Women's Writing*. Manchester: Manchester University Press, 2002.

Han, Arar, and John Hsu, eds. *Asian American X: An Intersection of Twenty-First Century Asian American Voices*. Ann Arbor: University of Michigan Press, 2004.

Ho, Jennifer Ann. *Consumption and Identity in Asian American Coming-of-Age Novels*. New York: Routledge, 2005.

Ho, Wendy. *In Her Mother's House: The Politics of Asian American Mother-Daughter Writing*. Lanham, Md.: AltaMira Press, 2000.

Huang, Betsy. *Contesting Genres in Contemporary Asian American Fiction*. New York: Palgrave, 2010.

Huang, Su-Ching. *Mobile Homes: Spatial and Cultural Negotiation in Asian American Literature*. New York: Routledge, 2006.

Hune, Shirley, ed. *Asian Americans: Comparative and Global Perspectives*. Pullman: Washington State University Press, 1991.

Isaac, Allan Punzalan. *American Tropics: Articulating Filipino America*. Minneapolis: University of Minnesota Press, 2006.

Jain, Anupama. *How to Be South Asian in America: Narratives of Ambivalence and Belonging*. Philadelphia: Temple University Press, 2011.

Kafka, Phillipa. *(Un)Doing the Missionary Position: Gender Asymmetry in Contemporary Asian American Women's Writing*. Santa Barbara: Praeger, 1997.

Kain, Geoffrey, ed. *Ideas of Home: Literature of Asian Migration*. East Lansing: Michigan State University Press, 1997.

Kang, Laura Hyun Yi. *Compositional Subjects: Enfiguring Asian/American Women*. Durham, N.C.: Duke University Press Books, 2002.

Kardux, Johanna, and Doris Einsiedel, eds. *Moving Migration: Narrative Transformations in Asian American Literature*. Berlin, Germany: Lit Verlag, 2011.

Kim, Daniel. *Writing Manhood in Black and Yellow: Ralph Ellison, Frank Chin, and the Literary Politics of Identity*. Stanford, Calif.: Stanford University Press, 2005.

Kim, Elaine H. *Asian American Literature: An Introduction to the Writings and Their Social Context*. Philadelphia: Temple University Press, 1982.

Kim, Jodi. *Ends of Empire: Asian American Critique and the Cold War*. Minneapolis: University of Minnesota Press, 2010.

Koshy, Susan. *Sexual Naturalization: Asian Americans and Miscegenation*. Stanford, Calif.: Stanford University Press, 2005.

Kurahashi, Yuko. *Asian American Culture on Stage: The History of the East West Players*. New York: Garland, 1999.

Lawrence, Keith, and Floyd Cheung, eds. *Recovered Legacies: Authority and Identity in Early Asian American Literature*. Philadelphia: Temple University Press, 2005.

Lee, Esther Kim. *A History of Asian American Theatre*. New York: Cambridge University Press, 2006.

Lee, Josephine, Imogene L. Lim, and Yuko Matsukawa, eds. *Re/Collecting Early Asian America: Essays in Cultural History*. Philadelphia: Temple University Press, 2002.

Lee, Julia. *Interracial Encounters: Reciprocal Representations in African and Asian American Literatures, 1896–1937*. New York: New York University Press, 2011.

Lee, Rachel C. *The Americas of Asian American Literature: Gendered Fictions of Nation and Transnation*. Princeton, N.J.: Princeton University Press, 1999.

Lee, Robert A. *Multicultural American Literature: Comparative Black, Native, Latino/a, and Asian American Fictions*. Jackson, Miss.: University Press of Mississippi, 2008.

Lee, Robert G. *Orientals: Asian Americans in Popular Culture*. Philadelphia: Temple University Press, 1999.

Li, David Leiwei. *Imagining the Nation: Asian American Literature and Cultural Consent*. Stanford, Calif.: Stanford University Press, 1998.

Lim, Shirley Geok-lin, John Blair Gamber, Stephen Hong Sohn, and Gina Valentino, eds. *Transnational Asian American Literature: Sites and Transits*. Philadelphia: Temple University Press, 2006.

Lim, Shirley Geok-lin, and Amy Ling, eds. *Reading the Literatures of Asian America*. Philadelphia: Temple University Press, 1992.

Ling, Amy. *Between Worlds: Chinese American Women Writers of Chinese Ancestry*. New York: Pergamon Press, 1990.

Ling, Jinqi. *Narrating Nationalism: Ideology and Form in Asian American Literature*. New York: Oxford University Press, 1998.

Lowe, Lisa. *Immigrant Acts: On Asian American Cultural Politics*. Durham, N.C.: Duke University Press, 1996.

Lye, Colleen. *America's Asia: Racial Form and American Literature, 1893–1945*. Princeton, N.J.: Princeton University Press, 2004.

Ma, Sheng-Mei. *Deathly Embrace: Orientalism and Asian American Identity*. Minneapolis: University of Minnesota Press, 2000.

———. *Immigrant Subjectivities: In Asian American and Asian Diaspora Literatures*. Albany: SUNY Press, 1998.

Mandal, Somdatta, ed. *The Diasporic Imagination: Identifying Asian-American Representations in America*. 2 vols. New Delhi: Prestige Books, 2000.

Mannur, Anita. *Culinary Fictions: Food in South Asian Diasporic Culture*. Philadelphia: Temple University Press, 2010.

Maria, Zamora C. *Nation, Race & History in Asian American Literature*. New York: Peter Lang, 2008.

Moy, James. *Marginal Sights: Staging the Chinese in America*. Iowa City: University of Iowa Press, 1993.

Nguyen, Viet Thanh. *Race and Resistance: Literature and Politics in Asian America*. New York: Oxford University, 2002.

Ninh, Erin Khuê. *Ingratitude: The Debt-Bound Daughter in Asian American Literature*. New York: New York University Press, 2011.

Oh, Seung Ah. *Recontextualizing Asian American Domesticity: From Madame Butterfly to My American Wife!* Lanham, Md.: Lexington Books, 2008.

Okihiro, Gary Y., ed. *Privileging Positions: The Sites of Asian American Studies*. Pullman: Washington State University Press, 1995.

Omi, Michael, and Dana Takagi, eds. *Thinking Theory in Asian American Studies*. Special issue of *Amerasia Journal* 21.1–2 (1995).

Ono, Ken A., ed. *Asian American Studies after Critical Mass*. New York: Blackwell, 2004.

Oster, Judith. *Crossing Cultures: Creating Identity in Chinese and Jewish American Literature*. Columbia, Mo.: University of Missouri, 2003.

Palumbo-Liu, David. *The Ethnic Canon: Histories, Institutions, and Interventions*. Minn.: University of Minnesota Press, 1995.

Pao, Angela C. *No Safe Spaces: Re-casting Race, Ethnicity, and Nationality in American Theater*. Ann Arbor: University of Michigan Press, 2010.

Park, Josephine. *Apparitions of Asia: Modernist Form and Asian American Poetics.* New York: Oxford University Press, 2008.

Pelaud, Isabelle Thuy. *This Is All I Choose to Tell: History and Hybridity in Vietnamese American Literature*. Philadelphia: American Literatures Initiative, 2010.

Ponce, Martin. *Beyond the Nation: Diasporic Filipino Literature and Queer Reading.* New York: New York University Press, 2012.

Revilla, Linda A., Gail M. Nomura, Shawn Wong, and Shirley Hune, eds. *Bearing Dreams, Shaping Visions, Asian Pacific American Perspectives*. Pullman: Washington State University Press, 1993.

Rody, Caroline. *The Interethnic Imagination: Roots and Passages in Contemporary Asian American Fiction*. New York: Oxford University, 2009.

Schlund-Vials, Cathy. *Modeling Citizenship: Jewish and Asian American Writing.* Philadelphia: Temple University Press, 2011.

Schultermandl, Silvia. *Transnational Matrilineage: Mother-Daughter Conflicts in Asian American.* Berlin, Germany: Lit Verlag, 2011.

Shah, Sonia, ed. *Dragon Ladies: Asian American Feminists Breathe Fire*. Boston: South End, 1997.

Shimakawa, Karen. *National Abjection: The Asian American Body Onstage*. Durham, N.C.: Duke University Press, 2002.

Song, Min Hyoung. *Strange Future: Pessimism and the 1992 Los Angeles Riots.* Durham, N.C.: Duke University Press, 2005.

Srikanth, Rajini. *The World Next Door: South Asian American Literature and the Idea of America.* Philadelphia: Temple University Press, 2004.

Steen, Shannon. *Racial Geometries of the Black Atlantic, Asian Pacific and American Theatre.* New York: Palgrave Macmillan, 2010.

Sumida, Stephen H. *And the View from the Shore: Literary Traditions of Hawai'i.* Seattle: University of Washington Press, 1991.

———. *Frontiers of Asian American Studies: Writing Research, and Criticism*. Pullman: Washington State University Press, 1989.

Szmanko, Klara. *Invisibility in African and Asian American Literature A Comparative Study.* New York: McFarland, 2008.

Trudeau, Lawrence J., ed. *Asian American Literature: Reviews and Criticism of Works by American Writers of Asian Descent*. Detroit, Mich.: Gale, 1999.

Tunc, Tanfer Emin, and Elisabetta Marino, eds. *Positioning the New: Chinese American Literature and the Changing Image of the American Literary Canon*. Newcastle upon Tyne, Great Britain: Cambridge Scholar Publishing, 2010.

Ty, Eleanor Rose. *The Politics of the Visible in Asian North American Narratives*. Toronto: University of Toronto Press, 2004.

———. *Unfastened: Globality and Asian North American Narratives.* Minneapolis: University of Minnesota Press, 2010.

Ty, Eleanor, and Donald C. Goellnicht, eds. *Asian North American Identities: Beyond the Hyphen.* Bloomington: Indiana University Press, 2004.

Ueki, Teruyo, and Gayle K. Sato, eds. *Reading Japanese American Literature: The Legacy of Three Generations*. Osaka, Japan: Sogensha, 1999.

Wong, Mitali P., and Zia Hasan. *The Fiction of South Asians in North America and the Caribbean: A Critical Study of English-Language Works since 1950*. Jefferson, N.C.: McFarland, 2004.

Wong, Sau-ling C. *Reading Asian American Literature: From Necessity to Extravagance.* Princeton, N.J.: Princeton University Press, 1993.

Xu, Wenying. *Eating Identities: Reading Food in Asian American Literature*. Honolulu: University of Hawaii Press, 2008.

Yamamoto, Traise. *Masking Selves, Making Subjects: Japanese American Women, Identity, and the Body*. Berkeley: University of California Press, 1999.

Yao, Steven G. *Foreign Accents: Chinese American Verse from Exclusion to Postethnicity.* New York: Oxford University, 2010.

Yin, Xiao-huang. *Chinese American Literature since the 1850s*. Champaign: University of Illinois, 2006.

Young, Mary E. *Mules and Dragons: Popular Culture Images in the Selected Writings of African-American and Chinese-American Women Writers*. Westport, Conn.: Greenwood Press, 1993.

Young, Morris. *Minor Re/Visions: Asian American Literacy Narratives as a Rhetoric of Citizenship.* Carbondale: Southern Illinois University Press, 2004.

Yu, Timothy. *Race and the Avant-Garde: Experimental and Asian American Poetry since 1965.* Stanford, Calif: Stanford University Press, 2009.

Zamora, Maria C. *Nation, Race & History in Asian American Literature*. New York: Peter Lang Publishing, 2008.

Zhan, Benzi. *Asian Diaspora Poetry in North America*. New York: Routledge, 2007.

Zhou, Xiaojing. *The Ethics and Poetics of Alterity in Asian American Poetry*. Iowa City: University of Iowa Press, 2006.

Zhou, Xiaojing, and Samina Najmi, eds. *Form and Transformation in Asian American Literature*. Seattle: University of Washington Press, 2005.

SELECTIVE BIBLIOGRAPHY FOR SPECIFIC WRITERS

Ai

Ai. "Movies, Mom, Poetry, Sex and Death: A Self-Interview." *Onthebus* 3–4.2–1 (1991): 240–48.

Becker, Robin. "The Personal Is Political Is Postmodern." *American Poetry Review* 23.6 (1994): 23–26.

Erb, Lisa. "An Interview with Ai: Dancing with the Madness." *Manoa: A Pacific Journal of International Writing* 2.2 (1990): 22–40.

Ingram, Claudia. "Writing the Crises: The Deployment of Abjection in Ai's Dramatic Monologues." *LIT: Literature Interpretation Theory* 8.2 (1997): 173–91.

Kilcup, Karen L. "Dialogues of the Self: Toward a Theory of (Re)Reading Ai." *Journal of Gender Studies* 7.1 (1998): 5–20.

Leavitt, Michele. "Ai's 'Go.'" *Explicator* 54.2 (1996): 126–27.

Mintz, Susannah B. "A 'Descent toward the Unknown' in the Poetry of Ai By." *Sage: A Scholarly Journal on Black Women* 9.2 (1995): 36–46.

Wilson, Rob. "The Will to Transcendence in Contemporary American Poet Ai." *Canadian Review of American Studies* 17.4 (1986): 437–48.

Ali, Agha Shahid

Benevenuto, Christine. "Conversation with Agha Shahid Ali." *Massachusetts Review: A Quarterly of Literature, the Arts and Public Affairs* 43.2 (2002): 261–68.

Chiu, Jeannie. "Melancholy and Human Rights in a Nostalgist's Map of America and Midnight's Children." *LIT: Literature Interpretation Theory* 16.1 (2005): 25–39.

Ghosh, Amitav. "'The Ghat of the Only World': Agha Shahid Ali in Brooklyn." *Annual of Urdu Studies* 17 (2002): 1–19.

Islam, Maimuna Dali. "A Way in the World of an Asian American Existence: Agha Shahid Ali's Transmigrant Spacing of North America and India and Kashmir." In *Transnational Asian American Literature: Sites and Transits*, ed. Shirley Geok-lin Lim et al. Philadelphia: Temple University Press, 2006. 257–73.

Kabir, Ananya Jahanara. "Sheikh-Ul-Alam, Zainab, Ishmael, Shahid: Emotion, Authority, and Islam in Agha Shahid Ali's Poetry." *Moving Worlds: A Journal of Transcultural Writings* 8.1 (2008): 139–52.

Mattawa, Khaled. "Writing Islam in Contemporary American Poetry: On Mohja Kahf, Daniel Moore, and Agha Shahid Ali." *PMLA* 123.5 (2008): 1590–95.

Mattoo, Neerja. "Agha Shahid Ali as I Knew Him." *Indian Literature* 46.1 (2002): 175–79.

Needham, Lawrence. "Agha Shahid Ali." In *South Asian Writers in English*, ed. Fakrul Alam. Detroit, Mich.: Thomson Gale, 2006. 9–14.

———. "Agha Shahid Ali." In *The VERSE Book of Interviews: 27 Poets on Language, Craft, and Culture*, ed. Brian Henry and Andrew Zawacki. Amherst, Mass.: Verse, 2005. 133–46.

———. "In Pursuit of Evanescence: Agha Shahid Ali's A Nostalgist's Map of America." *Kunapipi* 15.2 (1993): 123–27.

———. "'The Sorrows of a Broken Time': Agha Shahid Ali and the Poetry of Loss and Recovery." In *Reworlding: The Literature of Indian Diaspora*, ed. Emmanuel S. Nelson. Westport, Conn.: Greenwood Press, 1992. 63–76.

Newman, Amy. "'Separation's Geography': Agha Shahid Ali's Scholarship of Evanescence." *Hollins Critic* 43.2 (2006): 1–14.

Patke, Rajeev S. "Agha Shahid Ali (1949-2001)." In *World Writers in English, Volume I: Chinua Achebe to V. S. Naipaul*, ed. Jay Parini. New York: Scribner's, 2004. 41–57.

———. "Translation as Metaphor: The Poetry of Agha Shahid Ali." *Metamorphoses: Journal of the Five-College Seminar on Literary Translation* 8.2 (2000): 266–78.

Sabitha, T. P. "The Beloved Witness: A Homage to Agha Shahid Ali." *Indian Literature* 46.1 (2002): 180–83.

Shamsie, Kamila. "Agha Shahid Ali, Teacher." *Annual of Urdu Studies* 17 (2002): 23–27.

Smith, Hallie. "Poetic Form in Translation: Agha Shahid Ali's 'Real' American Ghazals." *Valley Voices: A Literary Review* 7.1 (2007): 38–43.

Suleri-Goodyear, Sara. "In Memory of Agha Shahid Ali." *Annual of Urdu Studies* 17 (2002): 20–22.

Tageldin, Shaden. "Reversing the Sentence of Impossible Nostalgia: The Poetics of Postcolonial Migration in Sakinna Boukhedenna and Agha Shahid Ali." *Comparative Literature Studies* 40.2 (2003): 232–64.

Werner, Louis. "A Gift of Ghazals." *Annual of Urdu Studies* 17 (2002): 28–35.

Woodland, Malcolm. "Memory's Homeland: Agha Shahid Ali and the Hybrid Ghazal." *English Studies in Canada* 31.2–3 (2005): 249–72.

Zaidi, Nishad. "Center/Margin Dialectics and the Poetic Form: The Ghazals of Agha Shahid Ali." *Annual of Urdu Studies* 23 (2008): 55–66.

Berssenbrugge, Mei-mei

Altieri, Charles. "Intimacy and Experiment in Mei-Mei Berssenbrugge's *Empathy*." In *We Who Love to Be Astonished: Experimental Women's Writing and Performance Poetics*, ed. Laura Hinton and Cynthia Hogue. Tuscaloosa: University of Alabama Press, 2002. 54–68.

Chiu, Jeannie. "Identities in Process: The Experimental Poetry of Mei-mei Berssenbrugge and Myung Mi Kim." In *Asian North American Identities: Beyond the Hyphen*, ed. Eleanor Ty and Donald C. Goellnicht. Bloomington: Indiana University Press, 2004. 84–101.

Fink, Thomas. "Poetry, Charm, and More: Billy Collins and Mei-Mei Berssenbrugge." *Talisman* 27 (2003): 100–107.

Fraser, Kathleen. "Overheard." *Poetics Journal* 4 (1984): 98–105.

Newman, Denise. "The Concretion of Emotion: An Analytic Lyric of Mei-Mei Berssenbrugge's *Empathy*." *Talisman* 9 (1992): 119–24.

Simpson, Megan. "Mei-mei Berssenbrugge's *Four Year Old Girl* and the Phenomenology of Mothering." *Women's Studies: An Interdisciplinary Journal* 32.4 (2003): 479–98.

Bulosan, Carlos

Alquizola, Marilyn. "The Fictive Narrator of *America Is in the Heart*." In *Frontiers of Asian American Studies*, ed. Gail Nomura, Stephen H. Suminda, Russell Endo, Russell C. Leong. Pullman: Washington State University Press, 1989. 211–17.

———. "Subversion or Affirmation: The Text and Subtext of *America Is in the Heart*." In *Asian Americans: Comparative and Global Perspectives*, ed. Shirley Hune, Hyung-chan Kim, Stephen S. Fugita, and Amy Ling. Pullman: Washington State University Press, 1991. 199–209.

Bernad, Miguel A. "Carlos Bulosan: The Issue of Honesty." *Manila Review* 1.5 (1975): 101–07.

Campomanes, Oscar. "Filipinos in the United States and Their Literature of Exile." In *Reading the Literatures of Asian America*, ed. Shirley Geok-lin Lim and Amy Ling. Philadelphia: Temple University Press, 1992. 49–78.

Campomanes, Oscar, and Todd Gernes. "Two Letters from America: Carlos Bulosan and the Act of Writing." *MELUS* 15.3 (1988): 15–46.

Daroy, Petronilo B. "Carlos Bulosan: The Politics of Literature." *Saint Louis Quarterly* 6 (1968): 193–206.

De Jesus, Melinda L. "Rereading History, Rewriting Desire: Reclaiming Queerness in Carlos Bulosan's *America Is in the Heart* and Bienvenido Santos' *Scent of Apples*." *Journal of Asian American Studies* 5.2 (2002): 91–111.

Evangelista, Susan. "Carlos Bulosan." In *Asian American Writers*, ed. Deborah L. Madsen. Detroit, Mich.: Gale, 2005. 10–18.

———. *Carlos Bulosan and His Poetry: A Biography and an Anthology*. Seattle: University of Washington Press, 1985.

———. "Subversion or Affirmation: The Text and Subtext of *America Is in the Heart*." In *Asian Americans: Comparative and Global Perspectives*, ed. Shirley Hune, Hyun-Chan Kim, Stephen S. Fugita, and Amy Ling. Pullman: Washington State University Press, 1991. 191–209.

Feria, Dolores S. "Carlos Bulosan: Gentle Genius." *Comment* 1 (1957): 57–64.

Gonzales, Gabriel Jose. "*America Is in the Heart* as a Colonial-Immigrant Novel Engaging the Bildungsroman." *Kritika Kultura* 8 (2007): 213–31.

Gotera, Vince. "Carlos Bulosan: Passion, Poetry, Politics." *Connecticut Review* 15.2 (1993): 11–23.

Grow, L. M. "*The Laughter of My Father*: A Survival Kit." *MELUS* 20.2 (1995): 35–46.

Higashida, Cheryl. "Re-Signed Subjects: Women, Work, and World in the Fiction of Carlos Bulosan and Hisaye Yamamoto." *Studies in the Literary Imagination* 37.1 (2004): 35–60.

Jaskoski, Helen. "Carlos Bulosan's Literary Debt to Richard Wright." In *Literary Influence and African-American Writers*, ed. Tracy Mishkin. New York: Garland, 1996. 231–43.

Libretti, Tim. "First and Third Worlds in U. S. Literature: Rethinking Carlos Bulosan." *MELUS* 23.4 (1998): 135–55.

Manarpaac, Danilo Victorino. "Desire and Loathing in Carlos Bulosan's *America Is in the Heart* and Bienvenido Santos's *The Man Who (Thought He) Looked Like Robert Taylor*." In *Embracing the Other: Addressing Xenophobia in the New Literatures in English*, ed. Dunjia M. Mohr. Amsterdam, Netherlands: Rodopi, 2008. 71–82.

Miller, Joshua L. "The Gorgeous Laughter of Filipino Modernity: Carlos Bulosan's *The Laughter of My Father*." In *Bad Modernisms*, ed. Douglas Mao and Rebecca L. Walkowitz. Durham, N.C.: Duke University Press, 2006. 238–68.

Morantte, P.C. *Remembering Carlos Bulosan: His Heart Affair with America*. Quezon City, Philippines: New Day Publishers, 1984.

Mostern, Kenneth. "Why Is America in the Heart?" *Hitting Critical Mass* 2.2 (1995): 35–65.

Orendain, Margarita. "Understanding the Dynamics of Third World Writing in Bulosan's *America Is in the Heart*." *Saint Louis Research Journal* 19.2 (1988): 365–75.

Ponce, Martin Joseph. "On Becoming Socially Articulate: Transnational Bulosan." *Journal of Asian American Studies* 8.1 (2005): 49–80.

San Juan, E., Jr. "Beyond Identity Politics: The Predicament of the Asian Writer in Late Capitalism." *American Literary History* 3.13 (1991): 542–65.

———. "Carlos Bulosan, Filipino Writer-Activist: Between a Time of Terror and the Time of Revolution." *The New Centennial Review* 8.1 (2008): 103–34.

———. *Carlos Bulosan and the Imagination of the Class Struggle*. New York: Oriole Editions, 1972.

———. "Carlos Bulosan: The Poetics and Necessity of Revolution." *The Researcher* 2 (1969): 113–23.

Santos, Marie Louise Kalaw. "The Bulosan Mosaic: Portrait of the Immigrant as American." *Diliman Review* 47.3–4 (1999): 77–84.

Slotkin, Joel. "Igorots and Indians: Racial Hierarchies and Conceptions of the Savage in Carlos Bulosan's Fiction of the Philippines." *American Literature* 72.4 (2000): 843–66.

Sonza, Jorshinelle. "The Stranger in Paradise: Portrait of the 'Filipino' in Bulosan's 'America.'" *Journal of English Studies* (Quezon City) 2.1 (1994): 84–102.

Sugisawa, Rieko. "Carlos Bulosan's Search for America and Himself: *America Is in the Heart*." *AALA Journal* 2 (1995): 1-11.

Tiempo, Edilberto K. "Carlos Bulosan Demystified: The Problem of Artistic Insensitivity." *Solidarity* (Manila) 130 (1991): 33–43.

Tolentino, Cynthia. "In the 'Training Center of the Skillful Servants of Mankind': Carlos Bulosan's Professional Filipinos in an Age of Benevolent Supremacy." *American Literature* 80.2 (2008): 381–406.

Tolentino, Delfin L. "Satire in Carlos Bulosan's *The Laughter of My Father*." *Philippine Studies* 34.4 (1986): 452–461.

Wesling, Meg. "Colonial Education and the Politics of Knowledge in Carlos Boulosan's *America Is in the Heart*." *MELUS* 32.2 (2007): 55–77.

Wong, Kong Luong Sheila. "The Asian Other in Carlos Bulosan's *America Is in the Heart*." In *Writing Asia: The Literatures in Englishes, Volume 1*, ed. Edwin Thumboo. Singapore: Ethos, 2007. 146–56.

Cao, Lan

Bacholle-Bošković, Michèle. "The Exiled Woman's Burden: Father Figures in Lan Cao's and Linda Lê's Works." *The Journal of Twentieth Century Contemporary French Studies* 6.2 (2002): 267–81.

Janette, Michele. "Guerrilla Irony in Lan Cao's *Monkey Bridge*." *Contemporary Literature* 42.1 (2001): 50–77.

Satterlee, Michelle. "How Memory Haunts: The Impact of Trauma on Vietnamese Immigrant Identity in Lan Cao's *Monkey Bridge*." *Studies in the Humanities* 31.2 (2004): 138–62.

Stocks, Claire. "Bridging the Gaps: Inescapable History in Lan Cao's *Monkey Bridge*." *Studies in the Literary Imagination* 37.1 (2004): 83–100.

Cha, Theresa Hak Kyung

Chang, Julia. "'Transform this Nothingness': Theresa Hak Kyung Cha's *Dictée*." *Hitting Critical Mass* 1.1 (1993): 75–82.

Cheng, Anne Anlin. "Memory and Anti-Documentary Desire in Theresa Hak Kyung Cha's *Dictée*." *MELUS* 23.4 (1998): 119–33.

Frost, Elisabeth A. "'In Another Tongue': Body, Image, Text in Theresa Hak Kyung Cha's *Dictée*." In *We Who Love to Be Astonished: Experimental Women's Writing and Performance Poetics*, ed. Laura Hinton, Cynthia Hogue, and Rachel Blau DuPlessis. Tuscaloosa: University of Alabama Press, 2002. 181–92.

Fusco, Serena. "'You See Only Her Traces': Theresa Hak Kyung Cha's *Dictée*, Or the Performance of a Voice." In *'Contact Zones': Rewriting Genre across the East-West Border*, ed. Donatella Izzo and Elena Spandri. Naples, Italy: Liguori, 2003. 175–96.

Grice, Helena. "Korean American National Identity in Theresa Hak Kyung Cha's *Dictée*." In *Representing Lives: Women and Auto/Biography*, ed. Alison Donnell and Pauline Polkey. New York: Macmillan, 2000. 43–52.

Guarino-Trier, Jennifer. "'From the Multitude of Narratives . . . for another Telling for Another Recitation': Constructing and Re-Constructing *Dictée* and Memory/All Echo." In *Screening Asian Americans*, ed. Peter X. Feng. New Brunswick, N.J.: Rutgers University Press, 2002. 253–72.

Kang, Laura Hyun Yi. "The 'Liberal Voice' of Theresa Hak Kyung Cha's *Dictée*." In *Writing Self/Writing Nation: Essays on Theresa Hak Kyung Cha's* Dictée, ed. Elaine H. Kim and Norma Alarcan. Berkeley, Calif.: Third Woman Press, 1994. 73–99.

Kim, Ae-Ju. "Historiographic Feminine Metafiction and *Dictée*." *Feminist Studies in English Literature* 11.1 (2003): 25–47.

Kim, Elaine H., and Norma Alarcon, eds. *Writing Self, Writing Nation: A Collection of Essays on* Dictée *by Theresa Hak Kyung Cha.* Berkeley, Calif.: Third Women Press, 1994.

Kim, Hyo. "Depoliticising Politics: Readings of Theresa Hak Kyung Cha's *Dictée*." *Changing English: An International Journal of English Teaching* 15.4 (2008): 467–75.

Kim, Sue J. "Apparatus: Theresa Hak Kyung and the Politics of Form." *Journal of Asian American Studies* 8.2 (2005): 143–69.

———. "Narrator, Author, Reader: Equivocation in Theresa Hak Kyung Cha's *Dictée*." *Narrative* 16.2 (2008): 163–77.

———. "Suspicious Characters: Realism, Asian American Identity, and Theresa Hak Kyung Cha's *Dictée*." *Journal of Narrative Theory* 32.2 (2002): 227–58.

Lee, Kun Jong. "Rewriting Hesiod, Revisioning Korea: Theresa Hak Kyung Cha's *Dictée* as a Subversive Hesiodic Catalogue of Women." *College Literature* 33.3 (2006): 77–99.

Lee, Min Jung. "Baring the Apparatus: *Dictée*'s Speaking Subject Writes a Response." *Hitting Critical Mass* 6.1 (1999): 35–50.

Lee, Sue-Im. "Suspicious Characters: Realism, Asian American Identity, and Theresa Hak Kyung Cha's *Dictée*." *Journal of Narrative Theory* 32.2 (2002): 227–58.

Lowe, Lisa. "Unfaithful to the Original: The Subject of *Dictée*." In *Writing Self/Writing Nation: Essays on Theresa Hak Kyung Cha's Dictée*, ed. Elaine H. Kim and Norma Alarcan. Berkeley, Calif.: Third Woman Press, 1994. 35–69.

Martin, Stephen-Paul. "Theresa Cha: Creating a Feminine Voice." In *Open Form and the Feminine Imagination: The Politics of Reading in Twentieth-Century Innovative Writing*. Washington, D.C.: Maisonneuve, 1988. 187–205.

McDaniel, Nicole. "'The Remnant Is the Whole': Collage, Serial Self-Representation, and Recovering Fragments in Theresa Hak Kyung Cha's *Dictée*." *ARIEL: A Review of International English Literature* 40.4 (2009): 69–88.

Miller, Joshua L. "Multilingual Narrative and the Refusal of Translation: Theresa Hak Kyung Cha's *Dictée* and R. Zamora Linmark's *Rolling the R's*." In *How Far Is America from Here?* ed. Theo D'haen et al. Amsterdam, Netherlands: Rodopi, 2005. 467–80.

Min, Eun Kyung. "Reading the Figure of Dictation in Theresa Hak Kyung's Cha's *Dictée*." In *Other Sisterhoods: Literary Theory and U.S. Women of Color*, ed. Sandra Kumamoto Stanley. Urbana: University of Illinois Press, 1998. 309–24.

Mukherjee, Srimati. "Nation, Immigrant, Text: Theresa Hak Kyung Cha's *Dictée*." In *Transnational Asian American Literature: Sites and Transits*, ed. Shirley Geok-lin Lim et al. Philadelphia: Temple University Press, 2006. 197–215.

Oh, Stella. "The Enunciation of the Tenth Muse in Theresa Hak Kyung Cha's *Dictée*." *LIT: Literature Interpretation Theory* 13.1 (2002): 1–20.

Park, Josephine Nock-Hee. "'What of the Partition': *Dictée*'s Boundaries and the American Epic." *Contemporary Literature* 46.2 (2005): 213–42.

Phu, Thy. "Decapitated Forms: Theresa Hak Kyung Cha's Visual Text and the Politics of Visibility." *Mosaic: A Journal for the Interdisciplinary Study of Literature* 38.1 (2005): 17–36.

Randall, Belle. "The Random Murder of Theresa Cha." *Common Knowledge* 7.3 (1998): 156–63.

Russell, Keith A. "'From a Far': Unifying Divisions in Theresa Hak Kyung Cha's *Dictée*." In *Moving Migration: Narrative Transformations in Asian American Literature*, ed. Johanna C. Kardux and Doris Einsiedel. Münster, Germany: Lit, 2010. 181–97.

Sakai, Naoki. "Distinguishing Literature and the Work of Translation: Theresa Hak Kyung Cha's *Dictée* and Repetition without Return." In *Translation and Subjectivity: On "Japan" and Cultural Nationalism*. Minneapolis: University of Minnesota Press, 1997. 18–39.

Shih, Shu-mei. "Nationalism and Korean American Women's Writing: Theresa Hak Kyung Cha's *Dictée*." In *Speaking the Other Self: American Women Writers*, ed. Jeanne Campbell Reesman. Athens: University of Georgia Press, 1997. 144–62.

Spahr, Juliana M. "Postmodernism, Readers, and Theresa Hak Kyung Cha's *Dictée*." *College Literature* 23.3 (1996): 23–43.

Swaner, Scott. "Frustrating Colonial Narratives: Writing and the Body in *Dictée*." *Atlantis: A Women's Studies Journal* 2 (2004): 54–63.

Tae, Heasook. "Writing the Body from Asian Diasporic Women's Locations: *The Woman Warrior* and *Dictée*." *Feminist Studies in English Literature* 11.1 (2003): 235–55.

Takada, Mayumi. "Annihilating Possibilities: Witnessing and Testimony through Cinematic Love in Theresa Hak Kyung Cha's *Dictée*." *LIT: Literature Interpretation Theory* 17.1 (2006): 23–48.

Twelbeck, Kirsten. "Otherness as Reading Process: Theresa Hak Kyung Cha's *Dictée*." In *Asian American Literature in the International Context: Readings on Fiction, Poetry, and Performance*, ed. Rocío G. Davis and Sämi Ludwig. Hamburg, Germany: Lit, 2002. 185–201.

Viray, Ma. "Diagrams and Declensions—A Reading of *Dictée*." *AmerAsia* 14.1 (1988): 143–47.

Wilson, Rob. "Falling into the Korean Uncanny: On Reading Theresa Hak Kyung Cha's *Dictée*." *Korean Culture* 12 (1991): 33–37.

Wolf, Susan. "Theresa Cha: Recalling Telling Retelling." *Aferimage* 14.1 (1986): 11–13.

Wong, Shelley Sunn. "Unnaming the Same: Theresa Hak Kyung Cha's *Dictée*." In *Feminist Measures: Soundings in Poetry and Theory*, ed. Lynn Keller and Cristanne Miller. Ann Arbor: University of Michigan Press, 1994. 43–68.

Chandra, G. S. Sharat

Das, Kamar. "Indian English Poetry by an Expatriate Indian: A Note on G. S. Sharat Chandra's *Heirloom*." *Literary Half-Yearly* 32.1 (1991): 34–42.

Natarajan, Nalini. "Reluctant Janeites: Daughterly Value in Jane Austen and Sarat Chandra Chatterjee's *Swami*." In *Post Colonial Jane Austen*, ed. Rajeswari Sunder Rajan. London: Routledge, 2000. 141–62.

Rao, Vimala. "Wanted New Directions: The Poetry of G. S. Sharat Chandra." *Chandrabhaga: A Magazine of World Writing* 6 (1981): 50–57.

Vasudeva, Mary. "Swallowing for Twenty Years/The American Mind and Body: An Interview with G. S. Sharat Chandra." *Journal of Commonwealth and Postcolonial Studies* 5.1 (1997): 9–17.

Chandra, Vikram

Alexandru, Maria-Sabina Draga. "Alternatives to the Novel Form: Oral Storytelling and Internet Patterns in Vikram Chandra's *Red Earth and Pouring Rain*." *Journal of Commonwealth Literature* 43.3 (2008): 43–58.

———. "Performance, Performativity, and Nomadism in Vikram Chandra's *Red Earth and Pouring Rain*." *Comparative Literature Studies* 45.1 (2008): 23–39.

———. "'Virtual Reality on Infinite Bandwidth': Vikram Chandra Interviewed." *Journal of Commonwealth Literature* 40.2 (2005): 5–21.

Chambers, Claire. "An Interview with Vikram Chandra." *Wasafiri: The Magazine of International Contemporary Writing* 53 (2008): 45–48.

———. "Postcolonial Noir: Vikram Chandra's 'Kama.'" In *Detective Fiction in a Postcolonial and Transnational World*, ed. Nels Pearson and Marc Singer. Farham, Great Britain: Ashgate, 2009. 31–46.

Ganapathy-Dore, Geetha. "The Story-Teller's Voice in Vikram Chandra's *Red Earth and Pouring Rain*." *Commonwealth Essays and Studies* 19.1 (1996): 102–10.

Mijares, Loretta M. "Mapping Hybridity: Historicizing Cultural and Racial Hybrids in Vikram Chandra's *Red Earth and Pouring Rain.*" *South Asian Review* 27.1 (2006): 30–52.

Salvador, Dora Sales. "As Time Goes By . . . Between Cultures? Vikram Chandra's Fictions and the Circle of Life." In *The Polemics of Ageing as Reflected in Literatures in English*, ed. Maria Vidal Grau, Nuria Casado Gual, and Brian J Worsfold. Lérida, Spain. Universitat de Lleida, 2004. 125–34.

———. "Forms, Representations, and Voices: Cultural Liminality in Vikram Chandra's Fiction." In *(Mis)Representations: Intersections of Culture and Power*, ed. Fernando Galvan, Juliu Canero Serrano, and Jose Santiago Fernandez Vazquez. Bern, Switzerland: Peter Lang, 2003. 57–73.

———. "Listening to Vikram Chandra: 'All Stories Have in Them the Seed of All Other Stories.'" *Miscelánea: A Journal of English and American Studies* 22 (2000): 201–13.

———. "The Passing of Time and the Flowing of Self: In Conversation with Vikram Chandra." *The Polemics of Ageing as Reflected in Literatures in English*, ed. Maria Vidal Grau, Nuria Casado Gual, and Brian J Worsfold. Lérida, Spain. Universitat de Lleida, 2004. 135–40.

———. "Vikram Chandra's Constant Journey: Swallowing the World." *Journal of English Studies* 2 (2000): 93–111.

———. "Vikram Chandra's Transcultural Narrative: *Red Earth and Pouring Rain*, Much More Than a Novel." In *Beyond Borders: Re-Defining Generic and Ontological Boundaries*, ed. Ramón Plo-Alastrué and María Jesús Martínez-Alfaro. Heidelberg, Germany: Carl Winter Universitätsverlag, 2002. 175–84.

Teverson, Andrew. "Vikram Chandra in Conversation." *Wasafiri: The Transnational Journal of International Writing* 37 (2002): 4–7.

Chin, Frank

Chang, Chin-ying. "Religion and Cultural Identity in Chinese American Literature: The Image of Gwan Gung in Writings by Frank Chin and David Henry Hwang." *Fiction and Drama* 19.2 (2009): 91–116.

Cheung, King-Kok. "The Deployment of Chinese Classics by Frank Chin and Maxine Hong Kingston." In *Querying the Genealogy: Comparative and Transnational Studies in Chinese American Literature*, ed. Jennie Wang. Shanghai, China: Shanghai Yiwen Press, 2006. 217–30.

Chiu, Jeannie. "Uncanny Doubles: Nationalism and Repression in Frank Chin's 'Railroad Standard Time'." *Hitting Critical Mass* 1.1 (1993): 93–107.

Cho, Fiona. "Daddy, I Don't Know What You're Talking About." *Hitting Critical Mass* 1.1 (1993): 57–61.

Chu, Patricia P. "Tripmaster Monkey, Frank Chin, and the Chinese Heroic Tradition." *Arizona Quarterly* 53.3 (1997): 117–39.

Davis, Robert Murray. "Frank Chin: An Interview with Robert Murray Davis." *Ameriasia* 14.2 (1988): 81–95.

———. "West Meets East: A Conversation with Frank Chin." *Amerasia Journal* 24.1 (1998): Fung, Eileen Chia-Ching. "'To Eat the Flesh of His Dead Mother':

Hunger, Masculinity, and Nationalism in Frank Chin's *Donald Duk*." *LIT: Literature Interpretation Theory* 10.3 (1999): 255–74.

Goldstein-Shirley, David. "'The Dragon Is a Lantern': Frank Chin's Counter-Hegemonic *Donald Duk*." *49th Parallel: An Interdisciplinary Journal of North American Studies* 6 (2000): (no pagination).

Kim, Daniel Y. *Writing Manhood in Black and Yellow: Ralph Ellison, Frank Chin, and the Literary Politics of Identity*. Stanford, Calif.: Stanford University Press, 2005.

Kim, Elaine, H. "Frank Chin: The Chinatown Cowboy and His Backtalk." *Midwest Quarterly* 20 (1978): 78–91.

Kim, Peter Kearly. "It's 'Ah Sin' to be Yellow in America: Theatrics of Racial Humor in Protesting Injustice." *Studies in American Humor* 3.18 (2008): 25–37.

Ku, Robert Ji-Song. "'Beware of Tourists if You Look Chinese' and Other Survival Tactics in the American Theatre: The Asian(Cy) of Display in Frank Chin's *The Year of the Dragon*." *Journal of American Drama and Theatre* 11.2 (1999): 78–92.

Lau, Joseph S. M. "The Albatross Exorcised: The Rime of Frank Chin." *Tamkang Review* 12.1 (1981): 93–105.

Lee, Robert A. "Bad Boy, Godfather, Storyteller: The China Fictions of Frank Chin." In *China Fictions/English Language: Literary Essays in Diaspora, Memory, Story*, ed. Robert Lee. Amsterdam, Netherlands: Rodopi, 2008. 79–100.

Leonard, Suzanne. "Dreaming as Cultural Work in *Donald Duk* and *Dreaming in Cuban*." *MELUS* 29.2 (2004): 181–203.

Li, David Leiwei. "The Formation of Frank Chin and Formations of Chinese American Literature." In *Asian Americans: Comparative and Global Perspectives*, ed. Shirley Hune et al. Pullman: Washington State University Press, 1991. 211–23.

Madsen, Deborah L. "Chinese American Writers of the Real and the Fake: Authenticity and the Twin Traditions of Life Writing." *Canadian Review of American Studies* 36.3 (2006): 257–71.

Peters, Ingo. "Passion, Plainness, Allegory: Frank Chin, American Literary Tradition, and the Question of Style." *A Quarterly of Language, Literature and Culture* 56.1 (2008): 49–60.

Richardson, Susan B. "The Lessons of *Donald Duk*." *MELUS* 24.4 (1999): 57–76.

Taylor, Gordon O. "'Adding on,' Not 'Giving Up': Ceremonies of Self in Frank Chin's *Donald Duk*." In *Asian American Literature in the International Context: Readings on Fiction, Poetry, and Performance*, ed. Rocío G. Davis and Sämi Ludwig. Hamburg, Germany: Lit, 2002. 57–66.

Xu, Wenying. "Masculinity, Food, and Appetite in Frank Chin's *Donald Duk* and 'The Eat and Run Midnight People.'" *Cultural Critique* 66 (2007): 78–103.

Chin, Marilyn

"An Interview with Marilyn Chin." *Indiana Review* 26.1 (2004): 112–20.

Gery, John. "'Mocking My Own Happiness': Authenticity, Heritage, and Self-Erasure in the Poetry of Marilyn Chin." *LIT: Literature Interpretation Theory* 12.1 (2001): 25–45.

Matsumoto, Tarisa. "Foxtrot with Marilyn: An Interview." In *Page to Page: Retrospectives of Writers from the Seattle Review*, ed. Colleen J. McElroy and Brenda Peterson. Seattle: University of Washington Press, 2006. 203–17.

McCormick, Adrienne. "'Being Without': Marilyn Chin's 'I' Poems as Feminist Acts of Theorizing." *Hitting Critical Mass* 6.2 (2000): 37–58.

Zhou, Xiaojing. "Breaking from Tradition: Experimental Poems by Four Contemporary Asian American Women Poets." *Revista Canaria de Estudios Ingelses* 37 (1998): 199–218.

———. "Marilyn Chin's Poetry of 'Self as Nation': Transforming the 'Lyric I,' Reinventing Cultural Inheritance." In *Asian American Literature in the International Context: Readings on Fiction, Poetry, and Performance*, ed. Rocío G. Davis and Sämi Ludwig. Hamburg, Germany: Lit, 2002. 111–35.

———. "Rearticulating 'Otherness' Strategies of Cultural and Linguistic Differences in Asian American Women's Poetry." In *Asian American Studies: Identities, Images, Issues Past and Present*, ed. Esther Mikyun Ghymn. New York: Peter Lang, 2000. 151–77.

Chong, Ping

Carroll, Noel. "A Select View of Earthlings: Ping Chong." *Drama Review* 27.1 (1983): 72–81.

Frieze, James. "The Mess behind the Veil: Assimilating Ping Chong." *Theatre Research International* 31.1 (2006): 84–100.

Knopf, Robert. "Truth and Beauty, Mystery and Utility: An Interview with Ping Chong." *Forum Modernes Theater* 17.1 (2002): 65–72.

Kurahashi, Yuko. "Search for Home and Identity: Ping Chong and Michael Rohd's Undesirable Elements—Berlin." *Journal of the Midwest Modern Language Association* 38.1 (2005): 85–100.

Martinovich, Kay. "Haunted Landscapes: Ping Chong's East/West Productions." In *Querying Difference in Theatre History*, ed. Scott Magelssen and Ann Haugo. Newcastle upon Tyne, Great Britain: Cambridge Scholars, 2007. 86–92.

Neely, Kent. "Ping Chong's Theatre of Simultaneous Consciousness." *Journal of Dramatic Theory and Criticism* 6.2 (1992): 121–35.

Sandla, Robert. "Practical Visionary: Ping Chong." *Theater Week* 2.20 (1989): 26–33.

Wehle, Philippa. "Citizen of the World: Ping Chong's Travels." *PAJ: A Journal of Performance and Art* 26.1 (2004): 22–32.

———. "What's Fiction When You Have Real Life? Ping Chong's Undesirable Elements Project." *Theatre Forum* 21 (2002): 37–42.

Westfall, Suzanne. "Ping Chong's *Terra In/Cognita*: Monsters on Stage." In *Reading the Literature of Asian America*, ed. Shirley Geok-lin and Amy Ling. Philadelphia: Temple University Press, 1992. 359–73.

Chu, Louis Hing

Chen, Xiangyang. "Constructions of Chinese Identity in *Eat a Bowl of Tea* and Chinese Box." In *Re-Reading America: Changes and Challenges*, ed. Weihe Zhong and Rui Han. Cheltenham, Great Britain: Reardon, 2004. 215–26.

Chua, Cheng Lok. "Golden Mountain: Chinese Version of American Dream in Lin Yutang, Louis Chu, and Maxine Hong Kingston." *Ethnic Group* 4 (1982): 33–59.

Hsiao, Ruth Y. "Facing the Incurable: Patriarchy in *Eat a Bowl of Tea*." In *Reading Literatures of Asian America*, ed. Shirley Geok-lin Lim and Amy Ling. Philadelphia: Temple University Press, 1992. 151–62.

Li, Shu-yan. "Otherness and Transformation in *Eat a Bowl of Tea* and *Crossings*." *MELUS* 18.4 (1993/1994): 99–111.

Ling, Jinqi. "Reading for Historical Specificities: Gender Negotiations in Louis Chu's *Eat a Bowl of Tea*." *MELUS* 20.1 (1995): 35–52.

Chuang, Hua

Chiu, Monica. "Motion, Memory, and Conflict in Chuang Hua's Modernist *Crossings*." *MELUS* 24.4 (1999): 107–23.

Douglass, Lesley Chin. "Finding the Way: Chuang Hua's *Crossings* and Chinese Literary Tradition." *MELUS* 20.1 (1995): 53–65.

Ho, Wen-ching. "Negotiating the Past: Gender Inequality in Chuang Hua's *Crossings*." *Concentric: Literary and Cultural Studies* 34.2 (2008): 155–75.

———. "Representing Diaspora and Identity Quest in Chuang Hua's *Crossings*." In *Seeking the Self-Encountering the Other: Diasporic Narrative and the Ethics of Representation,* ed. Tuomas Huttunen, Kaisa Ilmonen, et al. Newcastle upon Tyne, Great Britain: Cambridge Scholars, 2008. 151–67.

Lee, Karen A. "John Ford's *The Searchers* (1956) in Chuang Hua's *Crossings*: A Chinese American Woman's Categorical Liminality in a Cold War Society." *Hitting Critical Mass* 4.2 (1997): 79–86.

———. "A Rumble in the Silence: *Crossings* by Chuang Hua." *MELUS* 9.3 (1982): 29–37.

Pehkoranta, Anna. "Shifting the Center: Emotional Exile and the Aesthetic of Displacement in Chuang Hua's *Crossings*." In *Positioning the New: Chinese American Literature and the Changing Image of the American Literary Canon*, ed. Tanfer Emin Tunc and Elisabetta Marino. Newcastle upon Tyne, Great Britain: Cambridge Scholars, 2010. 69–82.

Wang, Veronica C. "In Search of Self: The Dislocated Female Émigré Wanderer in Chuang Hua's *Crossings*." In *Multicultural Literatures through Feminist/Poststructuralist Lenses*, ed. Barbara Frey Waxman. Knoxville: University of Tennessee Press, 1993. 22–36.

Desani, Govindas Vishnudas

Aravamudan, Srinivas. "Postcolonial Affiliations: *Ulysses* and *All about H. Hatterr*." In *Transcultural Joyce*, ed. Karen R. Lawrence. Cambridge: Cambridge University Press, 1998. 97–128.

Bardoph, Jacqueline. "Language and Madness in G. V. Desani's *All about H. Hatterr.*" *Commonwealth Essays and Studies* 8.1 (1985): 1–13.

Goers, Peter. "King's English: Whole Language and G. V. Desani's *All about H. Hatterr.*" *New Literature Review* 4 (1978): 30–40.

Naik, M. K. "Colonial Experience in *All about H. Hatterr*: A Philosophical Comedy." In *Studies in Indian Fiction in English*, ed. G. S. Balarama Gupta. Gulbarga, India: JIWE Publications, 1981. 25–35.

———. "Colonial Experience in *All about H. Hatterr.*" *Commonwealth Novel in English* 1.1 (1982): 37–49.

Riemenschneider, Deiter. "G. V. Desani's *All about H. Hatterr* and the Problem of Cultural Alienation." *The Literary Criterion* 20.2 (1985): 23–35.

Sharrad, Paul. "Musings on the Hats of the Hatterr." *ACLALS Bulletin* 7.4 (1986): 79–85.

Srinath, C. N. "G. V. Desani: *All about H. Hatterr.*" *The Literary Criterion* 9.3 (1970): 40–56.

Stilz, Gerhard. "'Truth? Hell, You Will Get Contrast, and No Mistake!': Sanitizing the Intercultural Polylemma in G. V. Desani's *All about H. Hatterr* (1948/72)." In *Hybridity and Postcolonialism: Twentieth-Century Indian Literature*, ed. Monika Fludernik. Tubingen, Germany: Stauffenburg, 1998. 79–101.

Williams, Haydn. "Hatterr and Bazza: Post-Colonial Picaros." *Commonwealth Review* 2.1–2 (1990–1991): 204–11.

Divakaruni, Chitra Banerjee

Davis, Rocío G. "Everyone's Story: Narrative You in Chitra Bannerjee Divakaruni's 'The World Love.'" In *Asian American Literature in the International Context: Readings on Fiction, Poetry, and Performance*, ed. Rocío G. Davis and Sämi Ludwig. Hamburg, Germany: Lit, 2002. 173–83.

Field, Robin. "'Through This Experience I Connect with You': An Interview with Chitra Banerjee Divakaruni." *South Asian Review* 29.4 (2008): 85–96.

Jahan, Husne. "Colonial Woes in Post-Colonial Writing: Chitra Divakaruni's Immigrant Narratives." *South Asian Review* 24.2 (2003): 149–69.

Knowles, Nancy. "Dissolving Stereotypical Cultural Boundaries: Allusions to Virginia Woolf in Chitra Banerjee Divakaruni's *Sister of My Heart.*" In *Virginia Woolf Out of Bounds: Selected Papers from the Tenth Annual Conference on Virginia Woolf*, ed. Jessica Berman and Jane Goldman. New York: Pace University Press, 2001. 67–73.

McConigley, Nina Swamidoss. "A South Asian American Writer's Perspective: An Interview with Chitra Banerjee Divakaruni." In *Other Tongues: Rethinking the Language Debates in India*, ed. Nalini Iyer and Bonnie Zare. Amsterdam, Netherlands: Rodopi, 2009. 97–104.

Rajan, Gita. "Chita Divakaruni's *The Mistress of Spices*: Deploying Mystical Realism." *Meridians: Feminism, Race, Transnationalism* 2.2 (2002): 215–36.

Rasiah, Dharini. "Chitra Banerjee Divakaruni." In *Words Matter: Conversations with Asian American Writers*, ed. King-Kok Cheung. Honolulu: University of Hawai'i Press, 2000. 140–53.

Ross, Robert. "Dissolving Boundaries': The Woman as Immigrant in the Fiction of Chitra Banerjee Divakaruni." In *Missions of Interdependence: A Literary Directory*, ed. Gerhard Stilz. Amsterdam, Netherlands: Rodopi, 2002. 247–54.

Selvam, Veena. "Mistresses and Sisters—Creating a Female Universe: The Novels of Chitra Banerjee Divakaruni." *Literary Criterion* 40.2 (2005): 53–66.

Shankar, Lavina Dhingra. "Not Too Spicy: Exotic Mistresses of Cultural Translation in the Fiction of Chitra Divakaruni and Jhumpa Lahiri." In *Other Tongues: Rethinking the Language Debates in India*, ed. Zare Iyer and Bonnie Nalini. Amsterdam, Netherlands: Rodopi, 2009. 23–52.

Singh, Ranjini Jothi. "A Feminist Critique: Woman's Struggle for Freedom in Chitra Banerjee Divakaruni's *Arranged Marriage*." *Indian Writing in English* 34.1 (2006): 15–23.

Srikanth, Rajini. "Chitra Banerjee Divakaruni: Exploring Human Nature under Fire." *Asian Pacific American Journal* 5.2 (1996): 94–101.

Vega-González, Susana. "Negotiating Boundaries in Divakaruni's *The Mistress of Spices* and Naylor's *Mama Day*." *CLCWeb: Comparative Literature and Culture: A WWWeb Journal* 5.2 (2003).

Xu, Wenying. "Reading Feminine Mysticism in Chitra Banerjee Divakaruni's *Queen of Dreams*." *South Asian Review* 31.1 (2010): 186–207.

Eaton, Edith Maude (Sui Sin Far)

Beauregard, Guy. "Reclaiming Sui Sin Far." In *Re/Collecting Early Asian America: Essays in Cultural History*, ed. Josephine Lee et al. Philadelphia: Temple University Press, 2002. 340–54.

Chapman, Mary A. "'Revolution in Ink': Sui Sin Far and Chinese Reform Discourse." *American Quarterly* 6.4 (2008): 975–1001.

Cho, Yu-Fang. "'Yellow Slavery,' Narratives of Rescue, and Sui Sin Far/Edith Maude Eaton's 'Lin John' (1899)." *Journal of Asian American Studies* 12.1 (2009): 35–63.

Chung, June Hee. "Asian Object Lessons: Orientalist Decoration in Realist Aesthetics from William Dean Howells to Sui Sin Far." *Studies in American Fiction* 36.1 (2008): 27–50.

Cutter, Martha J. "Sex, Love, Revenge, and Murder in 'Away Down in Jamaica': A Lost Short Story by Sui Sin Far (Edith Eaton)." *Legacy: A Journal of American Women Writers* 21.1 (2004): 85–89.

———. "Smuggling across the Borders of Race, Gender, and Sexuality: Sui Sin Far's 'Mrs. Spring Fragrance.'" In *Mixed Race Literature*, ed. Jonathan Brennan. Stanford, Calif.: Stanford University Press, 2002. 137–64.

———. "Sui Sin Far's Letters to Charles Lummis: Contextualizing Publication Practices for the Asian American Subject at the Turn of the Century." *American Literary Realism* 38.3 (2006): 259–75.

Degenhardt, Jane Hwang. "Situating the Essential Alien: Sui Sin Far's Depiction of Chinese-White Marriage and the Exclusionary Logic of Citizenship." *MFS: Modern Fiction Studies* 54.4 (2008): 654–88.

Dong, Larraine, and Marlon K. Hom. "Defiance or Perpetuation: An Analysis of Characters in *Mrs. Spring Fragrance*." In *Chinese America: History and Perspectives*, ed. Him Mark Lai, Ruthanne Lum McCunn, and Judy Young. San Francisco: Chinese Historical Society of America, 1987. 139–68.

Doyle, James. "Sui Sin Far and Onoto Watanna: Two Early Chinese Canadian Authors." *Canadian Literature* 140 (1994): 50–58.

Dupree, Ellen. "Sui Sin Far's Argument for Biculturalism in *Mrs. Spring Fragrance*." In *Asian American Studies: Identity, Images, Issues Past and Present*, ed. Esther Mikyung Ghymn. New York: Peter Lang, 2000. 77–100.

Ferens, Dominika. *Edith and Winnifred Eaton: Chinatown Missions and Japanese Romances*. Champaign: University of Illinois Press, 2002.

———. "Edith Eaton/Sui Sin Far: The Politics of Chinatown Reporting and Storytelling." In *Postcolonial Subjects: Canadian and Australian Perspectives*, ed. Mirosława Buchholtz. Toruń, Poland: Wydawnictwo Uniwersytetu Mikołaja Kopernika, 2004. 61–79.

———. "Tangled Kites: Sui Sin Far's Negotiations with Race and Readership." *Amerasia Journal* 25.2 (1999): 116–44.

Goudie, Sean X. "Toward a Definition of Caribbean American Regionalism: Contesting Anglo-America's Caribbean Designs in Mary Seacole and Sui Sin Far." *American Literature* 80.2 (2008): 293–322.

Jirousek, Lori. "Spectacle Ethnography and Immigrant Resistance: Sui Sin Far and Anzia Yezierska." *MELUS* 27.1 (2002): 25–52.

Li, Wenxin. "Sui Sin Far and the Chinese American Canon: Toward a Post-Gender-Wars Discourse." *MELUS* 29. 3–4 (2004): 121–31.

Lim, Shirley Geok-lin. "Sibling Hybridities: The Case of Edith Eaton/Sui Sin Far and Winnifred Eaton/Onoto Watanna." *Life Writing* 4.1 (2007): 81–99.

Ling, Amy. "Creating One's Self: The Eaton Sisters." In *Reading the Literatures of Asian America*, ed. Shirley Geok-lin Lim and Amy Ling. Philadelphia: Temple University Press, 1992. 305–18.

Martin, Quentin E. "Sui Sin Far's Railroad Baron: A Chinese of the Future." *American Literary Realism* 29.1 (1996): 54–61.

McCann, Sean. "Connecting Links: The Anti-Progressivism of Sui Sin Far." *Yale Journal of Criticism* 12.1 (1999): 73–88.

Ouyang, Huining. "Rewriting the Butterfly Story: Tricksterism in Onoto Watanna's *A Japanese Nightingale* and Sui Sin Far's 'The Smuggling of Tie Co.'" In *Alternative Rhetorics: Challenges to the Rhetorical Tradition*, ed. Laura Gray-Rosendale and Sibylle Gruber. Albany: State University of New York Press, 2001. 203–17.

Pan, Arnold. "Cosmopolitics from Below: Autobiography and Collective Identity in Sui Sin Far's 'Leaves from the Mental Portfolio of an Eurasian.'" In *Querying the Genealogy: Comparative and Transnational Studies in Chinese American Literature*, ed. Jennie Wang. Shanghai, China: Shanghai Yiwen Press, 2006. 141–50.

———. "Transnationalism at the Impasse of Race: Sui Sin Far and U.S. Imperialism." *Arizona Quarterly* 66.1 (2010): 87–114.

Peterson, Rachel. "Performing Ethnography and Identity in Sui Sin Far's Short Fiction." In *Positioning the New: Chinese American Literature and the Changing*

Image of the American Literary Canon, ed. Tanfer Emin Tunc and Elisabetta Marino. Newcastle upon Tyne, Great Britain: Cambridge Scholars, 2010. 158–74.

Pryse, Marjorie. "Linguistic Regionalism and the Emergence of Chinese American Literature in Sui Sin Far's 'Mrs. Spring Fragrance.'" *Legacy: A Journal of American Women Writers* 27.1 (2010): 83–108.

Roh-Spaulding, Carol. "Beyond Biraciality: 'Race' as Process in the Work of Edith Eaton/Sui Sin Far and Winnifred Eaton/Onoto Watanna." In *Asian American Literature in the International Context Readings on Fiction, Poetry, and Performance*, ed. Rocío G. Davis and Sämi Ludwig. Hamburg, Germany: Lit Verlag, 2002. 21–35.

———. "'Wavering' Images: Mixed-Race Identity in the Stories of Edith Eaton/Sui Sin Far." In *Ethnicity and the American Short Story*, ed. Julia Brown. New York: Garland, 1997. 155–76.

Shih, David. "The Seduction of Origins: Sui Sin and the Race for Tradition." In *Form and Transformation in Asian American Literature*, ed. Xiaojing Zhou and Samina Najmi. Seattle: University of Washington Press, 2005. 48–76.

Solberg, S. E. "Sui Sin Far/Edith Eaton: First Chinese-American Fictionist." *MELUS* 8.1 (1981): 27–39.

Song, Min Hyoung. "Sentimentalism and Sui Sin Far." *Legacy: A Journal of American Women Writers* 20.1–2 (2003): 134–52.

Tonkovich, Nicole. "Genealogy, Genre, Gender: Sui Sin Far's 'Leaves from the Mental Portfolio of an Eurasian.'" In *Beyond the Binary: Reconstructing Cultural Identity in a Multicultural Context*, ed. Timothy B. Powell. New Brunswick, N.J.: Rutgers University Press, 1999. 236–60.

Wang, Bo. "Rereading Sui Sin Far: A Rhetoric of Defiance." In *Representations: Doing Asian American Rhetoric*, ed. Luming Mao et al. Logan: Utah State University Press, 2008. 244–65.

White-Parks, Annette. "Intersections of Gender and Cultural Difference as Both Impediment and Inspiration to Sui Sin Far, a Canadian/American Writer." In *Intersexions: Issues of Race and Gender in Canadian Women's Writing*, ed. Coomi S. Vevaina and Barbara Godard. New Delhi, India: Creative, 1996. 197–218.

———. "A Reversal of American Concepts of 'Other-ness' in the Fiction of Sui Sin Far." *MELUS* 20.1 (1995): 17–34.

———. *Sui Sin Far/Edith Maude Eaton: A Literary Biography*. Urbana: University of Illinois Press, 1995.

———. "'We Wear the Mask': Sui Sin Far as One Example of Trickster Authorship." In *Tricksterism in Turn-of-the-Century American Literature: A Multicultural Perspective*, ed. Elizabeth Ammons and Annette White-Parks. Hanover, N.H.: University Press of New UK, 1994. 1–20.

Yin, Xiao-Huang. "Between the East and West: Sui Sin Far—the First Chinese-American Woman Writer." *Arizona Quarterly* 47.4 (1991): 49–84.

Eaton, Winnifred (Onoto Watanna)

Birchall, Diana. *Onoto Watanna: The Story of Winnifred Eaton*. Urbana: University of Illinois Press, 2001.

Birkle, Carmen. "Orientalisms in Fin-de-Siècle America." *Amerikastudien/American Studies* 51.3 (2006): 323–42.

Cole, Jean Lee. *The Literary Voices of Winnifred Eaton: Redefining Ethnicity and Authenticity.* New Brunswick, N.J.: Rutgers University Press, 2002.

———. "Newly Recovered Works by Onoto Watanna (Winnifred Eaton): A Prospectus and Checklist." *Legacy: A Journal of American Women Writers* 21.2 (2004): 229–34.

Doyle, James. "Sui Sin Far and Onoto Watanna: Two Early Chinese-Canadian Authors." *Canadian Literature* 140 (1944): 50–58.

Dupree, Ellen. "China and the Fad for Japan in Onoto Watanna's Chinese-Japanese Cook Book." *Popular Culture Review* 18.1 (2007): 85–89.

Ferens, Dominika. *Edith and Winnifred Eaton: Chinatown Missions and Japanese Romances*. Champaign: University of Illinois Press, 2002.

———. "Winnifred Eaton/Onoto Watanna: Establishing Ethnographic Authority." In *Form and Transformation in Asian American Literature*, ed. Samina Najmi and Xiaojiing Zhou. Seattle: University of Washington Press. 304–47.

———. "Winnifred Eaton's 'Japanese' Novels as a Field Experiment." In *Middlebrow Moderns: Popular American Women Writers of the 1920s*, ed. Meredith Goldsmith and Joan Shelley Rubin. Boston: Northeastern University Press, 2003. 65–84.

Ihara, Rachel. "Gentlemen Publishers and Lady Readers: Winnifred Eaton's Negotiations with the Literary Marketplace." In *Popular Nineteenth-Century American Women Writers and the Literary Marketplace*, ed. Mary De Jong and Earl Yarington. Newcastle, Great Britain: Cambridge Scholars, 2007. 466–84.

Lee, Katherine Hyunmi. "The Poetics of Liminality and Misidentification: Winnifred Eaton's *Me* and Maxine Hong Kingston's *The Woman Warrior*." *Studies in the Literary Imagination* 37.1 (2004): 17–33.

Lim, Shirley Geok-lin. "Sibling Hybridities: The Case of Edith Eaton/Sui Sin Far and Winnifred Eaton/Onoto Watanna." *Life Writing* 4.1 (2007): 81–99.

Ling, Amy. "Creating One's Self: The Eaton Sisters." In *Reading the Literatures of Asian America*, ed. Shirley Geok-lin Lim and Amy Ling. Philadelphia: Temple University Press, 1992. 312–13.

———. "Revelation and Mask: Autobiographies of the Eaton Sisters." *a/b: Auto/Biography Studies* 3.2 (1987): 46–52.

———. "Winnifred Eaton: Ethnic Chameleon and Popular Success." *MELUS* 11.3 (1984): 5–15.

Matsukawa, Yuko. "Cross-Dressing and Cross-Naming: Decoding Onoto Watanna." In *Tricksterism in Turn-of-the Century U.S. Literature*, ed. Elizabeth Ammons and Annette White-Parks. Hanover, N.H.: University Press of New UK, 1994: 106–25.

Murphy, Gretchen. "How the Irish Became Japanese: Winnifred Eaton's Racial Reconstructions in a Transnational Context." *American Literature* 79.1 (2007): 29–56.

Najmi, Samina. "White Woman in Asia: Racial Fluidity as Rebellion in Onoto Watanna's *The Heart of Hyacinth*." In *Re-Placing America: Conversations and Contestations: Selected Essays*, ed. Ruth Hsu et al. Honolulu: University of Hawaii Press, 2000. 82–91.

Oishi, Eve. "'High-Class Fakery': Race, Sex, and Class in the Screenwriting of Winnifred Eaton (1925–1931)." *Quarterly Review of Film and Video* 23.1 (2006): 23–36.

Ouyang, Huining. "Ambivalent Passages: Racial and Cultural Crossings in Onoto Watanna's *The Heart of Hyacinth*." *MELUS* 34.1 (2009): 211–29.

———. "Behind the Mask of Coquetry: The Trickster Narrative in *Miss Numè of Japan: A Japanese-American Romance.* In *Double Plots: Romance and History*, ed. Susan Strehle and Mary Paniccia Carden. Jackson: University Press of Mississippi, 2003. 86–106.

———. "Rewriting the Butterfly Story: Tricksterism in Onoto Watanna's *A Japanese Nightingale* and Sui Sin Far's 'The Smuggling of Tie Co.'" In *Alternative Rhetorics: Challenges to the Rhetorical Tradition*, ed. Laura Gray-Rosendale and Sibylle Gruber. Albany: State University of New York Press, 2001. 203–17.

Roh-Spaulding, Carol. "Beyond Biraciality: 'Race' as Process in the Work of Edith Eaton/Sui Sin Far and Winnifred Eaton/Onoto Watanna." In *Asian American Literature in the International Context Readings on Fiction, Poetry, and Performance*, ed. Rocío G. Davis and Sämi Ludwig. Hamburg, Germany: Lit Verlag, 2002. 21–35.

Shea, Pat. "Winnifred Eaton and the Politics of Miscegenation in Popular Fiction." *MELUS* 22.2 (1997): 19–32.

Sheffer, Jolie A. "'Citizen Sure Thing' or 'Jus' Foreigner'? Half-Caste Citizenship and the Family Romance in Onoto Watanna's Orientalist Fiction." *Journal of Asian American Studies* 13.1 (2010): 81–105.

Shih, David. "The Self and Generic Convention: Winnifred Eaton's *Me, a Book of Remembrance*." In *Recovered Legacies: Authority and Identity in Early Asian American Literature*, ed. Floyd Cheung and Keith Lawrence. Philadelphia: Temple University Press, 2005. 41–59.

Skinazi, Kareb E. H. "'As to Her Race, Its Secret Is Loudly Revealed': Winnifred Eaton's Revision of North American Identity." *MELUS* 32.2 (2007): 31–53.

Woo, Miseong. "Onoto Watanna's *A Japanese Nightingale*: Shifting Identities of the Pioneer Asian American Woman Writer." *Feminist Studies in English Literature* 10.2 (2002): 331–53.

Gotanda, Philip Kan

Cho, Nancy. "*Yankee Dawg You Die* by Philip Kan Gotanda." In *A Resource Guide to Asian American Literature*, ed. Stephen H. Sumida and Sau-ling Cynthia Wong. New York: Modern Language Association of America, 2001. 185–92.

Dunbar, Ann-Marie. "From Ethnic to Mainstream Theater: Negotiating 'Asian American' in the Plays of Philip Kan Gotanda." *American Drama* 14.1 (2005): 15–21.

Hurwitt, Robert. "Song of a Sansei Playwright: An Interview with Philip Kan Gotanda and Richard Seyd." In *West Coast Plays 21/22*, ed. Robert Hurwitt. Los Angeles: California Theatre Council, 1987. 166–74.

Hwang, David Henry. "Philip Kan Gotanda." *Bomb* (Winter 1998): 20–26.

Ito, Robert B. "Philip Kan Gotanda." In *Words Matter: Conversations with Asian American Writers*, ed. King-Kok Cheung. Honolulu: University of Hawaii Press, 2000. 173–85.

Kurahashi, Yuko. "Philip Kan Gotanda's Personal Saga, *A Song for a Nisei Fisherman*." In *Asian American Culture on Stage: The History of the East West Players*. New York: Garland, 1999. 162–66.

Moy, James. "David Henry Hwang's *M. Butterfly* and Philip Kan Gotanda's *Yankee Dawg You Die*: Repositioning Chinese American Marginality on the American Stage." *Theatre Journal* 42 (1990): 48–56.

———. "Flawed Self Representations: Authenticating Chinese American Marginality." In *Marginal Sights: Staging the Chinese in America*. Iowa City: University of Iowa Press, 1993. 115–29.

Vorlicky, Robert. "Realizing Freedom: Risk, Responsibility, and Individualization." In *Act like a Man: Challenging Masculinity in American Drama*. Ann Arbor: University of Michigan Press, 1995. 190–200.

Hagedorn, Jessica

Aguilar-San Juan, Karin. "The Exile within/the Question of Identity: Jessica Hagedorn." In *The State of Asian America: Activism and Resistance in the 1990s*, ed. Karin Aguilar-San Juan. Boston: South End Press, 1994. 173–82.

Arriola, Joyce L. "*Dogeaters*: Films as Subtext in Transposed and Invented History." *Ideya: Journal of the Humanities* 6–7.2–1 (2005): 105–17.

Bonetti, Kay. "An Interview with Jessica Hagedorn." *Missouri Review* 18.1 (1995): 90–113.

Casper, Leonard. "Bangungot and the Philippine Dream in Hagedorn." *Solidarity: Current Affairs, Ideas and the Arts* 127 (1990): 152–57.

Chang, Juliana. "Masquerade, Hysteria, and Neocolonial Femininity in Jessica Hagedorn's *Dogeaters*." *Contemporary Literature* 44.4 (2003): 637–63.

Chen, Shu-ching. "(Trans)National Imaginary and Tropical Melancholy in Jessica Hagedorn's *Dogeaters*." *Concentric: Literary and Cultural Studies* 31.1 (2005): 95–121.

Collins, Michael. "'I'm Interested as a Writer in Less Exalted Persons': An Interview with Jessica Hagedorn." *Callaloo* 31.4 (2008): 1217–28.

Covi, Giovanna. "Jessica Hagedorn's Decolonization of Subjectivity: Historical Agency beyond Gender and Nation." In *Nationalism and Sexuality: Crises of Identity*, ed. Yiorgos Kalogeras and Domna Pastourmatzi. Thessaloníki, Greece: Hellenic Association of American Studies, Aristotle University, 1996. 63–80.

De Manuel, Maria Teresa. "Jessica Hagedorn's *Dogeaters*: A Feminist Reading." *Likha* 12.2 (1990): 10–32.

Doyle, Jacqueline. "'A Love Letter to My Motherland': Jessica Hagedorn's *Dogeaters*." *Hitting Critical Mass* 4.2 (1999): 1–26.

Evangelista, Susan. "Jessica Hagedorn and Manila Magic." *MELUS* 18.4 (1993–1994): 41–52.

———. "Jessica Hagedorn: Pinay Poet." *Philippine Studies* 35.4 (1987): 475–87.

Fuh, Shyh-jen. "'At Home in the World': Transnationalism and the Question of Belonging in Jessica Hagedorn's *Dream Jungle*." *Tamkang Review* 40.2 (2010): 21–40.

Gairola, Rahul K. "Deterritorialisations of Desire: 'Transgressive' Sexuality as Filipino Anti-Imperialist Resistance in Jessica Hagedorn's *Dogeaters*." *Philament* 7 (2005): 22–41.

Gillian, Jennifer. "Border Perceptions: Reading U.S. Intervention in Roosevelt and Hagedorn." In *The Image of the Frontier in Literature, Media, and Society*, ed. William Wright et al. Pueblo: University of Southern Colorado, 1997. 121–25.

Hau, Caroline S. "*Dogeaters*, Postmodernism, and the 'Worlding' of the Philippines." In *Philippine Post-Colonial Studies: Essays on Language and Literature*, ed. Christina Pantoja-Hidalgo and Priscelina Patajo-Legasto. Quezon City: University of the Philippines, 1993. 113–27.

Lee, Suk-hee. "Cultural Colonization and Resistance: Jessica Hagedorn's *Dogeaters*." *Studies in Modern Fiction* 10.2 (2003): 219–41.

Mendible, Myra. "Desiring Images: Representation and Spectacle in *Dogeaters*." *Critique* 43.3 (2002): 289–304.

———. "Dictators, Movie Stars, and Martyrs: The Politics of Spectacle in Jessica Hagedorn's *Dogeaters*." *Genders* 36 (2002): 51 paragraphs.

Mendoza, Victor. "A Queer Nomadology of Jessica Hagedorn's *Dogeaters*." *American Literature* 77.4 (2005): 815–45.

Pearlman, Mickey, ed. "Jessica Hagedorn." In *Listen to Their Voices: Twenty Interviews with Women Who Write*. New York: Norton, 1993. 134–42.

San Juan, E., Jr. "Transforming Identity in Postcolonial Narrative: An Approach to the Novels of Jessica Hagedorn." *Post Identity* 1.2 (1998): 5–28.

See, Sarita. "Southern Postcoloniality and the Improbability of Filipino-American Postcoloniality: Faulkner's *Absalom, Absalom!* And Hagedorn's *Dogeaters*." *Mississippi Quarterly* 57.1 (2003/2004): 41–54.

Sohn, Stephen Hong. "From Discos to Jungles: Circuitous Queer Patronage and Sex Tourism in Jessica Hagedorn's *Dogeaters*." *MFS: Modern Fiction Studies* 56.2 (2010): 317–48.

Twelbeck, Kirsten. "Beyond a Postmodern Denial of Reference: Forms of Resistance in Jessica Hagedorn's *Dogeaters*." *Amerikastudien/American Studies* 51.3 (2006): 425–37.

Vizcaya Echano, Marta. "'you like to mix things up on purpose . . .? hoy, what are you trying to prove?': Representations of Recent (Hi)stories in Jessica Hagedorn's *The Gangster of Love*." *Feminist Review* 85 (2007): 70–82.

Werrlein, Debra T. "Legacies of the 'Innocent' Frontier: Failed Memory and the Infantilized Filipina Expatriate in Jessica Hagedorn's *Dogeaters*." *Journal of Asian American Studies* 7.1 (2004): 27–50.

Zamora, Maria. "Female Embodiment and the Politics of Representation in Jessica Hagedorn's *Dogeaters*." *Atenea* 26.2 (2006): 167–82.

Hahn, Kimiko

Casper, Robert N. "On 'The Tosa Diary': An Interview." *Jubilat* 17 (2009–2010): 55–61.

Chang, Juliana. "'I Cannot Find Her': The Oriental Feminine, Racial Melancholia, and Kimiko Hahn's *The Unbearable Heart*." *Meridians: Feminism, Race, Transnationalism* 4.2 (2004): 239–60.

Grotjohn, Robert. "Kimiko Hahn's 'Interlingual Poetics' in *Mosquito and Ant*." In *Transnational Asian American Literature: Sites and Transits*, ed. Shirley Lim, John Blair Gamber, et al. Philadelphia: Temple University Press, 2006. 219–34.

Kalamaras, George. "To Adore a Fragment: An Interview with Kimiko Hahn." *Bloomsbury Review* 19.2 (1999): 13–14.

Zhou, Xiaojing. "Two Hat Softeners 'In the Trade Confession': John Yau and Kimiko Hahn." In *Form and Transformation in Asian American Literature*, ed. Samina Najmi. Seattle: University of Washington Press, 2005. 168–89.

Hartmann, Sadakichi

Haslam, Gerald W. "The Exotics: Yone Noguchi, Shiesei Tsuneishi, and Sadakichi Hartmann." *CLA Journal* 19.3 (1976): 362–73.

Hill, Richard. "The First Hippie." *Swank International* 16 (1969): 16–18.

Knox, George. "A Complex Fate: Sadakichi Hartmann, Japanese-German Immigrant-Writer and Artist." *Journal of German-American Studies* 7 (1974): 38–49.

———. "Sadakichi Hartmann's The Last Thirty Days of Christ." *Christianity and Literature* 21.4 (1972): 23–29.

Knox, George, and Harry W. Lawton. *The Life and Times of Sadakichi Hartmann, 1867–1944.* Riverside: University of California Riverside Library and Riverside Press-Enterprise, 1970.

Tuerk, Richard. "Sadakichi Hartmann's 'How Poe Wrote the Raven': A Biochemical Explanation." *Markham Review* 3 (1973): 81–85.

Weaver, Jean Calhoun. "Introduction." In *Sadakichi Hartman: Critical Modernist.* Berkeley: University of California Press, 1991. 1–44.

Hongo, Garrett

Colley Sharon. "An Interview with Garrett Hongo." *Forkroads: A Journal of Ethnic American Literature* 4 (1996): 47–63.

Evan, Alice. "A Vicious Kind of Tenderness: An Interview with Garrett Hongo." *Poets and Writers Magazine* 20.5 (1992): 36–46.

Filipelli, Laurie. *Garrett Hongo*. Boise, Idaho: Boise State University Press, 1997.

"Garrett Hongo, Poet." Interview. In *Yellow Light: The Flowering of Asian American Arts*, ed. Amy Ling. Philadelphia: Temple University Press, 1999. 103–10.

Gunew, Sneja. "Gendered Reading Tactics: Public Intellectuals and Community in Diaspora." *Resources for Feminist Research* 29.1–2 (2001–2002): 57–71.

Jarman, Mark. "The Volcano Inside." *Southern Review* 32.2 (1996): 337–43.

Kamada, Roy. "Heterogeneity, Hybridity, and Multiplicity in *Volcano*: Garrett Hongo's Interventionist Poetics and the Intersectionality of Asian-American Identity." In *The Diasporic Imagination: Identifying Asian-American Representations in America*, ed. Somdatta Mandal. 2 vols. New Delhi: Prestige Books, 2000. 182–97.

Lee, A. Robert. "Ethnicities: The American Self-Tellings of Leslie Marmon Silko, Richard Rodriguez, Darryl Pickney, and Garrett Hongo." In *Writing Lives: American Biography and Autobiography*, ed. Hans Bak and Hans Krabbendam. Amsterdam, Netherlands: VU University Press, 1998. 122–35.

McCormick, Adrienne. "Theorizing Difference in Asian American Poetry Anthologies." *MELUS* 29.3–4 (2004): 59–80.

Sato, Gayle K. "Cultural Recuperation in Garrett Hongo's *The River of Heaven*." *Studies in American Literature* 37 (2001): 57–74.

Slowik, Mary. "Beyond Lot's Wife: The Immigration Poems of Marilyn Chin, Garrett Hongo, Li-Young Lee, and David Mura." *MELUS* 25.3–4 (2000): 221–43.

Tabios, Eileen. "Garrett Hongo: *Feeling* Knowing, Knowing *Feeling*." *Asian Pacific American Journal* 5.1 (1996): 139–71.

Witonsky, Trudi. "Twilight Conversations: Multicultural Dialogue." In *Asian American Studies: Identity, Images, Issues Past and Present*, ed. Esther Mikyung Ghymn. New York: Peter Lang, 2000. 217–29.

Hosseini, Khaled

Aubry, Timothy. "Afghanistan Meets the Amazon: Reading *The Kite Runner* in America." *PMLA: Publications of the Modern Language Association of America* 124.1 (2009): 25–43.

Jefferess, David. "To Be Good (Again): *The Kite Runner* as Allegory of Global Ethics." *Journal of Postcolonial Writing* 45.4 (2009 Dec): 389–400.

Lux, Elaine. "Images of Salvation and Healing in Shusaku Endo's Silence and Khaled Hosseini's *The Kite Runner*." In *Making Peace in Our Time*, ed. Joan F. Hallisey and Mary-Anne Vetterling. Weston, Mass.: Peace, with Regis College, 2008. 121–29.

Houston, Jeanne Wakatsuki

Chappell, Virginia. "But Isn't This the Land of the Free?: Resistance and Discovery in Student Responses to *Farewell to Manzanar*." In *Writing in Multicultural Settings*, ed. Carol Severiono et al. New York: MLA, 1997. 172–88.

Davis, Rocio G. "National and Ethnic Affiliation in Internet Autobiographies of Childhood by Jeanne Watasuki Houston and George Takei." *Amerikastudien/American Studies*. 51.3 (2006): 255–68.

Dong, Lan. "Eating Different, Looking Different: Food in Asian American Childhood." *Critical Approaches to Food in Children's Literature*, ed. Kara K. Keeling and Scott T. Pollard. New York: Routledge, 2009. 137–47.

Okamura, Raymond Y. "*Farewell to Manzanar*: A Case of Subliminal Racism." *Amerasia Journal* 3.2 (1976): 143–47.

Sakurai, Patricia A. "The Politics of Possession: The Negotiation of Identity in *American in Disguise*, *Homebase*, and *Farewell to Manzanar*." In *Privileging Positions: The Sites of Asian American Studies*, ed. Gary Y. Okihiro et al. Pullman: Washington University Press, 1995. 157–70.

Yamamoto, Traise. *Masking Selves, Making Subjects: Japanese American Women, Identity, and the Body*. Berkeley: University of California Press, 1999.

Houston, Velina Hasu

Haedicke, Susan. "'Suspended between Two Worlds': Interculturalism and the Rehearsal Process for Horizons Theatre's Production of Velina Hasu Houston's *Tea*." *Theatre Topics* 4.1 (1994): 89–103.

Hoang, Hahn. "Amazing Grace: Valina Hasu Houston Draws Strength and Inspiration from the Hard Adventure of Growing Up Black and Japanese." *Transpacific* July/August (1991): 37–45.

Janette, Michele. "Out of the Melting Pot and into the Frontera: Race, Sex, Nation, and Home in Velina Hasu Houston's *American Dreams*." In *Mixed Race Literature*, ed. Jonathan Brennan. Stanford, Calif.: Stanford University Press, 2002. 88–106.

Jew, Kimberly. "Dismantling the Realist Character in Velina Hasu Houston's *Tea* and David Henry Hwang's *FOB*." In *Literary Gestures: The Aesthetic in Asian American Writing*, ed. Rocio G. Davis and Sue-Im Lee. Philadelphia: Temple University Press, 2006. 187–202.

Kawarazaki, Yasuko. "Women's Struggles in Velina H. Houston's *Tea*." *AALA Journal* 2 (1995): 47–55.

Ling, Amy. "Velina Hasu Houston, Playwright and Poet." In *Yellow Light: The Flowering of Asian American Arts*, ed. Amy Ling. Philadelphia: Temple University Press, 1999. 236–40.

Usui, Masami. "Creating a Feminist Transnational Drama: *Oyako Shinju* (Parent-Child Suicide) in Velina Hasu Houston's *Kokoro* (True Heart)." *Japanese Journal of American Studies* 11 (2000): 173–98.

———. "Dreams and Nightmares, Nightmares and Dreams in Velina Hasu Houston's *American Dreams*." *Kansai American Journal* 35 (1998): 32–53.

———. "Japan's Post-War Democratization—Agrarian Reform and Women's Liberation in Velina Hasu Houston's *Asa Ga Kimashita* (Morning Has Broken)." *AALA Journal* 5 (1998): 11–25.

———. "Voices from the 'Netherworld': Japanese International Brides in Velina Hasu Houston's *Tea*." *Chu-Shikoku Studies in American Literature* 34 (1998): 45–64.

Hwang, David Henry

Alvarez López, M. Esther. "Gender and Genre Illusion: Man/Woman, Theatre, and *M. Butterfly*." In *Proceedings of the 20th International AEDEAN Conference*, ed. Guardia and J. Stone. Barcelona, Spain: Universitat de Barcelona, 1997. 347–52.

Bacalzo, Dan. "A Different Drum: David Henry Hwang's Musical 'Revisal' of *Flower Drum Song*." *Journal of American Drama and Theatre* 15.2 (2003): 71–83.

Bak, John S. "*Vestis virum reddit*: The Gender Politics of Drag in Williams's *A Streetcar Named Desire* and Hwang's *M. Butterfly*." *South Atlantic Review* 70.4 (2005): 94–118.

Bollobás, Eniko. "Making the Subject: Performative Genders in Carson McCullers' *The Ballad of the Sad Café* and David Hwang's *M. Butterfly*." *Americana: E-Journal of American Studies in Hungary* 4.1 (2008). (no pagination)

Botelho, Teresa. "The Dramatization of Cross-Identity Voicing, and the Poetics of Ambiguity." *Hungarian Journal of English and American Studies* 15.1 (2009): 79–97.

———. "Redefining the Dramatic Canon: Staging Identity Instability in the Work of David Henry Hwang and Chay Yew." In *Positioning the New: Chinese American Literature and the Changing Image of the American Literary Canon*, ed. Tanfer Emin Tunc and Elisabetta Marino. Newcastle upon Tyne, Great Britain: Cambridge Scholars, 2010. 128–42.

Boyd, Melinda. "Re-Orienting' the Vision: Ethnicity and Authenticity from Suzuki to Comrade Chin." In *A Vision of the Orient: Text, Intertexts, and Contexts of Madame Butterfly*, ed. Jonathan Wisenthal et al. Toronto: University of Toronto Press, 2006. 59–71.

Burgwinkle, William. "Negotiating Masculinity: Gendering within Sex." In *Translations/Transformations: Gender and Culture in Film and Literature East and West: Selected Conference Papers*, ed. Valerie Wayne, Cornelia Morre, and Wimal Dissanayake. Honolulu: University of Hawaii Press, 1993. 3–14.

Cavell, Richard. "Madame Butterfly and the Absence of Empire." In *A Vision of the Orient: Text, Intertexts, and Contexts of Madame Butterfly*, ed. Jonathan Wisenthal et al. Toronto: University of Toronto Press, 2006. 155–69.

Chang, Chin-ying. "Religion and Cultural Identity in Chinese American Literature: The Image of Gwan Gung in Writings by Frank Chin and David Henry Hwang." *Fiction and Drama* 19.2 (2009): 91–116.

Chang, Hsiao-hung. "Cultural/Sexual/Theatrical Ambivalence in *M. Butterfly*." *Tamkang Review* 23 (1992): 735–55.

Chang, Williamson B. C. "*M. Butterfly*: Passivity, Deviousness, and the Invisibility of the Asian-American Male." In *Bearing Dreams, Shaping Visions, Asian Pacific American Perspective*, ed. Linda A. Revilla et al. Pullman: Washington State University Press, 1993. 181–84.

Chen, Tina. "Betrayed into Motion: The Seduction of Narrative Desire in *M. Butterfly*." *Hitting Critical Mass* 1.2 (1994): 129–54.

Cheng, Anne Anlin. "Race and Fantasy in Modern America: Subjective Dissimulation/Racial Assimilation." In *Multiculturalism and Representation: Selected Essays*, ed. John Rieder and Larry E. Smith. Honolulu: University of Hawaii Press, 1996. 175–97.

Choi, Young-Joo. "Creating an Anti-Colonial Discourse: Women and Culture in *Madam Butterfly*, *Miss Saigon*, and *M. Butterfly*." *Feminist Studies in English Literature* 7.1 (1999): 87–113.

Clericuzio, Alessandro. "Labyrinths of Language and Race in L. Jones's *Dutchman* and D. H. Hwang's *Bondage*." In *America Today: Highways and Labyrinths*, ed. Gigliola Nocera. Siracusa, Italy: Grafià, 2003. 116–23.

Cody, Gabrielle. "David Hwang's *M. Butterfly*: Perpetuating the Misogynist Myth." *Theatre* 20.2 (1989): 24–7.

Cooperman, Robert. "Across the Boundaries of Cultural Identity: An Interview with David Henry Hwang." In *Staging Difference: Cultural Pluralism in American Theatre and Drama*, ed. Marc Maufort. New York: Peter Lang, 1995. 365–73.

———. "New Theatrical Statements: Asian Western Mergers in the Plays of David Henry Hwang." In *Staging Difference: Cultural Pluralism in American Theatre and Drama*, ed. Marc Maufort. New York: Peter Lang, 1995. 201–13.

Davis, Rocio G. "Desperately Seeking Stereotypes: David Henry Hwang and *M. Butterfly*." *Revista de Estudios Norteamericanos* 3 (1994): 53–64.

———. "'Just a Man': Subverting Stereotypes in David Henry Hwang's *M. Butterfly*." *Hitting Critical Mass* 6.2 (2000): 59–74.

Deeney, John J. "Of Monkeys and Butterflies: Transformation in M. H. Kingston's *Tripmaster* Monkey and D. H. Hwang's *M. Butterfly*." *MELUS* 18.4 (1993): 21–39.

Degabriele, Maria. "From *Madame Butterfly* to *Miss Saigon*: One Hundred Years of Popular Orientalism." *Critical Arts: A Journal of Cultural Studies*, 10.2 (1996): 105–18.

De Wagter, Caroline. "Performing the American Multi-Ethnic 'Other' in Hwang's *Bondage* and Geiogamah's *Foghorn*." *BELL: Belgian Journal of English Language and Literature* 4 (2006): 81–92.

Dickey, Jerry R. "'Myths of the East, Myths of the West': Shattering Racial and Gender Stereotypes in the Plays of David Henry Hwang." In *Old West-New West: Centennial Essays*, ed. Barbara Howard Meldrum. Moscow: University of Idaho Press, 1993. 272–80.

DiGaetani, John Louis. "*M. Butterfly*: An Interview with David Henry Hwang." *TDR: The Drama Review* 33.3 (1989): 141–53.

Ditor, Rachel. "*M. Butterfly*: Staging Choices and Their Meanings." In *A Vision of the Orient: Text, Intertexts, and Contexts of Madame Butterfly*, ed. Jonathan Wisenthal et al. Toronto: University of Toronto Press, 2006. 227–37.

Eng, David. "In the Shadows of a Diva: Committing Homosexuality in David Henry Hwang's *M. Butterfly*." *Amerasia Journal* 20.1 (1994): 93–116.

Frockt, Deborah. "David Henry Hwang." In *The Playwright's Art: Conversations with Contemporary Dramatists*, ed. Jackson R. Bryer. New Brunswick, N.J.: Rutgers University Press, 1995. 123–46.

Garber, Marjorie. "The Occidental Tourist: *M. Butterfly* and the Scandal of Transvestitism." In *Nationalisms and Sexualities*, ed. Andrew Parker et al. New York: Routledge, 1992. 121–46.

Geraths, Armin. "Asian-American Drama and the Unavoidable predominance of the Western Theatrical Code: D. H. Hwang's *M. Butterfly*." In *Word and Action in Drama: Studies in Honor of Hans-Jürgen Diller on the Occasion of His 60th Birthday*. Trier, Germany: Wissenschaftlicher, 1994. 213–23.

Grace, Sherrill. "Playing Butterfly with David Henry Hwang and Robert Lepage." In *A Vision of the Orient: Text, Intertexts, and Contexts of Madame Butterfly*, ed. Jonathan Wisenthal et al. Toronto: University of Toronto Press, 2006. 136–51.

Haedicke, Janet. "David Henry Hwang's *M. Butterfly*: The Eye on the Wing." *Journal of Drama Theory and Criticism* 7.1 (1992): 27–44.

Han, Yongjae. "The Theater of Law and the Law of Theater in *M. Butterfly*." *Journal of Modern British and American Drama* 23.1 (2010): 209–33.

Hanawa, Yukiko. "Inciting Sites of Political Interventions: Queer 'n Asian." In *A Queer World: The Center for Lesbian and Gay Studies Reader*. New York: New York University Press, 1997. 39–62.

Haney, William S., II. "The Phenomenology of Nonidentity and Theatrical Presence in *M. Butterfly*." *Reconstruction Studies in Contemporary Culture* 6.2 (2006). (no pagination)

Hawthorne, Melanie C. "'Du Du That Voodoo': *M. Venus* and *M. Butterfly*." *Esprit Créateur* 37.4 (1997): 58–66.

Hornbuckle, Calley. "Values and Parody in Giancomo Puccini's *Madama Butterfly* and David Henry Hwang's *M. Butterfly*." *Exit 9: The Rutgers Journal of Comparative Literature* 4 (2002): 11–17.

Hwang, David Henry. "A Conversation with David Henry Hwang." In *Bearing Dream, Shaping Visions: Asian Pacific American Perspectives*, ed. Linda A. Revilla et al. Pullman: Washington State University Press, 1993. 185–91.

Irmscher, Christoph. "'The Absolute Power of a Man'? Staging Masculinity in Giacomo Puccini and David Henry Hwang." *Amerikastudien/American Studies* 43.4 (1998): 619–28.

Jeong, Eun-sook. "The Endangered White Heterosexual Masculine American National Identity in David Henry Hwang's *M. Butterfly*." *Journal of English Language and Literature* 56.2 (2010): 187–217.

Jew, Kimberly M. "Dismantling the Realist Character in Velina Hasu Houston's *Tea* and David Henry Hwang's *FOB*." In *Literary Gestures: The Aesthetic in Asian American Writing*, ed. Rocí G. Davis and Sue-Im Lee. Philadelphia: Temple University Press, 2006. 187–202.

Kang, Hyeong-min. "Unmasking the Colonial Politics of Violence: David Henry Hwang's *M. Butterfly*." *Journal of Modern British and American Drama* 18.1 (2005): 23–46.

Kang, Taekyeong. "Who's Afraid of Madame Butterfly? The Broadway Reception of *M. Butterfly*." *Journal of English Language and Literature* 48.1 (2002): 25–52.

Kehde, Suzanne. "Engendering the Imperial Subject: The (De)Construction of (Western) Masculinity in David Henry Hwang's *M. Butterfly* and Graham Greene's *The Quiet American*." In *Fictions of Masculinity: Crossing Cultures, Crossing Sexualities*. New York: New York University Press, 1994. 241–54.

Kerr, Douglas. "David Henry Hwang and the Revenge of Madame Butterfly." In *Asian Voices in English*, ed. Mimi Chan and Roy Harris. Hong Kong: Hong Kong University Press, 1991. 119–30.

Koh, Karlyn. "(Dis)Placing Identities: Cultural Transvestism in David Henry Hwang's *M. Butterfly*." *West Coast Line* 28.13–14 (1994): 246–54.

Kondo, Dorinne K. "Interview with David Henry Hwang." In *About Face: Performing Race in Fashion and Theater*. New York: Routledge, 1997. 221–25.

———. "*M. Butterfly*: Orientalism, Gender, and a Critique of Essentialist Identity." *Cultural Critique* 16 (1990): 5–29.

Kong, Foong Ling. "Pulling the Wings off Butterfly." *Southern Review* 27.4 (1994): 418–31.

Lin, Hsiu-Chen. "Staging Orientalia: Dangerous 'Authenticity' in David Henry Hwang's *M. Butterfly.*" *Journal of American Drama and Theatre* 9.1 (1997): 26–35.

Liu, Cecilia Hsueh Chen. "Writing Back to the Empire: From *M. Butterfly* to *Madame Butterfly.*" In *Re-Imagining Language and Literature for the 21st Century,* ed. Suthira Duangsamosorn. Amsterdam: Rodopi, 2005. 331–44.

Loo, Chalsa. "*M. Butterfly*: A Feminist Perspective." In *Bearing Dreams, Shaping Visions, Asian Pacific American Perspectives*, ed. Linda A. Revilla et al. Pullman: Washington State University Press, 1993. 177–80.

Lye, Colleen. "*M. Butterfly* and the Rhetoric of Anti-Essentialism: Minority Discourse in an International Frame." In *The Ethnic Canon: Histories, Institutions, and Interventions*, ed. David Palumbo-Liu. Minneapolis: University of Minnesota Press, 1995. 260–89.

Lyons, Bonnie. "'Making His Muscles Work for Himself': An Interview with Davie Henry Hwang." *Literary Review* 42.2 (1999): 230–44.

Ma, Sheng-mei. "David Henry Hwang's *M. Butterfly*: From Puccini to East/Western Androgyny." *Tamkang Review: A Quarterly of Comparative Studies between Chinese and Foreign Literatures* 21.3 (1991): 287–96.

Martin, Robert K. "Gender, Race, and the Colonial Body: Carson McCuller's Filipino Boy and David Henry Hwang's Chinese Woman." *Canadian Review of American Studies* 23.1 (1992): 95–106.

McInturff, Kate. "That Old Familiar Song: The Theatre of Culture in David Henry Hwang's *M. Butterfly.*" In *A Vision of the Orient: Text, Intertexts, and Contexts of Madame Butterfly*, ed. Jonathan Wisenthal et al. Toronto: University of Toronto Press, 2006. 72–88.

Morris, Rosalind. "*M. Butterfly*: Transvestism and Cultural Cross Dressing in the Critique of Empire." In *Gender and Culture in Literature and Film East and West: Issues of Perception and Interpretation*, ed. Chicana Nagavajara et al. Honolulu: University of Hawaii Press, 1994. 40–59.

Moss-Coane, Mary, and John Timpane. "David Henry Hwang." In *Speaking on Stage: Interviews with Contemporary American Playwrights*, ed. Philip C. Kolin and Colby H. Kullman. Tuscaloosa: University of Alabama Press, 1996. 277–90.

Moy, James. "David Henry Hwang's *M. Butterfly* and Philip Kan Gotanda's *Yankee Dawg You Die*: Repositioning Chinese American Marginality on the American Stage." *Theatre Journal* 42 (1990): 48–56.

Neely, Kent. "Intimacy or Cruel Love: Displacing the Other by Self Assertion." *Journal of Dramatic Theory and Criticism* 5.2 (1991): 167–73.

Pao, Angela. "The Critic and the Butterfly: Sociocultural Contexts and the Reception of David Henry Hwang's *M. Butterfly.*" *Amerasia Journal* 18.3 (1992): 1–16.

Remen, Kathryn. "The Theatre of Punishment: David Henry Hwang's *M. Butterfly* and Michael Foucault's *Discipline and Punish.*" *Modern Drama* 37.3 (1994): 391–400.

Ross, Deborah L. "On the Trail of the Butterfly: D. H. Hwang and Transformation." In *Beyond Adaptation: Essays on Radical Transformation of Original Works*, ed. Phyllis Frus and Christy Williams. Jefferson, N.C.: McFarland, 2010. 111–22.

Rossini, Jon D. "From *M. Butterfly* to *Bondage*: David Henry Hwang's Fantasies of Sexuality, Ethnicity, and Gender." *Journal of American Drama and Theatre* 18.3 (2006): 54–76.

Saal, Ilka. "Performance and Perception: Gender, Sexuality, and Culture in David Henry Hwang's *M. Butterfly*." *Amerikastudien/American Studies* 43.4 (1998): 629–44.

Savran, David. "David Henry Hwang." In *Their Own Words: Contemporary American Playwrights*. New York: Theatre Communications Group, 1988. 117–31.

Seguro, Gómez. "*M. Butterfly* as Total Theatre." *BELLS: Barcelona English Language and Literature Studies* 15 (2006): 1–12.

Selim, Yasser Fouad A. "The Theatre of David Henry Hwang: From Hyphenation to the Mainstream." In *Positioning the New: Chinese American Literature and the Changing Image of the American Literary Canon*, ed. Tanfer Emin Tunc and Elisabetta Marino. Newcastle upon Tyne, GREAT: Cambridge Scholars, 2010. 114–27.

Shimakawa, Karen. "'Who's to Say?' or, Making Space for Gender and Ethnicity in *M. Butterfly*." *Theatre Journal* 45.3 (1993): 349–61.

Shin, Andrew. "Projected Bodies in David Henry Hwang's *M. Butterfly* and *Golden Gate*." *MELUS* 27.1 (2002): 177–97.

Skloot, Robert. "Breaking the Butterfly: The Politics of David Henry Hwang." *Modern Drama* 33.1 (1990): 59–66.

Street, Douglas. *David Henry Hwang*. Boise, Idaho: Boise State University, 1989.

Testa, Bart. "Late Mutations of Cinema's Butterfly." In *A Vision of the Orient: Text, Intertexts, and Contexts of Madame Butterfly*, ed. Jonathan Wisenthal et al. Toronto: University of Toronto Press, 2006. 91–122.

Volkmann, Laurenz. "David Henry Hwang, *M. Butterfly*." In *Drama, Part I*, ed. Susanne Peters et al. Trier, Germany: Wissenschaftlicher, 2006. 179–202.

Wantanabe, Yuriko. "Why *Madame Butterfly* Matters: From Modernity to Postmodernity." In *The Image of Europe in Literature, Media, and Society*, ed. Will Wright and Steven Kaplan. Pueblo: University of Southern Colorado, 2001. 64–70.

Wong, William. "*M. Butterfly*: A Symbol of Mainstream Success or Selling Out?" *East/West News* 4 (1988): 6–9.

Woo, Misseong. "Gender Trouble in Asian American Literature: David Henry Hwang's *The Sound of a Voice*." *Feminist Studies in English Literature* 11.2 (2003): 291–317.

Xie, Jingjing. "*M. Butterfly*: A Subversive Performance of Icon." In *Re-Reading America: Changes and Challenges*, ed. Weihe Zhong and Rui Han. Cheltenham, Great Britain: Reardon, 2004. 158–72.

Inada, Lawson Fusao

Balestrini, Nassim W. "Between California and Camp: Space and Structure in the Multipart Poems of Lawson Fusao Inada." In *Ideas of Order in Contemporary*

American Poetry, ed. Diana von Finck et al. Würzburg, Germany: Königshausen & Neumann, 2007. 173–93.

Burt, Ryan. "Interning America's Colonial History: The Anthologies and Poetry of Lawson Fusao Inada." *MELUS* 35.3 (2010): 105–30.

Chang, Juliana. "Time, Jazz, and the Racial Subject: Lawson Inada's Jazz Poetics." In *Racing and (E)Racing Language: Living with the Color of Our Words*, ed. Ellen J. Goldner and Safiya Henderson-Holmes. Syracuse, N.Y.: Syracuse University Press, 2001. 134–54.

Salisbury, Ralph. "Dialogue with Lawson Fusao Inada." *Northwest Review* 20.2–3 (1982): 60–75.

Sato, Gayle K. "Lawson F. Inada." In *Reading Japanese American Literature: The Legacy of Three Generations*, ed. Teruyo Ueki and Gayle K. Sato. Osaka, Japan: Sogensha, 1999. 168–75.

———. "Lawson Inada's Poetics of Relocation: Weathering, Nesting, Leaving the Bough." *Amerasia Journal* 26.3 (2000–2001): 139–60.

Yogi, Stan. "Yearning for the Past: The Dynamics of Memory in Sansei Internment Poetry." In *Memory and Cultural Politics: New Approaches to American Ethnic Literatures*, ed. Amritjit Singh et al. Boston: Northeastern University Press, 1996. 245–65.

Zhou, Xiaojing. "Spatial Construction and Management of the 'Enemy Race': US Concentration Camps." In *The Camp: Narratives of Internment and Exclusion*, ed. Colman Hogan and Marta Marín Dòmine. Newcastle upon Tyne, Great Britain: Cambridge Scholars, 2007. 92–114.

Jen, Gish

Ahokas, Pirjo. "Migrating Multiculturalisms in Zadie Smith's *On Beauty* and Gish Jen's *Mona in the Promised Land.*" In *Moving Migration: Narrative Transformations in Asian American Literature*, ed. Johanna C. Kardux et al. Münster, Germany: Lit, 2010. 161–77.

Arfaroui, Siham. "A Quest for a 'House with no Walls between the Rooms': An Ethnic Approach to Gish Jen's *Mona in the Promised Land.*" *Interactions: Ege University Journal of British and American Studies* 17.1 (2008): 15–27.

Brada-Williams, Noelle "Interethnic Relationships in Chang-rae Lee's Native Speaker and Gish Jen's Birthmates." In *Close Encounters of an Other Kind: New Perspectives on Race, Ethnicity, and American Studies*, ed. Roy Goldblatt et al. Joensuu, Finland: University of Joensuu Press, 2005. 18–25.

Byers, Michele. "Material Bodies and Performative Identities: Mona, Neil, and the Promised Land." *Philip Roth Studies* 2.2 (2006): 102–20.

Chen, Fu-jen. "The Parallax Gap in Gish Jen's *The Love Wife*: The Imaginary Relationship between First-World and Third-World Women." *Critique: Studies in Contemporary Fiction* 51.4 (2010): 394–415.

———. "Postmodern Hybridity and Performing Identity in Gish Jen and Rebecca Walker." *Critique: Studies in Contemporary Fiction* 50.4 (2009): 377–96.

Chen, Shu-ching. "Disjuncture at Home: Mapping the Domestic Cartographies of Transnationalism in Gish Jen's *The Love Wife*." *Tamkang Review: A Quarterly of Literary and Cultural Studies* 37.2 (2006): 1–32.

Feddersen, R. C. "From Story to Novel and Back Again: Gish Jen's Developing Art of Short Fiction." In *Creative and Critical Approaches to the Short Story*, ed. Noel Harold Kaylor, Jr. Lewiston, N.Y.: Edwin Mellen, 1997. 345–58.

Feng, Pin-chia. "Reinventing a Chinese American Women's Tradition in Gish Jen's *Mona in the Promised Land*." *EurAmerica: A Journal of European and American Studies* 32.4 (2002): 675–704.

Freedman, Jonathan. "'Who's Jewish?': Some Asian-American Writers and the Jewish-American Literary Canon." *Michigan Quarterly Review* 42.1 (2003): 230–54.

Furman, Andrew. "Immigrant Dreams and Civic Promises: (Con-)Testing Identity in Early Jewish American Literature and Gish Jen's *Mona in the Promised Land*." *MELUS* 25.1 (2000): 209–26.

Huang, Betsy. "The Redefinition of the 'Typical Chinese' in Gish Jen's *Typical American*." *Hitting Critical Mass* 4.2 (1997): 61–77.

Lee, A. Robert. "Imagined Cities of China: Timothy Mo's London, Sky Lee's Vancouver, Fae Myenne Ng's San Francisco and Gish Jen's New York." *Hitting Critical Mass* 4.1 (1996): 103–19.

Lee, Don. "About Gish Jen." *Ploughshares* 26.2–3 (2000): 217–22.

Lee, Rachel. "Failed Performances of the Nation in Gish Jen's *Typical American*." In *Navigating Islands and Continents: Conversations and Contestations in and around the Pacific*, ed. Cynthia Franklin et al. Honolulu: University of Hawaii, 2000. 63–79.

———. "Gish Jen." In *Words Matter: Conversations with Asian American Writers*, ed. King-Kok Cheung. Honolulu: University of Hawaii Press, 2000. 215–32.

Lin, Erika T. "Mona on the Phone: The Performative Body and Racial Identity in *Mona in the Promised Land*." *MELUS* 28.2 (2003): 47–57.

Ling, Amy. "Cultural Cross-Dressing in *Mona in the Promised Land*." In *Asian American Literature in the International Context: Readings on Fiction, Poetry, and Performance*, ed. Rocío G. Davis and Sämi Ludwig. Hamburg, Germany: Lit, 2002. 227–36.

Matsukawa, Yoko. "*MELUS* Interview with: Gish Jen." *MELUS* 18.4 (1993/1994): 111–20.

Mok, Nelly. "Sabotaging the 'Cultural Bridge,' Dropping the Hyphen: Love and Sexuality as Escape Routes in Gish Jen's *Mona in the Promised Land*." In *Positioning the New: Chinese American Literature and the Changing Image of the American Literary Canon*, ed. Tanfer Emin Tunc and Elisabetta Marino. Newcastle upon Tyne, Great Britain: Cambridge Scholars, 2010. 39–51.

Partridge, Jeffrey F. L. "Gish Jen's Mona in the Promised Land." In *American Writers: Classics, Volume II*, ed. Jay Parini. New York: Scribner's, 2004. 215–32.

———. "Re-Viewing the Literary Chinatown: Hybridity in Gish Jen's *Mona in the Promised Land*." In *Complicating Constructions: Race, Ethnicity, and Hybridity in American Texts*, ed. David S. Goldstein and Audrey B. Thacker. Seattle: University of Washington, 2007. 99–120.

Satz, Martha. "Writing about the Things That Are Dangerous: A Conversation with Gish Jen." *Southwest Review* 78.1 (1993): 132–40.

Tang, Weming. "Translating and Transforming the American Dream: Jade Snow Wong's *Fifth Chinese Daughter* and Gish Ren's *Typical American*." In *China Abroad: Travels, Subjects, Spaces, Hong Kong*, ed. Elaine Yee Lin Ho and Julia Kuehn. Hong Kong: Hong Kong University Press, 2009. 123–37.

TuSmith, Bonnie. "Success Chinese American Style: Gish Jen's *Typical American*." *Proteus: A Journal of Ideas* 11.2 (1994): 21–26.

Wang, Chih-ming. "'An Identity Switch': A Critique of Multiculturalism in Gish Jen's *Mona in the Promised Land*." In *Crossing Oceans: Reconfiguring American Literary Studies in the Pacific Rim*, ed. Noelle Brada-Williams and Karen Chow. Hong Kong: Hong Kong University Press, 2004. 139–54.

———. "'An Onstage Costume Change': Modernity and Immigrant Experience in Gish Jen's *Typical American*." *NTU Studies in Language and Literature* 11 (2002): 71–96.

———. "Writing on the Slash: Experience, Identification, and Subjectivity in Gish Jen's Novels." *Sun Yat-sen Journal of Humanities* 13 (2001): 103–17.

Wong, Sau-Ling Cynthia. "But What in the World Is an Asian American? Culture, Class and Invented Traditions in Gish Jen's *Mona in the Promised Land*." *Eur America: A Journal of European and American Studies* 32.4 (2002): 641–74.

Zhou, Xiaojing. "Becoming Americans: Gish Jen's *Typical American*." In *The Immigrant Experience in North American Literature: Carving Out a Niche*, ed. Katherine B. Payant and Toby Rose. Westport, Conn.: Greenwood, 1999. 151–63.

Jin, Ha

Geyh, Paula E. "An Interview with Ha Jin." *Boulevard* 17.3 (2002): 127–40.

Hofmann, Bettina. "Ha Jin's *A Free Life*: Revisiting the Kunstlerroman." In *Moving Migration: Narrative Transformations in Asian American Literature*, ed. Johanna C. Kardux and Doris Einsiedel. Hamburg, Germany: Lit, 2010. 199–212.

Juncker, Clara. "The New Americans: Ha Jin's Immigration Stories." In *Positioning the New: Chinese American Literature and the Changing Image of the American Literary Canon*, ed. Tanfer Emin Tunc and Elisabetta Marino. Great Britain: Cambridge Scholars, 2010. 216–28.

Nelson, Liza. "Ha Jin: An Interview with Liza Nelson." *Five Points: A Journal of Literature and Art* 5.1 (2000): 52–67.

Oh, Seiwoong. "Cultural Translation in Ha Jin's *Waiting*." In *Querying the Genealogy: Comparative and Transnational Studies in Chinese American Literature*, ed. Jennie Wang. Shanghai: Shanghai Yiwen Press, 2006. 420–27.

Parascandola, Louis J. "Love and Sex in a Totalitarian Society: An Exploration of Ha Jin and George Orwell." *Studies in the Humanities* 32.1 (2005): 38–49.

Shan, Te-hsing. "In the Ocean of Words: An Interview with Ha Jin." *Tamkang Review* 38.2 (2008): 135–57.

Sturr, Robert D. "The Presence of Walt Whitman in Ha Jin's *Waiting*." *Walt Whitman Quarterly Review* 20.1 (2002): 1–18.

Varsava, Jerry. "An Interview with Ha Jin." *Contemporary Literature* 51.1 (2010): 1–26.

Walsh, William. "Shakespeare's Lion and Ha Jin's Tiger: The Interplay of Imagination and Reality." *Papers on Language and Literature* 42.4 (2006): 339–59.

Zhang, Hang. "Bilingual Creativity in Chinese English: Ha Jin's *In the Pond*." *World Englishes* 21.2 (2002): 305–15.

Zhang, Mindy. "A Conversation with Ha Jin." *Valley Voices: A Literary Review* 8.1 (2008): 29–34.

Zhou, Xiaojing. "Writing Otherwise Than as a 'Native Informant': Ha Jin's Poetry." In *Transnational Asian American Literature: Sites and Transits*, ed. Shirley Geok-lin Lim et al. Philadelphia: Temple University Press, 2006. 274–94.

Kang, Younghill

Huh, Joonok. "'Strangest Chorale': New York City in *East Goes West* and *Native Speaker*." In *The Image of the Twentieth Century in Literature, Media, and Society*, ed. Will Wright and Steven Kaplan. Pueblo, Colo.: Society for the Interdisciplinary Study of Social Imagery, University of Southern Colorado, 2000. 419–22.

Kim, Joanne H. "Mediating Selves: Younghill Kang's Balancing Act." *Hitting Critical Mass* 6.1 (1999): 51–9.

Knadler, Stephen. "Unacquiring Negrophobia: Younghill Kang and Cosmopolitan Resistance to the Black and White Logic of Naturalization." In *Recovered Legacies: Authority and Identity in Early Asian American Literature*, ed. Keith Lawrence and Floyd Cheung. Philadelphia: Temple University Press, 2005. 98–119.

Lee, Kun Jong. "The African-American Presence in Younghill Kang's *East Goes West*." *CLA Journal* 45.3 (2002): 329–59.

Lee, Kyhan. "Younghill Kang and the Genesis of Korean-American Literature." *Korea Journal* 31.4 (1991): 63–78.

Lew, Walter K. "Grafts, Transplants, Translation: the Americanizing of Younghill Kang." In *Modernism, Inc.: Body, Memory, Capital*, ed. Jani Scandura and Michael Thurston. New York: New York University Press, 2001. 171–90.

Min, Jinyoung. "Study on Younghill Kang's *The Grass Roof*—Focusing on Its Writing Strategies." *British and American Fiction to 1900* 15.2 (2008): 185–211.

Solberg, S.E. "*Clay Walls*: Korean-American Pioneers." *Korean Culture* (1986): 30–35.

Sorensen, Leif. "Re-Scripting the Korean-American Subject: Constructions of Authorship in New Il Han and Younghill Kang." *Genre* 39.3 (2006): 141–55.

Szmanko, Klara. "America Is in the Head and on the Ground: Confronting and (Re-) Constructing 'America' in Three Asian American Narratives of the 1930s." *Interactions: Aegean Journal of English and American Studies* 15.2 (2006): 113–23.

Yun, Chung-Hei. "Beyond *Clay Walls*." In *Reading the Literatures of Asian America*, ed. Shirley Geok-lin Lim and Amy Ling. Philadelphia: Temple University Press, 1992. 79–95.

Keller, Nora Okja

Cho, Sungran. "Adieu: The Ethics of Narrative Mourning—Reading Nora Okja Keller's *Comfort Woman.*" *Studies in Modern Fiction* 10.1 (2003): 89–104.

Chu, Patricia P. "'To Hide Her True Self': Sentimentality and the Search for an Intersubjective Self in Nora Okja Keller's *Comfort Woman.*" In *Asian North American Identities: Beyond the Hyphen*, ed. Eleanor Ty and Donald C. Goellnicht. Bloomington: Indiana University Press, 2004. 61–83.

Chuh, Kandice. "Discomforting Knowledge: Or, Korean 'Comfort Women' and Asian Americanist Critical Practice." *Journal of Asian American Studies* 6.1 (2003): 5–23.

Dong, Lan. "Teaching Nora Okja Keller's *Comfort Woman* in a Comparative Literature Classroom." In *Teaching the Novel across the Curriculum: A Handbook for Educators*, ed. Colin C. Irvine. Westport, Conn.: Greenwood, 2008. 84–93.

Kim, Jodi. "Haunting History: Violence, Trauma, and the Politics of Memory in Nora Okja Keller's *Comfort Woman.*" *Hitting Critical Mass* 6.1 (1999): 61–78.

Koo, Eunsook. "The Colonized Female Body, Nationalism and Colonialism: Nora Okja Keller's *Comfort Woman.*" *Journal of English Language and Literature* 47.2 (2001): 471–86.

Lee, Kun Jong. "Princess Pari in Nora Okja Keller's *Comfort Woman.*" *Positions: East Asia Cultures Critique* 12.2 (2004): 431–56.

Lee, Seonju. "Nora Okja Keller's Tentative Approach to Kijichon Prostitution Women." *Studies in Modern Fiction* 12.2 (2005): 99–123.

Lee, So-Hee. "The Alternative Diaspora and Female Body in *Fox Girl.*" *Feminist Studies in English Literature* 15.1 (2007): 81–106.

———. "Cultural Citizenship as Subject-Making in *Comfort Woman* and *A Gesture Life.*" *Feminist Studies in English Literature* 14.2 (2006): 91–123.

———. "A Study of First-Person Narrative in *Comfort Woman*: From a Perspective of Women's Speaking and Writing." *Feminist Studies in English Literature* 10.2 (2002): 163–88.

Lee, Sung-Ae. "Re-Visioning Gendered Folktales in Novels by Mia Yun and Nora Okja Keller." *Asian Ethnology* 68.1 (2009): 131–50.

Lee, Young-Oak. "Nora Okja Keller and the Silenced Woman: An Interview." *MELUS* 28.4 (2003): 145–65.

Madsen, Deborah L. "Nora Okja Keller: Telling Trauma in the Transnational Military-(Sex)Industrial Complex." *Interactions: Aegean Journal of English and American Studies* 15.2 (2006): 75–84.

Najmi, Samina. "Decolonizing the Bildungsroman: Narratives of War and Womanhood in Nora Okja Keller's *Comfort Woman.*" In *Form and Transformation in Asian American Literature*, ed. Zhou Xiaojing. Seattle: University of Washington Press, 2005. 209–30.

Schultermandl, Silvia. "Hooked on the American Dream? Transnational Sexual Labor in Nora Okja Keller's *Fox Girl.*" *Feminist Studies in English Literature* 15.2 (2007): 159–84.

———. "Of Princesses Pari and Fox Girls: Nora Okja Keller's Transnational Performance of Korean Histories and Myths." In *Transnationalism and the Asian American Heroine: Essays on Literature, Film, Myth and Media*, ed. Lan Dong. Jefferson, N.C.: McFarland, 2010. 9–25.

———. "Writing Rape, Trauma, and Transnationality onto the Female Body: Matrilineal Em-body-ment in Nora Okja Keller's *Comfort Woman*." *Meridians: Feminism, Race, Transnationalism* 7.2 (2007): 71–100.

Usui, Masami. "Sexual Colonialism in Korea/Japan/America Spheres in Nora Okja Keller's *Comfort Woman* and *Fox Girl*." *Journal of American Studies* 36.1 (2004): 255–83.

Kim, Myung Mi

Chiu, Jeannie. "Identities in Process: the Experimental Poetry of Mei-Mei Berssenbrugge and Myung Mi Kim." In *Asian North American Identities: Beyond the Hyphen*, ed. Eleanory Ty and Donald C. Goellnicht. Bloomington: Indiana University Press, 2004. 84–101.

Jeon, Joseph Jonghyun. "Speaking in Tongues: Myung Mi Kim's Stylized Mouths." *Studies in the Literary Imagination* 37.1 (2004): 127–48.

Keller, Lynn. "An Interview with Myung Mi Kim." *Contemporary Literature* 49.3 (2008): 335–56.

Kim, Eui Young. "'Here, This Speck and This Speck That You Missed': A Poetics of the Archive in Myung Mi Kim's Commons." *Journal of English Language and Literature* 56.6 (2010): 1119–133.

Lee, James Kyung-Jin. "Interview with Myung Mi Kim." In *Words Matter: Conversations with Asian American Writers*, ed. King-Kok Cheung. Honolulu: University of Hawaii Press, 2000. 92–104.

Liu, Warren. "Making Common the Commons: Myung Mi Kim's Ideal Subject." In *American Poets in the 21st Century: The New Poetics*, ed. Claudia Rankine and Lisa Sewell. Middletown, Conn.: Wesleyan University Press, 2007. 252–66.

Park, Josephine Nock Hee. "'Composed of Many Lengths of Bone': Myung Mi Kim's Reimagination of Image and Epic." In *Transnational Asian American Literature: Sites and Transits*, ed. Shirley Geok-lin Lim et al. Philadelphia: Temple University Press, 2006. 235–56.

Schultz, Kathy Lou. "Kathy Lou Schultz on Myung Mi Kim." In *Women Poets on Mentorship: Efforts and Affections*, ed. Arielle Greenberg and Rachel Zucker. Iowa City: University of Iowa Press, 2008. 207–16.

Zhou, Xiaojing. "'What Story What Story What Sound': The Nomadic Poetics of Myung Mi Kim's Dura." *College Literature* 34.4 (2007): 63–91.

Kim, Richard E.

Galloway, David D. "The Love Stance: Richard E. Kim's *The Martyred*." *Critique* 7 (1964–1965): 163–71.

Kang, Jung In. "Politics and Truth: An Analysis of Richard E. Kim's Novel, *The Martyred.*" *Korea Journal* 47.2 (2007): 184–207.

Lawrence, Keith. "Toshio Mori, Richard Kim, and the Masculine Ideal." In *Recovered Legacies: Authority and Identity in Early Asian American Literature*, ed. Keith Lawrence and Floyd Cheung: Philadelphia: Temple University Press, 2005. 207–28.

Sung, Ae-Lee. "History and Displacement: Liminal Subjectivity in Narratives from and about Korea." In *Remaking Literary History*, ed. Helen Groth, Helen and Paul Sheehan. Newcastle upon Tyne, Great Britain: Cambridge Scholars, 2010. 179–90.

Kingston, Maxine Hong

Ahokas, Pirjo. "Constructing Diasporic Chinese American Masculinities in Maxine Hong Kingston's *China Men.*" In *Seeking the Self-Encountering the Other: Diasporic Narrative and the Ethics of Representation*, ed. Tuomas Huttunen, Kaisa Ilmonen, Janne Korkka, and Elina Valovirta. Newcastle upon Tyne, Great Britain: Cambridge Scholars, 2008. 106–35.

Arfaroui, Silham. "The Double-Voiced Undone: Maxine Hong Kingston's *The Woman Warrior*: *Memoirs of a Girlhood among Ghosts* and Fae Myenne Ng's *Bone*." *Interactions: Aegean Journal of English and American Studies* 16.2 (2007): 1–11.

———. "Feeding the Memory with Culinary Resistance: *The Woman Warrior*: *Memoirs of a Girlhood among Ghosts*, *The Joy Luck Club* and *The Kitchen God's Wife*." *Interactions: Aegean Journal of English and American Studies* 15.2 (2006): 37–48.

Banerjee, Mita. "The Asian American in a Turtleneck: Fusing the Aesthetic and the Didactic in Maxine Hong Kingston's *Tripmaster Monkey.*" In *Literary Gestures: The Aesthetic in Asian American Writing*, ed. Rocio G. Davis and Sue-Im Lee. Philadelphia: Temple University Press, 2006. 55–69.

———. "Black Bottoms, Yellow Skin: From Ma Rainey to Maxine Hong Kingston's *Tripmaster Monkey.*" *Amerikastudien/American Studies* 45.3 (2000): 405–23.

Bolaki, Stella. "'It Translated Well': The Promise and the Perils of Translation in Maxine Hong Kingston's *The Woman Warrior.*" *MELUS* 34.4 (2009): 39–60.

Cen, Lok Chua. "Two Chinese Versions of the American Dream: The Golden Mountain in Lin Yutang and Maxine Hong Kingston." *MELUS* 8.4 (1981): 61–70.

Chen, Fu-jen. "Asian-American Literature and a Lacanian Reading of Maxine Hong Kingston's *Tripmaster Monkey.*" *Comparatist: Journal of the Southern Comparative Literature Association* 31 (2007): 105–29.

Cheung, King-kok. "The Deployment of Chinese Classics by Frank Chin and Maxine Hong Kingston." In *Querying the Genealogy: Comparative and Transnational Studies in Chinese American Literature*, ed. Jennie Wang. Shanghai, China: Shanghai Yiwen press, 2006. 217–30.

———. "'Don't' Tell': Imposed Silences in *The Color Purple* and *The Woman Warrior.*" *PMLA* 103 (1988): 162–74.

———. "Provocative Silence: *The Woman Warrior* and *China Men*." In *Articulating Silences: Narrative Strategies in Hisaye Yamamoto, Maxine Hong Kingston, and Joy Kogawa*. Ithaca, N.Y.: Cornell University Press, 1993. 74–124

———. "*The Woman Warrior* versus the *Chinaman Pacific*: Must a Chinese-American Critic Choose between Feminism and Heroism?" In *Conflicts in Feminism*, ed. Marianne Hirsch and Evelyn Fox Keller. New York: Routledge, 1990. 234–51.

Chin, Frank. "This Is Not an Autobiography." *Genre* 18 (1985): 109–30.

Chin, Marilyn. "A MELUS Interview: Maxine Hong Kingston." *MELUS* 16.4 (1989–1990): 57–74.

Chiu, Jeannie. "Fox Spirits in Hualing Nieh's *Mulberry and Peach* and Maxine Hong Kingston's *China Men*." *Notes on Contemporary Literature* 33.1 (2003): 3–5.

Chiu, Monica. "Being Human in the Wor(l)d: Chinese Men and Maxine Hong Kingston's Reworking of *Robinson Crusoe*." *Journal of American Studies* 34.2 (2000): 187–206.

Christie, Stuart. "Centrifugal Tendencies around the Rim: Reading Maxine Hong Kingston's *The Woman Warrior* in the Hong Kong University Classroom." In *English and Globalization: Perspectives from Hong Kong and Mainland China*, ed. Tam Kwok-kan and Timothy Weiss. Hong Kong: Chinese University Press, 2004. 85–89.

Chu, Patricia. "'The Invisible World the Immigrants Built': Cultural Self-Inscription and the Antiromantic Plots of *The Woman Warrior*." *Diaspora: A Journal of Transnational Studies* 2.1 (1992): 95–115.

Chun, Gloria. "The High Note of the Barbarian Reed Pipe: Maxine Hong Kingston." *The Journal of Ethnic Studies* 19.3 (1991): 85–94.

Crafton, Lisa Plummer. "'We Are Going to Carve Revenge on Your Back': Language, Culture, and the Female Body in Kingston's *The Woman Warrior*." In *Women as Sites of Culture: Women's Roles in Cultural Formation from the Renaissance to the Twentieth Century*, ed. Susan Shifrin. Aldershot, Great Britain: Ashgate, 2002. 51–63.

Crow, Charles L. *Maxine Hong Kingston*. Boise, Idaho: Boise State University, 2004.

De La Vars, Lauren P. "*The Woman Warrior* and the Hero's Journey." In *The Hero's Journey*, ed. Harold Bloom and Blake Hobby. New York: Bloom's Literary Criticism, 2009. 215–23.

Den Tandt, Christophe. "Pragmatic Commitments: Postmodern Realism in Don DeLillo, Maxine Hong Kingston and James Ellroy." In *Beyond Postmodernism: Reassessments in Literature, Theory, and Culture*, ed. Klaus Stierstorfer. Berlin, Germany: de Gruyter, 2003. 121–41.

Farrell, Mary. "Fractured Frames: From Memory to Memoir, Perec and Kingston." In *A Place That Is Not a Place: Essays in Liminality and Text*, ed. Isabel Soto. Madrid: Gateway, 2000. 95–114.

Fishkin, Shelley Fisher. "Interview with Maxine Hong Kingston." *American Literary History* 3.4 (1991): 782–91.

Gao, Yan. *The Art of Parody: Maxine Hong Kingston's Use of Chinese Sources*. New York: Peter Lang, 1996.

Gardam, Sarah C. "'Maggots in the Rice': Women as a Sex-Class in *The Woman Warrior.*" In *Narratives of Community: Women's Short Story Sequences*, ed. Roxanne Harde. Newcastle, Great Britain: Cambridge Scholars, 2007. 286–304.

Gil, Isabel Capeloa. "'Arms and the Woman I Sing . . .': *The Woman Warrior* Reloading the Can(n)on?" In *Memory, Haunting, Discourse*, ed. Maria Holmgren Troy and Elisabeth Wenno. Karlstad, Sweden: Karlstads Universitet, 2005. 229–42.

Goellnicht, Donald C. "Father Land and/or Mother Tongue: The Divided Female Subject in Kogawa's *Obasan* and Hong Kingston's *The Woman Warrior.*" In *Redefining Autobiography in Twentieth-Century Women's Fiction: An Essay Collection*, ed. Janice Morgan and Colette T. Hall. New York: Garland, 1991. 119–34.

———. "Tang Ao in America: Male Subject Positions in *China Men.*" In *Reading the Literatures of Asian America*, ed. Shirley Geok-lin Lim and Amy Ling. Philadelphia: Temple University Press, 1992. 191–214.

Grice, Helena. "'The Beginning Is Hers': The Political and Literary Legacies of Maxine Hong Kingston and Amy Tan." In *China Fictions/English Language: Literary Essays in Diaspora, Memory, Story*, ed. Robert A. Lee. Amsterdam: Rodopi, 2008. 33–55.

Griffiths, Jennifer. "Uncanny Spaces: Trauma, Cultural Memory, and the Female Body in Gayl Jones's *Corregidora* and Maxine Hong Kingston's *The Woman Warrior.*" *Studies in the Novel* 38.3 (2006): 353–70.

Gsoels-Lorensen, Jutta. "Impossibilized Subjects in Maxine Hong Kingston's *China Men*: Thoughts on Migrancy and the State of Exception." *Mosaic: A Journal for the Interdisciplinary Study of Literature* 43.3 (2010): 103–18.

Haynes, Rosetta R. "Intersections of Race, Gender, Sexuality and Experimentation in the Autobiographical Writings of Cherrie Moraga and Maxine Hong Kingston." In *Women of Color: Defining the Issues, Hearing the Voices*. Diane Long Hoveler and Janet K. Boles. Westport, Conn.: Greenwood, 2001. 133–45.

Holaday, Woon-Ping Chin. "From Ezra Pound to Maxine Hong Kingston: Expressions of Chinese Thought in American Literature." *MELUS* 5.2 (1978): 15–24.

Hsu, Shounan. "Writing, Event, and Peace: The Art of Peace in Maxine Hong Kingston's *The Fifth Book of Peace.*" *College Literature* 37.2 (2010): 103–24.

Huntley, E. D. *Maxine Hong Kingston: A Critical Companion.* Westport, Conn.: Greenwood, 2001.

Izgarjan, Aleksandra. "Language as a Means of Shaping New Cultural Identity in Maxine Hong Kingston's *The Woman Warrior.*" *Gender Studies* 1.7 (2008): 7–16.

Juhasz, Suzanne. "Maxine Hong Kingston: Narrative Technique and Female Identity." In *Contemporary American Women Writers*, ed. Catherine Rainwater and William J. Scheick. Lexington: University Press of Kentucky, 1985. 173–90.

Lan, Feng. "The Female Individual and the Empire: A Historicist Approach to Mulan and Kingston's *Woman Warrior.*" *Comparative Literature* 55.3 (2003): 229–45.

Lee, Katherine Hyunmi. "The Poetics of Liminality and Misidentification: Winnifred Eaton's *Me* and Maxine Hong Kingston's *The Woman Warrior.*" In T*ransnational Asian American Literature: Sites and Transits*, ed. Shirley Geok-lin Lim et al. Philadelphia: Temple University Press, 2006. 181–96.

Lee, Ken-fan. "Cultural Translation and the Exorcist: A Reading of Kingston's and Tan's Ghost Stories." *MELUS* 29.2 (2004): 105–27.

Lee, Robert G. "*The Woman Warrior* as an Intervention in Asian American Historiography." In *Approaches to Teaching Kingston's "The Woman Warrior*," ed. Shirley Geok-lin Lim. New York: MLA, 1991. 52–63.

Lei, Daphne P. "The Blood-Stained Text in Translation: Tattooing, Bodily Writing, and Performance of Chinese Virtue." *Anthropological Quarterly* 82.1 (2009): 99–127.

Leonard, John. "Of Thee Ah Sing." *The Nation* (June 5, 1989): 768–72.

Li, David Leiwei. "*China Men*: Maxine Hong Kingston and the American Canon." *American Literary History* 2.3 (1990): 482–502.

Li, Juan. "Pidgin and Code-Switching: Linguistic Identity and Multicultural Consciousness in Maxine Hong Kingston's *Tripmaster Monkey*." *Language and Literature: Journal of the Poetics and Linguistics Association* 13.3 (2004): 269–87.

Lim, Jeehyum. "Cutting the Tongue: Language and the Body in Kingston's *The Woman Warrior*." *MELUS* 31.3 (2006): 49–65.

Lim, Shirley Geok-lin, ed. *Approaches to Teaching Kingston's "The Woman Warrior*." New York: MLA, 1991.

———. "Reading Back, Looking Forward: A Retrospective Interview with Maxine Hong Kingston." *MELUS* 33.1 (2008): 157–70.

———. "The Tradition of Chinese American Women's Life Stories: Thematics of Race and Gender in Jade Snow Wong's *Fifth Chinese Daughter* and Maxine Hong Kingston's *The Woman Warrior*." In *American Women's Autobiography: Fea(s)ts of Memory*, ed. Margo Culley. Madison: University of Wisconsin Press, 1992. 252–67.

Lim, Walter S. H. "Under Eastern Eyes: Ghosts and Cultural Haunting in Maxine Hong Kingston's *The Woman Warrior* and *China Men*." In *Crossing Oceans: Reconfiguring American Literary Studies in the Pacific Rim*, ed. Noelled Brada-Williams and Karen Chow. Hong Kong: Hong Kong University Press, 2004. 155–63.

Lin, Patricia. "Clashing Constructs of Reality: Reading Maxine Hong Kingston's *Tripmaster Monkey: His Fake Book* as Indigenous Ethnography." In *Reading the Literatures of Asian America*, ed. Shirley Geok-lin Lim and Amy Ling. Philadelphia: Temple University Press, 1992. 333–48.

———. "The Icicle in the Desert: Perspective and Form in the Works of Two Chinese-American Women Writers." *MELUS* 6.3 (1979): 51–71.

Ling, Amy. "Chinese American Women Writers: The Tradition behind Maxine Hong Kingston." In *Redefining American Literary History*, ed. A. LaVonne Brown Ruoff and Jerry W. Wand Jr. New York: MLA, 1990. 219–36.

Liu, Toming Jun. "The Problematics of Kingston's 'Cultural Translation': A Chinese Diasporic View of *The Woman Warrior*." *Journal of American Studies of Turkey* 4 (1996): 15–30.

Ludwig, Sami. "Celebrating Ourselves in the Other, Or: Who Controls the Conceptual Allusions in Kingston?" In *Asian American Literature in the International Context: Readings on Fiction, Poetry, and Performance*, ed. Rocio G. Davis and Sami Ludwig. Hamburg, Germany: Lit, 2002. 37–55.

Mackin, Jonna. "Split Infinities: The Comedy of Performative Identity in Maxine Hong Kingston's *Tripmaster Monkey*." *Contemporary Literature* 46.3 (2005): 511–34.

Madsen, Deborah L. "Chinese American Writers of the Real and the Fake: Authenticity and the Twin Traditions of Life Writing." *Canadian Review of American Studies* 36.3 (2006): 257–71.

Maini, Irma. "Writing the Asian American Artist: Maxine Hong Kingston's *Tripmaster Monkey: His Fake Book*." *MELUS* 25.3–4 (2000): 243–64.

Maxey, Ruth. "'The East Is Where Things Begin': Writing the Ancestral Homeland in Amy Tan and Maxine Hong Kingston." *Orbis Litterarum: International Review of Literary Studies* 60.1 (2005): 1–15.

McBride, Dwight A. "The Ghosts of Memory: Representing the Past in *Beloved* and *The Woman Warrior*." In *Re-Placing America: Conversations and Contestations: Selected Essays*, ed. Ruth Hsu et al. Honolulu: College of Languages, Linguistics and Literature, University of Hawaii, with East-West Center, 2000. 162–71.

Mylan, Sheryl A. "The Mother as Other: Orientalism in Maxine Hong Kingston's *The Woman Warrior*." In *Women of Color: Mother-Daughter Relationships in 20th-Century Literature*, ed. Elizabeth Brown-Guillory. Austin: University of Texas Press, 1996. 132–52.

Na, Wu. *Constructing Chinese Americans' National Identity: Reading Kingston's Text*. Cheltenham, Great Britain: Reardon, 2003.

Narcisi, Lara. "Wittman's Transitions: Multivocality and the Play of *Tripmaster Monkey*." *MELUS* 30.3 (2005): 95–111.

———. "From Lone Monkey to Family Man: Wittman's Evolving Inclusion in *Tripmaster Monkey*." *Connotations* 12.2–3 (2002–2003): 249–80.

Pearson, J. Stephen. "*The Monkey King* in the American Canon: Patricia Chao and Gerald Vizenor's Use of an Iconic Chinese Character." *Comparative Literature Studies* 43.3 (2006): 355–74.

Petit, Angela. "'Words So Strong': Maxine Hong Kingston's 'No Name Woman' Introduces Students to the Power of Words." *Journal of Adolescent and Adult Literacy* 46.6 (2003): 482–90.

Pezzulich, Evelyn. "Shifting Paradigms: The Reemergence of Literary Texts in Composition Classrooms." In *Teaching Composition/Teaching Literature: Crossing Great Divides*, ed. Michelle M. Tokarczyk and Irene Papoulis. New York: Peter Lang, 2003. 26–40.

Priborkin, Klarina. "Cross-Cultural Mind-Reading, or, Coming to Terms with the Ethnic Mother in Maxine Hong Kingston's *The Woman Warrior*." In *Toward a Cognitive Theory of Narrative Acts*, ed. Frederick Luis Aldama. Austin: University of Texas Press, 2010. 161–78.

Rabine, Leslie W. "No Lost Paradise: Social Gender and Symbolic Gender in the Writings of Maxine Hong Kingston." *Signs* 12 (1987): 471–92.

Royal, Derek Parker. "Literary Genre as Ethnic Resistance in Maxine Hong Kingston's *Tripmaster Monkey*: *His Fake Book*." *MELUS* 29 (2004): 141–56.

San Juan, E., Jr. "Dialectics of Aesthetics and Politics in Maxine Hong Kingston's *The Fifth Book of Peace*." *Criticism* 51.2 (2009): 181–209.

Sato, Gayle K. Fujita. "Ghosts as Chinese-American Constructs in Maxine Hong Kingston's *The Woman Warrior*." In *Haunting the House of Fiction: Feminist Perspectives on Ghost Stories by American Women*, ed. Lynette Carpenter and Wendy K. Kolmar. Knoxville: University of Tennessee Press, 1991. 193–214.

Schueller, Malini. "Questioning Race and Gender Definitions: Dialogic Subversions in *The Woman Warrior*." *Criticism* 31.4 (1989): 421–37.

———. "Theorizing Ethnicity and Subjectivity: Maxine Hong Kingston's *Tripmaster Monkey* and Amy Tan's *The Joy Luck Club*." *Genders* 15 (1992): 72–85.

Schultermandl, Silvia. "'What Am I, Anyhow?' Ethnic Consciousness, Matrilineage and the Borderlands—Within Maxine Hong Kingston's and Rebecca Walker's Autobiographies." In *Close Encounters of an Other Kind: New Perspectives on Race, Ethnicity, and American Studies*, ed. Roy Goldblatt et al. Joensuu, Finland: Faculty of Humanities, University of Joensuu, 2005. 3–17.

———. "Writing against the Grain: The Cross-Over Genres of Maxine Hong Kingston's *The Woman Warrior*, *China Men*, and *The Fifth Book of Peace*." *Interactions: Aegean Journal of English and American Studies* 16.2 (2007): 111–22.

Shan, Te-Hsing. "Life, Writing, and Peace: Reading Maxine Hong Kingston's *The Fifth Book of Peace*." *Journal of Transnational American Studies* 1.1 (2009): 1–22.

Shapiro, Elliott H. "Authentic Watermelon: Maxine Hong Kingston's American Novel." *MELUS* 26.1 (2001): 5–28.

Shounan, Hsu. "Writing, Event, and Peace: The Art of Peace in Maxine Hong Kingston's *The Fifth Book of Peace*." *College Literature* 37.2 (2010): 103–24.

Simmons, Diane. "Maxine Hong Kingston's *Woman Warrior* and Shaman: Fighting Women in the New World." *FEMSPEC* 2.1 (2000): 49–65.

Skandera-Trombley, Laura E., ed. *Critical Essays on Maxine Hong Kingston*. New York: G. K. Hall, 1998.

Skenazy, Paul, and Tera Martin, eds. *Conversations with Maxine Hong Kingston*. Jackson: University Press of Mississippi, 1998.

Sledge, Linda Ching. "Maxine Hong Kinston's *China Men*: The Family Historian as Epic Poet." *MELUS* 7.4 (1980): 3–22.

———. "Oral Tradition in Kingston's *China Men*." In *Redefining American Literary History*, ed. A. LaVonne Brown Ruoff and Jeff W. Wand, Jr. New York: MLA, 1990. 142–54.

Slowik, Mary. "When the Ghosts Speak: Oral and Written Narrative Forms in Maxine Hong Kingston's *China Men*." *MELUS* 19.1 (1994): 73–88.

Smith, Jeanne Rosier. *Writing Tricksters: Mythic Gambols in American Ethnic Literature*. Berkeley: University of California Press, 1997.

Smith, Sidonie. "Maxine Hong Kingston's *Woman Warrior*: Filiality and Woman's Autobiographical Storytelling." In *A Poetics of Women's Autobiography: Marginality and the Fictions of Self-Representation*. Bloomington: Indiana University Press, 1987. 150–73.

Storhoff, Gary. "'Even Now China Wraps Double Binds around My Feet': Family Communication in *The Woman Warrior* and *Dim Sum*." In *Reading the Family Dance: Family Systems Therapy and Literary Study*, ed. John V. Knapp and Kenneth Womack. Newark: University of Delaware Press, 2003. 71–92.

Szmanko, Klara. “Beyond Black and White: Striving for Visibility in *Tripmaster Monkey* by Maxine Hong Kingston and *Native Speaker* by Chang-rae Lee.” In *Close Encounters of an Other Kind: New Perspectives on Race, Ethnicity, and American Studies*, ed. Roy Goldblatt et al. Joensuu, Finland: University of Joensuu, 2005. 26–31.

Tang, Weimin. “Zone of Negotiation: Storytelling, Intersubjectivity and Transcultural Metamorphosis. Reading the Ethnic Texts *The Woman Warrior* and *The Bonesetter's Daughter*.” In *Oral and Written Narratives and Cultural Identity: Interdisciplinary Approaches*, ed. Francisco Cota Fagundes and Irene Maria F. Bayer. New York: Peter Lang, 2007. 153–71.

Tokarczyk, Michelle M. *Class Definitions: On the Lives and Writings of Maxine Hong Kingston, Sandra Cisneros, and Dorothy Allison.* Selinsgrove, Penn.: University Press, 2008.

Vandersee, Charles. “Naming in Novelizing the Nation: Intertextualities of Ellison, Vonnegut, and Kingston.” *Onoma* 38 (2003): 305–24.

Whalen-Bridge, John. “A Conversation with Charles Johnson and Maxine Hong Kingston.” *MELUS* 31.2 (2006): 69–93.

Wong, Sau-ling Cynthia. “Kingston's Handling of Traditional Chinese Sources.” In *Approaches to Teaching Kingston's "The Woman Warrior,"* ed. Shirley Geok-lin Lim. New York: MLA, 1991. 26–36.

———. *Maxine Hong Kingston's "The Woman Warrior": A Casebook.* New York: Oxford University Press, 1999.

———. “Necessity and Extravagance in Maxine Hong Kingston's *The Woman Warrior*: Art and the Ethnic Experience.” *MELUS* 15 (1988): 3–26.

Woo, Deborah. “Maxine Hong Kingston: The Ethnic Woman Writer and the Burden of Dual Authenticity.” *Amerasia* 16.1 (1990): 173–200.

Woo, Eunjoo. “‘The Beginning Is Hers, the Ending, Mine’: Chinese American Mother/Daughter Conflict and Reconciliation in Maxine Hong Kingston's *The Woman Warrior*.” *Studies in Modern Fiction* 9.1 (2002): 297–314.

Wu, Na. “Beyond the Celebration of Hybridity: On Kingston's *Tripmaster Monkey*.” In *Re-Reading America: Changes and Challenges*, ed. Weihe Zhong and Rui Han. Cheltenham, Great Britain: Reardon, 2004. 263–69.

Wu, Pei-Ju. “Translating Mother's Tongue(s) and Traveling Bodies: Palimpsest and Diaspora in Maxine Kingston's *The Woman Warrior*.” In *Transnationalism and the Asian American Heroine: Essays on Literature, Film, Myth and Media*, ed. Lan Dong. Jefferson, N.C.: McFarland, 2010. 203–19.

Yang, Caroline H. “Indispensable Labor: The Worker as a Category of Critique in *China Men*.” *MFS: Modern Fiction Studies* 56.1 (2010): 63–89.

Ziarkowska, Joanna. “Improvisations on the Genre: Maxine Hong Kingston's and Leslie Marmon Silko's (Auto)Biographical Writings.” *Americana: E-Journal of American Studies in Hungary* 2.1 (2006). (no pagination)

Lahiri, Jhumpa

Caesar, Judith. “Gogol's Namesake: Identity and Relationships in Jhumpa Lahiri's *The Namesake*.” *Atenea* 27.1 (2007): 103–19.

Einsiedel, Doris. "Colonial Recall in Motion: Migration Acts in *Desirable Daughters* and *The Namesake*." In *Moving Migration: Narrative Transformations in Asian American Literature*, ed. Johanna C. Kardux and Doris Einsiedel. Münster, Hamburg, Germany: Lit, 2010. 19–43.

Karttunen, Laura. "A Sociostylistic Perspective on Negatives and the Disnarrated: Lahiri, Roy, Rushdie." *Partial Answers: Journal of Literature and the History of Ideas* 6.2 (2008): 419–41.

Waisserová, Hana. "The Identities of Critical Cosmopolitans in Arundhati Roy's *God of Small Things* and Jhumpa Lahiri's *The Namesake*." *Litteraria Pragensia: Studies in Literature and Culture* 20.39 (2010): 115–31.

Lee, Chang-rae

Arac, Jonathan. "Violence and the Human Voice: Critique and Hope in *Native Speaker*." *Boundary 2* 36.2 (2009): 55–66.

Brada-Williams, Noelle. "Interethnic Relationships in Chang-rae Lee's *Native Speaker* and Gish Jen's 'Birthmates'." In *Close Encounters of an Other Kind: New Perspective on Race, Ethnicity, and American Studies*, ed. Amritjit Singh. Joensuu, Finland: Faculty of Humanities, University of Joensuu, 2005. 18–25.

Carroll, Hamilton. "Traumatic Patriarchy: Reading Gendered Nationalism in Chang-Rae Lee's *A Gesture Life*." *MFS: Modern Fiction Studies* 51.3 (2005): 592–616.

Chen, Tina Y. "Impersonation and Other Disappearing Acts in *Native Speaker* by Chang-rae Lee." *MFS: Modern Fiction Studies* 48.3 (2002): 637–67.

———. "Recasting the Spy, Rewriting the Story: The Politics of Genre in *Native Speaker* by Chang-Rae Lee." In *Form and Transformation in Asian American Literature*, ed. Xiaojing Zhou and Samina Najmi. Seattle: University of Washington Press, 2005. 249–67.

Cheng, Anne Anlin. "Passing, Natural Selection, and Love's Failure: Ethics of Survival from Chang-rae Lee to Jacques Lacan." *American Literary History* 17.3 (2005): 553–74.

Chuh, Kandice. "Discomforting Knowledge: Or, Korean 'Comfort Women' and Asian Americanist Critical Practice." *Journal of Asian American Studies* 6.1 (2003): 5–23.

Corley, Liam. "'Just Another Ethnic Pol': Literary Citizenship in Chang Rae-Lee's *Native Speaker*." *Studies in the Literary Imagination* 37.1 (2004): 61–81.

Dwyer, June. "Speaking and Listening: The Immigrant as Spy Who Comes in from the Cold." In *The Immigrant Experience in North American Literature: Carving Out a Niche*, ed. Katherine B. Payant and Toby Rose. Westport, Conn.: Greenwood, 1999. 73–82.

Engles, Tim. "'Visions of Me in the Whitest Raw Light': Assimilation and Doxic Whiteness in Chang-Rae Lee's *Native Speaker*." *Hitting Critical Mass* 4.2 (199): 27–48.

Hong, Terry. "Flying Aloft with Chang-rae Lee: A Conversation." *Bloomsbury Review* 24.5 (2004): 23–24.

Huang, Betsy. "Citizen Kwang: Chang-rae Lee's *Native Speaker* and the Politics of Consent." *Journal of Asian American Studies* 9.3 (2006): 243–69.

Huang, Joan. "Oral Fixations: An Exploration of *Native Speaker*." *Hitting Critical Mass* 6.1 (1999): 79–87.

Huh, Joonok. "'Strangest Chorale': New York City in *East Goes West* and *Native Speaker*." In *The Image of the Twentieth Century in Literature, Media, and Society*, ed. Will Wright and Steven Kaplan. Pueblo: Society for the Interdisciplinary Study of Social Imagery, University of Southern Colorado, 2000. 419–22.

Jerng, Mark C. "Nowhere in Particular: Perceiving Race, Chang-rae Lee's *Aloft*, and the Question of Asian." *MFS: Modern Fiction Studies* 56.1 (2010): 183–204.

———. "Recognizing the Transracial Adoptee: Adoption Life Stories and Chang-rae Lee's *A Gesture Life*." *MELUS* 31.2 (2006): 41–67.

Kim, Daniel Y. "Do I, Too, Sing America? Vernacular Representations and Chang-rae Lee's *Native Speaker*." *Journal of Asian American Studies* 6.3 (2003): 231–60.

Kim, Jodi. "From Mee-Gook to Gook: The Cold War and Racialized Undocumented Capital in Chang-rae Lee's *Native Speaker*." *MELUS* 34.1 (2009): 117–37.

Koh, Boo Eung. "The Identity of Empty Signifier in Chang-rae Lee's *Native Speaker*." *Journal of English Language and Literature* 48.3 (2002): 619–38.

Kwon, Teckyoung. "*A Gesture Life* as Gaze: The Multiculture Ethnics of Lacan and Chang-Rae Lee." *Journal of English Language and Literature* 48.1 (2002): 243–61.

Lee, James Kyung-Jin. "Where the Talented Tenth Meets the Model Minority: The Price of Privilege in Wideman's *Philadelphia Fire* and Lee's *Native Speaker*." *A Forum on Fiction* 35.2–3 (2002): 231–57.

Lee, Kun Jong. "Towards Interracial Understanding and Identification: Spike Lee's *Do the Right Thing* and Chang-rae Lee's *Native Speaker*." *Journal of American Studies* 44.4 (2010): 741–57.

Lee, Rachel C. "Reading Contests and Contesting Reading: Chang-rae Lee's *Native Speaker* and Ethnic New York." *MELUS* 29.3-4 (2004): 341–52.

Lee, So-Hee. "Cultural Citizenship as Subject-Making in *Comfort Woman* and *A Gesture Life*." *Feminist Studies In English Literature* 14.2 (2006): 91–123.

Lee, Young-oak. "Gender, Race, and the Nation in *A Gesture Life*." *Critique: Studies in Contemporary Fiction* 46.2 (2005): 146–59.

———. "Transcending Ethnicity: Diasporicity in *A Gesture Life*." *Journal of Asian American Studies* 2.1 (2009): 65–81.

Ludwig, Sami. "Ethnicity as Cognitive Identity: Private and Public Negotiations in Chang-rae Lee's *Native Speaker*." *Journal of Asian American Studies* 10.3 (2007): 221–42.

Moraru, Christian. "The Other, the Namesake: Cosmopolitan Onomastics in Change-rae Lee's *A Gesture Life*." *Names: A Journal of Onomastics* 55.1 (2007): 17–35.

———. "Speakers and Sleepers: Chang-rae Lee's *Native Speaker*, Whitman, and the Performance of Americanness." *College Literature* 36.3 (2009): 66–91.

Narkunas, J. Paul. "Surfing the Long Waves of Global Capital with Chang Rae-Lee's *Native Speaker*: Ethnic Branding and the Humanization of Capital." *MFS: Modern Fiction Studies* 54.2 (2008): 327–52.

Rhee, Suk Koo. "A Symptomatic Reading of 'Discrimination' and 'Difference' in *A Gesture Life*." *Journal of English Language and Literature* 56.5 (2010): 907–30.

Russell, Keith A., II. "Colonial Naming and Renaming in *A Gesture Life* by Chang-rae Lee." *Notes on Contemporary Literature* 35.4 (2006): 7–9.

Song, Min Hyoung. "A Diasporic Future? *Native Speaker* and Historical Trauma." *LIT: Literature Interpretation Theory* 12.1 (2001): 79–98.

Szmanko, Klara. "Beyond Black and White: Striving for Visibility in *Tripmaster Monkey* by Maxine Hong Kingston and *Native Speaker* by Chang-rae Lee." In *Close Encounters of an Other Kind: New Perspectives on Race, Ethnicity, and American Studies*. Joensuu, Finland: Faculty of Humanities, University of Joensuu, 2005: 25–31.

———. "The Conflict between African Americans and Korean Americans in Chang-rae Lee's *Native Speaker*." In *Transitions: Race, Culture, and the Dynamics of Change*, ed. Hanna. Vienna, Austria: Lit, 2006. 67–90.

———. "Immigrant Invisibility in Chang-rae Lee's *Native Speaker*." In *Interiors: Interiority/Exteriority in Literary and Cultural Discourse*, ed. Sonia Front and Katarzyna Nowak. Newcastle upon Tyne, Great Britain: Cambridge Scholars, 2010. 147–61.

Wu, Yung-Hsing. "*Native Sons* and *Native Speakers*: On the Eth(n)ics of Comparison." *PMLA* 121.5 (2006): 1460–74.

Lee, Gus

Hawley, John C. "Gus Lee, Chang-Rae Lee, and Li-Young Lee: The Search for the Father in Asian American Literature." In *Ideas of Home: Literature of Asian Migration*, ed. Geoffrey Kain. East Lansing: Michigan State University Press, 1997. 183–95.

Malcolm, Cheryl Alexander. "Going for the Knockout: Confronting Whiteness in Gus Lee's *China Boy*." *MELUS* 29.3–4 (2004): 413–26.

Nguyen, Viet Thanh. "The Remasculinization of Chinese America: Race, Violence, and the Novel." *American Literary History* 12.1–2 (2000): 130–57.

Otano, Alicia. "Rituals of Mothering: Food and Intercultural Identity in Gus Lee's *China Boy*." In *Asian American Literature in the International Context: Readings on Fiction, Poetry, and Performance*, ed. Rocío G. Davis and Sami Ludwig: Hamburg, Germany. Lit, 2002: 215–26.

Shen, Yichin. "The Site of Domestic Violence and the Altar of Phallic Sacrifice in Gus Lee's *China Boy*." *College Literature* 29.2 (2002): 99–113.

So, Christine. "Delivering the Punch Line: Racial Combat as Comedy in Gus Lee's *China Boy*." *MELUS* 21.4 (1996): 141–55.

Lee, Li-Young

Basford, Douglas. "Sexual Desire and Cultural Memory in Three Ethnic Poets." *MELUS* 29.3–4 (2004): 243–56.

Bilyak, Dianne. "Interview with Li-Young Lee." *Massachusetts Review* 44.4 (2003–2004): 600–612.

Chan, Kenneth. "Diasporic Desires: Narrating Sexuality in the Memoirs of Shirley Geok-lin Lim and Li-Young Lee." In *China Abroad: Travels, Subjects, Spaces*, ed. Elaine Yee Lin and Julia Kuehn. Hong Kong: Hong Kong University Press, 2009. 139–54.

Engles, Tim. "Lee's 'Persimmons.'" *Explicator* 54.3 (Spring 1996): 191–92.

Fluharty, Matthew. "An Interview with Li-Young Lee." *Missouri Review* 23.1 (2000): 81–99.

Hand, Meadhbh. "In the Shadow of *The Woman Warrior*—Li-Young Lee's *The Winged Seed*: A Remembrance." In *Positioning the New: Chinese American Literature and the Changing Image of the American Literary Canon*, ed. Tanfer Emin Tunc and Elisabetta Marino. Newcastle upon Tyne, Great Britain: Cambridge Scholars, 2010. 192–203.

Hawley, John C. "Gus Lee, Chang-Rae Lee, and Li-Young Lee: The Search for the Father in Asian American Literature." In *Ideas of Home: Literature of Asian Migration*, ed. Geoffrey Kain. East Lansing: Michigan State University Press, 1997. 183–95.

Hesford, Walter A. "*The City in Which I Love You:* Li-Young Lee's Excellent Song." *Christianity and Literature* 46.1 (1996): 37–60.

Hsu, Ruth. "Li-Young Lee." In *American Poets since World War II: Fourth Series*, ed. Joseph Conte. Detroit, Mich.: Thomson Gale, 1996. 139–46.

Jenkins, Tricia. "Forming Personal and Cultural Identities in the Face of Exodus: A Discussion of Li-Young Lee's Poetry." *South Asian Review* 24.2 (2003): 199–210.

Kajiware, Teruko. "'The Art of Memory': The Creation of Memory, the Subject, and Poetic Language in the Poetry of Li-Young Lee." *Studies in English Literature* 50 (2009): 123–42.

Kolosov, Jacqueline. "Poetries of Transformation: Joy Harjo and Li-Young Lee." *Studies in American Indian Literatures* 15.2 (2003): 39–57.

Lee, James Kyung-Jin. "Li-Young Lee." In *Words Matter: Conversations with Asian American Writers*, ed. King-Kok Cheung. Honolulu: University of Hawaii Press, 2000. 270–80.

Lorenz, Johnny. "The Way a Calendar Dissolves: A Refugee's Sense of Time in the Work of Li-Young Lee." In *Asian American Literature in the International Context: Readings on Fiction, Poetry, and Performance*, ed. Rocío G. Davis and Sämi Ludwig. Hamburg, Germany: Lit, 2002. 157–69.

Malandra, Marc. "Fugitive Visions: Exile, Silence, and Song in Li-Young Lee's 'Furious Versions.'" In *Exile and the Narrative/Poetic Imagination*, ed. Agnieszka Gutthy. Newcastle upon Tyne, Great Britain: Cambridge Scholars, 2010. 61–73.

———. "'Little Candle in the Pulpit': The Sacred Legacy of Memory and Genealogy in Li-Young Lee's *Book of My Nights*." *English Language Notes* 44 (2006): 19–27.

Marshall, Tod. "To Witness the Invisible: A Talk with Li-Young Lee." *Kenyon Review* 22.1 (2000): 129–47.

Moeser, Daniel. "Lee's 'Eating Alone.'" *Explicator* 60.2 (2002): 117–19.

Partridge, Jeffrey F. L. "The Politics of Ethnic Authorship: Li-Young Lee, Emerson, and Whitman at the Banquet Table." *Studies in the Literary Imagination* 37.1 (2004): 101–26.

Teruko, Kajiware. "'The Art of Memory': The Creation of Memory, the Subject, and Poetic Language in the Poetry of Li-Young Lee." *Studies in English Literature* 50 (2009): 123–42.

Xu, Wenying. "An Exile's Will to Canon and Its Tension with Ethnicity: Li-Young Lee." In *Multiethnic Literature and Canon Debates*, ed. Mary Jo Bona and Irma Maini. Albany: State University of New York Press, 2006. 145–64.

———. "Transcendentalism, Ethnicity, and Food in the Work of Li-Young Lee." *boundary 2* 33.2 (2006): 129–57.

Yao, Steven G. "The Precision of Persimmons: Hybridity, Grafting and the Case of Li-Young Lee." *LIT: Literature Interpretation Theory* 12.1 (2001): 1–23.

Yu, Timothy. "Form and Identity in Language Poetry and Asian American Poetry." *Contemporary Literature* 41.3 (2000): 422–61.

Zhou, Xiaojing. "Inheritance and Invention in Li-Young Lee's Poetry." *MELUS* 21.1 (1996): 113–32.

———. "'Your Otherness Is Perfect as My Death': The Ethics and Aesthetics of Li-Young Lee's Poetry." In *Textual Ethos Studies or Locating Ethics*, ed. Anna Fahraeus and Ann Katrin Jonsson. New York: Rodopi, 2005. 297–314.

Lim, Shirley Geok-lin

Chan, Kenneth. "Diasporic Desires: Narrating Sexuality in the Memoirs of Shirley Geok-lin Lim and Li-Young Lee." In *China Abroad: Travels, Subjects, Spaces*, ed. Elaine Ho, Elaine Yee Lin, and Julia Kuehn. Hong Kong: Hong Kong University Press, 2009. 139–54.

Chang, Joan Chiung-huei. "When Third-World Expatriate Meets First-World Peace Corps Worker: Diaspora Reconsidered in Shirley Lim's *Joss and Gold*." *Concentric: Literary and Cultural Studies* 31.1 (2005): 149–62.

Cetintas, S. Bilge Mutluay. "Diasporic (Dis)Connections: Shirley Geok-lin Lim's *Among the White Moon Faces*." In *Positioning the New: Chinese American Literature and the Changing Image of the American Literary Canon*, ed. Tanfer Emin Tunc and Elisabetta Marino. Newcastle upon Tyne, Great Britain: Cambridge Scholars, 2010. 204–15.

Davis, Rocío G. "Academic Autobiography and Transdisciplinary Crossings in Shirley Geok-lin Lim's *Among the White Moon Faces*." *Journal of American Studies* 43.3 (2009): 441–57.

———. "Reading Asian American Academic Autobiographies: Migration and Transdisciplinary Border Crossings in Shirley Lim and Yi-Fu Tuan." In *Narrative Transformations in Asian American Literature*, ed. Johanna C. Kardux and Doris Einsiedel: Münster, Germany. Lit, 2010. 235–52.

Feng, Pin-chia. "Chinese Malaysian English Writing in Diaspora: Shirley Geok-lin Lim's *Joss and Gold*." *Sun Yat-sen Journal of Humanities* 16 (2003): 33–46.

Fox, Timothy. "Just Another Cell in the Beehive: Interview with Shirley Geok-lin Lim Feminist Scholar, Teacher and Poet." *Intersections: Gender, History, and Culture in the Asian Context* (2000): 4–43.

Manaf, Nor Faridah Abdul. "Interview with Shirley Geok-lin Lim." *CRNLE Reviews Journal* 1.2 (1995): 7–17.

Means, Laurel. "The 'orient-ation' of Eden: Christian/Buddhist Dialogics in the Poetry of Shirley Geok-lin Lim." *Christianity and Literature* 43.2 (1994): 189–203.

Ng, Andrew Hock-Soon. "Malaysian Gothic: The Motif of Haunting in K. S. Maniam's 'Haunting the Tiger' and Shirley Lim's 'Haunting.'" *A Journal for the Interdisciplinary Study of Literature* 39.2 (2006): 75–87.

———. "The Maternal Imagination in the Poetry of Shirley Lim." *Women: A Cultural Review* 18.2 (2007): 162–81.

Powell, Katrina. "The Embodiment of Memory: The Intellectual Body in Shirley Geok-lin Lim's *Among the White Moon Faces*." In *New Essays on Life Writing and the Body*, ed. Christopher Stuart and Stephanie Todd. Newcastle upon Tyne, Great Britain: Cambridge Scholars, 2009. 154–67.

Quayum, Mohammad A. "'My Country'/'Our Country': Race Dynamics and Contesting Nationalisms in Lloyd Fernando's *Green Is the Colour* and Shirley Geok-lin Lim's *Joss and Gold*." *Crossroads: An Interdisciplinary Journal of Southeast Asian Studies* 18.2 (2007): 65–89.

———. "Nation, Gender, Identity: Shirley Geok-lin Lim's *Joss and Gold*." *Sun Yat-sen Journal of Humanities* 16 (2003): 15–32.

———. "Shirley Geok-lin Lim: An Interview." *MELUS* 28.4 (2003): 83–100.

Sawatsky, Chingyen. "Home and Exile in Hualing Nieh's *Mulberry and Peach* and Shirley Geok-lin Lim's *Among the White Moon Faces*." In *Querying the Genealogy: Comparative and Transnational Studies in Chinese American Literature*, ed. Jennie Wang. Shanghai, China: Shanghai Yiwen Press, 2006. 326–35.

Singh, Kirpal. "An Interview with Shirley Geok-lin Lim." *ARIEL: A Review of International English Literature* 30.4 (1999): 135–41.

Tay, Eddie. "Hegemony, National Allegory, Exile: The Poetry of Shirley Lim." *Textual Practice* 19.3 (2005): 289–308.

Yeow, Agnes S. K. "'Transformed by the Land's Rolling Green': Ecological Consciousness in the Poetry of Shirley Geok-lin Lim." *Tamkang Review* 39.1 (2008): 41–65.

Louie, David Wong

Gómez-Vega, Ibis. "Losing Everything in David Wong Louie's 'In a World Small Enough.'" *Short Story* 16.2 (2008): 63–77.

Hirose, Stacey Yukari. "David Wong Louie." In *Words Matter: Conversations with Asian American Writers*, ed. King-Kok Cheung. Honolulu: University of Hawaii Press, 2000. 189–214.

Ho, Wen-ching. *"Caucasian Partners and Generational Conflicts—David Wong Louie's Pangs of Love*." *EurAmerica: A Journal of European and American Studies* 34.2 (2004): 231–64.

Parikh, Crystal. "'The Most Outrageous Masquerade': Queering Asian-American Masculinity." *Modern Fiction Studies* 48.4 (2002): 858–98.

Partridge, Jeff. "Toward a More Worldly World Series: Reading Game Three of the 1998 American League Championship and David Wong Louie's 'Warming Trends.'" *American Studies International* 38.2 (2000): 115–25.

Sarkar, Sheila. "Cynthia Kadohata and David Wong Louie: The Pangs of a Floating World." *Hitting Critical Mass* 2.1 (1994): 79–97.

Wong, Sau-ling Cynthia. "Chinese/Asian American Men in the 1990s: Displacement, Impersonation, Paternity, and Extinction in David Wong Louie's *Pangs of Love*." In *Privileging Positions: The Sites of Asian American Studies*, eds. Gary Y. Okihiro, Marilyn Alquizola, Dorothy Fujita Rony, and Scott K. Wong. Pullman: Washington State University Press, 1995. 181–91.

Xu, Wenying. "Class and Cuisine in David Wong Louie's *The Barbarians Are Coming*." In *Eating Identities: Reading Food in Asian American Literature*. Honolulu: University of Hawaii Press, 2008. 62–93.

Lum, Darrell

Okawa, Gail Y. "Resistance and Reclamation: Hawaii 'Pidgin English' and Autoethnography in the Short Stories of Darrell H. Y. Lum." In *Ethnicity and the American Short Story*, ed. Julie Brown. New York: Garland, 1997. 177–96.

Sato, Gayle K. Fujita. "The Island Influence on Chinese American Writers: Wing Tek Lum, Darrell H. Y. Lum, and Eric Chock." *Amerasia Journal* 16.2 (1990): 17–33.

Usui, Masami. "Local Hawai'i as Home in Darrell H. Y. Lum's Plays." *Doshisha Literature* 46 (2003): 55–78.

Watanabe, Sylvia. "A Conversation with Darrell Lum and Eric Chock." In *Into the Fire: Asian American Prose*, ed. Sylvia Watanabe and Carol Brushac. New York: Greenfield Review Press, 1996. 85–98.

McCunn, Ruthanne Lum

Cheung, King-kok. "Self-Fulfilling Visions in *The Woman Warrior* and *Thousand Pieces of Gold*." *Biography: An Interdisciplinary Quarterly* 13.2 (1990): 143–53.

Hesford, Walter. "*Thousand Pieces of Gold*: Competing Fictions in the Representation of Chinese-American Experience." *Western American Literature* 31.1 (1996): 49–62.

Terry, Patricia. "A Chinese Woman in the West: *Thousand Pieces of Gold* and the Revision of the Heroic Frontier." *Literature Film Quarterly* 22.4 (1994): 222–26.

Min, Anchee

Hayot, Eric. "Immigrating Fictions: Unfailing Mediation in *Dictée* and *Becoming Madame Mao*." *Contemporary Literature* 47.4 (2006): 601–35.

Jolly, Margaretta. "Coming Out of the Coming Out Story: Writing Queer Lives." *Sexualities: Studies in Culture and Society* 4.4 (2001): 474–96.

Lai, Amy Tak-yee. *Chinese Women Writers in Diaspora: Jung Chang, Xinran, Hong Ying, Anchee Min, Adeline Yen Ma.* Newcastle upon Tyne, Great Britain: Cambridge Scholars, 2007.

———. "Images of Theatre and Theatricality in Anchee Min's Works." *Tsing Hua Journal of Chinese Studies* 36.2 (2006): 543–82.

Larson, Wendy. "Never This Wild: Sexing the Cultural Revolution." *Modern China* 25.4 (1999): 423–50.

Somerson, Wendy. "Under the Mosquito Net: Space and Sexuality in *Red Azalea*." *College Literature* 24.1 (1998): 98–115.

Xu, Ben. "A Face That Grows into a Mask: A Symptomatic Reading of Anchee Min's *Red Azalea*." *MELUS* 29.2 (2004): 157–80.

Xu, Wenying. "Agency via Guilt in Anchee Min's *Red Azalea*." *MELUS* 25.3–5 (2000): 203–19.

Yue, Ming-Bao. "Nostalgia for the Future: Cultural Revolution Memory in Two Transnational Chinese Narratives." *China Review* 5.2 (2005): 43–63.

Mirikitani, Janice

Grotjohn, Robert. "Remapping Internment: A Postcolonial Reading of Mitsuye Yamada, Lawson Fusao Inada, and Janice Mirikitani." *Western American Literature* 38.3 (2003): 247–69.

Hong, Grace Kyungwon. "Janice Mirikitani." In *Words Matter: Conversations with Asian American Writers*, ed. King-Kok Cheung. Honolulu: University of Hawaii Press, 2000. 123–39.

Lashgari, Deirdre. "Disrupting the Deadly Stillness: Janice Mirikitani's Poetics of Violence." In *Violence, Silence, and Anger: Women's Writing as Transgression*, ed. Deirdre Lashgari. Charlottesville: University Press of Virginia, 1995. 291–304.

Usui, Masami. "'No Hiding Place, New Speaking Space': Janice Mirikitani's Poetry of Incest and Abuse." *South Asian Literature* 32 (1996): 56–65.

Yamamoto, Traise. *Masking Selves, Making Subjects: Japanese American Women, Identity, and the Body*. Berkeley: University of California Press, 1999.

Yogi, Stan. "Yearning for the Past: The Dynamics of Memory in Sansei Internment Poetry." In *Memory and Cultural Politics: New Approaches to American Ethnic Literatures*, ed. Amritjit Singh et al. Boston: Northeastern University Press, 1996. 245–65.

Mori, Toshio

Arakawa, Suzanne. "Suffering Male Bodies: Representations of Dissent and Displacement in the Internment-Themed Narratives of John Okada and Toshiro Mori." In *Recovered Legacies: Authority and Identity in Early Asian American Literature*, ed. Floyd Cheung and Keith Lawrence. Philadelphia: Temple University Press, 2005. 183–206.

Bedrosian, Margaret. "Toshio Mori's California Koans." *MELUS* 15.2 (1988): 47–55.

Hassell, Malve von. "Ethnography, Storytelling and the Fiction of Toshio Mori." *Dialectical Anthropology* 4 (1994): 401–18.

Lawrence, Keith. "Toshio Mori, Richard Kim, and the Masculine Ideal. In *Recovered Legacies: Authority and Identity in Early Asian American Literature*, ed. Floyd Cheung and Keith Lawrence. Philadelphia: Temple University Press, 2005. 207–28.

Mayer, David R. "Akegarasu and Emerson: Kindred Spirits of Toshio Mori's 'The Seventh Street Philosopher.'" *Amerasia Journal* 16.2 (1990): 1–10.

———. "The Philosopher in Search of a Voice: Toshio Mori's Japanese-Influenced Narrator." *AALA Journal* 2 (1995): 12–24.

———. "The Short Stories of Toshio Mori." *Fu Jen Studies* 21 (1988): 73–87.

———. "Toshio Mori and Loneliness." *Nanzan Review of American Studies* 15 (1993): 20–32.

———. "Toshio Mori's '1936': A True and a False Prophecy." *Academia: Bungaku Gogaku Hen/Literature and Language* 67 (1999): 69–81.

———. "Toshio Mori's Neighborhood Settings: Inner and Outer Oakland." *Fu Jen Studies* 23 (1993): 100–115.

Palumbo Liu, David. "Silent Survivor: Toshio Mori's *Woman from Hiroshima*." *Academia: Bungaku Gogaku Hen/Literature and Language* 77 (2005): 219–48.

———. "Toshio Mori and the Attachments of Spirit: A Response to David R. Mayer." *Amerasia Journal* 17.3 (1991): 41–47.

———. "Universalism and Minority Culture." *Differences: A Journal of Feminist Cultural Studies* 7.1 (1995): 188–208.

Mukherjee, Bharati

Ahokas, Pirjo. "The Female Protagonist's Diasporic Identity Process: Bharati Mukherjee's *Desirable Daughters*, Monica Ali's *Brick Lane*." *Acta Litteraria Comparativa: Kultūros Intertekstai/Cultural Intertexts* 2 (2006): 28–36.

Alam, Fakrul. *Bharati Mukherjee*. New York: Twayne, 1996.

Alessandrini, Anthony C. "Reading Bharati Mukherjee, Reading Globalization." In *World Bank Literature*, ed. Amitava Kumar. Minneapolis: University of Minnesota Press, 2003. 265–79.

Aneja, Anu. "*Jasmine*, the Sweet Scent of Exile." *Pacific Coast Philology* 28.1 (1993): 72–80.

Bahri, Deepika. "Always Becoming: Narratives of Nation and Self in Bharati Mukherjee's *Jasmine*." In *Women, America, and Movement: Narratives of Relocation*, ed. Susan L. Roberson. Columbia: University of Missouri Press, 1998. 137–54.

Boxille, Anthony. "Women and Migration in Some Short Stories of Baharati Mukherjee and Neil Bossoondath." *Literary Half-Yearly* 32.2 (1991): 43–50.

Brewster, Anne. "A Critique of Bharati Mukerjee's Neo-nationalism." *SPAN* 34–35 (1992–1993): 50–59.

Burkhart, Matt. "Rewriting the West(ern): Shane, Jane, and Agricultural Change in Bharati Mukherjee's *Jasmine*." *Western American Literature* 43.1 (2008): 5–22.

Carter-Sanborn, Kristin. "'We Murder Who We Were': *Jasmine* and the Violence of Identity." *American Literature* 66 (1994): 573–93.

Chua, C. L. "Passages from India: Migration to America in the Fiction of V. S. Naipaul and Bharati Mukerjee." In *Reworlding: The Literature of the Indian Diaspora*, ed. Emmanuel S. Nelson. Westport, Conn.: Greenwood, 1992. 51–62.

Crane, Ralph J. "Of Shattered Pots and Sinkholes: (Female) Identity in Bharati Mukerjee's *Jasmine*." *SPAN* 36 (1993): 122–30.

Davé, Shilpa. "The Doors to Home and History: Post-Colonial Identities in Meena Alexander and Bharati Mukherjee." *Amerasia Journal* 19.3 (1993): 103–13.

Edwards, Bradley, ed. *Conversation with Bharati Mukharjee.* Jackson: University Press of Mississippi, 2009.

Farebrother, Rachel. "Testing the Limits of the Transcultural: Travel, Intertextuality and Tourism in Bharati Mukherjee's *The Holder of the World* and Anita Desai's *The Zigzag Way*." *Interactions: Aegean Journal of English and American Studies* 15.2 (2006): 61–74.

González, Laura Peco. "Rewriting Tradition in the Old and New World: *The Holder of the World* and *The Tree Bride* by Bharati Mukherjee." In *New Literatures of Old: Dialogues of Tradition and Innovation in Anglophone Literature*, ed. Jose Ramon Prado-Pérez and Didac Llorens Cubedo. Newcastle upon Tyne, Great Britain: Cambridge Scholars, 2008. 136–43.

Hawley, John C. "Assimilation and Resistance in Female Fiction of Immigration: Bharati Mukherjee, Amy Tan, and Christine Bell." In *Rediscovering America, 1492–1992: National, Cultural, and Disciplinary Boundaries Re-examined.* Baton Rouge: Louisiana State University Press, 1992. 226–34.

Hestetun, Øyunn. "Migration and Self-Transformation in Bharati Mukherjee's *Jasmine* and Kiran Desai's *The Inheritance of Loss*." In *Moving Migration: Narrative Transformations in Asian American Literature*, ed. Johanna C. Kardux and Doris Einsiede. Münster, Germany: Lit, 2010. 81–94.

Kehde, Suzanne. "Colonial Discourse and Female Identity: Bharati Mukherjee's *Jasmine*." In *International Women's Writing: New Landscapes of Identity*, ed. Anne E. Brown. Westport, Conn.: Greenwood, 1995. 70–77.

Lauret, Maria. "Bharati Mukherjee's English: The Multilingualism of an American Novelist." In *Post-National Enquiries: Essays on Ethnic and Racial Border Crossings*, ed. Jopi Nyman. Newcastle upon Tyne, Great Britain: Cambridge Scholars, 2009. 170–90.

Low, Gail Ching-liang. "In a Free State: Postcolonialism and Postmodernism in Bharati Mukherjee's Fiction." *Women: A Cultural Review* 4.1 (1993): 8–17.

Luo, Shao-Pin. "Rewriting Travel: Ahdaf Soueif's *The Map of Love* and Bharati Mukherjee's *The Holder of the World*." *Journal of Commonwealth Literature* 38.2 (2003): 77–104.

Mackay, Polina. "'There Are No Harmless Ways to Remake Oneself': Re-Invention of Self in Bharati Mukherjee." In *Rites of Passage in Postcolonial Women's Writing*, ed. Pauline Dodgson-Katiyo and Gina Wisker. Amsterdam, Netherlands: Rodopi, 2010. 113–26.

Maxey, Ruth. "'Who Wants Pale, Thin, Pink Flesh?': Bharati Mukherjee, Whiteness, and South Asian American Writing." *Textual Practice* 20.3 (2006): 529–47.

Nelson, Emmanuel S., ed. *Baharati Mukherjee: Critical Perspectives*. New York: Garland, 1993.

———. "Kamala Markandaya, Bharati Mukherjee, and the Indian Immigrant Experience." *Toronto South Asian Review* 9.2 (1991): 1–9.

Nishimura, Amy N. "Re-Imagining Happily-Ever-After in Bharati Mukherjee's *Jasmine*." In *Transnationalism and the Asian American Heroine: Essays on Literature, Film, Myth and Media*, ed. Lan Dong. Jefferson, N.C.: McFarland, 2010. 118–33.

Nyman, Jopi. "Ethnosexual Encounters in the Fiction of Bharati Mukherjee." In *Post-National Enquiries: Essays on Ethnic and Racial Border Crossings*, ed. Jopi Nyman. Newcastle upon Tyne, Great Britain: Cambridge Scholars, 2009. 148–69.

———. "Resisting the Resistor: Bharati Mukherjee, Memory, and the Murder of Gandhi." In *Postcolonialism and Cultural Resistance*, ed. Jopi Nyman and John A. Stotesbury. Joensuu, Finland: Faculty of Humanities, University of Joensuu, 1999. 158–67.

Olson, Daniel. "Smiling with Blood on the Tongue: Acceptable Sacrifices and the Annihilating Feminine in Bharati Mukherjee's *Jasmine*." *Commonwealth Essays and Studies* 30.2 (2008): 74–84.

Pandya, Sudha. "Bharati Mukherjee's *Darkness*: Exploring the Hyphenated Identity." *Quill* 2.2 (1990): 68–73.

Sen, Krishna. "America as Diaphor: Cultural Translation in Bharati Mukherjee's *The Holder of the World*." In *American Fiction of the 1990s: Reflections of History and Culture*, ed. Jay Prosser. London: Routledge, 2008. 46–59.

Shankar, Lavina Dhingra. "Activism, 'Feminisms,' and Americanization in Bharati Mukherjee's *Wife* and *Jasmine*." *Hitting Critical Mass* 3.1 (1995): 61–84.

Sullivan, Victoria. "Depictions of East-Indian Immigrant Women in Bharati Mukherjee's Mid-Career Fiction." In *Hybrid Americas: Contacts, Contrasts, and Confluences in New World Literatures and Cultures*, ed. Josef Raab and Martin Butler. Hamburg, Germany: Lit, 2008. 265–75.

Tapping, Craig. "South Asia Writers North America: Prose Fictions and Autobiographies from the Indian Diaspora." In *Reading the Literatures of Asian America*, ed. Shirley Geok-lin Lim and Amy Ling. Philadelphia: Temple University Press, 1992. 285–301.

Wickramagamage, Carmen. "Relocation as Positive Act: The Immigrant Experience in Bharati Mukherjee's Novels." *Diaspora* 2.2 (1992): 171–200.

Mura, David

Dong, Lan. "Turning Japanese, Turning Japanese American: David Mura's *Memoirs of a Sansei*." *Anachronist* 10 (2004): 143–52.

Franklin, Cynthia. "Turning Japanese/Returning to America: Problems of Gender, Class, and Nation in David Mura's Use of Memoir." *LIT: Literature Interpretation Theory* 12.3 (2001): 235–65.

Gidmark, Gill. "David Mura: Tearing Down the Door." *Asian America: Journal of Culture and the Arts* 2 (1993): 120–29.
Moyers, Bill. Interview. In *The Language of Life*, ed. James Haba. New York: Doubleday, 1995. 301–18.
Rossi, Lee. "David Mura." *Onthebus* 2.2-3.1 (1990/1991): 263–73.
Slowik, Mary. "Beyond Lot's Wife: The Immigration Poems of Marilyn Chin, Garrett Hongo, Li-Young Lee, and David Mura." *MELUS* 25.3–4 (2000): 221–42.
Taylor, Gordon. "'The Country I Had Thought Was My Home': David Mura's Turning Japanese and Japanese-American Narrative since World War II." *Connotations: A Journal for Critical Debate* 6.3 (1996–1997): 283–309.
Zhou, Xiaojing. "A Poetics of Identity: David Mura's Poetry." *MELUS* 23.3 (1998): 145–66.
———. "Race, Sexuality, and Representation in David Mura's *The Colors of Desire*." *Journal of Asian American Studies* 1.3 (1998): 245–67.

Murayama, Milton

Chang, Joan Chiung-huei. "Social Stratification and Plantation Mentality: Reading Milton Murayama." *Concentric: Literary and Cultural Studies* 30.2 (2004): 155–72.
Hiura, Arnold. "Comments on Milton Murayama." In *Writers of Hawaii: A Focus on Our Literary Heritage*, ed. Eric Chock and Jody Manabe. Honolulu: Bamboo Ridge, 1981: 56–67.
Najita, Susan. "Pleasure and Colonial Resistance: Translating the Politics of Pidgin in Milton Murayama's *All I Asking for Is My Body*." In *Imagining Our Americas: Toward a Transnational Frame*, ed. Sandhya Shukla and Heidi Tinsman. Durham, N.C.: Duke University Press, 2007. 111–37.
Sumida, Stephen H. "*All I Asking for Is My Body* by Milton Murayama." In *A Resource Guide to Asian American Literature*, ed. Sau-ling Cynthia Wong and Stephen H. Sumida. New York: MLA, 2001. 130–39.
———. "Japanese American Moral Dilemmas in John Okada's *No-No Boy* and Milton Murayama's *All I Asking for Is My Body*." In *Frontiers of Asian American Studies: Writing Research, and Criticism*. Pullman: Washington State University Press, 1989. 222–33.
Wilson, Rob. "The Language of Confinement and Liberation in Milton Murayama's *All I Asking for Is My Body*." In *Writers of Hawaii: A Focus on Our Literary Heritage*, ed. Eric Chock and Jody Manabe. Honolulu: Bamboo Ridge, 1981. 62–65.

Ng, Fae Myenne

Aldama, Frederick Luis. "Spatial Re-Imaginations in Fae Myenne Ng's Chinatown." *Hitting Critical Mass* 1.2 (1994): 85–102.
Arfaoui Abidi, Siham. "The Double-Voiced Undone: Maxine Hong Kingston's *The Woman Warrior*: *Memoirs of a Girlhood among Ghosts* and Fae Myenne Ng's

Bone." *Interactions: Aegean Journal of English and American Studies* 16.2 (2007): 1–11.

———. "Messing with Metonymic and Synecdochic Selves: A Reading of Female Subject-Making in Fae Myenne Ng's *Bone*." *Interactions: Ege University Journal of British and American Studies* 18.2 (2009): 15–24.

Chang, Juliana. "Melancholic Remains: Domestic and National Secrets in Fae Myenne Ng's *Bone*." *MFS: Modern Fiction Studies* 51.1 (2005): 110–33.

Chang, Yoonmee. "Chinese Suicide: Political Desire and Queer Exogamy in Fae Myenne Ng's *Bone*." *MFS: Modern Fiction Studies* 56.1 (2010): 90–112.

Chin, Vivian Fumiko. "Finding the Right Gesture: Becoming Chinese American in Fae Myenne Ng's *Bone*." In *The Chinese in America: A History from Gold Mountain to the New Millennium*, ed. Susie Lan Cassel. Walnut Creek, Calif.: AltaMira, 2002. 365–77.

Davis, Rocío G. "'Backdaire': Chinatown as Cultural Site in Fae Myenne Ng's *Bone* and Wayson Choy's *The Jade Peony*." *Revista Canaria de Estudios Ingleses* 43 (2001): 83–99.

Gee, Allen. "Deconstructing a Narrative Hierarchy: Leila Leong's 'I' in Fae Myenne Ng's *Bone*." *MELUS* 29.2 (2004): 129–40.

Goellnicht, Donald C. "Of Bones and Suicide: Sky Lee's *Disappearing Moon Cafe* and Fae Myenne Ng's *Bone*." *MFS: Modern Fiction Studies* 46.2 (2000): 300–330.

Kim, Thomas W. "'For a Paper Son, Paper Is Blood': Subjectivation and Authenticity in Fae Myenne Ng's *Bone*." *MELUS* 24.4 (1999): 41–56.

LeBlanc, Diane C. "Neologism as Oppositional Language in Fae Myenne Ng's *Bone*." *Rocky Mountain Review of Language and Literature* 54.1 (2000): 11–22.

Lee, Amy. "Chinatown and the Politics of Language in Fae Myenne Ng's *Bone*." In *Querying the Genealogy: Comparative and Transnational Studies in Chinese American*, ed. Jennie Wang. Shanghai, China: Shanghai Yiwen Press, 2006. 286–96.

Lee, A. Robert. "Imagined Cities of China: Timothy Mo's *London*, Sky Lee's *Vancouver*, Fae Myenne Ng's *San Francisco* and Gish Gen's *New York*." *Hitting Critical Mass* 4.1 (1996): 103–19.

Madsen, Deborah L. "Bearing the Diasporic Burden: Representations of Suicide in Sky Lee's *Disappearing Moon Café*, Fae Myenne Ng's *Bone*, and Hsu-Ming Teo's *Love and Vertigo*. In *China Fictions/English Language: Literary Essays in Diaspora, Memory, Story*, ed. A. Robert Lee. Amsterdam, Netherlands: Rodopi, 2008. 101–17.

Rhee, Michelle Young-Mee. "Reading Chinese in Fae Myenne Ng's *Bone*." In *Positioning the New: Chinese American Literature and the Changing Image of the American Literary Canon*, ed. Tanfer Emin Tunc and Elisabetta Marino. Newcastle upon Tyne, Great Britain: Cambridge Scholars, 2010. 52–68.

Ueki, Teruyo. "A Reading of Fae Myenne Ng's *Bone*." *AALA Journal* 2 (1995): 56–62.

Waller, Nicole. "Past and Repast: Food as Historiography in Fae Myenne Ng's *Bone* and Frank Chin's *Donald Duk*." *Amerikastudien/American Studies* 40.3 (1996): 485–502.

Noguchi, Yone

Duus, Masayo. *The Life of Isamu Noguchi: Journey without Borders*. Princeton, N.J.: Princeton University Press, 2004.

Graham, Don B. "Yone Noguchi's 'Poe Mania.'" *Markham Review* 4 (1974): 58–60.

Hakutani, Yoshinobu. "Ezra Pound, Yone Noguchi, and Imagism." *Modern Philology* 90.

———. "Father and Son: A Conversation with Isamu Noguchi." *Journal of Modern Literature* 17.1 (1990): 13–33. (1992): 46–69.

———. "Yone Noguchi's Poetry: From Whitman to Zen." *Comparative Literature Studies* 22.1 (1985): 67–79.

Haslam, Gerald W. "Three Exotics: Yone Noguchi, Shiesei Tsuneishi, and Sadakichi Hartmann." *College Language Association Journal* 19 (1976): 362–73.

Marx, Edward. "'A Different Mode of Speech': Yone Noguchi in Meiji America." In *Re/Collecting Asian America: Readings in Cultural History*, ed. Josephine Lee, Imogene L. Lim, and Yuko Matsukawa. Philadelphia: Temple University Press, 2002.

———. "A Slightly-Open Door: Yone Noguchi and the Invention of English Haiku." *Genre: Forms of Discourse and Culture* 39.3 (2006): 107–26.

Rao, K. S. Narayana. "The Poet as Cultural Ambassador: Yone Noguchi's *Indian Poems*." *Visvabharati Quarterly* 10.3 (2001): 9–16.

Sato, Hiroaki. "Yone Noguchi: Accomplishments and Roles." *Journal of American and Canadian Studies* 13 (1995): 105–21.

Yamasaki, Nobuko. "The Letters between Tagore and Noguchi, 1938." In *Rabindranath Tagore: Universality and Tradition*, ed. Patrick Colm Hogan and Lalita Pandit. Madison, N.J.: Fairleigh Dickinson University Press, 2003. 41–48.

Nunez, Sigrid

Beidler, Philip D. "Enlarging the Vietnam Canon: Sigrid Nunez's *For Rouenna*." *Michigan Quarterly Review* 43.4 (2004): 705–19.

Davis, Rocío G. "Identity in Community in Chinese American Short Story Cycles: Sigrid Nunez's *A Feather on the Breath of God*." *Hitting Critical Mass* 3.2 (1996): 115–33.

Fachinger, Petra. "German Mothers, New World Daughters: Angelika Fremd's *Heartland* and Sigrid Nunez's *A Feather on the Breath of God*." *Critique: Studies in Contemporary Fiction* 46.3 (2005): 253–66.

Schlote, Christiane. "(Sub)Urban Storytelling: Sigrid Nunez." In *Voces de América/American Voices: Entrevistas a escritores americanos/Interviews with American Writers*, ed. Laura Alonso Gallo. Cádiz, Spain: Aduana Vieja, 2004. 603–21.

Okada, John

Arakawa, Suzanne. "Suffering Male Bodies: Representations of Dissent and Displacement in the Internment-Themed Narratives of John Okada and Toshiro Mori."

In *Recovered Legacies: Authority and Identity in Early Asian American Literature*, ed. Keith Lawrence and Floyd Cheung. Philadelphia: Temple University Press, 2005. 183–206.

Bush, Harold K. "A Passion for the Impossible: Richard Rorty, John Okada, and James Baldwin." In *The Gift of Story: Narrating Hope in a Postmodern World*, ed. Emily Griesinger and Mark Eaton. Waco, Tex.: Baylor University Press, 2006. 171–86.

Kim, Daniel Y. "Once More, with Feeling: Cold War Masculinity and the Sentiment of Patriotism in John Okada's *No-No Boy*." *Criticism: A Quarterly for Literature and the Arts* 47.1 (2005): 65–83.

Ling, Jinqi. "Writing the Novel, Narrating Discontents: Race and Cultural Politics in John Okada's *No-No Boy*." In *Narrating Nationalism: Ideology and Form in Asian American Literature*. New York: Oxford University Press, 1998. 31–52.

McDonald, Dorothy Ritsuko. "After Imprisonment: Ichiro's Search for Redemption in *No-No Boy*." *MELUS* 6.3 (1979): 19–26.

Palumbo-Liu, David. "Discourse and Dislocation: Rhetorical Strategies of Asian-American Exclusion and Confinement." *LIT* 2 (1990): 1–7.

Park, Jinim. "The Portrait of a Japanese American in *No-No Boy* by John Okada." *Studies in Modern Fiction* 10.2 (2003): 155–75.

Sato, Gayle Fujita. "Momotaro's Exile: John Okada's *No-No Boy*." In *Reading the Literatures of Asian America*, ed. Shirley Geok-lin Lim and Amy Ling. Philadelphia: Temple University Press, 1992. 259–81.

Storhoff, Gary. "'A Prisoner of Forever': Cognitive Distortions and Depressions in John Okada's *No-No Boy*." *Interdisciplinary Literary Studies* 6.1 (2004): 1–20.

Sumida, Stephen H. "Japanese American Moral Dilemmas in John Okada's *No-No Boy* and Milton Murayama's *All I Asking for Is My Body*." In *Frontiers of Asian American Studies: Writing Research, and Criticism*. Pullman: Washington State University Press, 1989. 222–33.

Usui, Masami. "An Issei Woman's Suffering, Silence, and Suicide in John Okada's *No-No Boy*." *Amerasia Journal* 19.1 (1993): 121–33.

Xu, Wenying. "Sticky Rice Balls or Lemon Pie: Enjoyment and Ethnic Identity in *No-No Boy* and *Obasan*." *LIT: Literature Interpretation Theory* 13.1 (2002): 51–68.

Yeh, William. "To Belong or Not to Belong: The Liminality of John Okata's *No-No Boy*." *Amerasia Journal* 19.1 (1993): 121–33.

Yogi, Stan. "'You Had to be One or the Other': Oppositions and Reconciliation in John Okada's *No-No Boy*." *MELUS* 21.2 (1996): 63–77.

Rosca, Ninotchka

Casper, Leonard. "Social Realism in the Stories of Edilberto Tiempo and Ninotchka Rosca." *Solidarity* 8.1 (1973): 68–74.

Davis, Rocío G. "Postcolonial Visions and Immigrant Longings: Ninotchka Rosca's *Versions of the Philippines*." In *Twayne Companion to Contemporary World Literature: From the Editors of World Literature Today*, ed. Pamela A. Genova. New York: Thomson Gale, 2003. 761–68.

Fajutagana, Leonora M. "The Wild Woman Archetype in Contemporary Philippine Novels: The Empowered Filipina in Joaquin, Rosca and Yuson." In *The Likhaan Book of Philippine Criticism*, ed. J. Neil C. Garcia. Quezon City, Philippines: University of the Philippines Press, 2000. 257–74.

Manuel, Dolores de. "Decolonizing Bodies, Reinscribing Souls in the Fiction of Ninotchka Rosca and Linda Ty-Casper." *MELUS* 29.1 (2004): 99–118.

Maraan, Connie J. "Twice Blessed, Twice Oppressed: Ninotchka Rosca Writes Back." In *The Likhaan Book of Philippine Criticism*, ed. J. Neil C. Garcia. Quezon City, Philippines: University of the Philippines Press, 2000. 275–96.

Mendible, Myra. "The Politics and Poetics of Philippine Festival in Ninotchka Rosca's *State of War*." *International Fiction Review* 29.1–2 (2002): 30–39.

Nguyen, Viet. "The Postcolonial State of Desire: Homosexuality and Transvestitism in Ninotchka Rosca's *State of War*." *Critical Mass* 2.2 (1995): 67–93.

Santos, Bienvenido N.

Bascara, Victor. "Up from Benevolent Assimilation: At Home with the Manongs of Bienvenido Santos." *MELUS* 29.1 (2004): 61–78.

Bresnahan, Roger J. "The Midwestern Fiction of Bienvenido N. Santos." *Society for the Study of Midwestern Literature Newsletters* 13.2 (1983): 28–37.

Carpio, Rustica C. "Bienvenido Santos and *Brother, My Brother*." *Solidarity* 5.12 (1970): 58–64.

———. "Greater Shouting and Greater Silence: The Novels of Bienvenido Santos." *Solidarity* 3.10 (1968): 76–84.

———. "Paperboat Novels: the Later Bienvenido N. Santos." *Amerasia Journal* 13.1 (1986–1987): 163–70.

Cheung, King-Kok. "Bienvenido Santos: Filipino Old-timers in Literature." *Markham Review* 15 (1986): 49–53.

Davis, Rocío G. "Bienvenido Santos's *What the Hell for You Left Your Heart in San Francisco* and the Filipino Immigrant Dream." *Revista de Estudios Norteamericanos* 4 (1995): 139–45.

De Jesús, Melinda L. "Rereading History, Rewriting Desire: Reclaiming Queerness in Carlos Bulosan's *America Is in the Heart* and Bienvenido Santos' *Scent of Apples*." *Journal of Asian American Studies* 5.2 (2002): 91–111.

Grow, L. M. *The Novels of Bienvenido N. Santos.* Quezon City, Philippines: Giraffe, 1999.

———. "The Poet and the Garden: The Green World of Bienvenido N. Santos." *World Literature Written in English* 29.1 (1984): 136–45.

Manarpaac, Danilo Victorino. "Desire and Loathing in Carlos Bulosan's *America Is in the Heart* and Bienvenido Santos's *The Man Who (Thought He) Looked Like Robert Taylor*." In *Embracing the Other: Addressing Xenophobia in the New Literatures in English*, ed. Dunja M. Mohr. Amsterdam, Netherlands: Rodopi, 2008. 71–82.

Puente, Lorenzo. "Split-Level Christianity in *The Praying Man*." *Philippine Studies* 40.1 (1992): 111–20.

Reyes, Soledad S. "Death-in-Life in Santos's *Villa Magdalena*." In *Essays on the Philippine Novel in English*, ed. Joseph A. Galdon. Quezon City, Philippines: Ateneo de Manila University Press, 1979. 125–49.

Rico, Victoria S. "Themes in the Poetry of Bienvenido Santos." *Philippine Studies* 42.4 (1994): 452–74.

———. "*You Lovely People*: The Texture of Alienation." *Philippine Studies* 42.1 (1994): 91–104.

Valdez, Maria Stella. "The Myth and the Matrix in Bienvenido N. Santos' *Scent of Apples*: Searching for Harmony among Incongruities." *Dlsu Dialogue* 25.1 (1991): 73–82.

Ty, Eleanor. "A Filipino Prufrock in an Alien Land: Bienvenido Santos's *The Man Who (Thought He) Looked Like Robert Taylor*." *LIT: Literature Interpretation Theory* 12.3 (2001): 267–83.

Sidhwa, Bapsi

Abnoux, Cynthia. "A Study of the Stepfather and the Stranger in the Pakistani Novel: *The Bride* by Bapsi Sidhwa." *Commonwealth Essays and Studies* 13.1 (1990): 68–72.

Bruschi, Isabella. "Making Up with Painful History: The Partition of India in Bapsi Sidhwa's Work: Bapsi Sidhwa Interviewed." *Journal of Commonwealth Literature* 43.3 (2008): 141–49.

Didur, Jill. "Cracking the Nation: Gender, Minorities, and Agency in Bapsi Sidhwa's '*Cracking India*.'" *ARIEL: A Review of International English Literature* 29.3 (1998): 43–64.

Hai, Ambreen. "Border Work, Border Trouble: Postcolonial Feminism and the Ayah in Bapsi Sidhwa's *Cracking India*." *MFS: Modern Fiction Studies* 46.2 (2000): 379–426.

Jaidka, Manju. "Hyphenated Perspectives on the Cracking of India: Bapsi Sidhwa's *Ice-Candy-Man*." *South Asian Review* 25.2 (2004): 43–50.

Kain, Geoffrey. "Rupture as Continuity: Migrant Identity and 'Unsettled' Perspective in Bapsi Sidhwa's *An American Brat*." In *Asian American Literature in the International Context: Readings on Fiction, Poetry, and Performance*, ed. Rocío G. Davis and Sami Ludwig. Hamburg, Germany: Lit, 2002. 237–46.

Montenegro, David. "Bapsi Sidhwa: An Interview." *Massachusetts Review* 31.4 (1990): 513–33.

Sen, Asha. "Re-Visioning Bapsi Sidhwa's *Cracking India* in a Post-National Age." *Kunapipi: Journal of Postcolonial Writing* 31.1 (2009): 66–82.

Singh, Preeti. "My Place in the World: Bapsi Sidhwa." *Alif: Journal of Comparative Poetics* 18 (1998): 290–98.

Singh, Sujala. "Postcolonial Children: Representing the Nation in Arundhati Roy, Bapsi Sidhwa and Shyam Selvadurai." *Wasafiri: The Transnational Journal of International Writing* 41 (2004): 13–18.

Zaman, Niaz. "Bapsi Sidhwa." In *South Asian Writers in English*, ed. Fakrul Alam. Detroit, Mich.: Thomson Gale, 2006. 352–61.

Sone, Monica

Cooper, Janet. "A Two-Headed Freak and a Bad Wife Search for Home: Border Crossing in *Nisei Daughter* and *The Mixquiahuala Letters*." In *Literature and Ethnicity in the Cultural Borderlands*, ed. Jesus Benito and Ana Maria Manzanas. Amsterdam: Rodopi, 2002. 159–73.

Hoffman, Warren. "Home, Memory, and Narrative in Monica Sone's *Nisei Daughter*." In *Recovered Legacies: Authority and Identity in Early Asian American Literature*, ed. Keith Lawrence and Floyd Cheung. Philadelphia: Temple University Pres, 2005. 229–48.

Lim, Shirley Geok-lin. "Japanese American Women's Life Stories: Maternality in Monica Sone's *Nisei Daughter* and Joy Kogawa's *Obasan*." *Feminist Studies* 16.2 (1990): 288–312.

Rayson, Ann. "Beneath the Mask: Autobiographies of Japanese-American Women." *MELUS* 14.1 (1987): 43–57.

Sumida, Stephen H. "Protest and Accommodation, Self-Satire and Self-Effacement, and Monica Sone's *Nisei Daughter*." In *Multicultural Autobiography: American Lives*, ed. James Robert Payne. Knoxville: University of Tennessee Press, 1992. 207–47.

Yamamoto, Traise. "*Nisei Daughter* by Monica Sone." In *A Resource Guide to Asian American Literature*, ed. Sau-ling C. Wong and Stephen H. Sumida. New York: MLA, 2001. 151–58.

Song, Cathy

Chang, Juliana. "Reading Asian American Poetry." *MELUS* 21.1 (1996): 81–98.

Chen, Fu-Jen. "Body and Female Subjectivity in Cathy Song's *Picture Bride*." *Women's Studies: An Interdisciplinary Journal* 33.5 (2004): 577–612.

Choo, David. "Cathy's Song: Interview with Cathy Song." *Honolulu Weekly* 15 June, 1994: 6–8.

Fujita-Sato, Gayle K. "'Third World' as Place and Paradigm in Cathy Song's *Picture Bride*." *MELUS* 15.1 (1988): 49–72.

Usui, Masami. "Women Disclosed: Cathy Song's Poetry and Kitagawa Ukiyoe." *Studies in Culture and the Humanities* (1995): 1–19.

Van Dyne, Susan R. "Snapshots in History: Re-Reading Ethnic Subjects in Cathy Song." In *Re-Placing America: Conversations and Contestations: Selected Essays*, ed. Ruth Hsu et al. Honolulu: University of Hawaii, 2000. 181–98.

Wallace, Patricia. "Divided Loyalties: Literal and Literary in the Poetry of Lorna Dee Cervantes, Cathy Song, and Rita Dove." *MELUS* 18.3 (1993): 3–19.

Suleri, Sara

Adams, Timothy Dow. "Private Parts of Pakistan: Food and Privacy in Sara Suleri's *Meatless Days*." *Revista Canaria de Estudios Ingleses* 58 (2009): 67–75.

Bizzini, Silvia C. "Sara Suleri's *Meatless Days* and Maxine Hong Kingston's *The Woman Warrior*: Writing History and the Self after Foucault." *Women: A Cultural Review* (1996): 55–65.

Davis, Rocío G. "A Task of Reclamation: Subjectivity, Self-Representation, and Textual Formulation in Sara Suleri's *Meatless Days*." In *Asian North American Identities: Beyond the Hyphen*, ed. Eleanor Ty and Donald Goellnicht. Bloomington: Indiana University Press, 2004: 117–29.

———. "Writing Fathers: Auto/biography and Unfulfilled Vocation in Sara Suleri Goodyear's *Boys Will Be Boys* and Hanif Kureishi's *My Ear at His Heart*." *Life Writing* 6.2 (2009): 229–41.

Dayal, Samir. "Style Is (Not) the Woman: Sara Suleri's *Meatless days*. In *Between the Lines: South Asian and Postcoloniality*, ed. Deepika Bahri. Philadelphia: Temple University Press, 1996. 250–69.

Ganapathy-Doré, Geetha. "A Mouthful of Stones in a Mango Leaf: History, Womanhood and Language in Sara Suleri's *Meatless Days*, a Memoir." *Commonwealth Essays and Studies* 24.1 (2001): 31–40.

Grewal, Inderpal. "Autobiographic Subjects and Diasporic Locations: *Meatless Days* and *Borderlands*." In *Scattered Hegemonies: Postmodernity and Transnational Feminist Practices*, ed. Inderpal Grewal and Karen Kaplan. Minneapolis: University of Minnesota Press, 1994. 231–54.

Hirsiaho, Anu. "Devouring Grief: Mourning and the Embodied Politics of Memory in Sara Suleri's *Meatless Days*." *Atlantic Literary Review* 3.2 (2002): 188–209.

Koshy, Susan. "Mother-Country and Fatherland: Re-Membering the Nation in Sara Suleri's *Meatless Days*." In *Interventions: Feminist Dialogues on Third World Women's Literature and Film*, ed. Brinda Rose et al. New York: Garland, 1997. 45–61.

Kruckels, Birgit. "'Men Live in Homes, Women Live in Bodies': Body and Gender in Sara Suleri's *Meatless Days*." In *Hybridity and Postcolonialism: Twentieth-Century Indian Literature*, ed. Monika Fludernik. Tübingen, Germany: Stauffenburg, 1998. 167–86.

Lovesey, Oliver. "'Postcolonial Self-Fashioning' in Sara Suler's *Meatless Days*." *Journal of Commonwealth Literature* 32.2 (1997): 35–50.

Oed, Anja. "Aspects of (Self)-Representation in Sara Suleri's *Meatless Days*; or, What Does it Mean to Write a Book beyond What It Is About." In *Hybridity and Postcolonialism: Twentieth-Century Indian Literature*, ed. Monika Fludernik. Tubingen, Germany: Stauffenburg, 1998. 187–97.

Rahman, Shazia. "Orientalism, Deconstruction, and Relationality: Sara Suleri's *Meatless Days*." *LIT: Literature Interpretation Theory* 15.4 (2004): 347–62.

Ray, Sangeeta. "Memory, Identity, Patriarchy: Projecting a Past in the Memoirs of Sara Suleri and Michael Ondaatje." *Modern Fiction Studies* 39.1 (1993): 37–58.

Scanlon, Mara. "Mother Land, Mother Tongue: Reconfiguring Relationship in Suleri's *Meatless Days*." *LIT: Literature Interpretation Theory* 12.4 (2001): 411–25.

Sutherland, Katherine G. "Land of Their Graves: Maternity, Mourning and Nation in Janet Frame, Sara Suleri, and Arundhati Roy." *Canadian Review of Comparative Literature* 30.1 (2003): 201–16.

Warley, Linda. "Assembling Ingredients: Subjectivity in *Meatless Days*." *Autobiography Studies* 7.1 (1992): 107–23.

Tan, Amy

Adams, Bella. "Identity-in-Difference: Re-Generating Debate about Intergenerational Relationships in Amy Tan's *The Joy Luck Club*." *Studies in the Literary Imagination* 39.2 (2006): 79–94.

Bhattacharya, Chidananda. "The Spectrum of Diaspora in *The Joy Luck Club*." *Journal of Indian Writing in English* 36.2 (2008): 47–54.

Bow, Leslie. "Cultural Conflict/Feminist Resolution in Amy Tan's *The Joy Luck Club*." In *New Visions in Asian American Studies: Diversity, Community, Power*, ed. Franklin Eng et al. Pullman: Washington State University Press, 1994. 235–47.

Braendlin, Bonnie. "Mother/Daughter Dialog(ic)s in, around, and about Amy Tan's *The Joy Luck Club*." In *Private Lives: Women Speak on the Literary Life*, ed. Nancy Owen Nelson. Denton: University of North Texas Press, 1995. 111–24.

Caesar, Judith. "Patriarchy, Imperialism, and Knowledge in *The Kitchen God's Wife*." *North Dakota Quarterly* 62.4 (1994): 164–74.

Chang, Ya-Hui Irenna. "Food Consumption and the Troubled Self in Kingston's *The Woman Warrior*, Walker's *The Color Purple*, Tan's *The Joy Luck Club*, and Erdrich's *Love Medicine*." In *You Are What You Eat: Literary Probes into the Palate*, ed. Annette M. Magid. Newcastle upon Tyne, Great Britain: Cambridge Scholars, 2008. 345–66.

Chen, Leilei. "Resisting American Orientalism: Rereading Amy Tan as a Counter-Discourse of American Mainstream Ideology." In *Re-Reading America: Changes and Challenges*, ed. Weihe Zhong. Cheltenham, Great Britain: Reardon, 2004. 270–81.

Cheng, Sinkwan. "Fantasizing the Jouissance of the Chinese Mother: *The Joy Luck Club* and Amy Tan's Quest for Stardom in the Market of Neo-Racism." *Savoir: Psychanalyse et analyse culturelle* 3.1–2 (1997): 95–133.

David, Rocio G. "Wisdom (Un)heeded: Chinese Mothers and American Daughters in Amy Tan's *Joy Luck Club*." *Cuadernos de Investigacion Filologica* 19–20 (1993–1994): 89–100.

Dunick, Lisa. "The Silencing Effect of Canonicity: Authorship and the Written Word in Amy Tan's Novels." *MELUS* 31.2 (2006): 20.

Elbert, Monika. "Retrieving the Language of the Ghostly Mother: Displaced Daughters and the Search for Home in Amy Tan and Michelle Cliff." In *Ghosts, Stories, Histories: Ghost Stories and Alternative Histories*, ed. Sladja Blazan. Newcastle upon Tyne, Great Britain: Cambridge Scholars, 2007. 159–72.

Evans, Robert C., ed. *The Joy Luck Club by Amy Tan*. Pasadena, Calif.: Salem, 2010.

Foster, M. Marie Booth. "Voice, Mind, Self: Mother-Daughter Relationships in Amy Tan's *The Joy Luck Club* and *The Kitchen God's Wife*." In *Women of Color: Mother-Daughter Relationships in 20th Century Literature*, ed. Elizabeth Brown-Guillory. Austin: University of Texas Press, 1996. 208–27.

Hawley, John C. "Assimilation and Resistance in Female Fiction of Immigration: Bharati Mukherjee, Amy Tan, and Christine Bell." In *Rediscovering America, 1492–1992: National, Cultural, and Disciplinary Boundaries Re-examined*, ed. Leslie Bary et al. Baton Rouge: Louisiana State University Press, 1992. 226–34.

Heller, Dana. "A Possible Sharing: Ethnicizing Mother-Daughter Romance in Amy Tan's *The Joy Luck Club*." In *Family Plots: The De-Oedipalization of Popular Culture*, ed. Dana A. Heller. Philadelphia: University of Pennsylvania Press, 1995. 113–28.

Heung, Marina. "Daughter-Text / Mother-Text: Matrilineage in Amy Tan's *Joy Luck Club*." *Feminist Studies* 19.3 (1993): 597–616.

Ho, Wendy. "Swan-Feather Mothers and Coca-Cola Daughters: Teach Tan's *The Joy Luck Club*." In *Teaching American Ethnic Literatures: Nineteen Essays*, ed. John R. Maitino and David R. Peck. Albuquerque: University of New Mexico Press, 1996. 327–45.

Huntley, E. D. *Amy Tan: A Critical Companion*. Westport, Conn.: Greenwood, 1998.

Korpez, Esra Coker. "Revisiting the Amy Tan Phenomenon: Storytelling and Ideology in Amy Tan's Children's Story *The Moon Lady*." *Interactions: Aegean Journal of English and American Studies* 16.2 (2007): 87–95.

Lux, Elaine. "Narrative Bones: Amy Tan's *Bonesetter's Daughter* and Hugh Cook's *Homecoming Man*." In *The Gift of Story: Narrating Hope in a Postmodern World*, ed. Mark Eaton. Waco, Tex.: Baylor University Press, 2006. 117–32.

McAllister, Melanie. "(Mis)Reading *The Joy Luck Club*." *Asian America: Journal of Culture and the Arts* 1 (1992): 102–18.

Mountain, Chandra Tyler. "'The Struggle of Memory against Forgetting': Cultural Survival in Amy Tan's *The Joy Luck Club*." In *The World of Amy Tan: Special Issue of Paintbrush* 22 (1995): 39–50.

Olson, Carol Booth, and Pat Clark. "Using Amy Tan's *The Moon Lady* to Teach Analytical Writing in the Multicultural Classroom." *The World of Amy Tan: Special Issue of Paintbrush* 22 (1995): 85–98.

Reid, E. Shelley. "'Our Two Faces': Balancing Mothers and Daughters in *The Joy Luck Club* and *The Kitchen God's Wife*." *The World of Amy Tan: Special Issue of Paintbrush* 22 (1995): 20–38.

Rho, Heongyun. "Teaching Amy Tan from the Perspective of Comparative Cultural Studies." *British and American Fiction to 1900* 16.2 (2009): 29–48.

Schueller, Malini Johar. "Theorizing Ethnicity and Subjectivity: Maxine Hong Kingston's *Tripmaster Monkey* and Amy Tan's *The Joy Luck Club*." *Genders* 15 (1992): 72–85.

Shear, Walter. "Generation Differences and the Diaspora in *The Joy Luck Club*." *Critique: Studies in Contemporary Fiction* 34.3 (1993): 193–99.

Shen, Gloria. "Born of a Stranger: Mother-Daughter Relationships and Storytelling in Amy Tan's *The Joy Luck Club*." In *International Women's Writing: New Landscapes of Identity*, ed. Anne E. Brown and Maryann E. Gooz. Westport, Conn.: Greenwood, 1995. 233–44.

Somogyi, Barbara, and David Stanton. "Amy Tan: An Interview." *Poets and Writers Magazine* (September–October 1991): 24–32.

Souri, Stephen. "Only Two Kinds of Daughters: Inter-Monologue Dialogicity in *The Joy Luck Club.*" *MELUS* 19.2 (1994): 99–123.

Wang, Qun. "The Dialogic Richness of *The Joy Luck Club.*" *The World of Amy Tan: Special Issue of Paintbrush* 22 (1995): 76–84.

Wong, Cynthia F. "Asymmetries: Loss and Forgiveness in the Novels of Amy Tan." In *Asymmetries: Loss and Forgiveness in the Novels of Amy Tan*, ed. Robert A. Lee. Amsterdam, Netherland: Rodopi, 2008. 57–78.

Wong, Sau-ling Cynthia. "'Sugar Sisterhood': Situating the Amy Tan Phenomenon." In *The Ethnic Canon: Histories, Institutions, and Interventions*, ed. David Palumbo-Liu. Minneapolis: University of Minnesota Press, 1995. 174–210.

Woo, Eunjoo. "'The Things I Must Not Forget': Chinese American Mother/Daughter Conflict and Reconciliation in Amy Tan's *The Bonesetter's Daughter.*" *Feminist Studies in English Literature* 12.1 (2004): 129–49.

Xu, Ben. "Memory and the Ethnic Self: Reading Amy Tan's *The Joy Luck Club.*" *MELUS* 19.1 (1994): 3–18.

Xu, Wenying. "A Womanist Production of Truths: The Use of Myth in Amy Tan." *The World of Amy Tan: Special Issue of Paintbrush* 22 (1995): 56–66.

Ty-Casper, Linda

Lim, Jaime An. "*The Three-Cornered Sun*: Portraits of the Revolution." *Philippine Studies* 40.2 (1992): 255–66.

Manuel, Dolores de. "Decolonizing Bodies, Reinscribing Souls in the Fiction of Ninotchka Rosca and Linda Ty-Casper." *MELUS* 29.1 (2004): 99–118.

Martinez-Sicat, Maria Teresa. "The Exceptional Son in Linda Ty-Casper's *The Three-Cornered Sun.*" In *Imagining the Nation in Four Philippine Novels*. Quezon City, Philippines: University of Philippines Press, 1994. 70–91.

Villa, José Garcia

Arcellana, Francisco. "Jose Garcia Villa." In *Brown Heritage: Essays on Philippine Cultural Tradition and Literature*, ed. Antonio G. Manuud. Quezon City, Philippines: Ateneo de Manila University Press, 1967. 714–21.

Chua, Jonathan. "A Reaction to Rajeev S. Patke's 'Modernist Poetic Practices in English Poetry from Southeast Asia: A Comparison between Jose Garcia Villa and Arthur Yap.'" *Kritika Kultura* 9 (2007): 7, 27–33.

———, ed. *The Critical Villa: Essays in Literary Criticism by Jose Garcia Villa.* Quezon City, Philippines: Ateneo de Manila University Press, 2002.

Chua, Jonathan, and Luis Cabalquinto. "Interview with the Tiger." *Pen and Ink* 1 (1997): 10–15.

Cowen, John Edwin. "Doveglion—The E. E. Cummings and José Garcia Villa Connection." *The Journal of the E. E. Cummings Society* 10 (2001): 102–9.

Cruz, Denise. "José García Villa's Collection of 'Others': Irreconcilabilities of a Queer Transpacific Modernism." *MFS: Modern Fiction Studies* 55.1 (2009): 11–41.

Holden, Philip. "Unbecoming Rizal: José Garcia Villa's Biographical Translations." *Life Writing* 6.3 (2009): 287–302.

Patke, Rajeev S. "Modernist Poetic Practices in English Poetry from Southeast Asia: A Comparison between Jose Garcia Villa and Arthur Yap." *Kritika Kultura* 9 (2007): 11–26.

San Juan, E, Jr. "Homage to Jose Garcia Villa." In *The Anchored Angel: Selected Writings by Jose Garcia Villa*, ed. Eileen Tabios. New York: Kaya Press, 1999. 191–216.

———. "Jose Garcia Villa: Vicissitudes of Neocolonial Art-Fetishism and the 'Beautiful Soul' of the Filipino Exile." *Kritika Kultura* 13 (2009): 5–22.

Tinio, Rolando S. "Villa's Values; or, The Poet You Cannot Always Make Out, or Succeed in Liking Once You Are Able To." In *Brown Heritage: Essays on Philippine Cultural Tradition and Literature*, ed. Antonio G. Manuud. Quezon City, Philippines: Ateneo de Manila University Press, 1967. 722–38.

Veric, Charlie Samuya. "The Radical José Garcia Villa." *Pilipinas: Journal of Philippine Studies* 44 (2005): 49–57.

Yu, Timothy. "'The Hand of a Chinese Master': José Garcia Villa and Modernist Orientalism." *MELUS* 29.1 (2004): 41–59.

Wong, Jade Snow

Blinde, Patricia Lin. "The Icicle in the Desert: Perspective and Form in the Work of Two Chinese-American Women Writers." *MELUS* 6.3 (1979): 51–71.

Cobb, Nora. "Food as an Expression of Cultural Identity in Jade Snow Wong and *Songs for Jadina*." *Hawaii Review* 12 (1988): 12–16.

Douglas, Christopher. "Reading Ethnography: The Cold War Social Science of Jade Snow Wong's *Fifth Chinese Daughter* and Brown v. Board of Education." *In Form and Transformation in Asian American Literature*, ed. Xiaojing Zhou and Samina Najmi. Seattle: University of Washington Press, 2005. 101–24.

Kim, Elaine. "*Fifth Chinese Daughter*." In *Asian American Literature: An Introduction to the Writings and Their Social Context*. Philadelphia: Temple University Press, 1982. 66–72.

Koo, Eunsook. "African/Asian Diasporic Women's Autobiographies: Zora Neale Hurston and Jade Snow Wong." *Studies in Modern Fiction* 12.1 (2005): 7–38.

Lim, Shirley Geok-lin. "The Tradition of Chinese American Women's Life Stories: Thematics of Race and Gender in Jade Snow Wong's *Fifth Chinese Daughter* and Maxine Hong Kingston's *The Woman Warrior*." In *American Women's Autobiography: Fea(s)ts of Memory*, ed. Margo Culley. Madison: University of Wisconsin Press, 1992. 252–67.

Ling, Amy. "Jade Snow Wong and Maxine Hong Kingston." In *Between Worlds: Women Writers of Chinese Ancestry*. New York: Pergamon Press, 1990. 119–30.

Madsen, Deborah L. "The Oriental/Occidental Dynamic in Chinese American Life Writing: Pardee Lowe and Jade Snow Wong." *Amerikastudien/American Studies* 51.3 (2006): 343–53.

Piep, Karsten H. "'As If They Thought She Were Deaf or Dumb': The Reproduction of Dominant Discourses in Jade Snow Wong's *Fifth Chinese Daughter*." *Philament* 6 (2005): (no pagination).

Sue, Karen. "Jade Snow Wong's Badge of Distinction in the 1990s." *Hitting Critical Mass* 2 (1994): 3–52.

Tang, Weiming. "Translating and Transforming the American Dream: Jade Snow Wong's *Fifth Chinese Daughter* and Gish Jen's *Typical American*." In *China Abroad: Travels, Subjects, Spaces*, ed. Elaine Yee Lin Ho and Julia Kuehn. Hong Kong: Hong Kong University Press, 2009. 123–37.

Tolentino, Cynthia. "Crossings in Prose: Jade Snow Wong and the Demand for a New Kind of Expert." In *Afroasian Encounters: Culture, History, Politics*, ed. Heike Raphael-Hernandez and Shannon Steen. New York: New York University Press, 2006. 34–49.

Yin, Kathleen Loh Swee, and Kristoffer F. Paulson. "The Divided Voice of Chinese American Narration: Jade Snow Wong's *Fifth Chinese Daughter*." *MELUS* 9 (1982): 53–9.

Yamamoto, Hisaye

Cheng, Ming L. "The Unrepentant Fire: Tragic Limitations in Hisaye Yamamoto's *Seventeen Syllables*." *MELUS* 19.4 (1994): 91–107.

Cheung, King-kok. *Articulating Silences: Narrative Strategies in Hisaye Yamamoto, Maxine Hong Kingston, and Joy Kogawa*. Ithaca, N.Y.: Cornel University, Press, 1993.

———. "Double-Telling: Intertextual Silence in Hisaye Yamamoto's Fiction." *American Literary History* 3.2 (1991): 277–93.

———. "Thrice Muted Tale: Interplay of Art and Politics in Hisaye Yamamoto's *The Legend of Miss Sasagawara*." *MELUS* 17.3 (1991–1992): 109–25.

Chiu, Monica. "Japanese American Internment, National Pathology, and Intra-racial Strife in Hisaye Yamamoto's *The Legend of Miss Sasagawara*." *Notes on Contemporary Literature* 39.2 (2009): 8–10.

Crow, Charles L. "A MELUS Interview: Hisaye Yamamoto." *MELUS* 14.1 (1987): 73–84.

Elliott, Matthew. "Sins of Omission: Hisaye Yamamoto's Vision of History." *MELUS* 34.1 (2009): 47–68.

Higashida, Cheryl. "Re-Signed Subjects: Women, Work, and World in the Fiction of Carlos Bulosan and Hisaye Yamamoto." *Studies in the Literary Imagination* 37.1 (2004): 35–60.

Hong, Grace Kyungwon. "Something Forgotten Which Should Have Been Remembered: Private Property and Cross-Racial Solidarity in the Work of Hisaye Yamamoto." *American Literature* 71.2 (1999): 291–310.

McDonald, Dorothy Ritsuko. "Relocation and Dislocation: The Writings of Hisaye Yamamoto and Wakako Yamauchi." *MELUS* 7.3 (1980): 21–38.

Mullins, Maire. "Esther's Smile: Silence and Action in Hisye Yamamoto's *Wilshire Bus*." *Studies in Short Fiction* 35.1 (1998): 77–84.

———. "Imagining Community: Language and Literacy in Hisaye Yamamoto's *Seventeen Syllables*." *Journal of Asian American Studies* 13.2 (2010): 219–41.

Osborn, William P. "A Conversation with Hisaye Yamamoto." *Chicago Review* 39.3–4 (1993): 34–43.

Payne, Robert M. "Adapting (to) the Margins: Hot Summer Winds and the Stories of Hisaye Yamamoto." *East-West Film Journal* 7.2 (1993): 39–53.

Sugiyama, Naoko. "Issei Mothers' Silence, Nisei Daughters' Stories: The Short Fiction of Hisaye Yamamoto." *Comparative Literature Studies* 33.1 (1996): 1–14.

Yogi, Stan. "Legacies Revealed: Uncovering Buried Plots in the Stories of Hisaye Yamamoto." *Studies in American Fiction* 17.2 (1989): 169–181.

———. "Rebels and Heroines: Subversive Narratives in the Stories of Wakako Yamauchi and Hisaye Yamamoto." In *Reading the Literatures of Asian America*, ed. Shirley Geok-lin Lim and Amy Ling. Philadelphia: Temple University Press, 1992. 131–50.

Usui, Masami. "Prison, Psyche, and Poetry in Hisaye Yamamoto's Three Short Stories: 'Seventeen Syllables,' 'The Legend of Miss Sasagawara,' and 'The Eskimo Connection.'" *Studies in Culture and the Humanities* 6 (1997): 1–29.

Yamanaka, Lois-Ann

Cheung, Floyd. "The Language of Mourning in Lois-Ann Yamanaka's *Blue's Hanging*." *CLA Journal* 49.3 (2006): 305–12.

Chew, Kristina. "The Disabled Speech of Asian Americans: Silence and Autism in Lois-Ann Yamanaka's *Father of the Four Passages*." *Disability Studies Quarterly* 30.1 (2010): (no pagination).

Davis, Rocío G. "Short Story Cycle and Hawai'i Bildungsroman: Writing Self, Place, and Family in Lois-Ann Yamanaka's *Wild Meat and the Bully Burgers*." In *Form and Transformation in Asian American Literature*, ed. Xiaojing Zhou and Samina Najmi. Seattle: University of Washington Press, 2005. 231–48.

Inserra, Incoronata. "Spreading Traditions: Lois-Ann Yamanaka's Bildungsroman." In *'Contact Zones': Rewriting Genre across the East-West Border*, ed. Donatella Izzo and Elena Spandri. Naples, Italy: Liguori, 2003. 197–226.

Kim, Chang-Hee. "A Traumatic Face of Colonial Hawai'i: The 1998 Asian American Event and Lois-Ann Yamanaka's *Blu's Hanging*." *Journal of English Language and* 56.6 (2010): 1311–37.

Rie, Makino. "Under the Father's Slaughter: The Gendered Politics between Local Father and Subaltern Daughter in Lois-Ann Yamanaka's *Wild Meat and the Bully Burgers*." *AALA Journal* 11 (2005): 153–66.

Russell, Emily. "Locating Cure: Leprosy and Lois-Ann Yamanaka's *Blu's Hanging*." *MELUS* 31.1 (2006): 53–80.

Shea, Renee H. "Pidgin Politics and Paradise Revised." *Poets and Writers* 26.5 (1998): 32–39.

Shim, Rosalee. "Power in the Eye of the Beholder: A Close Reading of Lois-Ann Yamanaka's *Saturday Night at the Pahala Theater*." *Hitting Critical Mass* 3.1 (1995): 85–91.

Usui, Masami. "Sexual Colonialism in a Postcolonial Era in Lois-Ann Yamanaka's Novels: *Wild Meat and the Bully Burger*, *Blu's Hanging*, *Name Me Nobody*, *Heads by Harry*, and *Father of the Four Passages*." *Doshisha Literature* 47 (2004): 27–51.

Wilson, Rob. "Bloody Mary Meets Lois-Ann Yamanaka: Imagining Asia/Pacific—from South Pacific to Bamboo Ridge." In *Transnational Asia Pacific: Gender, Culture, and the Public Sphere*, ed. Shirley Geok-lin Lim et al. Urbana: University of Illinois Press, 1999. 92–110.

Wu, Cynthia. "Revisiting *Blu's Hanging*: A Critique of Queer Transgression in the Lois-Ann Yamanaka Controversy." *Meridians: Feminism, Race, Transnationalism* 10.1 (2010): 32–53.

Yamauchi, Wakako

Cheung, King-Kok. "Hisaye Yamomoto and Wakako Yamauchi." In *Words Matter: Conversations with Asian American Writers*, ed. King-Kok Cheung. Honolulu: University of Hawaii Press, 2000. 343–82.

Holliday, Shawn. "And the Soul Shall Dance: Thomas Wolfe's Influence on Wakako Yamauchi." *Thomas Wolfe Review* 31.1–2 (2007): 11–21.

Osborn, William P. "A MELUS Interview: Wakako Yamauchi." *MELUS* 23.2 (1998): 101–10.

Osumi, M. Dick. "Jungian and Mythological Patterns in Wakako Yamauchi's *And the Soul Shall Dance*." *Amerasia Journal* 27.1 (2001): 87–96.

Sumida, Stephen H. "*And the Soul Shall Dance* by Wakako Yamauchi." In *A Resource Guide to Asian American Literature*, ed. Sau-ling Cynthia Wong and Stephen H. Sumida. New York: MLA, 2001. 221–32.

Yogi, Stan. "Rebels and Heroines: Subversive Narratives in the Stories of Wakako Yamauchi and Hisaye Yamamoto." In *Reading the Literatures of Asian America*, ed. Shirley Geok-lin Lim and Amy Ling. Philadelphia: Temple University Press, 1992. 131–50.

Yau, John

Foster, Edward. "John Yau and the Seductions of Everything That Used to Be." *MultiCultural Review* 3.1 (1994): 36–39.

Lagapa, Jason. "Parading the Undead: Camp, Horror and Reincarnation in the Poetry of Frank O' Hara and John Yau." *Journal of Modern Literature* 33.2 (2010): 92–113.

Lee, Merton. "A Canon of Alterity: John Yau's Corpse and Mirror." In *Positioning the New: Chinese American Literature and the Changing Image of the American Literary Canon*, ed. Tanfer Emin Tunc and Elisabetta Marino. Newcastle upon Tyne, Great Britain: Cambridge Scholars, 2010. 143–55.

Mar, Christine. "The Language of Ethnicity: John Yau's Poetry and the Ethnic/Aesthetic Divide." In *Literary Gestures: The Aesthetic in Asian American Writing*, ed. Rocío G. Davis and Sue-Im Lee. Philadelphia: Temple University Press, 2006. 70–85.

Morris, Daniel. "Strangers and Oneself: John Yau's Writings on Contemporary Art." *Talisman* 21–22 (2001): 45–57.

Wald, Priscilla. "'Chaos Goes Uncourted': John Yau's Dis(-)orienting Poetics." In *Cohesion and Dissent in America*, ed. Carol Colatrella and Joseph Alkana. Albany: State University of New York Press, 1994. 133–58.

Wang, Dorothy J. "Undercover Asian: John Yau and the Politics of Ethnic Self-Identification." In *Asian American Literature in the International Context: Readings on Fiction, Poetry, and Performance*, ed. Rocío G. Davis and Sämi Ludwig. Hamburg, Germany: Lit, 2002. 135–55.

Zhou, Xiaojing. "Postmodernism and Subversive Parody: John Yau's 'Genghis Chan: Private Eye' Series." *College Literature* 31.1 (2004): 73–102.

———. "Two Hat Softeners 'In the Trade Confession': John Yau and Kimiko Hahn." In *Form and Transformation in Asian American Literature*, ed. Xiaojing Zhou and Samina Najmi. Seattle: University of Washington Press, 2005. 168–89.

Yew, Chay

Botelho, Teresa. "Redefining the Dramatic Canon: Staging Identity Instability in the Work of David Henry Hwang and Chay Yew." In *Positioning the New: Chinese American Literature and the Changing Image of the American Literary Canon*, ed. Tanfer Emin Tunc and Elisabetta Marino. Newcastle upon Tyne, Great Britain: Cambridge Scholars, 2010. 128–42.

Cho, Nancy. "Beyond Identity Politics: National and Transnational Dialogues in Anna Deavere Smith's *Twilight: Los Angeles, 1992* and Chay Yew's *A Beautiful Country*." *Journal of Dramatic Theory and Criticism* 20.1 (2005): 65–81.

De Wagter, Caroline. "Re-Configuring Cultural Memory in Chay Yew's *Wonderland* and M. J. Kang's *Blessings*." In *Signatures of the Past: Cultural Memory in Contemporary Anglophone North American Drama*, ed. Marc Maufort and Caroline De Wagter. Brussels, Belgium: Peter Lang, 2008. 273–90.

Diehl, Heath. "Beyond the Silk Road: Staging a Queer Asian America in Chay Yew's *Porcelain*." *Studies in the Literary Imagination* 37.1 (2004): 149–67.

Drake, David. "Fusion: David Drakes Interviews Playwright Chay Yew." *Lambda Book Report: A Review of Contemporary Gay and Lesbian Literature* 7.4 (1998): 6–8.

Drukman, Steven. "Chay Yew: The Importance of Being Verbal." *American Theatre* (November 1995): 58–60.

Lim, January. "Father Knows Best: Reading Sexuality in Ang Lee's *The Wedding Banquet* and Chay Yew's *Porcelain*." In *Reading Chinese Transnationalisms: Society, Literature, Film*, ed. Maria N. Ng and Philip Holden. Hong Kong: Hong Kong University Press, 2006. 143–60.

SOURCE BOOKS

Adams, Bella. *Asian American Literature (Edinburgh Critical Guides to Literature)*. Scotland: Edinburgh University Press, 2008.

Burn, Lucy. *Asian American Playwrights: A Bio-Bibliographical Critical Sourcebook.* Westport, Conn.: Greenwood Press, 2002.

Day, Frances Ann. *Multicultural Voices in Contemporary Literature: A Resource for Teachers.* London: Heinemann, 1994.

Cheung, King-Kok, ed. *An Interethnic Companion to Asian American Literature.* Cambridge: Cambridge University Press, 1997.

———, ed. *An Interethnic Guide to Asian American Literature.* New York: Cambridge University Press, 1997.

Cheung, King-Kok, and Stan Yogi. *Asian American Literature: An Annotated Bibliography.* New York: MLA, 1988.

Criddle, Joan D. *Bamboo and Butterflies: From Refugee to Citizen.* Dixon: East/West, 1992.

Hiura, Arnold T., and Stephen H. Sumida. *Asian American Literature of Hawaii: An Annotated Bibliography.* Honolulu: Japanese American Research Center and Talk Story, 1979.

Huang, Guiyou, ed. *Asian American Autobiographers: A Bio-Bibliographical Critical Sourcebook.* Westport, Conn.: Greenwood Press, 2001.

———, ed. *Asian American Literary Studies (Introducing Ethnic Studies).* Edinburg, Scotland: Edinburg University Press, 2005.

———, ed. *Asian American Poets: A Bio-Bibliographical Critical Sourcebook.* Westport, Conn.: Greenwood Press, 2002.

———, ed. *Asian American Short Story Writers: An A-to-Z Guide.* Westport, Conn.: Greenwood Press, 2003.

———, ed. *The Columbia Guide to Asian American Literature since 1945.* New York: Columbia University Press, 2006.

———, ed. *The Greenwood Encyclopedia of Asian American Literature.* Westport, Conn.: Greenwood Press, 2008.

Kamp, Jim, ed. *Reference Guide to American Literature.* Detroit, Mich.: St. James Press, 1994.

Leonard, George J., ed. *The Asian Pacific American Heritage: A Companion to Literature and the Arts.* New York: Garland, 1999.

Li, David Leiwei, ed. *Asian American Literature.* New York: Routledge, 2011.

Madsen, Deborah L. *Literary Topics V9 Asian American Literature.* Farmington Hills, Mich.: Thomson Gale, 2002.

———, ed. *Asian American Writers.* Detroit, Mich.: Gale, 2005.

———, ed. *Dictionary of Literary Biography: Asian American Writers.* Detroit, Mich.: Gale, 2005.

Nelson, Emmanuel S, ed. *Asian American Novelists: A Bio-Bibliographical Critical Sourcebook.* Westport, Conn.: Greenwood Press, 2000.

——— Westport, Conn.: Greenwood Press, 2005.

———, ed. *Reworlding: The Literature of the Indian Diaspora.* Westport, Conn.: Greenwood Press, 1992.

———, ed. *Writers of the Indian Diaspora: A Bio-Bibliographical Critical Sourcebook.* Westport, Conn.: Greenwood Press, 1993.

Oh, Seiwoong. *Encyclopedia of Asian-American Literature.* New York: Facts On File, 2007.

Peterson, Jane T., and Susanne Bennett, eds. *Women Playwrights of Diversity: A Bibliographical Sourcebook.* Westport, Conn.: Greenwood Press, 1997.

Valeros, Florentino B., and Estrellita Valeros-Gruenberg. *Filipino Writers in English: A Biographical and Bibliographical Directory.* Quezon City, Philippines: New Day Publishers, 1987.

Wong, Sau-ling Cynthia and Stephen H. Sumida, eds. *A Resource Guide to Asian American Literature.* New York: MLA, 2001.

WEBSITES

http://www.aatrevue.com/AATR-1.html

Run by Roger W. Tang, this site centers on Asian American theater, offering a bibliography of plays and a list of Asian American theaters.

http://www.aaww.org/

This is the official site of Asian American Writers' Workshop; it features a large number of writers and advertises literary events.

http://www.adoptvietnam.org/books/books-vn-americans.htm

This site offers summaries of a list of Vietnamese American writings.

http://wwwlibrary.csustan.edu/pcrawford/asianlit/

Compiled by Paula J. Crawford and maintained by Annie Hor, this link provides bibliographies of various subgroups in Asian American literature.

http://alumni.eecs.berkeley.edu/~manish/

Run by Manish Vij, this site offers samples of South Asian American authors, books, bookstores, films, etc.

http://english.emory.edu/Bahri/Filipino.html

The Department of English at Emory University runs this site that provides a brief history on Filipino Americans and a selection of Filipino American writings.

http://filamread.tripod.com/

Calling itself the Filipino and Filipino–American Cyber Library, this site offers a bibliography of fiction, poetry, and anthologies.

http://immigration-online.org/358-asian-american-literature.html

This link offers histories of Asian immigrants and Asian American literature.

http://koreanamericanliterature.com/

This site provides resources and bibliography of Korean American literature.

http://legacy.www.nypl.org/branch/features/index2.cfm?PFID=184

A site maintained by New York Public Library, it provides lists of Asian American literary anthologies and criticism.

http://www.mastersdegree.net/blog/2010/20-essential-works-of-asian-american-literature/

This site features 20 well-known Asian American works.

http://mockingbird.creighton.edu/worldlit/works/chamer.htm

Run by Creighton University, this site offers a short bibliography and a number of resource links on Asian American Literature.

http://palhbooks.blogspot.com/2007/06/filipino-american-literature.html

Philippine American Literary House's (PALH) Blog was founded in 1994 to serve the Philippine and Filipino American communities. It offers an extensive bibliography of Filipino American novels, poetry, children's books, plays and screenplays.

http://www.pawainc.com/directory.html

This site belongs to Philippine American Writers and Artists, Inc., and it posts events, articles, and links to other related sites.

http://sasialit.org/

This site offers an impressive reading list of works of South Asian Diaspora, including South Asian writers in the United States, Canada, Great Britain, the Caribbean, India, Pakistan, Sri Lanka, etc. This site also provides many useful resource links for South Asian American literature.

http://scholar.google.com/scholar?q=chinese+american+literature&hl=en&as_sdt=0&as_vis=1&oi=scholart

This is a Google Scholar site that offers a selective bibliography of Chinese American literary criticism.

http://www.sjsu.edu/faculty/awilliams/AsianAmResources.html

Run by Dr. Noelle Brada-Williams of San José State University, this site offers an extensive list of links to journals, scholarly books, publishers, bookstores, and programs related to Asian American literary studies.

http://www.wingluke.org/bibliography.html

Run by the Wing Luke Museum in Seattle, this site offers bibliographies of Asian American writings for adults and children.

About the Author

Wenying Xu was born in Shanghai, China. After she received her B.A. in English from Hebei University, China, she came to the United States to pursue graduate studies. She received her M.A. in English from West Virginia University and Ph.D. in English from University of Pittsburgh. Currently professor of English and associate dean of the College of Arts and Letters at Florida Atlantic University, she has authored two books: *Ethics and Aesthetics of Freedom in American and Chinese Realism* (2003) and *Eating Identities: Reading Food in Asian American Literature* (2008). Her essays on Asian American Literature have appeared in anthologies and journals, including *boundary 2*, *Cultural Critique*, *MELUS*, *LIT*, *Modern Language Studies*, *South Asian Review*, *Asian American Literature: Discourse & Pedagogies*, and *Journal of Contemporary Literature.* She has also published short fiction in *Prairie Schooner*, *Sistersong*, *A Room of One's Own*, and *American Intercultural Magazine*. She served as president of the Society for the Study of Multi-Ethnic Literature of the United States (MELUS) from 2009 to 2012.

CPSIA information can be obtained at www.ICGtesting.com
Printed in the USA
BVOW071333040412

286785BV00003B/3/P